The
Psychology Research Handbook

Second Edition

To Sandy, Kate, and Emily, whose love I cherish each day.
F.T.L.L.

To Jennifer Renée Austin and to Marilyn Marie Willhoff for their love.
J.T.A.

The **Psychology Research Handbook**
Second Edition

A Guide for
Graduate
Students and
Research
Assistants

Frederick T. L. Leong
University of Tennessee, Knoxville

James T. Austin
The Ohio State University

SAGE Publications
Thousand Oaks ▪ London ▪ New Delhi

For information:

Sage Publications, Inc.
2455 Teller Road
Thousand Oaks, California 91320|
E-mail: order@sagepub.com

Sage Publications Ltd.
1 Oliver's Yard
55 City Road
London, EC1Y 1SP
United Kingdom

Sage Publications India Pvt. Ltd.
B-42, Panchsheel Enclave
Post Box 4109
New Delhi 110 017 India

Printed in the United States of America

Library of Congress Cataloging-in-Publication Data

The psychology research handbook: A guide for graduate students and research assistants / edited by Frederick T.L. Leong and James T. Austin. — 2nd ed.
     p. cm.
Includes bibliographical references and index.
ISBN 0-7619-3021-3 (hardcover) — ISBN 0-7619-3022-1 (pbk.)
   1. Psychology—Research—Methodology. I. Leong, Frederick T. L. II. Austin, James T.
BF76.5.P795 2006
150′.72—dc22   2005009534

This book is printed on acid-free paper.

05   06   07   08   09   8   7   6   5   4   3   2   1

Acquisitions Editor:	Jim Brace-Thompson
Editorial Assistant:	Karen Ehrmann
Production Editor:	Diane S. Foster
Copy Editor:	Robert Holm
Typesetter:	C&M Digitals (P) Ltd.
Proofreader:	Kevin Gleason
Indexer:	Molly Hall
Cover Designer:	Ravi Balasuriya

CONTENTS

FOREWORD

The first edition of *The Psychology Research Handbook: A Guide for Graduate Students and Research Assistants,* published in 1996, quickly established itself as a standard text and reference work for students seeking to master research methods and procedures in psychology. Now, almost a decade later, the editors, Frederick Leong and James Austin, have produced a second edition with new chapters, chapter authors, and expanded coverage of material that will once again place the volume among those works that are essential reading for psychology students seeking to understand the complexities of research.

Like the first edition, the second offers a comprehensive guide for understanding and informing the entire research process. It's all here in clear and lucid prose: From identifying a research topic to applying for research grants, the reader is treated to an intellectually stimulating and fun-filled journey into the world of psychology research. The second edition volume contains 34 chapters, 5 more than the prior edition. As was the practice for the first edition, many of the chapters are coauthored by advanced graduate students all too familiar with pains and joys of conducting research.

Like the first edition, the chapters in the second edition follow the flow of the research process from the initial concern for a topic to the eventual endpoint of negotiating with journal editors. The second edition offers chapters on some of the new developments in research conceptualization and data processing, including multilevel research, computational modeling, and meta-analyses. The sequential flow of the research process offers the reader a natural accumulation of information, each chapter building on the material of the prior one and preparing the reader for the following one. This organization makes the handbook an ideal text for psychology students. Yet, I found that although the collection and flow of chapters is the volume's strength, any chapter can be pulled from the rest and can stand independently for those seeking information about some specific aspect of the research process. For example, anyone wanting to better understand qualitative methods would consult Chapter 17 on qualitative methods for an updated overview of the many developments in this important approach that is reshaping our notions about data collection, interpretation, and analysis.

Unlike other research handbooks that are filled with arcane material and ponderous writing that frighten the budding researcher because they assume levels of conceptual and technical sophistication that are far beyond the skills and talents of newcomers to the research process, the second edition of *The Psychology Research Handbook* is written and designed for students. The complexities and challenges of research are there and cannot be denied, but they are explicated and readily understandable. This volume has the potential to spark a lifelong love affair with the psychology research process. Of special value are a dozen chapters on topics typically missing from other texts, including cross-cultural research (Chapter 31), dealing with journal editors and reviewers

(Chapter 26), conducting meta-analyses (Chapter 21), and using archival data sets (Chapter 22).

In my opinion, this is the book of choice for introducing the psychology research process to students and research assistants. But you know what? The more I think of it, although this volume was developed for students, experienced researchers would find this volume to be a useful refresher course, capable of reigniting their own initial delight with the inquiry process, a delight that may have become dulled by years of routine and unchallenged ideas. This volume opens the mind to what is possible through systematic inquiry and, in doing so, will advance and broaden the field of psychology. Can't ask for more than that!

—Anthony J. Marsella

Atlanta, Georgia

ACKNOWLEDGMENTS

We began this second edition project with the same goal of explicating the research process so that psychology and related faculty could instruct graduate and undergraduate students in its intricacies. In completing this volume, we have come to the realization that a project like this could never have been completed in a timely manner without the contributions of numerous individuals, whom we wish to acknowledge here. First, our respective universities (Tennessee, Ohio State) provided support in the environment that fosters such contributions to scholarship and to training the next generation of researchers and practitioners. Our colleagues at Ohio State and at Tennessee have been a consistent source of stimulation and support, and several of these colleagues have contributed to this volume. We also wish to acknowledge all of the graduate students and undergraduates with whom we have worked over the years at Ohio State and at Tennessee. You served as the impetus for this book.

The staff at Sage Publications labored mightily to help this second edition take flight, to turn it into reality from our fledgling prospectus to this finished product. Among them are James Brace-Thompson and Karen Ehrmann, as well as their colleagues who worked behind the scenes. The contributors themselves, and especially those who worked heroically within time constraints, deserve the lion's share of the accolades. Without their expertise, willingness, and responsiveness, this project could not have been completed. Those scholars in the field who provided other reviews and advice also deserve our special gratitude. Finally, we would like to thank our spouses and significant others for their patience and support as we labored on this project over the last 2 years.

As editors, we wish to thank all of these individuals and also the many others who helped in the process of turning this second edition into reality.

INTRODUCTION

Scripts for Research: Thoughts on the Organization of the Psychology Research Handbook

JAMES T. AUSTIN

FREDERICK T. L. LEONG

What is the overarching frame around this handbook in its second edition? Briefly, researchers have directed substantial attention to the content, structure and process, and development of competence among scientists (Aiken, West, Sechrest, & Reno, 1990; Azmitia & Crowley, 2001; Kuhn, Amsel, & O'Loughlin, 1988; Nisbett, 1993; Tweney, Doherty, & Mynatt, 1981). Bradshaw, Langley, and Simon (1983) outlined the use of computer simulation to study scientific discovery. Anderson (1982), about the same time, proposed that the process of becoming an expert in any field involves converting a declarative knowledge network into a procedural network, largely through an intermediate stage of compilation (involving composition and generation processes with basic scripts as building blocks). Gholson and Shadish (1989) early on, and Feist and Gorman (1998) recently, have reviewed the psychology of science, a relative newcomer next to philosophy or sociology of science. Giere (2002) recently proposed a distributed architecture for scientific cognition. There are many other research studies in this domain that we harness for conceptualizing the acquisition of research knowledge and skills.

Using this work about knowledge and skill as a starting point, We have organized the issues involved in conducting research and in learning the domain. As a result, the key organizing principle behind *The Psychology Research Handbook* (*PRH*) is our conviction that cognitive scripts can be applied to the acquisition of higher-order research skills (cf. Hershey, Wilson, & Mitchell-Copeland, 1996). The application of scripts involves consideration of the research process as a procedural knowledge structure (Abelson, 1981; Galambos, Abelson, & Black, 1986; Schank & Abelson, 1977). Such a knowledge structure serves to sequence the activities involved in uneventful "normal science" research and also provides sufficient flexibility to accommodate changes in technology, conceptual structure, or immediate situation.

It is indeed useful to take a developmental-educational perspective on scripts for research. The research script is a function of exposure and activity. It is first acquired formally, for most, during undergraduate psychology classes. It can be amplified thereafter through graduate school, other research experiences, and either conducting or consuming research. Working from this plausible initial assumption, it should be possible to assess how well different individuals, at different stages of their training, possess scripts for conducting various types of research. Hershey et al. (1996) published a study to evaluate the plausibility of scripts for research. Their study involved asking different groups of participants to generate the "steps" of the research process within an interval bounded by two phrases: "get a research idea" and "publish a paper." Using four groups sampled along a novice-expert continuum (e.g., introductory psychology students, graduate students, assistant professors, full professors), their results indicated qualitative and quantitative differences in the scripts generated. Specifically, the scripts generated by novices (undergraduate students) differed from those who are presumably more expert (professors).

Another application of the script concept to research consists of elaborating individual differences in expertise. How might the same general cognitive structure be manifested differentially across scientists? How might development proceed from novice to expert over a period of 10 years or more? The final chapter of this handbook by Richard Petty, "Research Scripts: One Researcher's View," elaborates the overarching script concept from the perspective of a well-published, influential investigator of attitudes. Expertise can be inferred from number of publications (articles, books), leadership positions (academic, publication), and awards.

In this handbook, we have ourselves conducted a procedural analysis of the scientific research process that was used to generate the schematic for this handbook. As the chapter by Hershey and associates indicates, the research script is substantiated by empirical studies (Hershey et al., 1996) and is applicable to the teaching process (Wilson & Hershey, 1996).

One of the initial stages of research involves acquiring an idea and expanding it into a research topic, then a study design, then pilot studies and completed studies, and then a research report for presentation or publication. From that study or set of studies can flow an entire program of research. The structure of this book matches the script sequence. This concept is sequenced from "Research Planning" through "Design, Instrument Selection, and Sampling"; "Data Collection"; "Data Analyses"; and "Research Writing." A sixth section on special topics, for example the social organization of research groups as well as several advanced methodological concepts, provides coverage of unusual and contextual issues in the concluding section of the handbook. We now turn to the changes designed into this second edition.

CHANGES BETWEEN EDITIONS

What changes were made between editions? New coauthors were added by existing chapter contributors, six chapters were added, and two existing chapters were integrated into a single chapter. The new chapters were based on our judgment about important topics. The next chapter, by Douglas Hershey, Joy Jacobs-Lawson, and Thomas Wilson, introduces and substantiates the research script, and the last chapter by Richard Petty applies and ties together advanced use of the research script. These two chapters are bookends on the script framework. Concepts of statistical power are a perennial issue for research, and thus we now provide a chapter by Brett Myors on this topic. Multilevel analysis and computational modeling are two areas that are providing a new way to

NEW CHAPTERS	
Chapter	*Authors*
Research as a Script	Douglas Hershey, Joy Jacobs-Lawson, Thomas Wilson
Program Evaluation	James Altschuld, James Austin
Scale and Test Development	John Lounsbury, Lucy Gibson, Rich Saudargas
Statistical Power	Brett Myors
Multilevel Research	David Chan
Computational Modeling	Michael Zickar
The Research Script: One Researcher's View	Richard Petty

think across the social sciences. Thus we are fortunate to present chapters by David Chan and by Michael Zickar on these two topics. Program evaluation, that "worldly science" (Cook & Shadish, 1986), is becoming a function that psychologists increasingly encounter, and thus the chapter by James Altschuld and James Austin presents this domain to the reader. We asked John Lounsbury, Lucy Gibson, and Rich Saudargas to integrate scale development across multiple domains in their chapter. Titles of the new chapters, and authors, are presented in the accompanying table.

Because of the importance of the Internet and related technology for social life and research (Bargh & McKenna, 2004; Birnbaum, 2004), chapter authors were explicitly asked to address the effects of technology on their domains. Exercises were solicited and provided by most authors with the aim of helping motivated readers to further engage the material. As before, the book consists of chapters that fall into a categorical sequence of research, although we recognize that the sequence might be flexibly represented in a mental model of research. In Part I, the focus is research planning. Following the Hershey, Jacobs-Lawson, and Wilson chapter on research scripts, Frederick Leong and Douglas Muccio address finding a research topic. Once the topic is narrowed, a chapter by Jeffrey Reed and Pam Baxter covers bibliographic research necessary to identify what has been done in the area. Reviewing and evaluating a research article is the title of the chapter by Kathryn Oleson and Robert Arkin, in which a schema for critical thinking is applied to the research article. Last, program evaluation, including comparisons to research, is addressed by James Altschuld and James Austin. Each of these authors presents tasks and exercises for readers to try on their own.

In the next phase of the script, the focus is on design, instrument selection or development, and sampling that establish a context for data collection. The first chapter in Part II by Bruce Wampold discusses the design of research studies by analogy to car design. Wampold is followed by Madonna Constantine and Joseph Ponterotto's chapter on evaluating and selecting research instruments; Robert Goddard and Peter Villanova's chapter on designing surveys and questionnaires for research; John Lounsbury, Lucy Gibson, and Richard Saudargas's chapter on scale and test development; William McCready's chapter on sampling procedures; and the new chapter by Brett Myors on statistical power.

Next, the focus shifts to data collection. The first chapter in Part III by Don Dell, Lyle Schmidt, and Naomi Meara covers the important topic of applying for approval to conduct research with human participants. The next three chapters address different methods of data collection. One, on conducting mail and Internet surveys, is authored by Alan Vaux and Chad Briggs. It is followed by a chapter on conducting telephone surveys authored by Peter Chen and Yueng Huang. The last chapter in this part discusses collecting data in groups and was authored by Steven Zaccaro, Meredith Cracraft, and Michelle Marks.

Moving along, the emphasis shifts to analysis of both quantitative and qualitative data in Part IV. An important chapter on cleaning up data and running preliminary analyses contributed by David DiLalla and Stephen Dollinger leads off this section. Qualitative analysis techniques are addressed by Howard Pollio, Thomas Graves, and Michael Arfken. Charles Scherbaum then presents readers with a guide to statistical research and discovery, defined as planning and selecting statistical analyses. Basic statistical analyses are addressed by David Dickter, followed by advanced statistics by Lisa Steelman and Paul Levy. A method for conducting a meta-analysis is elaborated by Harris Cooper, Jorgi Robinson, and Nancy Dorr. A concluding chapter for this section by Barbara Zaitzow and Charles Fields covers archival data sets.

Research writing is the essence of scientific communication and ensures that the results of research are available for dissemination. In the first chapter of Part V on writing in APA style, Robert Calderón and James Austin review the mechanics and provide a meta-template of a research article for self-review. Getting started by writing rough drafts is treated by Christopher Peterson, and revising a research manuscript is addressed by Donna Nagata and Steven Trierweiler. Dealing with journal editors and reviewers by Samuel Osipow is the final chapter in this section.

Seven chapters on special topics in Part VI address a mixture of the practical, interpersonal, and methodological. The first, by Dennis Molfese and colleagues, concerns coordinating a research team. It is followed by two chapters of a methodological nature, the first by David Chan on multilevel research and the next by Michael Zickar on computational modeling. It is critical to possess skills in applying for research grants, and this topic is ably addressed by John Borkowski and Kimberly Howard. Next, cross-cultural research methodology is presented by Kwok Leung and Fons Van de Vijver. Charles Gelso discusses applying theories in research: the interplay of theory and research in science. We conclude with a chapter by an expert researcher, Professor Richard Petty. He identifies four contributions and illuminates them with examples from his own research scripts developed in and since graduate school.

REFERENCES

Abelson, R. P. (1981). Psychological status of the script concept. *American Psychologist, 36,* 715–729.

Aiken, L. S., West, S. G., Sechrest, L., & Reno, R. R. (1990). Graduate training in statistics, methodology, and measurement in psychology. *American Psychologist, 45,* 721–734.

Anderson, J. R. (1982). Acquisition of a cognitive skill. *Psychological Review 89,* 369–406.

Azmitia, M., & Crowley, K. (2001). The rhythms of scientific thinking: A study of collaboration in an earthquake microworld. In K. Crowley, C. D. Schunn, & T. Okada (Eds.), *Designing for science: Implications for everyday, classroom, and professional settings* (pp. 47–77). Mahwah, NJ: Lawrence Erlbaum.

Bargh, J. B., & McKenna, K. Y. A. (2004). The Internet and social life. *Annual Review of Psychology, 55,* 573–590.

Birnbaum, M. E. (2004). Human research and data collection via the Internet. *Annual Review of Psychology, 55,* 803–832.

Bradshaw, G. L., Langley, P. W., & Simon, H. A. (1983). Studying scientific discovery by computer simulation. *Science, 222*(4627), 971–975.

Cook, T. D., & Shadish. W. R. (1986). Program evaluation: The worldly science. *Annual Review of Psychology, 37,* 193–232.

Feist, G. J., & Gorman, M. E. (1998). The psychology of science: Review and integration of a nascent discipline. *Review of General Psychology, 2*(1), 3–47.

Galambos, J. A., Abelson, R. P., & Black, J. B. (Eds.). (1986). *Knowledge structures.* Hillsdale, NJ: Lawrence Erlbaum.

Gholson, B., & Shadish, W. R., Jr. (Eds.). (1989). *Psychology of science: Contributions to metascience.* Cambridge, UK: Cambridge University Press.

Giere, R. N. (2002). Scientific cognition as distributed cognition. In P. Carruthers, S. P. Stich, & M. Siegal (Eds.), *The cognitive basis of science* (pp. 285–299). Cambridge, UK: Cambridge University Press.

Hershey, D. A., Wilson, T. L., & Mitchell-Copeland, J. M. (1996). Conceptions of the psychological research process: Script variation as a function of training and experience. *Current Psychology: Developmental, Learning, Personality, Social, 14,* 293–312.

Kuhn, D., Amsel, E., & O'Loughlin, M. (1988). *The development of scientific thinking skills.* San Diego, CA: Academic.

Nisbett, R. E. (1993). *Rules for reasoning.* Hillsdale, NJ: Lawrence Erlbaum.

Schank, R. C., & Abelson, R. P. (1977). *Scripts, plans, goals, and understanding: An inquiry into human knowledge structures.* Hillsdale, NJ: Lawrence Erlbaum.

Tweney, R. D., Doherty, M. E., & Mynatt, C. R. (1981). *On scientific thinking.* New York: Columbia University Press.

Wilson, T. L., & Hershey, D. A. (1996). The research methods script. *Teaching of Psychology, 23,* 97–99. (Reprinted in M. E. Ware & C. L. Brewer, Eds., *Handbook for teaching statistics and research methods,* 2nd ed., pp. 193–196. Mahwah, NJ: Lawrence Erlbaum)

PART I

RESEARCH PLANNING

1

Research as a Script

Douglas A. Hershey
Joy M. Jacobs-Lawson
Thomas L. Wilson

Two questions often arise near the beginning of any course on research methods:
Why is it important to have sound
research skills? How are research skills
acquired? Answers to both questions are multifaceted, a point that will be reinforced throughout the opening chapter of this handbook.
Before attempting to answer those two questions, however, imagine the following scenario:

Two first-year graduate students were talking
about psychology late one evening. During the
course of their discussion, the two came up with
what they believed to be a fascinating research
idea, so they designed an empirical study to
explore the topic. Over the course of the following
year, they collected and analyzed data and prepared a manuscript for publication. The day they
dropped the manuscript in the mail to the journal
editor, the two were overjoyed by the fact that they
had accomplished this major task without assistance from their advisors. They were certain the
paper would be published, and they could hardly
wait for the editor's confirmation.

When the envelope containing reviews of their
manuscript arrived 10 weeks later, imagine their
surprise when they read the opening sentence of
the editor's letter: "We regret to inform you that
after soliciting three different reviews of your

work, we find your manuscript unsuitable for
publication." Enclosed were three detailed sets
of comments pointing out numerous critical flaws
in their work. One reviewer pointed out that a
number of studies had already been published on
this same topic and that the students' findings
failed to offer new insights. Another identified
methodological flaws in the design of the study
that failed to rule out alternative interpretations,
thus calling into question the authors' conclusions. And all three reviewers mentioned that the
statistics used to analyze the data were inappropriate given the nature of the research questions
that had been asked. Furthermore, in her cover letter, the editor indicated that the manuscript was a
poor fit given the interests of the readers of the
journal. Seriously disappointed, the two students
went to see their advisors to discuss what they
should have done differently.

Before reading further, take a minute or two
and think about what the students might have
done differently. What additional steps could
they have taken to help ensure a successful outcome? The students spent a year working on the
project, but from the gist of the reviews, it was
clear that several important steps of the research
process had been overlooked. It appears that not
only did they fail to conduct a thorough review

of the literature before beginning the project, but they also failed to critically evaluate the design for weaknesses or flaws. Moreover, the students would have been well served by consulting with a quantitative specialist (or their advisor) about the analysis plan, and they would have benefited by contacting the editor of the journal (or looking through back issues) to determine whether their paper represented an appropriate fit in light of the journal's audience.

In answer to the first question posed at the beginning of this chapter, it is important to possess a sound understanding of the research process because it allows us to work more efficiently. In conducting their study, the two students presumably learned important lessons about the research process, but at what cost? Think of the hundreds of hours that were wasted: time contributed by members of the institutional review board, the participants, the journal editor, reviewers, and the investigators themselves. Think of how just a bit more knowledge on their part, and assistance from others, might have led to a different, more positive outcome. Answers to the second question posed above (How are research skills acquired?) will be spelled out in detail later in the chapter when student learning and the development of expertise are discussed.

Most veteran researchers would not have experienced the same difficulties our two hypothetical graduate students encountered; in fact, errors, flaws, omissions, and conceptual gaps are not uncommon when it comes to conducting research in the social sciences. Even experienced researchers make critical errors, as suggested by the high rejection rates among top journals (in some instances greater than 90%). One key to avoiding mistakes is to develop a strong understanding of the complex set of steps involved in the research process, which, from the perspective of the novice investigator, may initially seem relatively straightforward.

Some of you may now be thinking: "Okay, so learning about the research process will help me to earn my degree and publish scientific papers, but will I benefit in other ways?" The answer is a resounding *yes!* First, strong research skills will allow you to better understand and evaluate the work of others. Second, from a more applied perspective, a good working knowledge of research methods will help you become not only a better scholar but also a better mentor, practitioner, or professor (depending on your career goals). Third, a solid set of research skills will help you to contribute quality scientific findings to the cutting edge of the psychological literature. Finally, a thorough grounding in research methods will make you a more careful and critical observer of the world around you. That is, knowledge of the scientific method will allow you to more accurately evaluate advertising claims, critically evaluate stories that appear in the press, and separate fact from fiction when participating in an intellectual debate. For these reasons (and many others), it is strongly in your best interests to actively work at developing your skills as a methodologist, not only during your graduate school years but on an ongoing basis throughout the remainder of your career.

SCOPE OF PRESENT CHAPTER

The primary goal of this chapter is to introduce you to the concept of a research method script. In its most basic form, a script is a series of ordered steps or events that occur when completing a task. More specifically, one can think of a script as a compiled mental event sequence, containing those activities typically associated with a commonly experienced event. In previous studies, individuals have been shown to possess psychological scripts for a variety of everyday events such as doing the grocery shopping (Light & Anderson, 1983), solving financial planning problems (Hershey, Jacobs-Lawson, & Walsh, 2003), attending a lecture, and visiting the dentist (Bower, Black, & Turner, 1979). In conducting a psychological study, the research script dictates the various stages of work that will take place and the sequence in which those stages should be completed. As will be discussed below, individuals' research scripts tend to evolve with experience over time; therefore, the script that currently guides your research efforts will likely differ from the one you follow 5 years from now. At this point, it is recommended that you turn to the end of the chapter and complete the first exercise, which is designed to elicit your current research script.

A second goal of this chapter is to provide a general overview of the procedures involved in a typical psychological research project. The processes and concepts presented in this chapter will be amplified and discussed in greater detail in subsequent chapters. This handbook is organized into a five-stage framework that includes (a) research planning; (b) design, instrument selection, and sampling; (c) data collection; (d) data analyses; and (e) research writing. It is no coincidence that these five stages correspond to the major goals of a psychological research project. Also note that the structural model introduced later in this chapter is organized around these same five general topics. This handbook concludes with a section on special topics not typically considered part of the research process per se, such as working as part of a research team (Chapter 27), grantsmanship (Chapter 30), and the role of theory in research (Chapter 32). Although these topics may not be central to the empirical research process, they are, as you will see, important areas to understand for those who aspire to become productive psychologists.

As will be revealed throughout this book, computers have become an indispensable tool in the research process, and as such, computer-based tasks are prominently represented in the research methods script. Long gone are the days when researchers manually searched through dusty paper files and bound journals to locate articles, wait for hours (or even days) for the results of statistical analyses, or use manual typewriters to prepare manuscripts. We can now conveniently locate, download, and print articles from the comfort of our offices; we obtain statistical findings at the click of a mouse; and we can even edit, submit, and revise manuscripts working from a laptop at the local coffee shop. Although the technological advances brought about by computers have unquestionably improved the quality of our science, learning how to effectively use computers can be difficult and can try one's patience. Take for example the fairly common experience of getting 1,000 or more hits when conducting a literature review on PsycINFO, a search engine for psychological research papers. You revise your search by adding one or two additional keywords, only to receive the frustrating message "No articles could be found—try broadening your search."

Learning the tricks of the trade when it comes to getting computers to do what you want, whether it involves conducting a literature review, specifying a complex statistical analysis, or drawing a figure that conforms to APA style, will necessarily take time and practice. As you read the chapters that follow, you will not only increase your knowledge of research methods but you will also come to better appreciate the integral role of computers in each stage of the research process.

In the following section, the psychological research process is described in further detail. It is characterized as a complex, highly varied, and extended problem-solving task that requires the application of specific and effective solution strategies. One such strategy, an empirically derived *expert script* of the psychological research process, is introduced. Presentation of this script is accompanied by a discussion of what it means to be an expert research psychologist.

EXPERTISE AND THE RESEARCH SCRIPT

Psychological Research as a Problem-Solving Endeavor

From an information processing perspective, the act of engaging in scientific research can be thought of as a complex problem-solving endeavor (Hunt, 1991). In a problem-solving situation, the task is to transform an initial state into a qualitatively different goal state through the application of a series of steps leading to a solution (sometimes referred to as *operators*). In a psychological research context, the *initial state* often consists of an existing theory and its base of empirical findings. The *goal state* is typically some extension of that theory based on findings from a new investigation. From this perspective, the ability to reach one's research goal depends on the selection and application of an appropriate set of operators (Newell & Simon, 1972). Stated in terms of the empirical research process, conducting a proper experiment will involve making a series of critical decisions about *how* your study should be carried out. When the research process is considered from this point of view, it almost goes without saying that one's methodological knowledge will determine, to a great extent, whether or not those critical decisions will be made in an intelligent fashion.

In discussing the concept of a research methods script, it is useful to distinguish between a structural model of the research process and an individual's mental representation of that same process. A *structural model* is a veridical and relatively complete representation of the various solutions that are applicable in a particular problem-solving context (Merrienboer, Clark, & Croock, 2002). Thus, a structural model of the research process would represent the various investigative approaches one might adopt, different data analytic strategies, methods used to disseminate findings, and so on. *Mental representations* (referred to by some as mental models) of the research process, in contrast, almost always fall short of a structural model. Mental representations in all but the simplest of domains tend to be incomplete or contain misspecifications, perceptual biases, or other types of distortions. One of the key objectives of this handbook is that the reader develop his or her mental model of the research process into a reasonable approximation of a structural model. Of particular relevance to this chapter is the fact that structural models have been shown to be valuable tools for training individuals to become more efficient and competent problem solvers (Hershey & Walsh, 2000/2001). It is on the combined mental models of experts that these structural models are based.

In one empirical investigation, Hershey, Wilson, and Mitchell-Copeland (1996; see also Wilson & Hershey, 1996) examined the research scripts of 49 "expert" psychologists, each of whom held appointments at major academic institutions. Participants were considered experts by virtue of their high level of training in research methods and the fact that all were actively engaged in research as a condition of their employment. As characterized in the article, a *psychological script* is a specialized type of procedural knowledge representation containing an ordered set of actions that are linked together in long-term memory (Abelson, 1975; Schank & Abelson, 1977). In the Hershey et al. (1996) study, participants were asked to list about twenty actions or steps that characterize

the process psychologists go through when working on a research problem. In order to establish common anchor events (across individuals) at the two ends of the event sequence, the phrase "Get Idea for Project" was printed at the top of the response form, and "Publish the Research Paper" was printed at the bottom.

A composite research script is shown in Table 1.1 that is based on the individual scripts of the 49 psychologists. This composite representation contains 23 of the most commonly mentioned events that occur over the course of a psychological investigation. Five different high-consensus events (printed in all capital letters in the table, mentioned by more than 60% of respondents) were identified: read literature, design experimental methods, data collection, data analysis, and write a draft of the paper. Notably, this set of events forms what might be thought of as a "meta-script" of the research process. That is, there is evidence to suggest that scripts are hierarchically organized, with major events representing superordinate procedural goals (Abelson, 1981; Galambos, 1986) and minor events representing subgoals. Presumably, when a superordinate goal is triggered, the scripts for various subordinate goals are activated in a prespecified order until the entire subroutine of constituent tasks has been carried out (Merrienboer et al., 2002). At that point, the next superordinate goal is activated, and a new series of steps in the overall event sequence is enacted.

The Expert Researcher

One of the hallmarks of expertise in a problem-solving domain is possession of a well-specified semantic and procedural knowledge network (Ericsson & Smith, 2002; Glaser & Chi, 1988). This does not suggest there is a single best solution for every problem or there exists a gold standard against which one's problem-solving efforts can be compared. That is because when dealing with ill-structured problems (such as how to conduct a psychological investigation), there are many different methodological approaches from which to choose, a myriad of ways to examine the data, countless ways to communicate the results, and so on. This last point suggests that there is no single research methods script that will *always* lead to

Table 1.1   Composite Research Script Based on Responses From 49 Psychology Professors

Get idea for project (anchor)

READ LITERATURE ON TOPIC

Discuss idea with colleagues

Conceptualize project

Determine appropriate subject population

Formulate Hypotheses

DESIGN EXPERIMENTAL METHODS

Obtain available materials and measures

Construct experimental materials and measures

Obtain research assistants

Pilot Test Procedures and Measures

Refine experiment based on pilot results

Obtain Subjects

DATA COLLECTION

Code and organize data

DATA ANALYSIS

Determine if hypotheses were supported

Make a conference or brown-bag presentation

Conduct a final literature review

WRITE DRAFT OF PAPER

Get feedback on paper

Submit Paper for Publication

Make post-review revisions

Publish the research paper (anchor)

SOURCE: Hershey et al., 1996.

NOTE: High-consensus events (mentioned by more than 60% of professors) are shown in capital letters. Moderate-consensus events (mentioned by 40–59% of professors) are shown in upper and lower case. Low-consensus events (mentioned by 20–39% of professors) are shown in italics.

an optimal outcome. Rather, the knowledge structures of experts are dynamic and contextually organized and thus able to accommodate subtle differences in environmental and situational demands (e.g., resource availability, participant considerations, ethical concerns) when the goal is to select and apply an appropriate solution strategy.

Moreover, an expert's knowledge base is constantly growing and changing to accommodate new advances in the field. To that end, a well-qualified empiricist must stay abreast of methodological developments, read about new data collection and analysis techniques as they become available, and learn about new and different ways to communicate findings to peers. That said, it is worth pointing out that expert status is not a goal state in and of itself. Rather, it may be better conceptualized as a life-long attitude toward learning. Certainly, possessing a large body of knowledge about research is a prerequisite to being considered an expert, but the humble and accomplished investigator realizes that the sine qua non of expertise involves a sincere commitment to a never-ending learning process.

As mentioned above, one of the chief objectives of this chapter is to present a detailed structural representation of the psychological research script. This structural script expands on the 23-item expert script shown in Table 1.1 to include a much broader set of issues involved in conducting a psychological investigation. One caveat should be raised, however, before proceeding. Until this point, it has implicitly been suggested that the research script is based on a linear process, a process in which one activity naturally and logically follows from the one that precedes it. Unfortunately, the sequence of steps involved in conducting real-world psychological research is not always unambiguous and straightforward. There are instances when two or more tasks within a script may be simultaneously enacted. For example, one might choose to pilot test a new measure while concurrently developing an application for the institutional review board. There may even be times when an investigator might need to leave a step out of the research process, such as the task of debriefing subjects when working with animals or recruiting subjects when conducting naturalistic observations. To further complicate matters, in some studies certain stages of the research process may be carried out in a recursive fashion. For instance, if during the data analysis stage one finds a statistical test has yielded insufficient power, then the investigator may return to the data collection phase of the process in an attempt to increase power.

As you read about the elements of the research process described on the following pages, it is important to recognize that the condensed structural model presented is not intended to be prescriptive in all cases. The structural model of the research script is designed to have heuristic value as a foundation for the set of activities associated with most empirical investigations. Therefore, deviations from the structural model that appears on the following pages might not be unreasonable if particular methodologies are adopted.

STRUCTURAL ELEMENTS OF THE RESEARCH SCRIPT

Let us walk through the research methods script and focus on each of the higher-level event sequences, or phases of research, in logical order. As a generalized event sequence of the scientific process, the research script begins with a representation of the scientific problem and ends with the goal of publishing the results of the investigation. Alternatively stated, the scientific process typically begins with an idea or question that requires an empirical answer, and in most cases it ends with the scientist publicly disseminating major findings in writing (see Chapter 23), and pointing out the implications.

As indicated earlier, the research events that transpire between a script's beginning and ending can vary depending on purpose, methodology, and resources. Very often a single project intended to test one or more hypotheses is part of a larger program of research that includes multiple projects that are either planned or simultaneously underway. Thus, most research projects do not end with the publication of one's data; rather, public presentation starts the script all over again, as the investigator continues on to another project and then another within the same general research program. For much of the remainder of this chapter, we will present a structural model of the research process. In the section that follows, we describe the five major stages of the research process, with each stage represented by a corresponding figure. Let us now turn to the first stage of the process, which involves formulating a viable research idea.

Formulating the Idea

For any given research project, the process begins when the researcher entertains a question to be put to scientific test (see Figure 1.1). At that point, an investigation has been launched. Sources for research ideas include one's specific knowledge of the scientific literature in a given domain and one's general knowledge of the ideas of other theorists. In terms of modern philosophy of science, the researcher is aware of the theoretical network within which the initial question resides. Experienced researchers know that each project begins at this rather broad conceptual level. There are often significant unanswered questions related to currently held theories and novel hypotheses that may be proposed to account for specific effects. In fact, the true source of research ideas, that is, the source of one's scientific inspiration, is considered by some to be an area of research in and of itself. Many original ideas come from scientists' private observations of phenomena in the world; others frame scientific questions by attempting to extend existing knowledge. Whether a researcher's project idea grows out of contradictions in the scientific literature, incredulity regarding the conclusions drawn from another study, the need to replicate previous findings, or private experience, the original project idea is the starting point that will largely determine the scripted events that follow.

Before selecting an appropriate methodology to address the research question of interest, it is necessary to be familiar with the body of work concerning the domain one plans to investigate. Most researchers tend to work in one or two specific domains, so they may already possess this knowledge. In fact, perhaps it was one of the investigator's previous findings that led to the new project idea in the first place; however, irrespective of the source of the inspiration, even leading theorists in a field must review the relevant and current literature. Others, in contrast, including a majority of students, may be preparing to conduct research in an area that is unfamiliar. To a large extent, when one is working in a novel research area, the literature review can reveal to the investigator dominant paradigms and possible methodologies. In Chapters 2–4, information is presented about how one might arrive at project ideas, how to conduct literature searches, and how to effectively evaluate the existing body of scientific work.

One benefit of representing research activities as a carefully planned script is that it

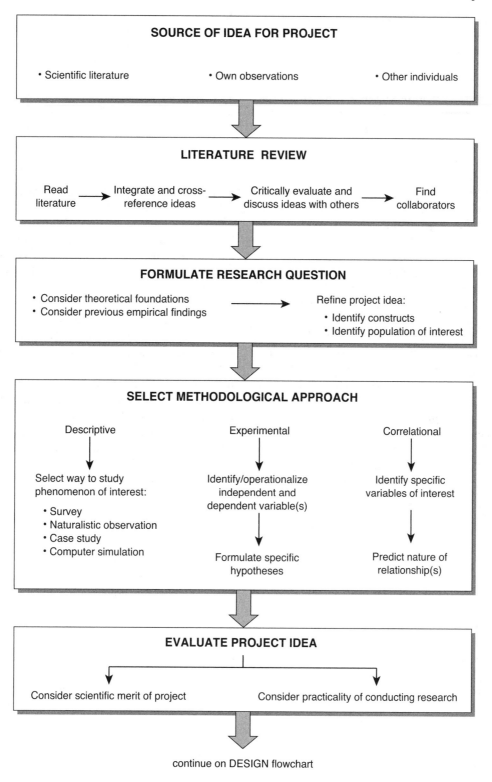

Figure 1.1   Stages Involved in Formulating the Research Idea

increases the likelihood of producing findings that will be valued by the scientific community. Therefore, reading the literature, integrating results across laboratories and studies, and critically evaluating the work of others will all help the researcher to determine whether a project idea has merit. Often the literature review leads one back to a new starting question, or it may even lead to relationships with others who will contribute valuable ideas and refinements to the project.

With a project idea and the pertinent literature now in hand, it is time to formulate the original research question into a clearly specified hypothesis. To formulate a hypothesis, a few specific activities are in order. First, the researcher must identify two or more theoretical constructs that take center stage in relation to the original idea. Second, the researcher attempts to specify *how* these constructs are related to one another in order to answer the original research question. Is a difference among groups expected on the dependent measure? Is a linear relationship anticipated, or will a quadratic trend emerge? Are there assumptions regarding the direction and magnitude of effects?

Identification of constructs at this point is not yet definition at the empirical level (i.e., at the level of an operational definition); the researcher simply wants to formulate an empirically verifiable proposition regarding the theoretical constructs. That is, at this stage the researcher should be able to make a purely conceptual statement about one possible answer to the original research question, and that statement should afford meaning specification at the empirical level. The proposition must be, according to the principles of the scientific method, testable. In addition, this "conceptual hypothesis" should provide clues about the population to which the eventual findings will generalize. From this conceptual development stage, the researcher has now identified the central constructs, predicted relationships, and the population in question. As one can see, much development can take place at a purely conceptual level, perhaps leading the researcher back to the literature again for further review and discussion with colleagues. Conceptual formulation is, therefore, a critical step that precedes the selection of a method and the formation of operational definitions.

The task of selecting a methodological approach may be rather straightforward at this point in the research process; it certainly must be accomplished before consideration of the study's practicality and merit. Whether the question is best addressed with a descriptive approach, using survey methods, questionnaires, observations or simulations, or best answered by experimental manipulations and controls, the conceptual work of selecting a scientific approach is clearly crucial for the remainder of the enterprise. Often researchers focus attention on the variables of interest in order to select the approach, by considering how constructs may be operationalized to address the project idea.

As every student of research methodology learns, the approach one takes will determine the kinds of inferences one will be able to draw from the study. Perhaps this is why most researchers include this conceptual step of method selection in their script, prior to the formal design and preparation of materials. The typical result of method selection is the transformation of conceptual hypotheses into specific hypotheses or predictions that will later be empirically tested. With a decision made regarding the methodological approach, one can begin to evaluate whether the project idea is developing appropriately in light of specific working hypotheses and the ultimate purpose of the research.

Experienced researchers often engage in a predesign stage during which the project idea is evaluated along two dimensions: merit and practicality. Considerations of merit include, among other things, whether one will be able to draw valid conclusions, whether the study will have external or ecological validity, and ultimately whether the findings will contribute to the scientific literature. With respect to practicality, it is clear that most research is neither cheap nor easy to conduct. Therefore, investigators must evaluate the project idea in terms of existing resources, potential sources of funding, equipment, and laboratory costs. Concerns about practicality may also include ethical considerations. Does the project idea pose any severe ethical dilemmas? Do the potential benefits of the study outweigh any anticipated risks? Thus, before moving on to the design stage, the researcher must balance the contributive value, resource value, and ethical value of the study in order to determine the best possible course of action.

Formulating the Design

Suppose one has done the conceptual work and thoroughly considered the potential of the project in terms of merit and practicality. It is then time to move on to more formal aspects of the research design (see design flowchart, Figure 1.2). At this stage of the research process, there is often a second level of project conceptualization, but this time at a more concrete level. In the design stage of the research methods script, questions regarding treatment groups, the appropriateness of the experimental task, and a variety of procedural details are addressed. (Chapter 6 presents a thorough look into the formal designs used in research studies.) Furthermore, there are two essential types of variables that are evaluated at this time: independent variables (IVs, or *predictors*) and dependent variables (DVs, or *criterion measures*). When considering IVs, it is necessary to identify all possible confounding variables and experimental biases that could reduce the internal validity of the investigation. In terms of DVs, for the research to pass any form of peer review, the measures must be both *reliable* and *valid*. It also behooves the investigator to use measures that are sufficiently *sensitive* to reveal meaningful relationships in the data. Often, researchers address these issues under a separate preparation period. For example, developing standardized procedures and writing survey questions are represented in the preparation phase of the method. Many of the considerations dealt with at this stage are treated in Chapters 8 and 9 of this handbook.

When the specific design characteristics of the investigation are clear (including decisions about variables, measures, and the sequencing of experimental events), then researchers can determine the number of participants to recruit for the study. Most investigators make preliminary specifications regarding the sample, long before the recruiting process begins. Well before advertisements are posted and classroom solicitations

are scheduled, researchers typically develop a plan for their analyses that corresponds to the hypotheses they plan to entertain. These decisions regarding statistical procedures will help to inform decisions regarding the number of participants in the study and any special characteristics of the sample that will ultimately be drawn. It is becoming increasingly common to conduct an a priori power analysis to help determine the size of the sample in relation to the magnitude of the anticipated effect. Such an analysis is a particularly important step for those who seek external funding inasmuch as review panels have come to expect this information in major grant applications. Chapter 18 guides the reader through the statistical planning process, and Chapter 11 presents ways to conceptualize and maximize statistical power.

Note the activities researchers engage in as part of the preparation phase. In addition to developing materials and making logistical arrangements for the work, the investigator must submit a plan of the proposed research for review by the institutional review board (IRB) to ensure adequate protections are met. A good description of this approval process and suggestions for preparing a successful IRB proposal are given in Chapter 12. With IRB approval and materials ready, the research script indicates one other activity prior to data collection. Very often a period of preliminary research takes place that is designed to fine-tune measures and try out new experimental methods. This step is commonly referred to as "pilot testing." During this process researchers carefully evaluate the appropriateness of their method and the adequacy of the procedures they have planned. Often a small (and perhaps known to be biased) sample is used solely for purposes of timing experimental events, testing for instruction comprehension, and identifying undesired demand characteristics. Although pilot testing involves the collection of data, this step is not generally recognized by investigators to be part of the data collection process. Rather, it is conceived of as a preliminary step aimed at refining elements of the material and procedure.

Data Collection

The research methods script places the subject recruitment process squarely within the

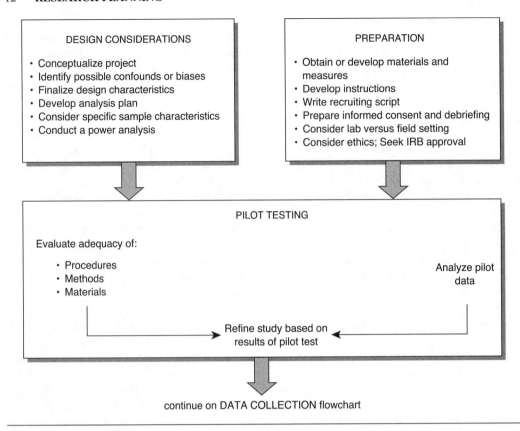

Figure 1.2   Stages Involved in Designing the Study

data collection phase. Applications of sampling procedures are the topic of Chapter 10. As seen in Figure 1.3, the period of actually collecting the data and the stage at which the data are coded and organized logically follow the recruitment phase. Chapters 13, 14, and 15 present a variety of considerations related to the data collection process. Whatever method of sampling is used, be it naturalistic observation, surveys, phone calls, or use of a subject pool, the event is clearly represented as part of the general data collection process. Researchers almost always have specific subgoals nested within the act of observation, such as obtaining informed consent, checking to see that subjects complete the task, and ensuring that all participants are treated fairly and ethically.

Once sufficient data have been obtained, they can be coded and entered into a database for analysis. Responses to surveys, questionnaires, verbal protocols, and tests containing subscales all must be coded for analysis. When this process is complete, the experimenter examines the data, checking for any input errors or unintentional mistakes in the assigned values. Double data entry procedures may be used (in which two different individuals code and enter the same data set) to help ensure the reliability of the data entry process. Chapter 16 presents ways in which data can be cleaned up and refined; Chapter 17 introduces the reader to various qualitative research techniques.

Data Analysis

Researchers often begin the data analysis phase by refamiliarizing themselves with the original hypotheses and the general data analysis plan (see Figure 1.4). The formal analysis begins with the computation of descriptive statistics (which may include computing measures of central tendency and variability and graphing

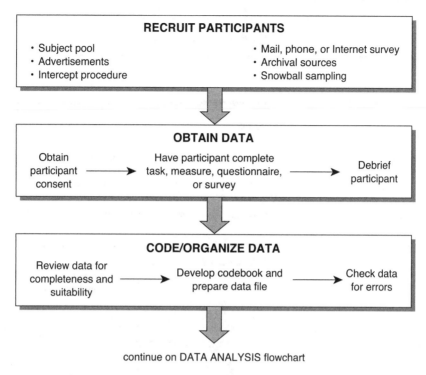

Figure 1.3   Stages Involved in the Data Collection Phase of a Project

scatterplots and frequency distributions). This step is carried out not only to determine whether there are outliers among the data but also to ensure that the skew and kurtosis of the data distributions are not unreasonable. When applicable, an item analysis is performed. A discussion of these basic analyses can be found in Chapter 19. Most of these preliminary computations are intended to evaluate the adequacy of the method, and they may include assessments of reliability, cross-validation of measures, and analysis of manipulation check items. Thus, a significant part of the process at this stage is to verify that the method and procedures were, in fact, successful in terms of their intended purpose. At this point, measurement weaknesses in the study can be identified and addressed, including problems brought on by low levels of interrater or observer reliability, selection biases, and order effects.

Following the preliminary analyses, advanced statistical analyses are carried out (see a discussion of advanced analyses in Chapter 20). Most investigators perform *planned* tests first, after which any number of follow-up tests may be performed. Examples of follow-up tests include post hoc comparisons, trend analyses, and residual analysis. At this stage, the researcher may seek to determine power levels and effect sizes for individual tests, assess whether the Type I error rate may be inflated, and evaluate whether key statistical assumptions have been met. Chapters 19–21 address the variety of tests and mathematical models available to researchers in the formal analysis stage of the research process.

Unplanned, or a posteriori, hypotheses are then tested when appropriate. In the research script, it is clear that investigators often discover new hypotheses suggested by the results of the advanced analysis. Students are often taught to avoid "hypothesis myopia" and encouraged to examine the data beyond their primary hypotheses. This is done to reveal other potentially interesting aspects of the study that have not yet been brought to light. The results of such unplanned analyses may reveal implications about the a priori hypotheses and suggest new hypotheses for future research. The sequence of preliminary analysis, advanced analysis, and

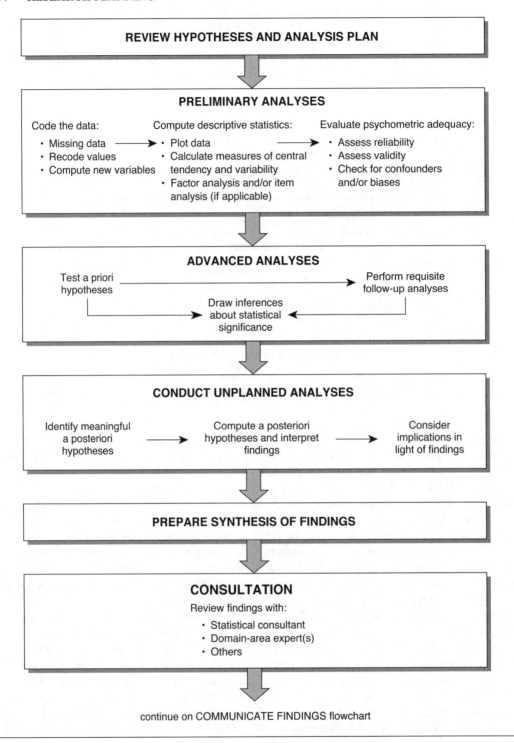

Figure 1.4   Stages Involved in the Data Analysis Phase of an Investigation

unplanned analysis often produces such a mass of results that there becomes a need to synthesize and cross-reference findings (organizationally, diagrammatically, or in written form) in order to return the focus of one's attention back to the question or questions that originally inspired the research. This particular step in the data analysis process can often yield "big-picture" insights about the work not previously recognized when one is in the midst of analyzing the data. The data analysis phase often ends with some informal sharing of the results of the study with consultants, peers, and other experts in the theoretical domain.

Communication of Findings

It is wise to begin the communication phase of the work by reflecting on the results of the study on a number of different levels (see Figure 1.5). Both depth of thought and integrative conceptual analysis are critical at this stage of the process, as both are necessary in order to tell an accurate and interesting story about the research. Investigators do well to critically evaluate their own studies and report any known difficulties or limitations to the consumers of the research. Considerations here may include the level of reliability of observations, the strength of treatment and control, and the generalizability of the findings. In addition, it is important for investigators to describe their work in relation to the existing body of research. Other reflections may include thoughts regarding the implications of the findings at the theoretical and applied levels. Engaging in reflective thought at this stage of the research process will serve to improve the quality of one's discussion when findings are communicated to members of the scientific community.

A year or more may elapse between the time an investigation is launched and the time one seeks to formally communicate the findings. In light of this fact, many researchers include a final literature review step in the final stage of the research process. The ability to discuss your work in relation to the most recently published findings will help to locate your efforts on the cutting edge and, at the same time, help advance scientific research at a more rapid pace. One may chose to share findings orally with a small group, such as at a brown-bag presentation, or in a larger, more formal setting, such as at a regional or national conference. For most investigators, however, the ultimate goal of the research is publication of a peer-reviewed manuscript. To accomplish this goal, the author must decide which journal or periodical would serve as the best home for the work. This includes considering not only factors such as the scope, quality,

and focus of different journals but also any special editorial objectives a journal may have (e.g., an upcoming special issue on your topic) or unique manuscript preparation guidelines.

The chapters in Part V of this handbook, "Research Writing," contain valuable information about manuscript preparation in the final communication phase. Generally speaking, the manuscript preparation phase entails developing a draft of a paper that is then shared with colleagues. The manuscript is then typically revised based on the comments and suggestions of others, at which point it is ready for submission and peer review. Following that review, the best case scenario would be one in which the author receives word that the paper has been accepted; however, acceptance letters following first-time submissions are rare, and they generally should not be expected. If the peer review process results in a rejection, the researchers then are faced with a choice. They can decide to scrap the project, choosing to start the process again from scratch, or they may attempt to publish the paper in a different journal (sometimes without making substantive changes). Alternatively, the editor may return the manuscript following peer review requesting that revisions be made prior to its being accepted. In this case, the author makes postreview changes to the manuscript and often includes with the second submission a detailed letter outlining specific modifications that were made to address reviewers' concerns. Secondary review of the manuscript will almost invariably result in either the disappointment of rejection or the satisfaction of reading an editor's letter of congratulations. In either case, the research methods script begins all over again with a search for new project ideas.

This concludes the structural description of the research methods script. In the next section, we address the issue of how one learns the research script, with a focus on how instruction and practice influence the development of methodological expertise.

INSTRUCTION, EXPERIENCE, AND THE DEVELOPMENT OF EXPERTISE

At the beginning of this chapter, we introduced the notion of a research script, followed by a discussion of the research scripts of experts.

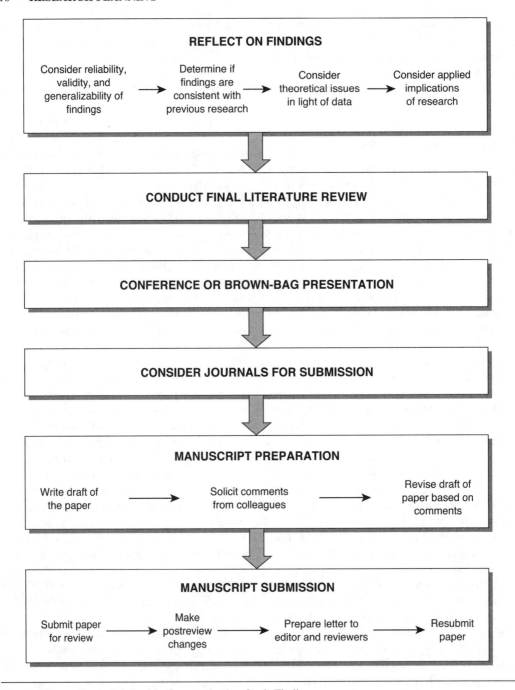

Figure 1.5   Stages Involved in Communicating One's Findings

Next, we presented a structural model of the research process, which outlined key events that are part of a typical psychological investigation. Inasmuch as this handbook is intended as a primer for graduate students and research assistants, it is worth discussing how individuals learn about the research process. What are the different sources of instruction when it comes to learning about the research process? What effect will hands-on experience have on the development of individuals' research scripts? And by what mechanisms do the scripts of novices develop into those of experts? Each of these questions will be addressed in this final section of the chapter.

Learning and Instructional Support

Fortunately, none of us start out from scratch when it comes to learning many of the fundamental principles of the research process. Long before our first formal introduction to the topic, we develop rudimentary schemata (i.e., knowledge structures) about science, and represented within those schemata are ideas about how research is typically conducted. By the time students enter college, noticeable differences in scientific skills and aptitudes are evident. At the collegiate level, the chief goals of research methods instruction are to fill in gaps, correct mistaken ideas, foster critical-thinking abilities, and connect scientific questions with solution paths. Taken together, this will serve to broaden the student's base of thinking about the workings of the investigative process.

Perhaps the most readily thought of source of instructional support is classroom instruction. Those reading this book will probably have completed at least one course in research methods and a second in introductory statistics. Both of these courses will help to lay the groundwork for acquisition of a detailed psychological research script. Those who have taken research methods at the graduate level are likely to have gone well beyond this basic stage of knowledge acquisition. At the graduate level, students have undoubtedly read journal articles that focus on specific methodological paradigms, and they have been privy to stimulating discussions about the philosophy of science. Methods courses at this level of education go well beyond fact building to forge deep conceptual linkages that cut across designs, empirical objectives, and sometimes even academic disciplines.

Numerous additional sources of learning about the research process can be found beyond the classroom. One source of learning is from role models, such as an instructor, advisor, or peer. By observing the research practices of others, we can discover much about the specifics of the process, such as how to properly debrief a participant or how to make an effective brown-bag presentation. It can be particularly beneficial to talk with more advanced investigators about the obstacles and opportunities associated with the research process. A second source of learning beyond the classroom involves hands-on research experiences. This may involve working in an established psychological laboratory or testing a research idea of your own. From a learning perspective, working in an academic lab can be a uniquely valuable experience because research activities are often well structured and clearly defined. Lab manuals are sometimes provided that describe critical project-related tasks and responsibilities and give the student a big picture of where the research program has come from and where it's headed. One other valuable source of learning about the research process comes from observing formal presentations made by one's peers in a research methods course or by professionals at a colloquium or a regional or national psychological conference. By fostering an interest in a wide range of research topics, you increase your breadth of knowledge, not only about the field but also about the variety of methods and procedures that are available to you as an investigator.

Most undergraduate psychology programs and the apprenticeship model of research training at the graduate level have been designed and refined over the years to facilitate the acquisition of the research script. From an instructional design perspective, cognitive learning objectives are typically *scaffolded* (i.e., sequentially ordered into what educational psychologists refer to as *zones of proximal development*) so as to build on themselves (Goldman, Petrosino, & Cognition and Technology Group at Vanderbilt, 1999; Samaras & Shelly, 1998). The goal of this progressive set of learning experiences is to ensure that one acquires the competence to conduct independent research by the time graduate school is completed.

In most cases, the uninitiated freshman psychology major transitions into a skilled and proficient researcher over a 7- to 10-year period. To maximize the success of this training objective, specific procedures associated with clearly defined research tasks are presented at precisely the right time in the student's cognitive development (Kester, Kirschner, van Merrienboer, & Baumer, 2001). Provision of this procedural information, coupled with supportive assistance during the student's practice of the new skill, appears to lead to the most efficient learning (Kester, Kirschner, & van Merrienboer, 2004). A fading process is built into the educational experience in order to facilitate this transition toward independence. This means that many sources of instructional support (e.g., formal course work) are gradually phased out over time (Merrienboer, Kirschner, & Kester, 2003) in favor of more individualized types of research experiences. Consequently, sources of learning about the research process normally change or shift in import as the student progresses through an extended program of studies.

Experience and Script Development

As the old story goes, a New York City tourist asked the violin virtuoso, "How do you get to Carnegie Hall?"

"Practice, my good man, practice!" he was advised.

The story may be corny, but the take-away message is clear: The skill acquisition process is rarely, if ever, easy. In most real-world problem-solving domains, practice is the key to learning a complex set of procedures, based in large part on the principle of learning by doing (Anzai & Simon, 1979). Moreover, the constructivist learning perspective suggests that individuals' schemata are built-up through the process of induction (Merrienboer et al., 2002), which in the psychological research context suggests students cull general lessons from the range of different problems they encounter. "Mindful abstraction" of the salient elements of different psychological studies results in the differentiation of one's research scripts. This, in turn, leads to the formation of specialized scripts, each with its own unique triggering conditions and application. Also, with practice, elements of scripts that occur frequently with one another become bundled into a unit, or compiled, so that they may be efficiently retrieved from long-term memory as a set (Anderson, 1996; Anderson & Lebiere, 1998). Moreover, repetitive application of a particular script leads to the strengthening of a procedural representation, thus increasing the probability that script will be appropriately applied in the future.

Any discussion of the role of experience in acquiring the research script would be incomplete without also discussing the importance of performance feedback. Feedback, whether it comes from an instructor, peers, or perhaps a review panel, can help shape individuals' thinking about the research process. Constructive criticism, in particular, can sometimes broaden, other times fine-tune, or fill in gaps in one's mental model of the scientific method. At this stage, however, two problems may arise. First, sometimes feedback is destructively offered; and second, performance feedback in psychology is often delayed. This can make it difficult to evaluate the quality of one's project-related decisions when one is immersed in the research process. The difficulties associated with making the right decisions when designing (and for that matter, carrying out) psychological investigations have been referred to by Jung (1971, 1982) as the experimenter's dilemma. Fortunately, acquiring expertise in the scientific process will help one meet the challenges that we all face as researchers.

The Development of Expertise

Early in this chapter, an expert script of the research process was introduced, although relatively little was said at that point about what it means to be an expert from an information-processing perspective. What *does* it mean to be an expert? There seems to be no debate on one key point: that experts possess a larger declarative knowledge base than novices and that they perceive and represent problems in their domain at a deeper (more principled) level (Glaser & Chi, 1988; Goldman et al., 1999). Moreover, relative to novices, experts have the ability to think creatively (Holyoak, 1991). This flexibly in thinking benefits experienced researchers in two different ways: It allows them to construct and apply new scripts as needed (Merrienboer et al., 2002), and it allows them to adjust existing problem-solving strategies to adapt to the unique demands of the situation (Dennis & Sternberg, 1999; Hatano & Inagaki, 1986).

Not only do experts process information differently than novices when solving a problem, but there is evidence that they learn differently as well. In an investigation of the development of skilled nursing abilities, Daley (1999) found that novices prefer more passive approaches to learning (e.g., learning from textbooks and lectures). Experts, in contrast, were more likely to engage in self-initiated learning approaches (e.g., making direct contact with other experts, actively seeking out information at conferences). Moreover, Daley found novices spent a great deal of time forming new concepts and assimilating information into their existing schemata. Experts, in contrast, spent time forging "blueprints in their minds" of what it would take to solve qualitatively different types of problems. Consistent with this observation, Scardamalia and Bereiter (1991) concluded that experts use a knowledge-building schema that lends itself to provisional interpretations, open-mindedness, and to the active pursuit of fuller understanding. This helps to explain why, when planning and designing psychological investigations, expert researchers are able to see subtleties across methodologies not perceived by novices.

By all accounts, the development of expertise in the psychological research arena is not something that comes quickly. Contemporary views of expertise suggest that the learning process is nonmonotonic with respect to time. That is, as individuals' knowledge structures grow and change, they pass through a series of qualitatively different developmental stages, each characterized by different skills and abilities (cf., Patel & Groen, 1991; Holyoak, 1991).

CONCLUSION

In this chapter, we presented the psychological research methods script and its specific components. Our goal was to characterize the research process as a coherent and coordinated set of activities. Ideally, you will have read this chapter and completed the accompanying exercises before exploring other parts of this handbook, as it was designed to lay a foundation for the sections that follow.

Any psychologist-in-training who is reading this handbook is already well on the way to becoming a skilled researcher. As you develop your investigative skills, we trust you will find the research process provides excitement, challenges, and intellectual rewards. By way of closing, we encourage you to reflect on the changing nature of your research scripts as they grow and expand over the years. Doing so will not only provide you with an appreciation of milestones in your own development but, at the same time, provide insights into where your scientific thinking may lead.

EXERCISES

1. Write at the top of a blank sheet of paper *Get Idea for Project,* and at the bottom write the words *Publish Paper.* Then list as many activities involved in the research process as you can think of that occur between these anchors, placing them in what you believe to be the correct serial order. Make this list now, before reading further.

Next, reflect on the nature of your mental representation of the research process. Can you group events in your research methods script into general categories, in much the same way the flowcharts in this chapter are organized? Are all superordinate events in the process (e.g., design, data collection) represented in your script? Compare your research methods script with the empirically derived expert script presented in Table 1.1. Are there differences in the ordering of the scripts? Do the scripts differ in terms of their level of specificity?

2. Look through the previous pages of this chapter and write down 20 or so research script events on separate slips of paper. Fold the slips and place them in a bowl or hat, shake, then withdraw them one at a time at random. For each event, write down the event in the research methods script that immediately precedes it and the event that follows. Check your answers against the structural script presented in the five flow diagrams. Compared with the serially ordered script generation task in Exercise 1, did you find it easier or more difficult to generate elements of the script when they were taken out of order?

Next, reflect on *why* it is important for the earlier event to precede the event drawn from the hat, and why it is important for the later event to follow.

3. Visit with colleagues, professors, or researchers in your field to discuss the idea of research as a form of scripted knowledge. Informally interview the individual to discover elements of his or her research script. Ask the person to describe the activities a researcher goes through for one or more of the higher-level event sequences, such as data analysis or communication of findings. For instance, one might ask, "What have you found takes place during the data analysis phase of research? What do you do first, and what goals are you trying to accomplish?" Notice the extent to which there are commonalities across individuals in terms of the big-picture dimensions of the script and how differences begin to emerge when it comes to specifying the individual elements that make up those major dimensions.

RECOMMENDED READINGS

A variety of both basic and advanced readings on the research methods process can be found in the literature. For a more detailed discussion of the research methods script, see Hershey et al. (1996) and Wilson and Hershey (1996). A classic and lucid discussion of the procedural aspects of the research process can also be found in Runkel and McGrath (1972). Theirs is a cyclic model of the research process, which includes a number of major steps that overlap with those outlined in this chapter. Moreover, good basic coverage of many elements of the psychological research process can be found in most undergraduate level, experimental-methods textbooks. At the more technical end of the spectrum, Kirk's text, titled *Experimental Design* (1994) provides an excellent treatment of the topic, as does Maxwell and Delaney's book, titled *Designing Experiments and Analyzing Data* (2004). In contrast, a highly readable introduction to the research process is found in the text *Research Methods in Psychology* (2002) by Elmes, Kantowitz, and Roediger. The book *Experimental and Quasi-Experimental Designs for Research* by Campbell and Stanley (1963) is considered by many to be a classic primer on research design, still well worth reading in spite of its age. An updated version of many of the key ideas outlined in Cambell and Stanley (1963) can be found in a recent book by Shadish, Cook, & Campbell (2002). And finally, an advanced treatment of validity in designing and conducting social science experiments is contained in an edited volume by Bickman (2000).

In addition to the readings on the topic of research methods listed above, numerous informative Web sites exist. Four of the better sites include Web Center for Social Research Methods, hosted by Cornell University (www.socialresearchmethods.net); Centre for Psychology Resources, maintained by Athabasca University (psych.athabascau.ca/html/aupr/tools.shtml); Research Methods Resources on the WWW, hosted by the University of British Columbia (www.slais.ubc.ca/resources/research_methods/measurem.htm); and for a first-rate statistical site, visit www.statistics.com.

REFERENCES

Abelson, R. P. (1975). Concepts for representing mundane reality in plans. In D. G. Bobrow & A. C. Collins (Eds.), *Representation and understanding: Studies in cognitive science* (pp. 273–309). New York: Academic.

Abelson, R. P. (1981). Psychological status of the script concept. *American Psychologist, 36,* 715–729.

Anderson, J. R. (1996). ACT: A simple theory of complex cognition. *American Psychologist, 51,* 355–365.

Anderson, J. R., & Lebiere, C. (1998). *The atomic components of thought.* Mahwah, NJ: Lawrence Erlbaum.

Anzai, Y., & Simon, H. A. (1979). The theory of learning by doing. *Psychological Review, 86,* 124–140.

Bickman, L. (Ed.). (2000). *Validity and social experimentation: Donald Campbell's legacy.* Thousand Oaks, CA: Sage.

Bower, G. H., Black, J. B., & Turner, T. J. (1979). Scripts in memory for text. *Cognitive Psychology, 11,* 177–220.

Campbell, D. T., & Stanley, J. C. (1963). *Experimental and quasi-experimental designs for research.* Boston: Houghton Mifflin.

Daley, B. J. (1999). Novice to expert: An exploration of how professionals learn. *Adult Education Quarterly, 49,* 133–147.

Dennis, M. J., & Sternberg, R. J. (1999). Cognition and instruction. In F. T. Durso, R. S. Nickerson, R. W. Schavndveldt, S. T. Dumais, D. S. Lindsay, & M. T. H. Chi (Eds.), *Handbook of applied cognition* (pp. 571–593). New York: Wiley.

Elmes, D. G., Kantowitz, B. H., & Roediger, H. L. III. (2002). *Research methods in psychology* (7th ed.). Belmont, CA: Wadsworth.

Ericsson, K. A., & Smith, J. (2002). Prospects and limits of the empirical study of expertise: An introduction. In D. J. Levitin (Ed.), *Foundations of cognitive psychology: Core readings* (pp. 517–550). Cambridge: MIT Press.

Galambos, J. A. (1986). Knowledge structures for common activities. In J. A. Galambos, R. P. Abelson, & J. B. Black (Eds.), *Knowledge structures* (pp. 21–47). Hillsdale, NJ: Lawrence Erlbaum.

Glaser, R., & Chi, M. T. H. (1988). Overview. In M. T. H. Chi, R. Glaser, & M. J. Farr (Eds.), *The nature of expertise* (pp. xv–xxviii). Hillsdale, NJ: Lawrence Erlbaum.

Goldman, S. R., Petrosino, A. J., & Cognition and Technology Group at Vanderbilt (1999). Design principles for instruction in content domains: Lessons from research on expertise and learning. In F. T. Durso, R. S. Nickerson, R. W. Schavndveldt, S. T. Dumais, D. S. Lindsay, and M. T. H. Chi (Eds.), *Handbook of applied cognition* (pp. 595–627). New York: Wiley.

Hatano, G., & Inagaki, K. (1986). Two courses of expertise. In H. Stevenson, H. Azuma, & K. Hakuta (Eds.), *Child development and education in Japan* (pp. 262–272). New York: Freeman.

Hershey, D. A., Jacobs-Lawson, J. M., & Walsh, D. A. (2003). Influences of age and training on script development. *Aging, Neuropsychology, and Cognition, 10,* 1–19.

Hershey, D. A. & Walsh, D. A. (2000/2001). Knowledge versus experience in financial problem-solving performance. *Current Psychology, 19,* 261–291.

Hershey, D. A., Wilson, T. L., & Mitchell-Copeland, J. M. (1996). Conceptions of the psychological research process: Script variation as a function of training and experience. *Current Psychology: Developmental, Learning, Personality, Social, 14,* 293–312.

Holyoak, K. J. (1991). Symbolic connectionism: Toward third-generation theories of expertise. In K. A. Ericsson & J. Smith (Eds.), *Toward a general theory of expertise* (pp. 301–335). New York: Cambridge University Press.

Hunt, E. (1991). Some comments on the study of complexity. In R. J. Sternberg & P. A. Frensch (Eds.), *Complex problem solving: Principles and mechanisms* (pp. 383–395). Hillsdale, NJ: Lawrence Erlbaum.

Jung. J. (1971). *The experimenter's dilemma.* New York: Harper & Row.

Jung, J. (1982). *The experimenter's challenge: Methods and issues in psychological research.* New York: Macmillan.

Kester, L., Kirschner, P. A., & van Merrienboer, J. J. G. (2004). Timing of information presentation in learning statistics *Instructional Science, 32,* 233–252.

Kester, L., Kirschner, P. A., van Merrienboer, J. J. G., & Baumer, A. (2001). Just-in-time information presentation in the acquisition of complex cognitive skills. *Computers in Human Behavior, 17,* 373–391.

Kirk, R. E. (1994). *Experimental design: Procedures for behavioral sciences.* Belmont, CA: Wadsworth.

Light, L. L., & Anderson, P. A. (1983). Memory for scripts in young and older adults. *Memory and Cognition, 11,* 435–444.

Maxwell, S. E., & Delaney, H. D. (2004). *Designing experiments and analyzing data: A model comparison approach* (2nd ed.). Mahwah, NJ: Lawrence Erlbaum.

Merrienboer, J. J. G., Clark, R. E., & Croock, M. B. M. (2002). Blueprints for complex learning: The 4C/ID-Model. *Educational Technology, Research & Development, 50,* 39–64.

Merrienboer, J. J. G., Kirschner, P. A., & Kester, L. (2003). Taking the load off a learner's mind: Instructional design for complex learning. *Educational Psychologist, 38,* 5–13.

Newell, A., & Simon, H. A. (1972). *Human problem solving.* Englewood Cliffs, NJ: Prentice Hall.

Patel, V. L., & Groen, G. J. (1991). The general and specific nature of medical expertise: A critical look. In K. A. Ericsson & J. Smith (Eds.), *Toward a general theory of expertise* (pp. 93–125). New York: Cambridge University Press.

Runkel, P. J., & McGrath, J. E. (1972). *Research on human behavior: A systematic guide to methods.* New York: Holt, Rinehart & Winston.

Samaras, A. P., & Shelly, G. (1998). Scaffolds in the field: Vygotskian interpretation in a teacher education program. *Teaching and Teacher Education, 14,* 715–733.

Scardamalia, M. U., & Bereiter, C. (1999). Literate expertise. In K. A. Ericsson & J. Smith (Eds.), *Toward a general theory of expertise: Prospects and limits* (pp. 172–194). New York: Cambridge University Press.

Schank, R. C., & Abelson, R. P. (1977). *Scripts, plans, goals, and understanding.* Hillsdale, NJ: Lawrence Erlbaum.

Shadish, W. R., Cook, T. D., & Campbell, D. T. (2002). *Experimental and quasi-experimental designs for generalized causal inference.* Boston: Houghton Mifflin.

Wilson, T. L., & Hershey, D. A. (1996). The research methods script. *Teaching of Psychology, 23,* 97–99. Reprinted in M. E. Ware & C. L. Brewer (Eds.), *Handbook for teaching statistics and research methods* (2nd ed., pp. 193–196). Mahwah, NJ: Lawrence Erlbaum.

2

FINDING A RESEARCH TOPIC

FREDERICK T. L. LEONG

DOUGLAS J. MUCCIO

The basic premise of this book is that conducting psychological research, as a novice or as an expert, is guided by a series of cognitive scripts. Based on the editors' concept of research as cognitive script, we present the procedures that one can use to find an appropriate research topic using this framework. In the Introduction to this volume, the editors argue that skill acquisition is dependent on the building of these scripts through practice. In a linear research project, finding a topic is the first basic script. Other scripts for subsequent stages in the research process include choosing a research design, selecting research instruments, applying sampling procedures, and conducting data analyses. The skill of finding a research topic is developed by experience, but learning about how others find topics is also helpful. The purpose of this chapter is to illuminate the components of the "finding a research topic" script for less-experienced researchers by using examples of how other psychologists find topics for study.

What does and does not interest each of us is the result of a combination of different factors that vocational psychologists have been researching a long time (e.g., see Osipow & Fitzgerald, 1996). In some sense, finding a research topic is a matter of personal interest and preference in the same way that music and food preferences are personal matters. Given individual differences in what constitutes an interesting topic for research, the best approach to providing guidance on the process of finding a research topic would be to use the "menu approach." Using the food metaphor again, if there are significant individual differences in which types of foods are interesting and appealing, then a restaurant with a diverse menu of foods cooked in many different ways would be most likely to satisfy the most individuals. In the same way, different individuals will exhibit a wide variety of preferences in how they find research topics that are of interest to them. Such an approach also takes into account the reader's different learning and cognitive styles (e.g., see Pintrich & Johnson, 1990). Therefore, we will offer in this chapter a whole series of different strategies for finding research topics.

Despite individual differences in preferences for research strategies, we strongly recommend that the reader make use of multiple strategies rather than just rely on one preferred strategy. As Einstein once said, "Chance favors the prepared mind." The best way to find an interesting and important research topic is to be prepared to consider a wide range of options, at least at the beginning of the search process. The initial stage of finding a research topic is really a multifaceted process requiring openness to new ideas and problems rather than simply reprocessing well-developed research topics. Art Fry,

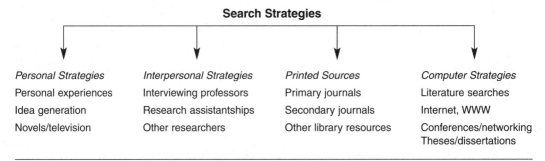

Figure 2.1   Search Strategies for Finding a Research Topic

the inventor of 3M's ubiquitous Post-it note, came upon his brilliant idea when he was able (and open) to link the nonbinding glue discovered by a junior colleague and the bookmarks that kept falling out of his church hymnals. The rest, as they say, is history.

Another reason to use multiple strategies for finding a topic is time urgency. Time urgency is a factor in many research projects. From the master's thesis to the first six publications as an assistant professor, a person usually experiences some urgency when attempting to find an exciting and feasible research topic that would also make a significant contribution to her or his field. Often, using a problem-focused approach helps us identify certain problems that are of interest and relevance to us. For example, if one were to have a close friend or relative who suffers from depression, then one might be interested in researching depression as a major mental health problem. Yet, having identified depression as a problem to be researched, there are many different directions to which one's attention could be focused. A multiple-strategy approach would aid in deciding which direction to take. The rest of this chapter will present multiple strategies for finding a specific research topic.

Finding a research topic can be broken down into two stages: search strategies and narrowing and refining the topic. Some authors have referred to this first stage as identifying the general area in which you want to do research (Cone & Foster, 1993). According to our current scheme, the first stage is finding a topic area. There are four general categories of search strategies: (a) personal, (b) interpersonal, (c) printed sources, and (d) computer resources

(See Figure 2.1). We will discuss each of these categories of strategies in turn.

SEARCH STRATEGIES

Personal Strategies

Personal experience and observation are sources of general research topics that are readily accessible to everyone. Many psychologists study the forms of human behavior that have become meaningful to them through their personal experience. For example, an African American social psychologist may be more apt to select research topics that clarify the processes of racial stereotyping than a European American social psychologist. A clinical psychologist who has lived abroad may be more prone to examine the cross-cultural differences in manifestations of schizophrenia. Another psychologist who grew up as an only child may become curious as to how personality develops when there is one child in a family versus multiple children in a family.

Personal observation can lead to new insights as well. A psychologist who has the opportunity to observe human behavior over long periods of time will have many chances to recognize possible research topics. For example, a counselor who notices that children of alcoholic parents have shorter attention spans may want to explore this relationship to determine if it is genetically or environmentally based. Obviously, you do not need to be a fully trained psychologist in order to take advantage of your personal observations as a source of ideas for research. By attending to your observations and writing them down, you too can generate research topics almost without effort. Research ideas can come from such personal experiences as noticing how your family members cope with illnesses or how sibling rivalry varies across the families of people you know. Or, you might become intrigued with group dynamics after watching the classic Henry Fonda movie, *Twelve Angry Men,* in which one person was able to sway the decision-making process of a jury.

Creativity in idea generation, the second personal search strategy, is helpful for finding a research topic when an assignment is very broad or when other strategies are not working. One way to generate creative ideas is by brainstorming. This general process of idea generation starts by writing down all topics that come to mind, independent of an immediate judgment of each idea's worth. Only after a substantial list of ideas has been produced should you allow yourself to eliminate an idea. The process of elimination should edit all ideas that are implausible or cannot be adequately addressed within the confines of the research at hand. If you have an assignment to write about the development of children, write down all ideas you have about the processes by which children develop or the types of behaviors children display as they mature. When you are satisfied with your list, examine the feasibility of each idea, the availability of research in the area, and your motivation to stick with each topic. By eliminating ideas in this way, you will choose a topic that is plausible and enjoyable.

Another creative strategy for idea generation is to use the "Martian perspective" as a cognitive device. By asking yourself to imagine how a Martian, who just landed on Earth, would view a particular problem or a particular situation, you may uncover interesting topics not considered by others. For example, if we adopted this Martian perspective, it would become quite evident that our fascination with automobiles in this country goes beyond an interest in cars merely as a form of transportation. Further, as Martians, we may notice that many earthlings prefer to solve conflicts by harming others physically or materialistically rather than attempting to deal with the underlying issues that generated the dispute. Using this type of exploration, we may be able to discover an area that greatly interests us and which has not yet been fully explored in psychology.

Reading novels, listening to the radio, or watching television can also lead to research topics. These sources of information reveal problems that may need research to aid in their resolution. For example, when the news tells us of the plight of servicemen and women as they adjust to civilian life after returning from an armed conflict, a person may realize that what is currently known in the area of post-traumatic stress disorder (PTSD) is not sufficient for providing a full explanation of their adjustment problems. After hearing a newscast, a student who is interested in clinical psychology may want to research in more detail the real and imagined barriers these people have when adjusting to civilian life. The key aim of the personal search strategy is to be aware of and analyze your personal experiences in order to identify unanswered questions.

Interpersonal Strategies

Other people are also good sources of ideas for research topics. One good source is a college professor. We suggest that you view your professors as resource persons and use a series of strategies to tap their knowledge and expertise. An interview with a professor who works in your general interest area regarding his or her current research can be very helpful. Most college professors are knowledgeable of discrepancies in research findings and gaps in the current literature that can be explored. Taking a course with a particular professor is another way to find out about possible research topics. Either during or after the course, you may ask the professor to recommend important articles to read for a comprehensive review of your potential research area. The type of course you choose could range from a commonly offered, formal course or one that is directed specifically to your interests or needs. One type of directed study is the specialized reading course, which may be available to most advanced undergraduate and graduate students. Reading courses provide an opportunity to be personally supervised in a particular topic area in which a professor specializes. Another way to use a professor as a resource is to ask a professor to share some of his or her reprints with you in order to learn more about that professor's research (Cone & Foster, 1993).

After reading a professor's reprints or speaking with a professor, you might discuss the possibility of becoming a research assistant for that professor. Research assistantships are very good sources of research topics. As a research assistant, you may become aware of current research topics and be able to make useful contributions to the literature by extending the research of the professor with whom you are working. Through assistantships, you may become immersed in a particular literature that may help you find areas of research that are congruent with your interests and need further exploration. The research assistantship experience not only affords you the opportunity to become familiar with a professor's research project, it may also provide a chance to develop your own research topic if you are able to creatively extend your professor's research to another level or problem. For example, you may be helping a professor with a project aimed at identifying the family dynamics associated with drug abuse. Having become familiar with that project, you might be able to explore potential racial or ethnic and gender differences in the relationships found by your professor.

Besides college and university professors, other active researchers can also serve as sources of research ideas. Applied researchers may be able to describe important problems that require research. For example, applied researchers may tell you their opinion regarding the public's current attitudes toward AIDS. You may decide to follow up this idea by studying how attitude change toward the HIV virus may reduce discriminatory actions taken against people diagnosed with HIV. Researchers can also be found in business settings. For example, researchers for insurance companies may examine how people react to risk factors or attempt to determine the personality characteristics of individuals who would make good insurance salespeople. Federal and state governments also support a wide range of researchers. These researchers deal with topics such as public health and voting behavior. Telephone or personal interviews with researchers outside your university may provide you with additional research topics.

Two other useful strategies for finding research topics are attending conferences and networking. Presentations and poster sessions at conferences can expose you to the wide range of ideas currently being explored by a discipline. Listening and reading about the ideas developed by others may lead you to a research topic. Combining others' research with your own ideas and extending their research into a new area are effective strategies for developing ideas and finding a research topic. Networking at conferences or getting to know professors and students within your institution is also a helpful search strategy. Listening to others' ideas and current areas of interest is a way to broaden your views and scope of ideas. Networking is a way to become acquainted with others who have similar research interests and may be helpful for suggesting possible areas of research.

Printed Sources

Printed sources are also beneficial for generating research ideas. The most immediately available and relevant sources of research topics are primary scientific journals. Browsing through recent issues of these journals may reveal topics of current concern. Briefly read the table of contents and abstracts of the articles found in three or four consecutive years of a relevant journal. To determine the most relevant scientific journal to examine, first decide the area in which you are most interested, then find a highly regarded journal in that area of psychology. For example, to find ideas about counseling, choose the *Journal of Counseling Psychology;* for industrial and organizational psychology, look at the *Journal of Applied Psychology;* for social psychology, scan the *Journal of Personality and Social Psychology.*

Those who cannot decide which area of psychology interests them may wish to consult *Journals in Psychology* (American Psychological Association [APA], 1993). This publication lists many of the leading journals in psychology (more than 360 in the fourth edition, 1993) and provides a brief summary of their editorial policies (i.e., what types of articles are appropriate and what topics are covered by the journal). This publication also provides a very useful classified index that allows readers to identify journals in different subject areas (e.g., *consulting/clinical, criminal and legal issues,* and *developmental*) as well as subtopics (e.g., *health psychology* under *consulting/clinical* and *aging* under *developmental*). Browsing through this publication may help you select journals to review in more detail for research topics.

Another approach to reviewing primary scientific journals may be to scan the specialized abstracting periodicals offered by the APA. As a service to busy researchers and clinicians, the APA has produced periodicals that reproduce the table of contents from a collection of journals that are clustered around a particular theme. For example, there is one on clinical psychology, one on applied psychology, and one on psychoanalysis. These periodicals are produced on regular intervals and provide a quick and convenient way to get a general view of the research being conducted in a particular area. Similar resources such as "Current Contents" are published by other organizations and may be available in your university library as well. The reader should consult the chapter by Reed and Baxter (this handbook) for further details on these library resources, or their book (Reed & Baxter, 2003).

Primary journal sources come in two types. We have been discussing primary scientific journals as a source of research ideas. Another valuable source of ideas is primary clinical journals. There are many journals that publish clinical information such as case discussions and formulations that can be useful for generating research ideas. For example, there was an article in one of these journals that described several cases in which male patients had rather unusual sexual phobias (Beit-Hallahmi, 1985). Specifically, these men had a fear that women's vaginas had teeth (i.e., *vagina dentata*) and that they would be severely injured if they were to have a sexual relationship with a woman. According to psychoanalytic theory, *vagina dentata* (or the fantasy of a vagina with teeth) symbolizes men's castration anxiety (Eidelberg, 1968). Whether or not one believes in Freud's concept of castration anxiety, this particular example serves as a good illustration of how clinically oriented journals contain many interesting human problems and can serve as a valuable resource for research ideas that should not be overlooked.

Secondary sources consist of materials that summarize primary source materials for dissemination to other readers. One example of a type of secondary source is textbooks. When conducting research, it is often best to consult primary sources for information about the finding of studies on your research topic and how these studies were conducted. Secondary sources, such as introductory textbooks and specialized texts, however, are valuable sources of ideas for research topics as well. They are especially helpful if you know little about your topic area. For example, if you are given a broad topic area to choose from, "any topic in cognitive psychology," a good place to start to get a general idea of what topics are covered in cognitive psychology would be the table of contents of a cognitive psychology textbook. The summary sections within specialized textbooks are also useful for generating research topics because they give you a quick overview of the issues and challenges currently facing a particular research area.

After examining the chapters that are of interest to you in a text book and eliminating those which are not, look at the studies and topic areas within each chapter to determine those you would like to explore in more detail. Finding the studies that have been cited by that chapter may quickly reveal whether or not that topic area will be interesting to look at in depth. Specialized texts, such as the *Annual Review of Psychology,* are also helpful because they review a topic area and point out areas that could benefit from further research. These texts also cite studies that are considered classics in the field and may provide necessary background information for your research. Other types of specialized texts that provide general yet useful overviews of topics are the various handbooks and encyclopedias that are available in libraries. These handbooks and encyclopedias are excellent places to start to browse in order to quickly find out about all the different topics within a specific field (e.g. Eidelberg's *Encyclopedia of Psychoanalysis*).

Besides introductory textbooks and specialized or professional texts, there are other sets of materials that serve as valuable secondary sources of information. These include technical reports, white papers (called consensus papers at the National Institutes of Health) and conference proceedings. Many of these special reports, which can be found in the federal government depositories sections of university libraries, are underutilized sources of research ideas. These reports, like primary scientific journals, contain cutting-edge materials in many different areas of psychology. They give the reader an added advantage by being in a summary form that can be readily reviewed. For example, the publication titled "Special Report: Schizophrenia 1993" (National Institute of Mental Health, 1993) summarizes the cutting-edge research being conducted on schizophrenia. It summarizes in 90 pages what might take an individual schizophrenia researcher years of reading and reviewing. A similar source of information and overview of behavioral medicine is provided by the report, "New Research Frontiers in Behavioral Medicine: Proceedings From the National Conference" (National Institute of Mental Health, 1994).

Beyond primary and secondary sources of research, theses and dissertations are useful for finding ideas. Theses and dissertations are somewhat unusual because they are not published scientific studies, yet are widely available. These sources are especially helpful to students who are in the process of determining a research topic for a thesis or dissertation or some other type of research. By examining theses and dissertations that have been written by other students, you may get an idea of the breadth and depth of the topics usually explored by these kinds of research. Also, many of these theses and dissertations contain a literature review chapter that contains useful ideas for future research. As a detailed review of a particular area of psychology, these literature reviews often contain much more in-depth information about various studies than those found in the introduction sections of journal articles, which are necessarily brief. Most university libraries will serve as a depository for all the theses and dissertations that have been completed at that university. You could also search the *Dissertations Abstracts International,* which is a serial abstracting of many of the dissertations completed in the United States annually.

Another printed source of research ideas is print media, such as newspapers and magazines. Many newspapers now carry articles about various aspects of psychology and psychological research. For example, *USA Today* printed a summary of the first author's research study

(Leong & Schneller, 1993, showing a relationship between boredom proneness and dogmatic styles of coping) within their "Lifestyle" section. The article included some implications of how to deal with boredom in the workplace. Although these sources do not provide sufficient depth of coverage to properly evaluate the nature of a study, they can point to interesting investigations that can be followed up by tracking down the primary sources. This would be especially true for magazines that have a strong psychological emphasis such as *Psychology Today* or *Skeptical Inquirer.* Therefore, browsing through newspapers and magazines can serve as an additional source of ideas for potential research topics.

Computer Strategies

The final category of search strategies consists of using computer resources. No matter how creative we are or how knowledgeable our consultants are, personal and interpersonal search strategies can never match the computer in terms of memory, comprehensiveness, and speed. We are referring to the computer databases that can be searched for various topics by entering particular key words (see the Reed & Baxter chapter in this volume). Within the field of psychology, the primary computer database is the PsycLit database produced by the APA.

Like other indexing systems, the PsycLit database started out as a paper medium in which selected journals in psychology were abstracted, indexed, and published beginning in 1927 as a library periodical entitled *Psychological Abstracts.* With the increasing availability of personal computers and CD-ROM drives, the PsycLit database was eventually developed as a more efficient computerized version of *Psychological Abstracts.* The PsycLit database is available in most university libraries either in the CD-ROM version or via a telephone dial-up connection (e.g., DIALOG).

When trying to identify a research topic in psychology, it is useful to begin with the PsycLit database, but you should not limit your search to only one database because each is limited to a selected set of journals. Articles on the particular topic you are most interested in may be in a journal that is not indexed by a specific database. The other mainstream databases that are useful for psychological research include ERIC (educational journals), Medline (medical and health sciences journals), and Sociological Abstracts (sociology journals). For example, if you were interested in exploring a topic in behavioral medicine, a search of both the PsycLit and the Medline database would give you a much more comprehensive set of studies than would be provided by just one database.

Besides the mainstream databases that are available in most university libraries, there are other specialized databases you should know about. It would not be possible for us to list all of these specialized databases, however, because there are so many of them and because they are not widely available. It is important for you to realize that there are other specialized databases available and that you should check in your university library or computing center to determine if there are alternative databases related to your topic, in addition to the mainstream databases. Other examples of specialized databases include one on alcoholism and drug abuse maintained by Dartmouth Medical School and one on the Myers-Briggs Type Indicator (i.e., a personality instrument based on Carl Jung's theory) maintained by the Center for Applications of Psychological Type in Gainesville, Florida.

Another helpful database is the Social Science Citation Index (SSCI). Although it is a widely available database, it is quite different from others and provides a separate advantage. Instead of indexing specific articles, the SSCI indexes the citations of specific articles. For example, if you were interested in Bandura's theory of self-efficacy, you could use the SSCI database to identify all the different studies that have cited Bandura's original presentation of his model in *Psychological Review.* Alternatively, if you were interested in what studies Bandura used to formulate his model, you could use the SSCI to find all the references cited in Bandura's *Psychology Review* article. The disadvantage of the SSCI is that the computerized version is quite expensive and only available in selected university libraries. The paper version of the SSCI in the form of a periodical is available in a larger number of libraries, but it does not have the advantages of a computerized database.

With any computerized database, it is usually best to begin with the thesaurus or manual that comes with the database. The thesaurus or manual will tell you which journals are abstracted in that particular database as well as the terms used to index those journals. It is quite important to use correct terms when searching for a topic because the use of unacceptable terms may result in a lower than expected output from the search. For example, if you were interested in the topic of *career goals* and searched the PsycLit (1990–1995) using those terms, you may end up with very few articles and conclude that there has not been a great deal of research on that topic during the last 5 years. On the other hand, if you had consulted the *Thesaurus of Psychological Index Terms* (APA, 1994), you would have discovered that the acceptable term in PsycLit is *occupational aspirations.* Using those acceptable terms, you would have found that there were 207 studies on the topic of *occupational aspirations* between 1990 and 1995 instead of the 38 studies found using the term *career goals.* Therefore, it is highly advisable to spend some time with the thesaurus or manual of a particular database planning your search and using the correct search terms.

Furthermore, the thesaurus or manual also serves another valuable function, namely as a stimulus for new ideas. In reviewing the thesaurus, one could examine the various concepts and constructs within psychology and begin cross-classifying different variables to check out potential research questions. For example, in browsing through the thesaurus, having found that *occupational aspirations* is the correct term to use in the PsycLit database, one may stumble on the interesting concept of psychological androgyny and wonder if there might be a relationship between psychological androgyny and occupational aspirations: Do androgynous women have different occupational aspirations than feminine women? Armed with these different concepts and search terms, one can then begin searching for studies that have examined these questions.

In addition to these computerized databases, the computer can also be a useful strategy for finding research topics through another avenue, namely the Internet. There is a series of guidebooks on the Internet (i.e., Wiggins, 1995). A large part of the Internet is its collection of news groups and electronic discussion groups. There are many of these groups that one can tap into as a source of research ideas. For example, if one were interested in ethnic identity among Asian Americans, one could log onto the Soc.Culture.Asian.American newsgroup and find out about some of the issues facing Asian American youths and young adults (e.g., pros and cons of interracial dating and how much to Americanize and become a "Banana"—yellow on the outside and White on the inside). Alternatively, if one were interested in John Bowlby's theory of attachment, one could subscribe to a special discussion group that addresses the clinical and research implications of attachment theory. Another example is the HRNet (Human Resources) maintained by the Academy of Management. It is quite a common practice for persons belonging to these news and discussion groups to post messages asking for help with different problems or questions. For example, someone may post a message asking if anyone on the network knows of a particular scale to measure ethnic identity. Others may post messages asking for help in identifying articles related to specific topics.

Another recent development within the Internet is the World Wide Web (WWW), which is a collection of multimedia sites that are linked together via hypertext for easy access. Hypertext is based on a special computer language (hypertext markup language, HTML), which allows users to jump from one information source directly into another simply by clicking on specially designated text. One could use the WWW to access different psychology department home pages to check out what different faculty members are researching, or one could log onto the National Institute of Mental Health's home page to find out what types of research grants are available. Many of these sites have reports that can be downloaded and read or printed on your computer. For example, there is a Federal Glass Ceiling Commission maintained by Cornell University on the WWW with some very interesting reports on occupational discrimination against women and minorities. Most WWW browsers and Internet programs have search engines, which allow you to search various databases for information on the topic that you are interested in. That is how we found that site on the Glass Ceiling Commission on the WWW. A useful way to learn about the WWW would be to browse through recent issues of the *Internet World* magazine, which is available in most public and university libraries. Alternatively, one could easily "Google" a particular topic and find literally hundreds of sites providing definitions, essays, references, class lecture notes, PDFs, and PowerPoint slides related to that topic.

At this point, we will illustrate how integrating and using the different strategies discussed in this chapter may prove worthwhile. Suppose that you are interested in abnormal psychology in general and post-traumatic stress disorder (PTSD) specifically. You conduct a computerized literature search using PsycLit and Medline and find quite a few articles produced by researchers affiliated with the National Center for PTSD, which is part of the Veterans Administration. On reviewing these articles, you find that Dr. Matthew Friedman is a frequent author, and he is the director of the National Center for PTSD headquartered at the White River Junction VA Medical Center in Vermont. You decide to use an interpersonal strategy as well, so you arrange a telephone interview with Dr. Friedman to discuss your research ideas. During the interview, he informs you that the National Center for PTSD also maintains its own computerized database on the worldwide literature on PTSD, and he arranges for you to search that database. Through this specialized database, you are able to find many more articles related to your topic than those generated by PsycLit and Medline.

Here is a list of Internet links helpful in finding a research topic:

www.library.cornell.edu/olinuris/ref/research/topic.html

www.pc.maricopa.edu/departments/library/guides/topicselect.html

www.lib.duke.edu/libguide/choosing.htm

http://library.weber.edu/ref/guides/howto/topic selection.cfm

www.unl.edu/mcnair/Handouts/FindingResearch Topic.htm

www.msjc.edu/sjclibrary/research/topicideas.htm

www.edwdebono.com/

www.educationau.edu.au/archives/cp/04i.htm

www.brainstorming.co.uj/tutorials/creativethinking contents.html

Creative Strategies

Researchers have constructed methods and exercises for enhancing individuals' creativity and increasing their ability to develop ideas. These methods focus on creativity from both a right- and left-brain perspective, taking into account both the intuitive-philosophical and verbal-analytical components.

Creativity via right-brain function can be achieved through exercises such as the investment theory, which states that the major task in achieving creativity is actually making the decision to be creative (Sternberg, 2003). Sternberg outlines 21 techniques that can be utilized to enable an individual to make the decision to be creative.

Sternberg's first technique involves redefining problems and essentially mirrors the cliché of thinking out of the box. Sternberg outlines an example of redefining a problem and reaching a creative solution in his story of an employee who disliked his boss. The employee went to a headhunter looking for a new job for himself, when he realized an opportunity to redefine the problem. At that point, the employee had the headhunter find a new job for his boss. The employee stayed in his current company, didn't have to work for the boss he disliked, and was promoted to his former boss's job.

Sternberg's second method for choosing to be creative requires that you question and analyze your assumptions. Everyone has assumptions, and creativity cannot be achieved until those assumptions are challenged. Many of the great innovators throughout history, such as Galileo, Christopher Columbus, and the Wright Brothers, would have never achieved their creative accomplishments without questioning the beliefs of their societies.

The techniques of concept mapping (Novak, 2004) and lateral thinking (deBono, 1971) can be used to improve creativity while focusing on the language and analysis components of the left brain. *Concept maps* serve as aids to arrange

and characterize knowledge. These consist of two key elements: concepts and propositions (Novak, 2004) and are based on the work of Ausubel (1963, 1968, 1978, cited in Novak, 2004), which stated that combining new concepts and propositions allows new knowledge to come forth. The concept refers to "a perceived regularity in events or objects, or records of events or objects, designated by a label" (Novak, 2004, p. 1). In the concept map, the concepts are represented visually by enclosing them in boxes. These concept boxes are then attached by lines to different propositions, or "statements about some object or event in the universe, either naturally occurring or constructed" (Novak, 2004, p. 1). Propositions also "contain two or more concepts connected with other words to form a meaningful statement" (Novak, 2004, p. 1). A relationship between the concept and proposition is denoted by drawing a line connecting the two.

The format of the concept map depicts a hierarchal structure, moving from more broad concepts on the top to more detailed concepts on the bottom of the map (see Figure 2.2). Relationships between two different concepts are indicated through *cross-links*. The first step in constructing a concept map is to select a specific area of knowledge, then pinpoint the main concepts that apply to this area. Once this is accomplished, the main concepts can be ranked from most general to most specific. Post-it notes can be very helpful in organizing the hierarchal rankings of the concepts from top (most general) to bottom (most specific), as they can be easily adjusted until your hierarchy is appropriate. When the conceptual hierarchy is established, cross links can be drawn to illustrate conceptual relationships from one area to another. Figure 2.2 is an example of a concept map in its final form:

The *dance of the boxes* (Figure 2.3) is a simpler exercise that students can utilize to stimulate their creative process (Gordon, 1974). This exercise enables the individual to combine the right-brain processes of concept framing with brainstorming and the left-brain processes of lateral thinking. In the dance of the boxes, a broad or general topic or idea is placed in the box at the top of the figure. Once having done that, you think of the first two words that come to mind related to the general topic and place

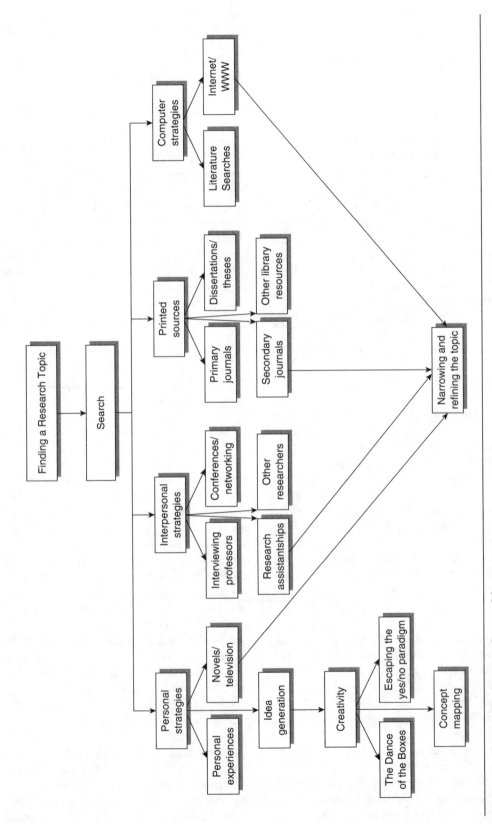

Figure 2.2 Creative Strategy: Concept Map

those words in the two boxes below. You then repeat this step, breaking each of the two new ideas into two more new ideas. A step-by-step example using the general topic *career* is provided to help illustrate the process. As you can see in Figure 2.3, *career* was broken down into *work* and *unemployment.*

Work is broken into *long* and *money,* and *unemployment* is broken into *poor* and *stress.* Now that the four boxes in the middle of the graph have been filled with words, the next task is to come up with a word that summarizes the three words on the left side and the right side. On the left side, *work, long,* and *money* are summarized by *success.* On the right side, *unemployment, poor,* and *stress* are summarized by *government services* (see Figure 2.4).

The last step involves bringing the final two word boxes together to formulate a topic. Using the example above, a possible conclusion could be "The success rate of government unemployment services in finding careers for displaced workers"; deBono (1971) describes his concept of lateral thinking as a planned and organized process leading to new ideas. Using lateral thinking entails following a two-step process of escape and provocation. deBono explains *escaping* as attempting to determine one's own dominant ideas and assumptions on an issue, followed by making a conscious effort to seek out different ideas to resolve that issue. Finding different ideas is more important than finding the best

idea, as gathering your creative thoughts will lead to an abundance of possibilities.

This idea involves putting aside all philosophies, theories, and concepts designed to categorize and organize thought. In doing so, lateral thinking takes the opposite approach to creativity than that of concept mapping, advocating the escape of the restrictiveness of concepts and truly emphasizing the exercise of "thinking outside the box." Once you have escaped from the restrictiveness of these traditional concepts and philosophies, you discover that many different routes exist to the solution of a problem.

Achieving deBono's second phase of *provocation* necessitates the division of thinking of new ideas and assessing them. This can be achieved by focusing on an idea's potential rather than whether it is right or wrong. deBono advocates this type of active creativity, asserting that many times a wrong idea at one point leads to a solution in the future. Ultimately, this active creativity prescribed by lateral thinking enables one to formulate a new direction of one's own, rather than to blindly adhere to an old one.

NARROWING AND REFINING THE TOPIC

In the first stage of finding a research topic, you are primarily interested in identifying a general topic area such as masked depression or job satisfaction among women. Having found a

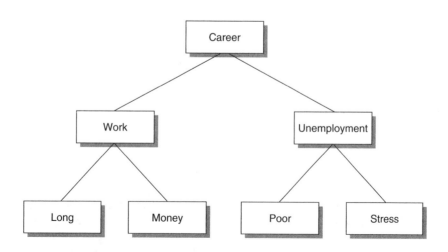

Figure 2.3   Creative Strategy: The Dance of the Boxes, Part I

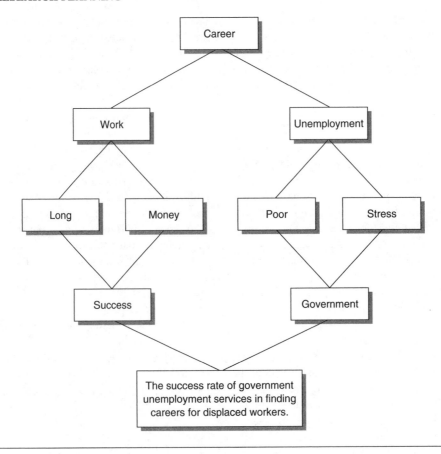

Figure 2.4   Creative Strategy: The Dance of the Boxes, Part II

general topic area that interests you by using the strategies outlined above, the next stage is to narrow and refine the topic. As suggested by Cone and Foster (1993), a useful way to narrow your topic is to develop a research question from your general topic. They point out that a research question consists of three characteristics. First, it should be a question—you need to phrase what you would like to study in the form of a question (e.g., Do men and women react differently to violence in movies?). Second, the research question should propose a relationship between variables that needs to be examined (e.g., Are adolescents with higher self-esteem less likely to become addicted to drugs than are adolescents with lower self-esteem?). Third, the research question should use terminology that allows it to be tested empirically (e.g., *self-esteem* and *drug addiction* versus a vague idea such as *adolescents who come from good homes*).

Just as you were able to use and combine the initial search strategies to help you find a general research topic, you can also use the same search strategies to help you narrow and refine your topic into a research question. For example, if your initial search led you to the topic of gifted children, you may be able to seek out professors in education (personal strategies) who can tell you more about that area of research. Professors who are actively involved in research in a particular area can usually guide you to some promising areas for additional research. Following on some leads from the personal strategies, you could do a computer literature search using PsycLit (computer strategies) to determine if any research has been conducted on the relationship between birth order and giftedness among children. Alternatively, you may wish to proceed directly to the printed sources and begin reading different textbooks on special education to get a sense of the major research questions in the topic of educating gifted children. Having familiarized yourself with the major theories and issues, you may then use computer strategies and start searching different topics related to gifted children on your own. Regardless of how you mix and match the different search strategies, your goal in this stage of finding a topic is to narrow your general topic down to a research question that is specific, empirically testable, doable within a certain time frame, and likely to make a significant contribution to the scientific knowledge base.

Once you have narrowed your general topic down to a research question, the next step is to formulate one or more hypotheses from your research question (Cone & Foster, 1993). Because the goals of science are to understand, explain, predict, and control phenomena, one of the major functions of psychological research is to be able to predict human behavior. A hypothesis is a prediction about the relationship between certain variables (e.g., adolescents with low self-esteem will be more likely to become addicted to various drugs). Testing and confirming hypotheses about human behavior is how psychological science progresses. In general, we use null and research hypotheses to test our research questions. Null hypotheses are necessary because they are the ones we can test directly. The research hypothesis is usually a converse of the null hypothesis, in that the latter stipulates *no* relationship between the variables and the former proposes that there *is* a relationship. For example, a null hypothesis might be as follows: There is no relationship between adolescents' level of self-esteem and their drug use and addiction. Therefore, a research hypothesis would be as follows: There is a negative relationship between adolescents' level of self-esteem and their drug use and addiction. In addition to specifying the variables (e.g., self-esteem and drug addiction), hypotheses also specify the nature of the relationship (i.e., positive, negative, curvilinear).

Both your research questions and hypotheses can come from the four categories of search strategies we have outlined above. For example, you may be able to identify a general research topic from reading a textbook (printed resources), and the professor with whom you are working as

a research assistant may help you find a specific research question (interpersonal strategies). Moreover, you may have identified some specific hypotheses to test from the articles you were able to locate using the PsycLit computer database (computer strategies).

Finally, we would like to offer several conceptual frameworks or strategies that might be useful in helping you narrow and refine your research topics. Within the field of psychology, a common conceptual scheme for understanding human behavior is the ABC model. When using this model, psychologists first identify a specific behavior that is of particular interest to them for further research. The behavior of interest can range from bed-wetting among grade school children to the functioning of military personnel under highly stressful conditions. The ABC model places a target behavior within the three-part model (i.e., antecedents-behavior-consequences). Within this model, the target behavior is supposed to have identifiable antecedents, sometimes assumed to be causal, and also certain consequences. Using bed-wetting as the target behavior, the antecedent might be familial stress, such as the parents undergoing a divorce, and one of the consequences may be the redirection of the parents' attention from conflict with each other to the stress experienced by the child.

It is sometimes useful to apply the ABC model to a general topic that you have selected in order to identify some research questions for exploration. Using an earlier example, assuming that you have become very interested in the general topic of job satisfaction among women, you may apply the ABC model by asking what are the various antecedents of job satisfaction among women. As you use this model to search for more literature, you may discover that a common variable in the existing career literature is whether women are in traditional (overrepresentation of women) or nontraditional (underrepresentation of women) careers. You could then narrow your general topic to a research question on traditionality of career choice as a significant antecedent of women's job satisfaction level. You might then hypothesize that women in traditional careers will have higher levels of job satisfaction than women in nontraditional careers.

Another conceptual scheme or strategy that might be useful in narrowing your research topic is to look for potential moderators. According to Baron and Kenny (1986), a *moderator* is "a qualitative (e.g., sex, race, class) or quantitative (e.g., level of reward) variable that affects the direction and/or strength of the relation between an independent and a dependent or criterion variable" (p. 1174). In a correlational analysis framework, the moderator would be a third variable that affects the zero-order correlation between two other variables. In an analysis of variance framework, the moderator would be represented by the interaction terms between the independent and dependent variables (see chapters by Scherbaum (18), by Dickter (19), and by Steelman & Levy (20), this volume, for more details on data analyses).

The recent polls showing major differences in African Americans' and White Americans' perceptions of the O. J. Simpson verdict illustrated that race is a significant moderator of perceptions of the police and justice systems in this country. Other researchers have tried to identify different variables that represent culture as a major moderator variable in psychology. Returning to the women's job satisfaction example, using the concept of a moderator (i.e., not all women in traditional careers will be highly satisfied with their jobs), you might notice that sex role orientation seems to be a significant variable in that research area. Could it be that the relationship between the traditionality of women's career choice and their level of job satisfaction is moderated by their sex role orientation? The sex role literature would suggest that highly feminine women would be more likely to enter and enjoy traditional careers, whereas androgynous women would be less likely to be satisfied with such career positions. Applying the concept of a moderator, you may then propose a research study to test this moderated relationship between the traditionality of women's career choices and their job satisfaction level.

Another useful conceptual scheme that we have found helpful in narrowing down a research topic and identifying a research question is to look for possible cross-fertilization between specialties (e.g., social psychology and industrial-organizational psychology). Often there are natural and logical links between the research topics being examined by different specialties that require only a small amount of creativity and innovation to combine in order to develop a research question worth further pursuit. For example, let us assume that you are interested in industrial-organizational psychology and more specifically in gender bias in performance appraisals as a possible factor underlying the glass-ceiling effect (see Morrison, White, & Van Velsor, 1987). Briefly, the *glass-ceiling effect* is a hypothesized barrier to occupational advancement for women in corporations due to their being female. To use the strategy of cross-fertilization of specialties, you may decide to review of the leading social psychology journals during the last few years. In your review, you discover that the area of social cognition is a new and exciting area of research in social psychology. Specifically, you are intrigued by the *out-group homogeneity effect* (e.g., see Mullen & Hu, 1989; Park, Judd, & Ryan, 1991) This robust effect, which has been discovered by social psychologists, consists of the tendency in human beings to perceive greater homogeneity in out-groups (e.g., Most African Americans seem to have greater musical talent or most women are terrible drivers) and greater heterogeneity in in-groups. It is argued that it is this out-group homogeneity effect that underlies the stereotyping process. You realize that the out-group homogeneity effect may be a possible factor underlying occupational stereotyping, and you decide to test the hypothesis that this effect may be operative in performance appraisals and may indeed account for the gender biases that contribute to the glass-ceiling effect reported by others.

The final conceptual framework or strategy we would recommend to help you narrow and refine your research topic is to search for new constructs in other areas of psychology. When using the strategy of cross-fertilization of specialties, you may find concepts and constructs that are new to you but that have been around for a while within another specialty (e.g., social cognition). When trying to find new constructs in psychology, you are trying to locate constructs, and the measures associated with them, that have been recently developed. For example, in the area of counseling and clinical psychology, there has been a great deal of research on the help-seeking process or service utilization patterns among racial and ethnic minorities (see Leong, Wagner, & Tata, 1995, for a review). Many previous studies have examined variables such as accessibility of the mental health services as well as the theoretical orientation of the clinicians and counselors. In a 1995 study, Leong, Wagner, and Kim decided to test the role of a new construct in psychology—the culturally based concept of loss of face—as a possible factor in the attitudes of Asian Americans toward seeking group counseling. Efficient ways to identify new constructs in psychology are to review recent issues of journals (printed sources) as well as attend conferences where these new ideas and measures are presented (interpersonal strategies).

In our opinion, there are two essential components underlying the strategies described above for finding a research topic. These components are mastery of the subject and creativity. There is no getting around the fact that one must have a certain level of mastery in a subject matter in order to come up with important and significant new research studies. *Mastery* of a subject matter can only come from investing the time and energy to learn about a research topic by identifying and studying the relevant sources of information on the topic.

Building on this mastery of the subject, the second component for finding and conducting an important study is *creativity.* Although it remains controversial whether creativity is a personality trait or a skill that can be learned, we believe that creativity is probably a combination of nature and nurture. There is a series of books that offer suggestions for improving our current level of creativity (e.g., Adams, 1986; Sternberg, 1988; Weisberg, 1993). There are also articles that offer similar suggestions, and one by Wicker (1985) serves as an excellent example. It would be worthwhile to spend some time, especially for those with an interest in a research career, to learn about the nature and process of creativity and how you might improve your level of creative ability and thus your ability to generate important research ideas.

In conclusion, we hope that the search strategies as well as the conceptual schemes for narrowing and refining your research topic that we have offered here will prove to be helpful in your search for a meaningful and important research study.

EXERCISES

1. Using the Thesaurus

In addition to serving as a guide to computer literature searches, the thesaurus from PsycINFO can also serve as a good source of ideas for possible research. For this exercise, you need to locate the latest version (10th ed.) of the *Thesaurus of Psychological Index Terms* (2005) published by the APA. You can find it in the library, or perhaps your faculty advisor would have a copy.

Start at the beginning of the thesaurus where there will be an appendix describing the content classification system (e.g., *developmental psychology, social processes, social psychology, personality psychology, psychological and physical disorders,* etc.). Browse through those headings to see what interests you most. Once you have identified the area that seems most interesting (e.g., *eating disorders* under the *psychological and physical disorders*), then you can go to the alphabetical section to read more about it (e.g., the section on *eating* will list *eating attitudes, binge eating,* and *appetite disorders*).

Because research is primarily about discovering relationships, it is important to identify other terms and concepts that you would like to relate to the area that you have just identified. For example, you may be interested in cultural influences; therefore you would look up the appropriate search term for that variable (e.g., *cross-cultural differences*) in the thesaurus. You can then search for those terms in the PsycINFO database in the library (e.g., *eating disorders* and *cross-cultural differences*). Scanning those results would then enable you to further refine what aspects of this topic most interest you. Taking this example further, you may discover that several studies have examined the relationship between eating disorders and acculturation, and you want to pursue that topic further. You would check the thesaurus for the appropriate terms and then go back to PsycINFO and search the terms *eating disorders* and *cultural assimilation.*

Alternatively, you could begin your exploration either at the rotated alphabetical section or the cluster section (toward the back of the thesaurus). There is no one right way to identify a research topic that interests you. Pick up the thesaurus and try either one of these routes with the follow-up procedures suggested above, and happy browsing!

2. Using Magazines

As indicated in the chapter, newspapers and magazines can also be a good source of research ideas. You can undertake this exercise by using either the print version or the Web version of *Psychology Today.* For our illustration, we will describe the Web version. Go to Google and type in "Psychology Today" as your search term and follow the link to the magazine's home page (Note: we could provide the actual URL but this may change in the next month or a year down the road). Once you are at the home page, you can click on the current links and then follow your natural tendencies, pursuing whatever current topics seem to interest you.

Using the current links (November 28, 2004), I followed the story entitled "Surviving Holiday Hell," which indicated that people become unhappy during the holidays because they create expectations that the holidays should be perfect. Because that seldom occurs, many people suffer unfulfilled fantasies and expectations. The idea that caught my eye was the notion that people expected the holiday event to be perfect. Therefore, I went back to the home page and searched for *perfectionism* and found more articles to read. The story "Surviving Holiday Hell" may lead you to track down other leads. Whatever interests you from the first article, you can always search the terms further on that Web page. Just keep following the leads until you come to a puzzle that you find so personally meaningful that you would like to research further.

Besides following the latest links or stories on the current Web page of *Psychology Today,* you can also use the established links. On the left frame of their Web page, you will find a list of topics. You can start there and keep following your natural tendencies. For example, if the topic of *relationships* interests you and you click on that link, you will find about 65 specific topics to explore. Let us assume that the topic *infidelity* intrigues you. You click on that link, which takes you to about half a dozen articles, columns, and quizzes related to infidelity. You can then follow those links to see what aspects of infidelity might be worth researching. I followed the link entitled "Beyond Betrayal: Life after Infidelity" and found that the author had classified infidelity into those that were "accidental, romantic, marital arrangements, and philandering." The idea of "philandering" intrigued me and given my interest in personality, I am going to explore if research has been conducted to examine the relationship between personality type (e.g., Big Five model) and philandering.

Your interests will probably take you down a different path, but go ahead and start with *Psychology Today* and see where the exploration takes you.

3. Escaping the Yes/No Paradigm

deBono offers an exercise to facilitate the development of lateral thinking in which the syllable *PO* is substituted for the word *NO.* The word *NO* represents a common concept of pessimism and one that supports the rejection and restriction of ideas. Using *PO* continues to build on the idea of escaping from concepts of conformity. In this case, *PO* allows for "the escape from the Yes/No system" of our society (deBono, 1971, p. 134). By escaping from the hold of the Yes/No concept, one can more easily realize the full capacity of an idea, rather than focusing on what is right or wrong. Whereas Yes/No serves as a belief or conclusion, PO is a proposal that can lead to the formulation of ideas beyond the limits of one's own experience. Thus, one can replace *NO* with *PO* in order to shift one's thinking from that of judging a situation as right or wrong (via Yes/No) to hypothesizing to uncover the potential possibilities. This lateral thinking allows you to overcome the assumptions and ideas of current theories and concepts, which deBono terms as the *Intermediate impossible.* Here are two examples that deBono (1971, p. 141) provides:

A. Problem: To reduce traffic congestion in cities.
   Intermediate impossible: *PO* automobiles should have square wheels.
   Idea: Cars could not move—road would have to move.

B. Problem: To reduce supermarket thefts.

   Intermediate impossible: *PO* all food should be given away free.

   Idea: Free food but entrance fee to store.

Using *PO* and rejecting the assumptions of our Yes/No society enabled these creative solutions to problems to be conceived. Here is an example of using *PO* in your search for a research topic:

C. Problem: To improve availability of counseling services to low socioeconomic clients.

   Intermediate impossible: *PO* counseling services should be provided in the homes of clients.

   Idea: Evaluate the effectiveness of home therapy visits.

RECOMMENDED READINGS

Readers interested in learning more about finding research topics may wish to read the relevant chapters in Cone and Foster's (1993) book titled, *Dissertations and Theses From Start to Finish: Psychology and Related Fields,* which is published by the APA. Useful information on finding a research topic can also be found in Chapter 2 of Long, Convey, and Chwalek's (1985) *Completing Dissertations in the Behavioral Sciences and Education.* Another useful resource is the chapter on "Selecting a Problem" in Dixon, Bouma, and Atkinson's (1987) *Handbook of Social Science Research.* Finally, the book titled, *What to Study: Generating and Developing Research Questions* by Campbell, Daft, and Hulin (1982) is also a very useful reference for finding a research topic (especially the last two chapters).

REFERENCES

Adams, J. L. (1986). The care and feeding of ideas: A guide to encouraging creativity. Reading, MA: Addison-Wesley.

American Psychological Association. (1993). *Journals in psychology* (4th ed.). Washington, DC: APA.

American Psychological Association. (1994). *Thesaurus of psychological index terms* (7th ed.). Washington, DC: APA.

American Psychological Association. (2005). *Thesaurus of psychological index terms* (10th ed.). Washington, DC: APA.

Baron, R. M., & Kenny, D. A. (1986). The moderator-mediator variable distinction in social psychological research: Conceptual, strategic, and statistical considerations. *Journal of Personality and Social Psychology, 51,* 1173–1182.

Beit-Hallahmi, B. (1985). Dangers of the vagina. *British Journal of Medical Psychology, 58,* 351–356.

Campbell, J. P., Daft, R. L., & Hulin, C. L. (1982). *What to study: Generating and developing research questions.* Beverly Hills, CA: Sage.

Cone, J. D., & Foster, S. L. (1993). *Dissertations and theses from start to finish: Psychology and related fields.* Washington, DC: APA.

deBono, E. (1971). *Lateral thinking for management: A handbook of creativity.* New York: McGraw-Hill.

Dixon, B. R., Bouma, G. D., & Atkinson, G. B. J. (Eds.). (1987). *Handbook of social science research.* New York: Oxford University Press.

Eidelberg, L. (1968). *Encyclopedia of psychoanalysis.* New York: Free Press.

Gordon, W. J. J. (1974). *Making it strange* (Books 1–4). New York: Harper & Row.

Leong, F. T. L., & Schneller, G. (1993). Boredom proneness: Temperamental and cognitive components. *Personality and Individual Differences, 14,* 233–239.

Leong, F. T. L., Wagner, N. S., & Kim, H. (1995). Group counseling expectations among Asian

Americans: The role of culture-specific factors. *Journal of Counseling Psychology, 42,* 217–222.

Leong, F. T. L., Wagner, N. S, & Tata, S. P. (1995). Racial and ethnic variations in help-seeking attitudes. In J. Ponterotto, J. M. Casas, L. Suzuki, & C. Alexander (Eds.), *Handbook of multicultural counseling* (pp. 415–438). Thousand Oaks, CA: Sage.

Long, T. J., Convey, J. J., & Chwalek, A. R. (1985). *Completing dissertations in the behavioral sciences and education.* San Francisco: Jossey-Bass.

Morrison, A., White, R., & Van Velsor, E. (1987). *Breaking the glass ceiling: Can women reach the top in America's largest corporations?* Reading, MA: Addison-Wesley.

Mullen, B., & Hu, L. (1989). Perceptions of in-group and out-group variability: A meta-analytic integration. *Basic and Applied Social Psychology, 10,* 233–252.

National Institute of Mental Health. (1993). *Special report: Schizophrenia 1993* (NIH Publication No. 93–3499). Rockville, MD: Author.

National Institute of Mental Health. (1994). New research frontiers in behavioral medicine. *Proceedings from the National Conference.* (NIH Publication No. 94–3772). Rockville, MD: Author.

Novak, J. D. (2004). The theory underlying concept maps and how to construct them. Retrieved May 19, 2005, from http://cmap.coginst.uwf .edu/info

Osipow, S. H., & Fitzgerald, L. F. (1996). *Theories of career development* (4th ed.). Boston: Allyn & Bacon.

Park, B., Judd, C. M., & Ryan, C. S. (1991). Social categorization and the representation of variability information. In W. Stroebe & M. Hewstone (Eds.), *European review of social psychology* (Vol. 2, pp. 211–245). New York: Wiley.

Pintrich, P. R., & Johnson, G. R. (1990). Assessing and improving students' learning strategies. In M. D. Svinicki (Ed.), *The changing face of college teaching* (pp. 83–92) (New Directions for Teaching and Learning, No. 42). San Francisco: Jossey-Bass.

Reed, J. G., & Baxter, P. M. (2003). *Library use: A handbook for psychology* (3rd ed.). Washington, DC: APA.

Sternberg, R. J. (1988). *The nature of creativity: Contemporary psychological perspectives.* New York: Cambridge University Press.

Sternberg, R. J. (2003). *Wisdom, intelligence, and creativity synthesized.* New York: Cambridge University Press.

Weisberg, R. W. (1993). *Creativity: Beyond the myth of genius.* New York: W. H. Freeman.

Wicker, A. W. (1985). Getting out of our conceptual ruts: Strategies for expanding our conceptual frameworks. *American Psychologist, 40,* 1094–1103.

Wiggins, R. W. (1995). *The Internet for everyone: A guide for users and providers.* New York: McGraw-Hill.

3

BIBLIOGRAPHIC RESEARCH

JEFFREY G. REED
PAM M. BAXTER

Reading, understanding, and reviewing prior work on your research topic are critical steps in the research process. The work that people have already reported will lay the foundation for your research by helping to describe what is known and unknown. Previously published work will also help to identify gaps in research and areas of controversy.

Prior chapters have discussed the planning of your research (Chapter 1) as well as selecting and refining your topic (Chapter 2). It is especially important to understand your topic clearly, define its major points, and narrow it sufficiently to permit a successful review of the literature. Succeeding chapters will discuss critical evaluation of sources (Chapter 4) and writing your paper (Chapters 23–26). This chapter provides an overview of bibliographic research: the process of using the library and bibliographic resources to locate information relevant to your topic.

Our primary purpose in writing this chapter is to help you locate information on your topic. We begin with the types of sources you might consult and how each will be useful in your search process. Second, we discuss both the methods of access to bibliographic sources (databases and indexes) that will help you locate research reports and the search process itself. The chapter closes with some suggestions for recording and organizing the information you discover.

SOURCES

This section describes types of sources that may be found in the personal (materials within your personal possession), institutional (materials available through your college or university library), or virtual library (materials available anywhere). For each type of source, we describe the purpose and format (what it is), how it is used in research, its typical location (personal vs. institutional vs. virtual library) and provide examples. For additional information, extensive listings of sources, and specific examples of how to use particular tools not included here, refer to Baxter (1993), McInnis (1982), Reed and Baxter (2003), or Sternberg (2003). In this chapter, we will focus on the field of industrial and organizational (I/O) psychology to provide examples of sources.

Textbooks

Purpose and Format

Textbooks perform an instructional function and are organized to support an educational program. Introductory textbooks provide a broad overview of a field such as industrial and organizational psychology (e.g., Landy & Conte, 2004; Levy, 2003; Muchinsky, 2003). They summarize key principles, theories, research findings, and trends in the field. Intermediate and advanced textbooks provide more detailed treatment of a subfield, such as work motivation (e.g., Porter, Bigley, & Steers, 2003).

Use in Research

Every good textbook should refer to key sources related to the topics it covers. Thus a textbook may provide an entry into the literature of the field. Recognize, however, that a textbook is a secondary source, summarizing and reporting the work of others. Despite the advantage of providing a summary and overview of a field, the risk is always that as a secondary source, a textbook may misinterpret, oversimplify, or ignore research findings.

Location

Most professionals maintain a small collection of introductory textbooks in their personal library pertaining to each area of significant interest, as well as a larger collection of advanced textbooks relating to their areas of specialization. Although libraries tend not to acquire textbooks, focusing instead on primary sources, most institutional libraries have one or several textbooks on major topics of interest. The reference department of your college or university library, or the virtual library, should be able to provide information about most textbooks.

Monographs

Purpose and Format

In every field, there are book-length sources that go beyond the textbook. They communicate the results of original research and therefore make a unique contribution to a field. In time, some become classic works in the field with which every practitioner in that field is expected to be familiar. Some of these classic works become the textbooks of graduate courses and have an impact on the work of future generations of psychologists, as the examples below illustrate.

Use in Research

To the extent that classic monographs provide critical new approaches to a field, they become primary sources and furnish a starting point for further investigation. Several examples follow: Campbell, Dunnette, Lawler, and Wick (1970) stimulated numerous studies on managers. The work of Katz and Kahn (1966) on organizations as systems stimulated the thinking of subsequent organizational psychologists. March and Simon's (1958) work is recognized as a point of departure for many subsequent works on organizational theory, structure, and conflict. Work by Kahneman, Slovic, and Tversky (1982) on judgment and heuristics provided the foundation for later work on judgment and decision making.

Location

As in the case of the advanced textbook, practitioners tend to have several key classic monographs in their personal library. Because some seminal works are out of print and difficult to obtain, they may be available only in the institutional library or in some cases must be accessed through the virtual library.

Handbooks

Purpose and Format

At intervals, persons decide (and publishers agree) to prepare a comprehensive reference work that summarizes a field. At the time it is published, a handbook provides a comprehensive assessment of the state of the art in a particular field, including theory, research, methodology, and issues. This is typically offered as a multichapter handbook with numerous contributors, each a specialist or expert in his or her particular chapter topic.

Use in Research

A handbook chapter provides an overview of a topic; it usually also offers an extensive bibliography of important sources in that area. It can be an excellent starting point for further investigation. In addition, a handbook will point to key variables that have been investigated, and the absence of a chapter in a handbook may indicate areas lacking in extensive research.

Location

The *Handbook of Industrial and Organizational Psychology* (Dunnette, 1976) was considered an important statement of the state of the art at the time of its publication. Many professionals in the field acquired copies for their personal libraries. Many graduate students used it as a key source in work on advanced degrees. Some professors even viewed it as a textbook for graduate students. The subsequent four-volume second edition updated and expanded the original, making it even more valuable in the personal professional library (Dunnette & Hough, 1990–1994). The more recent handbook by Anderson (2001–2002) provides an update in some areas of the field. Because we all have limits on our finances, we might rely on the college or university library for related or more specialized handbooks such as *Bass and Stogdill's Handbook of Leadership* (Bass, 1990) or the *Handbook of Leadership Development* (McCauley & Van Velsor, 2004). The virtual library provides information about, and access to, additional handbooks.

Annual Reviews

Purpose and Format

Reviews present selective and evaluative review of the status and recent progress in main areas of the field. Volumes such as the *Annual Review of Psychology,* published each year since 1950, follow a master plan for regular review of topics in the field. Some topics, including those in which there are especially active research programs, receive more frequent review chapters.

Use in Research

Each *Annual Review of Psychology* volume contains about 20 chapters and each is authored by an expert on the field covered. Each chapter includes an extensive reference list, providing a good starting point for many research projects. An advantage of a review is that such compendia may be issued annually and provide updates more frequently than handbooks. Some areas within psychology are supported by more specialized reviews.

Location

Some academic professionals receive each volume in an annual series to ensure awareness of work such as that of O'Reilly (1991). Many larger institutional libraries include complete sets of volumes of annual reviews. In addition, some reviews such as the *Annual Review of Psychology* are also available online to subscribing libraries. A very specialized source, particular to I/O, is the *International Review of Industrial and Organizational Psychology,* an annual publication first issued in 1986, which provides authoritative reviews of topics in the field (Cooper & Robertson, 1986+). You may have to rely on the virtual library for more specialized review monographs.

Professional Directories

Purpose and Format

These sources provide brief biographical information on individuals, including current address, workplace, and educational background. There are numerous directories, and most associations maintain a directory of their members (e.g., the American Psychological Association [APA] *Directory*).

Use in Research

Directories can both facilitate communication among researchers by providing location information and indicate a researcher's background by listing credentials of biographees.

Location

A benefit of membership in most associations is a membership directory. Many psychologists will have directories in their personal library for associations of which they are members. Institutional libraries may carry directories of major national organizations (e.g., the APA *Membership Directory*) but will not own all directories of all associations. Many institutional libraries tend to focus on nondisciplinary directories of distinguished individuals, for example, *Who's Who in America.* The virtual library expands the scope and reach of printed directories. Many academic institutions make their campus directories, telephone books, and electronic mail directories available for remote searching on the Internet. Some provide in-depth information about the ongoing research in their departments. In addition, more faculty and researchers maintain their own Web pages that include a list of current publications, areas of current research interests, and conference papers presented. If copyright restrictions permit, some researchers provide copies of unpublished papers, presentations, and data sets for downloading. Such information is helpful if you want to review a researcher's work in progress or contact someone whose research interests closely parallel your own.

Journals

Purpose and Format

Most published research in psychology appears as articles in journals. There are hundreds of journals of interest to psychologists. The field of industrial, organizational, and engineering psychology has dozens of potentially relevant journals focused on the interests of the practitioners in particular areas. The most reputable journals are refereed; that is, articles accepted for publication undergo a review process such as described in Part V.

Use in Research

The thorough, competent researcher conducts a careful, retrospective search of previously published work in his or her area of interest while defining the scope of a research project and before beginning the data collection phase. This is done to benefit from the findings of other researchers, to ensure that relevant variables are being addressed, to relate the proposed project to relevant trends in the field, and to determine that the proposed project makes a unique contribution (unless the intent is to replicate a particular study).

Location

Most psychologists subscribe to a few key journals for their personal library that represent their primary interests (e.g., *Journal of Applied Psychology*). The institutional library will contain a larger collection of potentially relevant journals (e.g., *Organizational Behavior and Human Decision Processes*) as well as journals covering closely related disciplines (e.g., *American Management Review*). Institutional libraries, like individuals, have limited budgets to acquire all journals needed for their users, especially those that are more specialized (e.g., *Organizational Dynamics*). Thus the researcher may need to tap the virtual library through methods such as interlibrary loan for full coverage of a topic. Since the early 1990s, an increasing number of refereed journals are beginning to appear in electronic form. As a result, your institution may have access to many electronic journals through joint purchasing agreements with other universities or by subscribing to indexing services that also provide the full text of articles, as described below.

Abstracts and Indexes

Purpose and Format

Most indexing and abstracting tools provide author, title, and subject access to articles within journals. Some more specialized sources index published conference papers and proceedings, book chapters, dissertations and master's theses, federal and state publications, and technical reports. Although they can be in a printed publication or an electronic searchable format, some are available only in an electronic format.

Although most indexes began as printed volumes (published on a monthly or quarterly basis), the significant ones are now searchable as bibliographic databases. Not only are they updated more frequently, they permit more flexible search strategies; for example, the ability to search for words in the title or an accompanying abstract. Some database producers provide a link from a bibliographic citation to the full text of an article. When libraries subscribe to indexes that supply articles as well, they can increase the scope of journals they provide to their own researchers.

Use in Research

Indexes and abstracts provide coverage of thousands of journal titles and access to articles in many languages. Their breadth of coverage brings publications to the attention of researchers who might not otherwise have the time or money to peruse very specialized journals or those in disciplines tangential to their own. A significant function that they provide is retrospective bibliographic searching, the ability to search the journal literature in a field to locate important, relevant sources, even if local institutional libraries do not own all the publications indexed.

Location

Until the 1980s, many psychologists relied either on the printed *Psychological Abstracts* to conduct searches of the literature or on the services of a librarian to perform a computer search of the PsycINFO database. Increasingly, availability of this information in electronic formats using relatively easy search software means that researchers can initiate their own computer searches and, in many cases, can do so from offices or homes. Some government-sponsored databases, such as ERIC and Medline, can be searched from publicly accessible Web sites. Some databases have the ability to link from a citation to the full text of an article, although the availability of this feature varies widely from one database to another or among individual campuses.

Dissertations and Theses

Purpose and Format

A requirement of almost all scholarly doctoral programs (e.g., PhD) and of many research-oriented master's programs is the completion of a thesis or dissertation. The dissertation or thesis is expected to be an original piece of research in the discipline that demonstrates one's knowledge of the literature in an area, ability to use appropriate methods and tools in conducting research, and skill in communicating and defending the content and merits of the research contribution to the field.

Use in Research

Because dissertations or theses contain an extensive review of relevant literature, they can be useful in identifying prior research. Because most research raises new questions as well as answers prior questions, a dissertation or thesis can provide ideas for future research. Reviewing completed dissertations or theses can provide guidance in completing one's own project.

Location

Academic programs typically require the degree candidate to file a copy of the dissertation or thesis in the college or university library. In the case of doctoral dissertations, most universities also require that a copy be submitted to University Microfilms International (UMI). UMI makes an archival microfilm copy of each dissertation received, announces its availability in the *Dissertation Abstracts International* (or the electronic Dissertation Abstracts Online), and sells copies of dissertations to individuals and institutions.

Conference Papers

Purpose and Format

Presentations at conferences take many forms, including reports of research, symposia or discussions, and invited addresses. Researchers often use the conference paper to provide the earliest public report of the most recent results of their research program.

Use in Research

Conference papers may contain important findings of research, significant new theoretical approaches, or reflections on the progress in a field. Symposia may provide a discussion of several alternative theoretical approaches or data from different studies on the same topic.

Location

Some conferences issue a proceedings book that contains the text of presentations, but these are not formal publications, and the papers are more often represented by abstracts. Formal publication of conference proceedings as a journal article, special journal issue, or book chapter is rare. Many conference papers never appear in print within the journal literature of a field for a variety of reasons; for example, they are not submitted for publication by their authors or are not accepted for journal publication. A small number of authors submit their conference papers to a service that accepts unpublished manuscripts, such as ERIC's *Resources in Education.* But many conference papers never find their way into an indexing or abstracting database; they become part of what is known as the "fugitive literature" in psychology. Unless you search the programs of conferences of the APA, American Psychological Society, Psychonomic Society, Midwestern Psychological Association, Society for Industrial and Organizational Psychology, and many others (most of which are not indexed by PsycINFO), you will not know about an important paper. Some authors have begun to provide copies of their presentations for download from their Web sites, especially if they do not plan to publish them.

Research Reports

Purpose and Format

Research reports provide results of a research project conducted by a center or institute. These report on ongoing projects of research funded by a grant or foundation. The reports themselves are often issued by the sponsoring research institute or research center as part of a series of publications.

Use in Research

Because they provide reports of research, they may provide valuable data and conclusions. They may be a preliminary report, which might appear later in a slightly different format as a published article or a conference presentation, or simply the results of a funded study, so that the written product will be the only one produced.

Location

They are often unpublished; they have not been through any type of peer review process and do not appear in a journal, nor are they likely to be indexed in bibliographic databases. As in the case of the conference paper, research reports are difficult to identify, locate, and

acquire, making them part of the fugitive literature. Some research centers or institutes provide copies through their Web sites.

Government Documents

Purpose and Format

Government documents are publications issued by federal, state, local, and international organizations. Governmental agencies issue statistical reports, annual reports on their programs, regularly appearing magazines, and reports on special topics. Governmental agencies issue thousands of publications each year; one of the largest publishers in the world is the U.S. Government Printing Office. These publications may be on any topic in which a governmental body has an interest, for example, hearings of a U.S. Senate subcommittee on mental health and aging, a publication by the Administration for Children and Families reporting national statistics on mistreatment of children, an OSHA standard on safety with video display terminals, or the quarterly *Schizophrenia Bulletin,* published since 1969 by the U.S. Center for Studies of Schizophrenia.

Use in Research

Depending on your research topic, a governmental publication may have a great deal or little to offer. It may contain statistical summaries, public opinion or policy positions, or information on government programs. Some areas, especially more applied fields such as educational and applied psychology, are more likely to be the focus of government publications than others.

Location

Many of these publications are available in hardcopy as well as in microform, and some are available electronically. Thousands of documents are acquired each year by hundreds of government depository libraries in each state across the country. Many are available for sale from the Superintendent of Documents or a Government Printing Office bookstore. Increasingly, such publications are available electronically on the Internet.

Access to federal government publications is available through the Catalog of U.S. Government Publications (CGP). This service is available online through the GPO Access Web site at www.gpoaccess.gov and indexes federal government publications starting in 1994.

State government publications are handled separately by each entity. As of this writing, documents issued by some states, such as Missouri, Nebraska, New Jersey, and Washington, can be located online by using a Web index to that state's publications. States generate a wide variety of publication formats (reports, legislative hearings, statistical publications, and data sets) reflecting varying levels of peer review and scrutiny from the research community.

Data Archive

Purpose and Format

Data archives exist to collect and preserve data that are made available to researchers. Archives tend to specialize in particular topics or disciplines, for example, longitudinal or qualitative studies and public opinion surveys.

Use in Research

As with government documents, availability and utility of data archives for your research will depend on your subdiscipline and research topic. You are much more likely to find a relevant data archive on topics in applied areas. Data archives are becoming increasingly important as researchers find the cost of collecting or acquiring data prohibitive. Additionally, researchers are seeing increasing value in sharing data with other laboratories to compare findings. Large data repositories, such as the Inter-university Consortium for Political and Social Research and the Economic and Social Data Service (University of Essex), collect, process, and distribute public use data for use by researchers.

Location

Some, such as the National Data Archive on Child Abuse and Neglect, are maintained by a university (the Family Life Development Center in the College of Human Ecology at Cornell University, Ithaca, NY). Others are maintained by government entities, such as the U.S. Bureau of Labor Statistics, a Division of the U.S. Department of Labor, the primary federal government data collection body for information on labor economics. For additional information, consult Chapter 22 on use of archival data sets, and Chapter 21 on conducting a meta-analysis.

Web Site

Purpose and Format

It is probable that almost every reader of this chapter has used the Internet and has visited many Web sites. Web sites provide information in an electronic form that is available on the Internet. They are made available in many ways: by professional organizations (e.g., APA), by publishers of electronic materials (e.g., Elsevier Science), by consultants wishing to advertise their services, and by individuals who wish to offer information to the public or to make a statement.

Web sites have a number of advantages. They can be very current. Some offer information that is not provided elsewhere (it is unique). Web sites can be accessed at almost any time.

They also have a number of potential disadvantages. There is no mechanism that controls what information can be offered on a Web site. Although some are very reliable and authoritative, others promote a particular social or political agenda and may contain information that is either strongly biased or just downright incorrect.

You must use information gained from a Web site with care. Beck (1997), Kirk (1996), and others have offered a variety of criteria you should use in evaluating Web sites. Among the most important are the following:

- Authority—Who is responsible for the information contained in the Web site, and is this a reliable source?
- Accuracy—Is the information accurate, and can it be verified?
- Objectivity—Is the information relatively free of bias, or is there a clear political, social, economic, or commercial agenda underlying the message?

- Currency—Is the information still available and up to date?
- Coverage—Is this site a duplicate of something available in print or elsewhere, or is the information uniquely available here?

Use information contained in Web sites with care. Although some are excellent sources of information, others are not. You must always use good judgment when evaluating information, and this is especially important when investigating Web-based material.

Use in Research

Web sites are varied and numerous. Established publishers are making more of their products available electronically (e.g., materials to support publishers' textbooks and electronic versions of printed magazines). These trends make it hard to generalize, but on the Web you may find data, scholarly articles, reviews, and other information that will assist your research project.

Location

What can we say other than, hop on the Internet with your favorite Web browser. Again, be cautious as you search. Web browsers differ in their capabilities. Our favorites today are metasearch engines (e.g., MetaCrawler) and Web spiders (e.g., Google). See Gowan and Spanbauer (2001) for more information.

In summary, sources such as textbooks, handbooks, and reviews can be useful in defining and narrowing your research topic (see Chapter 1 of this volume for details). Abstracts and indexes enable you to perform a thorough retrospective literature search, which we have discussed. Much of the advice contained in Chapter 4 on evaluating manuscripts will be useful as you evaluate the papers, articles, reports, and other materials identified in your search.

ACCESS TO SOURCES

Over the past 30 years, access to information has changed radically. In 1975, if you wanted research information (e.g., an article, book, or research report), you had to get that information in the form of a physical document. Your options were few. You could own the material yourself in your personal library. You could rely on the resources of your college, university, or local public library. Or you could make use of interlibrary loan (if it was available to you) to get what you needed from another library. Often what you needed was either difficult to locate, because the print indexes were difficult and cumbersome to search, or took weeks to acquire from other libraries through interlibrary loan.

Many researchers still rely heavily on their personal library and the resources of their college or university library. The increasing cost of journal subscriptions and the expanding array of potentially relevant publications, however, make local availability of all relevant resources increasingly challenging.

The advent of the digital age and advances in technology have opened vast new avenues leading to information resources. The virtual library, "all the stuff out there," can consist of library resources, databases, and electronic archives, wherever they are. Many libraries now provide their catalog of monographic materials (books) in an electronic form that is searchable through a Web browser interface. State library resources (e.g., WISCAT) and national resources (e.g., Library of Congress) are available to be searched online, and agreements among libraries to share resources can make access to these materials easier for researchers.

Bibliographic databases and indexes to journals, research reports, and technical reports, once only available in print form are now available electronically. Many of these materials are available through computer interfaces to libraries and subscribers. Your college or university library subscribes to a variety of abstracting and indexing services that provide electronic access to their databases, and these are described in more detail below. An increasing number of journals are becoming available in an electronic form— either as an Adobe portable document format (pdf) image of the article or as a hypertext markup language (HTML) file of the article. One important example is JSTOR, an electronic archive of hundreds of scholarly journals that focuses on historical, retrospective coverage.

The implication of this is that you can locate information that resides in a library or database in another part of the globe by using the computer in your home.

In the next section, we will describe some of these key indexing and abstracting tools. Then we will briefly discuss information available on the Internet. Last, we will address the search process itself, that is, how to most effectively use these sources.

Bibliographic Databases

Databases that index the content of journals, books, and other publication formats are the most efficient way to conduct a comprehensive literature search. There are a large number of abstracting and indexing services. Some provide very specific coverage, such as *Child Development Abstracts* or *Social Work Abstracts.* Others provide information on the contents of thousands of journals and books within one discipline and related disciplines. Among these broader indexes, five titles are the most germane to psychology. These are PsycINFO (also published as the printed *Psychological Abstracts*), ERIC, Sociological Abstracts, Business Source Elite/Premier, and Medline (also published as *Index Medicus*).

PsycINFO

Produced by the APA, the PsycINFO database indexes the contents of about 1,900 journal titles from all fields of psychology as well as related disciplines such as sociology, medicine, management, and education. In addition, it indexes books and book chapters, dissertations, and research reports. The coverage afforded by PsycINFO is unique in several respects: its international coverage of the research literature; the retrospective indexing, with some entries dating back to the 1880s; and the detail with which entries are analyzed. From 1967 forward, most entries contain lengthy abstracts and have detailed subject indexing based on the *Thesaurus of Psychological Index Terms*—which is regularly revised—and other standardized terms such as age group, grade level, language and country of publication, and species. Cited references attached to articles, books, and chapters were added to entries in 2002, with some cited

references added retrospectively to 1988. Although a rich source of information on published literature, its long publication history and evolving indexing strategies since it was first produced in 1967 necessitate a well-prepared search strategy before using the database. A careful review of PsycINFO coverage and indexing approaches is necessary if you plan to conduct a literature review spanning decades.

ERIC

Begun in 1966 under the auspices of the U.S. Department of Education's Educational Resources Information Center, this database is composed of two types of indexing. One is to the journal literature of education and related disciplines, and ERIC currently indexes approximately 980 such titles. (The journal index component is also published as the printed index, *Current Index to Journals in Education.*) The second component consists of an index to research reports, conference papers, curriculum guides, and other unpublished material. This function is published as the printed *Resources in Education* (formerly *Research in Education*). The database's structure is similar to PsycINFO, in that entries provide nonevaluative abstracts and extensive indexing based on a controlled vocabulary, which is revised regularly (*Thesaurus of ERIC Descriptors*). In addition, most of the unpublished reports indexed are also reproduced and distributed by ERIC. In the past, such documents were distributed in microfiche to about 800 libraries and information centers in the United States and sold directly to individuals on a cost-recovery basis; recent ones are provided on the Internet at no charge. Like Medline (described below), ERIC can be searched at no charge from several Web sites. In 2004, ERIC as an organization was restructured, and changes in document delivery and support services were implemented. Production and distribution of microfiche were discontinued, and more nonjournal material is distributed from the ERIC Web site (http://eric.ed.gov/).

Sociological Abstracts

In many ways, Sociological Abstracts (SA) is the sociology counterpart to PsycINFO. It indexes approximately 2,600 journal titles, as well as books, dissertations, and conference papers in the discipline. Because its indexing goes back to 1953 (with article abstracts since 1974), its retrospective coverage is not as complete. In addition, it uses its own controlled vocabulary, *Thesaurus of Sociological Indexing Terms.*

Business Source

Many aspects of psychology have applications in business: communication, groups, leadership, learning, motivation, stress, and so forth. EBSCO Information Services offers several versions of its Business Source database. Academic libraries most commonly subscribe to *Business Source Elite* or *Business Source Premier,* providing access to information in accounting, banking, economics, human resources, management, marketing and sales, and related business disciplines. The difference between the two is scope and coverage. Both index peer-reviewed journals, provide abstracts, and link to full text where available. As of January, 2005, *Business Source Elite* provided coverage of over 1,800 abstracted and indexed journals, over 1,100 full-text journals, over 900 peer-reviewed journals, and over 500 full-text, peer-reviewed journals. The coverage of *Business Source Premier* is broader and adds business trade journals, general business magazines, selected monographs, and other sources (EBSCO Information Services, 2005).

Medline

Medline is produced by a unit of the federal government, the National Library of Medicine, and can be searched at no charge as part of the library's PubMed service. At present, the Medline database contains over 11 million citations from the 1960s forward and uses the Medical Subject Headings List (MeSH) as its source of controlled vocabulary. Its strengths include extensive international coverage of foreign language journals and breadth of coverage in medicine and related biomedical areas, including mental health and psychiatry, public and community health, and psychopharmacology.

The content and organization of indexing and abstracting tools, especially those produced over a long period of time and that began their production lives as printed products, can be complex to use. Using PsycINFO as an example, dissertations have been cited in the database for many years, although abstracts have been included for those entries only since 1995. Citations to materials before 1967 present a special challenge because they do not use the *Thesaurus*-controlled vocabulary and, therefore, you cannot rely on the same search strategy as that used for more recent material. Fortunately, database producers provide a variety of information sheets and tutorials that discuss the organization, content, and use of their products. Libraries also produce guides to commonly used databases that cover features specific to their local environment, including instructions on downloading search results and linking to the full text of articles.

SEARCH PROCESS EXAMPLES

Leadership

As already noted, before consulting the resources, preliminary work must be done to prepare for a computer search. We need to define our topic, narrow it, identify possible search terms, and structure our search. The example below provides a very brief illustration of this process.

One topic of great interest within industrial and organizational psychology is the area of leadership. Thousands of books and articles have been written on this subject. Our first activity must be to define our topic and narrow it to a reasonable scope.

Defining and Narrowing the Topic

A significant issue in leadership over the past few years has been the ethics of senior managers and executives. Numerous Fortune 500 companies have faced huge challenges due to what appear to be questionable practices of their senior managers—Enron CEO Kenneth Lay, Tyco Chairman Dennis Kozlowski, and Adelphia head John Rigas (Greenberg, 2003; Novack, 2003). In part as a result of such problems, Van Yoder (2003) asserts that it is becoming more difficult to recruit chief financial officers to corporations. The Sarbanes-Oxley law was passed in 2002 by the U.S. Congress in an attempt to respond to ethical challenges (Sayther, 2003). But Barry (2002) suggests that a legalistic response is not necessarily the best approach to ethics. And Rogel (2003) suggests steps organizations and leaders can take to bolster trust and confidence in business organizations.

From a research perspective, there are many questions for the psychologist. How do senior managers develop values and ethics? How are these business leaders socialized? What personality attributes might dispose leaders to unethical behavior? What characteristics of the organizational environment support apparent lapses in business ethics? What might be done to better develop stronger ethical practices among emerging senior leaders?

We settled on a focus for our research in the following topic question: "How are ethics developed in senior managers of organizations?"

Search Term Identification

Our next step is to identify search terms that might be used to find prior publications on our topic. For each key term in our topic question, we will identify synonyms and related terms. The list follows:

> *ethics.* Also: *values, morals*
>
> *developed.* Also: *development, socialization, change*
>
> *senior managers.* Also: *leaders, CEO, president, chair, CFO*
>
> *organization.* Also: *business, corporation.*

Search Structure

Our next step is to structure our computer search, before starting with an index or database or the Internet. We will define our search using Boolean operators found in most search engines. Boolean operators (**AND, OR, NOT**) establish relationships between search concepts, allowing you to tailor your search and the resulting list of references to closely match your topic. We will employ the Boolean **OR** operator to retrieve any one of the terms in a set of

synonyms. We will also employ the Boolean **AND** operator, requiring a member of each set to be present in our search. Because some terms may be very similar and use the same root word (e.g., *develop* and *development*), we will use the asterisk (*) as a wild card to locate these terms (i.e., using *develop** would also retrieve references to *development* and *developing*). The following is our proposed initial search structure:

(ethics **OR** moral* **OR** value*)
AND (develop* **OR** social* **OR** change)
AND (CEO **OR** president **OR** CFO **OR** chair* **OR** lead*)

Note that this search structure uses three sets of terms. A source retrieved must have at least one term from each group, as required by the **AND**. For further information on Boolean structures and searching, consult Reed and Baxter (2003).

Database Selection

In the preceding section, we reviewed several widely available bibliographic databases. Our next step is to ascertain which bibliographic resources we should consult. Which are most likely to identify articles and other media that we will find useful? As PsycINFO is the most important bibliographic source in psychology, we will start there.

The Database Search

We entered our library's online version of PsycINFO to conduct our search. Using our library's access through EBSCO, we selected the Advanced Search option in PsycINFO. (Our search was conducted on December 6, 2003.) Our first pass retrieved 3,701 citations. Because it would be very difficult to review all of these citations, we need to narrow our search. In reviewing this search, we note that it included doctoral dissertations and several other publication formats in which we are not interested, so we successively modified our search. Table 3.1 provides examples of several of the searches we conducted and indicates the ways in which we modified them.

Table 3.1   Comparison of Results of Search Strategy Alternatives

#	Modification	Search Structure		Citations
1	Original search		(ethics **OR** moral* **OR** value*)	3701
		AND	(develop* **OR** social* **OR** change)	
		AND	(CEO **OR** president **OR** CFO **OR** chair* **OR** lead*)	
2	Limit to journal articles; add -er to lead		(ethics **OR** moral* **OR** value*)	973
		AND	(develop* **OR** social* **OR** change)	
		AND	(CEO **OR** president **OR** CFO **OR** chair* **OR** leader*)	
3	Delete value; Delete change		(ethics **OR** moral*)	305
		AND	(develop* **OR** social*)	
		AND	(CEO **OR** president **OR** CFO **OR** chair* **OR** leader*)	
4	Add **AND** business		(ethics **OR** Moral*)	10
		AND	(develop* **OR** social*)	
		AND	(CEO **OR** president **OR** CFO **OR** chair* **OR** leader*)	
		AND	business	

As you can see from Table 3.1, the way in which a search is defined can make a huge difference in what is retrieved. Making such small changes as selecting only journal articles, or using the word *leader* instead of *lead** can make huge differences in the number of citations retrieved in a search. Also be aware that the search engine used and timing of the search can change the results. Using the WebSPIRS service (rather than EBSCO), conducting a search using the original search strategy on December 8, 2004 (1 year later), retrieved 4,720 sources (vs. 3,701). Conducting the most restricted search again (example four in Table 3.1) on February 9, 2005, yielded 19 sources (vs. 10 a year earlier), some of which were due to growth in the literature.

We start reviewing our citations. Several look very interesting and relevant to our topic. For example, one is an article by Agle, Mitchel, and Sonnenfeld, titled "Who Matters to CEO's? An Investigation of Stakeholder Attributes and Salience, Corporate Performance and CEO Values," appearing on pages 507 through 525 of the October 1999 issue of the *Academy of Management Journal*.

It would also be useful to consult an index to business literature such as *Business Source Elite*

for access to additional sources not covered by PsycINFO. In doing so, we used the same search strategy and terms as in PsycINFO (see Table 3.1, line 4), but the results were very different. Limiting our search to full-text, peer-reviewed journals, we uncovered 117 citations that satisfied our search strategy, more than five times the number in our final pass using PsycINFO. One of the more interesting was an article on strategic leadership of ethical behavior in business. Thomas, Schermerhorn, and Dienhart (2004) argue that leaders have a great deal of power to guide behavior within their organizations. Responding to numerous recent instances of high-profile corporate fraud in the United States in another article, Hill, Stephens, and Smith (2003) explore its impact. Examining organizations recognized as socially responsible, they argued that there are significant positive benefits to positive corporate social behavior.

But we are not finished. After reviewing these citations, we may elect to modify our search strategy and do it again. Possibly we wish to cast our net more broadly, to organizations other than for-profit business organizations. We could also select another relevant database that indexes a different set of literature. ERIC, mentioned above, might provide some insight on educational leadership. Finally, we might also search the World Wide Web.

Eyewitness Testimony—Another Search Example

For many years psychologists have been concerned about the reliability and accuracy of memory. The review chapter on memory by Koriat, Goldsmith, and Pansky (2000) considered many types of distortions and limitations that may occur in memories (e.g., false recall, misattributions, and source errors). In his popular book on memory, Daniel Schacter (1996, ch. 4) recounted instances of memory distortions involving mistaken identity, and recollection of events that never happened.

A popular topic has been the accuracy of eyewitness testimony. The justice system relies heavily on eyewitnesses and places a great deal of weight on their testimony in a court room. Cases of eyewitness errors, however, led some psychologists to question the limits of reliance on eyewitnesses. Since the 1970s, researchers have been conducting systematic studies on factors affecting eyewitness accounts (e.g., Aronstam & Tyson, 1980; Blonstein & Geiselman, 1990; Loftus, 1975; Loftus & Palmer, 1974; Smith & Ellsworth, 1987).

Suppose we wished to learn more about the limits of eyewitness testimony. After reading a good overview on the topic (e.g., Wells & Olson, 2003), we restrict the scope of our topic. We could focus on variables such as the witness, the event, or how questions are asked (Loftus, 2003).

As in the prior example, we should be concerned about how we structure our search and the terms we use. For example, in PsycINFO controlled vocabulary, the term *witnesses* is used instead of *eyewitness*. Knowing the names of key researchers who have conducted research on our topic enables location of other articles by the same authors (e.g., Phoebe Ellsworth, R. C. L. Lindsay, Elizabeth Loftus, Elizabeth Olson, Vicki Smith, S. L. Sporer, and Gary Wells).

Conducting a search of PsycINFO, using the search terms *witness* **AND** *testimony,* and limiting the search to peer-reviewed articles, yielded 80 citations. In one, the influence of gender

stereotypes is the focus of research reported by McKimmie, Newton, Terry, & Schuller (2004).

Conducting an additional search of PsycINFO for peer-reviewed sources, this time seeking citations authored by the prominent researcher Elizabeth Loftus, we retrieved 161 citations. Reviewing the list, we learn that Ms. Loftus has been involved in many areas of memory research. Some are not directly relevant to our specific topic, such as the article on the impact of advertising on memories by Braun, Ellis, and Loftus (2002).

The retrieval of large numbers of citations, and many not related to our specific topic, underscores how critical it is to have a well-defined search strategy with carefully selected search terms. Reviewing hundreds of sources to find the few that are directly related to our research topic consumes significant time and a great deal of effort.

LIBRARIES OF THE FUTURE

What does the future hold for libraries? Scholarly research and communication are in the midst of significant trends that will shape how people acquire and use information in the future:

• The cost of print materials and information can be expected to continue to increase. At the same time, the volume of information available continues to expand. If current trends continue, this may result in increasing pressure on both personal and institutional library budgets, forcing increased reliance on nonlocal information sources.

• Electronic publishing and the use of electronic media in publishing are occurring with increasing frequency. Increasing numbers of sources are available as electronic documents. Encyclopedias, almanacs, atlases, and even journals are being produced in some electronic form in addition to—or instead of—their paper counterparts. Production of research tools in an electronic medium, whether it is CD or Web-based, can allow flexibility for users to search, format, and extract the information.

• Data sets from researchers and research institutions may become increasingly available directly from authors, agencies, or research organizations in electronic form. This will result in increased distribution of scholarly output, including fugitive literature. It will also disperse access to research output; that is, more publications will be found outside the traditional publication formats (books, journals).

• Use of the Internet has exploded since the early 1990s. Graphical user interfaces such as Internet Explorer and Netscape allow rapid electronic written communication worldwide and afford increasing flexibility in the type and format of information shared among researchers.

• Scanning of hard copy documents for preservation and electronic delivery may mean an increasing retrospective information base accessible in electronic form.

The availability of full-text sources online will mean greater access to information. Electronic formats will also allow faster communication of that information among geographically dispersed researchers. Users, however, will face a number of obstacles in use of the virtual library: For example, the quantity of information will be imposing and difficult to negotiate effectively, and monetary charges will increasingly be levied for retrieval of information from remote sites.

RECORDING AND ORGANIZING YOUR INFORMATION

There are many sources of information on this topic. Among these are the APA *Publication Manual* (2001); Booth, Colomb, and Williams (2003); and Sternberg (2003). Basic steps in this process are detailed below.

Taking Notes

Searching for and locating material appropriate to your research topic are among the first steps, followed by reading, organizing, and synthesizing the information. One step in this process is to use a systematic approach to taking notes and organize them in a coherent manner.

There are several ways to accomplish complete and accurate notes. One is to use the index card method. This is accomplished by recording bibliographic information about each source on a small index card (for example, 3" × 5") with notes on corresponding 5" × 7" cards. This system has several advantages. It is portable. Cards can be sorted as you develop your outline and flesh out the paper. The process of recording notes can help you focus on the salient points of the item you're examining.

Another approach is to use software designed to record or collect bibliographic information, many such programs also allow you to record notes and outline your project. These include Reference Manager, EndNote, and Library Master, although there are others; see Chapter 23 by Calderon and Austin. Such software takes bibliographic information and reformats it for the reference list in your paper. Some software will import citations from databases such as PsycINFO and ERIC, placing bibliographic information in the correct fields and then exporting those references into standardized publication formats. Some software runs not only on desktop and laptop computers but also on palm-sized computers or personal digital assistants (PDAs).

As you examine each item (e.g., book, chapter, journal article, research report), record basic bibliographic information about it. This includes author(s), title, publisher information, date of publication, pages, journal in which it appeared, and enough location information so that you can find it again if needed (such as a library call number or URL). Even if the source is not germane to your topic, recording this information serves as a reminder that an item has been examined and has been discarded. Recording information in a standardized publication format such as APA will insure the information is complete and will save time later on.

Selecting the key points from a publication and summarizing those points are important skills. Read the item in its entirety and think about the contributions it contains. Then in your own words summarize those concepts and how they contribute to your own project. Resist the temptation to simply photocopy or print an article or chapter, highlighting those sections that are important. This will not help you synthesize the material into your own research. In the case of electronic media, resist the urge to cut and paste large sections of text from a publication, even if you enclose it in quotation marks. This approach does not allow you to summarize the content and, more important, can lead to plagiarism, even if it is unintentional. Think about what you read, isolate the important points, and summarize those points in your own words. Save direct quotes for short excerpts, using the APA *Publication Manual* as a guide.

Outline Your Project

Creating an outline for your own paper can take many forms. Some people begin by constructing a very detailed outline, a skeleton fleshed out by the content you have synthesized in the course of reviewing the research of others and discovered in the course of your own research. The ability to create detailed outlines is sometimes integrated into word processing software or note-taking software.

Alternatively, some people are more comfortable with a very loose content outline, no more detailed than the structure of a research article described in Chapter 23. This outline can be fleshed out by relying on the *spewing out* method described in Chapter 24, "Writing Rough Drafts," followed by a series of rewrites to add structure. Whatever method reflects your personal style, it's important to be flexible as your research project and paper develop.

RECOMMENDED READINGS

Several recent publications cover research paper topic selection and definition. Now in its fourth edition, Sternberg's *The Psychologist's Companion* (2003) details the process from topic selection and outlining content to reporting research results. *The Craft of Research* (Booth, Columb, & Williams, 2003) also includes the processes of identifying, planning, and designing the research project, as well as communicating results.

Library Use: Handbook for Psychology (Reed & Baxter, 2003) not only covers selecting and refining the research topic, it extends those activities into the literature search process. Specific examples from a variety of subfields illustrate use of important finding tools in psychology and related disciplines. It provides expanded discussion of publication types seldom covered elsewhere, such as locating published tests, government publications as sources of research activities, and using cited reference literature searching. Two volumes retrospectively survey the literature of reference materials relevant to psychology. Although dated, *Research Guide to Psychology* (McInnis, 1982) and *Psychology: A Guide to Reference and Information Sources* (Baxter, 1993) are annotated bibliographies covering indexes and abstracting services, directories, journal literature, and other tools to access research communication and the information on the profession of psychology.

As the basic style guide used in psychology, *Publication Manual of the American Psychological Association* (APA, 2001) is an essential reference for all writers in the discipline for its tips on content organization, reference and paper formatting, and the process of preparing one's research for publication.

EXERCISES

1. Narrow the topic. Identify a key source, such as an annual review or handbook article on your topic. Read the source. Select an aspect of the topic that sounds interesting. Reduce the scope of your topic to a size that might be manageable for your research and bibliographic review. Write a topic statement or topic question.

You might consider one of the following sources as a starting point:

[Abnormal] Joiner, T. E., Brown, J. S., & Wingate, L. R. (2005). The psychology and neurobiology of suicidal behavior. *Annual Review of Psychology, 56,* 287–314.

[Creativity] Runco, M. A. (2004). Creativity. *Annual Review of Psychology, 55,* 657–687.

[Learning] Domjan, M. (2005). Pavlovian conditioning: A functional perspective. *Annual Review of Psychology, 56,* 179–206.

[Perception] Logan, G. D. (2004). Cumulative progress in formal theories of attention. *Annual Review of Psychology, 55,* 207–234.

[Personality] Mischel, W. (2004). Toward an integrative science of the person. *Annual Review of Psychology, 55,* 1–22.

[Women's Studies] Stewart, A. J., & McDermott, C. (2004). Gender in psychology. *Annual Review of Psychology, 55,* 519–544.

2. Develop a topic search strategy. Identify your topic. Review a relevant source. Develop the search terms that you will use to conduct your search.

You might begin by selecting one of the sources you considered in Exercise 1 above or a source such as one below:

[Clinical] Witkiewitz, K., & Marlatt, G. A. (2004). Relapse prevention for alcohol and drug problems: That was Zen, this is Tao. *American Psychologist, 59(4),* 224–235.

[Intelligence and Race] Sternberg, R. J., Grigorenko, E. L., & Kidd, K. K. (2005). Intelligence, race, and genetics. *American Psychologist, 60(1),* 46–59.

[Judgment and Decision Making] Kahneman, D. (2003) A perspective on judgment and choice: Mapping bounded rationality. *American Psychologist, 58*(9), 697–720.

[Religion] Miller, W. R., & Thoresen, C. E. (2003). Spirituality, religion, and health: An emerging research field. *American Psychologist, 58*(1), 24–35.

[Social Conflict] Eidelson, R. J., & Eidelson, J. I. (2003). Dangerous ideas: Five beliefs that propel groups toward conflict. *American Psychologist, 58*(3), 182–192.

3. Conduct a search. Start with a search strategy and terms you have identified that are related to a topic of interest. Identify a relevant database such as PsycINFO, Business Source Elite, or ERIC. Conduct your search. Review and evaluate the results of your initial search. How relevant are the results of your search to what you were seeking?

Modify your search strategy to restrict the search. Add required parameters such as a subject population, age period, or specific aspect of the topic. Perform the search again. Compare the results from this new search with results of your initial search.

(If your search yielded no results, expand your search strategy by adding synonyms and related terms. Then perform the search again.)

You might begin by selecting one of the topics noted above, or you might use one of the sample topics suggested below. In each topic below, you would probably need to restrict your search to narrow its focus.

[Clinical] Posttraumatic stress disorder

[Cognitive development] Neural pruning

[Education] Teacher expectations, Pygmalion effect

[Ergonomics] Human-computer interaction

[Learning] Spontaneous recovery

[Sleep disorders] Insomnia

REFERENCES

Agle, B. R., Mitchell, R. K., & Sonnenfeld, J. A. (1999). Who matters to CEOs? An investigation of stakeholder attributes and salience, corporate performance and CEO values. *Academy of Management Journal, 42*(5), 507–525.

American Psychological Association. (2001). *Publication manual of the American Psychological Association* (5th ed.). Washington, DC: Author.

Anderson, N. (2001–2002). *Handbook of industrial, work, and organizational psychology* (Vols. 1, 2). Thousand Oaks, CA: Sage.

Aronstam, D., & Tyson, G. A. (1980). Racial bias in eyewitness perception. *Journal of Social Psychology, 110*(2), 177–182.

Barry, M. (2002). Why ethics and compliance programs can fail. *Journal of Business Strategy, 23*(6), 37–40.

Bass, B. M. (1990). *Bass and Stogdill's handbook of leadership* (3rd ed). New York: Free Press.

Baxter, P. M. (1993). *Psychology: A guide to reference and information sources.* Englewood, CO: Libraries Unlimited.

Beck, S. (1997). *The good, the bad & the ugly: or, why it's a good idea to evaluate Web sources.* Las Cruces: New Mexico State University Library. (http://lib.nmsu.edu/instruction/eval.html)

Blonstein, R., & Geiselman, R. E. (1990). Effects of witnessing conditions and expert witness testimony on credibility of an eyewitness. *American Journal of Forensic Psychology, 8*(4), 11–19.

Booth, W. C., Columb, G. G., & Williams, J. M. (2003). *The craft of research* (2nd ed.). Chicago: University of Chicago Press.

Braun, K. A., Ellis, R., & Loftus, E. F. (2002). Make my memory: How advertising can change our memories of the past. *Psychology & Marketing, 19*(1), 1–23.

Campbell, J. P., Dunnette, M. D., Lawler, E. E., & Wick, K. E. (1970). *Managerial behavior, performance, and effectiveness.* New York: McGraw-Hill.

Cooper, C. L., & Robertson, I. T. (Eds.). (1986+). *International review of industrial and organizational psychology* (Vol. 1 +) [Annual]. New York: Wiley.

Dunnette, M. D. (Ed.). (1976). *Handbook of industrial and organizational psychology.* Chicago: Rand McNally.

Dunnette, M. D., & Hough, L. M. (1990–1994). *Handbook of industrial and organizational psychology* (Vols. 1–4, 2nd ed.). Consulting Psychologist's Press.

EBSCO Information Services. (2005). *Bibliographic and full text databases.* Retrieved February 6, 2005, from www.epnet.com/academic/default.asp

Gowan, M., & Spanbauer, S. (2001). Find everything faster. *PC World, 19*(9), 109–111.

Greenberg, H. (2003, April 28). Enron never happened. *Fortune, 147*(8), 128.

Hill, R. P., Stephens, D., & Smith, I. (2003). Corporate social responsibility: An examination of individual firm behavior. *Business and Society Review, 108*(3), 339–364.

Kahneman, D., Slovic, P., & Tversky, A. (1982). *Judgment under uncertainty: Heuristics and biases.* New York: Cambridge University Press.

Katz, D., & Kahn, R. L. (1966). *Social psychology of organizations.* New York: Wiley.

Kirk, E. E. (1996). *Evaluating information found on the Internet.* Baltimore: Sheridan Libraries of Johns Hopkins University. (www.library.jhu.edu/researchhelp/general/evaluating/index.html)

Koriat, A., Goldsmith, M., & Pansky, A. (2000). Toward a psychology of memory accuracy. *Annual Review of Psychology, 51*, 481–537.

Landy, F. J., & Conte, J. M. (2004). *Work in the 21st century: An introduction to industrial and organizational psychology.* New York: McGraw-Hill.

Levy, P. E. (2003). *Industrial/organizational psychology: Understanding the workplace.* Boston: Houghton Mifflin.

Loftus, E. F. (1975). Leading questions and the eyewitness report. *Cognitive Psychology, 7*, 560–572.

Loftus, E. F. (2003). Make-believe memories. *American Psychologist, 58*, 867–873.

Loftus, E. F., & Palmer, J. C. (1974). Reconstruction of automobile destruction: An example of the interaction between language and memory. *Journal of Verbal Learning and Verbal Behavior, 13*, 585–589.

March, J. G., & Simon, H. A. (1958). *Organizations.* New York: Wiley.

McCauley, C. D., & Van Velsor, E. (Eds.). (2004). *Center for creative leadership handbook of leadership development.* San Francisco: Jossey-Bass.

McInnis, R. G. (1982). *Research guide for psychology.* Westport, CT: Greenwood.

McKimmie, B. M., Newton, C. J., Terry, D. J., & Schuller, R. A. (2004). Jurors' responses to expert witness testimony: The effects of gender stereotypes. *Group Process & Intergroup Relations, 7*(2), 131–143.

Muchinsky, P. M. (2003). *Psychology applied to work: An introduction to industrial and organizational psychology* (7th ed.). Belmont, CA: Thompson/Wadsworth.

Novack, K. (2003, June 23). CEO Scandals: Get your scorecard. *Time, 151*(25), 26.

O'Reilly, C. A. (1991). Organizational behavior: Where we've been, where we're going. *Annual Review of Psychology, 42,* 427–258.

Porter, L. W., Bigley, G. A., & Steers, R. M. (2003). *Motivation and work behavior* (7th ed.). Boston: McGraw-Hill/Irwin.

Reed, J. G., & Baxter, P. M. (2003). *Library use: Handbook for psychology* (3rd ed.). Washington, DC: APA.

Rogel, S. (2003). Business ethics and the Boy Scout code. *Vital Speeches of the Day, 69*(13), 403–406.

Sayther, C. (2003). Report card on Sarbanes-Oxley: One year later. *Financial Executive, 19*(7), 6.

Schacter, D. L. (1996). *Searching for memory: The brain, the mind, and the past.* New York: Basic Books.

Smith, V. L., & Ellsworth, P. C. (1987). The social psychology of eyewitness accuracy: Misleading questions and communicator expertise. *Journal of Applied Psychology, 72,* 294–300.

Sternberg, R. J. (2003). *The psychologist's companion: A guide to scientific writing for students and researchers* (4th ed.). New York: Cambridge University Press.

Thomas, T., Schermerhorn, J. R., & Dienhart, J. W. (2004). Strategic leadership of ethical behavior in business. *Academy of Management Executive, 18*(2), 56–66.

Van Yoder, S. (2003). Latest board challenge: Recruiting CFOs. *Financial Executive, 19*(7), 42–44.

Wells, G. L., & Olson, E. A. (2003). Eyewitness testimony. *Annual Review of Psychology, 54,* 277–295.

4

REVIEWING AND EVALUATING A RESEARCH ARTICLE

KATHRYN C. OLESON
ROBERT M. ARKIN

Reading a research article is as much an art and science as writing one. In this chapter, we touch on many aspects of the skill of critical reading. Before we begin, though, we hasten to advocate that you read and think about Chapters 23 through 26 in this handbook, too, as you develop your approach to the reading of research. Learning to read about research is so intimately linked with learning to write about it that to us the two seem inseparable. Effective reading and writing are both reflections of comparable critical thinking skills (e.g., Squire, 1983). Both also involve communication, in one case of the "transmitter" variety and, in the other, the "receiver" variety. The principles of effective transmission and effective receiving are mirror images of one another. To be a good transmitter of information, it is key to imagine yourself in the role of receiver; to be an effective receiver, it is key to imagine what the author is trying to transmit. Additionally, we encourage you to read the first chapter of this book, "Research as a Script." It provides an overall framework for understanding the research process that will prove helpful in your reviewing and critiquing others' research.

Our central mission in this chapter is to describe a set of tools to use in reading, reviewing, and evaluating research. Some of these tools are more like delicate instruments than like spades and drills. It takes a great deal of experience and a deep appreciation of research to use the delicate instruments well. For instance, the tools needed to dissect a research design and to consider the various statistical approaches a researcher might use are something that even experienced researchers are continually learning about. Learning how to select and use proper statistical procedures and methods is a moving target with new approaches and techniques being developed. There is even a relatively new journal, *Psychological Methods*, published by the American Psychological Association (APA), devoted to these advances. Because

AUTHORS' NOTE: This research was supported in part by faculty development funds provided by Reed College. We are indebted to a large number of teachers and colleagues who, over the years and while we were writing this chapter (and the first edition of it), talked with us about the various ways to think about, review, and evaluate empirical research. In addition, we thank Cameron Brick, Paige Ramsdell, and Leigh Wensman, as well as several graduate students, for reading an earlier version of this chapter.

improvements occur often and trends and strategies grow and change, even experienced researchers must stay alert and change as well. Other tools are more of the garden-variety sort with which you are already familiar, such as checking the logic and internal consistency of the arguments in a research paper.

In our experience as teachers, it is almost as common for beginners to be anxious and frustrated in reading research as it is for them to be paralyzed by the prospect of writing about it. Our metaphor about delicate instruments and garden tools is intended to help you put some of those concerns aside. There are many levels of critical reading, and one can do a good job at many of those levels before completing "Delicate Instruments of Research Design and Statistical Analysis 101."

PURPOSE AND AUDIENCE

The crucial starting point actually occurs before you read one word of an article. You are headed for greater efficiency and greater effectiveness if you ask yourself a couple questions: (a) What is my purpose in reading the article? (b) What is the audience for the assessment I will make?

Sometimes people read psychology articles for the pure pleasure of it. More often, you will have some purpose in mind, and it will involve informing someone about the research or communicating your evaluation of it.

Your purpose will range from informal to formal and will also depend on whether you are reading just one study or surveying a literature (see Table 4.1). For a class assignment, you may be asked to describe a study, or set of studies, from beginning to end. You might also be expected to offer a brief evaluation of the strengths and weaknesses of the research. Your task is to find your way around the research article, to gain a general sense of the story it tells, and to offer some critical analysis.

On other occasions, your purpose is to read and synthesize a range of articles (the literature review). Toward that end, your first reading has a specific purpose, in addition to learning the lay of the land in a research literature, such as (a) finding studies that all use the same method, (b) locating studies that uncover the same general finding, or (c) identifying studies that stem from the same theory. The digital revolution has changed entirely the ways one can access and use information. Literature searches are more convenient and more complete because of the

Table 4.1   Your Purpose and Audience in Reading Research

	Number of Articles	
	One or a Few	*Many*
Informal Educational purpose: Your goal is to learn Audience: Classmates, advisor, or colleague Mode: Often oral presentation or conversation	Class assignment (e.g., oral report) Background reading	Literature review Meta-analysis
Formal Professional purpose: Your goal is to assess or decide Audience: Author(s), editor, and other reviewers Mode: Written	Journal review	You've just been named editor of *Journal of Good Ideas and Good Research*

availability of search engines such as PsycINFO and the Social Science Citation Index. These enable one to search by topic, author, and keywords, and consequently to see the linkages across studies in the psychological literature. (See Chapters 2 and 3 in this handbook for helpful suggestions on ways to find a research topic and conduct bibliographic research.) Search engines such as Google are also commonly available and provide a quick and often useful panorama of themes and names of prominent researchers (and their Web sites) and topics that can lead to valuable connections. As we write, a new version of Google (called Google Scholar) is being tested (beta version) and should be implemented widely soon.

In addition to completing informal reviews of articles, you may be asked by a journal's editor (or associate editor) to provide a formal review of a manuscript being considered for publication. The purpose of the review is ordinarily (a) to make a recommendation to the editor about whether the paper should be published in the journal and (b) to provide some commentary about your assessment of the article, judging its merits—ranging from theoretical contribution to the specifics of research design and statistical analysis (see also Chapter 26 of this book).

THE LIGHT SURVEY

Once you have identified your purpose and audience, you are ready to read. But here, we suggest again that you avoid the temptation to "Just Do It!" Start with a light survey.

Those who specialize in the study of reading and writing recommend that you begin reading a book with the preface and foreword to gain background information about the authors. Next, a survey of the chapter headings throughout the book can reveal the main themes and show how the author will proceed to develop them (Rheingold, 1994). Only then do you read the first chapter—*followed by the last!* Together, these steps in your survey will convey a fairly complete sense of the book as a whole. If your appetite has been whetted, the first and last paragraphs of the intervening chapters will be next, along with a survey of the index, a rereading of the table of contents, and a careful reading of the middle of the book last, if at all (Rheingold, 1994). In just a few hours, you will have uncovered the main idea of the book, become familiar with the author's style, and you will have placed the book in context. Most important, you will have gauged the relevance of the book to your purposes and interests in a progressive way; at each step, you could abort your survey and move to your next learning task. This strategy is both efficient and effective.

You can easily export the same survey techniques to the reading of empirical research articles. The effective light survey does not always rigidly adhere to the time-honored flow from Introduction, through Method and Results, to Discussion. First, start with the abstract. It acts like an executive summary for those without time or inclination to go further. It provides you with context and landmarks and even foreshadows specifics. The first paragraph of the Introduction then provides more detailed background, and the first paragraph or two of the Discussion usually summarizes the findings and reveals how well the study met its goals. The specifics of the hypotheses (usually at the end of the Introduction) might be next, followed by a general scanning of the Results and then a scanning of the Method section. Whatever your preferred order, your approach will likely change to fit your specific purpose (e.g., literature review or formal review). Regardless of your purpose, though, we think a good trick for a quick and effective survey is to first read the abstract and then the first sentence of every paragraph (usually the topic sentence) in the article, in order. Generally, this highly manageable task requires only a few minutes, and it conveys a remarkable amount of information about the article and a sense of whether a more detailed reading will be profitable.

We urge you to try these strategies as an exercise (see Exercise 1 at the end of the chapter). You might locate a journal that includes brief articles to give you a manageable start (e.g., *Basic and Applied Social Psychology, Health Psychology, Journal of Consulting and Clinical Psychology, Journal of Experimental Social Psychology, Psychological Science*), but then try this with journals that include longer articles as well (e.g., *Developmental Psychology, Journal of Educational Psychology, Journal of*

Experimental Psychology, Personality and Social Psychology Bulletin). Try the first-sentence strategy a few times for each type of journal. It does not always work, particularly if the article is not well written, but we think that you will be impressed with how much you can gain with this small expenditure of time and effort. Now try to see how quickly you can locate the essential theory involved, the specific independent variable, or the general finding for several additional empirical articles. This exercise should help you develop your skills in finding your way around a research article in psychology.

REVIEWING A RESEARCH ARTICLE

Here, we turn to specific suggestions that can guide your in-depth review of an article, be it for an informal class project or to assess a manuscript under consideration for publication.

Generally speaking, when evaluating a manuscript, you ask of the author's work the very same questions that would guide you in conducting research and writing your own manuscript to report it (see Chapters 1 and 6, "Research as a Script" and "Designing a Research Study," and Chapters 23 to 26 on research writing; see also Bem, 2004). In a formal review of research you have two purposes: (a) assessing the quality of content and making a recommendation about whether the research merits publication and (b) providing commentary to the author and the editor about strengths and shortcomings you perceive in the manuscript and advice about how the manuscript might be improved. A classroom assignment version of this task might be briefer and might be presented orally, and of course, author and editor would not be the audience. The fifth edition of the *Publication Manual* of the APA (APA, 2001) provides a nice abstract (executive summary) of the questions that comprise this task, for whatever audience:

Is the research question significant, and is the work original and important?

Have the instruments been demonstrated to have satisfactory reliability and validity?

Are the outcome measures clearly related to the variables with which the investigation is concerned?

Does the research design fully and unambiguously test the hypothesis?

Are the participants representative of the population to which generalizations are made?

Did the researcher observe ethical standards in the treatment of participants—for example, if deception was used for humans?

Is the research at an advanced enough stage to make the publication of results meaningful? (p. 6)

The list of potential criteria to answer these questions is quite long, however. Gottfredson (1978) identified 83 attributes that editors and reviewers use in evaluating manuscripts; Lindsey (1978) narrowed the evaluation task to 12 dimensions. Perhaps it is no surprise, then, that statistical analyses of reviewers' agreement with one another show only a modest relationship (e.g., Fiske & Fogg, 1990).

Reviewer Agreement?

But saying that two reviewers do not agree does not imply that they disagree. Instead, analyses of reviewers' commentaries and recommendations show that they tend to write about different topics, each making points that are appropriate and accurate (Fiske & Fogg, 1990). Fiske and Fogg's (1990) search for statements about weaknesses in submitted manuscripts showed that, across the reviews, the number of points cited ranged from 0 to 37. The mean number cited was 8.6. For your purposes, the mean number (fewer than 10) may be the most informative number to remember as you search for a model review as a prototype against which to match your own effort (see Appendix 5.1 at the end of this chapter). As we will discuss later, one should focus on finding the set of key weaknesses rather than creating a long laundry list. The range (none to many) is also revealing, however. At times, a longer or shorter list of critiques is appropriate. It is also important to note that editors are familiar with nonoverlap in commentaries. Indeed, they expect it. Editors pick reviewers of different types (older, younger; expert, wise generalist; sympathetic, dispassionate, unsympathetic; etc.) and expect that they will emphasize different kinds of points.

Form 4.1   A Typical Evaluation Form for a Journal Reviewer

Journal of Good Ideas and Good Research

1. Overall appraisal of the manuscript (place a check mark):
   _____ Accept
   _____ Accept, with revisions as indicated
   _____ Reject, with invitation to resubmit in revised form
   _____ Reject, for reasons indicated in the enclosed critique

2. Confidential appraisal of the manuscript:

   A. On a scale of 1-10, with 10 representing excellence, rate this paper with respect to the following:
      Adequacy of the literature review   _____
      Theoretical importance   _____
      Adequacy of quantitative analysis   _____
      Sophistication of methodology   _____
      Clarity of communication   _____
      Likelihood of being cited in future   _____

   B. Additional comments for the editor:

Whether two reviewers agree or do not agree that a paper should be published, they may weight their reasons differently. A groundbreaking study on a novel question may have the potential for high impact but be flawed from a design or analysis perspective (Perlman & Dean, 1987), and the weighting of these two factors is to a great extent a reflection of the reader's values. The editor, in turn, must weigh the recommendations and commentary and apply his or her own cognitive gymnastics to the equation and conclusion. The process requires expert and balanced judgment, and editors are selected on that basis. You might be relieved to know that there rarely is just one right answer in reviewing; your job as a reviewer is to do the best job you can, be balanced, and to bring your own skills and perspectives to bear on the task.

Form 4.1 is a typical rating form used by a reviewer in making a recommendation to an editor.

On a separate page, the reviewer ordinarily includes a commentary about facets of the manuscript that seem notable, whether positive or negative. These commentaries vary dramatically, depending on the nature of the manuscript and the type of the journal as well as the style of the reviewer; however, one clear dimension that emerges in these critiques is that they range from broad to narrow. The *narrow* type is focused on methodological matters and statistical procedure—the delicate instruments dissection. The *broad* type deals more with the ideas at hand, the importance of the theory under study, how persuasive or compelling the hypothesis is, the excitement the work might generate, and the work's novelty. These two types of reviews are exemplified in starkly contrasting reviewers' commentaries in Appendix 5.1. Most important, reviews of articles are usually a mix of narrow matters of procedure and broader matters of the theoretical importance, interest value, and judgments of the paper's likely impact.

Pitfalls for the Novice Reviewer

Interestingly, novice reviewers show three tendencies: First, they tend to be picky at times, noting shortcomings or outright mistakes—but ones that are not very consequential (see Review B, Appendix 5.1). This is a bit ironic because the novice is attempting delicate dissection. The art of dissection, however, is distinguishing the benign from the malignant, and that requires experience. Second, novices tend to be overly critical at times. The newcomer to reviewing is more likely than the seasoned reader to zero in on deficiencies like a laser and to weight them heavily. More experienced evaluators know that all research is flawed, and they are usually predisposed to forgive the minor, inconsequential errors and dwell only on the crucial. Finally, novice reviewers tend to write much longer, more detailed commentaries than do seasoned reviewers. Naturally, the lengthier the commentary, the more helpful it might be to the editor and author who read and try to learn from it. Lack of confidence, however, often leads novices to take a shotgun approach, hoping that some criticism will hit the target. When extreme, this approach, coupled with a tendency to be harsh and narrow, can lead to a laundry list of shortcomings that is more likely to hurt the author's feelings than to provide constructive criticism.

One important goal of reviews of research is to be supportive of the author. The author's hard work in bringing the research and manuscript to completion should be commended. The author's risk in exposing his or her work to evaluation should be rewarded, not punished. Civility is a very important quality of any review for an author's consumption. Constructive criticism balanced with positive commentary is the most effective way to review a paper.

No research article is perfect. You need to be able to identify flaws when reviewing research articles; however, the key matter is to rest your evaluation on whether the flaws are consequential. If you have a firm understanding of the paper's main purpose, the conceptual questions the paper sets out to address, the methods used, the clarity of the conclusions, and the extent to which they follow from the findings, you are equipped to understand whether the paper's shortcomings are fatal flaws or garden variety problems of little import. Conceptual shortcomings are the most fatal; if the research questions or theoretical assumptions are illogical or flawed, then even brilliant empirical realizations of variables may not matter.

For instance, take a researcher who is investigating the impact of self-awareness on ethical behavior. If the researcher introduced an operating video camera in one condition versus a non-operating (broken) video camera in the other as a way to arouse feelings of high self-awareness and low self-awareness respectively, there might be a consequential problem with the translation from concept to operation. The presence of an operating video camera has been shown to create self-awareness. In this setting, however, it might also elicit ethical behavior for reasons of self-presentation (i.e., being videotaped makes everything pretty public). Now, to illustrate an inconsequential flaw, consider another researcher who introduces a mirror to the participant's environment. In one condition, the participant can see her or his own reflection in the mirror (high self-awareness). In the other condition, the participant can only see a reflection of the experimenter (low self-awareness). It might have been a bad idea to have the participant see a reflection of the experimenter in the low self-awareness condition. It makes you wonder what seeing a reflection of an experimenter might do, psychologically. But there is no evidence on this question. So the presence of the experimenter's reflection in the low self-awareness condition is, probably, inconsequential—a flaw perhaps, but not a fatal flaw.

Flaws in the empirical aspects of research are fatal only to the degree they influence the paper's conclusions. Further, as we said above, it is every bit as important to search for and mention strengths as to search for shortcomings.

More Detail on How to Evaluate the Sections of a Research Paper

We now expand on the *Publication Manual* abstract by discussing in more detail how to evaluate each of the sections of a research paper: Introduction, Method, Results, and Discussion/Conclusions. It is important to note that we are both social psychologists, so some issues that we consider key may be less relevant to other domains of psychology. Take this into account. For each section, we list some important issues that you should consider, but keep in mind that each section should be assessed within the overall framework of the paper and its objectives. As we will say a number of times, it is the big picture that matters.

The Abstract and Introduction

Your concerns here are

Objectives of the paper

Importance of the research questions

Research idea at the conceptual level

What you are assessing/How to assess it. Read the abstract and introduction with the goal of understanding why the research was conducted. You are trying to gain a sense of the big picture. Ask yourself, "What is the goal of this research, this paper?" "What is the hypothesis?" "Is the question clearly presented?"

Begin by determining the research question and then consider its importance. Is the question significant? If answered, would it change how we think about human behavior? Also consider how the current research question relates to previous research. Does the researcher accurately and usefully convey past research in this area? Is the researcher familiar with past work, and is the description complete? Does the current work change or add to our theoretical understanding of the problem? Does it add to our general knowledge, and will it lead others to do more research in this area? After reading the review of previous research, think about what findings you would predict. Making your own predictions will help you assess the author's hypothesis and also cause you to think about possible alternative explanations for the findings.

Pop quiz. When you have finished reading the paper, you should be able to describe it and assess its importance in no more than two or three sentences. A colleague of one of the authors often asks her students to present the main ideas of a research article in a way that their grandmothers would understand. Quiz yourself by seeing if you can in clear, simple terms ("grandmotherese") convey the research article's big picture, including its main ideas and their importance (see also Bem, 2004, who stresses that this is how one should approach writing a research article.) For instance, if you

were reading the self-serving bias article reviewed in Appendix 5.1, you might note that the study is trying to understand whether someone takes more personal responsibility for positive than negative things that they do. This work is important because it could help us understand the different ways that people hold themselves accountable, an understanding that could improve personal relationships. Without this understanding, people might believe that others hold themselves just as accountable for negative as for positive outcomes. They don't. In a group performance context, for instance, a set of individuals might each take 40% of the responsibility for a group success (collectively, 200% responsibility in a five-person group); however, a set of individuals might each take only 10% of the responsibility for a group failure (where, collectively, only 50% of the responsibility is then accounted for).

We recommend that you try this today (see Exercise 2) by obtaining a recent copy of *Psychological Science.* You can likely find *Psychological Science* in your college library; it is available in print and electronically. (If you have not already learned to use the Internet to obtain an article so efficiently in our digital age, downloading the electronic version of the journal article is an eye-opener.) Select an article of interest and then proceed through the steps we suggest. You should have an understanding of the conceptual logic of the paper. You should also be able to convey to someone whether the paper convincingly addressed the questions posed. Try this pop quiz on yourself at every opportunity. It's a test of your growing ability to move easily from the receiver to the transmitter mode.

The Method Section

Your concerns here are

Internal validity

Construct validity

External validity

What you are assessing. When reading the Method section, once again keep the big picture in mind. Think about what ideas the author is trying to test at the conceptual level and what steps would be required to realize those ideas operationally. Have the researchers successfully translated their conceptual variables into concrete operations? By evaluating the methods carefully, you are trying to determine whether the research is valid (Aronson, Brewer, & Carlsmith, 1985; Campbell & Stanley, 1966; Cook & Campbell, 1979; Shadish, Cook, & Campbell, 2002). You are considering whether it accomplishes the goals that it set out to reach. In particular, you are assessing three types of validity: internal, construct, and external (see Shadish et al., 2002, for a more detailed discussion of these three types of validity; see also Chapters 6 through 10 in this handbook.)

In assessing *internal validity*, you examine whether factors *other than the independent variables* could have caused the effects on the dependent measures. Are there elements in the procedure that accompanied the independent variables and therefore could have caused, or at least influenced, the results? Two major factors to consider when assessing a study's internal validity are whether participants were randomly assigned to conditions and whether the proper control or comparison groups were included in the experimental design. For instance, suppose that in the self-serving bias study reviewed in Appendix 5.1, all of the success participants were run in the study during their *morning* psychology class and all of the failure participants were run in the study during their *afternoon* psychology class. Participants were not randomly assigned. Instead, the time of day accompanies the independent variable and therefore could be the cause of the differences rather than the manipulation of success and failure. Additionally, this study did not include a comparison group in which the participants did not succeed or fail, making it impossible to understand if, under success, one takes more credit, or if, under failure, one takes less credit. A neutral (e.g., moderate success or no information about success or failure) condition is necessary to understand the directionality of the effect.

If you believe an experiment has *construct validity,* you judge that, within their experiment, the researchers are actually testing the conceptual hypotheses they pose. In other words, have the researchers operationalized their hypotheses in ways that capture the concepts they are trying to study? Finally, if the research has *external validity,* then the findings may be generalized to the populations and settings to which the experimenters wish them to apply. With external validity, the results have application to other people and situations. In addition, when evaluating the methods used, you should always consider whether the researchers treated their participants ethically.

How to assess it. First, consider the overall research design of the studies presented, focusing on internal validity. What experimental groups did the researchers include and are they adequate to test the research questions? Were participants randomly assigned to conditions? Are there appropriate control or comparison groups? You are examining here, based on common sense and what is known about research design, whether this experiment allows the researchers to test their hypotheses without artifact or ambiguity.

Next, think about the experimental situation created in the study. Try on for size the perspective of the participants in the study. How would it feel to participate in this study? Does the procedure seem to make sense? Are participants apt to guess the hypotheses? If so, were checks on suspicion taken? Also, look at the experimental situation from the viewpoint of the experimenter. Were steps taken to control for biases? Were the experimenters kept blind to condition and so forth? In thinking about the experimental situation, keep in mind that problems or biases are important to the extent that they affect the validity of the study, including internal, construct, and external validity. That is, could these problems or biases, instead of the independent variables, have caused the effects measured and observed on the dependent variables of interest? Also, do various problems seem to influence whether the conceptual variables are realized in a meaningful way or whether the results can be generalized to other populations?

Next, to assess construct validity directly, examine the way that the experimenters realized their conceptual variables. How did the researchers operationalize the variables of their hypotheses? Do these operationalizations seem appropriate? Do you have enough information from the paper to understand how the variables were manipulated? Is there independent evidence (e.g., manipulation checks) that the operationalizations were reasonable? Do you believe that the manipulated variables accurately capture the phenomena of interest? Why or why not? If you think that the operationalization is not reasonable, consider whether there are better ways to manipulate the variables. Have the researchers captured the variables in the best ways possible given current research? Keep in mind that researchers who are conducting exploratory studies on exciting new topics may have less of a basis for operationalizing their variables. The standards for assessment should necessarily be more stringent when researchers are using well-established paradigms than novel, home-cooked strategies. Finally, when assessing construct validity, consider the dependent measures used. As with the manipulations, do you believe that these measures accurately capture the phenomena of interest? Are the measures reliable and valid? Why or why not?

Next, to assess the external validity of the studies, take into account the sample of participants. How large was the sample size (N)? What were the demographics (gender, race) of the sample? Are these demographics appropriate to this research? In asking these questions, you are considering whether the results generalize to other situations. If so, what situations?

Finally, assess whether the researchers treated their participants ethically. For instance, if deception was used, were the participants debriefed? Did the researchers seem to take the perspective of their participants and treat them in a sensitive and ethical way?

The Results Section

Your concern here is

Statistical conclusion validity

What you are assessing/How to assess it. In the results section, you are assessing the *statistical conclusion validity,* or the validity of the conclusions that are drawn from the data (see Shadish

et al., 2002). First, you should reconsider the sample size of the study. Keep in mind that the number of participants in the study affects how easy it is to find a result (see Chapter 11, "Statistical Power," for a fuller discussion). With small samples, it is difficult to find an effect, whereas with extremely large samples, it is much easier. Was the sample size adequately large for finding a result? Was it so large that a result, although statistically significant, may have little practical significance? By examining the size of the sample, you are considering not only whether the study was sensitive enough to detect a relationship between the independent and dependent variable but also the size of the effect.

Next, consider the statistical tests that were run on the sample. Are the analyses valid and appropriate? If possible, assess whether they meet the necessary statistical assumptions and whether they use the appropriate error terms. If the statistical tests are inappropriate, then you should consider how they seem to affect the conclusions drawn from the data. (See Part IV, and particularly Chapters 18 through 20 for more detailed discussions of statistical analyses.)

Finally, consider the results reported. Are the data presented clearly? Do the researchers seem to be ignoring parts of the data? Did they drop some participants? If so, why? Is their rationale appropriate? If so, the paper should still report what the results look like with dropped participants included. How strong are the results—both by p values and absolute values? (See also Part IV on data analysis.) Are the measures reliable?

Pop quiz. The Results section of a research article is often the most difficult to assess, particularly for a beginner. Again, we recommend your trying out these new skills of assessing the Results section by using a *Psychological Science* article (see Exercise 3). Ask a friend to do the same, and then you can act as the audience for each other's report. Have you said something in your formal review or class presentation that you could not support in a pop quiz? We have identified many things to note while reviewing this section of the paper, but where the matter we identify outstrips your base of knowledge and experience, you should seek more information for your review rather than do a feeble (or downright incorrect) job of dealing with it. In a formal review, when you lack expertise or feel unqualified to address a matter, say so! Your observation can be judged in that light. If you are not sure about something, either acknowledge it or skip over it. You may miss an obvious or subtle point to make, but when formally reviewing, it is often better to make an error of omission than to step outside the bounds of your knowledge and experience and make an error of commission. Similarly, in a classroom presentation, there is wisdom in acknowledging your limitations before others strive to point them out.

The Conclusion/Discussion Section

Your concern here is

Validity of conclusions

What you are assessing/How to assess it. In the Discussion section, you are evaluating whether the researchers found significant results and are stating their results fairly. As with each section of the paper, assess the conclusions in terms of the big picture. Given the objectives of the paper, the questions it set out to address, and the methods that were used, do their findings follow? Have the authors put their findings back into the theoretical framework with which they began? Did the authors consider alternative explanations for their data? How do the data fit with their theory? How do the data fit with conflicting data from other research? It is obviously best if the data uniquely fit the authors' theory. Have they discussed the limitations of their data, such as possible artifacts or problems? After reading the Discussion, take a moment to consider the overall paper, trying to

reconstruct its overall meaning and flow. To test yourself, you could try to write the abstract for the article (see Exercise 4).

CONCLUSION

If your goal is to be a psychologist, then we recommend that you take every opportunity to try out and improve your research assessment skills. By becoming a better consumer of others' research, you will be better equipped to develop your own research topics. Our goal in this chapter was to provide you with a set of tools to use in reading, reviewing, and evaluating research. We hope that you apply these tools, expand on them, and eventually develop your own style or approach. As your critical skills expand and are refined, we think you will also see growth in your efforts as a theorist, methodologist, and author. In sum, becoming immersed in evaluating existing research on particular topics helps set the stage to think critically about important new questions, and the critical skills associated with reading, reviewing, and evaluating research provide the foundation for designing and implementing one's own research ideas effectively. Don't be easily frustrated. Experienced scholars will sometimes struggle with a research article, trying to decide about its merits or trying to sense the context for its contribution and sometimes take hours or even days to make up their minds about a manuscript. One editor once said that she inferred the "magnitude of contribution" of a work only when, after a day or two had passed, she could recall clearly the point of the study and the essentials of its methods. There is no premium in being very sure of yourself and your judgment too quickly. As you learn to be both critic and author, take your time. It takes time. And the reward is growth in your scholarship, which is well worth both the time and the effort. Good luck!

EXERCISES

1. The Light Survey

Locate a recent copy of the journal *Psychological Science*. You can likely find this journal in your library, either in print or electronically. Select an article from it that sounds interesting to you. Read the abstract first to gain a general sense of the ideas and approaches. Then try the first-sentence strategy. Keep in mind that it does not always work, particularly if the article is not well written; however, we think that you will be impressed with how much you can gain with this small expenditure of time and effort. Now using the same article, go back to read the first paragraph of the Introduction and the first paragraph or two of the Discussion. Next turn to reading the hypotheses (typically presented at the end of the Introduction), and then scan the methods and results sections. Finally, stop to quiz yourself to see if you have a basic understanding of the research questions, the hypotheses and their importance, the methods, and the results. If not, go back to scanning various sections to determine these. This exercise should help you develop your skills in finding your way around a research article in psychology.

2. Describing Main Ideas in 2–3 Sentences

Once again, find a recent copy of *Psychological Science*. Select an article of interest to practice describing it and its importance in no more than two or three sentences. See if you can, in clear, simple terms, convey the research article's big picture, including its main ideas and their importance. We recommend that you do this with a partner. Each of you should read a different article and then transmit this key information to each other. Then, read each other's article and try to transmit that information to your partner. Compare the information that you each conveyed to develop your skills in pulling out the key concepts.

3. Summarizing and Assessing the Key Results

Find a recent copy of *Psychological Science*. Select an article of interest to practice summarizing and assessing its key results; you could use the same article that you used for Exercise 2. See if you can explain, in clear, simple terms, the key results and then present your assessment of them. We recommend that you do this with a partner. Each of you should read a different article and then provide each other with a summary and assessment of the key results. Then, read each other's article and try to transmit that information to your partner. Compare the information that you each conveyed to develop your skills in summarizing and assessing research findings.

4. Writing an Abstract for the Paper

Take the *Psychological Science* article you used for Exercise 1. Carefully read it. Now without looking at the abstract for the article, write its abstract, acting as though you were the author. Authors typically write their abstract last. This exercise is one that helps you to improve your skills in being both an author and a careful reader. Authors often go to their research articles to select sentences that are critical to the meaning and flow of the work. They then revise those sentences and weave them together into the abstract to capture the essence of the research questions, the method, the chief finding, and the core interpretation. After writing your abstract, compare it with the one the authors wrote to determine similarities and differences.

APPENDIX 5.1: SAMPLE REVIEWER COMMENTARIES

This appendix presents two abbreviated, illustrative reviewer commentaries. Both commentaries are reviews of the same hypothetical manuscript, written by the hypothetical authors K. C. Oleson and R. M. Arkin.

The first review was written to illustrate a fairly balanced, useful review, one typical of those an editor would be pleased to receive. The second was written to exemplify a number of the pitfalls of the novice reviewer, the unmotivated or careless reviewer, or the nasty reviewer. Editors cringe when they receive these sorts of reviews, and some editors have the strength of character to hold them back from the author. Sometimes editors will seek additional reviewers' commentaries as substitutes or to offset such a poor or unhelpful review. In any event, publishers (including the APA) instruct editors to take a point of view indicating which reviewers' observations they agree with and which they do not. Most editors write decision letters to authors (whether acceptances or letters of rejection) that spell out some of their own views alongside summaries of the reviewers' collective wisdom.

We know that these two prototype reviews do not exhaust the list of attributes of a quality article review—or the unhelpful, picky, or negative review. They merely serve as examples to start you on the path to strong article reviews that reflect your own skills and style. Do not read them for content; instead they are most useful if you speed-read them for format and style.

The following are a few notable qualities you can find in these two reviews. We number the key points from Review A because they could serve in part as a checklist for what you are trying to accomplish in your review. Review B, on the other hand, is not one that you should use as a model.

Reviewer A's Review:

1. The review begins with a useful summary of the study. The summary shows that the reviewer understands the study, and it helps the reviewer, editor, and author grasp the essence of what they are communicating about.

2. Next, the review assesses the manuscript's handling of general conceptual issues, discussing both its strengths and weaknesses. It focuses on alternative explanations for the data, but it suggests how they might be addressed.

3. The review then lays out smaller concerns, such as methodological issues that may have influenced the findings.

4. Finally, the review ends with a general evaluation of the manuscript, one that places the work in context.

5. Throughout, the reviewer makes a variety of constructive comments, including ways to improve the research design and to improve and clarify the dependent measures. Last, the reviewer notes future research avenues to explore.

6. The review is critical, yet constructive, and balanced throughout.

Reviewer B's Review:

Reviewer B's commentary reflects both errors of omission (i.e., it is missing most of the positive qualities we noted in Reviewer A's commentary) and many errors of commission. Review B is nasty, narrow, and picky. The review is more a laundry list of complaints than a constructive, supportive review. There are unsupported allegations (some of which might be supportable), and the reviewer seems to have extended the criticism well beyond his or her base of expertise.

REVIEWER A

Journal of Good Ideas and Good Research

Reviewer's Commentary

"Is There a Self-Serving Bias in Self-Attribution for Outcomes?"

Kathryn C. Oleson and Robert M. Arkin

Ms #04–777

Date: January 1, 2005

This interesting work was designed to investigate whether there is a tendency for individuals to assume greater personal responsibility for successful than for failing outcomes, a phenomenon the authors say would reflect a "self-serving bias." The work reported here seems to be a reasonable and potentially important first step in systematically demonstrating this phenomenon, one that seems to have both theoretical and practical implications. The study involves two conditions: Participants learned that they had either succeeded (85th percentile) or failed (15th percentile) on a supposed "social sensitivity test" (feedback was "false"). Participants in the success condition were much more likely to attribute the outcome to themselves (their ability and effort) than was the case for participants who failed. Failing participants were much more likely than were successful participants to cite task difficulty and bad luck in explaining the outcome.

This one study seems like a useful first demonstration of this self-serving-bias phenomenon; however, the one study alone does little to pin down the precise process underlying this result. Consequently, although this intriguing demonstration of the difference in self-attribution for success and failure outcomes may be heuristic and novel enough to justify publication, it was disappointing that this initial finding was not taken further into the realm of examining the psychological processes involved. A couple of points stem from this concern.

First, the present finding does not clarify the directionality: Is the result due to heightened responsibility for success, lessened responsibility for failure, or both? Without a neutral or control group, the precise source of the phenomenon is unclear. The control group might reflect either "moderate success" (say 60%) or no information about outcome at all—or both groups could be included.

The absence of this control condition is linked with a theoretical issue that bothered me as well. Although the authors' "motivational" (i.e., self-serving) explanation of the attributional difference is plausible, there may be other explanations equally plausible. For instance, success typically covaries with one's effort—and with one's ability, and it could be that participants merely based their guesses about the causes of success on this typical covariation (or on actual covariation they perceived in this experimental setting); this would be more of an information-processing interpretation of this finding than a motivationally based interpretation. Kelley and others have written a good deal on this covariation idea, and there is good research by Cunningham on this point.

Second, could it be that the participants in this study—who were closely observed—were merely presenting themselves favorably (and did not, in their private perceptions, believe what they were portraying in their questionnaire responses)? There are other, related alternative interpretations, too. I think this initial demonstration of the self-serving bias would be much, much stronger if this sort of "process" evidence was provided and if the interpretation of the findings was clearer and more compelling. The present study has more of a preliminary investigation feeling to it than is desirable.

In addition to these general concerns, I have three smallish concerns to raise:

1. It seems problematic that the attribution measure is anchored on one scale, ranging from self-attribution to task-attribution. This strategy clouds whether the result might be mostly or solely in the self-attribution domain or in the task-attribution domain (but not both). In the future, I'd separate these into two separate scales to find out.

2. The experimenter's delivery of the false feedback worried me for two reasons. First, the experimenter was not kept blind to the induction, and the description (requiring lots of good acting ability) presented plenty of opportunity for experimenter bias. Second, it was difficult to tell from the manuscript if participants were fully, sensitively, and carefully debriefed; this raised ethical concerns for me.

3. The Discussion section could be trimmed a bit. It rambles in places, and several opportunities to foreshadow applications of this work and its implications were overlooked. These could be included, and in even less space. Some of the implications are as follows: (a) Could interpersonal conflict result from the self-serving bias, as when a small group of people might divide credit for a collective success (or blame for a collective failure)? (b) Is the effect qualified by any motive for

modesty that prevails in our culture? Would participants still engage in a self-serving bias if modesty were at a premium? (c) Are there individual differences in self-serving-bias tendencies, and could these help explain things like dysphoria, moodiness, or unhappiness?

Conclusion. In general, I think the logic of the work is well thought out and presented. The research is truly groundbreaking in certain ways; there isn't anything published on this topic— at least as far as I am aware. I think the researchers captured the key conceptual elements in their paradigm; however, at the same time, I really wish the authors had conducted replication work to include the crucial sort of control conditions I described and the distinguishing of the dependent measures, too. With those two additions, this work would constitute a fine contribution to the literature. At this point, however, I do not think that the paper makes enough of a contribution to warrant publication.

Reviewer B

Journal of Good Ideas and Good Research

Reviewer's Commentary

"Is There a Self-Serving Bias in Self-Attribution for Outcomes?"

Kathryn C. Oleson and Robert M. Arkin

Ms #04–777

Date: January 1, 2005

This research seems to be inherently flawed. The authors start out with a fairly obvious idea—one derived from little more than common sense: People take more responsibility for success than they do for failure—and then the authors fail to shed a whole lot of light on it.

As I read the manuscript, I had a number of specific problems I found in it and in the research it reports:

1. The number of subjects is too small. They need to have a larger sample size.

2. There are a number of typos, two on one page!

3. The statistics used (a *t*-test to compare the two conditions) are inappropriate for the comparison. They should be more careful about their use of statistics.

4. They did not include all necessary control groups. I can't believe they didn't include a control condition in which no feedback was included or in which a moderate level of success was described. We learn nothing from this one finding without that.

5. The experimental protocol or paradigm seems flawed. Scoring at the 15% seems so low; did subjects even believe that? I wouldn't. I think that the failure should have been higher, or more plausible—maybe at 40% or something.

6. The authors did not consider alternate explanations for their findings. What is the precise mechanism behind the effect? Does it have to be a "self-serving bias"?

7. Manuscript needs to be much shorter in length.

8. The research does not seem to be that rigorous. I suppose two conditions in a study might be elegant in some ways, but this much simplicity seems more like simple than simplicity.

9. The authors did not seem to know about other studies that have already been conducted on this topic, and although I can't think of them just now, I know there are some.

10. The measures used seemed invalid.

11. The authors did not counterbalance the different ratings that they had subjects make, and I have this nagging feeling that they haven't reported all their findings.

I don't think there is a contribution of any scope or magnitude here. I don't think there is much merit in the whole area of motivation anyway. This paper doesn't qualify as cognitive social psychology, and that is clearly where the field is going. So the research here seems more old-fashioned than anything. I can't see publishing the paper, and I don't think very many readers would be interested in reading it. There aren't even any applied questions raised, and the theoretical implications seem uninteresting.

RECOMMENDED READINGS

We recommend a number of guides to assist you in the task of article reviewing. For instance, Jordan and Zanna (1999) present how one should initially approach reading a journal article in social psychology. They do not focus primarily on critiquing and reviewing research, but rather they help one understand the structure of a journal article. Maher (1978) and Schwab (1985) also present ways to tackle reviewing articles. Maher (1978), then editor of an important journal, offers a "reader's, writer's, and reviewer's guide to assessing research"; the title of his offering reminds us of our opening observation about the intimate link between learning to read about research and learning to write about it. In that vein, we also commend you to the *Publication Manual of the APA* (2001) and Bem's (2004) paper on writing empirical papers. These sources can serve as much as handbooks for reviewers as for authors; your growth as an author will likely yield commensurate, collateral development in your critical skills in reviewing. In our experience, the "causal arrow" also points in the opposite direction from developing critical reviewing skills to increasing one's skills as a writer. We also recommend that you read various books on evaluating research, including Aronson, Ellsworth, Carlsmith, and Gonzales (1990) and Shadish, et al. (2002). These books focus on the fundamentals of research design and issues of validity. In addition, we recommend books on conducting research, like a recent text by Pelham and Blanton (2003).

Bem (2004): An engaging useful perspective on how to write an empirical journal article. He provides general suggestions about writing in addition to detailed advice about each section of the empirical article.

Jordan and Zanna (1999): A beginner's guide to how to approach reading a journal article in social psychology. They provide a user-friendly framework for understanding the structure (as they call it, "the anatomy") of a journal article.

Pelham and Blanton (2003): An up-to-date text focusing on conducting research. They offer an engaging and readable approach to research design and writing up research. Furthermore, they provide an extensive list of Web sites relevant to the conducting and reviewing of research.

Shadish, Campbell, & Cook (2002): A recent update to Cook and Campbell's classic text. It is an essential guide to understanding issues of validity. We also recommend the earlier texts by Campbell and Stanley and by Cook and Campbell.

REFERENCES

American Psychological Association. (2001). *Publication Manual of the American Psychological Association* (5th ed.). Washington, DC: Author.

Aronson, E., Brewer, M., & Carlsmith, J. M. (1985). Experimentation in social psychology. In G. Lindzey & E. Aronson (Eds.), *The handbook of social psychology* (3rd ed.). New York: Random House.

Aronson, E., Ellsworth, P. C., Carlsmith, J. M., Gonzales, M. H. (1990). *Methods of research in social psychology* (2nd ed.). New York: McGraw-Hill.

Bem, D. (2004). Writing the empirical journal article. In J. M. Darley, M. P. Zanna, & H. L. Roediger, III (Eds.), *The compleat academic: A career guide* (2nd ed., pp. 185–219). Washington, DC: APA.

Campbell, D. T., & Stanley, J. C. (1966). *Experimental and quasi-experimental designs for research.* Chicago: Rand McNally.

Cook, T. D., & Campbell, D. T. (1979). *Quasi-experimentation: Design and analysis issues for field settings.* Chicago: Rand McNally.

Fiske, D. W., & Fogg, L. (1990). But the reviewers are making different criticisms of my paper. *American Psychologist, 45,* 591–598.

Gottfredson, S. D. (1978). Evaluating psychological research reports: Dimensions, reliability, and correlates of quality judgments. *American Psychologist, 33,* 920–934.

Jordan, C. H., & Zanna, M. P. (1999). Appendix: How to read a journal article in social psychology. In R. F. Baumeister (Ed.), *The self in social psychology* (pp. 461–470). Philadelphia: Taylor & Francis.

Lindsey, D. (1978). *The scientific publication system in social science: A study of the operation of leading professional journals in psychology, sociology, and social work.* San Francisco: Jossey-Bass.

Maher, B. A. (1978). A reader's, writer's, and reviewer's guide to assessing research reports in clinical psychology. *Journal of Consulting and Clinical Psychology, 46,* 835–838.

Pelham, B. W., & Blanton, H. (2003). *Conducting research in psychology: Measuring the weight of smoke* (2nd ed.). Belmont, CA: Thomson Learning.

Perlman, D., & Dean, E. (1987). The wisdom of Solomon: Avoiding bias in the publication review process. In D. N. Jackson & J. P. Rushton (Eds.), *Scientific excellence.* Newbury Park, CA: Sage.

Rheingold, H. (1994). The psychologist's guide to an academic career. Washington, DC: APA.

Schwab, D. P. (1985). Reviewing empirically based manuscripts: Perspectives on process. In L. L. Cummings & P. J. Frost (Eds.), *Publishing in the organizational sciences.* Homewood, IL: Irwin.

Shadish, W. R., Cook, T. D., & Campbell, D. T. (2002). *Experimental and quasi-experimental designs for generalized causal inference.* Boston: Houghton Mifflin.

Squire, J. R. (1983). Composing and comprehending: Two sides of the same basic process. *Language Arts, 60,* 581–589.

5

PROGRAM EVALUATION

Concepts and Perspectives

JAMES W. ALTSCHULD
JAMES T. AUSTIN

At first it might seem strange or even somewhat misplaced that a handbook dealing with research in psychology would contain a chapter on evaluation. After all, evaluation is an activity that is carried out for a purpose quite different from that of research, that is, to guide practical decision making in applied settings. Add to this the fact that although there is scientific study of evaluation, many scholars and empirical researchers still tend to look with disdain at the topic. It is perceived to be poor research, that is, research often conducted with much less control than the norm in articles in prestigious, refereed academic journals. Beyond these issues is the further concern that evaluation is usually not based on theoretical understandings. For these reasons collectively, some social scientists may not ascribe much value to evaluation.

So we must begin by addressing the subtle, implicit questions in the first paragraph. Why should evaluation be in this book, and why is it of importance and value for practicing psychologists, psychology students, educational psychologists, and for that matter, others in social science? We will provide several answers to this question.

A first answer is that psychologists in a variety of environments (businesses, government organizations, educational institutions, etc.), in the course of their work, might be called on to evaluate an activity or a program whether or not they have been trained as evaluators or have indepth comprehension of it. Davidson (2002), for instance, shows how this could occur for industrial-organizational psychologists. They are there in the situation, and they have had methodological training, so they must be able to do it. Essentially, this is a reason by default. Secondly, evaluation has a number of unique methodological and substantive content areas that would be useful for psychologists to understand and be able to use in their work. A third answer is that some psychologists will undoubtedly lead or participate in evaluations as their main professional focus.

Therefore, the purposes of this chapter are to provide an overview of the nature of evaluation, to define it conceptually, to show its relationship to research, and to give a sense of what might have to be done to conduct an evaluation. Specifically, the chapter is organized as follows: Some background related to defining evaluation is described; defining evaluation with a comparison of evaluation and research, based on the definition, comes next; and implications of the definition for practice and generic types of evaluation are the latter parts of the text. Last, a hands-on exercise, which helps in pulling together ideas, will form the chapter conclusion.

TOWARD A DEFINITION OF EVALUATION

In 2002, the lead author (Altschuld, 2002) wrote about a presentation that he had attended at an annual meeting of the American Evaluation Association (www.aea.org), a presentation that is relevant for defining evaluation. In a panel conducted by individuals who were nearing completion of graduate programs or who had just received their degrees, perspectives and views of the quality of the educational experience were being shared and examined. The panelists explained their backgrounds and then briefly discussed what they thought about their graduate education in terms of learning and preparation for the job market.

One participant, a recent graduate, elaborated about his extensive coursework in statistics and measurement and the skills he had gained in these areas. Later when questions from the audience were appropriate, the coauthor asked him what in this set of courses would constitute training for the practice of evaluation. Stated alternatively, what really is evaluation, what does it mean to be an evaluator, what does an evaluator do, how should one train for work as an evaluator, what should an evaluator know, and what specific skills should an evaluator have? After all, would it not be better to think of what he had taken as simply methodology and just call it that? Further, he was asked if he had any courses that could be somehow thought of or construed as specifically emphasizing evaluation concepts, whatever those concepts might be, even if they were distantly related to evaluation.

He pondered for a moment and to his credit replied that he had never considered this line of inquiry, and in reality, his background could not be viewed as actually dealing with evaluation. There was nothing specific in it related to, or called, evaluation.

The point here is not to discount being well grounded in methodology or that evaluators need sound methodological understandings in order to be successful in the field. That is neither an issue nor debatable. Indeed, our advisees are required to take many quantitative and qualitative methods courses. Rather, methodology, although necessary and critically important for evaluation, constitutes, by itself, an insufficient condition for being adequately trained in the field and understanding its substance.

Evidence to support the above assertion can be found in international studies of evaluation training conducted by Altschuld, Engle, Cullen, Kim, and Macce (1994) and by Engle and Altschuld (2003/2004). Also, the writing of individuals concerned with the training of evaluators is pertinent here. For example, see Scriven (1996), Altschuld (1995, 2002), Mertens (1994), and the recent work of King, Stevahn, Ghere, and Minnema (2001) in regard to the critical skill domains required to be an evaluator.

In 1994, Altschuld and his colleagues identified 47 university-based evaluation training programs, and in a repeat of the same study in 2001, Engle and Altschuld found 29 programs. Although the number of programs is smaller, it is also apparent from studying trends across the two time periods that there has been a slow, steady, and noticeable emergence of a unique set of courses with specialized evaluation content. That content is quite distinct from research and/or measurement methodology. Examples include evaluation theory and models, applied evaluation design for field settings, evaluation and program planning, evaluation and its relationship to the formation of policy, cost-benefit analysis, readings and research in evaluation, and others (Engle, Altschuld, & Kim, 2005). Nearly all of these topics are not covered in traditional methodology offerings or other courses in psychology and other social science disciplines, or they are covered only tangentially.

Several writers have discussed the skill sets needed for evaluation work. Mertens (1994) presented a taxonomy derived rationally from literature reviews and discussions with colleagues. It consisted of grouping the knowledge and skills into the following areas: research methodology, borrowed from other areas, and unique to specific disciplines. The work of King and her associates (King et al., 2001) is particularly relevant because of its combination of rational and empirical methods. King et al. (2001) engaged 31 individuals representing a diverse set of backgrounds and contexts of practice in rating the relative importance for 69 domains or items of evaluation capability. Using what they describe as a multiattribute consensus-building process, they reported that they achieved significant agreement on 54 of the 69 (78%) competencies. King et al. (2001) proposed four skill domains in which evaluators must be successful, not only doing evaluations but obtaining the results of evaluations accepted and used in making decisions. Those domains are (a) systematic inquiry, (b) competent evaluation practice, (c) general skills for evaluation practice, and (d) evaluation professionalism. Stevahn, King, Minnema, and Ghere (2005) followed up with additional research and refinement. Finally, a project by the Canadian Evaluation Society (CES) that focused on advocacy and professional development also addressed capacity building. The literature review by McGuire (2002) focused on the benefits, outputs, processes, and knowledge elements of evaluation.

Given the nature of emerging curricula, the evolving dimensions of evaluative thinking, and the skill domains, what is evaluation? In what ways does it differ from research, and in what ways is it similar?

Defining Evaluation and Some Useful Distinctions

From many sources (Scriven, 1991; Stufflebeam, 1971, 1980, 2002; Worthen, Sanders, & Fitzpatrick, 1997), there are common features to the definition of evaluation. Synthesizing across these authors, we could define or think of *evaluation* as a process or set of procedures for providing information for judging decision alternatives or for determining the merit and worth of a process, product, or program.

Imbedded in this collated, conceptual definition are subtleties that help us to distinguish between research and evaluation, as well as to explain the practice of evaluation. In Table 5.1, evaluation and research are briefly compared in terms of several dimensions emanating from the definition. When examining the table, keep in mind that the comparisons are somewhat exaggerated to aid the discussion and your understanding. Probably a better way to think about

the linkage between evaluation and research is to use Venn diagrams with areas of overlap as well as areas of uniqueness.

In Table 5.1, evaluation is presented as being conducted in field situations to guide and facilitate the making of decisions. This immediately implies that evaluators must identify who the decision makers and key stakeholding groups are, the degree of their influence on the entity being evaluated, and how their value positions and perspectives will affect the evaluation. This point is so important that audience identification for results and involvement in the process of evaluation is highlighted as the first standard in the *Program Evaluation Standards* (American Evaluation Association, 1995). Evaluators essentially work at the behest of decision makers, and the needs of multiple decision-making audiences have to be factored into all evaluations. Evaluators have to carefully maintain their objectivity and avoid being co-opted (handling their results to favor a political or vested position), given the social and political environments in which they exist.

Researchers, on the other hand, in the best of all possible worlds, are not working on someone else's priorities but more in terms of their own curiosity about phenomena. Their wonderment, their questioning, their desire to know and understand, and even their awe are what drives the enterprise, not what someone else wants. This is an ideal point of view, but at the same time, we recognize that politics and values can influence research. Political forces frequently push certain substantive areas or stress what methodologies might be acceptable at a point in time. Despite that, the ideal is one that we should strive for and cherish with regard to research.

Looking at the comparisons in the second row of the table, the relationship of evaluation to theory is not as strong or prominent as it is in research. Although there are theory-driven evaluations and the idea of theory in a variety of forms and connotations does affect evaluation (see Chen, 1990), for the most part evaluations are directed toward practical concerns of decision makers and stakeholders, not toward theory. "Proving" (demonstrating) the validity of a theory or proposition versus depicting how well something works in a field setting (its

Table 5.1   A Comparison of Evaluation and Research on Selected Dimensions

Dimensions	Evaluation Craft	Research Craft
Driving force for endeavor	Interests of decision makers and other stakeholders	Personal interest and curiosity of the researcher
	Value/political positions of multiple groups/individuals come into play	
Purposes	Facilitate decision making	Understand phenomena
	Show how well something did or did not work	Develop theory (ultimately) or to "prove" a proposition
	Improve real world practice	Add to body of knowledge
Degree of autonomy	Variable to possibly very limited, with evaluator always directly in midst of the decision-making milieu	Ideally, autonomy should be very high (production of knowledge should be unfettered)
Generalizability	Often limited to the specific local environment	The greater the generalizability (over time, location, and situation) the better
Methodological stance	Tends to be multimethod or mixed method in approach	Tends to be less multimethod in orientation

SOURCES: Adapted from Worthen and Sanders (1973, 1987); Worthen, Sanders, and Fitzpatrick (1997); Altschuld (2002).

impact or effect) and then describing what its implementation entailed is a critical distinction between research and evaluation. Evaluation looks at program performance and how it might be improved in subsequent use and has less of a theory orientation than does research.

It is fairly obvious that the evaluator, due to being imbedded in the complex and political realities of schools and organizations, may have limited ability to be an independent and autonomous actor (or sense that that is the case—see the third row of the table). Furthermore, the evaluator may have to assume a political role in his or her work (Fitzpatrick, 1989). On the other hand, it is absolutely imperative for the researcher to be autonomous. Do we, in our kind of society, want drug or tobacco companies to be able to control what the researcher does, what methods the researcher uses, and what, in turn, can be said publicly about the findings and results of the research? This comparison is purposely exaggerated, to a degree. On numerous occasions, evaluators will experience relatively minor constraints on the conduct of their business, and in some instances the researchers may feel intense political heat and pressure.

Entries in the last two rows of the table further aid in seeing distinctions. Evaluations are many times localized, and thus the results do not generalize. The interests of the decision makers, the evaluators, or both do not relate to generalizability of results, and it often is not foremost in the minds of the evaluators. Evaluation stress is more on the localized findings and how they can affect change and improvement within a specific and narrow context.

Conversely, researchers in the social sciences are more attentive to the generalizability concept. They have a need to publish in journals for reasons of advancement and salary, as well as professionalism. Part of the scrutiny of those journals will be external validity, in the Campbell and Stanley meaning of the phrase. External validity, although not unimportant to the evaluator, will be of more prominence to the researcher. As far as methods go (see the fifth row), the demands of evaluation will tend to require the utilization of multiple or mixed methods applications. In fact, numerous writings have dealt with how mixed methods can be incorporated into evaluation and needs assessment strategies (Altschuld & Witkin, 2000;

Caracelli, 1989; Greene & Caracelli, 1997; Mark & Shotland, 1987; Tashakkori & Teddlie, 2002; Witkin & Altschuld, 1995).

On balance, based on these brief comparisons, it may seem that research would be the preferred activity. Just predicated on autonomy and the driving force underlying the endeavor, wouldn't people prefer to be researchers rather than evaluators?

But evaluation has its advantages as well. Evaluation is closer to decision making, the formulation of policy, and program or project improvement. Evaluators may more directly and rapidly see the impact of their work on organizations and, in turn, those who are the recipients of the services organizations offer. In contrast, the gratification from research is most likely long-term in realization. Finally, it should not be overlooked that evaluators conduct research on their field or incorporate research into their evaluation activities, and many publish their findings in very reputable evaluation journals with rather high rejection rates (e.g. *Evaluation Review, Evaluation and Program Planning, Educational Evaluation and Policy Analysis,* and *American Journal of Evaluation*).

IMPLICATIONS OF THE DEFINITION FOR PRACTICE

How do evaluators go about their work? What may seem to be a simple process can become complex as we probe beneath the surface of our conceptual definition. Using that definition as our anchor, what must evaluators consider as they plan and conduct evaluations? Table 5.2 contains a sampling of implications drawn from an analysis of the definition. The sampling, although incomplete, does reveal why some evaluations are not easy to implement (and the subtle, almost hidden decisions that have to be made in virtually any evaluation).

Keep in mind that, and we must emphasize that, the table is just a sampling of what the evaluator must think about when working with the highly varied consumers of his or her work. Furthermore, most evaluators do not have the luxury of doing evaluations in just one area (e.g., math education programs, training and development, social service delivery).

Professional evaluators tend to be eclectic, having to apply their knowledge of the practice of evaluation and their experience to evaluate programs in many settings and specialized subject matter fields. For example in our own backgrounds, we have conducted evaluations in science education, reading, corporate training and development, team-building projects, and so forth.

A couple of the row entries are not dealt with in any great detail. As one example, the nature of what is being evaluated (row 3) can be extremely variable and may necessitate working with a subject matter expert. Consider the case of evaluating a new reading program or evaluating a health care delivery system from the perspective of a person who is seeking assistance for an elderly relative and trying to navigate the maze of our current health care system. Another example is multiple methods, which is a very substantial topic. Both of these rows are important and could be explored in depth. Treating them to any appreciable degree far exceeds the scope of this chapter.

Most of the rest of Table 5.2 is self explanatory, so we will point out only several issues. In the first row, merit and worth decisions are noted. Merit refers to the quality of the idea underlying a new program or project. When we evaluate merit, we are assessing (usually via expert review and judgment) whether or not there is intrinsic value in an idea or proposed entity. Worth, on the other hand, refers to the outcomes achieved by a project. Are they substantial and of value? Cost-benefit analysis and return-on-investment methods can be used in the investigation of this aspect of evaluation decision making.

In the second row, an essential and early part of any evaluation is ascertaining who the decision makers are, their relative order in terms of importance, and if multiple levels of decision makers with differing information needs are apparent. If the latter is the case and if there are disparate requirements for information, the skills of the evaluator may be sorely taxed, and tight evaluation budgets might be stretched to the limit. In educational situations, the evaluator may be asked to provide data for high-level decisions and the formation of policy and, at the same time, be pressed for detailed and very

Table 5.2   Sampling of Implications for Practice as Derived From the Definition of Evaluation

Implication Focus	Description	Comments
Decisions to be made	What are our needs? Does our plan have merit? How can we improve? What outcomes were achieved? (Does our program have worth?) How cost-beneficial is this effort? What are the long-term outcomes? Should we continue or discontinue this effort?	Multiple levels of decision makers may have different information needs. Evaluators facilitate the process of identifying possible decisions.
Decision maker identification	Who are the decision makers? Are there multiple levels? Who are the key stakeholders? How influential are the different levels? How do we prioritize across the different levels?	Multiple levels of decision makers may have different information needs Evaluation reports may be used by key stake holding groups who do not directly make decisions
Nature of what is being evaluated	Service delivery programs Multiple service delivery programs Educational projects Public awareness campaigns Staff development endeavors	Programs and projects are similar yet different Complex programs may require different evaluation designs for subsystems within them
Multiple time points for conducting the evaluation	Is there a need for a program or intervention? Should a program or project be undertaken? Analysis of inputs and design before beginning Pre–data collection at start Collection of data during process of implementation Post–data collection Follow-up data collection	Many possibilities exist, so evaluators must carefully weigh time points and data collection against available dollar, time, and human resources
Multiple Methods	Most likely, multiple methods will have to be used for the evaluation if data are to be used for varied types of decisions or time points of the data collection, or both	Evaluations are often conducted under the demands of the knowledge and understanding required to implement multiple methods
Utilization of Evaluation Results	Three types of utilization possible: Instrumental Conceptual Persuasive	Beware of the subtle influence of politics if and when results are utilized, but note politics isn't necessarily negative

NOTE: All of these activities implied by these questions would take place before the start of a new program or intervention.

specific suggestions for improvement by curriculum developers. Test data, which will satisfy the first level, seldom provides much of use for the second.

In the fourth row, it is important to determine the time phase of the entity being evaluated. This point has routinely been noted by numerous writers and in their evaluation models. The well-known CIPP model, proposed by Stufflebeam in 1971, is predicated on four time phases going from the start of a project to its completion. In *context* evaluation, the need for the endeavor is assessed (and *needs assessment* now tends to be recognized as an important aspect of evaluation). *Input* evaluation is concerned with the adequacy of resources and strategies for resolving the need; *process* evaluation looks at how the solution is being implemented and what is working and what must be modified to make the solution work better; and finally the purpose of *product* evaluation is to find out what outcomes were achieved and the level to which they were achieved. Similar notions of time can be found in the work of Kirkpatrick (1959, 1998) and Holton, Bates, and Naquin (2000) in the development and evaluation of training programs and Altschuld and Kumar (1995, 2002) in the evaluation of science and technology education programs.

The last row underscores the fact that evaluation, at its core, is oriented toward the utilization of findings. Without utilization, evaluation would be an empty activity, devoid of value and meaning (an activity of little merit). But what is utilization and how does it come about in complex organizations with internal and external power bases and the interplay of political forces and expediencies? These are not easy matters to explain.

Leviton and Hughes (1981) observed that there are three types of utilization: instrumental, conceptual, and persuasive. *Instrumental* is utilization that occurs as a direct result of the findings and recommendations of an evaluation. Ideally, this is what evaluators hope for and expect to occur. Unfortunately, for the most part in evaluation thinking, conceptual rather than instrumental utilization is what takes place. *Conceptual* utilization occurs when the ideas in the evaluation, the concepts imbedded in it, and the findings come together to begin to affect the

thinking and emerging understandings of decision makers. Slowly, the evaluation is inculcated into the deliberation process and influences decisions that will occur much later. The effect of the evaluation is there, but it is interacting in the process of change in almost indiscernible ways. This makes it difficult to trace the impact or effect of evaluation. *Persuasive* utilization is utilization intended to foster a political purpose, even one that is predisposed before the evaluation is undertaken. Obviously this last type of utilization is to be avoided if possible.

In 1993, Altschuld, Yoon, and Cullen studied the direct and conceptual utilization of administrators who had participated in needs assessments (NAs). They found that conceptualization was indeed more prominent than instrumental utilization to the administrators, although they had been personally involved in the NA process. This study would tend to confirm that conceptual is more the norm than instrumental.

More must be said about persuasive use. Certainly, the evaluator has to be aware of the potential for this negative situation and do his or her best to avoid it. If one is an external evaluator, a contract can always be turned down. If one is internal, then an advisory group for the evaluation can ameliorate the political pressure to some degree.

But is politics always bad? Political concerns can, and in some circumstances do, play an important positive role in evaluation. Political pressure from opposing points of view can lead to balanced support for an evaluation of a controversial project or program. Legislators and others might simply want to know what is taking place and how well a program is working. They may desire to implement good public policy that helps rather than hinders.

Further, due to politics, the financial underwriting of the evaluation might be greater than otherwise would be the case, making a better (not financially constrained) evaluation possible. The controversy can help to illuminate issues to be emphasized in the evaluation and can even lead to more enthusiasm and ultimately "buy-in" for the implementation of results. So the evaluator must monitor the political factors (positives and negatives) of any evaluation and be prepared to deal with them as they arise.

GENERIC TYPES OF EVALUATION

Reviewing the prior sections of this chapter, we find that different types of evaluation have been woven into or alluded to in the discussion. Other classifications of evaluation are possible with the one given below having been used in the teaching of evaluation classes at The Ohio State University. For another example of a classification scheme see the Worthen, Sanders, and Fitzpatrick (1997) text cited earlier.

In Table 5.3, an informal listing of types of evaluation is offered. It is intended to convey the range of activities often conducted under the rubric or title of evaluation. With the entries in the table, a more comprehensive picture (in conjunction with the definition of evaluation, its comparison to research, and key aspects of what evaluators do) should now be coming into view.

The entries in the table are, for the most part, self explanatory with perhaps the exception of needs assessment (NA). *Need* is defined as the measurable discrepancy between the "what-is" status and the "what-should-be" status of an entity. Generally, the what-should-be status comes from collective value judgment. Examples

Table 5.3   Some Types of Evaluation

Evaluation Type	Nature of Type	Commentary
Theoretical	Development of evaluation theories and models	Most often emanating from university researchers and writers about evaluation
Needs assessment	Evaluation and planning hybrid Essential condition for program planning and evaluation	To a great extent more of a program planning mechanism than evaluation but now viewed as integral to evaluation
Formative and summative	Formative evaluation is focused on monitoring the implementation of programs and describing processes Summative deal with the outcomes or results of programs (the bottom line decisions)	Formative and summative evaluation, although more traditional ways of thinking about evaluation, are still useful
Accountability	Looking at the overall results, often associated with the results or outcomes of systems Also might include the idea of systems (inputs, thru puts, outputs and even long-term outcomes)	May have a negative, harsh connotation in that someone could be held accountable for failure, especially in complex systems
Accreditation	A review by an external accrediting body that leads to accreditation (a "Good-Housekeeping-Seal-of-Approval" -type of public acknowledgement)	May not lead to change or anything other than the seal At times, in the past, has tended to be process rather than process and summative focused
Staff or personnel	Evaluation of staff from initial selection procedures to work performed Many purposes (performance improvement, rewarding performance, changing jobs, etc.)	Often perceived negatively—no one likes to be evaluated

would be the following: What should be the outcomes of a high school education? What should be the wellness level of the U.S. population? What constitutes reasonable and cost-feasible access to drug therapies? And so forth. Current or what-is status can be ascertained from a variety of methods including records, surveys, observations, databases, and so forth. Numerous methodological approaches are available for assessing needs, and over the last 20 years many texts have been written describing the nature of needs and procedures for assessing them (Altschuld & Witkin, 2000; McKillip, 1998; Witkin & Altschuld, 1995).

After the states have been determined, the process continues with prioritizing the resulting needs or discrepancies and transforming the high priorities needs into organizational action plans to resolve or reduce the problem underlying or causing the discrepancy. In other words, decisions to design and implement programs should be based on clearly delineated needs. From some perspectives, needs assessment might appear to be more of a planning topic type of activity, so why was it placed in Table 5.3 as a type of evaluation work?

Several reasons support such placement. A well-implemented NA illuminates major problems, what key variables relate to them or are causing them, and what likely solutions might be. It is the essential condition for designing and implementing good programs; and by virtue of its analytic properties, it should enhance the overall evaluation of solution strategies that are developed and used. Therefore, one of the reasons is that evaluation and NA are inextricably intertwined; they are two ends of one continuum.

A second reason is basically an offshoot of the first. A small (almost informal) national group of needs assessors felt that they could not survive as a small group; therefore, in the late 1980s they began to cast about for a larger society with which to affiliate. They chose the American Evaluation Association (AEA), based on the recognition that evaluation and NA were highly related. Now, as a partial outgrowth of that event, most evaluators see NA as important to the practice of evaluation. Other entries in Table 5.3 could have been discussed in a similar fashion. Needs assessment was singled out as an exemplar to demonstrate the thought process.

TOWARD THE FUTURE

As we near the end of this exposition, consider for a moment evaluation as a profession. As a discipline, evaluation emerged in psychology and in education during the 1930s. Ralph Tyler's Eight-Year Study and notions of curriculum evaluation were pioneer landmarks in education, and Rossi, Lipsey, and Freeman (2004) point to field studies of evaluation conducted by Kurt Lewin and other social psychologists. Nonetheless, these were isolated instances and were not formalized in terms of department or area status, curriculum, journals, and professional organizations. Rossi et al. (2004) went on to define a boom period in evaluation following World War II and pointed out its emergence as a specialized area during the 1970s. Their indicators of emergence included books, journals, and associations. The books that have shaped the discipline are numerous. They include pioneering classics (Suchman, 1967), methodological contributions (Campbell & Stanley, 1966; Cook & Campbell, 1979), and textbooks across multiple editions (Fitzpatrick, Sanders, & Worthen, 2003; Rossi et al., 2004). Prominent journals devoted to evaluation range from the first, *Evaluation Review* (since 1976), to the *American Journal of Evaluation* (since 1978), and *Evaluation and Program Planning* (since 1980). Two key professional associations in the United States are the American Evaluation Association (www.eval.org), created in 1986 through a merger between the Evaluation Network (ENet) and the Evaluation Research Society (ERS), and the American Educational Research Association Evaluation Division (http://aera.net). Many other professional organizations exist across nations, including the Canadian Evaluation Association (www.evaluationcanada.ca/), the European Evaluation Society (www.europeanevaluation.org), the U.K. Evaluation Society (www.evaluation.uk), and the Australasian Evaluation Society (www.parklane.com.au/aes). Instances of these features are depicted in Table 5.4.

Table 5.4   A Sampling of Several Features of Evaluation as a Discipline

Books	Journals	Professional Associations
Rossi, Lipsey, & Freeman (2004)	*American Journal of Evaluation (AJE)*	American Evaluation Association
Fitzpatrick, Sanders, & Worthen (2003)	*Evaluation and Program Planning (E&PP)*	AERA Evaluation Division
Altschuld & Witkin (2000)	*Evaluation Review (ER)*	Canadian Evaluation Association
Bickman & Rog (1998)	*Educational Evaluation and Policy Analysis (EEPA)*	European Evaluation Society
Chelimsky & Shadish (1997)	*Studies in Educational Evaluation (SEE)*	U.K. Evaluation Society
Herman (1997)	—	Australasian Evaluation Society
Witkin, Altschuld (1995)	—	—
Wholey, Hatry, & Newcomer (1994)	—	—
Chen (1990)	—	—

Why focus on the future of evaluation? We might reply, "For one major reason." The demand for evaluation is increasing rapidly, even as university-based training programs are tending to disappear (Engle, Altschuld, & Kim, in process). Thus, a priority need is to resuscitate graduate or other types of training in this important discipline. Perhaps the multidisciplinary nature of program evaluation contributes to training issues due to the fact that evaluation training is housed in varied colleges and departments (education, psychology, social work, public policy, and management). Clearly, affiliation between psychologists and evaluators could be valuable for both groups. Davidson (2002), in the aforementioned article, indicated that there is a great interest in the evaluation community about industrial-organizational psychology issues and that many opportunities exist for forms of involvement. Edwards, Scott, and Raju (2003) edited a wide-ranging application of evaluation to human resource management. Consider further that the major professional society for evaluators, the American Evaluation Association, runs a major international discussion list, EVALTALK (http://bama.ua.edu/

archives/evaltalk.html). An informal group that coalesced at a recent Society for Industrial Organizational Psychology conference, the Strategic Evaluation Network, also runs an electronic mailing list specifically for people who do evaluation in organizational settings (see http://evaluation.wmich.edu/archives). The American Evaluation Association has a Business and Industry (B & I) Topical Interest Group on evaluation (www.evaluationsolutions.com/aea-bi-tig), which welcomes presentation proposals (and audience members!) for the annual conference each November (details at http://eval.org).

Other features of the field include knowledge dissemination and globalization. The Evaluation Center at Western Michigan University is a professional clearinghouse for information, including bibliographies and checklists. The checklist project provides a number of useful checklists for various evaluation functions (www.wmich.edu/evalctr/checklists/). The checklists are organized under categories: evaluation management, evaluation models, evaluation values and criteria, metaevaluation, and other. There is even a checklist for developing checklists by Stufflebeam (www.wmich.edu/evalctr/checklists/cdc.htm). Globalization is clearly evident at the Canadian Evaluation Association's Web site (http://consultation.evaluationcanada.ca/resources.htm). There are links to evaluation standards, for example from associations (Joint Committee on Standards for Educational Evaluation, 1994) and from nations (Germany, Canada, United States).

CONCLUSION

In this postscript, we attempt to tie together the strands of evaluation presented in this chapter. First, the placement of evaluation in a psychology research handbook makes good sense for several reasons. Readers may be called on to consume or produce evaluations. Respectively, these two terms mean reading and reacting to evaluation reports or designing, conducting, and reporting a program evaluation. An individual trained in social psychology, for instance, might be asked to conduct a needs assessment in order to design and evaluate a community-based collaborative conflict resolution program. On the other hand, an industrial-organizational psychologist might be charged with doing a training needs assessment in order to design a leadership development program for middle and top managers.

Second, the nature of evaluation can be viewed as dynamic with exciting emergent dimensions and twists. Third, using the definition of evaluation as a "process or set of procedures for providing information for judging decision alternatives or for determining the merit and worth of a process, product, or program," we presented useful distinctions as to several types of evaluation (Table 5.3). Fourth, we discussed the structure of evaluation as a profession in a limited way to provide some context. Two key sets of professional standards are the five AEA "Guiding Principles" (1995) and the *Program Evaluation Standards* (Joint Committee on Standards for Educational Evaluation, 1994). Fifth and finally, we have provided three brainstorming exercises to tie your new understandings together into a scaffolded mental model. As you practice evaluation, read evaluation research, and talk to evaluation practitioners, this scaffolding will eventually disappear, and you will be able to use the mental model for practice and research.

EXERCISES

Pulling Your Understandings Together

In evaluation workshops conducted for the National Association of School Psychologists, Altschuld and Ronning (2000) developed a brainstorming activity that fits well with the content of this chapter. To do this exercise, pretend that you are in the specialized area of school psychology or modify the activity in accord with the psychological work context that has most meaning for you. The activity consists of three brainstorming or idea-generating parts and then examples of responses to them. Do not peek ahead, but rather try your hand at the activity before glancing at our ideas about possible responses. We believe that the activity constitutes an interesting, different, and good way to summarize the concepts contained in this chapter.

Spend a minute or two thinking about the possibilities for school psychologists to become involved in program evaluation (or substitute for *school psychologists* your particular interest in psychology). Additional material on evaluation exercises and activities may be found in Mertens (1989).

For example, what decisions are various stakeholders in your district facing? Are there specific paperwork demands, time limits on referrals, or accountability reports? Do you work under local guidelines and restrictions, the values of which are questionable? Are your methods, results, and roles being scrutinized or changed erratically?

First, fill in the blanks from your experiences. These responses may vary widely as each person works in, or will work in, different settings under different rules and regulations and with different administrations and colleagues.

Step 1: List up to 10 reasons why you might be called upon or wish to conduct an evaluation. Reflect back on what was presented in the chapter, what evaluators do, and the various types of evaluations. There are no wrong or right answers. Rather the purpose here is to encourage you to think about all of the possibilities for conducting an evaluation. Later, when you examine the reasons we supplied, please note that they are not definitive answers but come from a brainstorming activity very similar to what we asked you to do.

1. _____

2. _____

3. _____

4. _____

5. _____

6. _____

7. _____

8. _____

9. _____

10. _____

Step 2: In the spaces provided below, identify as many programs as you can in which evaluations could be conducted. What programs are you or your colleagues currently involved with that may be appropriate for using evaluation techniques to determine their worth or merit? For example, school psychologists in private practice may link closely with community agencies and schools to provide mental health services. Is this more effective than having the school psychologist assigned to specific buildings provide this service? Or, you may be responsible for grief counseling of children in cooperation with the local hospitals. List program titles in the appropriate space, or use a short phrase to describe the program. List as many as you can.

Program Titles or Descriptive Phrases

1. _____   11. _____

2. _____   12. _____

3. _____   13. _____

4. _____   14. _____

5. _____   15. _____

6. _____   16. _____

7. _____   17. _____

8. _____   18. _____

9. _____   19. _____

10. _____   20. _____

Step 3. Speculate about the types of activities evaluators might do in the course of an evaluation and briefly describe them below.

1. _____

2. _____

3. _____

4. _____

5. _____

6. _____

7. _____

8. _____

9. _____

10. _____

Sampling of Responses to Brainstorming Activity

Step 1. List reasons why you might be called upon or wish to conduct an evaluation.

Increased pressure for accountability of dollars spent for testing
1. _____

Use as a lever for increasing various services
2. _____

Effectiveness of teacher development efforts
3. _____

To showcase effective programs during school levy (tax) time
4. _____

To get rid of ineffective programs
5. _____

To streamline a districtwide intervention program (e.g., peer tutoring)
6. _____

To justify additional training in certain areas
7. _____

To pick up one of two methods of providing certain types of instruction for the district
8. _____

I want to do something out of the ordinary, and I want to show that it works.
9. _____

To guide implementation of a community conflict resolution program
10. _____

Step 2: What programs are you or your colleagues currently involved with that may be appropriate for using evaluation techniques to determine their worth or merit?

1. Community involvement programs
2. Districtwide proficiency interventions
3. Reading evaluation (primary)
4. Provision of school psychological services
5. Therapy outcomes in conjunction with other providers (e.g., AA)
6. Career planning or experience program
7. Reporting test results to parents, etc.
8. Parenting programs
9. Special education programs
10. Multihandicapped programs severely disturbed (behavioral and emotional) youth

11. Community outreach programs
12. Efficacy of multiage classrooms
13. School-based provision of health benefits
14. Head Start
15. All day, everyday kindergarten
16. Preschool programs
17. Districtwide testing program
18. Statewide testing program
19. Effectiveness of research efforts
20. Effectiveness of local efforts to serve

Step 3. What types of activities do program evaluators do in the course of an evaluation?

Evaluation design

1. _____

Sampling of information and stakeholders

2. _____

Generating, analyzing, and interpreting data

3. _____

Use the results of the evaluation for program change

4. _____

Work with a variety of groups effectively

5. _____

Clarify values of different stakeholders

6. _____

Use administrative skills for planning, scheduling, and managing the finances of an evaluation

7. _____

Use results to help analyze educational policies

8. _____

Help decide appropriate audiences and information for feedback

9. _____

Determine the needs of a building to improve instruction

10. _____

RECOMMENDED READINGS

The field of evaluation includes educational researchers and psychological researchers. Among the resources for further understanding are the following: Witkin and Altschuld (1995); the *Encyclopedia of Evaluation* (Mathison, 2004); and Rossi et al. (2004). Bickman and Rog (1998) provide an edited collection of applied research methods relevant to evaluation; Chelimsky and Shadish (1997) provide an edited collection of forward-looking chapters on evaluation topics. Caron (1993) presents a Canadian perspective on the body of knowledge for evaluation practice; Mark, Henry, and Julnes (1999) articulated a framework for evaluation practice. The 1987 program evaluation tool kit from Sage is another valuable resource. The evaluation tool kit at the Web site of the W. K. Kellogg Foundation is exceptionally valuable as a distance resource (it can be accessed at www.wkkf.org/).

REFERENCES

Altschuld, J. W. (1995). Developing an evaluation program: Challenges in the teaching of evaluation. *Evaluation and Program Planning, 18*(3), 259–265.

Altschuld, J. W. (2002). The preparation of professional evaluators: Past tense and future perfect. *Japanese Journal of Evaluation Studies, 2*(1), 1–9.

Altschuld, J. W., Engle, M., Cullen, C., Kim, I., & Macce, B. R. (1994). The 1994 directory of evaluation training programs. *New Directions in Program Evaluation, 62,* 71–94.

Altschuld, J. W., & Kumar, D. D. (1995). Program evaluation in science education: The model perspective. *New Directions for Program Evaluation, 65,* 5–17.

Altschuld, J. W., & Kumar, D. D. (2002). *Evaluation of science and technology education at the dawn of a new millennium.* New York: Kluwer/Plenum.

Altschuld, J. W., & Ronning, M. (2000). *Program evaluation: Planning a program evaluation.* Invited Workshop presented at 32nd annual convention of the National Association of School Psychologists, New Orleans, LA.

Altschuld, J. W., & Witkin, B. R. (2000). *From needs assessment to action: Transforming needs into solution strategies.* Thousand Oaks, CA: Sage.

Altschuld, J. W., Yoon, J. S., & Cullen, C. (1993). The utilization of needs assessment results. *Evaluation and Program Planning, 16,* 279–285.

American Evaluation Association. (1995). Guiding principles for evaluators. *New Directions for Program Evaluation, 66,* 19–26.

Bickman, L., & Rog, D. (Eds.). (1998). *Handbook of applied social research.* Thousand Oaks, CA: Sage.

Campbell, D. T., & Stanley, J. C. (1966). *Experimental and quasi-experimental designs for research.* Chicago: Rand McNally.

Caracelli, V. J. (1989). Structured conceptualization: A framework for interpreting evaluation results. *Evaluation and Program Planning, 12,* 45–52.

Caron, D. J. (1993). Knowledge required to perform the duties of an evaluator. *Canadian Journal of Program Evaluation, 8,* 59–79.

Chelimsky, E., & Shadish, W. R. (Eds.). (1997). *Evaluation for the 21st century: A handbook.* Thousand Oaks, CA: Sage.

Chen, H-T. (1990). *Theory-driven evaluations.* Newbury Park, CA: Sage.

Cook, T. D., & Campbell, D. T. (1979). *Quasi-experimentation: Design and analysis issues for field settings.* Chicago: Rand McNally.

Davidson, E. J. (2002, October). The discipline of evaluation: A helicopter tour for I/O psychologists. *Industrial/Organizational Psychologist, 40*(2), 31–35.

Edwards, J. E., Scott, J. C., & Raju, N. S. (Eds.). (2003). *The human resources program evaluation handbook.* Thousand Oaks, CA: Sage.

Engle, M., & Altschuld, J. W. (2003/2004). An update on university-based training. *Evaluation Exchange, 9*(4), 13.

Engle, M., Altschuld, J. W., & Kim, Y. C. (2005). *Emerging dimensions of university-based evaluator preparation programs.* Manuscript in progress. Corvallis: Oregon State University.

Fitzpatrick, J. L. (1989). The politics of evaluation: Who is the audience? *Evaluation Review, 13*(6), 563–578.

Fitzpatrick, J. L., Sanders, J. R., & Worthen, B. R. (2003). *Program evaluation: Alternative approaches and practical guidelines* (3rd ed.). Boston: Allyn & Bacon.

Greene, J. C., & Caracelli, V. J. (Eds.). (1997). *Advances in mixed-method evaluation: The challenges and benefits of integrating diverse paradigms.* San Francisco: Jossey-Bass.

Holton, E. F., III, Bates, R. A., & Naquin, S. S. (2000). Large-scale performance-driven training needs assessment: A case study. *Public Personnel Management, 29,* 249–268.

Joint Committee on Standards for Educational Evaluation. (1994). *The program evaluation standards* (2nd ed.). Thousand Oaks, CA: Sage.

King, J. A., Stevahn, L., Ghere, G., & Minnema, J. (2001). Toward a taxonomy of essential evaluator competencies. *American Journal of Evaluation, 22,* 229–247.

Kirkpatrick, D. L. (1959). Techniques for evaluating training programs. *Journal of the American Society for Training and Development, 13,* 3–32.

Kirkpatrick, D. L. (1998). *Evaluating training programs: The four levels* (2nd ed.). San Francisco: Berrett-Koehler.

Leviton, L. C., & Hughes, E. F. X. (1981). Research on the utilization of evaluations: A review and synthesis. *Evaluation Review, 5,* 525–548.

Mark, M. M., Henry, G. T., & Julnes, G. (1999). Toward an integrative framework for evaluation practice. *American Journal of Evaluation, 20,* 193–212.

Mark, M. M., & Shotland, R. L. (Eds.). (1987). *Multiple methods in program evaluation* (New Directions in Program Evaluation, Vol. 35). San Francisco: Jossey-Bass.

Mathison, S. (Ed.). (2004). *Encyclopedia of evaluation.* Thousand Oaks, CA: Sage.

McGuire, M. (2002, October). *Canadian Evaluation Society project in support of advocacy and professional development: Literature review.* Toronto: Zorzi.

McKillip, J. (1998). Needs analysis: Processes and techniques. In L. Bickman & D. Rog (Eds.), *Handbook of applied social research* (pp. 261–284). Thousand Oaks, CA: Sage.

Mertens, D. (1994). Training evaluators: Unique skills and knowledge. *New Directions for Program Evaluation, 62,* 17–27.

Mertens, D. M. (1989). *Creative ideas for teaching evaluation: Activities, assignments, and resources* (Evaluation in Education and Human Services Series). New York: Kluwer.

Rossi, P. H., Lipsey, M. W., & Freeman, H. E. (2004). *Evaluation: A systematic approach* (7th ed.). Thousand Oaks, CA: Sage.

Scriven, M. (1991). *Evaluation thesaurus* (4th ed.). Newbury Park, CA: Sage.

Scriven, M. (1994). The final synthesis. *Evaluation Practice, 15,* 367–382.

Scriven, M. (1996). Types of evaluation and evaluators. *Evaluation Practice, 17,* 151–161.

Stevahn, L., King, J. A., Ghere, G., & Minnema, J. (2005). Establishing essential competencies for program evaluators. *American Journal of Evaluation, 26*(1), 43–59.

Stufflebeam, D. L. (1971). The relevance of the CIPP evaluation model for educational accountability. *Journal of Research and Development in Education, 5*(1), 19–25.

Stufflebeam, D. L. (1980). An EEPA interview with Daniel L. Stufflebeam. *Educational Evaluation and Policy Analysis, 4,* 85–90.

Stufflebeam, D. L. (2002). The CIPP model for evaluation. In T. Kellaghan & D. L. Stufflebeam (Eds.), *International handbook of educational evaluation.* Dordrecht: Kluwer.

Suchman, E. A. (1967). *Evaluative research: Principles and practice in public service of social action programs.* New York: Russell Sage Foundation.

Tashakkori, A., & Teddlie, C. (Eds.). (2002). *Handbook of mixed methods for the social and behavioral sciences.* Thousand Oaks, CA: Sage.

Wholey, J. S., Hatry, H. P., & Newcomer, K. E. (Eds.). (1994). *Handbook of accreditation standards for practical program evaluation.* San Francisco: Jossey-Bass.

Witkin, B. R., & Altschuld, J. W. (1995). *Planning and conducting needs assessments: A practical guide.* Thousand Oaks, CA: Sage.

Worthen, B. R., & Sanders, J. R. (Compilers). (1973). *Educational evaluation: Theory and practice.* Worthington, OH: C. A. Jones.

Worthen, B. R., & Sanders, J. R. (1987). *Educational evaluation.* New York: Longman.

Worthen, B. R., Sanders, J. R., & Fitzpatrick, J. L. (1997). *Program evaluation: Alternative approaches and guidelines* (2nd ed.). New York: Longman.

PART II

DESIGN, INSTRUMENT SELECTION OR DEVELOPMENT, AND SAMPLING

6

DESIGNING A RESEARCH STUDY

BRUCE E. WAMPOLD

As you approach the automobile dealer to buy the automobile of your dreams, the reality occurs that any car you purchase will not meet all of one's criteria. These criteria might involve reliability, utility, comfort, price, resale value, visual appeal, and so forth. Clearly there are trade-offs. One might want a Volvo but not be able to afford it. Moreover, one might want one automobile and realize that it wouldn't satisfy others (e.g., one's partner). Even after deciding to purchase a certain make and model, it is likely one will modify it by choosing various options and even then will make further additions by purchasing floor mats, trash receptacles, and so forth. Even the most sophisticated buyer will occasionally be disappointed, perhaps because of his or her weighted criteria or because of chance factors (the particular automobile had an unknown defect). Moreover, during the period of ownership, events transpire that frequently alter one's satisfaction with the automobile: Newer models have features that were not obtainable with the present model; one's needs and attitudes toward automobiles change; and the automobile deteriorates.

Designing a study and purchasing an automobile have many similarities. To select an appropriate design, one should have (a) the specific purpose that the design should accomplish, (b) the criteria for deciding whether the design has a high probability of accomplishing that

purpose, and (c) knowledge of the logic of the design so that the design can be modified to optimally accomplish the goal and avoid problems. As in purchasing an automobile, there is no perfect study, and choice of a particular design involves trade-offs of known factors; moreover, unexpected events will occur that will demand modification of the design and perhaps aborting the study and designing a different study. Some studies will become classics; others will be forgotten, the Dodge Darts of psychological research.

This chapter will outline the general considerations involved in designing a psychological study. Knowing the rules of research and applying them to one's area of interest will not lead linearly to the optimal design; designing research is a creative process. Ingenuity often is needed to find a parsimonious way to discover truths about behavior.

PURPOSE OF THE STUDY

The overarching guiding principle in designing a research study is to ensure that the study addresses the purpose of the research. In generic terms, the purpose of research is to discover knowledge, that is, to know something that was previously unknown. Research cannot be adequately designed unless the purpose of the research is carefully thought out and well stated.

In the received view of science, research is conducted to refine or reject extant theories or to develop new theories. The relation between theory and empirical research is complex and deeply embedded in philosophy of science. Nevertheless, a synopsis of this relation will be useful to understand how the design of a research study should be tied to theoretical propositions. One conception of a theory is that it is a general statement specifying the relations among psychological constructs. In order to conduct research that provides information about this theory, it is necessary to examine various implications of the theory. That is, if theory adequately explains the true situation, then it can be predicted that some event or series of events should occur in a specified context. For example, if depression is caused by a lack of reinforcers in the environment, then increasing these reinforcers should decrease depression of depressed people. Research is focused when this implication is stated as a specific prediction, known as a research hypothesis. Research is then designed such that an experimental result will fall into one of two categories: (a) the experimental result is consistent with the prediction, or (b) the experimental result is inconsistent with the prediction.

If the experimental result is consistent with the prediction, our faith in the theory that germinated the prediction is increased. On the other hand, if the experimental result is inconsistent with the prediction, then the theory is suspect. However carefully the research is designed, there will be flaws, and conclusions about theory should be made conservatively. Theories should be revised, rejected, or developed only when the research evidence is strong.

Knowledge accumulates by repeated studies. Every study that has investigated the connection between smoking behavior of humans and health was flawed, although the conclusion that smoking causes physical disease is inescapable given the totality of the results. The problems with one study were corrected in other studies, although these latter studies also had problems. No study is perfect, but the consistent accumulation of conclusions tends to rule out competing points of view.

It should be clear that the faith one places in the conclusions made from a study is related to the quality of the study. Consequently, to design a good study, one must be cognizant of the problems that can occur. *Validity* is the general descriptor that is used to discuss the "goodness" of research. If the validity of the study is high, then one places faith in the conclusions made from the study and will consider carefully the implications for theory. On the other hand, if the validity is low, then the conclusions are meaningless, and it would be foolish to adjust theory in any way. Validity is often discussed in terms of threats. Threats are possible explanations for a particular experimental result other than the one intended by the researcher. A valid study is one in which threats are few and minor.

Finding a research topic (Leong & Muccio, Chapter 2), using the library effectively to understand the literature in an area and systematically conducting the literature search (Reed & Baxter, Chapter 3), reviewing individual research articles (Oleson & Arkin, Chapter 4), and applying theory to research (Gelso, Chapter 32) are discussed elsewhere in this volume.

The following sections will discuss (a) steps in designing a study and drawing inferences from the research, (b) types of research design, and (c) a taxonomy of validities and the threats to these validities.

Design and Inference Steps

There are many stages of research, and critical inferences are made in each. Consider the following process of hypothesis testing. The first step is to develop a research hypothesis that reflects an implication of theory. Suppose that one has a theory that the stability of personality is caused, in part, by the selection of environments that are compatible with personality. One implication of this theory would be that extroverts would choose activities that allow them to interact with others, whereas introverts would choose solitary activities.

A research hypothesis is a specific prediction about how two or more constructs will be related. A hypothesis is of the general form: Under specific conditions, a phenomenon will be expected to occur. Development of the research hypothesis, in the minds of many, is the most creative and the most difficult step in research. Certainly, knowledge of the substantive area is a prerequisite for developing a hypothesis. Some hypotheses will be developed to extend knowledge in a small and deliberate way; other times, researchers will bring together disparate areas to develop a hypothesis that will profoundly influence the field by changing direction (Platt, 1964).

> Examining crucial hypotheses leads to the extension of knowledge, the winnowing of theories, the clarification of discrepancies, the identification of active ingredients of treatments, and so on, [whereas] inconsequential research hypotheses . . . do not produce resolution because they do not lead to a convergence of knowledge. (Wampold, Davis, & Good, 1990, p. 362)

In the second step, operations are chosen to represent the constructs referenced in the hypothesis. In the example of extroversion-introversion and choice of environments involving various degrees of social interaction, extroversion-introversion and the environmental choice must be operationalized to conduct the research. One might choose to use a paper-and-pencil test to measure extroversion-introversion (see Constantine & Ponterotto, Chapter 7, for a discussion of selecting instruments). Socialization in the environment could be designed into the experiment by having two activities that are similar in all respects other than degree of socialization and then giving the participants their choice of activities. For example, participants in the research might be led to believe that their problem-solving ability is being judged and then be given a choice of either participating in a group that solves the problem or solving the problem by themselves. The choice of solitary or group problem solving is then an operation intended to reflect choice of environments.

Third, the study is designed so that the covariation of the operations can be examined. That is, are the scores yielded by the operations of the constructs referenced in the hypothesis related in a systematic way? In the continuing example, one might test the extroversion-introversion of participants and then give them a choice of problem-solving situations; in that way, one could determine whether participants who scored high on extroversion would be more likely to choose group problem-solving situations more frequently than would participants who scored high

on introversion. This is to say, the researcher designs the study so that the covariation of measured variables can be examined. In an experimental study, the independent variable is manipulated so that the effect on the dependent variable can be observed.

Fourth, it is determined whether or not the measured variables do indeed covary as expected. That is, one examines the results to determine whether the results reflect the predictions. This examination is usually accomplished by applying a statistical test. Figure 6.1 reflects the general procedure of designing a study.

Having designed and conducted the study, the investigator reverses the direction of the sequence described above, making inferences along the way. Figure 6.1 illustrates how inferences are made from the statistical tests back up to theory. The measured variables do indeed covary; the independent variable was the cause of the concomitant covariation in the dependent variable; the independent variable and the dependent variable accurately reflect the constructs of interest; the results apply to various persons, settings, and times; and the results have implications for theory and/or practice.

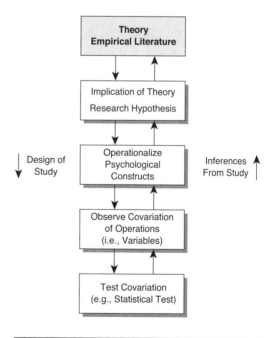

Figure 6.1 Steps to Designing and Making Inferences From a Psychological Study

Before explicating validity of research, various types of research designs will be discussed. Although there are many variations on the theme of research designs, a useful way to conceptualize research designs is to classify them as passive, experimental, or quasi-experimental.

Types of Research Designs

Passive Designs

Passive designs are designs in which the researcher examines the covariation of variables without manipulating some aspect of the study. Generally, there are two types of passive designs: correlational and between-group designs. As shown in Figure 6.2, the correlational design involves selecting a random sample from a population, measuring two variables on each subject, calculating the correlation coefficient r_{AB}, and

then testing whether or not the true (i.e., the population correlation) between these two variables is zero (H_o: $\Delta_{AB} = 0$) (see Dickter, Chapter 19, for a discussion of the logic of statistical tests). For example, a researcher may wish to know whether depression and anxiety covary in the general population. A random sample of subjects is drawn from a population, the levels of depression and anxiety are measured (perhaps with depression and anxiety inventories), and the correlation of the measured levels of depression and anxiety is calculated and tested. If the sample correlation is sufficiently large, the null hypothesis of a zero population correlation is rejected, and it is concluded that anxiety and depression covary in the population. Because this is a passive design, it is not possible to make causal statements from the design: Depression might cause anxiety; anxiety might cause depression; or each may be caused by a third construct.

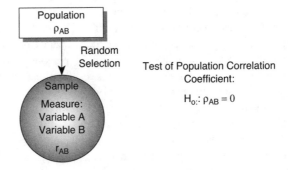

CORRELATIONAL PASSIVE DESIGN

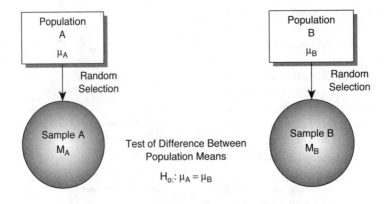

BETWEEN-GROUPS PASSIVE DESIGN

Figure 6.2   Passive Designs

The *between-groups* passive design involves taking random samples from two populations, as shown in Figure 6.2. The goal is to determine whether the true (i.e., population) means of two (or more) populations are the same. The sample means M_A and M_B are calculated, and if these sample means are sufficiently different, the null hypothesis that the population means are equal (i.e., H_o: $\mu_A = \mu_B$) is rejected (probably with the use of a *t*-test for two groups or an analysis of variance for three or more groups). One can then make the conclusions that the populations means differ. For example, one might want to test whether the ability of males and females to decode emotional expression differs. Again, because this is a passive design, no causal statements can be made; any differences found may be due to socialization, biological differences, motivation, or so forth.

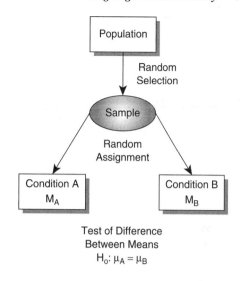

Figure 6.3   Experimental Designs

Experimental Design

In an *experimental design,* the researcher manipulates some variable so that the comparison between groups yields a causal statement about the manipulated variable. The goal of the experimental design is to create conditions (variously called groups, treatments, or levels) such that the conditions differ in only one aspect, the aspect intended by the researcher. This manipulation is called the *independent variable.* Figure 6.3 presents the simplest two-group experimental design. Subjects are randomly selected from a population and then randomly assigned to two conditions, A and B. In this way, any differences between the two conditions are due to chance. Then the researcher has the subjects in Condition A and Condition B do something that creates differences in these two conditions in the way planned by the researcher. Next, the subjects are assessed on the relevant variable, which is called the dependent variable, and sample means calculated (M_A and M_B); if the sample means are sufficiently different, then the null hypothesis of no population differences (i.e., H_o: $\mu_A = \mu_B$) is rejected, and it is concluded that the manipulation was the cause of the differences. For example, to examine the effect of evaluation on performance, a study might be designed in which the subjects in Condition A are led to believe that their performance on

some task will be evaluated by the research team, whereas the subjects in Condition B are led to believe that their performance will be evaluated by computer, and the research team will not be knowledgeable of individual performance. Ideally, the conditions differ only with respect to the belief by subjects that their performance is being evaluated by psychologists or not; in this way, differences in performance (the dependent variable) would be attributed to the effect of evaluation.

There are many variations on the experimental design theme. Of course, more than two conditions could be included (e.g., public evaluation, private evaluation, and no evaluation). The researcher might also want to include two independent variables, each with two or more levels. In the performance example, the researcher might want to make the difficulty of the task an independent variable (e.g., two groups, easy and difficult). Repeated designs, in which subjects are assessed in more than one condition of an independent variable, are often used. For example, the subjects in the performance experiment may complete both the easy and difficult task.

It is useful to emphasize the difference between passive and experimental designs. The key difference between the designs is that in the experimental design, the researcher determines the conditions and the groups differ only in the intended way. Passive and experimental designs might involve testing exactly the same statistical hypothesis (e.g., H_o: $\mu_A = \mu_B$) and use the same statistical test (e.g., t-test), but the logic is fundamentally different. To make matters more confusing, designs might have experimental as well as passive aspects; for example, the performance experiment might contain a nonexperimental variable, such as gender.

Quasi-experimental Designs

Often, true experimental designs are difficult to conduct because of ethical or practical constraints or because one wants to conduct research in the field to get a better feel of the "real world." Any design that approximates an experimental design is called a *quasi-experimental design*. Technically, any design that has one or more threats to validity (as described in the next section) is a quasi-experimental design. Sometimes one attempts to design an experimental study and various threats to validity creep in, creating a quasi-experimental design. In other instances, one cannot design an experimental design, and one deliberately designs a quasi-experimental design. In either case, the logic of the design is good enough to have reasonably good faith in the conclusions. Campbell and Stanley (1963) were the first to discuss the concept of quasi-experimentation and to describe such designs; Cook and Campbell (1979) discussed these issues further in the context of conducting field research.

Validity of Research

In the research process, the inferences made at each step may or may not be proper. If the validity of the study is high, then there are few rival interpretations, and they are relatively implausible; if the validity is low, there are many alternative and veridical explanations for an obtained result. The overall conclusion of a study is either that the inferences lead to support for the hypothesis (i.e., the obtained pattern of results was consistent with the prediction of the research hypothesis) or that the hypothesis was not supported (i.e., the obtained pattern of results was not consistent with the prediction of the hypothesis). If validity is high, then one

places faith in the inferences and the resulting conclusion about the hypothesis. Given high validity and confidence in the conclusion about the hypothesis, one can revise, reject, or develop theoretical propositions.

The seminal work of Campbell and Stanley (1963) explicated two types of validity, internal and external. Bracht and Glass (1968) expanded on the external validity theme. Concerned about drawing inferences in field settings, Cook and Campbell later (1979) divided both internal validity and external validity, yielding four types: statistical conclusion validity, internal validity, construct validity of putative causes and effects, and external validity, which were further refined (Shadish, Cook, & Campbell, 2002). Recently, Wampold et al. (1990) expanded the concept of validity by considering the theoretical context of research and proposed threats to hypothesis validity. A brief description of each type of validity follows.

Statistical Conclusion Validity

The first inference typically made in a study is whether or not the variables in a study truly covary. Typically, statistical tests are used to make this inference. When statistical tests are employed, the null hypothesis is that there is no relationship between (or among) variables in the population. When the null hypothesis is rejected, the decision is made that, in the relevant population, the two variables covary. For example, in a randomized treatment design, in which subjects are randomly assigned to a treatment condition and to a control group, a statistically significant t-test indicates that scores on the dependent variable covaried with the manipulation to the extent that it was unlikely that the obtained result would have occurred by chance had there been no true population relationship. In a design in which conditions are not manipulated by the researcher, one might want to examine the relationship between two variables, such as Graduate Record Examination—Quantitative scores and grades in statistics classes. In this instance, a statistically significant Pearson correlation coefficient would indicate that the observed linear relationship between GRE scores and grades in statistics was sufficiently large to conclude that it did not occur by chance and thus there is a true linear relation between these two variables.

Statistical inferences are based on probabilities such that one is never sure whether they are true or not. *Type I error* involves deciding that variables are related (i.e., rejecting the null hypothesis of no relationship), when in fact there is no true relationship. *Type II error* involves deciding that there is no relationship (i.e., variables do not covary), when in fact there is a relationship. *Alpha,* the probability of making a Type I error, and *beta,* the probability of making a Type II error, are indicators of statistical conclusion validity. If a study is designed so that alpha equals .05, then there are less than five chances out of 100 that the investigator has made an incorrect inference by concluding that the variables covary. Dickter (Chapter 19) and Steelman and Levy (Chapter 20) discuss the logic of statistical testing in more detail.

Threats to statistical conclusion validities are conditions that inflate the error rates. For example, if the assumptions of a statistical test are violated, the chances of falsely concluding that variables covary may be much greater than the nominal alpha set by the investigator. Similarly, if power is low, the probability of falsely concluding that there is no covariation is high (see Byors, Chapter 11). Threats to statistical conclusion are discussed more fully by Shadish et al. (2002).

Statistical conclusion validity applies to inferences about covariation, whether or not inferential statistics per se are used. For example, single-subject designs often are used to establish the *functional* relation between an intervention and behavior (Barlow & Hersen, 1984). Essentially, *functional relation* means that the independent variable (baseline vs. intervention) covaries with the dependent variable (typically some behavior). In this context, Type I and Type II errors continue to exist; for example, one might falsely conclude that there is a true functional relation.

Internal Validity

After it has been determined that two variables covary (or do not covary), a causal attribution typically is made. For example, in an experimental design, when the manipulation of the independent variable results in a concomitant change in the dependent variable, the treatment is said to be the cause of the change; however, the causal inference may be incorrect. For example, the participants who were not benefiting from treatment may have dropped out of the treatment group, raising the mean for this group; mortality (i.e., participants drop out of the study) is then an alternative explanation for the results. *Internal validity* refers to the degree to which an attribution of causality for a given relationship between variables is correct.

Internal validity is highest when subjects are randomly assigned to conditions, the conditions differ on only one dimension, and all treatments and assessments are given to the groups simultaneously; however, even under the best conditions (e.g., laboratory studies), threats to internal validity creep in. Nonrandomization presents special problems in that groups may not be comparable before the treatments are administered. Designs in which variables are not manipulated by the researcher (i.e., passive designs) present special challenges to causal inferences. For example, studies that have examined the causal link between smoking and health have been unable to randomly assign participants to a smoking and to a nonsmoking condition. Critics of the early smoking studies made the point that the poorer health of smokers may be due to factors other than smoking, such as general health behavior (e.g., smokers participating in riskier behavior), genetic predispositions (i.e., some people are predisposed to smoking and to poor health), diet, and so forth. Each of these alternative explanations presents threats to internal validity because the subjects were not randomly assigned to conditions, and consequently, selection of subjects may have resulted in systematic differences in the smoking and nonsmoking conditions other than smoking.

In any context in which causation is attributed, the trick is to rule out as many threats to internal validity as possible. An important aspect of internal validity is that it is related to the design of the study and not to the statistical procedure used (Cohen, 1968). For example, a regression analysis can be used just as well to analyze the data from a purely experimental design as it can to analyze the data from a passive design (Cohen, 1968; Cohen & Cohen, 1983; Kerlinger, 1986).

As discussed previously, studies in which subjects are not randomly assigned to conditions present special problems in causality. There is a saying that "correlation does not mean causation." A simple correlation coefficient indexes the degree of linear relationship between two variables, but it does not identify which is the cause of the other. Suppose that it is found that scores on a depression inventory and scores on a test of social perception are related such that relatively depressed people tend to falsely perceive that people do not like them at a higher rate than nondepressed people. Does the depression cause the misperceptions or do the misperceptions cause the depression; or does a third variable (e.g., a variable related to brain chemistry) cause both? In recent years, statistical methods have been developed to test various causal models from correlational data (e.g., structural equation modeling, Joreskog & Sorbom, 1988; see Steelman & Levy, Chapter 20, for a more complete discussion of using advanced statistical tests). Nevertheless, the most direct means to attribute causality is to experimentally manipulate a variable.

Construct Validity

Presumably, the measured variables in a study are reflective of psychological constructs. When measured variable X is thought to be the cause of measured variable Y, then one wants to infer that the construct operationalized by X is the cause of the construct operationalized by Y. *Construct validity* refers to all variables in a study, including the independent and dependent variables in an experimental study, and reflects the theoretical constructs described in the theory and referenced in the hypotheses.

With regard to the independent variable, the experimental manipulation needs to indicate some construct. Suppose that a social psychologist believes that people will be more likely to self disclose to close friends than to strangers. The task for this researcher is to design conditions of the manipulated variable so they differ on the object of the disclosure (friend vs. stranger) and on no other dimension. Clearly, it would be improper if the friends were female and the strangers were male because any differences between the conditions could be attributed to gender as easily as to closeness (friend vs. stranger). Other improper operationalizations may be more subtle. Suppose the researcher used pictures of persons who were either friends or strangers; it would then be vital that the pictures were matched on all attributes other than closeness, such as ethnicity, personal attractiveness, and age.

The dependent variable should also operationalize a construct. If a treatment is intended to affect depression, then any measures of the dependent variable used should reflect depression and not some other construct, such as social desirability. Lounsbury, Gibson, and Saudargas (Chapter 9) discuss how to construct tests to measure constructs, and Constantine and Ponterotto (Chapter 7) discuss how to evaluate and select the proper instruments to operationalize a construct.

When it is not clear whether the variable or variables in a study reflect one construct or another construct, a confound is said to exist. Explicitly, a *confound* is an alternative construct that cannot be logically or statistically differentiated from a hypothesized construct. In the self-disclosure study, if all friends were females and all strangers were male, then a complete confound exists between gender and friend or stranger. If an instrument intended to measure depression actually measures, to some degree, social desirability, then depression and social desirability are confounded.

Often, variables related to characteristics of people are naturally confounded. For example, in U.S. society, ethnicity is correlated with socioeconomic status (SES) and therefore attributions about ethnicity may more appropriately be made about SES. Sorting out naturally occurring confounds is problematic but can often be partially accomplished with statistical methods (see e.g., Cohen & Cohen, 1983).

External Validity

Shadish et al. (2002) focused their discussion on generalizability across types of units, settings, treatments, and outcomes. The central question in external validity is the degree to which the conclusions from a study apply equally to subsets of units, settings, treatments, and outcomes. Units are most often people but also could be some groups of people (e.g., families) or institutions (e.g., schools). Most often, it is generalizability across types of people that is most interesting. A recent study linking strenuous weekly exercise with reduced risk of cardiovascular disease was conducted on males only, leaving the important issue of whether this result generalized to females unanswered (and unanswerable). Inclusion of males and females in the study would have allowed the researchers to determine whether or not strenuous exercise was equally potent prophylactically for males and females. To determine whether a conclusion is equally applicable to subpopulations, the subpopulation must be a part of the design. Populations can be handled as a factor in a factorial design; interaction effects of the population factor with some other factor are evidence that the results vary as a function of the type of person. For example, the exercise study could be redesigned to include gender as a factor. An interaction between gender and exercise on the incidence of cardiovascular disease would indicate that exercise was not equally beneficial to males and females.

Possible choices for characteristics to examine vis-à-vis subpopulations are virtually unlimited. Important characteristics, from a policy or social perspective, include gender, ethnicity, SES, and age. Often there are theoretical or empirical reasons for examination of generalizability across various subpopulations. See McCready (Chapter 10) for a more complete discussion of sampling issues and generalizability.

Hypothesis Validity

Wampold et al. (1990), concerned about the relation of method to theory, discussed hypothesis validity. *Hypothesis validity* refers to the extent to which results elucidate theoretically derived predictions about the relations between or among constructs. Hypothesis validity involves four steps. First, the *research hypotheses,* which are statements about presumed relations among constructs, should be crucial to extending knowledge. This is the "Who Cares?" factor. Research may be beautifully designed and conducted, but unless it has important

implications for psychology, few will be interested in the results.

To have adequate hypothesis validity, the research hypothesis should be stated unambiguously and in a form that is falsifiable. If the hypothesis is ambiguous, it will be impossible to determine whether or not the obtained results are consistent with the hypothesis. Statements such as "The purpose of the present study is to explore the relation between . . . " lead to inferential problems because there are no predictions against which to compare the obtained results. Any study that examines the relationship between a set of two or more variables will inevitably "discover" a pattern of results, but it cannot be used to support or reject a theoretical proposition because none was offered (Wampold et al., 1990).

Hypothesis validity also involves the close association between research hypotheses and statistical hypotheses. Research hypotheses are stated in terms of relations among constructs; these constructs are then operationalized as observed variables; and the scores produced by these variables are then statistically tested. Underlying each statistical test is a statistical hypothesis. Rejection of the statistical hypothesis should be informative relative to the research hypothesis. Problems occur when multiple statistical tests are used to verify a single research hypothesis because it is likely some of those statistical tests will be statistically significant and some not. Is this evidence for or against the research hypothesis? Ideally, one statistical test will be focused on one research hypothesis (see Rosnow & Rosenthal, 1988).

CONCLUSION

In this chapter, the general considerations for designing a study were discussed. However carefully one designs a study, there will be threats to validity, just as there is no ideal automobile that can satisfy all one's dreams. Certainly, there are practical constraints, particularly in terms of researcher time, resources, availability of participants, and ethical considerations. We may all desire a Ferrari or a Rolls Royce, but need to settle for a Toyota or Ford. The important question is "Will the design get the job done?" If the design is adequate, the conclusion made will be believable (i.e., validity is reasonably good), although there will be various threats that cannot be ruled out. Future research is always needed to continue the quest for the understanding of behavior.

EXERCISES

1. In your area of interest, find two studies, one that used an experimental design and one that used a passive design.

    A. Identify the hypotheses of each of the studies.

    B. Identify the major conclusions made by the authors.

    C. Assess the validity of the conclusions by examining the statistical, internal, construct, external, and hypothesis validity of the study.

    D. Determine design features for each study that would have improved the validity of the study.

2. Design an experimental study. Explain how the independent variable will be manipulated to test its effect. What will be the various conditions, how will the conditions differ, and what safeguards will be needed to maintain internal validity?

3. Design a passive design. Describe the variables that will be used in the study and explain the conclusions that could be made from the study. What are the limitations to this study?

4. Discuss the trade-offs in designing a study. For instance, how does ensuring internal validity limit external validity? Which is more important in your area of interest? Have studies focused too much on one type of validity (e.g., are studies in your area conducted in a laboratory with little relevance to real world situations?)?

RECOMMENDED READINGS

There are many, many sources of information about research design and related topics, and the graduate student should seek advice from his or her advisor and methods instructors. Kerlinger (1986) presented a comprehensive overview of behavioral research that provides an excellent introduction to the many facets of research in the social sciences. Kirk (1982) has presented well the variants of the experimental design theme, as well as the statistical tests of each variation. For discussion of field research, Cook and Campbell (1979) discussed the many issues of conducting research outside of the laboratory. Keren and Lewis (1993) edited a volume that examined many of the current issues in behavioral research and quantitative methods inherent in such research. Shadish, Cook, and Campbell (2002) discuss the philosophical bases of research in the social sciences. For qualitative research, which was not discussed in this chapter, see Pollio, Graves, and Arfken (Chapter 17); Denzin and Lincoln (1994) have edited a collection of methods related to the qualitative paradigm. Methods applicable to specialized areas are discussed by metrologists in various subspecialties such as counseling (Heppner, Kivlighan, & Wampold, 1999) and clinical psychology (Kazdin, 1992). Researchers are advised to acquire specific knowledge of designs most applicable to their area of interest.

REFERENCES

Barlow, D. H., & Hersen, M. (1984). *Single case experimental designs: Strategies for studying behavior change* (2nd ed.). New York: Pergamon.

Bracht, G. H., & Glass, G. V. (1968). The external validity of experiments. *American Educational Research Journal, 5,* 437–474.

Campbell, D. T., & Stanley, J. C. (1963). *Experimental and quasi-experimental designs for research.* Chicago: Rand McNally College.

Cohen, J. (1968). Multiple regression as a general data-analytic strategy. *Psychological Bulletin, 70,* 426–443.

Cohen, J., & Cohen, P. (1983). *Applied multiple regression/correlation for the behavioral sciences* (2nd ed.). Hillsdale, NJ: Lawrence. Erlbaum.

Cook, T. D., & Campbell, D. T. (1979). *Quasi-experimentation: Design and analysis issues for field settings.* Boston: Houghton Mifflin.

Denzin, N. K., & Lincoln, Y. S. (Eds.). (1994). *Handbook of qualitative research.* Thousand Oaks, CA: Sage.

Heppner, P. P., Kivlighan, D. M., Jr., & Wampold, B. E. (1999). *Research design in counseling* (2nd ed.). Pacific Grove, CA: Brooks/Cole.

Kazdin, A. E. (1992). *Research design in clinical psychology* (2nd ed.). New York: Macmillan

Kerlinger, F. N. (1986). *Foundations of behavioral research* (3rd ed.). New York: Holt, Rinehart & Winston.

Joreskog, K., & Sorbom, D. (1988). LISREL 7: A guide to the program and applications. Chicago: SPSS.

Keren, G., & Lewis, C. (Eds.). (1993). *A handbook for data analysis in the behavioral sciences: Methodological issues.* Hillsdale, NJ: Lawrence Erlbaum.

Kirk, R. E. (1982). *Experimental design: Procedures for the behavioral sciences* (2nd ed.). Monterey, CA: Brooks/Cole.

Platt, J. R. (1964). Strong inference. *Science, 146,* 347–353.

Rosnow, R. L., & Rosenthal, R. (1988). Focused tests of significance and effect size estimation in counseling psychology. *Journal of Counseling Psychology, 35,* 203–208.

Shadish, W. R., Cook, T. D., & Campbell, D. T. (2002). *Experimental and quasi-experimental designs for generalized causal inference.* Boston: Houghton Mifflin.

Wampold, B. E., Davis, B., & Good, R. H., III. (1990). Hypothesis validity of clinical research. *Journal of Consulting and Clinical Psychology, 58,* 360–367.

7

Evaluating and Selecting Psychological Measures for Research Purposes

Madonna G. Constantine
Joseph G. Ponterotto

Even from the beginning of the research process, some individuals become overwhelmed or intimidated by the complex and intricate processes associated with conducting sound psychological inquiry. In particular, evaluating and selecting ideal psychological measures may be quite challenging in light of the broad array of tests currently available (e.g., Robinson, Shafer, & Wrightsman, 1991, 1999). Although some of these instruments are carefully designed and validated, many psychological measures are not carefully thought out and crafted. Unfortunately, we have found that a good number of researchers select measures out of convenience (e.g., no cost and easily available) rather than out of a systematic evaluation process (Ponterotto, 1996).

The most widely used psychological tests are self-report instruments. These measures typically are presented in the format of questionnaires or surveys wherein respondents share their feelings, attitudes, behaviors, or abilities regarding specific issues or constructs. Self-report scales may be valuable tools in assessing variables of interest for quantitative research purposes if proper analysis is applied to the process of selection, utilization, and evaluation of these instruments. We hope this chapter serves as a practical guide to researchers regarding some basic considerations in identifying, selecting, and using appropriate psychological self-report measures.

Locating Psychological Instruments for Research

Once researchers specify their constructs of interest, they must choose instruments that properly assess these attributes. Using published journal articles, reference books, and computer database searches might be helpful to them in locating possible scales. Subsequently, examining critical reviews of scales helps many investigators to narrow down from a larger group of instruments those most plausible for use.

Given the myriad journal articles and books in the field of psychology, as discussed by Reed and Baxter in Chapter 3, literature databases such as PsycINFO, PsycLIT, and ERIC can be used to locate appropriate references that discuss relevant research variables. For example, simply using keywords in the bibliographic PsycINFO database, which encompasses most of the published psychological research since 1872, researchers can view a collection of citations for journal articles, books, and doctoral dissertations in their areas of interest. An investigator interested in children's motivation regarding school performance, for example, might use the keywords *motivation, children,* and *school* in a PsycINFO search. After the results of this search present a potential list of citations related to various forms of children's school motivation, the researcher could retrieve and review articles, books, and dissertations that may be of interest (see Oleson & Arkin in Chapter 4 for more information). If such a search yielded an unwieldy number of entries, the investigator could further specify search criteria, such as focusing on elementary or secondary school children. If any of the aforementioned keywords in isolation were searched in the PsycINFO database, then a very large number of references would be listed for each term. This phenomenon could create difficulties for the researcher in terms of narrowing down his or her area of focus.

The American Psychological Association (APA) suggests using test reference books to locate psychological instruments. Four of the most well known of these books are *Tests in Print (TIP)*, the *Buros Mental Measurements Yearbook (MMY)*, *Tests* and *Test Critiques*. TIP is perhaps the most inclusive reference book because it contains the most entries per volume; the latest edition has 3,009 entries (APA, 2004). It describes scales' purposes, intended populations, publication dates, prices, authors, time needed to complete instruments, publishers, and test references. *TIP VI* (Murphy, Plake, Impara, & Spies, 2002) serves as the most recent index to *MMY*.

Additional reference books for locating instruments include the *Directory of Unpublished Experimental Measures; Dictionary of Behavioral Assessment Techniques; Measures of Psychological Assessment: A Guide to 3,000 Original Sources and Their Application; Measures of Personality and Social Psychological Attitudes; Measures of Political Attitudes; Measures for Clinical Practice: A Source Book; ETS Test Collection Catalogue; Handbook of Research Design and Social Measurement; A Sourcebook for Mental Health Measures;* and *Tests: A Comprehensive Reference for Assessments in Psychology, Education, and Business* (Ponterotto, 1996). Reading the reviews of a test also can provide useful information pertaining to the specific population for which the tool was created, as well as its intended purpose. Moreover, test reviews may enlighten readers about issues such as biases and flaws within measures.

Another APA (2004) recommendation for finding appropriate psychological instruments is the use of the Internet. For example, the *MMY*'s Web site (www.unl.edu/buros) sells over 4,000 commercial reviews that appear in the print version of that book. Each review can be ordered through the Web site for $15. In addition, the Educational Testing Service's Web site (http://ets.org) contains a database of abstracts of research reports and research memorandums that are available to view online free of charge. More specific information about these test review resources can be found in Table 7.1.

PRACTICAL CONSIDERATIONS IN SELECTING PSYCHOLOGICAL RESEARCH INSTRUMENTS

Cost

Researchers must take into account the cost to obtain tests from authors or publishers to ensure that it is not precluded by their budget. Some instruments may be free of charge, whereas others may be quite expensive. For-profit test publishers charge for the use of their copyrighted instruments. Prices for these measurements typically are listed in the publishers' catalogues. Many test authors, however, do not sell their copyright to for-profit test publishing companies, and these authors often allow free use of their measures to both graduate students and experienced researchers.

Permission and Responsibility for Using Instruments

It often is mandatory to receive permission from either the authors or publishers of psychological instruments before incorporating them into research studies. Often, permission is

Table 7.1   Test Review Resources

Test Review Source	Information Provided
Mental Measurements Yearbook The Buros Institute of Mental Measurement	Names of tests, summary of test purpose, intended population, test acronym, price, authors, publishers, and test reviews.
Tests in Print The Buros Institute of Mental Measurement	Names of over 3,000 published tests by subject index, summary of test purpose, intended population, test acronym, price, authors, publishers, and references of articles related to test.
Tests Pro-Ed, Inc.	Test titles, descriptions of tests, intended population, authors, tests' purpose, major test features, administration time, scoring methods, cost, availability, publishers, and information about self- or examiner-administered tests.
Test Critiques Pro-Ed, Inc.	Companion to *Tests*; includes information about test purposes, test reliability and validity, test norms, practical applications and uses, technical aspects, test critiques, authors, publishers, intended population, administration procedures, expert opinions regarding test adequacy, and user-friendly explanations of technical terms.
ETS Test Collection Catalogue Educational Testing Service	Describes over 10,000 instruments by subject index, including test titles, appropriate uses, authors, and publishers' addresses.

requested by sending a formal or e-mail letter to the authors or publishers of the instruments. It is common for publishing companies to list specific requirements of the purchasers (e.g., must possess a master's degree in psychology or a related field, or a supervisor's signature must be obtained, as in the case of a student or uncertified professional). Although requesting permission for the use of a scale might seem tedious to some researchers, the test authors' or publishers' selective distribution of these instruments can provide substantial security of test materials and prevent possible misuse. Nonetheless, it is virtually impossible to be certain that all tests will remain in qualified hands.

Because different tests require different levels of competence in their use and interpretation, researchers selecting and using psychological tests should have the requisite training and experience to use these scales (Ponterotto, 1996). In addition to minimum qualifications required for the use of certain measures, investigators have a responsibility to contribute to the profession by reporting relevant validity, reliability, and uses of the instruments they select. At times, some researchers are asked to provide raw data from

their studies to the instruments' developers in order to conduct large-scale validity studies.

Time and Length

The amount of time required to complete instruments and the length of these instruments are additional considerations in the selection of appropriate tests for research investigations. For example, if one of the scales in a survey packet includes an instrument containing 250 items, the study may attract fewer respondents because of the potential amount of time it would take to complete a scale or packet of scales perceived as lengthy. It may appear to be more intimidating than a shorter measure. Further, excessively long instruments may limit the number of constructs researchers may be interested in studying simultaneously. For example, in the same 40-minute period, research participants can complete either two lengthy scales (measuring two constructs) or five brief scales (measuring five constructs). Moreover, the more time-efficient a measurement, the more potential there is for respondents to complete all the items once they have begun the testing process. We have found, however, that if participants are compensated with money, food, course credit, or other types of incentives, they may not be as concerned with completing more lengthy instruments.

In addition to the aforementioned practical considerations in selecting psychological research instruments, it is important to ask yourself the following questions with regard to your potential scales:

1. To what degree do these scales address my primary constructs or variables of interest?

2. Based on previous researchers' assertions, what have been the chief strengths and limitations regarding how my constructs of interest have been assessed through these self-report measures?

3. What do I anticipate will be the strengths and limitations of my research study in light of my use of these self-report instruments?

PSYCHOMETRIC ISSUES

Reliability

Reliability is concerned with the degree to which test scores are free from measurement error. Although in most situations the results of tests are rarely exactly identical when repeated, the results generally should reflect some level of consistency from one trial to another (Carmines & Zeller, 1979; Thorndike, 1997). The lower the degree of measurement error in tests, the higher their reliability. Reliability estimates range from 0 to 1, and the appropriateness of reliability for a test depends on the purpose of the test (Thorndike, 1997). A reliability coefficient of at least .70 is typically considered to be acceptable (Loewenthal, 2001; Ponterotto, 1996). According to Carmines and Zeller (1979), a reliability coefficient of .80 or higher is viewed as satisfactory because it indicates that 80% or more of the variance relies on true test scores and substantially excludes the possibility of it being due to random measurement error.

Because there is more than one technique to calculate measurement error, it is essential for researchers to include details of the method employed. Test-retest, equivalent form, split-half, and internal consistency are the most widely used approaches to calculating reliability.

Test-Retest

In test-retest methods of calculating reliability, participants are given the same instrument to complete several times (Carmines & Zeller, 1979; Thorndike, 1997). Researchers then calculate the correlation coefficient by comparing scores from a test session with those of the next test session. When reporting test-retest reliability, noting the time interval between each test administration is recommended (Anastasi & Urbina, 1997). The time interval between measures could range from a few hours to a few months but preferably from 1 to 2 weeks (Pedhazur & Schmelkin, 1991). Intervals any longer than 2 weeks might assess substantial alterations within a person rather than random slight differences in test responding, thus altering more accurate representations of instruments' reliability (Anastasi & Urbina, 1997).

Even when the retest is given within the appropriate time interval, however, there are other difficulties associated with the test-retest method. Participants' previous exposure to the test may result in improved score because of a practice effect. In addition, if the time between test and retest is especially short, there is an increased likelihood of individuals remembering their previous responses and repeating them instead of rereading the same questions (Carmines & Zeller, 1979; Thorndike, 1997). Hence, the carryover effects of practice and memory may falsely increase consistency between tests scores (Pedhazur & Schmelkin, 1991). On the other hand, with an extended time interval, the difficulties associated with the longer time intervals noted above might occur. Furthermore, random variability within participants, such as illness, fatigue, stress, and worry, can account for differences between scores. Although appearing straightforward, the test-retest method for assessing reliability has several limitations and may not be the most appropriate technique to achieve this goal.

Equivalent or Alternate Form

Because of possible practice and memory biases associated with the test-retest reliability method, distributing an equivalent form (also referred to as an alternate form) of a test might reduce these problems. Using the same participants from the original instruments, equivalent forms intend to measure the identical attributes as the original test (Carmines & Zeller, 1979; Thorndike, 1997). The correlation between both measures represents an estimation of the instruments' reliability, which is expressed in the form of a reliability coefficient (Anastasi & Urbina, 1997; Pedhazur & Schmelkin, 1991).

Similar to the test-retest method, however, equivalent form reliability will reflect random differences within individuals from the original test to the alternate form (Pedhazur & Schmelkin, 1991). Subsequently, researchers should delineate the length of intervals between test administrations (Anastasi & Urbina, 1997). Unlike test-retest reliability, an alternate form may be administered immediately after the completion of an original test because researchers do not need to take into consideration memory and practice effects. Nonetheless, despite the optimistic prognosis of eliminating certain errors associated with the test-retest method, researchers must take into account the complexity of creating a satisfactory alternate form. There is limited availability of acceptable equivalent forms that truly measure the identical construct as the original form of an instrument (Thorndike, 1997).

Split-Half

In contrast to the two methods discussed above, the split-half reliability technique yields reliability estimations based on only one test administration. The split-half reliability process entails dividing one test into two equal parts. The correlation between the two distinct halves represents the reliability estimate. The Spearman-Brown correction formula is used to calculate split-half reliability, and this formula assumes that the instruments' two sections being compared are basically parallel (Pedhazur & Schmelkin, 1991). Although fairly convenient because it only requires one administration, the Spearman-Brown formula of computing split-half reliability has its limitations. For example, this method exhibits some difficulty in proving two test halves as equivalent. Furthermore, erratic scores could result for each of the halves, depending on the manner in which the instruments were divided (Thorndike, 1997). Therefore, the split-half

procedure and Spearman-Brown formula could lead to biased estimations of reliability, as well as neglecting reliability associated with stability over time (Anastasi & Urbina, 1997).

Internal Consistency

Similar to the split-half method, the internal consistency method of reliability is calculated following a single test administration (Ponterotto, 1996; Thorndike, 1997). The most commonly used coefficient in which internal consistency is expressed is the Cronbach's alpha (Carmines & Zeller, 1979). Unlike other methods of calculating reliability, Cronbach's alpha considers the average intercorrelation between every item of a given measure. Thus, the magnitude of alpha depends on the average inter-item correlation and the total number of items in a scale (Anastasi & Urbina, 1997; Ponterotto, 1996). For example, a driver's test that measures only specific skills on an enclosed course will have higher inter-item consistency in comparison with a driver's test that includes a written section, parallel parking skills, on-road driving, and an enclosed course section of the test. Although more homogeneous instruments may be considered preferable for determining reliability because the outcomes frequently yield more clarity, more heterogeneous tests may be more precise predictors of issues or behaviors involving a multifaceted construct (Anastasi & Urbina, 1997).

In addition, the more items on tests, the higher the reliability of those instruments (assuming the items do not reduce the inter-item coefficients); however, if there are excessive numbers of items on these measures, the overall reliability may be reduced substantially (Carmines & Zeller, 1979). Although alpha is sometimes more complicated to use compared with other reliability techniques because it compares all items with one another, it is a practical and efficient technique to calculate reliability, and it is considered to be the preferred measure of internal consistency reliability (Carmines & Zeller, 1979; Ponterotto, 1996).

Other Reliability Considerations

Determining the reliability of some instruments might be an easy task when the researchers are concerned with measuring something concrete and stable. But what happens when the subject of interest is constantly changing in moods, thoughts, knowledge, and attitudes? Working with human participants in research can be quite complicated, not only because they are always changing but also because the actual measurement process might affect their behavior as well. For example, in the case of within-group reliability (consistency within one group from one time to the next), individuals completing a test at another time might be concerned with how they answered the questions previously rather than with their experience at that moment. Therefore, it is common to discuss salient characteristics of individuals within a given group, setting, or testing situation when estimating reliability. Pedhazur and Schmelkin (1991) have stressed the importance of researchers' exploring instruments' reliability and not overgeneralizing reliability from one study to another. Noting reliability from a previous investigation may be a beneficial comparison tool, as long as investigators realize that samples may vary from study to study. Finally, it is pertinent for researchers to present their own evaluation of measures' reliability by indicating this information in their findings.

Validity

Validity is one of the most important factors to consider when evaluating instruments' efficacy in measuring a specific construct (Ponterotto, 1996; Thorndike, 1997). An instrument is considered *valid* when it properly evaluates what it is intended to measure. The correlation between a test score and a criterion measure is known as its *validity coefficient.* Validity estimates also range from 0 to 1. In general, validity is classified into three basic types: content validity, criterion-related validity, and construct validity (Anastasi & Urbina, 1997).

Content Validity

Content validity examines the extent to which instruments properly measure the defined domain of interest. For example, scales designed to measure social anxiety would not have an acceptable content validity if they only examined situations pertaining to anxiety in the work environment and neglected inquiries reflecting anxiety in nonwork situations. Content validity requires a thorough exploration of the constructs of interest to assure that no vital aspects are excluded in the content of the measures.

Criterion-Related Validity

Criterion-related validity occurs when the instruments' results can be connected to one or more outcomes. More specifically, it relates to the extent to which an outcome may be predicted based on the scores obtained on a measure (Thorndike, 1997). Criterion-related validity is not concerned with *why* something occurs but rather *if it predicts* it will occur.

When evaluating criterion-related validity, both concurrent and predictive methods may be applied depending on the construct of interest (Ponterotto, 1996). When a criterion exists in the present, concurrent validity is assessed by correlating an instrument with the criterion at an identical point in time (Anastasi & Urbina, 1997); however, when the instruments regard a future criterion, predictive validity correlates this future criterion with the current scales (Carmines & Zeller, 1979). For example, concurrent validity may be applicable to instruments concerned with reactions after an earthquake, administered directly following the earthquake. In contrast, predictive validity would apply when a work performance measure completed before work begins is correlated with a work evaluation measure completed after a certain amount of work was completed.

Construct Validity

Construct validity is concerned with the extent to which an instrument is appropriately measuring the variable of interest. There are two primary types of construct validity: convergent and discriminant validity. To determine *convergent validity,* a scale must correlate significantly and positively with other instruments designed to measure the same construct. To show *discriminant validity,* also known as *divergent validity,* a scale should not correlate significantly with other measures with which theory suggests it should not correlate.

COMMON FLAWS OF SELF-REPORT MEASURES

Self-report psychological instruments are not error free and have several potential shortcomings. According to Laing (1988), these measures may fail to address adequately researchers' areas of interest, or they may be too costly or inefficient for widespread use. Moreover, some self-report questionnaires are unclear as to their intent. For example, a questionnaire's item might read, "How often do you communicate with your mother?" The author of this measure could expect respondents to answer the question according to how often they have a verbal conversation with their mother; however, respondents also could answer this question in reference to the degree to which there was e-mail communication, verbal communication, and even in-person interactions with their mother. Because of the possible variety of ways in which such a question could be interpreted by respondents, the responses to some psychological instruments might lead to self-report inconsistencies that ultimately are reflected in the conclusions of the study.

Another problem with self-report measures may be related to participants' not knowing information required to respond to a question. For example, a question asking about the earned income of their household may inquire about information not accessible to dependent participants still living with their parents. Therefore, respondents could choose to leave this item unanswered or even wager a guess to this question, although they could be providing inaccurate information in the latter case.

Besides the possibility of incorrect information being reported, it is plausible to consider that some individuals might answer self-report questions inaccurately in order to look more socially acceptable (Holtgraves, 2004). This is referred to as social desirability (Paulhus, 1984). Impression management, a form of social desirability, can occur when individuals respond to questions in the hopes of having others view them as competent or healthy in some fashion. Social desirability also may emerge unintentionally when some

individuals are unaware they are reporting fictitious information but believe their answers are true. In order to prevent both intentional and unintentional social desirability, some researchers include a social desirability scale, in addition to their primary instruments of interest, to assess the extent of participants' socially desirable responses (Anastasi & Urbina, 1997; Loewenthal, 2001).

Tests or scales that address potentially uncomfortable or anxiety-producing topics, such as sexual activity, drug use, weight, family conflict, or history of mental health, also may be more likely to be left unanswered. Participants may feel embarrassed or concerned about who might have access to their personal information or whether it can be traced back to them. With increased assurance of anonymity, however, it may be possible to increase the number of answered questions related to unpleasant subjects (Loewenthal, 2001).

Researchers' inability to understand the context in which the participants are reporting can represent another unfortunate limitation of self-report psychological instruments (Laing, 1988). For instance, when researchers assess participants' feelings of depression through self-report instruments, some respondents, who may recently have experienced the death of a loved one, might respond affirmatively to items on these instruments, as compared with other respondents who might not have experienced similar life circumstances. Thus, participants' life circumstances often are not taken into account when interpreting the results of some self-report psychological tests, which might affect the conclusions that some researchers make about data they obtain from respondents.

TECHNOLOGY AND RESEARCH

In many ways, today's investigators are fortunate because of numerous advances in technology that have occurred over the past 30 years. In particular, computers have contributed immensely to the ease of conducting sound psychological research (see Vaux & Briggs in Chapter 13 for more information). Computers can serve as vital tools to help investigators achieve their research goals and objectives from the preliminary to the final phases of their research studies.

Collecting Primary Information

In the initial stages of research, collecting background information about the constructs of interest and finding ideal measures to assess these constructs has never been easier than with the use of computers. Before the Internet was widely accessible, individuals primarily used library card catalogues to locate specific references. In many ways, the inconvenience and inefficiency of catalogues inhibited some researchers' access to newly published reference sources because it took many months to update these card catalogues. Today, we are fortunate that many psychology literature bases such as PsycINFO are updated nearly every week or two. With up-to-the-minute information at our fingertips, computer technology has improved and simplified the process of collecting a vast array of psychological knowledge, particularly regarding psychological tests.

Distributing Measures

Computers are not only valuable when retrieving background information pertinent to conducting research but also for dispensing information to potential participants. For instance, e-mail can be an excellent device to recruit possible participants for a study or to distribute actual research measures. Sending online surveys to potential respondents also can lower many of the costs associated with conducting research, and data can be collected from literally thousands of participants with minimal intervention on the part of researchers. Electronic surveys are becoming increasingly common, and some research comparing electronic versus postal surveys suggests that electronic survey results may not be significantly different from those obtained from postal surveys (Kraut et al., 2004).

Test Administration and Scoring

In addition to computers' usefulness in increasing the number of participants for psychological research studies, computers frequently can facilitate the testing or evaluation process

as well. For instance, some psychological measures feature a *narrative computer interpretation,* which generates an explanation detailing response patterns of the participants (Anastasi & Urbina, 1997). Measures such as the Minnesota Multiphasic Personality Inventory (MMPI), which has a narrative computer interpretation, provide important information about respondents' personality tendencies and emotional conditions (Anastasi & Urbina, 1997). Another computer application is the *interactive computer system,* which not only can assist researchers in the scoring process but also can allow respondents to complete research measures directly on the computer (as opposed to traditional paper-and-pencil methods).

Analyzing Data

Once psychological test scores are acquired, data analysis can begin (see Chapters 18–20 for more information). Although there are a variety of computer programs that can help in the data analysis process, there are at least three common components of most statistical software packages (Pedhazur & Schmelkin, 1991). The first component is *data description,* which includes techniques for defining and naming variables, identifying the format of data, assigning an external data file when needed, supplying extended labels for variables and/or values, and identifying absent values. The second common component of many statistical software packages includes *data transformation techniques,* which can categorize data by certain specified criteria, recode or transform data, generate new variables, and integrate two or more data files. The third common component includes *data analysis techniques,* which can provide means by which researchers can calculate descriptive and inferential statistics. Although there are variations from one statistical software program to another in terms of the types of analyses they can perform, three of the most commonly used programs among research psychologists are SPSS, SAS, and MINITAB (Pedhazur & Schmelkin, 1991).

Technical Difficulties

Researchers must consider that human error can occur when psychological data are being entered into computers. Another potential difficulty with computer programs includes "bugs," or problems with hardware or software of these programs. Such problems often go undetected, and the results could be detrimental to the accuracy of researchers' findings. Fortunately, because most statistical software programs are thoroughly critiqued by experts and because these programs are sometimes upgraded or modified by their developers, researchers are advised to remain updated about potential modifications or changes to these programs (Pedhazur & Schmelkin, 1991).

CONCLUSION

This chapter presents an overview of important considerations related to choosing appropriate self-report instruments for conducting psychological research. By thoroughly identifying literature related to topics of interest, reviewing possible self-report measures with regard to their reliability and validity, and integrating computer technology in the research process, investigators can maximize their likelihood of obtaining successful outcomes related to their psychological research.

EXERCISES

1. Read through a recent issue of one of the following three journals: *Educational and Psychological Measurement, Psychological Assessment,* or *Measurement and Evaluation in Counseling and Development.* Select an article that reports on the development and validation of a new psychological instrument. Write a one-page summary of the article and address the following questions:

A. What construct is the research team trying to measure, and do you believe the Introduction to the article presents a strong rationale for the need for this new instrument?

B. Describe how the researchers went about developing items for the instrument. Was this item development logical to you?

C. Describe briefly the sample(s) and procedures used in the study. Do you think the sample and procedures were appropriate given the purpose of the instrument?

D. Describe how the authors established levels of score validity and reliability for the instrument. Were you impressed by this aspect of the article? Why or why not?

E. Do you think score reliability and validity would hold up with another sample? Why or why not?

F. If you were conducting a study on this psychological construct, would you use this instrument? Why or why not?

2. Now that you have read this chapter, as well as a recent journal article on instrument development, consider a construct in psychology that you would like to measure. In one page or so, address the following questions:

A. What construct have you selected and why?

B. Using the Internet and various texts cited in this chapter, find out if there are already instruments measuring the construct you have selected. If so, write down their names.

C. Write five items that could be used to measure your construct. If instruments already exist that measure your construct of interest, then come up with a unique aspect of your instrument (for example, if there are already instruments for adolescents and adults that measure Attitudes Toward the Elderly, then come up with an instrument that measures Children's Attitudes Toward the Elderly). Your five items should be placed on a Likert-type scale (e.g., a *Strongly Agree* to *Strongly Disagree* continuum with a number of choice points).

D. Now that you have five new instrument items, discuss how you would go about establishing evidence for score validity and reliability for this new brief measure.

RECOMMENDED READINGS

Some recommended resources pertaining to topics highlighted in this chapter include Anastasi and Urbina's (1997) *Psychological Testing,* which is a comprehensive guide to understanding the use of psychological instruments. Pedhazur and Schmelkin's (1991) *Measurement, Design, and Analysis: An Integrated Approach* also is a thorough and well-written book that presents pertinent background and technical information related to psychological measures. For a thorough overview of reliability, we recommend Thompson's (2003) *Score Reliability: Contemporary Thinking on Reliability Issues.* Finally, Loewenthal's (2001) *An Introduction to Psychological Tests and Scales* is an outstanding resource that explains the basics of conducing psychological research using self-report measures.

REFERENCES

Anastasi, A., & Urbina, S. (1997). *Psychological testing* (7th ed.). Upper Saddle River, NJ: Prentice Hall.

American Psychological Association. (2004). FAQ/Finding information about psychological tests. Retrieved January 22, 2004, from www.apa.org/science/faq-findtests.html

Carmines, E. G., & Zeller, R. A. (1979). *Reliability and validity assessment.* Newbury Park, CA: Sage.

Holtgraves, T. (2004). Social desirability and self-reports: Testing models of socially desirable responding. *Personality and Social Psychology Bulletin, 30,* 161–172.

Kraut, R., Olson, J., Banaji, M., Bruckman, A., Cohen, J., & Couper, M. (2004). Psychological research online: Report of Board of Scientific Affairs' Advisory Group on the Conduct of Research on the Internet. *American Psychologist, 59,* 105–117.

Laing, J. (1988). Self-report: Can it be of value as an assessment technique? *Journal of Counseling and Development, 67,* 60–61.

Loewenthal, K. M. (2001). *An introduction to psychological tests and scales.* Philadelphia: Psychology Press.

McMillan, J. (2004). *Educational research: Fundamentals for the consumer* (4th ed.). Boston: Pearson.

Murphy, L. L., Plake, B. S., Impara, J. C., & Spies, R. A. (Eds.). (2002). *Tests in print VI: An index to tests, test reviews, and the literature on specific tests.* Lincoln: Buros Institute of Mental Measurements, University of Nebraska.

Paulhus, D. L. (1984). Two-component models of socially desirable responding. *Journal of Personality and Social Psychology, 46,* 598–609.

Pedhazur, E. J., & Schmelkin, L. P. (1991*). Measurement, design, and analysis: An integrated approach.* Hillsdale, NJ: Lawrence Erlbaum.

Ponterotto, J. G. (1996). Evaluating and selecting research instruments. In F. T. L. Leong & J. T. Austin (Eds.), *The psychology research handbook: A guide for graduate students and research assistants* (pp. 73–84). Thousand Oaks, CA: Sage.

Robinson, J. P., Shaver P. R., & Wrightsman L. S. (Eds.). (1991). *Measures of personality and social psychological attitudes* (Vol. 1). San Diego: Academic.

Robinson J. P., Shaver P. R., & Wrightsman L. S. (Eds.). (1999). *Measures of political attitudes* (Vol. 2). San Diego: Academic.

Thompson, B. (Ed.). (2003). *Score reliability: Contemporary thinking on reliability issues.* Thousand Oaks, CA: Sage.

Thorndike, R. M. (1997). *Measurement and evaluation in psychology and education* (6th ed.). Upper Saddle River, NJ: Prentice Hall.

8

DESIGNING SURVEYS AND QUESTIONNAIRES FOR RESEARCH

ROBERT D. GODDARD III

PETER VILLANOVA

S urveys and questionnaires are among the most frequently used research methods of the social sciences (Isaac & Michael, 1983). This popularity is really no surprise given that much of contemporary research, particularly in psychology, involves the study of individuals' perceptions of and beliefs about themselves, their immediate situation, and the relationship these perceptions and beliefs maintain with behavior. In this chapter, we provide a design primer to assist students in the development of survey and questionnaire instruments for research purposes. We've organized the chapter to facilitate your development of a cognitive script to understand survey and questionnaire design and administration. The chapter begins with an overview of survey methods and a description of the development process. This first section serves to orient you to the methods and provides a context in which to better understand the more specific issues and choices that follow. A second section takes up design issues in greater detail and is meant to reflect the variety of technical issues you might face once you've committed your project to the use of these methods. The final section reviews some alternatives to questionnaire methods of data collection.

ORIENTATION TO SURVEYS AND QUESTIONNAIRES

Design and Administration

What Is a Survey?

A survey is a method of collecting information from people for descriptive or predictive purposes. A survey can be used to gather information about the nation's population as a whole (the decennial census of the United States) or to assess the reactions of a sample of consumers to a new soft drink. Surveys can take the form of a questionnaire filled out by individuals, a one-on-one interview between the subject and the surveyor, or a telephone interview. Once the data have been collected, they may be archived so that other researchers may analyze them for their own purposes (see Zaitzow & Fields, "Archival Data Sets," Chapter 22).

Reasons for Surveys

There are many reasons for conducting a survey, including facilitating decisions, evaluating the effectiveness of current policies or programs, or satisfying a need for information about a research topic. Needs assessment and training needs assessment, to name two examples, rely on measurement through surveys, knowledge-skill-ability testing, and focus groups to provide input for program design. Altschuld and Austin discuss needs assessment as part of their presentation ("Program Evaluation," Chapter 5).

There are, of course, many ways of obtaining information from people. You could simply observe people to obtain the needed information. But what if the information needed is not behavioral? That is, one can observe behavior fairly simply, but what if the information you need is attitudinal or meta-cognitive in nature? We cannot observe attitudes, opinions, or beliefs, but we can ask people about their attitudes, opinions, or beliefs by using a survey.

Types of Surveys

The most commonly used forms of surveys are questionnaires, interviews, and telephone surveys (several chapters in the present handbook address these variations, including Vaux and Briggs on mail and Internet surveys in Chapter 13 and Chen and Huang on telephone interviews in Chapter 14). *Questionnaires* are written surveys that contain items that address the goals of the project. Questionnaires can be self-administered or they can be administered to groups of people by a trained administrator who explains the purpose of the survey, answers questions about the survey items and administrative procedures, and ensures that proper survey procedures are followed. A limitation of questionnaires is that the items are preset and respondents cannot fully express their opinions. The latter deficit can be partially remedied by providing a place for open-ended, spontaneous responses.

Interviews share many of the features of questionnaires, in that there may be a set of items the researcher uses to gather information. With interviews, however, it is possible to ask for explanations (to probe) and to provide information on the reactions of the respondents that cannot be obtained from a questionnaire.

Telephone surveys are interviews conducted by telephone. The researcher prepares a set of items to be asked and may have the flexibility to probe respondents' answers for elaboration.

Ethics

The choice between anonymity and confidentiality is often an issue when conducting a survey. Respondents may not wish to have their identities known when responding to a survey, and protecting their identities may result in more valid responses to survey questions. A self-administered questionnaire mailed in to the researcher can preserve anonymity, as no one knows just who the respondent is if there is no identifying information on the envelope or questionnaire. Interviews and telephone surveys, by their nature, do not offer respondents anonymity. Confidentiality is the more frequent level of protection given to survey respondents, whether they are responding to a questionnaire or to an interview. In the case of confidentiality, the specific individual's responses are identifiable to the researcher but are not disclosed to other parties. Frequently, researchers provide respondents with a pledge of confidentiality, and this is usually honored by securing all survey responses and reporting only aggregate (i.e., grouped) data that prohibits identification of individual responses to questions. Researchers more frequently assure confidentiality rather than anonymity to respondents because this allows researchers to establish that the responses were provided by individuals whom the researchers intended to represent in their study. In any case, whatever promise is made to respondents regarding disclosure of their responses, it is imperative that the researcher maintain procedures to satisfy this pledge. Dell, Schmidt, and Meara (this handbook, Chapter 12) address the rationale and mechanics of applying to an institutional review board in order to conduct research.

Survey or Questionnaire
Development Process

The process of developing a suitable survey or questionnaire (S/Q) involves several steps, with the success of each step dependent on how well the previous step was performed. The reader should note that software is increasingly available for managing surveys at all steps of the process (e.g., WinAsks Professional, www.assess .com/index.htm).

The first step in developing an S/Q requires the researcher to have clearly stated study goals and hypotheses that identify the information needed to conduct the study. One point of departure is to identify whether the study requires information about respondents' attributes (e.g., age, employment, and education), attitudes, beliefs, intentions, and/or behaviors. Subsequently, the aim is to more precisely identify what set of attributes are relevant to the research question. A table of specifications is one way to detail which items correspond to the attributes or other characteristics that the survey is designed to measure.

A *table of specifications* (Hopkins & Antes, 1978) is a two-dimensional matrix in which one dimension represents the domain of interest (e.g., job satisfaction, attitudes toward prison overcrowding, biographical data) and a second dimension represents the items or behaviors representative of these domains. A table of specification's brief and accurate summary of the entire S/Q can facilitate decisions about the appropriateness of the items, what items should appear together or apart, and the best order for the groups of items.

The second step involves identifying the *characteristics of respondents* that may serve as the sample for the study. This includes the respondents' ability to comprehend the terms appearing on the S/Q and their accessibility to the researcher. Is the population you wish to sample easily accessible? What arrangements need to be made to assure representation? At what level of reading skill should the questionnaire items be written in order to be understandable to the target population? McCready, in Chapter 10, discusses a variety of sampling procedures to increase the representativeness of your sample.

The third step involves the *form* that specific items should take in order to assure that the desired information is obtained. This step involves writing questionnaire items and response formats that yield information most compatible with the aims of the study. For example, is a simple ranking of respondent preferences for program alternatives all that you need, or do you wish to quantify their preference for alternatives using a continuous scale? Or, is a simple *yes* or *no* response—as to whether each program characteristic is desirable—sufficient for the purpose of your study?

The fourth step considers the *structure* of the S/Q. This includes such matters as the instructions for respondents, how items should be ordered, which items should be grouped together, and whether and how many discrete sections should appear on the S/Q. As a general rule, it is often advisable to proceed from more general information to more specific information. What is most important here is that the S/Q be ordered in the most user-friendly manner to the respondent. Sometimes, the most logical ordering of questions or sections of the questionnaire may not provide the best psychological sequence from the respondents' perspective. For example, some authors have recommended that demographic questions appear at the end of the survey because of the suspicion they may arouse (Frey, 1989; Miller, 1991).

Related to the physical design and appearance of the S/Q are the set of *procedures* to be followed during administration. It is essential to establish an administration protocol for any systematic research endeavor, including laboratory experiments or surveys. In the case of the survey, the protocol would include required materials for supporting data collection during a session, information that may need to be conveyed to respondents (such as what identifying code to include on their questionnaire or other factual data), instructions to be read to respondents, allowable answers to respondent questions about the items, and communicating an appropriate event script to respondents so that they can anticipate what follows with a minimum of confusion.

As a final step before going to the field with your survey, consider evaluating your effort as a package in a *pretest* prior to administration of the actual research sample. If pretesting suggests additional problems need to be worked out, then the entire process should be repeated until the survey meets the standards acceptable for research use. Pretesting is one of the most useful exercises you can engage in to identify potential problems and to produce a quality survey.

The different forms of pretesting basically invite different levels of respondent participation in the development of the S/Q. A *participating pretest* asks respondents to approach the S/Q as collaborators in the research project, in that they are fully briefed about the intentions of the study and the aims of different questions. As they complete the S/Q, respondents may encounter prompts about certain questions asking respondents to evaluate those items in terms of clarity, meaning, and prejudice. An *undeclared pretest* differs in that the respondents experience the same administration protocol as the "for-keeps" sample. Finally, a focus group discussion can follow the S/Q administration. A *focus group discussion* involves having the respondents form small groups of 6–8 people led by a member of the research team. The respondents are interviewed as a group about their reactions to, and questions about, the S/Q and the administration protocol. The focus group discussion can be structured according to an interview protocol that is prepared in advance, and it may also include opportunities for respondent initiated inquiry. Dillman (2000) uses the term "cognitive interview" to define this topic.

SURVEY DESIGN ISSUES

Format

How long should your survey be? The answer to this question depends on two things: the purpose of your survey and the method you chose for administration. Your purpose—what you are trying to accomplish with it—will determine the number of questions needed to ensure the credibility of the data.

The type of survey you choose, questionnaire, interview, or telephone survey, also affects the length of your survey. Because of time and attention considerations, telephone surveys are generally limited to 30 minutes or less. Interviews are also limited by time considerations but can last longer and contain more items than telephone surveys. Questionnaires administered by a trained researcher can also be longer than telephone surveys but should take no longer than 1 hour. Self-administered questionnaires, which are completed at the respondent's leisure, can be even longer but should not take more than 1–2 hours to complete. Of course, the time and the amount of contemplation required of respondents to answer each question on the survey needs to be considered. Wordy questions or those that require considerable thought to generate an answer will take more time than those that require respondents to indicate how strongly they agree or disagree with a statement. Heberlein and Baumgartner's (1978) quantitative review of mail questionnaires involving 98 studies found that the average mail questionnaire consisted of 72 questions appearing on seven pages and required about one-half hour to complete. It is possible that large-scale use of surveys in the intervening quarter century and the recent increase in Internet sampling have changed the perception of the public about surveys.

Design and Layout

Your survey should begin with an introduction describing its purpose and who you are. The introduction should not be long, probably no more than a paragraph. You might include an estimate of time to complete the survey, a statement as to why the respondent was chosen to participate in your survey, and an assurance of confidentiality or anonymity.

Item Ordering

The first survey item should be directly related to your purpose. After that, item order depends on your respondents. Some subjects may be more at ease when responding to objective items until they get used to the survey and its purpose. Your respondents may feel more comfortable if you order your survey items from most familiar to least familiar. Likewise, some thought should be given to the effect one survey item will have on the responses to succeeding items. People generally wish to be consistent in their behavior, and this tendency may artificially increase relationships among responses to different items. For this reason, it is sometimes wise to consider counterbalancing sections of the survey so that the questions appear in a different order for different respondents. This design feature allows you to conduct analyses that will indicate whether there are order effects as a result of placing items in different orders of appearance on the survey.

Scales

Establishing response scales that are appropriate for the goals of the survey and the type of items used is an important consideration for researchers. It is important to distinguish among the various types of response scales in order to properly code responses and to facilitate the application of statistical analyses. Scherbaum discusses what statistical analyses are appropriate for different data in Chapter 18, and Lounsbury and colleagues describe scale construction principles for personality traits that generalize to survey and questionnaire design in Chapter 9.

Nominal Scales. Nominal scales are categorical in nature. That is, the values associated with the variable of interest have no real numerical meaning but describe categories. The values cannot be added, subtracted, multiplied, or divided, but are more like labels used to describe the variable of interest (Kerlinger & Lee, 2000). Nominal scales are often used to gather factual information, such as demographic information; there are usually better response scales available to a researcher for the measurement of attitudes (*ordinal, interval*). The example below is a nominal scale:

My race is (check one)
(1) ___ African American
(2) ___ Asian American
(3) ___ Caucasian
(4) ___ Hispanic
(5) ___ Native American
(6) ___ Other

Ordinal. Ordinal scales indicate a rank ordering on a survey item. An ordinal scale indicates that there are differences among the responses but does not indicate the magnitude of those differences, nor does it suggest that the differences are the same across responses (Kerlinger & Lee, 2000; Pedhazur & Schmelkin, 1991). Below is an example of an ordinal scale:

The service on this airline flight is (check one):

(1) ___ Better than the service on my last flight
(2) ___ About the same as the service on my last flight
(3) ___ Worse than the service on my last flight

Interval. The most common interval scale used in surveys is the Likert or summated rating scale. Likert scaling is often used in attitude or opinion surveys that ask respondents to state their level of agreement or disagreement with an item. Responses are generally composed of five or more categories, as in the following example:

This company is a better place to work this year than it was last year.

(1) ___ Strongly Disagree
(2) ___ Disagree
(3) ___ Undecided or No Opinion
(4) ___ Agree
(5) ___ Strongly Agree

Respondents are asked to select one and only one response from the choices given. The response choices are mutually exclusive and collectively exhaustive, meaning that the respondent cannot select more than one category and that the choices cover all of the possible responses.

There is some controversy as to whether the continuum reflected in Likert scales is ordinal or interval and considerable research has been conducted to understand better what scale anchors provide a better approximation to interval data (e.g., Spector, 1992) and to lay out validity issues (e.g., Roberts, Laughlin, & Wedell, 1999).

Item Characteristics and Response Formats

There are several characteristics that distinguish good and bad items, just as with items in ability testing. Much of the distinction is determined by the kind of information one needs to obtain and the sample of respondents. Specific item characteristics can strongly influence response errors and biases (Bradburn, 1982).

Define Terms

An interviewer should be provided with definitions for any word(s) and/or phrase(s) in the survey instrument that might be ambiguous or unclear. This is accomplished with an additional description as illustrated below:

I am in favor of the death penalty (that is, I think death is an appropriate punishment for those who commit certain major crimes).

Do not assume that all members of the target sample share the same vernacular. When in doubt, provide the interviewer with definitions for any problematic words and phrases.

Questionnaires pose a greater challenge of equating item meaning across respondents. For example, without the advantage of an interviewer to define the term *fit,* the item below leaves the meaning of the word to the individual respondent.

To what extent do you believe each employee below fits the job she or he currently performs?

One respondent might consider *fit* to involve how well someone gets along with others in the workplace; someone else might take it to mean the extent to which one has the appropriate education and skills to qualify for the job; and yet another might believe the question asks if the employee is meeting work standards. Morrow, Eastman, and McElroy (1991) found that respondents' unfamiliarity with work attitude concepts resulted in considerable redundancy in responses in five different work attitude scales.

Item clarity can also be improved by providing verbal anchors along the response continuum that are specific and distinguishable. Bass, Cascio, and O'Connor (1974) and Spector (1976) provide helpful information about how different adjectival anchors (e.g., *occasionally, seldom, often, rarely*) are perceived to differ in absolute magnitude by respondents. The characteristics of anchors become increasingly important when the response involves some judgment of behavior observed by the respondent and when one wants to treat these responses as interval data.

Open- Versus Closed-Ended Questions

Generally, the more specific a survey question is, the more probable that the same interpretation of that question will be made by respondents and the more easily comparable and accurate the answers will be. On the other hand, open-ended questions allow respondents to give their own opinions about survey items; however, in order to set limits on just how subjects can respond, you can ask respondents to "list no more than three things" about the topic. Closed-ended questions consist of a stem in the form of a statement or question followed by several alternative choices:

Which issue is of greatest significance to you? Or alternatively, rank these issues from lowest (1) to highest (4) importance to you.

____ budget deficit
____ economic growth
____ health care
____ social justice

Open-ended questions are particularly useful in the early stages of research on some phenomenon that is poorly understood and for which you are seeking primarily descriptive information. Subsequent research might employ a closed-question format when the characteristics of the phenomenon (e.g., dimensions or the range of values along any dimension) are better understood.

Open-ended questions can also allow one to probe answers to closed-ended questions in order to gauge respondent familiarity with an issue. In the 1983 Detroit Area Study of attitudes toward welfare, for example, a significant majority of respondents agreed with the statement "Government is trying to do too many things that should be left to individuals and private businesses." However, when these respondents were asked the follow-up question, "What things do you feel should be left to individuals or private businesses," over 25% could not answer or give an example (Converse & Presser, 1986; Schaeffer & Presser, 2003).

Generally, closed questions require less administrative skill and facilitate data analysis. They also enhance the comparability of responses. Use of closed questions, however, assumes that the response choices accurately represent the breadth of people's opinions. It really comes down to whether respondents should be more or less constrained in their response alternatives. Imagine for example, a continuum ranging from absolutely free to absolutely constrained responses to questions.

At the free end of the continuum are open-ended questions or questions that instruct a respondent to "list those things you believe the government does well." At the other end, representing completely constrained alternatives, are the kinds of answers that lawyers often favor from witness testimony, *yes* or *no*; and of course, the question sounds something like "Does the government do anything right?" Somewhere between these extremes are questions that frame responses but allow the respondent some freedom of expression: "List no more than three things," "Rank this list in order of . . . ," and "Choose one from this list."

Filtering and Middle Alternative Responses

Don't assume that respondents are equally well informed or have an opinion about everything you might ask them. If you force an opinion by not offering a *No Opinion* option, then you may reduce the accuracy of your survey results. Aside from offering a *No Opinion* option, you could use a filtering question that asks respondents whether they have an opinion about an issue and if so, to indicate what it is:

Not everyone has an opinion about every world event. If you have no opinion, just say so. The statement is, "The United Nations is doing all it can to relieve suffering in the Sudan."

Do you have an opinion about this? If yes, do you agree or disagree with the statement?

Some researchers prefer that the *Undecided* or *No Opinion* category be eliminated, forcing the respondent to indicate an opinion one way or the other. Other researchers use the so-called *Neutral* category to determine the relative importance of the survey item. If many respondents indicate that they are neutral, it may indicate that the item is not of major concern to them or that they do not have enough information to take a position (Orlich, 1978). For instance, employees who have been with the company less than 1 year may indicate *Undecided* or *No Opinion* on the earlier example. Be careful in using *No Opinion* options, as research has found that between 10% and 30% of respondents elect it as a response (Schuman & Presser, 1981).

Likewise, if your aim is to measure the intensity of beliefs about an issue, you might want to consider omitting the middle alternative as a response option. For example, you might ask the following:

Should abortion in this state be easier to obtain, harder to obtain, or stay as it is now?

By doing so, you invite many respondents who don't feel strongly about the issue to indicate that it should stay the same. If, however, you were to limit responses to *Easier* or *Harder* and then followed up with a measure of how strongly respondents believed in their response, you would be better able to discriminate among respondents who hold less extreme beliefs.

Yet another alternative is to force a choice between alternatives that seem equally desirable but that, in fact, are at odds. For example, one could ask respondents to agree or disagree with the following statements:

(a) Government should guarantee health care for all individuals.

(b) It is the responsibility of individuals to provide for their medical care.

An agree response seems plausible for both statements (a) and (b), thus failing to distinguish between respondent preferences for one position or the other. A better alternative would be to combine the statements into one question, as in (c):

(c) Should the government be required to guarantee medical care for everyone, or should individuals be responsible for their own medical care?

Single Object, One Meaning

Avoid instances where more than one object is asked to be evaluated:

Do you agree or disagree with this statement: "Professors and students should determine the policies that affect their work?"

The question obviously begs for clearer definition of *policies* and *work* but also confuses the reader because two objects (*professors* and *students*) are mixed together. A better strategy would be to separate them into two items.

Edit items so that they have one meaning that can be directly interpreted by respondents. For example, asking for an agree or disagree response to the statement, "Professors should not be required to take class attendance," invites confusion. A disagree response may mean, "I do not agree that professors should not be required to take attendance." Try to word these kinds of statements in a positive direction: "Professors should be required to take attendance."

Don't Invite Response Acquiescence or Artificial Compliance

If your aim is to describe other people's opinions and beliefs, don't set them up to agree with a statement because it seems appropriate to do so. Avoid leading questions. For example, "Do you support President Bush's progressive foreign policy?" assumes that President Bush's foreign policy is "progressive"; moreover, does the respondent "support" the policy or the President? Also, note that such a question is begging for a filter question like the following:

Are you familiar with President Bush's foreign policy? Do you now have an opinion about it? If so, would you say that you support it or oppose it?

Similarly, avoid beginning a question with an obvious request for compliance, such as in, "Don't you agree that . . ."; you risk tilting the results toward agreement with a particular position.

ALTERNATIVES TO QUESTIONNAIRES

Interviews

Probably the most time-consuming and costly survey form to administer is the interview. Interviews have many advantages, however, including (a) allowing the respondent to reveal otherwise concealed attitudes, (b) revealing problems and their potential solutions through discussion, (c) encouraging free expression, (d) allowing for observation and recording of nonverbal communication, (e) discovery of personal information, attitudes, beliefs, and perceptions that a paper-and-pencil survey might not

uncover, (f) ensuring a high rate of participation, (g) allowing interviewers to probe or follow up on survey items, and (h) facilitating the participation of individuals who are visually handicapped or who cannot read or write (Orlich 1978, p. 8). It is feasible to apply universal design principles to surveys and questionnaires just as to tests (Thurlow & Johnson, 2000).

On the other hand, a trained staff of interviewers and extensive training may be required. The interviewers can affect survey results by directly influencing respondents' attitudes toward the survey itself; interviewers can alienate potential respondents in the way they present the survey to the subject. Second, interviewers must teach subjects how to respond to their survey. Finally, interviewers must conduct the interview in a standardized way to avoid possible bias in responses (Fowler, 2002).

If you are conducting the interview, you need to gain the cooperation of your subject. Good interviewers gain cooperation by being businesslike, confident, and assertive. Good interviewers also have the ability to tailor their presentations to focus on and become personally involved with the respondent.

Training can help interviewers present their study to the respondent, ask their questions in a standardized way, and probe subjects when responses are incomplete. Training can also aid interviewers in recording responses correctly and consistently. Training is particularly important in instances requiring the interpretation and classification of responses to open-ended questions.

Telephone Interviews

Perhaps you have watched a nightly news show in which the anchor casually asserts, "Fifty-three percent of those surveyed indicated that they believe the president of the United States is doing a fine job." In this high-tech world, an opportunistic means by which to collect information from large populations rests at our fingertips. Now, we can "reach out and touch someone" (if they have a phone, are home, and are willing to talk) and affect national policy by sharing the results with the television audience.

Telephone surveys use carefully constructed questions to obtain a variety of facts about people's attitudes and behavior—what they say they have done, or would do, in a variety of situations.

As noted by Fowler (2002), the decision to use telephone surveys has several advantages compared with other methodologies. These include (a) potentially lower costs, (b) random-digit dialing sampling of general populations, (c) access to certain populations, (d) potential for short data collection period, (e) interviewer administration advantages, (f) ease of interviewer staffing and management considerations, and (g) better response rate from a list sample (p. 65).

Telephone surveys can be less costly than other methodologies in terms of financial and personnel-related needs if the sample is in the local calling area and if the survey does not require a lot of training. Selection of the sample that will be contacted for the telephone interview is easily facilitated through random-digit dialing. This procedure ensures representativeness of the sample selected for inclusion. Of course, households without a telephone would be excluded, but as the estimate for this occurrence is small, researchers don't spend sleepless nights worrying about such omissions. Again, one must confront the issue of the usefulness of telephone surveys to the question being investigated. If you are hoping to find out what homeless people think about America's current domestic state (e.g., housing and job availability),

you will not find a list of names and phone numbers of such persons from which to obtain a representative sample. Here, an alternative data collection strategy would have to be devised; however, the use of telephone surveys to study community attitudes toward neighborhood development would surely be appropriate. You would have to obtain a telephone book from which potential respondents would be selected as part of the sample. Then, you might want to consult the appropriate chapters in this text to help develop a sampling strategy (see Chapter 10 by McCready) and conduct telephone surveys (see Chapter 14 by Chen and Huang).

CONCLUSION

This chapter has presented a considerable amount of information about survey and questionnaire design for you to consider. Despite our best efforts to include many important issues and describe their implications for S/Q design, some issues cannot be discussed adequately because of space limitations. We encourage you to consider additional sources (e.g., Dillman, 2000; our suggested readings list below, and our references list) to assist you with the development of your S/Q; and it is hoped that this chapter has prepared you for presentations of the material you may encounter in other sources.

EXERCISES

1. Develop and organize a list of best practices for survey or questionnaire item writing. Try to consider the influence of item writing for ability testing (Haladyna, Downing, & Rodriguez, 2002), as well as the ideas presented within this chapter (e.g., table of specifications).

2. You have been assigned the task of developing an attitude survey for your organization. The vice president for human resources asks you to head up the task force and to provide him with a rough outline of steps, as well as a detailed project plan. You have limited resources but a staff of two other individuals to assist (a total of three task force members). What would you do?

3. Scour the Internet using Google or some other search engine to find some samples of scales presented in technical reports. Develop a critique of the items in those scales. Make sure that you propose alternative wording to take care of common errors.

RECOMMENDED READINGS

For those readers interested in further information about this topic, please refer to the following sources: Fink and Kosecoff (1998); Guenzel, Berkmans, and Cannell (1983); Payne (1951); Rosenfeld, Edwards, and Thomas (1993); and Sudman and Bradburn (1982). Useful information is also available in the following articles: Gibson and Hawkins (1968); Hunt, Sparkman, and Wilcox (1982); Wiseman and Billington (1984); and Yu and Cooper (1983). Spector and Jex (1998) demonstrate scale construction in the domain of subjective perceptions of stress in their account of developing four self-report scales; and Hinkin (1995, 1998) illustrates a review of practice in the domain of organizational scales and provides a brief tutorial in scale construction. Recent work influenced by cognitive psychology of survey responses is best addressed by reading Sudman, Bradburn, and Schwarz (1996) or Tourangeau, Rips, and Rasinski (2000).

REFERENCES

Bass, B. M., Cascio, W. F., & O'Conner, E. J. (1974). Magnitude estimations of expressions of frequency and amount. *Journal of Applied Psychology, 59,* 313–320.

Bradburn, N. M. (1982). Question-wording effects in surveys. In R. Hogarth (Ed.), *New directions for methodology of the social and behavioral sciences: Question framing and response consistency* (pp. 65–76). San Francisco: Jossey-Bass.

Converse, J. M., & Presser, S. (1986). *Survey questions: Handcrafting the standardized questionnaire.* Newbury Park, CA: Sage.

Dillman, D. (2000). *Mail and internet surveys: The tailored design method.* New York: Wiley.

Fink, A., & Kosecoff, J. (1998) How to conduct surveys: A step-by-step guide (2nd ed.). Thousand Oaks, CA: Sage.

Fowler, F. J. (2002). *Survey research methods* (3rd ed.). Thousand Oaks, CA: Sage.

Frey, J. H. (1989). *Survey research by telephone* (2nd ed.). Newbury Park, CA: Sage.

Gibson, F., & Hawkins, B. (1968). Interviews versus questionnaires. *American Behavioral Scientist, 12,* NS-9–NS-11.

Guenzel, P., Berkmans, R., & Cannell, C. (1983). *General interviewing techniques.* Ann Arbor, MI: Institute for Social Research.

Haladyna, T. M., Downing, S. M., & Rodriguez, M. C. (2002). A review of multiple-choice item writing guidelines for classroom assessment. *Applied Measurement in Education, 15*(3), 309–334.

Heberlein, T. A., & Baumgartner, R. (1978). Factors affecting response rates to mailed questionnaires: A quantitative analysis of the published literature. *American Sociological Review, 43,* 447–462.

Hinkin, T. R. (1995). A review of scale development practices in the study of organizations. *Journal of Management, 21,* 967–988.

Hinkin, T. R. (1998). A brief tutorial on the development of measures for use in survey questionnaires. *Organizational Research Methods, 1,* 104–121.

Hopkins, C. D., & Antes, R. L. (1978). *Classroom measurement and evaluation.* Itasca, IL: Peacock.

Hunt, S. D., Sparkman, R. D., Jr., & Wilcox, J. B. (1982). The pretest in survey research: Issues and preliminary findings. *Journal of Marketing Research, 19,* 269–273.

Isaac, S., & Michael, W. B. (1983). *Handbook in research and evaluation* (2nd ed.). San Diego, CA: EDITS.

Kerlinger, F. N., & Lee, H. B. (2000). *Foundations of behavioral research* (4th ed.). New York: Holt, Rinehart & Winston.

Miller, D. C. (1991). *Handbook of research design and social measurement* (5th ed.). Newbury Park, CA: Sage.

Morrow, P. C., Eastman, K., & McElroy, J. C. (1991). Concept redundancy and rater naivety in organizational research. *Journal of Applied Psychology, 21,* 219–232.

Orlich, D. (1978). *Designing sensible surveys.* Pleasantville, NY: Redgrave.

Payne, S. (1951). *The art of asking questions.* Princeton, NJ: Princeton University Press.

Pedhazur, E., & Schmelkin, L. (1991). *Measurement, design, and analysis.* Hillsdale, NJ: Lawrence Erlbaum.

Roberts, J. S., Laughlin, J. E., & Wedell, D. H. (1999). Validity issues in the Likert and Thurstone approaches to attitude measurement. *Educational and Psychological Measurement, 59,* 211–233.

Rosenfeld, P., Edwards, J. E., & Thomas, M. D. (1993). *Improving organizational surveys: New directions, methods, and applications.* Newbury Park, CA: Sage.

Schaeffer, N., & Presser, S. (2003). The science of asking questions. *Annual Review of Sociology, 29,* 65–88.

Schuman, H., & Presser, S. (1981). *Questions and answers in attitude surveys.* New York: Academic.

Spector, P. E. (1976). Choosing response categories for summated rating scales. *Journal of Applied Psychology, 61,* 374–375.

Spector, P. E. (1992). *Summated rating scale construction.* Newbury Park, CA: Sage.

Spector, P. E., & Jex, S. M. (1998). Development of four self-report measures of job stressors and strain: Interpersonal Conflict at Work Scale, Organizational Constraints Scale, Quantitative Workload Inventory, and Physical Symptoms Inventory. *Journal of Occupational Health Psychology, 3*(4), 356–367.

Sudman, S., & Bradburn, N. (1982). *Asking questions.* San Francisco: Jossey-Bass.

Sudman, S., Bradburn, N. M., & Schwarz, N. (1996). *Thinking about answers: The application of cognitive processes to survey methodology.* San Francisco: Jossey-Bass.

Thurlow, M. L., & Johnson, D. R. (2000). High-stakes testing of students with disabilities. *Journal of Teacher Education, 51*(4), 305–314.

Tourangeau, R., Rips, L., & Rasinski, K. (2000). *The psychology of survey response.* Cambridge, UK: Cambridge University Press.

Wiseman, F., & Billington, M. (1984). Comment on a standard definition of response rates. *Journal of Marketing Research, 21,* 336–338.

Yu, J., & Cooper, H. (1983). A quantitative review of research design effects on response rates to questionnaires. *Journal of Marketing Research, 20,* 36–44.

9

SCALE DEVELOPMENT

JOHN W. LOUNSBURY
LUCY W. GIBSON
RICHARD A. SAUDARGAS

This chapter addresses the topic of scale development. Although much of what we present here can be applied to the topic of test development, our focus is not on measuring *maximal* performance assessed by tests of achievement, aptitude, and ability but on measuring *typical* performance assessed by personality instruments. Our emphasis is on personality scales, though much of our material is also applicable to attitude scales, measures of preference, and values. We will be relying primarily on reliability concepts drawn from classical test theory; more recent approaches, such as item response theory and confirmatory factor analysis, will not be covered here. We will cover seven main topics:

1. Reasons for developing a psychological scale

2. Purpose of a psychological scale

3. Construct specification strategies

4. Strategies for conceptualizing and writing items

5. Administering your scale

6. Psychometric scale analysis

7. Developing norms

REASONS FOR DEVELOPING A PSYCHOLOGICAL SCALE

In our experience, it is not difficult for researchers to develop useful new psychological scales. There are a variety of reasons for doing so. Usually, a researcher is interested either in creating a new scale that has not been developed or in constructing a scale that improves on an existing scale in some manner. We have frequently observed six rationales for developing scales:

1. To update an established scale that has become outmoded in terms of language and concepts

2. To revise an existing scale based on more refined psychometric processes, such as confirmatory factor analysis

3. To develop shortened versions of scales, as there is continuing pressure from many sources to reduce completion time and measure multiple dimensions when collecting data from subjects

4. To contextualize a general scale to more specific subgroups of people, usually defined by a demographic variable

5. To improve on an existing scale by making it more relevant to the construct under consideration

6. To create a new scale to fill a specific research purpose

For example, in an applied measurement project, the senior authors developed a measure of soft-selling orientation to assess a special sales style used by restaurant managers in a business setting where the strategy was to develop long-term personalized relationships with repeat customers (often retirees) by indirect, low-key methods.

Regarding contextualization, different versions of a scale measuring a personality construct may be required for groups that differ in terms of age (e.g., adolescent vs. adult), gender, language spoken and cultural identity, literacy, and cognitive ability. Similarly, a researcher may be interested in a particular domain of experience that could lead to a work-based version of a normal personality scale. As an example of this latter approach, Schmit, Ryan, Stierwalt, and Powell (1995) found that the job-related validity of the NEO Big Five measures could be improved by simply adding the phrase "at work" to each statement in the NEO Big Five scales. One of the graduate students in our psychology department is developing a "sexual extraversion" scale to measure extraversion in the context of sexual dynamics (which had not been developed previously). It is easy to imagine how different sexual extraversion scales could be developed for males and females, hetero- and homosexuals, college students and midlife adults, and individuals identifying with different ethnic groups, or how one could develop a Big Five scale for sexual behavior. There are endless possibilities for developing contextualized measures of existing scales, and in our view, contextualization of scales to measure a wide variety of constructs is a rapidly emerging area in the field of assessment.

PURPOSE OF A PSYCHOLOGICAL SCALE

Most scales are developed as research tools to measure a construct reliably so that validity relationships can be tested within a theoretical

framework. Scale reliability is a threat to the integrity of your scale that should be considered at the outset. Often college students respond to the scale, usually along with several other scales, for class credit or to fulfill a course requirement. From the standpoint of the person taking the scale, there are usually no contingencies for answering items carelessly or even randomly. There is no incentive for honest, accurate responding, other than acting in accord with one's personal standards or trying to help the researcher. The really busy student concerned with efficient time management may be motivated to simply complete a scale quickly by not reading the items and answering all items the same way, or answering randomly. We have found that in some cases when college students take our scales for extra credit, up to 10% of the sample answered in a way that was so careless or random that their entire set of answers had to be scrapped. We will return to some ways to detect such careless responders later in this chapter.

In contrast, there are a number of other scenarios in which the responses a person makes are consequential because some type of decision will be made based on how the person scores. For example, a decision to offer a person a job may be based, in part, on the person's scores on a personality scale. Similarly, a person's diagnostic status for the purpose of custody rights in a divorce case or determining workmen's compensation eligibility may depend on how the person answers a personality scale. Other examples could be drawn for a variety of practical situations in which decisions affecting a person are based on the person's responses to a psychological scale. The researcher who develops a scale that will be used for making important decisions should, from the outset, be concerned with the problem of social desirability bias. People who know that their responses will be scored and evaluated to make decisions affecting them, usually in an important way such as job selection, are almost always motivated to "fake good" and present themselves in a manner that will lead to favorable evaluations. For example, at one time we used this item to measure conscientiousness in preemployment screening:

It never bothers me to have to follow every single health and safety standard at work.

In repeated samples of job applicants, however, over 90% of the respondents agreed with this item, and it did not contribute to the validity of our conscientiousness scale, so we dropped it. When used with other populations, such as a college student sample, the response pattern was not so extreme. If a scale is going to be used in a situation in which you expect social desirability bias, the research to develop the scale should be based on the same population.

Social desirability or faking good will greatly influence what kinds of items the scale developer writes and the norms she or he generates for making normative score interpretations. Unfortunately, there is currently no good way to take social desirability into account to increase the validity of scales.

We note one other consideration when the purpose of a scale can have a substantive influence on the development process. Most psychological scales are designed to assess individual differences constructs that are used to characterize individuals (e.g., a therapist assessed her client Pat Smith as being depressed, based on Pat's responses to a depression scale) or that are used in correlational studies to evaluate hypotheses about construct relations (e.g., an assistant professor is conducting a study that asks, "How is self-esteem related to locus of control among high school students?"). In such cases, it is important for the scale to have fairly high reliability because errors of measurement have such a direct, negative effect on the accuracy of the measure. To return to our previous example, without adequate reliability, Pat may be assessed as depressed when taking the depression scale on a Tuesday morning but not depressed had Pat taken the scale Friday morning. Or, if the scales are not very reliable, the assistant professor may find a significant negative correlation between self-esteem and locus of control if the students had taken the scales on Monday morning, but she or he may find no significant relationship if the same scales were given to a similar group of students the next day.

On the other hand, some psychological scales are used to represent the average or composite score for a group of individuals. For example, a researcher might want to measure social alienation in community high schools for 10 years to monitor whether high school student alienation is changing over time. In this type of study, in which scores are combined across people to obtain estimates of the mean or median, it is less important to have highly reliable scales, because random errors of measurement will tend to cancel each other out, particularly when moderately large samples of students (e.g., more than 100) are available.

CONSTRUCT SPECIFICATION

Although it might seem obvious that one should define the construct to be measured by a scale before writing items and testing their psychometric properties, in our experience this phase of scale development is often given short shrift and not thought through very carefully. A well-defined construct can make it easier to write items that individually are faithful to the meaning of the construct and collectively can better represent the content domain of the construct. Without a well-defined construct at the beginning of the scale process, the items may well diverge from the original intent. Having a good construct specification at the outset is fundamental to developing psychological scales. It is basically the theory for the construct that guides item development.

For example, the trait of Gregariousness, which is measured by the 16 PF (one of the most extensively researched normal personality inventories), is defined by Cattell, Cattell, and Cattell, (1993) as "an emotional orientation toward other people" and "the degree to which contact with others is sought and found rewarding" (p. 12). Also, Cattell notes that more gregarious individuals enjoy doing things with other people and direct their energy toward social interaction. Given this conceptualization of Gregariousness, it would be relatively easy to write items consistent with the above meanings. Here are five Gregariousness items that we have written for the purpose of this chapter (and should not be construed as representing the 16 PF Gregariousness scale):

Examples of Gregariousness Items

I like doing things with other people.

I am usually energized by meetings with other people.

I enjoy going to big parties.

I feel completely comfortable being in a large crowd of people.

I would prefer to work as part of a team than work on a project by myself.

Note that Cattell's conceptualization of Gregariousness allows us to write items that vary in terms of both the setting, that is, *parties, meetings, crowds,* and *teams,* and the emotional or affective orientation, like *enjoy, energize,* and *feeling comfortable.* It would be easy to rewrite any of these items in the negative direction such as, "I dislike doing things with other people," or "I hate going to big parties." By writing items that refer to different settings in which Gregariousness can occur and items that express different affective orientations, we can more fully represent the domain of Gregariousness specified by Cattell's conceptualization. Also, it should be noted that we could easily contextualize this scale to a specific setting like work by slightly rephrasing the items to include work referents. The first three Gregariousness items above could be adapted to a work-based Gregariousness scale as follows:

Examples of Work-Related Gregariousness Items

I like working on projects with other people.

I am usually energized by team meetings at work.

I enjoy going to office parties with other employees.

In an effort to comprehensively represent the content domain of a psychological construct, some researchers include too much detail and write items that have too much specificity. For example, one might write the following Gregariousness items:

Examples of Overly Specific Gregariousness Items

I really enjoy going to large rock concerts.

I would rather play baseball than golf.

I like to go on picnics with a large group of friends.

I would like to go on a group tour of Iceland.

It is fun for me to watch quiz shows on TV with my friends.

Although agreement with each of the above statements could reflect Gregariousness, it may also be measuring a person's involvement in or feelings about the activity in question. If a person disagrees with the statement, it is not clear whether it is because the person is not gregarious or because he or she doesn't like to do the activity in question. For example, both a very gregarious person who hated rock concerts and a solitary person who loved rock concerts but hated doing things in groups might both disagree with the item "I really enjoy going to large rock concerts." The same problem applies to the other five items listed above.

When writing items to represent the content domain of a construct, it is important to write the items at a fairly general level and not be too specific, such that the item also taps a person's response concerning a particular behavior, activity, or setting. Also, it is important to remember this: *Do not write items where disagreement can be interpreted more than one way*—that is, where disagreement can reflect a low level of a trait or a negative orientation to what the item refers to.

Whereas Gregariousness is an example of what some would consider to be a narrow personality trait, other traits are viewed as broad constructs, encompassing a wider range of behaviors and settings. For example, the Big Five traits of Openness, Conscientiousness, Extraversion, Agreeableness, and Neuroticism (hint: if you want to remember the Big Five, think of the mnemonic device, O-C-E-A-N) are considered to be relatively broad traits. They are so broad that researchers differ on what to include in the construct specification. To illustrate, De Raad (2000) conceptualizes Conscientiousness as a disposition or tendency to be "Organized, Efficient, Systematic, Practical, and Steady," whereas Costa and McCrae (1985) specify six facets of Conscientiousness—Competence, Order, Dutifulness, Achievement Striving, Self-Discipline, and Deliberation. If one were to write one item for each of these characteristics, then 10 items would be needed just to reflect these qualities. And if we were to write items for two different aspects of each of these characteristics (e.g., for Order, two possible items are "I keep all of my belongings in a specific place," and "I like to do tasks and projects in an orderly, step-by-step manner"), 20 items would be required. In general, broad constructs like Extraversion and Conscientiousness will require more detailed construct specifications and a larger number of items to represent the content domain measured by the construct. Very narrow traits may need only a few items to sample the domain. As an extreme example, consider a measure of "Attitudes Toward Iguanas." This domain of affective orientation toward iguanas could probably be adequately represented by two or three items, such as "I really like iguanas," and "I would like to have an iguana in my home."

Below is a short, six-item scale (with responses on a five-point Likert scale ranging from *Strongly Disagree* to *Strongly Agree*) that the senior author of this chapter developed to measure the rather narrow trait of Career Decidedness, which usually shows a coefficient alpha (to measure internal consistency reliability) of .90 and above and has demonstrated meaningful correlations with other constructs (Lounsbury, Hutchens, & Loveland, 2005).

Career-Decidedness Items

1. I have made a definite decision about a career for myself.

2. I am having a difficult time choosing among different careers. (Reverse coded)

3. I am sure about what I eventually want to do for a living.

4. I go back and forth on what career to go into. (Reverse coded)

5. I know what kind of job I would like to have someday.

6. I am not sure what type of work I want to do when I get out of school. (Reverse coded)

Thus, we can see that the constructs measured by psychological scales vary in terms of their breadth and complexity, with broader traits requiring more items to represent the different aspects of the content domain than narrower traits.

STRATEGIES FOR CONCEPTUALIZING AND WRITING ITEMS

After construct specification, good items are the keys to good psychological scales. If you have clearly specified the construct of interest, you are ready to write the items for your scale. In the case of personality measures, the items typically take the form of statements, which is the focus of our discussion, although other formats are available, such as using adjectives or paragraph descriptions and scenarios for items.

One way to begin thinking of items is to consider the *different situations* in which the attribute being measured can be expressed and write items that refer to these different situations. For example, if you are interested in Achievement, think about the different areas where achievement can occur—such as at work, in school, in games and hobbies, sports, and recreation—and write items for these domains. You can also write some items that are not situation-specific.

Examples of Achievement Items Sampling Different Domains

I always try to be one of the best students in classes I take.

I try to win at every game I play.

When I exercise, I like to record my performance so that I can measure my improvement.

I like to play sports in which I can excel.

It is very important for me to be a high achiever at work.

When I learn a new skill, I am not happy until I can perform at a high level.

I enjoy competing with other students.

It really bothers me if I am not good at doing something when my performance can be compared with other people's.

Another way to generate ideas for items is to consider the meaning of the attribute for a person and one's attitude or *affective orientation* toward the kinds of behavior associated with the attribute. For example, one could write items with such phrases as these:

I really like ____.

____ is one of the most important things I do.

It bothers me if I can't regularly ____.

It makes me happy when I ____.

My friends would say I am very concerned with ____.

____ provides much personal satisfaction for me.

Some of the most satisfying experiences I have had in my life come from ____.

Another simple way to generate items is to frame them in terms of *frequency and duration of occurrence*. Items in many scales use phrases such as these:

I regularly ____.

I frequently ____.

I sometimes ____ for hours at a time.

I never ____.

My friends say I ____ too much.

One useful strategy for conceptualizing items is to think of the behaviors associated with the construct and *use different verbs* to portray different types of behavior. De Raad (1985) and Hofstee (2001) contend that in ordinary, everyday language, the personalities of individuals are commonly "discussed in terms of behavior denoted by verbs" (Hofstee, p. 23), more so than trait adjectives. Verbs usually refer to observable behaviors that distinguish one construct from another and one person from another. Here is a set of five statements we have developed to measure Adolescent Aggressiveness that use different verbs (italicized) to denote the construct. Incidentally, these five items by themselves form a reliable scale that we have found to be predictive of aggressive behavior in school and the grade point average (GPA) of middle and high school students.

Adolescent Aggressiveness Scale

1. If somebody pushes me too far, I get angry and *attack* that person.

2. I will *fight* another person if that person makes me really mad.

3. I sometimes feel like *smashing* things.

4. I would *hit* another student if they hit me first.

5. I would *fight* to keep from getting picked on by other students.

Presented below are some general suggestions and recommendations for how to write items for a personality scale. (The reader might also wish to consult Jackson's 1970 method for developing the Personality Research Form by means of a rational-empirical approach.)

1. Most items should deal with one idea or concept.

Don't write double-barreled items so that a person could agree with one part of the item and not the other, like this achievement motivation item: "I am a very ambitious and successful person." Below are three achievement motivation items for which people can get the same score, although they differ in terms of actual achievement motivation.

I am very ambitious, but young and not yet successful.

I am not very ambitious, but I am successful because I inherited a lot of money.

I am not ambitious and successful.

2. Use language that all respondents will understand and has a common meaning.

If a person does not know the meaning of a word and if the people responding to an item interpret it differently, the item will not be useful for a scale. We have two related recommendations:

a. Use words that have similar meanings for most people and avoid colloquialisms or idiomatic language. Even when people can define a word, it may have different connotations for different people. Examples of such words and phrases are in italics:

I get *hot under the collar* when I ____.

I can *relate* when other people say 'life is hopeless.'

I like *to get loaded* _____.

It would *be the bomb* for me to _____.

I frequently *get into a zone* out when I _____.

I like to *mess with* people who *put on airs*.

b. Don't use big words that are too complex. For example, we have seen scales that use such words as *obfuscate, intentionality, extemporize, vicissitude, empathize, dyadic, prevaricate, ruminate, epithet,* and *opaque*—which might not have been understood by many of the intended users. One rule of thumb is to try to keep the reading level at a high school level, such as the 10th grade or 11th grade. In Microsoft Word, you can readily check the Flesch-Kincaid grade level of the readability of your text by clicking Tools, Spelling & Grammar, Options, Readability Statistics. Or, you can compute this readability index by means of the following formula:

Flesch-Kincaid Index =
[(0.39)*(Average#Words/Sentences)] +
[(11.8)*(Avg#Syllables/Word)] − 15.59

3. Don't write items for which everybody gives the same response; or in statistical terms, don't write items for which there will be no variance or low variance of responses.

If everybody answers an item the same way, or about the same way, the variance (or standard deviation) of responses will be zero or close to zero. Items with no variance are useless in that they do not help the scale distinguish between people and they will not add to the variance of the total scale. Items must correlate with other items in a scale, and in some cases, with other variables, but there must be item variance for the item to correlate with any other items. Here are two examples to which everybody is likely to agree and that would produce little or no variance in responses.

I like to talk to some people more than others.

I sometimes dislike things that other people say to me.

Along this vein, another strategy is to write some items that maximize variance between people or to write items that about as many people agree with as disagree with. Increased item variance will help increase the variance of the total scale and may help increase the validity of the scale. Below is an example of a Conscientiousness item for adolescents for which there are nearly equal levels of agreement and disagreement for middle and high school students:

It is hard for me to keep my bedroom neat and clean.

If the purpose of your scale is to develop a normal distribution of total scores, it might be good to develop items with varying degrees of agreement-disagreement. You may want to have a few items that a small percentage of people agree with, a few items that most people agree with, and more items that have larger item variances, either by equal numbers agreeing or disagreeing or a moderate percentage, such as 20–30%, agreeing or disagreeing. In any event, once you have developed items, be sure to examine what percentage of the respondents chose each response as an answer and what the item variances are.

4. Write at least some negatively worded items; in some cases, you may want to write about the same number of positive and negatively worded items.

For most scales, your natural inclination will be to write items in a positively worded direction reflecting the meaning of the scale and for which agreement reflects a higher score (if items are written, say, on a five-point Likert scale ranging from 1-*Strongly Disagree,* 2-*Disagree,* 3-*Neutral/Undecided,* 4-*Agree,* 5-*Strongly Agree*). In our Career Decidedness scale above, items 1, 3, and 5 are positively worded, whereas items 2, 4, and 6 are negatively worded because people who are more "career-decided" will likely disagree with the item. One of the main reasons some researchers give for writing both positively and negatively worded items is that they reduce the likelihood of response bias. In this case, it might discourage a person from simply going down the right side and strongly agreeing with every item, which will lower the reliability and validity of a scale. In our experience, few respondents (e.g., undergraduates who are hurriedly completing a questionnaire for extra credit in a course) will mark their answers in such a biased way (i.e., by responding only on the right or left side of a scale).

Balancing positively and negatively worded items will not totally prevent intentional distortion by those respondents whose answers may affect their lives in a positive or negative way, such as people who are trying to look good on the dimension to increase their chance of being selected for a job, club, or organization.

We have occasionally developed scales in which negatively worded items did not work and only lowered the reliability of the scale, and we ended up with mainly or solely positively worded items. Such was the case for the Adolescent Aggressiveness scale noted above. When we tried to make an item negatively worded by qualifying the verb, as below, with the word *never,* it did not correlate as well with the other items:

> I would *never* fight to keep from getting picked on by other students.

Similarly, changing the meaning of an item (as shown below) to reflect a positive, accepting posture toward other people did not work either:

> I am always kind toward other people no matter how they treat me.

One possible reason why the above item did not work as a negatively worded Aggressiveness item is that Kindness is not opposite in meaning of Aggressiveness. But then we researchers could not agree on what is the opposite of Aggressiveness.

Incidentally, the negatively worded items have to be reverse-coded before adding up a person's responses and getting a total score for Career Decidedness. (And they also have to be recoded before examining the scale by the SPSS Reliability program, which we will describe below.) Thus, for example, if a person has made a definite career choice, his or her answers (shaded) will be as follows in the table below.

After reverse-scoring items 2, 4, and 6 (which you should always let the computer do—never do yourself—when entering answers onto a recording form, such as a data file), the person's average decidedness score will be $(5 + 5 + 5 + 5 + 5 + 5) / 6 = 5.0$.

	Strongly Disagree	Disagree	In-Between	Agree	Strongly Agree
1. I have made a definite decision about a career for myself.	1	2	3	4	5
2. I am having a difficult time choosing among different careers.	1	2	3	4	5
3. I am sure about what I eventually want to do for a living.	1	2	3	4	5
4. I go back and forth on what career to go into.	1	2	3	4	5
5. I know what kind of job I would like to have someday.	1	2	3	4	5
6. I am sure what type of work I want to do when I get out of school.	1	2	3	4	5

And what will the average Career Decidedness score be for someone who has no idea at all about what career to go into? Answer: 1.0

And what will the average Career Decidedness score be for someone who is about equally decided and undecided, or evenly split? Answer: 3.0

One other suggestion: It is easier to interpret individual scores and correlational results for your scale if you set up your response codes so that a larger number for the total scale score represents a higher level of the construct. For example, an average score of 4.99 on our Career Decidedness scale means that the person is much more decided about a career than the person scoring 1.99. One way to do this on a five-point Likert scale is to make the *Strongly Agree* response reflect a higher score on the construct.

How Many Items Should I Write for a Scale?

This question must be answered in two parts: First, the number of items you initially have to write to produce a reliable, valid scale will depend on how well you write items. To become good at writing items, we offer these recommendations: Know your construct well. Do extensive reading and qualitative research on your construct. Be very precise in your use of language. Keep practicing. Write several scales and revise them based on psychometric properties, and try to validate them.

Assuming that you are moderately skilled at writing items for a given construct, you may have to start out writing 50%–100% more items than you eventually want. Therefore, if you intend to have 8 items in your scale, you may need to write 12 to 16 items initially.

Second, the number of items you will need for your scale to be reliable and valid will depend on the breadth of the construct in question. Some very narrow constructs like the Adolescent Aggressiveness or Career Decidedness scales presented above required 5 and 6 items, respectively. In their full NEO-PIR scale, Costa and McCrae (1985) have six subscales with 8 items to represent their Big Five constructs. For example, their scale for measuring the broad trait of Conscientiousness is comprised of the six relatively narrow traits of Competence, Order, Dutifulness, Achievement Striving, Deliberation, and Self-Discipline, each of which has 8 items. In our own research and professional practice, *we typically find that we can measure narrow traits with 8 items or fewer.* On the other hand, the scales we have developed to measure broad constructs typically require about 12 to 14 items. It is interesting to note in this regard that in their short form of the NEO—the NEO Five Factor Inventory—Costa and McRae (1985) use 12 items to measure the broad traits of Openness, Neuroticism, Conscientiousness, Agreeableness, and Extraversion.

Before leaving the question of how many items to have in a scale, we want to argue, from a practical standpoint, against using long scales. Granted, longer scales, such as ones that have 25 to 40 items to measure a construct, may be highly reliable and demonstrate validity in terms of being related to other constructs or criterion, but we have found increasing pressure in most psychological measurement situations, especially in companies, to keep the measurement process as a whole as short as possible. For example, we have several client organizations that use our measures for preemployment screening that insist the total time it takes a candidate to take a measurement battery be less than 30 minutes, and in some cases less than 20 minutes. Similarly, many classroom instructors don't want measures to take up much class time, and undergraduate students having to take an inventory or questionnaire for class credit ordinarily want to spend as little time as possible completing it. In addition, many people are intolerant of inventories that take a long time to complete because of simple boredom. When this happens, it is not uncommon for respondents to simply give up in the middle of an assessment without completing it.

The demand for a 20- to 30-minute inventory would not be a problem itself for a long scale, but in most research or applied situations, you will want to measure a number of variables representing multiple scales, and you will probably also want to measure demographic or background information, which takes additional time, as do the administrative procedures—introducing and explaining it, answering questions (in live vs. online or mail administration), and gathering up the completed forms. Nevertheless, we find that a 60- to 90-item questionnaire, with most individual scales represented by 8–10 items, can be taken in about 15–20 minutes by most college students or job candidates. Of course, it must be pointed out that time pressure varies widely across measurement situations. We have observed that there generally seems to be much less assessment time pressure in clinical settings than industrial-organizational settings. For example, the widely used MMPI-2 inventory consists of 567 items to measure various psychopathology constructs and often takes individuals up to 90 minutes to complete (e.g., Butcher, Dahlstrom, Graham, Tellegen, & Kaemmer, 2004).

What Kind of Response Format Should I Use?

There are many different response formats one can use, and the number of response choices could range from 2 to 100 or more. Although item variances and therefore scale variances generally increase with more scale choice points, we recommend using a standard five-point Likert scale with score values coded from 1 to 5: 1-*Strongly Disagree,* 2-*Disagree,* 3-*Neutral/Undecided,* 4-*Agree,* and 5-*Strongly Agree.* We like to include a midpoint because we feel that is a valid option for some people. Also, an advantage of having five scale points is that it is easy to give each scale point a verbally meaningful descriptor. We don't know what verbal anchors we would give for each category in a 10- or 12-point scale.

ADMINISTERING YOUR SCALE

Administering Your Scale to a Sample of Respondents

In this section, we cover three important questions concerning the initial sample: Who should you give the scale to, what sample size do you need, and how do you name your scale?

Choosing the Sample

First, it is best to give the scale to the people for whom your scale will eventually be used. If your scale is intended to measure work-based Openness among adults, you would want to give it to working adults in various jobs. If your scale measures Sense of Identity for college students, you should give it to currently enrolled college students. On the other hand, many researchers initially give their scales to college students because they are easy to recruit and may earn course credit for taking the scale. In our experience, the biggest disadvantage of using college students to represent, say, adults, is that the means and standard deviations for items, and thus for the scale as a whole, often differ quite a bit for college students in comparison with, say, working adults. We have found that college students typically score higher on Neuroticism and lower on Conscientiousness than do working adults, but we have also found that the intercorrelations among the items in a scale and the factor structure of the scale are often fairly similar when based on different types of respondents, such as adolescents versus college students versus adults. Nevertheless, it is always better to try out your scale on a group representing the population for whom the scale is intended. As will be seen below, when your goal is to develop representative norms for an intended group, it is essential that your scale be given to the group of interest. One other important point: *Avoid double-dipping.* Use separate, independent samples for your reliability and validity analyses. Doing everything based on a single sample would greatly capitalize on error variance and lead to unreliable results. After you have achieved satisfactory reliability for your scale, use a new sample to evaluate the validity of the scale.

What Sample Size?

There are no hard-and-fast rules here, but it is generally true that larger samples produce better estimates of psychometric properties such as reliability. For practical purposes, and based on guidelines for factor analysis sample size (Bryant & Arnold, 1998), we recommend giving your scale to at least five times as many people as there are items in your scale. If you have 12 items in your Sensation-Seeking scale, try to give it to at least 60 people initially. One important reason why you want enough subjects is that your results may be utterly unreliable if you have too few subjects relative to the number of items. For example, if you correlate any two items in a 12-item scale based on only four subjects where you repeatedly draw four subjects at random from a larger group, you will find that the correlations are all over the board. On the other hand, if you were able to repeat this procedure with thousands of subjects, it is likely that your correlations will differ by only a few hundredths. A similar analogy applies to reliability (and validity) estimates based on small versus large samples. The larger the sample, the more stable will be your estimates of reliability (and validity). If you have a very large sample to begin with (e.g., over 1,000), you might want to randomly divide it in half and generate reliability estimates in both samples. If the estimates from the two samples are very similar or even identical, you will have demonstrated the robustness of your reliability estimate.

What Name Should You Give Your Scale?

When you present your scale in written or computerized form to your sample, you should name your scale, which typically appears as a center heading above your items. We recommend giving a general name for your scale that broadly encompasses the items you are measuring—such as Interpersonal Style Inventory, or Personal Beliefs Scale, or Personal Descriptive Index. Or you may choose to use a more neutral, ambiguous title like ISI or PDI scale. Some constructs evoke a strong reaction and predispose the respondents to give socially desirable answers, such as Antisocial Behavior Scale or Marital Infidelity Scale. If you label the scale by the name of the construct you are measuring, the people taking the scale may answer the items in a socially desirable manner or in a way that they feel is consistent with the title, rather than how they think they are on each individual item. Some of the most widely used personality scales reflect the choice of a nonspecific title such as 16 PF, NEO-PIR, MMPI, and PRF.

PSYCHOMETRIC SCALE ANALYSIS

To adequately cover the material for this topic would require a course in statistics and a course in psychometrics. We will condense our treatment

into a relatively small number of concepts that we consider to be the most important ones for psychometric analysis of your scale. We will introduce and explain elementary reliability and validity concepts as needed to describe a procedure. For this section, we will assume that you have entered the responses from your sample into a computer file, such as an SPSS (Statistical Package for the Social Sciences) data file. Our examples will rely on SPSS-Windows to generate statistics and illustrate statistical concepts.

The Importance of Reliability

Before learning how we use reliability in scale development, you should know a few key reliability concepts. *Reliability of measurement* refers to consistency of measurement. Other synonyms for reliability are *repeatability, reproducibility, precision, dependability, fidelity, accuracy,* and *generalizability.* Reliability is relative; there are many different types of reliability. Here are four important general reliability principles:

> *There is no single, universal reliability coefficient for any psychological measure.*
>
> *If psychological measures are not reliable, they will not be valid.*
>
> *Reliability is a minimum, but not a sufficient, criterion for validity.*
>
> *As the reliability of a measure decreases, validity usually decreases.*

When people speak of psychology being an inexact science, compared with say physics or chemistry, they are essentially saying that psychology is based on measures that have a lot of errors of measure. One index of the accuracy or precision of a measure is the *standard error of measurement,* which can be represented as:

$$\sigma_E = \sigma_O \sqrt{(1 - r_{xx'})}.$$

where σ_E is the standard error of measurement, σ_O is the observed score standard deviation, and $r_{xx'}$ is the reliability of the measure. If we examine the above formula, we can see that two factors directly influence the magnitude of the standard errors of measurement: reliability and the standard deviation. This leads to an important scale development implication: If we want to have smaller standard errors of measurement for our scale (i.e., make them more accurate), we should use scales with higher reliabilities. The above formula indicates that smaller standard deviations also lead to smaller standard errors of measurement, but we usually don't want to have smaller standard deviations of measures, which tends to lower reliability.

Internal Consistency Reliability and Coefficient Alpha

There are a number of different kinds of reliability that are important but, in the interest of brevity, will not be considered here. These include parallel forms, equivalent forms, test-retest, split-half, and interrater reliability. Our focus here is on internal consistency reliability as represented by coefficient alpha. One of the most important features of your scale is that it measures one construct, not several, and that it is internally consistent, meaning that the ideas measure the same thing, which in turn means that they are at least moderately, positively (after recoding) intercorrelated. In psychology journals, the most common statistical index of internal consistency reliability is Cronbach's coefficient alpha, named after the notable psychologist Lee J. Cronbach (Cronbach & Shavelson, 2004).

Cronbach's coefficient alpha typically ranges from 0 to 1.0, with higher magnitudes being more desirable. Although opinions differ somewhat, we recommend that any scale that you use in research or to make decisions in applied settings have a coefficient alpha (symbolized here as α) of at least .75 or higher. Moreover, you should try to achieve an α of at *least* .80 in the initial stage of scale development. The reason for this is that when you try to replicate your scale on a new sample, it will almost always shrink from the first value, sometimes only a few hundredths, but in some dismaying instances, the coefficient alpha α may shrink by two tenths or more.

The procedure for SPSS Windows Reliability Analysis (Scale/Reliability) presents coefficient alpha for a scale. It can also be used to conduct an *item analysis* for the scale to determine which items should be discarded and allows you to quickly recompute coefficient alpha to see if alpha increases after eliminating the item or items from the scale. To do so, we examine two very useful columns of information in the Item-Total Statistics summary: (a) the corrected item-total correlation, which is the correlation between that item and the sum (or mean) of all the other items combined and can be considered a form of item reliability—in general, we look for items that have a corrected item-total correlation of .40 or higher; (b) the value for each item in the column labeled "Alpha if Item Deleted," which tells you what coefficient alpha would be if the item on that row were deleted.

The following example is based on the Reliability procedure in SPSS Windows (if you are doing point and click, then click: Analyze, Scale, Reliability Analysis, Statistics, plus click all the boxes under Descriptives, Summaries, and Inter-Item). We performed the reliability procedure and item analysis on an eight-item, work-related Optimism scale developed by the first two authors (Lounsbury & Gibson, 2004), which is presented below along with a work-related Conscientiousness item added at the end for demonstration purposes.

1. I am basically a pessimistic person at work.	□ 1	□ 2	□ 3	□ 4	□ 5	I am basically an optimistic person at work.
2. I tend to agree more with the saying, "The glass is half empty."	□ 1	□ 2	□ 3	□ 4	□ 5	I tend to agree more with the saying, "The glass is half full."
3. When things aren't going my way at work, I tend to stay positive.	□ 1	□ 2	□ 3	□ 4	□ 5	When things aren't going my way at work, I tend to feel down.

4.	I do not have very high expectations for how my work will go next year.	□ □ □ □ □ 1 2 3 4 5	I have very high expectations for how my work will go next year.
5.	When the future is uncertain, I tend to anticipate positive outcomes.	□ □ □ □ □ 1 2 3 4 5	When the future is uncertain, I tend to anticipate problems.
6.	When bad things happen, I tend to look on the bright side.	□ □ □ □ □ 1 2 3 4 5	When bad things happen, I tend to dwell on them.
7.	I do not expect to be recognized as an outstanding performer in my occupational field.	□ □ □ □ □ 1 2 3 4 5	I expect to be recognized as an outstanding performer in my occupational field.
8.	I really believe in the saying, "Every cloud has a silver lining."	□ □ □ □ □ 1 2 3 4 5	I don't really believe in the saying, "Every cloud has a silver lining."
9.	If I broke my arm and had it set over the weekend, I would probably *not* go to work on Monday morning.	□ □ □ □ □ 1 2 3 4 5	If I broke my arm and had it set over the weekend, I would probably still go to work on Monday morning.

Note that we used a bipolar format rather than the usual five-point Likert scale where responses range from *Strongly Disagree* to *Strongly Agree*. Individuals taking the scale are asked to mark the box that best describes them on the scale ranging from the left-side statement to the right-side statement. Before conducting the reliability analysis, we recoded items 3, 5, 6, and 8 so that the higher score would reflect more optimism. Before turning to the results, we would expect that the last item will lower the coefficient alpha because it does not measure Optimism and would expect that the corrected item-total correlation for this item would be relatively low.

Based on a sample of over 500 candidates for nonmanagerial, salary positions (such as engineer, accountant, information technology specialist), the following corrected item-total correlations and alpha-if-item-deleted values were observed:

Left-Side Descriptor	*Right-Side Descriptor*	*Corrected Item-Total Correlation*	*Coefficient Alpha If Item Deleted*
1. I am basically a pessimistic person at work.	I am basically an optimistic person at work.	.49	.71
2. I tend to agree more with the saying, "The glass is half empty."	I tend to agree more with the saying, "The glass is half full."	.43	.73
3. When things aren't going my way at work, I tend to stay positive.	When things aren't going my way at work, I tend to feel down.	.58	.70
4. I do not have very high expectations for how my work will go next year.	I have very high expectations for how my work will go next year.	.48	.72

(Continued)

(Continued)

Left-Side Descriptor	Right-Side Descriptor	Corrected Item-Total Correlation	Coefficient Alpha If Item Deleted
5. When the future is uncertain, I tend to anticipate positive outcomes.	When the future is uncertain, I tend to anticipate problems.	.56	.70
6. When bad things happen, I tend to look on the bright side.	When bad things happen, I tend to dwell on them.	.62	.70
7. I do not expect to be recognized as an outstanding performer in my occupational field.	I expect to be recognized as an outstanding performer in my occupational field.	.27	.76
8. I really believe in the saying "Every cloud has a silver lining."	I don't really believe in the saying "Every cloud has a silver lining."	.42	.73
9. If I broke my arm and had it set over the weekend, I would probably *not* go to work on Monday morning.	If I broke my arm and had it set over the weekend, I would probably still go to work on Monday morning.	.08	.79

Coefficient alpha for the 9 items was .75. Note that the item-total correlations for item 7 and 9 were fairly low, especially for item 9, which is a Conscientiousness item. Note also that the far right column indicates the coefficient alpha for the scale would *decrease* if any of the other items were deleted, but it would *increase* if item 7 or item 9 were deleted. Therefore, we deleted items 7 and 9 from the scale and ran the reliability analysis again, which produced the following results:

Left-Side Descriptor	Right-Side Descriptor	Corrected Item-Total Correlation	Coefficient Alpha If Item Deleted
1. I am basically a pessimistic person at work.	I am basically an optimistic person at work.	53	.77
2. I tend to agree more with the saying "The glass is half empty."	I tend to agree more with the saying "The glass is half full."	.46	.78
3. When things aren't going my way at work, I tend to stay positive.	When things aren't going my way at work, I tend to feel down.	.59	.76
4. I do not have very high expectations for how my work will go next year.	I have very high expectations for how my work will go next year.	.45	.78
5. When the future is uncertain, I anticipate positive outcomes.	When the future is uncertain, I anticipate problems.	.58	.76
6. When bad things happen, I usually look on the bright side.	When bad things happen, I usually dwell on them.	.64	.75
7. I really believe in the saying "Every cloud has a silver lining."	I don't really believe in the saying "Every cloud has a silver lining."	.44	.79

Coefficient alpha for the above 7-item scale was .80. Notice that the coefficient alpha would not be higher than .80 if any of the items were deleted, so we decided to go ahead and use this 7-item revised scale to measure work-related Optimism, which we subsequently found to be positively related to job performance (Lounsbury & Gibson, 2002) and career satisfaction (Lounsbury, Loveland, et al., 2003).

If you cannot raise the coefficient alpha to an acceptable level by deleting items, you will need to write new items and repeat the reliability analysis. Before doing so, be sure to try to learn from your first item analysis which kinds of items are working and which ones aren't working.

Validity

Although there many types of reliability, there are even more different kinds of validity. Nevertheless, validity is a unitary concept, which always refers to the degree to which empirical evidence and theoretical rationales support each other. Validity is based on data supporting theory, and vice-versa. There is no one definitive index of validity. Rather, validity is supported by multiple forms of evidence. For good constructs, validity is never finished. We will now briefly describe eight important types of validity.

Content validity is evaluated by how well the content of a scale samples the class of behaviors and other psychological responses potentially represented by the construct. A content valid scale is a sample of items that is representative of the different ways the construct can be expressed by people. Unlike most of the other forms of validity, content validity is not measured by a statistic. It is usually assessed in terms of expert opinion. In the above example of the work-related Optimism scale, the item about breaking one's arm and still going to work would not have been considered initially as part of the scale, because it does not pertain to work-related optimism.

Criterion-related validity is evaluated by comparing scale scores with some criterion measure. For example, when we correlated our adolescent Conscientiousness scale with grade point average for middle school students (Lounsbury, Sundstrom, Gibson, & Loveland, 2003) and found a .31 correlation ($p < .01$), this demonstrated one form of criterion-related validity for our Conscientiousness scale.

Predictive validity indicates the extent to which the scores on a scale are related to future scores on a criterion or some other construct. *Concurrent validity* indicates the extent to which the scores on a scale are related to a criterion or some other construct measured at the same time. For example, if Conscientiousness for company employees measured on July 1 is found to be significantly positively correlated with their supervisor's ratings of each employee's current promptness in completing assignments, concurrent validity is demonstrated. If the same Conscientiousness scores are found to be significantly positively correlated with promptness in completing assignments in December of that same year, predictive validity will have been demonstrated.

Convergent validity is evaluated by the degree to which different (hopefully independent) methods of measuring a construct are related and produce similar results. For example, convergent validity would be demonstrated if self-reported Extraversion is related to Extraversion as reported by a spouse or as rated by an observer. A related concept is *convergence of indicators,* which refers to the extent to which measures of a common construct are related and display similar patterns of relationships. For example, if the NEO, 16 PF, Jackson PRF, and Myers-Briggs measures of Extraversion were all highly intercorrelated, convergence of indicators would be signified.

Discriminant validity is evaluated by the degree to which a construct is discriminable (e.g., uncorrelated) from, and nonredundant with, other constructs. Discriminant validity would be demonstrated if a new measure of Self-Esteem can be differentiated statistically from (though it can be mildly or moderately related to) a somewhat related measure of Neuroticism, and the new Self-Esteem measure is uncorrelated with unrelated measures, such as Openness and Conscientiousness.

Incremental validity refers to the degree to which a construct (or variable) significantly adds unique variance to the prediction of some construct or criterion above and beyond what is predicted by some other measure. This is often one of the most important forms of validity when you have developed a new and improved measure of some construct because you must show that your scale demonstrates incremental

Table 9.1   Results of a Hierarchical Multiple Regression Analysis to Predict Course Grade

Step	Variable	Multiple R	R^2	R^2 Change
1	General intelligence	.401**	.161**	.161**
2	Big Five personality measures	.477**	.227**	.067**
3	Work drive	.551**	268**	.041**

NOTE: ** $p < .01$

validity beyond the established measure(s). For example, as can be seen in the following summary of results for a hierarchical regression analysis, we (Lounsbury, Sundstrom, Loveland, & Gibson, 2003) showed that our new, narrow personality trait of Work Drive added significantly to the prediction of a psychology course grade after controlling first for General Intelligence and then the Big Five personality traits (see Table 9.1).

We can see that General Intelligence (a traditional predictor of academic performance) accounted for 16% of the variance in course grade, followed by the Big Five personality traits entered as a set, which added another 6.7% to the prediction of course grade. Then Work Drive was entered in the third step of the analysis, adding 4.1% of the variance in course grade, which was significant ($p < .01$), demonstrating the incremental validity of our new measure of Work Drive.

Known-group validation refers to predicting and verifying differences on a construct as a function of group membership when there is a high degree of a priori consensus about between-group differences on levels of the construct. For example, using independent samples t-tests, we (Lounsbury, Tatum, et al., 2003) found that the mean Conscientiousness scores for a group of high school leaders of student organizations were significantly higher than the mean Conscientiousness scores for "average" students and that the mean Emotional Stability scores for a group of high school students identified by teachers and counselors as being "at risk" were significantly lower than the mean Emotional Stability scores for "average" students.

Construct validity can be seen as encompassing all the other forms of validity. Ideally, there is a complete theory surrounding a construct, with hypothesized linkages to other constructs

and variables, every link of which is empirically verified in construct validation. Construct validation requires the integration of many studies and forms of evidence. If, for example, our adolescent Conscientiousness scale correlated substantively with established measures of Conscientiousness, such as the NEO-PIR, that form of convergence of indicators would contribute to the construct validity of our scale, as would the finding that it correlated significantly with the criterion of GPA (criterion-related validity) and if it added to the prediction of GPA above and beyond the NEO Conscientiousness scales (incremental validity).

Item Analysis to Increase Validity

In situations in which you have the appropriate data, you may want to examine the item validities of a scale; that is, the correlations between each item in the scale and the variable against which you are attempting to validate your scale. You can make decisions about which items to delete based on item validities in an attempt to increase the validity of the scale. In fact, you can examine item validities jointly with item reliabilities to make more informed decisions about which items to delete.

Table 9.2 shows nine items from a Neuroticism scale that we used on a sample of 188 sophomore, junior, and senior college students. The corrected item-total correlations and the item validities (i.e., the correlation between the score for each item and GPA) are shown in the columns to the right of each item.

The coefficient alpha for this 9-item scale is .84. The correlation between the Neuroticism scale score (which we computed by reverse coding the 7th and 9th items, then computing the average of the responses to the nine items) and GPA was $r = -.137$ (not significant).

Table 9.2   Corrected Item-Total Correlations and Item Validities for Neuroticism Scale

Neuroticism Scale Items	Corrected Item-Total Correlation	Item Validity
1. My mood goes up and down more than most people's.	.58	−.15
2. Sometimes I don't feel like I'm worth much.	.55	−.04
3. I often feel tense or stressed out.	.59	.01
4. I sometimes feel like everything I do is wrong or turns out bad.	.64	−.19
5. I feel like I can't handle everything that is going on in my life.	.57	−.23
6. I sometimes feel like I'm going crazy.	.58	−.15
7. It takes a lot to get me worried.	.35	.01
8. I sometimes feel sad or blue.	.55	.06
9. I feel good about myself most of the time.	.53	−.08

Let's suppose we wanted to increase the validity of the Neuroticism scale in relationship to GPA. Bear in mind that Neuroticism is usually negatively related to GPA; students who are more neurotic tend to have lower GPAs. If we look at the item validities, we see that three of the items—3, 7, and 8—are positively correlated with GPA (instead of negatively like the other items). In the case of item 7, the corrected item-total correlation is lower than the rest (and in fact is lowering the coefficient alpha). When we deleted these three items, the correlation between the revised Neuroticism scale and GPA increased to a significant level: $r = .20$ ($p < .01$). Also, the coefficient alpha for the revised 6-item scale was still respectable with coefficient alpha equaling .81.

Developing Norms

After establishing the reliability of your scale (which may involve replication, confirmatory factor analysis, and demonstrating different types of reliability) and accumulating a fair amount of validity evidence (which may involve any of the other above forms of validity and cross-validating your findings on independent samples), you may decide to make the use of your scale available to other researchers and practitioners, or you may want to provide feedback to individuals on their results after they have taken your scale. In either case, you may be motivated to construct norms for scores on your scale.

Here is one way (among many) to norm your scale. First, you should try to have a large

sample size (e.g., 400 or more would be quite desirable). Your norm group should be representative of the population of interest for making comparisons and generalizations. For example, in the preemployment assessment context, we often create local norms for scales rather than national norms, based on applicants who have applied for the specific job under consideration at the particular company that has the job. Although our emphasis in the preemployment situation is on a general norm group that does not consider demographic variables, in other contexts, it may be of interest to create separate norms for males and females, age groups, racial and ethic groups, or any other demographic variable.

The obtained sample should be described in terms of descriptive statistics—such as the mean, median, standard deviation, range, minimum and maximum score, and kurtosis—as well as information about how, when, where, and to whom the scale was administered. We would then recommend rank-ordering all grouping total scores and creating 10 "decile" groups, each of which represents 10% of the total sample. Then list the score ranges for each decile group. For example, for a Conscientiousness scale, the score ranges for the decile groups might be as follows:

Decile Scores

0–9%   Less than 2.31

10–19%   Greater than or equal to 2.31 and less than 2.67

20–29%	Greater than or equal to 2.67 and less than 3.14
30–39%	Greater than or equal to 3.14 and less than 3.67
40–49%	Greater than or equal to 3.67 and less than 4.03
50–59%	Greater than or equal to 4.03 and less than 4.18
60–69%	Greater than or equal to 4.18 and less than 4.32
70–79%	Greater than or equal to 4.32 and less than 4.51
80–89%	Greater than or equal to 4.51 and less than 4.78
90–99%	Greater than or equal to 4.78

In situations when you want to give feedback to individuals who have taken the scale, from an ethical psychometric standpoint you should not report a person's exact score (such as 4.11 or the 58th percentile) because all psychological measures have some error and the best we can say is that a person's true score lies within a range of scores. Thus, we recommend reporting of scores in terms of a confidence interval (such as we are 90% confident that Pat's score is at the 64th percentile plus or minus 5%) or in terms of a range of scores (such as the 50–59% range). Many scales also label a person's score (or score range) in five categories referencing the larger norm group:

Low, Below-Average, Average, Above Average, and *High.* One thing you have to be careful about in such labeling is to specify what the descriptor means statistically, as the label may seem to be inappropriate given the raw score. If you were norming a Conscientiousness score on a group of accountants, the *Low* group may have scores in the 4.20–4.30 range (which means that the person could have responded *Agree* or *Strongly Agree* to all items in the Conscientiousness scale, yet still have a lower score than 80% of their peers.

Conclusion

Scale development is a process that is characterized by a relatively integrated series of activities for which there are some common practices and some consensual criteria, but there is also a wide range of choices at each stage of development and many different ways to demonstrate reliability and validity. Good scale development starts with a sound theory about the construct, which leads to construct specification, item development, initial testing, psychometric analyses, and revision of the scale. These activities are repeated as the construct is extended to diverse settings and contexts. Ultimately and hopefully, this process culminates in construct validation (in all its many different representations), forms of evidence, and kinds of interpretation. Just as validation is never complete, scale refinement is never finished.

Exercises

1. Defining a Construct and Writing Items

Let's suppose you want to design a scale of your own to measure a personality construct. For practice, start with something familiar like Agreeableness or Jealousy or Self-Esteem. Your task is now to write items that tap your construct. But first try to define what you mean by, for example, the concept *agreeableness*. For this purpose, use a comprehensive dictionary or use Google on the Internet and search for meanings and definitions for the word you have chosen. After you have a working definition, usually one or two sentences, you can use a dictionary or Google or Microsoft Word (Tools, Language, Thesaurus) to search for synonyms (and antonyms) and meanings where the meanings are in a natural context. You might also search for articles in psychology journals using APA PsycINFO and look at how the authors describe the construct and associated contexts in the Introduction and in the Discussion sections. In the case of Agreeableness, the context is usually other people.

Then construct sentences, often starting with the word *I,* around the adjectives and use different situations. For example, "I am always pleasant toward other people." Or, "When somebody says something I don't agree with, I just let it go and don't say anything about it." After you have written a set of 10–12 items, go to somebody you know who really exemplifies the construct you are measuring—for example, the most agreeable, kindhearted, pleasant person you know—and explain to him or her what you are trying to do and ask for personal anecdotes and examples of when she or he was very agreeable. Use these as ideas for writing more items. After you have gone through your final list of items and eliminated phrases and words that are repetitive or redundant, look at the whole array of concepts and make sure that you have adequately represented the construct and range of situations, and included some negatively worded items. Then develop your final scale, give it a neutral title, make copies, and give it to a sample of 20–30 people. Tell some of the people who complete it what you are doing and ask for feedback on the wording of the items. Examine the responses and see how consistent the answers are and if there is a range of responses on each item. You might also want to do Exercise 2 below using the responses you have obtained in your sample to check out coefficient alpha for your scale and to see which items should be deleted to improve coefficient alpha.

2. Performing a Reliability Analysis Using SPSS

Suppose you have a four-item scale that purportedly measures Attitudes Toward Iguanas. Here are the items:

Item

1. I love iguanas.

2. I would like an iguana to live in my house.

3. Iguanas turn me on.

4. I like to repair engines and machinery.

We can see right away that item four looks odd and does not seem to measure Attitudes Toward Iguanas. But let's see what happens in the reliability analysis.

Assume we get four people—Mary, Ted, Alice, and Bill—to give their responses to these four items on a five-point scale on which 1 = *Strongly Disagree,* 2 = *Disagree,* 3 = *Neutral/Undecided,* 4 = *Agree,* and 5 = *Strongly Agree.* Here are their answers in a table form.

	Item 1	Item 2	Item 3	Item 4
Mary	1	2	1	3
Ted	5	4	5	3
Alice	3	3	2	5
Bill	2	1	3	4

It appears that Mary, who is majoring in accounting, does not like iguanas because she strongly disagreed with items 1 and 3, whereas Ted, who is a zoology major, strongly agreed with items 1 and 3.

Here is how we perform a reliability analysis using SPSS (Windows Versions 11 and above):

1. Launch SPSS by selecting it from the Start/Programs menu or clicking the on screen icon for SPSS:

2. Click on the Data menu and select Variable View (tab in lower left screen) and enter the *I1* on the first row for the first variable. Click the column Type of Variable and it should come up Numeric or drag down to Numeric for type of variable. Then go to the next row and repeat these steps for *I2,* then repeat for *I3* and *I4.* Then click Data View in lower left tab and fill in the data as displayed in above table, so that your screen looks like this:

	Item 1	Item 2	Item 3	Item 4
Mary	1	2	1	3
Ted	5	4	5	3
Alice	3	3	2	5
Bill	2	1	3	4

3. To run Reliability, click the following: Analyze, Scale, Reliability Analysis.

4. Then click all Variables from list at left into the Items box at right.

5. Click Statistics. Next click all options under Descriptives, Summaries, and Inter-Item.

6. Click Continue, and then click OK. This will generate output.

7. To read output, on the left under Reliability, click Reliability Statistics and you will see that

Cronbach Alpha = .71

This coefficient alpha is not bad, but let's examine the results further and try get a higher alpha.

8. Click Item-Total Statistics. Examine the Corrected Item-Total Correlation column, and you will see that the corrected item total correlation for I4 is .161. This is not good. Usually the corrected item-total correlations should be about .40 and higher. Also look at the far right column labeled "Cronbach's Alpha if Item Deleted" and note that the alpha would rise to .897 if the item were deleted. These results tell us that I4 does not belong in the scale, so we need to take it out. Here's what we do next:

9. Go back and open up the Data Editor by clicking Window on the top line of the screen and click *I4* in the Items box back into the Variables box, leaving *I1, I2,* and *I3* in the Items box.

Then, repeat Steps 3–7 above. You will now see, as forecast by the "Alpha if Item Deleted" result, that the Cronbach alpha for this scale does indeed equal .897, which is very good.

We will stop there and say that items 1–3 form a reliable scale to measure Attitudes Toward Iguanas. Here are two hints when running SPSS reliability analysis. All negatively worded items (e.g., "I hate iguanas" for the above scale) should be recoded before running reliability. Use Transform and Recode from top menu. Also, when you have your data entered satisfactorily, it is a good idea to save your data. You might save the above data as "iguanas.sav" for example.

RECOMMENDED READINGS

There are many different sources of information about scale development, ranging from elementary to quite complex, with the statistical techniques used to evaluate items and scale properties being one of the main contributors to complexity. A clear, sound introduction to scale construction is presented by Spector (1992), who emphasizes such key concepts as what makes a good scale, defining the construct, scale design, item analysis, reliability, validation, and norms. Although written for a slightly more advanced audience, another good introduction to scale development theory and application is provided by DeVellis (2003), who emphasizes classical measurement methods involving guidelines for scale development, reliability, and validity, but he also introduces the more advanced statistical procedure of factor analysis and furnishes an introduction to the more recent item response theory. Graduate students who want a more in-depth treatment of scale development in the context of psychometrics are well advised to read that classic in the field, Nunnally and Bernstein's (1994) *Psychometric Theory*. They offer practical suggestions and conceptual rationales for writing and evaluating items and provide a comprehensive overview of measurement issues, ranging from the purpose of measurement to the theory of measurement errors and assessment of reliability and validity, as well as exploratory and confirmatory factor analysis, scaling methods, and the analysis of categorical data.

Interested readers who would like more information about this topic may wish to read the following:

AERA/APA/NCME. (1999). *Standards for educational and psychological tests.* Washington, DC: Author.

DeVellis, R. F. (2003). *Scale development: Theory and application.* Thousand Oaks, CA: Sage.

Jackson, D. N. (1970). A sequential system for personality scale development. In C. D. Spielberger (Ed.), *Current topics in community and clinical psychology* (Vol. 2, pp. 61–96). Orlando, FL: Academic.

Jackson, D. N. (1971). The dynamics of structured personality tests. *Psychological Review, 78,* 229–248.

Messick, S. (1989). Validity. In R. Linn (Ed.) *Educational measurement* (pp. 3–103). London: Collier.

Nunnally, J. C., & Bernstein, I. H. (1994). *Psychometric theory.* New York: McGraw-Hill.

Ozer, D. J. (1999). Four principles for personality assessment. In L. A. Pervin & O. P. John (Eds.), *Handbook of personality: Theory and research* (2nd ed., pp. 671–686). New York: Guilford Press.

Spector, P. E. (1992). *Summated rating scale construction: An introduction.* Newbury Park, CA: Sage.

Web Site

Finally, anybody interested in developing or working with personality scales should peruse Lewis Goldberg's International Personality Item Pool (http://ipip.ori.org/), which currently has 2,036 items keyed to 280 personality scales, along with a wealth of information about labels, scoring keys, comparison tables, and translations to different languages.

REFERENCES

Bryant, F. B., & Arnold, P. R. (1998). Principal-components analysis and confirmatory factor analysis. In L. G. Grimm & P. R. Yarnold (Eds.), *Reading and understanding multivariate statistics* (pp. 99–136). Washington, DC: APA.

Butcher, J. N., Dahlstrom, W. G., Graham, J. R., Tellegen, A., & Kraemmer, B. (2004). MMPI-2 (revision). (http://www.pearsonassessments.com/tests/mmpi_2.htm)

Cattell, R. B., Cattell, A. K., & Cattell, H. K. (1993). *Sixteen personality factor questionnaire* (5th ed.). Champaign, IL: Institute for Personality and Ability Testing.

Costa, P., & McCrae, R. (1985). *The NEO Personality Inventory (NEO-PI-R) and the NEO Five-Factor Inventory (NEO-FFI) professional manual.* Odessa, FL: Psychological Assessment Resources.

Cronbach, L. J., & Shavelson, R. J. (2004). My current thoughts on coefficient alpha and successor procedures. *Educational and Psychological Measurement, 64*(3), 391–418.

De Raad, B. (2000). *The Big Five personality factors: The psycholexical approach to personality.* Seattle, WA: Hogrefe & Huber.

Hofstee, W. K. B. (2001). Intelligence and personality: Do they mix? In L. M. Collis & S. Messick (Eds.), *Intelligence and personality: Bridging the gap in theory and measurement* (pp. 43–60). Mahwah, NJ: Lawrence Erlbaum.

Jackson, D. N. (1970). A sequential system for personality scale development. In C. D. Spielberger (Ed.), *Current topics in community and clinical psychology* (Vol. 2, pp. 61–96). Orlando, FL: Academic.

Lounsbury, J. W., & Gibson, L. W. (2002, May). *An investigation of the job performance validity of optimism.* Paper presented at the 2002 Society for Industrial-Organizational Psychology Conference. Toronto, Ontario.

Lounsbury, J. W., & Gibson, L. W. (2004). *Personal Style Inventory: A work-based personality measurement system.* Knoxville, TN: Resource Associates.

Lounsbury, J. W., Hutchens, T., & Loveland, J. (2005). An investigation of Big Five personality traits and career decidedness among early and middle adolescents. *Journal of Career Assessment, 13*(1), 25–39.

Lounsbury, J. W., Loveland, J. M., Sundstrom, E., Gibson, L. W., Drost, A. W., & Hamrick, F.

(2003). An investigation of personality traits in relation to career satisfaction. *Journal of Career Assessment, 11*(3), 287–307.

Lounsbury, J. W., Sundstrom, E., Gibson, L. W., & Loveland, J. L. (2003). Broad versus narrow personality traits in predicting academic performance of adolescents. *Learning and Individual Differences, 14*(1), 65–75.

Lounsbury, J. W., Sundstrom, E., Loveland, J. M., & Gibson, L. W. (2003) Intelligence, "Big Five" personality traits, and work drive as predictors of course grade. *Personality and Individual Differences, 35,* 1231–1239.

Lounsbury, J. W., Tatum, H., Gibson, L. W., Park, S. H., Sundstrom, E. D., Hamrick, F. L., & Wilburn, D. (2003). The development of a Big Five adolescent personality scale. *Psychoeducational Assessment, 21,* 111–133.

Schmit, M. J., Ryan, A. M., Stierwalt, S. L., & Powell, A. B. (1995). Frame-of-reference effects on personality scale scores and criterion-related validity. *Journal of Applied Psychology, 80,* 607–620.

10

APPLYING SAMPLING PROCEDURES

WILLIAM C. MCCREADY

Sampling is a tool for solving specific problems in research. Because we cannot see all of reality in a single glance, we are restricted to viewing events one at a time. The purpose of sampling is to provide systematic rules and methods for allowing us to estimate how well our sample represents the reality we are studying.

For example, think of the people who first tried to study human beings from the inside. They had no idea what to expect. There was no map for them. The very earliest students of anatomy studied cadavers, the bodies of people who had died. By carefully describing what our circulatory systems and organ placements looked like, these early scientists provided an eventual map of the human body that became extremely useful in the development of Western medical science. The earliest practitioners of surgery followed this map and soon found that all human beings looked pretty much the same anatomically. Surgeons could generalize from this map created from a very small sample of the entire population to the entire population of humans because there is very little variation between humans when it comes to anatomical structures such as the circulatory system and the placement of our organs.

On the other hand, think of asking one person 10 questions about his or her goals in life. Does it seem reasonable to take that person's answers and assume that everyone else in the world will answer those questions the same way? Why does it make sense to use a very small sample to answer some types of questions when other questions require very large samples? Can you tell, other than by common sense, when you should use each method? Why do some scientists use sampling and others actually do not? Remember sampling is one of many research tools, and it is used only for specific purposes. That research tool is the subject of this chapter.

SAMPLING AND THE SCIENTIFIC METHOD

Representativeness

The whole purpose of drawing a sample is to have a small group of "things" that will accurately represent the properties and characteristics of the larger group of the same "things." The small group is the *sample* and the larger group is the *population*. How you select the sample is a key to how representative it will be of the population. Whether you are conducting an experiment with a control group and a treatment group or whether you are doing a community survey, you will want your sample to represent the populations you are studying. Sampling provides methods for measuring how representative the small group is of the larger group.

It is important to remember that you cannot reach perfect representation. The sample will never perfectly replicate the population. Representativeness in science is about estimates and approximations, not duplication. We're trying to make a sample that is the best estimate of the population under the conditions we face. The rules and methods of sampling are aimed at producing reliable and accurate estimates. For example, suppose we want to know how many people will decide to provide support for a disaster victim under each of two circumstances: The first is when the victim had no warning of the disaster, and the second is when the victim had a warning but failed to take any appropriate action. We can construct an experiment to test for this difference, but our experiment can never perfectly replicate the total reality. The rules and methods of sampling can provide a guideline so that our sample will come close to the reality by a known amount. That's the most we can expect from a sample.

Replication

One of the most essential aspects of science is conducting an investigation that can be repeated by another scientist who will obtain the same results you did—this is called *replication.* Different disciplines do this in different ways, but whether you are a biologist working in a laboratory investigating DNA or a social psychologist studying the connections between family life and community violence, you will want to conduct your study in such a way that its findings can be replicated.

Social scientists, for instance psychologists and sociologists, tend to deal with research questions that contain more variation than the problems our early anatomists solved. Human behaviors are incredibly complex and contain many variations. Therefore, you might think it was a simple matter of using very large samples so that we could make sure and capture all the varieties of the behavior we are studying. You would be wrong.

Experimental Method

One of the most powerful tools researchers have is the experiment. For some types of experiments you need large samples, but for other types you do not. As a matter of fact sometimes the experiment with the smaller sample is actually the more powerful of the two. The key to a powerful experiment is manipulating the conditions one at a time and observing the changes that occur. Many insights have been produced by this method. The famous American psychologist B. F. Skinner (1966) advised, "Study one rat for a thousand hours rather than a thousand rats for one hour each or one hundred rats for ten hours each." Sigmund Freud, from the other end of the psychological spectrum, also studied subjects in great depth rather than many subjects superficially. The experiment is particularly useful when testing strong theories, and detailed observation of a single subject is particularly useful when you've a reason to think all possible subjects are pretty much the same when it comes to what you are studying—like the human circulation system.

Experimental research frequently involves the random assignment of subjects to control and treatment groups. Members of the *control group* do not receive the experimental manipulation, and those in the *treatment group* do receive it. Subjects in the two groups are frequently matched on a number of variables such as gender, age, physique, and so forth so that the only thing being studied is the result of the experimental manipulation.

Population Estimation

On the other hand, there are research questions that do not lend themselves to being studied by conducting an experiment. For example, you may have no strong theory to test or you may suspect that there is a great deal of variation among the subjects in your sample. Sometimes the research question involves trying to ascertain what conditions are like in the larger population. For example, "How are people in a community predisposed toward environmental issues?" In such an instance, a sample of the community is required.

Chapter Overview

Sampling provides different tools for different jobs, and the type of sample depends on the job you want it to do. There is sampling for experiments and sampling for community surveys. There is sampling to produce a feasible number of subjects and sampling to project to population estimates. In the next section, we will discuss the different types and tools for sampling and offer some guidelines as to when to use them. Near the end, we turn to the new technologies of Internet and cell phone sampling and discuss the issues surrounding them.

There are two general types of sampling— nonprobability sampling and probability sampling—and each has its uses. We will discuss nonprobability sampling first because psychologists frequently use this method to select subjects for experiments. To remove the potentially pejorative implications of the preface *non,* we will describe various methods of selecting sample elements as judgmental sampling, purposive sampling, and matching sampling.

NONPROBABILITY SAMPLING TECHNIQUES

The Power of Relationships

C. James Goodwin (1995) writes,

Of course, the hope is that the results of these studies will extend beyond the subjects participating in it, but the researcher assumes that if the relationship studied is a powerful one, it will occur for most subjects within a particular population, regardless of how they are chosen. (p. 109)

This statement is an excellent description of the power attributed to the relationship between the variables being studied in many psychological experiments. Powerful relationships, such as that between obedience and the perceived legitimization of authority, will occur in the population regardless of how the participants in the experiments are chosen. In this type of research, various types of nonprobability samples are effective. There are several names for these samples, including *judgmental, ad hoc, convenience, purposive,* or *matching* samples.

The Participant Pool

There are those who would say that nonprobability sampling is not really sampling at all but rather involves systematic subject selection. For example, it is common practice for the subjects who volunteer for experiments at many university departments of psychology to be students in first-year psychology courses. These students form the *pool* from which researchers select participants. Although student subjects may be randomly drawn from the pool, the pool itself may or may not be representative of any larger population; however, for the purpose of the experiment, the selected subjects are indeed a sample of all the possible subjects available for that experiment.

Selecting and Assigning Participants

Participants in the pool should indeed be volunteers and, in order to ensure that ethical principles are maintained, should not be coerced in any way. Participants should not be allowed to volunteer for experiments but should be randomly assigned to either the control or the treatment group. These randomization procedures prevent bias from occurring due to previous experience or knowledge of the experiment or other potential causes by distributing it across the groups. Bias is one source of error in a sample, and if it is due to such causes as prior knowledge or disposition, it can usually be prevented during the selection process. The researcher frequently used his or her judgment about the characteristics of the members of the sample to assist in their selection. For example, if you were studying people for the presence of chronic fatigue syndrome, you would not be interested in people who at the outset of the interview said they had never felt tired a day in their lives. Your professional judgment would exclude these people from your sample.

Matching Samples

The ideal matched sample consists of identical twins, and twin registries in various countries have been used for research purposes. Putting one twin in a control group and the other twin in the experimental group goes about as far as possible in eliminating all the sources of experimental variation except the one we are studying, the one due to our experimental manipulation.

In most experiments, there are efforts to simulate the twinning process by matching members of the experimental and control group on as many salient characteristics as possible. Matching is usually done at the outset of the study when the sample is selected. Subject characteristics are tallied during the intake process and matches are created, and then random assignment to either the experimental or control group takes place. The result is that the control group and experimental group are as alike as can be, except for the administration of the experimental treatment or condition. Therefore, when we discover differences between the two groups on the experimental outcome, we can consider the difference to be the result of the experiment and not due to some other differences between the members of the groups.

Sampling "Error" in Nonprobability Samples: A Misnomer

Sampling error is a frequently misunderstood concept in the social sciences. The more appropriate term is sampling *variance,* and it has to do with the replicability of the measurements one obtains if one repeated the same sampling procedure many, many times. The use of the term *error* is unfortunate because there are many more sources of error than those that are due to sampling methods.

The issue here, and we will revisit it in the material on probability sampling as well, is whether or not you will get the same measurements or statistics from repeated samples of the type you are using. We estimate sampling variation by accumulating the variances in the measures derived from the repeated samples and taking the square root of that term. In other words, what some refer to as "sample error" is usually better described as the "standard deviation of the variances between the measurements from repeated samples."

We can compute this statistic for nonprobability samples, but interpretation is made difficult by the fact that the participant's probability of being selected is unknown. We will discuss this more in the following section, but because it is difficult to define the "population" for a nonprobability sample, it is also difficult to define the selection process in probabilistic terms. For these reasons, the subject of error is not usually discussed in those sampling contexts where

participants are recruited from pools for experiments.

Sample Size

The size of samples is a good bridge topic between nonprobability sampling and probability sampling because sample size is almost as frequently misunderstood as the concept of error. How large should a sample be for an experiment? In experimental methods, this has everything to do with how many trials and conditions and manipulations you plan to make and virtually nothing to do with the need to estimate values in a larger population. The situation is virtually reversed when it comes to doing probability sampling for a project like a community survey. That is, the precision of estimates of population parameters becomes paramount.

For nonprobability sampling, N (sample size) should be sufficient to allow reliable detection of expected changes in the experimental variable(s). A pragmatic rule of thumb for the beginning researcher to establish sample sizes is to adopt the sample sizes observed during the review of the research literature that invariably precedes an experimental project. In other words, when you review the literature in your area prior to designing your particular experiment, note the sample sizes being reported by others and use the mean of those as your guide. As a rough guideline, include projects conducted within the past 3 years or so. Typical experimental samples range between 50 and 200 participants. Additional detail on the sample size issue is provided by Scherbaum (Chapter 18) and by Myors (Chapter 11).

Clearly the cost of running participants in experiments also figures into the choice of sample size. How many assistants do you have? How long does it take for a participant to complete an experiment? How many participants can the experiment accommodate at one time? Whether you are retrospectively trying to fit the design to a grant budget, or prospectively trying to prepare a budget application, these are essential questions to consider. It is frequently possible to obtain useful information simply by querying colleagues who have conducted similar experiments. If that is not possible, a careful reading of the research literature will provide contacts for you to call.

PROBABILITY SAMPLING

The other major sampling procedure is *probability sampling,* in which members of a sample have known probabilities of membership. The probabilities may not be equal, but they are known.

Samples, Populations, and the Unit of Analysis

A *sample* is a portion of a population selected by some method that the researcher hopes will produce a smaller group representing the larger population. A population may consist of any elements. It may be people, families, schools, cities, crimes, graduations, financial transactions, events, decisions, tasks, or any other similar elements. An important part of the task in designing a survey is to define the population to be studied, and an important aspect of that process is to match the population to the unit of analysis for the project.

A typical unit of analysis problem occurs when trying to estimate how many persons were treated by medical facilities within a community during the past year. The governing agencies may keep counts of the number of times people were treated at the facilities, but unless there is a personal identifier attached to each element of the count, we cannot be sure how many persons are actually represented in the statistic. In this case, the researcher would have to decide whether to make the unit of analysis the "fact of being treated at a facility" or "the person being treated." There is data for the first unit of analysis—the event of being treated, but new data would have to be collected to study the second unit of analysis—the person being treated. In fact, need for this new data would necessitate a modification of the intake procedures to create a unique personal identifier for each participant.

Probability Theory

The key point contributed to sampling by probability theory is that it enables the researcher to know the odds, chances, or probabilities of a single respondent being selected in the sample. Why is this information useful? Because if you know the odds or probabilities of selection, you can also estimate the probabilities of nonselection and have a more precise estimate of the variation between repeated samples of the same design. By doing this you can assign a numeric or quantitative value to the concept of representation. For example, suppose we draw a sample of a community. After finding that 25% of our respondents agree that the community needs a new school and 75% disagree, we would like to have some assurances that this sample accurately represents the attitudes of the population in the community. What if we drew another sample? To what extent would we get the same results? *Sampling variance* answers this question with numerical results that can be compared, analyzed, and replicated. As we noted before, this procedure is frequently referred to as *sampling error,* but a more precise term is *sample variation* or *sample variance.*

It may simplify things for beginning researchers to remember that virtually all social science statistics have either one of two purposes. We're either trying to estimate how close together things are or how far apart they are. The first goes under the heading of *centrality* and the second under the heading of *variance.* Another way of thinking of this is that most social science research looks simply at how much alike or how much different subjects are, according to sets of properties or characteristics that we call *variables.* Whether the similarities or differences are relevant or important is usually determined by our theoretical statements. The task of the sample design is to provide a framework or a map that makes sure another researcher could replicate the way we selected participants for our study and that our findings are true for more than just one sample.

Probability theory is a specific field within mathematics, statistics, and philosophy and can be very complex. Probabilities are estimated for all sorts of events and happenings all the time. The reason that the news media provide point spreads for various athletic events is to facilitate gambling on those events, not just for fan information. Huge corporate marketing campaigns are based on the probabilistic estimates of groups of people with specific characteristics doing certain things. Your insurance rates are computed using probability methods. Probabilities frequently determine whether or not your tax return will be audited. Probabilities are all around us every day. We tend to accept statements such as, "It's more likely that you will die from being struck by lightning than in an airplane crash" without knowing very much at all about how those estimates are derived.

The key thing to remember about probability theory and sampling is that the theory provides a way of assigning known values to the event of respondent or participant selection. The advantage of having a specific value assigned to selection, such as a 1 in 258,765 chance, is that the value can be manipulated and compared with other values using the principles of mathematical statistics. Without such specific values, it is not possible to know with precision what would happen during repeated trials of the same sampling method. Without this knowledge, there is no precision to the replication, and without replication there is no scientific method.

The most common use of probability sampling is within survey research methodology because surveys are usually designed to use a sample of respondents to estimate the properties, characteristics, and parameters of a larger population. In a sense, although small samples for experiments can be selected nonprobabilistically without sacrificing precision, large samples are best selected using probability methods so that we can estimate their variation. A good expression of this phenomenon is provided by Kalton (1983). He observes that if you compare a small probability sample with a small judgmental or nonprobability sample, the sample variation for the probability sample will be so large as to make the sample virtually useless. Increasing the size of the probability sample reduces the sample variance and makes the sample useful.

On the other hand, because a sample variance for the nonprobability sample cannot be computed, the concern about bias grows as the sample gets larger because the larger sample size will magnify any bias due to errors of judgment in selecting the sample. Therefore, the small size of the nonprobability sample is not a liability, but rather it is actually a convenience. In a sense, it is like the relationship between a navigational inaccuracy and the distance being traveled. Over a short distance, an inaccuracy might result in a small error of a few hundred yards.

Over a longer distance, the same inaccuracy will produce a much larger error and you will miss your destination by many miles instead of a few yards. Using probability methods to select participants in larger samples ensures that we take advantage of the fact that the sample variance decreases as the sample size grows larger.

Sampling Frame

The listing of probabilities for each member in the population to be selected into the sample is the *sampling frame*. The frame is not simply all the members of the population, but rather it is the array or listing of all the individual members' probabilities of being chosen for the sample. In a simple random sample, each member of the population has the same probability of being selected, but how that number is computed may be different for different members of the population. And that is what is meant by the *sampling frame*.

Simple Random Sampling

A *simple random sample* is a selection from a population in which each element of the population has the same probability of being chosen for the sample and in which the selection is done all in one step or stage. For example, if we wanted to take a sample of a community that totaled 7,500 people, we would make it so that each person had a 1-in-7,500 chance of being selected, correct? That would be correct if we intended to include all the babies and children in our sample, but we probably do not wish to do that. If we had census information as to the number of people in the community in each age group, we could replace the 7,500 with the number of adults (however we agreed to define *adult*) and make our sample so that each adult had a 1-in-(the total number of adults) chance of being chosen. If, as is often the case, we do not have census information because the community is too small or the census is too old, we have to develop another strategy. That would probably involve doing one sampling to see what the distribution of ages was in the community and then doing another to actually select the adults for our study. The point here is that even simple random sampling gets complicated pretty quickly when we take it into the real world of project operations.

List or Systematic Sampling

A variation of a simple random sample is to randomly sample from a list of elements. In most instances this is a true simple random sample, unless there are unusual periodicities, cluster-ings, groupings, or fragmentations of the list. To randomly sample from a list, first compute the sampling fraction (*n*th) by dividing the size of the sample you desire into the total number of elements in the list. Then randomly choose a starting point and select every *n*th element, and you will produce a simple random sample of the members of the list. For example, suppose you have a class roster of Psych 100, and there are 300 students on it. You want a sample of 30 for your experiment. Create the sampling fraction (*n*th) by dividing 30 into 300 with the result being 10. Choose a random starting point and select every tenth student. (If you had wanted a sample of 25 you would have chosen every twelfth student.) A random starting point can be generated by numbering the students from 001 to 300 and, using a table of random numbers or the random-number generator function found on many scientific calculators, selecting the first number between 001 and 300 to appear. If the list is available in a format you can use on your computer, it is also a good idea to simply scram-ble the names alphabetically before making the random selection. Sometimes the elements of the list will come with their own ID numbers that can be perused by the random-number generator and used to select a starting point as well.

Block Quota Sampling

Strictly speaking, quota sampling is a non-probability method of judgmental sampling. In the early days of survey research, it was com-monly used. Interviewers would be told to select a specific number of respondents with certain char-acteristics. For example, the instruction might be that out of a cluster of 30 respondents, they were to get 15 men and 15 women and 7 of the men should be under 40 years of age and 8 should be over 40, whereas 8 of the women should be under 40 years old and 7 should be older.

As probability sampling began to dominate use, researchers would combine aspects of prob-ability selection with the older quota selection methods as a way of creating a cost-effective compromise. Residential blocks would be selected using probability methods, and once on a selected block, interviewers would use the quota method to select individual respondents from households. Some researchers still use this method on occasion for personal interviewing when costs have to be kept to a minimum.

Full-Probability Sampling

The usual difference between a block quota sample and a full-probability sample in personal interviewing is that the probabilistic selection of the respondent continues right down to the selection of the individual respondent. Once an interviewer reaches the household, he or she asks the person who answers the door how many people live in the household. The res-pondent for the survey is selected from that list by a probability method. Some variation of a Kish table is then used to identify to the inter-viewer the person in the household to be inter-viewed. A Kish table, named for the sampling pioneer Leslie Kish (1965) of the University of Michigan, is simply a table of randomly gener-ated numbers that tell the interviewer that "If there are two people in the household, select the oldest;" "if there are three people, select the youngest;" and "if there are four, select the sec-ond oldest;" and so on. The secret to the success of this method is that these tables are randomly generated, so they are different for each house-hold the interviewer visits. For example, the next time the interviewer called on the table, instead of what we saw above we might see, "If there are two people in the household, select the youngest;" "if there are three people, select the middle one;" and "if there are four, select the second youngest;" and so on. In this way, we guarantee that each person in the household has the same chance of being chosen for an inter-view, thereby fulfilling the goal of the full-probability sampling method. Samples in which each individual in the population has an equal chance of being selected are frequently referred to as *epsem* samples, for equal probability of selection of each member.

Another way of selecting respondents within a selected household is to ask for the "respondent who has had the last birthday." Birthdays are randomly distributed in the population, and this method provides a reasonable method of randomly selecting a respondent in a household.

Random-Digit-Dialing Sampling

Surveys are now being conducted over the telephone, and this is being done more and more as computer programs for the administration of surveys—CATI (computer assisted telephone interviewing) programs—have been developed. In a country like the United States where telephone coverage averages near 95%, telephone surveys represent a considerable cost savings over personal interviewing. Sampling for telephone surveys is usually done using some form of rdd, or random-digit dialing. Typically this consists of developing estimates for how many listed household numbers exist for each three-digit exchange in an area code and selecting a sample proportionate to that distribution.

Today many researchers who use CATI purchase the numbers they call from vendors such as Survey Sampling, Inc. or Genesys, Inc. These companies do all the statistical work of selecting the samples according to your specifications; and with the rapid changes in telecommunications technologies, such as cell phones, beepers, faxes, and new area codes, it is more and more difficult for the researcher who works on one project at a time to keep up with the technology. Chen and Huang provide additional details on this topic in Chapter 14.

Sample Size

One of the first questions a student usually asks about sampling is, "How do you know how large or small a sample to create?" The answer to this question is complex and requires understanding some of the points we have already covered. On the other hand, it is also an intuitively simple question because it seems that there should be a direct, positive relationship between sample size and sample quality. After all, isn't bigger better? Not always! It is absolutely crucial to remember that in sampling the salient question is not "How big is the sample? but rather "How are the elements of the sample selected?"

Although it does not seem to make intuitive sense, it takes the same number of respondents to provide identical estimates of precision and accuracy, whether our populations are the entire country, a specific state, a city, or a smaller community. In other words, if it takes 1,500 respondents in a national sample of the adult population of the United States to provide a 3% range of accuracy to survey questions with a 95% confidence interval, it will also take 1,500 respondents to depict the population of Cleveland, keeping to the same statistical specifications.

The *law of large numbers* (Mosteller, Rourke, & Thomas, 1961) describes the reason for this state of affairs. The law states that as the size of a sample increases, any estimated proportion rapidly approaches the true proportion that the estimate represents. For example, increasing the sample size from 500 to 1,000 will decrease the range of accuracy around a percentage from approximately 7% to 4%, and increasing the sample to 1,500 will reduce the range to about 3%. But after that, the decreases in the range are slight and are not usually worth the added cost of obtaining the extra cases. For example, doubling the sample to 3,000 respondents only reduces the range another 1.5 to 1.5%. This illustrates diminishing returns in action.

A more intuitive way to think about the law of large numbers is to imagine the following experiment. For the Fourth of July gala, I have emptied the swimming pool at the local park and filled it with ping-pong balls; some are red, some are white, and the rest are blue. I will award a prize of $500 to the person who gives the best estimate of the proportions of red, white, and blue balls. If you select 50 balls, and you see that 11 (22%) are red, 19 (38%) are white, and 20 (40%) are blue, are you very confident that you will win the prize? You shouldn't be. If another person does the same experiment, he or she may well come up with a different set of percentages.

If you select 500 balls, however, you are likely to be more convinced that the percentages you have will win you the prize, and you are even surer after you have picked 1,000 or 1,500 balls. If, however, you spend a lot more time and select a sample of 3,000 or 6,000 balls, you will find that your estimate hasn't changed very much, and it's hardly worth the extra effort. You are pretty well sure that the estimate you derive after 1,000 to 1,500 selections is as accurate as you're going to get—the law of large numbers has been at work.

Sample Variance

If you draw repeated samples of the same size and follow the same method, you will find that the samples will be different from one another. Seldom will they be exactly alike. The extent of the difference, the variation between samples, is the sample variance. This is sometimes called sampling error, but sample variance is actually the smallest component of total error in a sample. (The other components of total error, sample bias and response effects, are usually much larger. *Sample bias* has to do with making mistakes in the execution of the sample plan, and *response effects* are the result of the differences between the behaviors and attitudes that respondents report and respondents' true behaviors and attitudes.)

You can only compute sampling variances for probability samples, and that is one reason they are chosen over nonprobability samples for some research projects, such as those that require a population estimate.

Cluster Sampling

Some populations have members that are in close proximity to one another, such as students, and these can be sampled by drawing clusters and then sampling individual members within the clusters. For example, if we want to sample students, we can first randomly select schools because that is where students can be easily found. Then we can randomly sample students within the selected schools, and we will still have a known probability for each of the students in our sample. The advantage is that we can do this with considerably less expense and effort than if we tried to find students by randomly sampling households.

Stratified Sampling

Populations can also be divided into subgroups according to characteristics that are not geographically linked, like clusters. For example, we may decide to separate our population into four groups; males under 40, males 40 and over, females under 40, and females 40 and over. We may decide to do this because we are most interested in some aspect of the lives of females who are 40 and over, and we want to concentrate our sampling efforts on maximizing that information.

Stratified sampling is not always appropriate and should be used carefully. Sudman (1976) has an excellent discussion of the possible negatives in stratifying your sample. There are generally three reasons why you might stratify. First, the strata themselves are interesting topics within your research design. This can be true especially in survey work where demographic characteristics are important. Second, you may have good prior information about the differences between strata in terms of variances or other characteristics. Third, stratifying can generate cost savings, but one should take precautions that stratifying for cost reasons does not actually produce a less efficient and accurate sample.

Multistage Sampling

Most national survey samples are *multistage samples*, whether data are collected by personal interviewing or CATI interviewing. This simply means that sampling is done in several stages, starting with natural clusters and ending with selection of the individual respondent. Probabilities are assigned to the selection of each unit at each stage and can be combined to provide a known unique probability for the selection of every member of the final sample. Natural geographic clusters, like census tracts and area codes, are used to sort the population, and sampling proportionate to size is used within each to select individuals.

For example, if you live in a small town, your town will have a small chance of being in a national sample. (For many good national survey samples of 1,500 respondents or so, between 14 and 16 states are routinely left out because none of the towns in them make it to the final selection.) If your town is selected at the early stages, however, you personally have a much better chance of being selected in the national sample than someone who lives in a larger town.

Most beginning researchers will not need to know about multistage sampling. If you have the opportunity to work on a project using this technique, however, you will learn a good deal about the practical techniques of applied sampling, and it is worth doing. Applied sampling is best learned by being an apprentice to others who have been doing it for a long time. It's a skill that has been modified, refined, and handed down from one generation of samplers to the next—and that's the way to learn it best.

Other special-purpose sampling designs include sampling for longitudinal studies, cohort samples, cumulative sampling, aggregating across samples, and Bayesian sampling. Conceptual and operational treatments of such complex designs can be found in advanced treatments of sampling (Frankel, 1983; Sudman, 1983). Another advanced topic that is influential is technology, in the form of Internet and cell phone sampling.

Technology and Sampling: The Internet and Cell Phones

The Internet has grown from a patchwork of local linkages built by defense laboratories and academics into an international communication system that spans countries and continents. The U.S. Department of Commerce report, *A Nation Online,* states that the growth rate of Internet use in the United States is estimated at about half a million new users per month, and more than half of the nation (about 54%) is now online (NTIA, 2004). Given these figures, the potential for Internet surveys cannot be ignored. It is logical that social scientists and market research professionals would see it as an alternative sampling mechanism. The main virtue of using the Internet to conduct surveys is low cost. One can broadcast surveys to respondents and have them provide their answers without interviewers visiting homes or making repeated phone calls at inconvenient hours. The main limitation to using the Internet to conduct surveys is that THERE IS NO SAMPLE. This cannot be stressed often enough. There is currently no way to create a random-sampling algorithm for e-mail addresses. The permutations and structural variances defy sampling protocols, and there is no assurance that a person will have only one e-mail address. There are at least five significant disadvantages of Internet surveys from a sampling perspective.

No list. There is no known list of e-mail addresses such as there is for landline phones. It is therefore impossible to construct geographic area samples, and it is impossible to use the techniques of random assignment that produce samples with known statistical properties.

Inadequate coverage. About 35–40% of U.S. households do not have a personal computer (PC) that is connected to the Internet. It is a researchable question as to whether these are different from connected households, but the research obviously needs to be done without using the Internet as a sampling device. (During the 2000 election, there were data indicating that Internet users were more politically knowledgeable than nonusers; that is, 40% knew who Trent Lott was, but rather than a positive, this is a sampling negative. Clearly, this is not a representative group in society.)

Volunteering for surveys on favorite topics. A related issue is the fact that for many Internet surveys, respondents can volunteer for the types of surveys they take. This is sometimes referred to as the *opt-in bias,* in which respondents get to choose their survey topic. There is no real relationship between the respondent and the survey administrator in many cases, and this can lead to respondents tweaking their demographic characteristics to respond to surveys just to earn incentive points. (This can be similar to people who become professional focus group respondents to increase their weekly income.)

Respondent identity issues. People can and do have more than one e-mail address. They can also have more than one Internet protocol (IP) address, for example, home, work, and public places like libraries. Although this makes it very convenient to access the net and to engage in a variety of communication and surfing behaviors, it makes it impossible to create a sample with a unique, known unit of analysis. People have the ability to change their Internet identities frequently, and this means that a sampling protocol could never be sure who they were selecting from one time to another.

Calculation of meaningful response rates. It is usually impossible to compute response rates for online surveys because it is impossible to obtain a true denominator. In order to compute a response rate, you usually need to be able to classify the disposition of every case in your sample file, and this cannot be done with most online surveys. In sum, most Internet samples are simply "BOP"s (bunches of people). It's really no different than standing on a street corner waving a survey and asking, "Who wants to do a survey?" There is a place for this technique, as there is for mall intercept surveys, but it does not produce statistically valid and generalizable data.

Moving from disadvantages, there are also at least five significant advantages to Internet surveys from a practical point of view.

Use of audiovisuals. Surveys administered over the Internet can contain visuals, including photographs and, in some cases, video; and they can also incorporate audio under certain circumstances. Although relatively little use of this capability has been made to date, there are clearly ways in which this could enhance the quality of data obtained through the survey process. For example, it is much easier for respondents to respond to questions about proportions and risks if they can see the choice displayed graphically.

Response at any time. Respondents do not have to wait for an interviewer to call or visit; they can answer the survey at a time of their choosing. This sense of control may increase response rates, but that has not yet been determined. (However, at Knowledge Networks we have documented that a high proportion of our respondents complete their surveys outside the high-contact telephone survey times of 5 P.M. to 8 P.M.)

Convenient data entry. If the respondent answers a survey online, the respondent is becoming the data entry worker for that particular survey. As long as the survey program has been vetted for quality issues and the branching and skipping work properly, this is a considerable efficiency.

Access to respondents. The Internet provides easy access to millions of people, but this comes along with the sampling problems mentioned earlier. There are instances, however, when a researcher wants many respondents and is not worried very much about sample quality. These may be during pilot studies or exploratory research efforts.

Low cost. The Internet provides a lower cost option for data collection because there is no field staff to support, no data entry staff, and the cost of initiating a survey does not depend at all on the size of the sample being surveyed. (In other words, one can administer 500 surveys or 50,000 surveys for much the same outlay of operational cost.)

In sum, there are cost-convenience-methodology advantages to online surveys, but they must always be weighed against the lack of representative probabilistic sampling.

Conducting Quality Sample Surveys Online

In 1999, a company began to address the inherent sampling difficulties for online surveys by constructing the only "Internet-accessible panel" representative of the U.S. population that adhered to traditional probability sampling methodology. [Full disclosure: The author has worked for InterSurvey-Knowledge Networks since mid-1999. The name of the company was changed from InterSurvey to Knowledge Networks to reflect its broad design and analysis capabilities beyond conducting surveys.]

The Knowledge Networks panel-based approach is the only presently available method for conducting Internet-based survey research with a nationally representative probability sample (Couper, 2000; Krotki & Dennis, 2001). The Knowledge Networks panelists are recruited through a traditional random-digit-dialing protocol that produces a sample that represents the broad diversity and key demographic dimensions of the U.S. population. The panel tracks closely the U.S. population on age, race, Hispanic ethnicity, geographical region, employment status, and other demographic elements. The differences that do exist are small and are corrected statistically in survey data (i.e., by nonresponse adjustments).

The panel is comprised of both Internet and non-Internet households, and all were initially provided the same equipment (MSN TV) for participation in Internet surveys. This was the incentive for people to participate in the sample originally. Today households have the option of participating through their own Internet connection, if they wish, or through the device provided by the company.

There are four main factors responsible for the representativeness of what Knowledge Networks calls its "Web-enabled" research panel. First, the panel sample is selected using list-assisted random digit dialing telephone methodology, providing a probability-based starting sample of U.S. telephone households. Second, the panel sample weights are adjusted to U.S. Census demographic benchmarks to reduce error due to noncoverage of nontelephone households and to reduce bias due to nonresponse and other non-sampling errors. Third, samples are selected from the panel for individual studies using probability methods. Appropriate sample design weights for each study are calculated based on specific design parameters. Fourth, nonresponse and post-stratification weighting adjustments are applied to the final survey data to reduce the effects of nonsampling error (variance and bias).

Knowledge Networks provided households in the panel with free Web access and an Internet appliance, which used a telephone line to connect to the Internet and used the television as a monitor. (As mentioned earlier, households do have the option currently of participating through their own connection and earning points that can be exchanged for cash.) In return, panel members participate in 10- to 15-minute Internet surveys three to four times a month. Survey responses are confidential, with identifying information never revealed without respondent approval. When surveys are assigned to panel members, they receive notice in their password-protected e-mail account that the survey is available for completion. Surveys are self-administered and accessible any time of day for a designated period. Participants can complete a survey only once. Members may leave the panel at any time, and receipt of the MSN TV and Internet service is not contingent on completion of any particular survey. The current Web-enabled research panel consists of approximately 40,000 adults actively participating in research.

Knowledge Networks and TESS: A Resource for Graduate Student Research

An innovative program allows graduate students and faculty to use either a traditional telephone survey or the Knowledge Networks panel to gather data for a very modest cost. The National Science Foundation supports Time-Sharing Experiments for the Social Sciences (TESS). This program provides social scientists an opportunity to run studies on a random sample of the population that is interviewed via the Internet-MSN TV or via a telephone survey. The TESS project operates with six primary goals in mind:

1. To provide opportunities for original data collection

2. To promote innovative experiments

3. To increase the precision of measuring and understanding fundamental social, political, and economic dynamics

4. To increase the speed and efficiency of applying social scientific theory and analyses to critical social problems

5. To maximize financial efficiency by radically reducing the average cost per study

6. To create an Internet portal for people who want to learn about social science experimentation (www.experimentcentral.org/)

TESS collects data for researchers' experiments and quasi-experiments by providing access to two large-scale data collection instruments. One of these instruments is a series of national telephone surveys administered by the Indiana University Center for Survey Research (www.Indiana.edu/~csr/) where investigators can add their own original experiments. The other instrument, administered by Knowledge Networks, provides investigators an opportunity to run experiments on a random sample of the population that is interviewed via the Internet or MSN TV.

Research-oriented faculty and graduate students from the social sciences or fields related to the social sciences, such as law and public health, compete for time on one or both instruments. A comprehensive, online submission and review process screens proposals for the importance of their contribution to science and society. The Internet-based and telephone-based data collection platforms allow researchers to run novel experiments on representative samples drawn from the United States population in order to examine substantive or methodological hypotheses. Proposals may come from any substantive area within any discipline in the social sciences so long as they utilize experimental or quasi-experimental designs that make a significant contribution to knowledge.

Sampling and Cell Phones: An Evolving Scene

The expanding base of cell phone users poses important challenges for the survey research industry, and there will be a meeting in February 2005 to deliberate many cell phone sampling issues, such as coverage, frame, nonresponse, geographic screening, weighting, and so forth. More information on these issues as they develop can be obtained from the American Association for Public Opinion Research (www.aapor.org)

The essential problem is that researchers are currently prohibited from sampling cell phone numbers, and an unknown proportion of citizens are moving to a cell phone–only status. Estimates range from 3% to 7% of the population and up to 10% of specific demographic groups, such as young people. We do not currently know if this represents a long-term trend or if it is a short-term fad. If a significant portion of the population to be sampled is cell phone–only, then excluding them creates a bias.

Cell phones and the Internet, as well as technologies that are only now being developed (PDAs), will undoubtedly play an important role in future research.

Conclusion

In summary, this chapter contains a basic overview of sampling theory and procedures for the beginning researcher. Internet and cell phone samples were presented to illustrate the impact of technology on sampling for applied as well as for theoretical research. The importance of sampling for scientific research and for producing confidence in research findings served as an introduction. The distinction between nonprobability and probability sampling was used to organize a review of the major designs for experiments and surveys. The chapter also provides recommended readings. Finally, it is appropriate to conclude with a reminder of the ethical obligations of researchers and, in particular, sample designers. It is ethically sensitive to strive toward a goal of ensuring that all members of a defined population have a chance to appear in the sample of participants or respondents and share their views with researchers and policy makers. It is also ethically sensitive to ensure that the participation or response is provided voluntarily and without coercion or deception.

Finally, there are six associated exercises for the interested reader to complete. It is hoped that the combination of knowledge and skill will enable you to apply sampling wisely in your research and practice.

EXERCISES

1. Access the Web site for the U.S. Census Bureau (www.census.gov/) and explore the links to People, Business, and American FactFinder (the last is among the links on the left side) to familiarize yourself with the variables and proportions that characterize your hometown, state, and the United States as a whole. This builds a set of statistical expectations within your thinking that is based on accurate representational data that you can use to evaluate other sources of information.

2. Spend an hour several times a week observing the people who patronize the drive-up window of a local fast-food restaurant. Make a plan that includes lunchtime and dinner hours, and be sure to include some weekdays and weekends. Document the visitors during each hour in terms of predetermined variables, such as year and model of car; gender, race and approximate ages of occupants; time from arrival to departure with food; and so forth. Write a summary that includes profiles for weekday lunch and dinner and weekend lunch and dinner.

Contact the company's public affairs office, and see if they will provide you with some of their own profile data for comparison. This allows you to test your own sampling strategy with real data; and even if the company doesn't provide comparative data, you will learn about operationalizing a sampling plan in the real world.

3. Roll a pair of dice 10 times and write down each score. Repeat this 10 times so that you have 100 observations in 10 sets of 10. Compare the distributions and compute the average error between them. You can also use these data to compute various forms of deviation and estimates of error. You will gain facility in thinking about the ways error is used to characterize probabilistic events.

4. Ask your friends, family, and associates (approximately 25 people would be a good sample) several questions from a national survey (such as Gallup/CNN) and compare the results you get with what the national data reported. This will provide you a real-time experience in detecting bias.

5. Rent the video of the movie *Magic Town* (1947, directed by William A. Wellman) and write a summary (two pages at most, with bullets) describing its implications for today's market researcher.

6. Keep a log of TV dramas and sitcoms for a week (here's your chance to veg a little for science), and count the appearances of minorities, smoking, guns, thin fit people, and/or any other variables that are of interest to you. (Make your list of variables ahead of time.) After a week, tally the variables on your log and search data sites (like the Census) to see how TV compares with society. (A specific form of this that could probably produce publishable results would be to limit the input to TV reality shows.)

RECOMMENDED READINGS

Sampling is a vast topic, with many potential reference resources in theory and in practice. A classic resource is Sudman's (1976) *Applied Sampling*—which focuses on the costs of surveys and on maximizing the use of limited resources. Also see his chapter on applied sampling in the (Sudman, 1983) *Handbook of Survey Research.* The sampling theory chapter in that same handbook is also useful.

REFERENCES

Couper, M. P. (2000). Web surveys: A review of issues and approaches. *Public Opinion Quarterly 64*, 464–494.

Frankel, M. (1983). Sampling theory. In P. Rossi, J. Wright, & A. Anderson (Eds.), *Handbook of survey research* (pp. 21–67). New York: Academic.

Goodwin, C. J. (1995). *Research in psychology: Methods and design.* New York: Wiley.

Kalton, G. (1983). *Introduction to survey sampling.* Beverly Hills, CA: Sage.

Kish, L. (1965). *Survey sampling.* New York: Wiley.

Krotki, K., & Dennis, J. M. (2001, August). *Probability-based survey research on the Internet.* Presented at the conference of the International Statistical Institute, Seoul, Korea.

Mosteller, F., Rourke, R. E. K., & Thomas, G. B., Jr. (1961). *Probability with statistical applications.* Reading, MA: Addison-Wesley.

NTIA. (2004, September). *A nation online: Entering the broadband age.* Washington, DC: Author.

Skinner, B. F. (1966). Operant behavior. In W. K. Honig (Ed.), *Operant behavior: Areas of research and application* (p. 21). New York: Appleton-Century-Crofts.

Sudman, S. (1976). *Applied sampling.* New York: Academic.

Sudman, S. (1983). Applied sampling. In P. Rossi, J. Wright, & A. Anderson (Eds.), *Handbook of survey research* (pp. 145–194). New York: Academic.

Online Sources

Knowledge Networks can be accessed at www.knowledgenetworks.com

MSG, the vendor for GENESYS, can be accessed at www.m-s-g.com/

Survey Sampling, Inc. can be emailed at info@ssisamples.com

11

STATISTICAL POWER

BRETT MYORS

Psychological researchers have become increasingly aware of the importance of designing more powerful studies. In this context, *power* is a technical term that indicates the sensitivity of statistical significance tests used in the analysis of data. The power of a statistical test is the probability of rejecting the null hypothesis when the alternative hypothesis is true (i.e., when there is a real effect in the population). To put it simply, power is the probability of getting a significant result when you deserve to get one. Assuming you are seeking significant effects, so you will have something to talk about in your discussion, power is the probability that your experiment will work out the way you hope it will. Before power was routinely calculated, it was not uncommon to find studies carried out in the psychological and behavioral sciences with power of .50 or less (Cohen, 1962; Sedlmeier & Gigerenzer, 1989). When power is as low as .50, the chance of a successful research outcome is no better than the toss of a coin. When power is less than .50, you'd be lucky to get a significant result at all! With a bit of forethought, however, the odds of a significant result can be improved considerably, and methods for doing so fall under the rubric of power analysis.

Obviously power is something worth finding out about before you start collecting data. Most researchers are disappointed with nonsignificant results, especially after going to all the time and effort required to run their study; and it can be especially disappointing to realize that the odds were stacked against you right from the start. A power analysis during the planning stages of research is a good insurance policy against this kind of disappointment. Over the years, many commentators have lamented the low levels of power found in some areas of psychological and behavioral research (e.g., Cohen, 1962). This lamentation has led to increasing demands for research to be conducted with sufficient levels of power (Wilkinson & Task Force, 1999). Proper attention to power analysis during the early stages of research will lead to the design of better studies, and this can only be to the benefit of individual researchers, as well as to the long-term benefit of the discipline. If adequate power cannot be achieved, then the research proposal needs to be reconsidered or even abandoned.

The most comprehensive treatment of power analysis for the psychological and behavioral sciences is due to Cohen (1988), who recommends aiming for a power of .80, or in other words, an 80% chance of success. This recommendation has been widely accepted in the literature as providing a good balance between the various tradeoffs required to achieve acceptable levels of power. The main reason for not aiming above .80 is that higher levels of power become extremely costly in terms of the effort and resources required; see Chapter 18 for a further discussion of the relative costs of Type I and Type II errors.

What is Statistical Power?

The concept of statistical power follows from the logic of hypothesis testing, which aims to help researchers draw reasonable conclusions from their studies. In particular, researchers must *decide* whether the study they have conducted provides sufficient evidence to conclude in favor of the theory they are wishing to test or whether the results were more likely due to chance fluctuations in their data. See Chapter 19 on hypothesis testing for an elaboration of these concepts. Power can be seen as one of the outcomes of this decision. As shown in Figure 11.1, power is the probability of making a correct decision when the null hypothesis is, in fact, wrong. Power can also be defined as 1 minus the Type II error rate, β.

Increasing Power

A first step in increasing power is to use more powerful statistical tests. Often researchers are presented with a variety of analytical options, and one way to choose between them is to pick the most powerful one. For example, many situations can be analyzed using contingency tables, but this is not a particularly powerful technique. Similarly, parametric tests are generally more powerful than nonparametric ones, and F tests with one degree of freedom in the numerator, and their equivalent t-tests, are more powerful than multiple-degree-of-freedom F tests. Once the test is chosen, power is a function of three things: the Type I error rate, the effect size, and the sensitivity of the study.

As Chapter 19 explains, Type I and Type II error rates are inversely related, and it is never possible to completely avoid them. At best, we can only trade potential errors off against each other. As Type I errors are reduced, Type II errors increase; and, given that power = $1 - \beta$, reducing Type I errors also reduces power. This fact leads to the easiest method of increasing power: Use a less stringent α rate. Although, strictly speaking, α is within your control as the experimenter, long-held conventions in the scientific literature surround appropriate values of α, and it is difficult to gain acceptance for α rates above .05. In fact, more time is spent in statistics courses learning how to keep Type I errors at or below this level than on virtually any other topic. This is because Type I errors, rejecting the null hypothesis when it should have been retained, are seen as potentially very damaging to the scientific enterprise because they may lead many researchers to waste time exploring blind alleys. In contrast, large Type II error rates and low power are only likely to hurt individual researchers if they are imprudent enough to conduct studies with little chance of success, which is why choosing an appropriate topic and design are so important (see Chapter 6 by Wampold).

If you follow the recommendations in this chapter and aim for power equal to .80, then your Type II error rate will be no worse than .20, which treats Type II errors as one quarter as bad as Type I errors (.05 / .20 = .25). This ratio of 4:1 represents a reasonable balance for most

	Unbeknownst to you, H_0 is actually true, treatments really have no effect	Unbeknownst to you, H_0 is actually false, treatments really do have an effect
You decide not to reject H_0 because treatments didn't seem to have any effect	You made a correct decision to retain a true H_0 $(1 - \alpha)$	You made a Type II error (β)
You decide to reject H_0 because treatments appeared to be working	You made a Type I error (α)	You made a correct decision to reject a false H_0 $(1 - \beta = \text{power})$

Figure 11.1   Consequences of Statistical Decisions

researchers, but see Murphy and Myors (2004) for more rational methods of balancing Type I and Type II error rates.

Apart from setting a higher α level, another way to increase power is to look for larger effects because large effects are easier to detect than small ones. By *effect size* is meant the degree of departure of the alternative hypothesis from the null hypothesis. If there is little difference between the two hypotheses, then the effect size is, by definition, small. In experimental studies, effect size refers to the impact of treatments (i.e., how much difference they are expected to make). In correlational studies, effect size refers to how closely two variables are associated. Sometimes experimenters are able to induce large effects through their manipulations or through tight control over extraneous variables; or they can "top and tail" (i.e., select participants at extreme ends of the distribution on some dimension of interest). This can reduce the generalizability of the study, however, so it may be preferable to work with effect sizes closer to those encountered outside the laboratory. Nonexperimenters, on the other hand, have little or no control over the effect sizes they study. In correlational research, the effect size is determined by the nature of the phenomenon under investigation rather than by anything the researcher might do. In any case, studying very small effects may not be feasible, given the level of effort and resources required, unless one has a very large research budget. Good examples of this can be found in the biomedical literature. For example, the Physician's Aspirin Study, involving over 22,000 participants, helped establish the benefit of aspirin in reducing heart attacks. Although the effect was very small by the standards used here, $r = .034$ (Rosenthal, 1993, p. 538), the outcome variable, survival, is sufficiently important to make this small effect very practically significant indeed.

A variety of indices have been proposed for specifying effect sizes. In the simplest case of comparing two group means, the usual effect size index is the *standardized mean difference* given by $d = (M_T - M_C) / SD$, where M_T and M_C are the means for the treatment and control groups respectively and SD is the pooled standard deviation.[1] The above formula scales the difference between the two means in terms of

their common standard deviation so that diverse treatments can be compared using the common dimensionless scale of SD units. A d of 1.0 means that the treatment group differed from the control group by a full standard deviation; a d of .50 means that the difference was only half a standard deviation; and a d of .20 means a difference of a fifth of a standard deviation was found. For example, Lipsey and Wilson (1993) collated effect sizes from over 300 meta-analyses for treatments ranging from the educational benefit of grouping children in terms of ability, $d = .01$, to the effectiveness of assertiveness training, $d = 1.51$. A few of the effect sizes reported were negative, meaning that the treatment was actually detrimental.

A more general index of effect size is the *percentage of variance account for,*[2] which is a squared correlation denoted by r^2. It is worth remembering that you can always switch back and forth between d and r^2 using the following formulas:

$$r^2 = \frac{d^2}{d^2 + 4} \quad (11.1)$$

and

$$d = \frac{2r}{\sqrt{1 - r^2}} \quad (11.2)$$

although d makes most sense in the context of two group means. Equation 11.1 assumes a balanced design (i.e., that the sizes of the two groups are equal). A slight elaboration of Equation 11.1 allows us to handle unequal sample sizes within the groups. In this case

$$r^2 = \frac{d^2}{d^2 + \frac{1}{pq}} \quad (11.3)$$

where p and q are the proportion of the total sample in each group and $q = 1 - p$. For example, if I had 60 participants in one group and 40 in another, p would equal .6 and q would equal .4. Notice that for balanced designs $p = q = .50$ and $1 / (.50 \times .50) = 4$, which gives Equation 11.1.

Appropriate values for r^2 and d can often be determined from pilot studies or by studying the relevant research literature; however, in the absence of a clear indication, another set of conventions has been widely adopted as indicative of "small," "medium" and "large" effects commonly found in the psychological and behavioral sciences. These are given in Table 11.1. Although the values shown in Table 11.1 were somewhat arbitrarily proposed by Cohen (1988), they seem to have stood the test of time. For example, 85% of the d's reported by Lipsey and Wilson (1993) were above .20 (Cohen's definition of a small effect) and about half were greater than .50 (Cohen's definition of a medium-sized effect). It is preferable to give some thought as to the most likely effect size for your study before simply reaching for Table 11.1; nevertheless, these default values provide a useful fallback position. In general, larger effects are of more practical value, but the crucial difference between two competing theories may hinge on a very subtle phenomenon, so studying small effects can be very important in testing and developing new theory.

Table 11.1   Some Effect Size Conventions

	r^2	d
Small Effect	.01	.20
Medium Effect	.10	.50
Large Effect	.25	.80

Finally, power can be increased by improving the sensitivity of your study. *Sensitivity* is affected by several things, including the reliability of the measures and scales used, the degree of control you hold over extraneous variables that contribute to the error in your analysis, and how accurately you observed the outcome of interest (i.e., the dependent variable). Sensitivity is also improved by using larger samples. From a practical point of view, given that the conventions limiting α to .05 or less are hard to shift and the fact that effect sizes are primarily predetermined by nature, increasing the sensitivity of your research design usually offers the greatest potential for improving power. More reliable variables, greater control over the situation, and a larger sample size all contribute to making your study more sensitive and thus more powerful. In fact, it is in the determination of sample size that power analysis is probably of most use to researchers. You should aim for a power of .80 without overshooting or undershooting this value by too much.

Determining Sample Size

Many approaches have been employed for the determination of sample size. All are broadly similar and give approximately the same results. Cohen (1988) provides the most comprehensive treatment for the psychological and behavioral sciences, covering the most commonly used statistical tests. Kraemer and Thiemann (1987) developed a general framework based on the intraclass correlation coefficient. Lipsey (1990) used the t-test and Murphy and Myors (2004) used the noncentral F. Readers are referred to these sources if they wish to obtain specific power estimates or if they wish to determine the sample size required in complex experimental designs. This chapter focuses on a few simple methods for determining the sample size needed to achieve acceptable levels of power in some of the more common statistical analyses used by beginning researchers. These are one- and two-sample t-tests, tests of a significant correlation coefficient, and analysis of variance.

In addition to the books mentioned above, a number of computer programs have been written in recent years for determining sample size and power. Many of these programs are offered commercially, but some are available free. One of the most popular freely available programs is G*Power (Erdfelder, Faul, & Buchner, 1996), which covers t, F and χ^2 tests. R. Lenth has also written a number of add-in functions for Microsoft Excel—collectively known as PiFace, which can be used for power calculations—and has more recently developed an interactive Web site for power analysis located at www.stat.uiowa.edu/~rlenth/Power. Given the fact that computer software tends to be updated fairly regularly, it is difficult to provide a useful review of software programs for power analysis; however, a helpful, though somewhat dated review, was provided by Thomas and Krebs (1997).

In the absence of a computer or a book of tables, simple expressions for the sample size needed to reach the desired power of .80 are shown in Table 11.2. Because the equations in Table 11.2 both assume one degree of freedom in the numerator, they are very similar and differ only in terms of the effect size parameter in the denominator. Nevertheless, these two

Table 11.2 N_{needed} to Achieve Power of .80 With Two-Tailed Tests Assuming an α Level of .05

One-Sample Tests	Two-Sample Tests
$N_{needed} = \dfrac{7.85}{d^2}$	$N_{needed} = \dfrac{7.85}{r^2}$

expressions form the basis of a wide range of power analyses that can be used to answer specific research questions. In each case, the effect size must be specified up front, before your study begins. It represents your best guess as to the effect you are hoping to find or the smallest effect you are interested in. Post hoc power analysis based on the actual effect size observed on completion of a particular study is to be avoided because it contributes little to the understanding of the study that is not already contained in the significance tests performed (Hoenig & Heisey, 2001). Framing power analysis around N_{needed}, rather than in terms of power per se, puts the emphasis on planning good research rather than on post hoc analysis. Thus power analysis starts with an a priori estimate of effect size. Obviously, if you really knew the true effect size at the beginning of your study, you wouldn't need to do the research. You would already know whether it was greater than zero (i.e., significant) and if it was large enough to be of interest to anyone. Estimates of effect size can be obtained from prior research and experience in the area of study, from pilot studies, or from the conventional definitions of small, medium, or large effects shown in Table 11.1.

Because the effect size you specify in power analysis is really just a guess, it is very unlikely to equal the actual effect size you are investigating. In many respects, the true effect size can never be known for sure, no matter how many studies are done, because the population is effectively infinite (e.g., the population of all human beings). This, coupled with the fact that you can never really tell how well you met the assumptions of your significance test, makes power analysis a fairly inexact science. It follows then that we can never really know the true power of our studies. The power obtained by the

methods presented here, or by any other method, is always an approximation at best, and it is impossible to tell which approach is absolutely correct for any particular study. Nevertheless, all methods are likely to lead to similar decisions in planning research. All methods will give you a good indication of whether you should bother carrying out your study and roughly how large it should be, but don't read too much into specific values.

Example 1: One-Sample *t*-Test

To illustrate a number of power analyses, consider a study by Gillespie and Myors (2000) into the personality of rock and roll musicians. Gillespie and Myors (2000) administered the self-report form of the NEO-PI-R, Form S, (Costa & McCrae, 1992) to 100 rock-and-roll musicians living in the Sydney metropolitan area. The NEO-PI-R is a widely used personality test that measures the Big Five personality traits of Neuroticism, Extraversion, Openness to Experience, Agreeableness, and Conscientiousness, along with their 35 component facets. One aim of Gillespie and Myors's study was to determine the extent to which rock musicians differed from the rest of the adult population. To answer this question, the authors compared the mean scores of musicians in their sample on the Big Five traits with the general population norms supplied in the test manual. This comparison called for a series of one-sample *t*-tests.[3]

To ascertain the sample size needed to conduct this study, the authors noted that scores falling above or below half a standard deviation from the population mean on each trait were considered by Costa and McCrae (1992, p. 13) to be outside the average range. Now, half a standard deviation equals a *d* value of .50, which can be substituted into the first equation in Table 11.2 to yield a N_{needed} of 32[4] to achieve power of .80. Thus, with a sample size of 100, the authors had ample power to achieve one of the basic aims of their study, comparing rock musicians with the general population. Incidentally, rock musicians were found to be above average on Neuroticism and Openness, and below average on Agreeableness and Conscientiousness. Does this sound like any rock stars you know?

Example 2: Two-Sample *t*-Test

Suppose Gillespie and Myors also wanted to compare the personalities of singers and instrumentalists. In particular, they might have been interested in the idea that singers need to be more outgoing than instrumentalists in order to be the front person of their band. This hypothesis could be tested by comparing singers and instrumentalists on the trait of Extraversion. In an attempt to estimate the size of the effect they would need to detect, the authors noted that the reliability (r_{xx}) of Extraversion is given as .89 in the test manual (Costa & McCrae, 1992, p. 44). This value can be used to determine the standard error of the difference between two test scores (*SED*) (Gulliksen, 1950), which is just the standard error of measurement multiplied by $\sqrt{2}$ (i.e., $SED = SD \times \sqrt{1 - r_{xx}} \times \sqrt{2}$. In order to be 95% confident of a real difference in true scores, *SED* needs to be multiplied by 1.96, the value corresponding to a 5% level of chance. Thus the effect size to look for when comparing singers to instrumentalists on Extraversion is $d = SD \times \sqrt{1 - .89} \times \sqrt{2} \times 1.96 / SD = .92$, which is a difference of almost a full standard deviation. This value needs to be converted into r^2 via Equation 11.1 in order to use it in the second equation in Table 11.2. By Equation 11.1, $r^2 = .92^2 / (.92^2 + 4) = .17$ and the sample size needed to detect a significant difference in Extraversion between the two groups is $N_{needed} = 7.85 / .17 = 47$ according to the two-sample equation in Table 11.2. Thus Gillespie and Myors had plenty of power to observe a difference in Extraversion between singers and instrumentalists, assuming equal numbers of these musicians in their sample.

Example 3: Two-Sample *t*-Test With Unequal Sample Sizes

The previous example assumed that rock groups are made up of equal numbers of singers and instrumentalists; however, the typical four-person rock group is more likely to be composed of one lead singer and three instrumentalists (lead guitarist, bass guitarist, and drummer) for a ratio of instrumentalists to singers of 3:1. Thus Equation 11.3 would be more appropriate for converting *d* to r^2 than the use of Equation 11.1 in the previous example. As such $p = .25$ and $q = .75$ (i.e., about one quarter of the sample are expected to be singers, and the remaining three quarters are expected to be instrumentalists. In fact, there were 22 singers and 70 instrumentalists in Gillespie and Myors's sample, with 8 participants describing themselves primarily as songwriters. Assuming the same *d* as determined in Example 2, Equation 11.3 gives $r^2 = .92^2 / (.92^2 + 1 / (.25 \times .75) = .14$ and by the two-sample formula in Table 11.2, $N_{needed} = 7.85 / .14 = 57$. Ten more musicians are needed to achieve a power of .80 to compensate for the imbalance in the design. In any case, there was sufficient power in the study to detect this effect. As it turned out, singers *are* more extraverted than instrumentalists ($t(90) = 2.12, p < .05$).

Example 4: Matched-Sample *t*-Test

In the case of the matched-sample or repeated-measures *t*-test, there is an association between paired members in each group or between two scores obtained from the same individual. This association can be used to increase the power of the analysis. Such an analysis can be thought of as falling part way between the two equations shown in Table 11.2 and is handled by a slight adjustment to the one-sample formula. In this case, the one-sample formula is multiplied by a matching factor of $2(1 - \rho)$, where ρ is the estimated association (correlation) between the matched scores from each group. The matched-sample *t*-test is a special case of the one-sample *t*-test because members of each group are linked.

Suppose Gillespie and Myors wanted to test the hypothesis of Examples 2 and 3 that singers are more extraverted than instrumentalists, using musicians from the *same* band. In this case, participants in the study would be related by their common band membership. It is fairly likely that musicians are attracted to other musicians with similar tastes and interests, and this self-selection could result in bands whose members have somewhat similar personality traits. Suppose the correlation between personality traits of band members was thought to be small but positive, in the order of, say, .20. What sample size would Gillespie and Myors need to test for a difference between singers and instrumentalists on Extraversion in this case? From Example 2, we know the effect size we seek is .92, and we have just determined that $\rho = .20$, so incorporating the matching factor into the one-sample equation gives $N_{needed} = 7.85$ $/ .92^2 \times 2(1 - .20) = 15$ pairs of musicians. This would require a total sample of 30 participants in the study, which is less than the N_{needed} in Examples 2 and 3, illustrating the power of matching. Unfortunately, Gillespie and Myors did not collect information about band membership with which to perform a matched-sample analysis.

Example 5: Significance of a Correlation Coefficient

Intercorrelations between the five domains of the NEO-PI-R range between .02 and .53 (Costa & McCrae, 1992, p. 100). Suppose Gillespie and Myors wanted to look for correlations of similar magnitudes among the traits and facets of their rock musicians. What sample size would be required to sensibly look for such correlations with a reasonable chance of success? Applying the two-sample formula in Table 11.2, which uses a correlation as the effect size, when $r = .53$, $N_{needed} = 7.85 / .53^2 = 28$, whereas when $r = .02$, $N_{needed} = 7.85 / .02^2 = 19,625$. Clearly Gillespie and Myors had plenty of power for detecting correlations above .50, which would be considered large effects ($.50 \times .50 = .25$, see Table 11.1), but nowhere near enough power to detect very small correlations. From this result, you can readily see that no one should seriously look for correlations in the order of .02, which should probably be thought of as effectively zero. Even conventionally small correlations require sample sizes of almost 800 ($7.85 /$ $.01 = 785$).

Example 6: Analysis of Variance

A simple and effective way of determining the sample size needed in ANOVA is to identify the smallest simple effect of interest and work out the N_{needed} for that. By multiplying half the N_{needed} obtained by the number of cells in the design, the total sample required in the study can be found. For example, suppose you have a fairly complicated $2 \times 2 \times 3$ factorial design and have identified the comparison between the first and last cells as a meaningful question. You could estimate an appropriate value for d, or use one of the conventions supplied in Table 11.1, convert it into r^2, and apply it to the two-sample formula in Table 11.2. Half of the N_{needed} obtained from that calculation is the sample size needed in each cell, so this value can be multiplied by 12, the number of cells in the design, to obtain the total sample size required. This approach aims for a balanced design, which is always the most powerful.

For example, suppose Gillespie and Myors asked the instrumentalists in their sample to identify the instrument they played in the hope of finding personality differences between instrumentalists. The options provided in the questionnaire were guitar, keyboards, bass, drums, and other. This question could be answered by a series of one-way ANOVAs, one for each NEO-PI-R trait as the dependent variable and type of instrument as the independent variable. Such an approach is reasonable because the five traits are not highly correlated, so a multivariate analysis would not differ that much from a series of one-way ANOVAs. What sample size would be needed to detect personality differences among the different instrumentalists?

Example 2 above estimated the effect size in seeking a difference in Extraversion to be $d = .92$ and found $N_{needed} = 47$ for a simple two-group analysis. This results in $47 / 2 = 24$ for each cell in the current more complicated factorial design. Now there are five cells (guitarists, keyboard players, bass players, drummers, and others) with each cell requiring 24 musicians for a total sample of $5 \times 24 = 120$. Gillespie and Myors did not have 120 instrumentalists in their sample so did not achieve desired levels of power for this analysis.

Other Uses of Power Analysis

This chapter has emphasized the most practical application of power analysis, namely the determination of sample size for research. It should be evident that a number of other potentially useful applications also exist. Given that power analysis involves a system of four factors—power, sample size (N), effect size (ES) and α—four different applications of power analysis are possible in which any one factor is solved in terms of the other three. See Murphy and Myors (2004) for a detailed discussion of each application.

This chapter has deemphasized solving for power and α, preferring to leave them fixed at their conventional levels of .80 and .05; however, many researchers like to solve for power in order to determine how under- (or over-) powered their research actually is and how much larger (or smaller) their study needs to be in order to achieve more acceptable levels of power. The formulas in Table 11.2 can give an answer to this question, although they do not provide an actual power estimate. Instead of specifying the scope of the study in terms of power, the formulas scale the study in terms of N, which is probably the most meaningful unit anyway. For example, if you initially planned to access 100 participants and the two-sample formula suggests that you really need something closer to 150, you know that your study needs to be 50% larger than you had originally planned. Conversely, if the formula suggests that you only need 80 participants, you can reduce the scale of your participant recruiting effort by 20%. Whether specified directly in terms of power or in terms of N, this information helps researchers appreciate how under- or overpowered their research proposal actually is.

Another application of power analysis is to solve for ES, which tells you the smallest effect you can reasonably expect to find, given a particular sample size. This question can be answered by solving for ES for a given N in the formulas shown in Table 11.2. The value obtained represents the smallest ES (r^2 or d) you are likely to detect for the sample size given (see Exercise 7 below). You can then compare this ES with the conventions tabulated in Table 11.1 to determine whether it would be considered small, medium, or large.

Finally, it is possible to solve for α. Doing so will tell you the significance level you should aim for in order to achieve the level of power you desire, given a particular N and the ES in your particular area of research. Unfortunately, there is no way to do this using the methods presented here. Nevertheless, solving for α, given a desired level of power, is probably the best method of rationally

balancing Type I and Type II errors in any particular analysis. It should be acknowledged that departing from conventional levels of α may leave you vulnerable to criticism from reviewers and journal editors. Readers interested in solving for α or varying more than one factor in a power analysis simultaneously are referred to Murphy and Myors (2004) for appropriate methods.

SUMMARY

Power analysis has become an essential tool for planning effective research. Prior to the widespread appreciation of the importance of power, studies were often conducted with inadequate levels of power. This led some fields of research to become populated with small sample studies and a plethora of inconclusive results. The rise of meta-analysis has gone some way toward improving this situation by creating surrogate large-sample studies through the pooling of many smaller ones, but the best solution lies in the conduct of adequately powered primary research using larger samples. In general, larger samples are required when α is low, ES is small, and one is aiming for high power. The most practical application of power analysis lies in the determination of sample size, and this is a relatively straightforward process for a wide range of tests of specific hypotheses if one is prepared to adopt the convention of aiming for a power of .80. Such a level of power provides a reasonable balance between Type I and Type II errors for many purposes. Researchers who pay attention to power during the planning stages of their research are likely to design better studies, and this can only be to the long-term benefit of their particular field.

NOTES

1. If the treatment is believed to affect the dependent variable's variance as well as its mean, then the standard deviation of the control group should be used, without pooling.

2. You can think of *variance* as a generalization of the concept of *difference* because, if things don't differ, they are constant and therefore have no

variance. So *explaining* or *accounting for* variance amounts to explaining why your participants differed in various ways, such as because they had different treatments or because they scored differently on some variables. *Percentage of variance accounted for* is the extent to which we can explain, predict, or understand the differences we observe among our participants.

3. Because the population standard deviations as well as the population means were available from the test norms, the authors actually used *z*-tests. This does not really affect the current discussion, however, because *z*-tests are virtually identical to *t*-tests in samples of 100 or more.

4. The formula gives a value of 31.4, which must be rounded up to the next whole person.

EXERCISES

Exercise 1: One-Sample *t*-Test

Suppose Gillespie and Myors wanted to identify the personality traits for which rock musicians would be considered *very high* or *very low*. What sample size would they need to use to detect effects of this magnitude? Note that Costa and McCrae (1992, p. 13) define these extreme scores as those falling 1.5 standard deviations above or below the population mean.

ANSWER: 4

COMMENT: If Gillespie and Myors had sampled only four rock musicians, none of their results would have been significant because $d = 1.5$ is a highly unrealistic estimate of the true effect size in this field of study. On average, rock musicians' personalities are not that extreme.

Exercise 2: Two-Sample *t*-Test

What if the effect size for determining the difference in Extraversion between singers and instrumentalists was simply obtained by reference to the effect size conventions rather than through the analysis of *SED*? What would be the sample size needed to find a medium effect?

ANSWER: 134

COMMENT: Gillespie and Myors's study would benefit from a larger sample if an effect of this magnitude was sought.

Exercise 3: Two-Sample *t*-Test

What if Gillespie and Myors hypothesized that singers, on average, would exhibit more "attitude" than instrumentalists, given their higher profile on stage? Assuming that this hypothesis translates into the hypothesis that singers would be less agreeable than instrumentalists, what sample size would be needed to test for a significant difference in Agreeableness? Note that the reliability of the Agreeableness scale is .86 (Costa & McCrae, 1992, p. 44).

ANSWER:

$$d = \sqrt{1-.86} \times \sqrt{2} \times 1.96 = 1.04$$

$$r^2 = 1.04^2 / (1.04^2 + 4) = .21$$

$$N_{\text{needed}} = 7.85 / .21 = 38$$

COMMENT: Why do we need a smaller sample size to detect a less reliable difference? Because the difference we can detect with confidence needs to be larger.

Exercise 4: Two-Sample t-Test With Unequal Sample Sizes

Repeat the analysis in Exercise 3 using the more realistic assumption that instrumentalists outnumber singers by 3:1.

ANSWER:

$$p = .25 \text{ (singers)}$$

$$q = .75 \text{ (instrumentalists)}$$

$$r^2 = 1.04^2 / (1.04^2 + 1 / (.25 \times .75)) = .17$$

$$N_{needed} = 7.85 / .17 = 47$$

COMMENT: Incidentally, singers are less agreeable than instrumentalists ($t(90) = -2.05, p < .05$).

Exercise 5: Two-Sample t-Test With Unequal Sample Sizes

Repeat the analysis in Exercise 4 assuming that typical rock bands also contain keyboards.

ANSWER:
Now the ratio of instrumentalists to singers is 4:1 so $p = .20$ (singers) and $q = .80$ (instrumentalists).

$$r^2 = 1.04^2 / (1.04^2 + 1 / (.20 \times .80)) = .15$$

$$N_{needed} = 7.85 / .15 = 53$$

Exercise 6: Matched-Sample t-Test

Suppose the similarity between members of the same band was .50. What sample size would be needed to compare singers and instrumentalists in terms of Extraversion, assuming $d = .92$?

ANSWER: $N_{needed} = 7.85 / .92^2 \times 2(1 - .50) = 10$ pairs, or a total N of 20 musicians.

Exercise 7: Significance of a Correlation Coefficient

What was the smallest correlation coefficient that Gillespie and Myors could reasonably expect to detect with a sample of 100?

ANSWER: About $r = \sqrt{7.85/100} = .28$

COMMENT: Only 2 of the 10 correlations between NEO-PI-R traits were larger than .28: however, personality traits should exhibit divergent validity, so we would not expect them to be highly correlated.

Exercise 8: Analysis of Variance

Rather than deriving an effect size estimate from the reliability of the test, what if a moderate effect ($d = .50$) was sought? What would be the total sample size required to detect personality differences of this magnitude among instrumentalists in Gillespie and Myors's study using an analysis of variance?

ANSWER: This analysis involves the two-sample case because each instrumentalist is assumed to only fall in one cell of the design. As such, $r^2 = .50^2 / (.50^2 + 4) = .06$ by Equation 11.1. N_{needed} for a single cell = $7.85 / .06 / 2 = 66$ by the two-sample formula in Table 11.2, which gives a total sample size of $5 \times 66 = 330$ required for the study.

COMMENT: Gillespie and Myors's study was not sufficiently powerful to attempt this analysis.

RECOMMENDED READINGS

Cohen, J. (1988). *Statistical power analysis for the behavioral sciences* (2nd ed.). Hillsdale, NJ: Lawrence Erlbaum.

Cohen, J. (1992). A power primer. *Psychological Bulletin, 112,* 155–159.

Murphy, K. R. (2002). Using power analysis to evaluate and improve research. In S. G. Rogelberg (Ed.), *Handbook of research methods in industrial and organisational psychology* (pp. 119–137). Oxford, UK: Blackwell.

Murphy, K. R., & Myors, B. (2004). *Statistical power analysis: A simple and general model for traditional and modern significance tests.* Mahwah, NJ: Lawrence Erlbaum.

REFERENCES

Cohen, J. (1962). The statistical power of abnormal-social psychological research: A review. *Journal of Abnormal and Social Psychology, 69,* 145–153.

Cohen, J. (1988). *Statistical power analysis for the behavioral sciences* (Rev. ed.). Hillsdale, NJ: Lawrence Erlbaum.

Costa, P. T., Jr., & McCrae, R. R. (1992). *Revised NEO Personality Inventory (NEO-PI-R) and NEO Five-Factor Inventory (NEO-FFI) professional manual.* Odessa, FL: Psychological Assessment Resources.

Erdfelder, E., Faul, F., & Buchner, A. (1996). GPOWER: A general power analysis program. *Behavior Research Methods, Instruments & Computers, 28,* 1–11.

Gillespie, W., & Myors, B. (2000). Personality of rock musicians. *Psychology of Music, 28,* 154–165.

Gulliksen, H. (1950). *Theory of mental tests.* New York: Wiley.

Hoenig, J. M., & Heisey, D. M. (2001). The abuse of power: The pervasive fallacy of power calculations for data analysis. *The American Statistician, 55,* 19–24.

Kraemer, H. C., & Thiemann, S. (1987). *How many subjects?* Newbury Park, CA: Sage.

Lipsey, M. W. (1990). *Design sensitivity.* Newbury Park, CA: Sage.

Lipsey, M. W., & Wilson, D. B. (1993). The efficacy of psychological, educational and behavioral treatment: Confirmation from meta-analysis. *American Psychologist, 48,* 1181–1209.

Murphy, K. R., & Myors, B. (2004). *Statistical power analysis: A simple and general model for traditional and modern significance tests.* Mahwah, NJ: Lawrence Erlbaum.

Rosenthal, R. (1993). Cumulating evidence. In G. Keren & C. Lewis (Ed.), *A handbook for data analysis in the behavioral sciences: Methodological issues* (pp. 519–559). Mahwah, NJ: Lawrence Erlbaum.

Sedlmeier, F. L., & Gigerenzer, G. (1989). Do studies of statistical power have an effect on the power of studies? *Psychological Bulletin, 105,* 309–316.

Thomas, L., & Krebs, C. J. (1997). A review of statistical power analysis software. *Bulletin of the Ecological Society of America, 78,* 126–139.

Wilkinson, L., & Task Force. (1999). Statistical methods in psychology journals. *American Psychologist, 54,* 594–604.

PART III

DATA COLLECTION

12

Applying for Approval to Conduct Research With Human Participants

Don M. Dell
Lyle D. Schmidt
Naomi M. Meara

A task that is absolutely necessary for conducting research with human participants is having the proposed research reviewed by an institutional review board (IRB). This review is every bit as important as the substantive review your adviser or dissertation reading committee will provide, but the focus will be different. To accomplish the IRB review effectively and efficiently, it is helpful to know not only the specific procedures and forms used at your university but also the rationale behind the formation of IRBs and the ethical and deliberative aspects of their responsibilities.

Development of
Institutional Review Boards

Any institution in the United States in which research involving human participants is conducted, supported, or otherwise subject to regulation by almost any federal department or agency must have a procedure for protecting the research participants. The federal policy that regulates the procedure is presented in the Code of Federal Regulations, Title 45 CFR Part 46, as revised in 1991. This policy required that each institution "engaged" in federally supported human subjects research negotiate and have approved an "Assurance" of protection for human research participants. This assurance is filed with a unit within the Department of Health and Human Services (DHHS) that implements the regulations for the protection of human subjects. That unit is now called the Office for Human Research Protections (OHRP). Historically there were three types of such assurances, but recent legislative action has replaced all of these with a new Federal-wide Assurance (FWA) effective not later than December 31, 2003. The FWA is intended to

AUTHORS' NOTE: Except when the term *subjects* appears in the title of a document (e.g., the Belmont Report), we have instead adopted the use of the term *participants*.

create a new registry of institutional review boards and to streamline the assurance process. If your institution has negotiated an assurance with OHRP, you should find your institution listed on the OHRP Web site's list of institutions with OHRP-approved assurances (see http://www.hhs.gov/ohrp/assurances/assurances_index.html). Your own institution's directory should also include a listing under *Human Subjects (Participants) Review Committee,* or *Institutional Review Board for the Protection of Human Subjects (Participants),* or some combination of these terms. This office should be able to provide you the guidelines and materials necessary to apply for committee approval for research with human participants at your institution. In addition, your departmental colleagues or academic adviser may have not only this information but an understanding of the process based on their experiences in securing approval from the IRB.

The term most commonly used to identify the body charged with protection of human participants in research is *institutional review board* (IRB). This is an administrative body established to protect the rights and welfare of persons recruited to participate in research activities conducted within the institution. It may have one or more sections, which may be designated, for example, *Social and Behavioral Sciences Review Committee,* or *Biomedical Sciences Review Committee,* depending on the area of research to be reviewed and the size of your institution. The committees review research protocols, which you, the researcher, prepare following a format that the committee specifies. These protocols are descriptions of a research program or individual investigation presented in sufficient detail for the committee to (a) assess the nature of the requirements of the human participant in the research and (b) determine whether provisions have been made for adequate protection of the participants' rights and welfare.

Why have IRBs been established? Although regard for the welfare of human recipients of professional services, as in physicians' Hippocratic oath, is of long standing, the history of human subjects' protection in the United States began in 1947. Abuses of prisoners in Nazi concentration camps by physicians and scientists

conducting biomedical experiments were made public after the defeat of Nazi Germany in 1945. During the Nuremberg War Crimes Trials, the Nuremberg Code was drafted as a set of standards for judging physicians and scientists who had committed such offenses. The code became a model for later codes in the principles it set forth for the ethical treatment of human subjects who participate in research. First among these principles was that "the voluntary consent of the human subject is absolutely essential" (Office for Protection from Research Risks [OPRR], 1993, Ap. 6, p. A1). Other principles include a favorable risk-benefit ratio, the avoidance of harm and suffering, protecting participants from injury, the necessity that investigators be qualified scientists, and freedom for participants to withdraw at any time. An elaboration of these principles was made by the World Medical Association's Declaration of Helsinki in 1964 and revised in 1975, 1983, and 1989 (OPRR, 1993, Ap. 6, p. A3). Both the Nuremberg Code and Declaration of Helsinki were concerned with medical research.

Government regulations protecting human subjects in the United States first appeared in 1966 as National Institutes of Health policies for the protection of human subjects. Passage of the National Research Act in 1974 created the National Commission for the Protection of Human Subjects of Biomedical and Behavioral Research. The commission's final report was submitted in 1978 under the title of *The Belmont Report: Ethical Principles and Guidelines for the Protection of Human Subjects of Research.* The name came from the meeting place of the commission in the Belmont Conference Center of the Smithsonian Institution. The report is reprinted in what was then called the Office for Protection from Research Risks' 1993 publication: *Protecting Human Research Subjects,* Appendix 6. It can also be accessed from the OHRP Web site (see section titled "Policy Guidance" on that Web site).

The Belmont Report distinguished between research and practice and identified three basic ethical principles in research with humans. Research was considered "an activity designed to test an hypothesis, permit conclusions to be drawn, and thereby to develop or contribute to generalizable knowledge" (National Commission for the Protection of Human Subjects of Biomedical and Behavioral Research [NCPHS-BBR], 1979, p. 3). The report considered practice to refer to "interventions that are designed solely to enhance the well-being of an individual patient or client and that have a reasonable expectation of success" (p. 3). The three basic ethical principles discussed by the commission were respect for persons, beneficence, and justice. *Respect* involved two convictions: that persons should be treated as autonomous individuals and that persons with diminished autonomy should be protected. *Beneficence* was understood as an obligation to protect subjects by maximizing possible benefits and minimizing possible harms. *Justice* was concerned with the fair distribution of the burdens and benefits of research.

In response to the Belmont Report, the U.S. Department of Health and Human Services in 1981 revised its regulations. They were codified in 1981 as Title 45 Part 46 of the Code of Federal Regulations, Protection of Human Subjects (45 CFR 46). Revisions became effective in 1983 and 1991, the latter involving the adoption of the federal policy for the protection of human participants by 16 agencies of the federal government that support, conduct, or regulate research that involves human participants. Subpart A of this code, often referred to as "the Common Rule," applies "to all research involving human subjects conducted, supported or otherwise subject to regulation" by these agencies (45 CFR 46, 1991, p. 4). It is this Common Rule that is the basis for the activity of most IRBs and to which we give most of our attention. For completeness, however, we should also note that Subparts B–D of 45 CFR 46 comprise additional DHHS protections for special populations including pregnant women, prisoners, and children. Other sections of the CFR that have implications for research with humans are 21 CFR 50 and 51, regulations applying to research involving products regulated by the Food and Drug Administration, and 34 CFR 97, 98, and 99, Department of Education policies on the protection of human research subjects, protection of pupil rights, and Family Educational Rights and Privacy Act, respectively. We should also note the Health Insurance Portability and Accountability Act of 1996 (HIPAA), which applies to health information created or maintained by health providers.

What research requirements derive from the three basic ethical principles described in the Belmont Report? The first of these, respect for persons, underlies the requirement of informed consent. Research participants, to the extent they are capable, must be allowed to decide what shall or shall not happen to them. This process is said to contain the elements of information, comprehension, and voluntariness. Information ordinarily includes the research procedures, their purposes, risks and possible benefits, alternative procedures if treatment is involved, the opportunity for participants to ask questions, and a statement they may withdraw from the research at any time. Although it is impossible to know all related information, the standard is generally interpreted to mean that the information communicated to potential participants emphasizes factors important enough to influence a decision to participate. Such information would include what participants will be doing, how their data will be used, and, if the data are not anonymous, what measures are in place to assure confidentiality. Comprehension means that the information is conveyed in manner and context so that participants understand what is presented to them. Limited capacity to comprehend may require some persons (e.g., children) to be represented by third parties, and even then, such persons must be allowed to choose whether to participate or not (that is, to give assent rather than consent), unless the research involves a treatment that has some probability of success and is not otherwise available. Voluntariness requires that the consent to participate be given without coercion or undue influence. An example of undue influence is an excessive or unwarranted reward offered for participation.

The second basic ethical principle, beneficence, underlies the requirement of a risk-benefit analysis to minimize the probability and severity of possible harm to participants and balance any such potential harm against the probability and magnitude of anticipated benefits to health or welfare of the individual and possibly others. The analysis involves a systematic assessment of the nature and scope of risks and benefits. This offers researchers an opportunity to evaluate the research design and assist prospective participants in their decision to participate. Several considerations are necessary, among them the following:

- Brutal or inhumane treatment of human participants is never justified.
- Risks should be only at the level necessary to the research objective, and lower risk alternatives should be a major goal in research design.
- The appropriateness of involving vulnerable populations must be demonstrated.
- Risks and benefits must be made obvious in the consent process.

The third basic ethical principle, justice, underlies the requirement that there be fairness in the selection of participants to equitably distribute the burdens and benefits of research. At the individual level, this means not offering potentially beneficial research to only favored individuals (e.g., college students or young professionals) and risky research to less favored ones (e.g., persons on welfare or prison inmates). At the social level, justice may be served by a preferential order, such as adults before children, and by avoiding, when possible, some populations already burdened by their conditions or circumstances, such as institutionalized persons. Injustice may occur when participants are selected largely for convenience, as in the case of ethnic minorities, very ill persons, or students who happen to be in settings where research is conducted or whose conditions may make them more vulnerable to manipulation or likely to consent. In general, justice would suggest that those groups who may benefit from research also should be the ones approached to participate in it. Some would argue, however, that particularly when no risk is present, individuals have a moral duty to their community to participate in research that could benefit others.

The best known early code for conduct of social and behavioral research was *Ethical Principles in the Conduct of Research with Human Participants* first published by the American Psychological Association (APA) in 1973 and revised in 1982 (APA, 1973, 1982). The impetus for the development of these standards was professional and public criticism of

social science research following Milgrim's work (1965, 1974) and other studies where there were questions about the appropriateness of the deception used, informed consent, and harmful effects for participants (for a critique of such work, see Bok, 1989). These criticisms prompted the APA to conduct a comprehensive review of research ethics. Similar to the procedures employed for the development of the original APA ethics code (Hobbs, 1948), an empirical approach was implemented. APA members were surveyed and asked to describe research involving ethical questions. Approximately 5,000 such descriptions were received. Ethical principles derived from these samples and other sources were circulated for APA membership review, then revised and circulated again. The principles developed from this process formed the basis for the publication and its revision.

It should be noted, however, that the first publication of the APA ethics code, *Ethical Standards of Psychologists,* (APA, 1953) contained standards for research. These concerned the psychologists' responsibility for adequately planning and conducting research, reporting research results, and managing relations with research subjects. Specific principles included protecting subjects' welfare by not exposing them to unnecessary emotional stress and by removing harmful aftereffects, should any occur; fully informing subjects when a danger of serious aftereffects exists and giving them an opportunity to decline participation; withholding information or giving misinformation only when clearly required by the research problem and when the above principles are observed; not revealing the identity of research subjects without explicit permission; and fulfilling obligations to subjects that were offered in return for their cooperation in the research (Schmidt & Meara, 1984, p. 66).

Subsequent revisions of the APA ethics code maintain sections devoted to research and contain these same general principles. In addition, the APA Science Directorate Web page has a section on research ethics that includes links to federal legislation and regulations affecting research with humans, other professional ethics codes, training resources, and an extensive bibliography on these topics (see www.apa.org/science/researchethics.html).

The current code, "Ethical Principles of Psychologists and Code of Conduct" (APA, 2002) contains one specific section with 14 standards related to research with human participants. These standards cover many of the same topics as the 1953 and 1992 codes (APA, 1953, 1992), such as informed consent, deception, and honoring commitments. These sections, as well, are concerned with the same general principles as set forth in the Belmont Report (respect for persons, beneficence, and justice) and relate to the focal issues (discussed below) of an IRB review of research proposals. In addition to these standards, the current APA code (APA, 2002) contains several related to the integrity of researchers, including the topics of conflict of interest, plagiarism, publication credit, and responsibilities of professionals who review the research of others for publication. There is in the 2002 code a specific standard (Standard 8.01) dealing directly with institutional approval.

Where institutional approval is required, psychologists provide accurate information about their research proposals and obtain approval prior to conducting the research. They conduct the research in accordance with the approved research protocol (APA, 2002, p. 1069).

FOCAL POINTS OF AN IRB REVIEW

What are likely to be focal points of an IRB review of your protocol? They follow from the research requirements and their underlying ethical principles described above and are discussed in detail in the *Protecting Human Research Subjects: Institutional Review Board Guidebook* (OPRR, 1993). Your university's IRB will likely have a detailed checklist of the information and materials they require for a review.

Informed Consent

One focal point will be *informed consent.* The elements of information, comprehension, and voluntariness are important considerations for reviewers of protocols. Is the research described in sufficient detail so that prospective subjects can know what will occur to them and

in a manner that will allow them to understand what the description means? Are the circumstances of the invitation to participate such that the consent is freely given?

The federal requirements as to the information to be provided prospective participants are reported in the *Code of Federal Regulations* (45 CFR 46), in the *IRB Guidebook* (OPRR, 1993, also available on the OHRP Web site) and in the policy and procedures materials of your institutional IRB. Explicit reference to these requirements also is made in ethical Standard 8 of the APA code. The reviewers will examine your protocol to determine if you have satisfied these requirements according to your institutions' and the reviewers' interpretations of them. They may be especially concerned about the following: Is there adequate content in the consent process and is it expressed in language and format understandable to the potential participant? If English is not the first language of some or all of your participants, is the request for participation presented in language that will allow informed consent on their part? Have you provided for the appropriate documentation of the consent? If you are requesting a waiver of the requirement of written consent, have you provided sufficient justification, consistent with federal and your IRB's policies? If your research involves existing data records or proposes to videotape or film subjects without their knowledge, have you satisfied the special consent requirements of these situations? And if you propose to deceive subjects or only partially disclose what will occur to them, have you provided full justification of the necessity for this, consistent with IRB requirements?

Risk-Benefit Analysis

A second focal point will be *risk-benefit analysis.* If participants in research are exposed to risk, their participation should be justified by anticipated benefits to them or to society. Risk is the probability that physical, psychological, social, or economic harm will occur from participating in the research. *Minimal risk* is a probability of harm not greater than ordinarily present in daily life or in routine physical or psychological examinations or tests.

The members of IRBs are typically very concerned about any risks that accrue to the participants and what, if any, benefits the research can provide for the individual participants or society in general. As Beauchamp and Childress (1994) note,

> In submitting a research protocol involving human subjects to an institutional research board (IRB) for approval, an investigator is expected to array the risks to subjects and probable benefits to both subjects and society, and then to explain why the probable benefits outweigh the risks. (Beauchamp & Childress, 2001, p. 194)

The members of an IRB usually make a reasoned rather than a numerical or statistical assessment of the balance between risks and benefits. A risk-benefit analysis involves the principles of beneficence, respect for persons, and justice. For example, if the research appears to have no potential benefit, it is unlikely to be approved. Sometimes IRBs will note that a design is below acceptable scientific standards. Although such a study may not contain any significant risks, the interpretability of the results obtained can be so ambiguous that there are no apparent benefits either. Badly designed research also can waste participants' time and research pool resources and thus is not fair to either participants or other researchers who need individuals for more beneficial research. If consent forms do not show proper respect for subjects (for example, by containing misinformation or not clearly stating potential risks and benefits), the IRB will most likely ask you to revise the forms to meet this important criterion. In preparing your protocol, you will be asked not only to state the risks and benefits for the IRB members but also to demonstrate how the informed consent and other information you provide for subjects makes this information clear so that they can make informed decisions with respect to participating.

Privacy and Confidentiality

A third focal point of an IRB review will be privacy and confidentiality. *Privacy* has to do with one's control over the extent, timing, or circumstances of sharing physical, behavioral, or intellectual aspects of oneself with others. *Confidentiality* relates to what is done with information participants have disclosed in the course of their participation in your research. They have a right to expect that it will not be revealed to others except as specified in the original request for participation or unless specific, subsequent permission is obtained.

A research procedure that may seem routine and noninvasive to an investigator can require individuals to disclose information that is very personal if not interpersonally threatening to some participants. Often they are asked for information that they have revealed to no one else, or perhaps to one or two intimates whom they trust. Therefore issues of privacy and confidentiality are critical to sound research and the approval of your proposal.

Researchers have implicit contracts with participants to do what they say and to treat the information obtained in a manner to which they agreed in advance. It seems important to remember as well that although a person may have agreed to a certain use of the information, he or she has a right to remove identifiable information from a data set at any time. In general, it is better not to have any kind of identification in data files (electronic or hard copy) that could point to a specific person. When such identification is necessary, extra precautions must be taken that the data do not become available to anyone except those who have been specified in the original research agreement.

The APA code (APA, 2002) provides guidance with respect to invading one's privacy. Standard 8.03 raises special cautions in filming or recording subjects, and Standard 8.07 discusses circumstances under which deception may be permissible. A good general rule to follow is that potential participants have the right to be left alone and not be repeatedly asked to participate in research. Some will argue that however important the project or potential benefit, researchers should not pursue a prospective participant beyond a simple refusal. If the person says "no," the researcher does not have warrant to mount a sales campaign about the virtues of the project or the obligation of the individual. If individuals have a moral duty to help society, it is not up to researchers to badger them into it or make individual decisions about who ought to participate in a given project. The best attitude for a researcher to adopt would seem to be that if persons agree to participate in research, they are going beyond duty. Their motive may be to help the researcher or contribute to some larger good or secure some minor benefit for themselves, such as extra credit in a course. Whatever the motive, potential participants are free to refuse, and when they agree to participate, what they tell us should be used only for science. Information obtained through research should not be trivialized, used to demean individuals, be the source of gossip, or in other ways betray trust in the research enterprise.

Selection of Participants

A fourth focal point will be the *selection of participants.* IRBs attempt to determine that the selection is equitable with respect to fairness in the distribution of burdens and benefits of the research. There are likely to be questions such as the following: Will the burdens of participating fall on those groups most likely to benefit from it? Will repeated demands on any participating group be avoided when possible? Does the research justify a particular participant group? If vulnerable individuals are proposed as research participants, could the research be conducted on other less vulnerable persons?

Human research is time-consuming and often hard to manage. As a result, the temptation is to look to convenient, captive audiences—college students, school children, prisoners, and others who are institutionalized by the state or federal government—as a source of participants in our research. These—the poor, the uneducated, the dying (in the case of medical research), and others—may bear an undue burden in psychological research and may realize an insufficient share of the benefits. We are coming to realize as well that those who are culturally different may be put upon more than others to be research participants. Clarity about what is just and about one's own taken-for-granted scientific and everyday assumptions is critical for accurate science. Respect and sensitivity to these issues are essential for ethical science. Psychologists need to guard against the possibility that in using these readily identifiable populations we may violate the principle of justice. It is for these reasons that the special protections for

special populations of Subparts B–D of 45 CFR 46 were developed. As we discuss below, this issue can be more complicated when there are incentives for research. They need to be equally distributed but not be coercive, particularly with more vulnerable populations.

Incentives for Participation

A fifth focal point may be the *incentives* offered for participation. In order to ensure that subjects' decisions to participate in research are voluntary, IRBs will try to determine if consent has been solicited without coercion or undue influence. Are subtle or obvious threats present in the solicitation, or will participants be compensated so excessively their refusal is rendered unlikely?

A fine line exists between respecting and appreciating the time and effort of research participants (and thus offering some reward or incentive) and making the incentives so large that the result is undue influence. For example, offering extra credit in a psychology class seems appropriate if students can earn the same credit in other ways with approximately the same investment of time and energy. Requiring students to participate in research to earn a significant portion of their course grade (say 10 to 30%) may be coercive. It would be difficult to argue in such circumstances that one's agreement to participate is, in fact, voluntary; it seems more reasonable to argue that this important condition for informed consent is absent. The current APA code (APA, 2002) offers us guidance on these issues. For example, Standard 8.06(a) states the following:

> Psychologists make reasonable efforts to avoid offering excessive or inappropriate financial or other inducements for research participation when such inducements are likely to coerce participation. (p. 1070)

Researchers have to be cautious, as well, when they have a special relationship with potential subjects. For example, teachers and counselors have more power than students or clients and must be sensitive to that fact if they are recruiting participants from among their classes or clients. Such power differential can make potential participants believe that they have no real choice. The more powerful one is, the more careful he or she has to be to respect potential participants' right to refuse. There is a balance to be achieved between possibly changing the nature of a client-counselor relationship for some anticipated research benefit and being faithful to the implied contract that the therapeutic relationship represents (Meara & Schmidt, 1991). Again, the APA code (APA, 2002) might offer some assistance here. Standard 6.05 raises cautions and suggests guidelines with respect to the use of barter in exchange for psychological services, and Standard 8.05(b) speaks specifically to the issue of the psychologist's responsibilities when offering psychological services as incentives for research participation. For most graduate students conducting research, barter may be a less significant issue, as they are not usually in a position to offer excessive amounts of course credit or extended psychological services. Standard 8.04(a) (APA, 2002), however, is important as graduate students are often teaching assistants and need to be sensitive to how students may interpret requests or suggestions from their teachers. The standard reads as follows:

> When psychologists conduct research with clients/ patients, students or subordinates as participants, psychologists take steps to protect the prospective participants from adverse consequences of declining or withdrawing from participation. (p. 1069)

Members of an IRB will want to be certain that potential participants are protected in this regard. In short, they will look closely at research protocols to assure themselves that the procedures and precautions outlined do not treat subjects in a manner that is explicitly or implicitly exploitive or coercive.

PREPARATION FOR AN IRB REVIEW

One of the first things one can do in preparing an IRB proposal is to plan ahead. Without such planning, individuals often find that participants may be available and the project may be ready for data collection, but approval has not yet been granted. IRBs usually have regular meetings

about once per month. You need to know when yours meets and how far in advance of the meeting they need your protocol. Knowing these facts is an important consideration in scheduling your own work. Also, it is helpful, if you are a student, to know the policies of your adviser. University IRBs require that faculty members be listed as one of the investigators on student research. You need to know, therefore, how much time your sponsor will require to read your proposal and how long it might take you to revise it.

You have to know how to obtain IRB approval forms. Are they available online, or must you visit the IRB office? Each university develops its own forms, but you can see an example of such forms on the Web site of the Office of Responsible Research Practices at Ohio State University (www.orrp.ohio-state.edu/). After you complete the forms, you need to ask your sponsor or supervisor to review them. Be sure to allow time for possible revisions. If you are completing one for the first time, it is helpful if you can have access to a protocol in a similar area of research that has already been approved. Studying one that has been successful alerts you to how other individuals have addressed some of the focal issues we have discussed above and gives you information with respect to such things as different ways of expressing important issues in an informed consent document or describing your research instruments. Usually your adviser, other faculty members, or students may be willing to share examples of their protocols that have already been approved.

When you submit the protocol, you might ask if it is permissible for you to attend the meeting when your proposal is being reviewed. If not, it is helpful, if possible, to attend an IRB meeting before you complete your protocol, but after you are familiar with what the form requires.

The attitude with which one enters into the process of completing a research protocol is important. Often students, and some faculty as well, think that the IRB is an adversary or, at best, just one more time-consuming hurdle they have to surmount. It can be helpful to remember that, for the most part, members of the IRB want what you want: ethical, competent research. You try to achieve this through knowledge of your discipline and your research problem, methods, and design and by careful planning, as well as by studying the ethical principles that the government, your institution, and the APA think important. To this list, the IRB members add their experience of dealing with many proposals and the deliberative process during which viewpoints can be exchanged about the strengths and potential problems of proposals. Planning, attention to detail, modeling the work of others, watching the deliberations of an IRB, and understanding the communality of your goals with those of an IRB can facilitate the process of having your protocol approved. Such steps can make the process efficient, educational, and even enjoyable.

EXERCISES

1. Use the OHRP Web site to determine if your institution has a FWA. Does it have a registered IRB?

2. Use the OHRP Web site to access and read the Belmont Report.

3. Determine what special protections are required in order to obtain permission to use incarcerated persons as participants in research.

4. Determine what consent procedures are appropriate for non-English-speaking participants.

5. Log on to the OHRP Web site (www.hhs.gov/ohrp/ humansubjects/guidance/decisioncharts.htm) and review the decision charts presented there to determine if a project you are considering needs review and, if so, whether it qualifies for expedited review.

RECOMMENDED READINGS

Bok, S. (1989). Deceptive social science research. In *Lying: Moral choice in public and private life* (2nd ed., pp. 183–202). New York: Vintage Books.

The philosopher Sissela Bok critically examines the use of deception in social and behavioral science research. In particular, she focuses on how "disguises" and "cover stories" can interfere with a prospective research participant's right to an informed choice, harm both researchers and participants, and erode public trust in research.

Pritchard, I. A. (2002). Travellers and trolls: Practitioner research and institutional review boards. *Educational Researcher, 31,* 3–13.

Pritchard discusses some of the factors creating conflicts between those who engage in action-oriented, practitioner research (especially in educational settings) and IRBs.

Sales, B. D., & Folkman, S. (Eds.). (2000). *Ethics in research with human participants.* Washington, DC: APA.

Separate chapters consider the conduct of research with human participants, beginning with the planning of projects and continuing through recruitment of participants, dealing with issues of informed consent, respecting the confidentiality and privacy of participants, and issues related to the reporting of results.

Smith, M. B. (2003). Moral foundations in research with human participants. In A. E. Kazdin (Ed.), *Methodological issues and strategies in clinical research* (pp. 771–778). Washington, DC: APA.

M. Brewster Smith discusses the five moral principles that underlie both the federal regulations on the use of human participants in research and the principles developed by the APA and incorporated in their code.

Ethics in research. (1994). *Psychological Science, 5* [Special section], 127–143.

This section consists of a general article by Robert Rosenthal (Rosenthal, 1994) and four commentaries: Pomerantz (1994), Parkinson (1994), Gurman (1994), and Mann (1994). Rosenthal argues that science and ethics are closely related and that studies of poorer scientific quality are not as ethically defensible as studies of higher scientific merit.

Pomerantz is in general agreement with Rosenthal but believes that the cost-utility analysis Rosenthal brings to determining the ethicality of research might be too stringent. Such an analysis could leave one who is inefficient or who makes an honest mistake vulnerable to ethical challenge.

Parkinson takes issue with the scientific-ethical relationship explicated by Rosenthal and explains that he judges "the scientific quality of a study independent of the ethical quality of a study" (p. 137).

Gurman raises a concern with respect to the absence of debriefing for subjects who are excluded from a study based on preliminary questionnaire responses or other prescreening procedures.

Finally, Mann presents a study with college undergraduates assessing their comprehension of informed consent documents. Results indicate that after reading and signing the forms, subjects were not knowledgeable about critical aspects of the experiment (contained in the form) or some of the rights they retain when agreeing to participate. Mann argues for shorter, less legalistic forms, if not oral consent procedures.

References

American Psychological Association. (1953). *Ethical standards of psychologists.* Washington, DC: Author.

American Psychological Association. (1973). *Ethical principles in the conduct of research with human participants.* Washington, DC: Author.

American Psychological Association. (1982). *Ethical principles in the conduct of research with human participants* (Rev. ed.). Washington, DC: Author.

American Psychological Association. (1992). Ethical principles of psychologists and code of conduct. *American Psychologist, 47,* 1597–1611.

American Psychological Association. (2002). Ethical principles of psychologists and code of conduct. *American Psychologist, 57,* 1060–1073.

Beauchamp, T. L., & Childress, J. F. (2001). *Principles of biomedical ethics* (5th ed.). New York: Oxford University Press.

Bok, S. (1989). *Lying: Moral choice in public and private life* (2nd ed.). New York: Vintage Books.

Code of Federal Regulations, Title 45 CFR Part 46. (1981, 1983, 1991). Washington DC: Department of Health and Human Services, National Institutes of Health, Office for Protection from Research Risks.

Gurman, E. B. (1994). Debriefing for all concerned: Ethical treatment of human subjects. *Psychological Science, 5,* 139.

Hobbs, N. (1948). The development of a code of ethical standards for psychology. *American Psychologist, 3,* 80–84.

Kazdin, A. E. (Ed.). (2003). *Methodological issues and strategies in clinical research.* Washington, DC: APA.

Mann, T. (1994). Informed consent for psychological research: Do subjects comprehend consent forms and understand their legal rights? *Psychological Science, 5,* 140–143.

Meara, N. M., & Schmidt, L. D. (1991). The ethics of researching counseling/psychotherapy processes. In C. E. Watkins & L. J. Schneider (Eds.), *Research in counseling* (pp. 237–259). Hillsdale, NJ: Lawrence Erlbaum.

Milgrim, S. (1965). Some conditions of obedience and disobedience to authority. *Human Relations, 18,* 57–75.

Milgrim, S. (1974). *Obedience to authority.* New York: Harper & Row.

National Commission for the Protection of Human Subjects of Biomedical and Behavioral Research. (1979). *The Belmont report: Ethical principles and guidelines for the protection of human subjects of research.* (Reprinted from *Protecting human research subjects,* Appendix 6 (pp. A6–7 to A6–14) by Office for Protection from Research Risks, U.S. Department of Health and Human Services, 1993, Washington, DC.

Office for Protection from Research Risks, U.S. Department of Health and Human Services (1993). *Protecting human research subjects: Institutional review board guidebook.* (2nd ed.). Washington, DC: Author.

Parkinson, S. (1994). Scientific or ethical quality. *Psychological Science, 5,* 137–138.

Pomerantz, J. R. (1994). On criteria for ethics in science. *Psychological Science, 5,* 135–136.

Rosenthal, R. (1994). Science and ethics in conducting, analyzing, and reporting psychological research. *Psychological Science, 5,* 127–134.

Schmidt, L. D., & Meara, N. M. (1984). Ethical, legal and professional issues in counseling psychology. In S. D. Brown & R. W. Lent (Eds.), *Handbook of counseling psychology* (pp. 56–96). New York: John Wiley.

Web Sites

American Psychological Association Science Division: www.apa.org/science

Department of Health and Human Services, Office for Human Research Protections: www.hhs.gov/ohrp/

National Institutes of Health training module: http://ohsr.od.nih.gov/cbt/nonNIHpeople.html

13

CONDUCTING MAIL
AND INTERNET SURVEYS

ALAN VAUX

CHAD S. BRIGGS

Most research psychologists will need to conduct a survey of some kind during their careers, and for a substantial number, this will be a principal method of data collection. Yet formal training in survey methodology is very rarely part of the research curriculum of psychology graduate programs. This chapter is intended to provide a primer on the conduct of mail and Internet surveys. We will identify some key issues that need to be addressed by researchers using survey methods (or considering their use); we will outline options and their advantages and disadvantages; we will present empirical research on relevant methodological issues where available; and we will provide suggestions on how to conduct surveys competently. A research assistant—or, indeed, an experienced researcher who is new to survey methodology—should find sufficient information here to avoid making serious errors and to conduct a survey that meets general scientific standards. As with all research methods, however, exceptional performance requires experience, creativity, talent, and further study. In many instances, we identify issues about which empirical evidence is continually emerging. Valuable sources include Dillman (2000), Fink and Kosecoff (1985), Fowler (2001),

Goddard and Villanova (Chapter 8, this volume), Salant and Dillman (1994), Schaeffer and Presser (2003), Schwarz (1999), and Sudman and Bradburn (1982).

MAIL AND INTERNET SURVEYS

A very substantial portion of data collection in the social sciences involves the presentation of questions to which research participants reply. The context and mode of question delivery varies: in-person interviewing, telephone surveys (see Chen and Huang, Chapter 14, this volume), and mail and electronic surveys (this chapter). The latter two methods share some appealing features: (a) careful control of data collection through written presentation of structured questions and (usually) selection from written, structured response options and (b) the potential to collect data from a large, dispersed, and carefully selected sample of participants. The mail survey is an extremely adaptable method with a long history of widespread use in the social sciences. Indeed, it is such a common method that most people are very familiar with it—so much so that novice researchers often are seduced into thinking themselves expert.

Internet surveys represent a new and rapidly changing frontier in survey methodology. High-speed computers, printers, and sophisticated software have not only greatly facilitated mail survey design and implementation, but these and related technologies (Internet, electronic mail) have opened up entirely new methods of surveying. These currently include Web-based surveys and electronic mail (e-mail) surveys, methods that have enormous potential but that also present special challenges and require technical expertise, as well as familiarity with more general issues of competent survey design and implementation.

E-mail Surveys

With the advent of the Internet, surveys can be e-mailed directly to many potential respondents without the delays of "snail mail." A plain text version of a survey can be embedded in an e-mail message by using a word processor copy and paste function; however, this method has serious disadvantages—such as loss of formatting that can lead to response bias and lower response rates—and it is not recommended (Dillman, 2000; Salant & Dillman, 1994). A better alternative is to create an HTML (hypertext markup language) version of the survey using word processing software. The HTML file that is created can then be embedded in the body of an e-mail message by placing the cursor where the survey is to be located and adding the HTML survey as an attachment. For ease of responding, Dillman (2000) recommends providing brackets (e.g., [ ]) for categorical and continuous response options so that respondents have clearly demarcated locations for keying in their responses. Yet perhaps the best method is to create HTML surveys using special Web survey development software. Currently, this is preferable because compatibility issues (i.e., viewability across software and hardware platforms) will be minimized or eliminated, and useful design features associated with Web surveys (e.g., radio buttons) can be incorporated. Regardless of the embedding method, Dillman (2000) suggests that potential respondents should be given the option of printing the survey, filling it out as a paper survey, and returning it through the mail (obviously requiring the inclusion of a postal address). Participants should also be instructed to first select the Reply option in their e-mail program before typing in their responses to the survey.

Web Surveys

Instead of being sent through the postal or electronic mail, surveys may simply be made accessible to potential respondents at a unique URL location on the World Wide Web, created by the researcher or a Web consultant. Respondents may be informed of the URL address by mail (e.g., Yun & Trumbo, 2000), phone, or more typically by an e-mail containing a hyperlink to the introductory page of the survey. Access to the survey may be limited to sampled individuals through user IDs, passwords, or PIN numbers (see Heerwegh & Loosveldt, 2002, for a useful discussion on the utility of PIN numbers). Once the introductory page has been successfully navigated, the participant is required to make responses by using the mouse and keyboard.

Whether using a Web-survey or an e-mail survey, extensive pretesting is strongly recommended to make sure that the formatting and readability of the survey are manageable and consistent across different versions of Internet browsers, e-mail software, and hardware platforms. Dillman (2000) provides a caution for researchers considering the design of a Web survey: "The designers of Web questionnaires face an unusual challenge. Instead of designing at the cutting edge of their evolving science, there is a need for them to hold back on the incorporation of advanced features" (p. 375). Important issues that warrant consideration by Web survey designers include line length, screen resolution, programming language (e.g., HTML, Java, JavaScript), use of color, file size, selection of methods for responding, and placement of directions, among others. For sage advice on these issues, consult Dillman (2000) and Dillman and Bowker (2000).

Mixed-Mode Surveying

Surveys may utilize a combination of several contact modes: in-person, mail, telephone, Internet, and so forth. Still in its infancy, this is a promising area of survey methodology. Researchers are rapidly exploring options and conducting experiments on alternative methods. One of the unique features of this methodology is its flexibility and potential for creative implementation. For example, Schaeffer and Dillman (1998) randomly assigned participants to one of four conditions: (1) all paper contacts, (2) all e-mail contacts, (3) a paper pre-notice for an e-mail survey, and (4) a paper reminder for an e-mail survey. They theorized that using both mail and electronic contact modes would tap into mode preferences among respondents (i.e., some respondents may prefer paper surveys to Internet surveys); however, their findings suggested otherwise. Response rates were 57.5%, 58%, 48.2%, and 54.4%, respectively, leading them to suggest that respondents failed to cognitively connect paper contacts with electronic contacts, thereby limiting the utility of mixed-mode methodology. Yun and Trumbo (2000), however, implemented an alternative mixed-mode procedure involving four contacts: (a) a mailed pre-notice, (b) a paper version of the survey with a URL to the Web version of the survey, (c) an e-mail version of the survey with a hyperlink to the Web version of the survey, and (d) a reminder postcard sent by mail. This procedure yielded a good response rate (72%), suggesting the potential utility of mixed-mode surveying and highlighting the need for further experimental comparisons of mode combinations.

ADVANTAGES AND DISADVANTAGES OF THE SURVEY METHOD

As with all research methods, an impeccably conducted survey is no guarantee of an important contribution to knowledge, but otherwise exceptional research can be undermined by a poorly implemented survey. Survey methods can be examined most usefully in terms of internal validity, construct validity, statistical conclusion validity, and external validity (Cook & Campbell, 1979; Shadish, Cook, & Campbell, 2002).

Validity

Internal Validity

With respect to internal validity, mail and Internet surveys can be valuable as part of true experimental studies in which participants have been randomly assigned to different treatments. They are particularly valuable in large-scale field experiments in which large samples are exposed to complex, ongoing interventions. True experiments also can be implemented through surveys in which participants are randomly assigned to different conditions that involve manipulations within the survey (e.g., different information, vignettes, modes of administration). Opportunities for making strong inferences regarding causality are limited only by the manipulations that a creative researcher can make within a survey. *Differential* response rates across conditions, however, may yield a selection threat (i.e., groups may not be equivalent or may not remain so), undermining internal validity and reducing the study to a quasi-experiment. In sum, survey research may be most useful for descriptive research, passive observational research, or other situations in which internal validity is irrelevant, secondary, or otherwise unattainable. True experiments usually require more certain data collection than is possible with mail and Internet surveys, unless a 100% response rate can be approached.

Statistical Conclusion Validity

The likelihood of detecting an empirical relationship statistically depends on the many factors that influence power (see Myors, Chapter 11, this volume), but most relevant here is the reliability of measures. Mail and Internet surveys, per se, are no less reliable than any other mode. Care should be taken in the selection of instruments and in the subsequent assessment of their reliability. Because response rates show an inverse relationship with survey length—at least under certain circumstances (Heberlein & Baumgartner, 1978; Kellerman & Herold, 2001; Tomaskovic-Devey, Leiter, & Thompson, 1994; Yammarino, Skinner, & Childers, 1991), researchers must seek a survey length that provides optimal response rates and reliability.

Too often, researchers new to surveys forget elementary principles of reliability and rely on one or few items when multiple items are not only essential for reliability but also quite feasible. In short, standardized procedures (careful and clear wording), repeated measurement (multiple semiredundant items), and other procedures that enhance measurement reliability are neither less critical nor inherently less achievable in mail and Internet surveys than other methodologies.

Construct Validity

With respect to construct validity, surveys share the strengths and weaknesses of other self-report and other-report methods. There are many constructs of relevance to psychologists—beliefs, personality, attitudes, values, interests, activities—for which self-reports are an important measurement strategy. Also valuable are other-reports such as teacher ratings of students, supervisor ratings of workers, or clinician ratings of clients. Obviously, other relevant constructs—such as blood pressure or evoked potentials—cannot be measured directly through self- or other-report. Reliability and validity of survey measures can be examined, as with any other measure, and research findings support survey measurement of even sensitive constructs such as clinical problems (Fournier & Kovess, 1993). Additionally, monomethod bias can be assessed to some degree using a mixed-mode survey strategy by examining response variation across modes of administration. The key questions the researcher must ask are these: Is it reasonable to expect someone to provide the information of interest? Do relevant, reliable, and valid survey measures exist? Can an existing self-report measure be adapted to a mail or Internet survey method? Is it reasonable to expect reliable and valid data across different administration modes? Affirmative answers to these questions support the utility of survey methodology in a given case, and construct validity can be assessed in relation to other measures collected through surveys or other means.

External Validity

A key aspect of external validity has to do with participants: to whom can we generalize findings? A casual examination of journal articles in psychology will reveal that although participant samples are generally described in terms of number and demographic composition, they are usually volunteer convenience samples. Often, we know little about recruitment procedures, refusal rates, and so forth. In contrast, survey methods typically address issues of generalizability and representativeness explicitly through formal sampling procedures.

Sampling and Return Rates

Sampling

Shoddy sampling can ruin the external validity of survey research, and relevant issues are often overlooked or misunderstood. As with other methods, mail and Internet surveys can be conducted on convenience samples. Yet, representativeness is often important, and formal sampling can easily be incorporated into such surveys. To supplement the brief treatment here, see Shadish et al. (2002), Henry (1990), or McCready (Chapter 10, this volume). For many research purposes, sampling frames are available that represent populations of interest well. These *sampling frames* may be organizational mailing lists (postal or electronic), professional directories, community phone books, or lists generated from a synthesis of esoteric databases.

Formal sampling may be random, systematic, or more elaborate, such as stratified random sampling or cluster sampling (Cochran, 1977; Lohr, 1999). *Random sampling* involves the assignment of numbers to persons or sampling elements and their subsequent random selection (i.e., each person or element in the sampling frame has an equal probability of inclusion). *Systematic sampling* involves the selection of every nth person or element (where n is the ratio of sampling frame to desired sample size) and may be as convenient as selecting every tenth person in every fifth column of names. (Periodic random starts are useful to make sure that every nth person does not coincide with a specific type, such as organizational officers or residents with a corner apartment.) *Stratified random sampling* involves selection within specified strata: for example, randomly selecting psychologists from groups defined by sex, American Psychological Association (APA) division, and region of the country. *Cluster sampling* involves layers of selection: for example, randomly selecting states, then universities, then departments, and then professors. Each method has advantages and disadvantages, relevant to a given context. Regardless, the advantages of formal sampling depend on adequate return rates.

Internet surveys present special challenges with respect to sampling. Current Internet use is highly selective, so any Internet sample will be highly unrepresentative of the general population. A number of studies indicate that Internet users are disproportionately young, educated, White, male, urban, and of middle and upper socioeconomic classes (Dillman & Bowker, 2000; Duffy, 2002; Jackson et al., 1996; Naglieri et al., 2004; Pitkow & Kehoe, 1996; Yun & Trumbo, 2000). Moreover, Dillman and Bowker (2000) suggest that "it seems likely . . . that the 'weighting' of under-represented groups will introduce other errors, [for example], it will be assumed that those few low-income minority respondents who have Internet access are similar to such people who lack that access" (p. 5): that is, trying to correct one error may amplify another. Clearly, this is an important caveat for researchers interested in using Internet surveys. On the other hand, although the prevalence of Internet and e-mail access is still low, it is increasing quite rapidly (see studies reviewed in Dillman, 2000; Naglieri et al., 2004), particularly among some of the groups (e.g., women, older adults) who showed relatively low use early on (see studies reviewed in Yun & Trumbo, 2000). As more people gain access to the Internet, samples of Internet users will become increasingly representative of the general population. Also, Internet use is almost universal among some populations of interest.

More generally, sampling frames of Internet users are not always readily available, so researchers will be unable to assign every member of a target population a known probability of being selected, resulting in coverage error. Comprehensive lists that do exist (e.g., at a university) may have problems: e-mail users tend to change their addresses periodically, some users have multiple addresses, and some users infrequently check their e-mail, precluding them from making timely responses.

Response Rates

The benefits of formal sampling depend on good response rates, which vary widely.

Response rates may be enhanced through careful survey design and implementation, but knowledge of best practices is still evolving, particularly for Internet surveys. Although many studies have found higher response rates to mail surveys than to e-mail surveys (Bachmann, Elfrink, & Vazzana, 1996; Harewood, Yacavone, Locke, & Wiersema, 2001; Kiesler & Sproull, 1986; Kittleson, 1995; Paolo, Bonaminio, Gibson, Partridge, & Kallail, 2000; Schuldt & Totten, 1994; Sproull, 1986; Tse et al., 1995; Weible & Wallace, 1998), other studies have found e-mail survey response rates to be comparable with (Mehta & Sivadas, 1995; Schaeffer & Dillman, 1998; Truell, Bartlett, & Alexander, 2002), or even greater than (see studies reviewed in Matz, 1999; in Sheehan & McMillan, 1999; and in Sills & Song, 2002), mail survey response rates. Moreover, response rates to Internet surveys have ranged wildly from 0% (Pradhan, 1999, cited in Sills & Song, 2002) to 85.3% (Roselle & Neufeld, 1998). Little research has gone into comparing Web survey response rates with those of either mail surveys or e-mail surveys. One study (conducted by CustomerSat.com and cited in Slevin, 1997) found that e-mail (30%) yielded a slightly higher response rate than an identical Web survey (24%). Yun and Trumbo (2000) allowed respondents to complete their survey by mail, e-mail, or on the Web. The majority of the respondents completed and returned the survey by mail, and roughly equal proportions completed the survey by e-mail (14%) and Web (15%). These studies suggest that the two Internet contact modes may yield similar response rates, but further research is needed before solid conclusions can be made.

Improving Response Rates

A number of procedures can be used to enhance response rates. It is worth noting here that in proposing a mail or Internet survey (e.g., in a grant or a doctoral prospectus), the focus should be on procedures, not outcomes: that is, be very cautious about guaranteeing a given obtained sample size. Most important, the research literature on survey return rates is growing and should be consulted to weigh the costs and benefits of particular procedures in a given research context. This is particularly true for Internet surveys. At a minimum, a carefully designed survey with a good cover letter may be sent out bulk mail with a postage-paid return envelope, followed 2 weeks later by a postcard (sent to the entire sample) thanking those who participated and requesting those who have not to do so. The following procedures and survey characteristics have been shown to increase response rates above those for this basic procedure: first-class postage rather than bulk-mail (Dillman, 2000), certified mail (Dillman, 2000; Gitelson & Drogin, 1992), priority mail (Dillman, 2000), pre-notification (by letter, phone, or e-mail) (Dillman, 2000; Roselle & Neufeld, 1998; Schlegelmilch & Diamantopoulos, 1991), multiple follow-up reminders (by postcard, phone, or e-mail; Dillman, 2000; Nederhof, 1988), multiple contacts and replacement surveys for those who have not responded (Dillman, 2000), optimal survey length (Adams & Gale, 1982), personalized envelopes (Dillman, 2000; Kellerman & Herold, 2001), sponsorship (Fox, Crask & Kim, 1988), personalized cover letters (Yammarino et al., 1991), anonymity (Yammarino et al., 1991), salience of topic (Dillman, 2000), nonmonetary incentives, and monetary incentives (promised and included; Hopkins & Gullickson, 1992). The feasibility and cost of these procedures may vary dramatically with sample size, but research findings indicate that they may substantially improve return rates, at least under some circumstances. Altschuld and his colleagues (1992) have set the benchmark: They have attained return rates as high as 96%.

Choosing Among Mail, Internet, and Other Modes

Another relevant issue is choosing between mail survey, telephone survey, personal interview, and new options such as e-mail and Web-based surveys. Each of these methods has advantages and disadvantages that may recommend use in a particular situation. Several conditions argue against conducting a mail survey, including urgency of data collection, numerous open-ended questions, and most critically an elaborate system of contingent questions (i.e., the next question being determined by a previous

answer). These circumstances might suggest a telephone survey, in-person interviews, or an Internet survey. On the other hand, when time allows for the careful selection or development of a set of closed-ended questions, data may be collected on a very large sample in a relatively short period of time, and mail or Internet surveys may compare favorably in cost and data quality with telephone surveys (Fournier & Kovess, 1993; McHorney, Kosinski, & Ware, 1994). Notably, the advantages of mail surveys—relative ease of implementation and a large literature on best practices—should not be lightly dismissed.

Internet surveys have a number of advantages outlined below, but currently they also have a number of disadvantages (beyond the sampling and external validity issues noted above). Start-up costs (e.g., computer equipment and software) are diminishing, but Web survey designers still face technical difficulties that may be considerable. Issues such as browser type, e-mail software, programming language (e.g., HTML, Java, JavaScript), screen resolution, equipment age, and user skill all present problems that have to be dealt with prior to administering the survey to the population of interest (Dillman, 2000). Working out the kinks in the Internet survey requires pretesting, which may add a substantial investment of time at the beginning of a study. Also, incentives cannot easily be included in an e-mail survey. Evidence reported in a meta-analysis of 62 studies (Hopkins & Gullickson, 1992) and in a review of the literature (King, Pealer, & Bernard, 2001) suggests that the inclusion of monetary incentives substantially increases response rates over conditions offering no incentives (median response rate difference = 18.5%; Hopkins & Gullickson), nonmonetary incentives, and promised incentives (median response rate difference = 11.9%; Hopkins & Gullickson). The inability to include monetary incentives in a study using all e-mail contacts may therefore be crippling, especially in circumstances when high response rates are essential.

On the other hand, when a researcher wishes to conduct a survey with a population that has nearly ubiquitous access to the Internet (e.g., computer industry professionals, university faculty and students) and resources allow for careful survey development, this method may prove extremely advantageous. Commonly cited advantages include speed of distribution, speed of response, cost-efficiency, survey design flexibility (question presentation and response options), ease of data entry, and data quality.

In one of the more conservative estimates of electronic survey response speed encountered in the literature review for this chapter, Roselle and Neufeld (1998) reported that 27.5% of all their electronic survey returns were received by the end of the first week. Other promising findings follow and are presented as the percentage (or number) of all electronic responses received within a specified time period after sending an electronic survey: one return within 20 minutes (Berge & Collins, 1996, cited in Matz, 1999), 10% of all returns within 2 hours (Harewood et al., 2001), 39% of all returns within 24 hours (Meehan & Burns, 1997, cited in Matz, 1999), 50% of all returns within 3 days (Mehta & Sivadas, 1995), and 90% all returns within 4 days in a cross-national survey (Swoboda, Muhlberger, Weitkunat, & Schneeweib, 1997). Comparatively, e-mail responses are received an average of 6 days sooner than mail surveys (Schaeffer & Dillman, 1998; Sheehan & McMillan, 1999; Truell et al., 2002; Tse, 1998). Schaeffer and Dillman (1998) reported receiving 50% of all their electronic responses before they received the first response from their mail survey. In short, electronic surveys are without peer when data are needed very quickly.

The cost of an Internet survey has been estimated at between 5% and 20% of the cost of a mail survey. This reduction in cost is primarily due to the elimination of paper, duplicating, envelopes, and postage. Harewood et al. (2001) conducted a cost-efficiency analysis for an e-mail survey (70% response rate), a mail survey (85% response rate), and a telephone survey (90% response rate). They found the cost per completed survey to be $.71 for e-mail, $2.54 for mail, and $2.08 for telephone. Furthermore, most of the cost of an Internet survey is likely to be incurred at the beginning of a study when computer hardware and software may need to be purchased and technical assistance acquired for developing an effective Internet survey. Consequently, the cost of an Internet survey decreases substantially as the sample size increases. This advantage of Internet surveys becomes even more salient when compared with the costs of other modes over time. For example, to improve on the 70% response rate achieved in the e-mail survey noted above, Harewood et al. (2001) estimated that it would cost $6.86 per additional completed telephone survey.

Response option formats for Web surveys allow attractive ways to guide appropriate responses: offering radio buttons when only one response option must be selected, check boxes when multiple responses are allowed, drop-down boxes (one column is used to store numerous response options; e.g., selecting state of residence) for responding to closed-ended questions, and text boxes for responding to open-ended questions. Critically, skip patterns can be easily incorporated into the Web survey by having participants select a response[1] and then click on a spatially proximal hyperlink to take them to the next appropriate question in the skip pattern. Web surveys, then, combine advantages of mail surveys (written presentation of questions) with those of telephone or in-person interviews (flexible tailoring of questions).

Another striking advantage of Web surveys further exploits computer technology. Once the respondent completes the Web survey, responses are sent to and stored on the server holding the Web site. Responses can then be automatically added to a database, thereby eliminating the data entry phase and greatly reducing the time and resources needed prior to data analysis. The database can then be quickly called up—complete with variable labels—for analysis[2] using popular spreadsheets and statistical packages (e.g., Excel, SPSS, SAS).

Response quality has been measured by the frequency of item completion errors, frequency of omitted items, candid (vs. socially desirable) open-ended question responses, and response length for open-ended questions. E-mail surveys have been associated with fewer item completion errors (Kiesler & Sproull, 1986) and omitted items (Kiesler & Sproull, 1986; Schaeffer & Dillman, 1998; Truell et al., 2002). Responses to Internet surveys also tend to be more honest, less socially desirable, and more extreme than responses to mail or telephone surveys (Bachmann et al., 1999; Dillman, 2000; Kiesler & Sproull, 1986), even among marginalized populations such as gays and lesbians (Kauffman et al., 1997, cited in Matz, 1999). Responses to open-ended questions also tend to be longer (Kiesler & Sproull, 1986; Yun & Trumbo, 2000), with Schaeffer and Dillman (1998) reporting a fourfold increase in the amount of text used in e-mail responses compared with mail responses.

In summary, Internet surveys should be avoided when (a) the use of Internet and e-mail is not widespread in the population of interest; (b) no suitable sampling frame is available for the population of interest; (c) sufficient time, resources, or technical assistance are unavailable to create an effective Internet survey; and (d) incentives are crucial for obtaining acceptable response rates. When the research environment is favorable to an Internet survey, however, high-quality data can be gathered very quickly and cost efficiently from large samples.

Mixed-mode surveys should also be strongly considered. Using multiple modes of contact can have the effect of eliminating the disadvantages associated with each mode and amplifying their respective advantages. Specifically, a mixed-mode survey using both mail and e-mail contacts could engage the respective advantages and disadvantages of each method in the following ways: (a) when time and resources are sufficient, care can be taken in selecting or developing a set of closed-ended questions, and in effectively adapting a paper survey to the Web environment; (b) complex contingent questions and numerous open-ended questions can be included in the Internet version of the survey;[3] (c) general population sampling frames complete with mailing addresses can be used to help reduce coverage error in an Internet survey by sending replacement paper surveys to nonrespondents; (d) monetary incentives can be sent along with an initial mail contact to boost response rates; and, (e) costs can be reduced by creatively mixing modes. For example, one may use e-mail to make a first contact in a cross-sectional study and then use the postal service to deliver follow-up reminders and replacement surveys to those who have not replied. The initial use of an e-survey reduces cost compared with a postal mail survey, and the mailed follow-ups help increase response rates (Dillman, 2000). Costs can also be cut in panel research. For example, if e-mail addresses are unknown at Time 1, then a question on a mail survey can be used to quickly gather this information. E-mail addresses can then be used, as in the cross-sectional case, to make initial contacts at Time 2.

Furthermore, Dillman (2000) suggests that some respondents may prefer one type of mode over others. In other words, even if potential respondents have access to e-mail, they may prefer to fill out a paper survey. Yun and Trumbo (2000) used a mixed-mode, four-contact procedure to distribute a survey to 360 randomly selected individuals. The response rate was good (72%), with substantial variation in the selected mode of response (162 paper, 33 e-mail, and 35 Web). Yun and Trumbo also found that the electronic responders reported more social use of e-mail than the paper responders ($p < .10$), providing further evidence that there is an important amount of variation in mode preference. Using multiple modes to deliver copies of a survey, then, will likely increase response rates as researchers tap into particular mode preferences.

Last, we have seen that response quality (item completion errors, omitted items, and candid and lengthy responses to open-ended questions) may vary across response modes (Bachmann et al., 1999; Dillman, 2000; Kiesler & Sproull, 1986; Schaeffer & Dillman, 1998; Truell et al., 2002). The use of multiple modes, then, can help to both identify and minimize these sources of method bias.

Summarizing, there are important features and caveats associated with both mail and Internet surveys that need to be considered when carefully selecting a mode for survey delivery. Creatively combining the mail and Internet survey modes is an attractive alternative that can both minimize or eliminate the cons associated with each mode and increase the absolute number of pros. Therefore, a mixed-mode methodology is encouraged when time and human resources are available, when it is important to minimize costs, and when combining contact modes is expected to decrease coverage error and increase response rates.

Mailed Survey Envelopes

The outgoing envelope is the first contact that the potential respondent has with the study. Salant and Dillman (1994) paint a picture of the importance of the envelope by putting the researcher into the shoes of a potential respondent who has just spotted the survey envelope in a pile of mail. They ask, "Does [the envelope] strike you as a letter that should be opened and taken seriously?" (p. 137). Poorly designed envelopes are less likely to be returned (Dillman, 2000; King et al., 2001; Salant & Dillman, 1994). The function of the outgoing envelope is that of gatekeeper, and the relevant question is, "How can I get the potential respondent to open the envelope?" Personalization seems to be important. Written addresses (target and reply) have been found to increase response rates by 6.5% compared with printed computer labels (see King et al.). Paper stamps, especially large commemorative stamps, have also been shown to be effective in increasing response rates when compared with metered postage. Race- or ethnic group–specific stamps have not been shown to be effective for African American women (see King et al.), but more research is needed before a definitive answer on this issue can be given. The mode of delivery is also important. It may be cheap to send mail surveys by bulk mail, but it may be more cost-efficient (especially if multiple waves of the survey are sent to nonrespondents) to use first-class mail. Certified mail, although even more expensive, has been found to increase response rates by 16% over even first-class mail (see King et al.).

The reply envelope is also important. At a minimum, a self-addressed, stamped reply envelope should be included with the cover letter and survey in the initial mailing (Dillman, 2000). Handwritten return addresses also help demonstrate the researcher's effort, as well as the importance of the respondent's reply. Matching the stamp on the outgoing envelope with the stamp on the reply envelope has been shown to improve response rates compared with the use of a different stamp on each envelope (see King et al., 2001). Perhaps commemorative stamps on both the outgoing and reply envelopes would yield the highest response rates.

THE COVER LETTER

A common error made by novices is to pay too little attention to the cover letter, often a mere afterthought. Dillman (1978, 2000) reminds

survey researchers that they are asking a stranger to do them a favor, expending time and effort to complete the instrument and perhaps to share personal feelings, thoughts, or beliefs. Moreover, in mail surveys and Internet surveys the cover letter often represents one of the first contacts that the potential respondent has with the study. Thus, apart from being polite and professional, the letter must serve several key functions.

Importance of the Research

First, readers are likely asking themselves: "What is this and why should I bother with it?" Thus the first paragraph of the letter must introduce the research and characterize it as important, noting possible benefits and its relevance to the potential respondent. Depending on the topic, this may be done quite generally: for example, "Violence is a serious social problem in many American communities. This research is being conducted to help us understand the problem and to provide guidance to schools and police departments about how violence can be controlled in towns like yours." Or the topic may be of more immediate interest: for example, "Managed care is changing how psychotherapy is paid for and practiced. As a clinical psychologist in private practice, you may be concerned about these changes. This research is being conducted so that we can help your state professional association represent your interests and influence upcoming legislation." These and other examples are necessarily brief. See Dillman (1978, 2000) and other referenced sources for more complete examples.

Importance of the Respondent

Second, the reader may be asking, "Why me?" The letter must answer in two ways: explain how the potential respondent was selected and persuade the respondent of the importance of participation. This can be tricky if respondents are in the sample by chance! For example, "You were randomly selected as part of a relatively small group of residents in Yourtown to participate in the study. In order to get a complete picture of the issue, it is extremely important that we get your opinions on this topic. So, we would really appreciate it if you could take 15 minutes to complete the enclosed survey." Research in the area of appeals (reviewed by

King et al., 2001) has shown that egoistic appeals (e.g., "Your opinions on this topic are important to us") tend to yield higher response rates than altruistic appeals (e.g., "Providing your opinions on this topic will be beneficial to upcoming legislation changes.").

Privacy

Potential participants are likely to ask themselves, "Who will know how I answered these questions?" This is especially salient for surveys asking for sensitive information. The letter must tell potential respondents what degree of privacy they can expect and exactly how this will be achieved. In their review of the literature, King et al. (2001) communicate that a strong emphasis on confidentiality or anonymity for a survey that asks for sensitive information can increase response rates, but may decrease response rates when the content of the survey is not sensitive.

Anonymity is easiest to communicate. "This survey is anonymous. Return the completed survey in the enclosed envelope and do not write your name on the survey or envelope. There is no way that we can identify any person's answers or even who has or has not responded." Confidentiality is more difficult to communicate because the researcher is seeking the respondent's trust. "Your survey data will be kept completely confidential. Your name will never appear directly on your survey or with your survey data. You will note an identification number on your survey. This will be used only to link up the four surveys that we will be sending you over the next year. The list of names and corresponding numbers will be kept in a locked file drawer and destroyed when the project is complete." Researchers must be aware of, and give careful consideration to, relevant ethical issues. Betraying trust by covert identification of surveys or breaking confidentiality is a serious ethical breach. Omitting tricky confidentiality information in the hope of boosting return rates is ethically questionable and likely to backfire in any case (see APA, 2002).

Expectations of Respondent

Most cover letters let the participants know what will be expected of them. With Web surveys, researchers may want to emphasize in both the cover letter and the introductory survey Web page what information the respondent will need to complete the survey. Telling respondents that they will need particular information during the course of the survey may help to increase accuracy and prevent frustration and premature termination. Whether and how the respondents can save their responses halfway through for later completion should also be communicated to the respondent.

To summarize, the cover letter is critically important. It may be the first contact between the researcher and a potential participant, creating a crucial first impression. In separate paragraphs, the letter should communicate the importance of the project, the importance of this person's participation, and explain privacy procedures. A final paragraph may reiterate these points and encourage a phone call regarding any concerns. Researchers may find that a research ethics committee favors standard paragraphs or a format that runs counter to the recommendations here. These may include standard statements regarding risks, voluntary participation, committee approval, identification of researchers as students, and so forth. At times, such statements may mar a good cover letter, or even seriously undermine the credibility of a good survey, without in any way enhancing the ethical treatment of participants. The researcher must weigh issues and negotiate with the ethics committee.

GENERAL FORMAT

Survey design should reflect Dillman's (2000) point that the researcher is asking a favor of a stranger: It should facilitate rather than hinder participation. This is a statement of the obvious, yet novices often produce surveys that look untidy and disorganized, that seek information cryptically or impolitely, and that make it difficult for respondents to answer questions, even when they want to. In short, the survey should look professional, interesting, and easy to complete. Powerful personal computers, sophisticated software, and high-quality printers have dramatically altered the ease with which professional-looking surveys can be produced, although they also may have raised the standards for acceptable correspondence! The recommendations here are adapted from Dillman's (2000) tailored design method. They should be viewed as illustrative, though they appear to work very well. The main point is that the survey should follow *some coherent design style* and one that facilitates participation by a respondent.

Layout

The overall appearance of the survey, layout, fonts, colors, and so forth should look professional, legible, and easy to complete. If the potential respondent gets the impression either that the researcher has not taken much care in constructing the survey or that it will be onerous to complete, then participation is unlikely. In fact, the appearance of the survey has been found to affect response rates more than survey length (see King et al., 2001). Several tactics may be used to make a survey look good and easy to complete. Producing the survey in pamphlet form may make it look more professional and shorter, as well as reduce paper and possibly postal costs. Using current word processors with flexible control of fonts, a pamphlet can be produced quite easily and without photocopy reductions. Thus, one folded sheet of paper, printed front and back, yields four pages of questionnaire; two folded pages yield eight survey pages, and so on. Once the layout is correct, any copy shop can handle copying, stapling, and folding. Experienced researchers recommend that the face page contain only a project title or logo and that the last page be blank or be used for a final open-ended question and a statement of appreciation.

Every effort should be made to establish a consistent legible style for the survey, one that gives it a simple appearance with lots of space, that clearly distinguishes questions and answers, and that establishes a response set for how to answer questions. A section should begin with a transition paragraph that orients the reader to the topic (e.g., "Below is a series of statements regarding . . . "), asks the question ("To what extent do you agree or disagree with each of these statements?"), and provides instructions on how to respond (e.g., "Refer to the scale in the box below and, for each statement, circle one number that corresponds to your answer.").

Items and response options should be clearly distinguished: This can be done spatially, by distinct fonts, by shading, by boxing, or other means. A consistent procedure for answering questions should be established: This might be checking a box, circling a number, or some other procedure. Circling numbers has the advantage of simplifying coding to a data set. When many questions have a common set of response options (e.g., a four-point scale of agreement), a reference scale might be followed by items on the left with a corresponding scale to the right. When questions have different response options, Dillman (1978, 2000) recommends that each question have options listed vertically. This may seem to waste space, but usually space-saving formats are confusing and look cluttered. Although control of fonts can be invaluable in fitting question sets on pages, the common error of font chaos—using many different font sizes and types—should be carefully avoided. An advantage of Web surveys is that the researcher may restrict disallowed answers (e.g., attempts to check several rather than just one response).

The use of color may help or hurt the appeal of either a mail survey or an Internet survey. A color survey is easier to find in the middle of a stack of papers on a potential respondent's desk (see King et al., 2001). The use of a green mail survey has been associated with increases in response rates (Fox et al., 1988), but other colors and color combinations have either had no effect or have been detrimental to response rates in studies using both mail surveys and Internet surveys. Some colors and color schemes may make the survey less aesthetically appealing and more difficult to read, but more experimental research is needed to determine the effect of color and color schemes on response rates. For now, black on white is generally recommended and is the most conservative choice of colors (Dillman, 2000).

Organization of Questions

The survey should be organized into sections reflecting different topics, with brief transition statements to facilitate movement from section to section. The survey should begin with an engaging question that follows the cover letter.

Questions about a particular topic, with a similar format, or with a similar response format generally should be placed together. This will be, and will seem to be, easier for a participant to complete. Questions about demographics typically should come at the end rather than at the start of a survey.

Context

In organizing surveys, one should keep in mind the possibility that context, especially prior questions, may influence a participant's answer to a question. Tourangeau and Rasinski (1988) have proposed a cognitive model of how survey questions are answered involving four steps: identifying the attitude a question is about, retrieving relevant beliefs and feelings, using these to make a judgment, and using the judgment to select a response. They argue that contextual material such as prior questions may prime a topical cluster of beliefs, set a norm or standard for making later judgments, or create a demand to be consistent or to be moderate. Tourangeau and others have demonstrated how context items relevant to a particular belief can increase access to related beliefs (Tourangeau, Rasinski, & D'Andrade, 1991) and alter survey responses (Resinski & Tourangeau, 1991; Schwarz, 1999). This latter effect is especially prevalent when participants hold well-developed but conflicted views on a topic (ambiguity of response; Tourangeau, Rasinski, Bradburn, & D'Andrade, 1989), when the question is ambiguous or poorly worded (ambiguity of stimulus), or when the respondent does not have a well-developed view or lacks adequate information on the topic (Schwarz, 1999). The magnitude of these effects can be rather large. For example, Schwarz, Strack, and Mai (1991) asked respondents about their marital and life satisfaction. When asked about life satisfaction first, the correlation between marital and life satisfaction was equal to .32. When asked about marital satisfaction first, however, the correlation between marital and life satisfaction jumped to .67. Schwarz suggested that this finding "reflects that the marital satisfaction question brought marriage-related information to mind, which could be included in the representation formed of one's life as a whole" (p. 102).

In short, context effects may simply facilitate the answering of questions (by priming relevant beliefs), but they may alter responses too.

Several techniques have been developed to both identify and minimize context effects. Schwarz (1999) and Schaeffer and Presser (2003) suggest in-person interviews with extensive probing and use of "think-aloud" techniques (i.e., cognitive interviews) to help identify context effects. Manipulating question order and response option order can also aid the researcher in identifying and counterbalancing bias associated with context effects. Researchers using Internet surveys can either provide different hyperlinks to multiple forms of the survey, each with a different order, or they can program the computer to randomly change the question order for each respondent.

QUESTION DESIGN

Psychologists often will use or adapt established instruments for a mail or Internet survey. Yet, for a variety of reasons, surveys often will involve new questions, and these must be carefully designed. The treatment here is necessarily brief, and readers are encouraged to read further (Dillman, 2000; Fowler, 2001; Salant & Dillman, 1994; Schaeffer & Presser, 2003; Schwarz, 1999). Note that many of these suggestions apply to question design in modes other than mail survey; similarly knowledge from other modes often is pertinent to mail surveys. Large-scale ongoing surveys such as the General Social Survey (Davis & Smith, 1992) often involve studies of wording effects that yield useful information. Also, survey design increasingly involves consideration of the cognitive processes involved in survey participation: understanding questions, recalling information, making judgments, formulating answers, and so forth (Fienberg & Tanur, 1989; Schaeffer & Presser, 2003; see Schwarz, 1999, for a discussion of these processes). At present, knowledge generated by this approach has not yielded a set of simple guidelines for question design. In general, questions should be polite, clear, specific, unbiased, guided by appropriately specific and detailed instructions, and match specific research goals.

Politeness

Nothing will undermine a survey more quickly than asking questions in ways that are demanding, rude, disrespectful, or patronizing. Very common errors are the nonquestion question (e.g., "Age? ___"), the unnecessarily intrusive question (e.g., "Exactly what is your annual income? $___"), the overly demanding question (e.g., "Rank these 25 topics in order of importance"), the impossibly precise question (e.g., "How many times in the past year did you read a magazine?"), the presumptuous question (e.g., "When you travel overseas, . . . ?"), and the patronizing question (e.g., to a group of experienced scientists, "Publishing is a complex process. Manuscripts must be submitted for review and often revised before publication. How . . . ?"). Researchers may find a use for these types of questions from time to time (e.g., using a presumptive question to ask about a sensitive topic helps normalize the response). In general, however, inquiries should be in question form, be relatively easy to answer, not presume experience or knowledge, and seek personal information graciously and only to the degree necessary.

Clarity and Precision

Questions should be short, simple, and straightforward—brief but not cryptic. Ideally, all respondents will understand a question in the same way, an assumption that can be tested using in-person interviews, probing, and the think-aloud technique. Complex questions usually can be broken up (for examples see Schaeffer & Presser, 2003). Common errors include unnecessarily elaborate structure (e.g., "Some people think . . . , others that . . . , what do you think?"), double questions (e.g., "Do you think that the U.S. deficit is too big and that spending should be cut?"), and double negatives (e.g., "Current graduate training does not adequately teach students how not to make basic research errors.").

Language should be appropriate to the audience. Generally, this means using simple, short words rather than longer and more sophisticated words. Care must be taken to avoid abbreviations, acronyms, technical terms, and unconventional phrases with which a sample may be unfamiliar. On the other hand, an audience sophisticated in a given arena may experience the absence or misuse of technical terms and common abbreviations as patronizing or a sign of incompetence. In general, terms and phrases that may be unfamiliar to respondents should be clarified in a preamble, and an acronym should appear first in parentheses after the phrase for which it stands.

Precision requires clarity about the research questions at hand. Questions easily may be too vague to be useful (e.g., "Is psychotherapy of high quality?"). Often precision involves a compromise between what a researcher would like to know and what a person is capable of reporting, as when questions elicit fake precision (e.g., "Exactly how many movies did you attend last year?"). Care also should be taken to avoid asking questions that presume knowledge that respondents may not have (for a useful discussion of these issues, see Schaeffer & Presser, 2003).

Avoiding Bias

Care should be taken to avoid wording questions in a leading way (e.g., "Do you agree that the numerous and intrusive APA requirements make graduate training more difficult than necessary?"). Response options too should be balanced and not skewed (e.g., "To enhance graduate psychology training, should APA requirements be increased slightly, decreased slightly, decreased substantially, or eliminated?"). Selecting the right scale is critical because, according to Schwarz (1999), respondents tend to see a response scale like a normal distribution. Middle response options tend to be perceived as average or normal, whereas options located outside the middle represent extreme behaviors and attitudes. The implications of this perception are twofold: (a) a behavior or attitude will be overestimated on a high-frequency scale and underestimated on a low-frequency scale and (b) a high-end response on a low-frequency scale (or low-end response on a high-frequency scale) may alter subsequent responses. Schwarz, Hippler, Deutsch, and Strack (1985) provided evidence of the first implication by asking German respondents how much television they watched per day using both a low- and a high-frequency scale: 16% and 38% of respondents, respectively, reported that they watched 2.5 hours of television per day. Schwarz et al. also provide evidence for the second implication mentioned above. They found that respondents who marked a high-end response (i.e., watching 2.5 hours of TV per day) on a low-frequency scale reported being less satisfied with the activities they engage in during their leisure time than respondents who reported the same TV watching frequency on a high-frequency scale. Schwarz (1999) argued that the low-frequency scale suggests to the high-end respondents that they watch more TV than the majority of other individuals.

Seeking Sensitive Information

Psychological research often involves sensitive information, and material may seem more personal or private to others than to us. Questions may be made less intrusive by the use of broad response categories (e.g., a broad income range), by approaching the topic gradually through a series of questions (e.g., asking about general views on drugs in society, others' use of drugs, then the respondent's use of soft drugs), or by using more private modes of administration (e.g., self-administered mail or Internet surveys; Schaeffer & Presser, 2003). Findings on return rate noted earlier (see King et al., 2001) suggest that an appropriate emphasis on anonymity or confidentiality may facilitate trust and more candid responses. Thought should be given to balance the desire for detailed sensitive information with the possibility of nonparticipation!

Web Survey Software

Developments in computer software over the past decade have facilitated the preparation of mail surveys a great deal (contrast the 1978 and 2000 editions of Dillman). Yet the avenues that computer technologies have opened for electronic surveying are revolutionary. A quick Internet search on Google using the words, "free survey software" yielded a large number of potential sites offering free, demonstration, and commercial versions of survey software. Researchers at universities using university samples might also consider using the Web survey function available on WebCT or on similar versions of course management software. Potential respondents must be given log-in user names and passwords, which can be easily created by the campus WebCT administrator and included in the e-mail contacts along with a hyperlink to the introduction page of the survey. Like most versions of Web survey software, WebCT can incorporate skip patterns, multiple response option types, and run descriptive statistics for preliminary analyses. Note that the WebCT administrator can be a key resource for technical instruction and assistance. Other survey software products are listed at the end of this chapter.

Ethics and Security for Internet Surveys

Although the ethical principles and goals are the same in all modes of surveying, electronic surveys raise some special problems. Repeated unsolicited e-mail contacts present one unique problem. In response to this, human subjects committees may require that a line be added to the consent form that allows potential respondents to opt out of future mailings. A second issue with Internet surveys is the provision of confidentiality or anonymity. Anonymity presents more problems for researchers than confidentiality and may only be possible for Web surveys. E-mail surveys require that an electronic response be sent from the respondent's computer to the researcher's computer, but this is likely to transmit respondent identification information to the researcher. In keeping with anonymity, a researcher will either have to allow automatic access to a Web survey (i.e., no ID, password, or PIN number required) or provide sampled individuals with a generic ID, password, or PIN number (e.g., requiring all respondents to enter a generic password such as "Survey"). The latter option may work well but has been untested in the literature. One potential problem is that respondents will pass on the necessary log-in information to a nonsampled person. Evidence for the potential of this problem comes from a survey of oceanographers conducted by Walsh, Kiesler, Sproull, & Hesse (1992). They achieved a 76% response rate and had 104 additional requests from nonsampled individuals to participate in their study! Nonsampled individuals gaining access to a survey greatly compounds the selection problems arising from nonresponse because the researcher will not be able to identify or estimate the extent of this problem. Allowing automatic access to a survey presents similar problems and begs the question, "Who exactly is responding to my survey?" Obviously, this raises serious questions of external validity.

With regard to respondent security, Heerwegh and Loosveldt (2002) found a lower response rate for participants who were allowed automatic access (45%) compared with those who had to enter a unique four-digit PIN number (52%). In contrast, Crawford, Couper, and Lamias (2001) found a higher response rate for respondents who were allowed automatic access to a survey than for those who had to manually log in with a user ID and password. The different results may reflect the different log-in procedure, suggesting that although being required to provide some information to gain access to the survey may be comforting to respondents (e.g., by providing a stronger sense of security), the amount of information that is required of the respondent should be minimized. Consistent with this assumption, Heerwegh and Loosveldt (2002) found that respondents in the manual log-in condition completed significantly more sections in their survey and were less likely to choose the response options *No Answer* and *Don't Know* to sensitive questions about parental income than were respondents in the automatic log-in condition. Heerwegh and Loosveldt were also able to identify nine attempts to access their survey that were denied. They determined that seven of these failed attempts were due to respondents forgetting to enter their PIN, one failed attempt was due to a typing error, and the last failed attempt was likely an attempt to hack into the survey. The decision to keep Web survey respondents anonymous has to be carefully balanced with the need to limit multiple responses by the same individual, responses by unsampled individuals, and the sense of comfort that may be gained by requiring an access code.

CONCLUSION

Mail and Internet surveys are flexible, valuable, and widely used methods. When used properly, the survey may provide a relatively inexpensive way to collect data on large samples of geographically, organizationally, or socially remote persons. Mail and Internet surveys may be used to collect sensitive information and in some contexts may provide better data at lower cost than telephone or personal interviews. Formal sampling, a rarity in psychological research, can easily be incorporated into mail surveys and, with some populations, into Internet surveys. Return rates may be enhanced by a variety of procedures based on a growing research literature. High return rates and quality data depend primarily on personalization of mail envelopes and e-mail contacts, thoughtful cover letters, monetary incentives, topic salience, well-designed layouts, carefully crafted questions, survey length, and well-timed follow-up contacts. The basics of survey methodology can readily be mastered by a conscientious researcher. Form 13.1 presents a checklist of issues to address and tasks to complete in conducting a survey.

Form 13.1   A Mail and Internet Survey Checklist

Research Goals

_____ What are the principal research questions to be addressed?

_____ Does a mail, Internet, or mixed-mode survey fit the research design (e.g., manipulations, time frame)?

_____ Can principal variables be measured reliably and validly by self- or other report?

Mail, Internet, or Other Survey Method

_____ Does the research involve a large sample? (The larger the sample, the more valuable a mail or Internet survey will be over phone or in-person interviews.)

_____ Is sufficient time available to design a survey? (Mail surveys require careful preparation, though duplication is simple.)

_____ Is sufficient time available to develop an electronic version of a survey? (Internet surveys require careful preparation and pretesting.)

_____ Are the survey questions generally close-ended?

_____ Does the survey involve few contingent questions and easily followed skips? (More contingent questions favor an electronic survey over a mail survey.)

_____ Are there explicit instructions for completing the Internet survey (including how to respond to radio buttons, check boxes, drop-down boxes, text boxes, and contingent questions), and are they placed close enough to their referent questions?

Sampling

_____ What size sample do you need (given the research questions, design, power, etc.)?

_____ Are suitable sampling frames available? How complete are these?

_____ What sampling strategy will you use (random, systematic, etc.)?

_____ If a Web survey, will user IDs, passwords, or PIN numbers be needed to limit access to sampled individuals only?

Return Rates

_____ What procedures will you use to enhance return rates (prenotification, personalization, incentives, follow-up reminders, repeat surveys, etc.)?

_____ Would a 30% return rate be fatal for your design?

Cover Letter

_____ Have you carefully written your cover letter, providing information on the importance of the research, how the participant was selected, how privacy will be maintained, and, if an Internet survey, what information will be needed to complete the survey?

Organization

_____ Have you selected reliable and valid measures of key variables that have been used previously in mail or Internet surveys or that can be suitably adapted?

_____ Have you placed high-interest questions at the start of the survey and demographic questions at the end?

_____ Have you considered alternative options for the organization of material in the survey?

(Continued)

Form 13.1 (Continued)

_____ Are order or context effects likely to be a problem?

_____ Do the response options reflect reality (middle-response option equals the population average; low- and high-response options represent the extremes in the population)?

_____ Do the skip directions on an Internet survey encourage the respondents to first mark their responses (e.g., _Yes_ or _No_) to the questions before clicking on the hyperlink to the next question in the skip sequence?

_____ If the survey seems too long, can you substitute shorter, yet acceptable, instruments?

_____ Are the respondents given a progress graph or symbols to let them know how much of the survey they have completed and how much they have left?

Layout

_____ Have you considered format options (pamphlet, line length, screen resolution, etc.)?

_____ Have you established a coherent design style (margins, font type and size, etc.)?

_____ Are questions spatially or graphically distinct from answer options?

_____ Have you established a simple and consistent procedure for indicating answers?

_____ If a Web survey, is there an introductory Web page that is motivational, informs respondents of what they will need to complete the survey, emphasizes the ease with which the survey may be completed, and that has instructions for navigating to the next page?

_____ Are there differences in the formatting and layout (e.g., wrapping text) of the questions and response options across different screen configurations, operating systems, browsers, e-mail software, or on tiled versus full screens?

_____ If a mixed-mode survey, are the mail and Internet surveys comparable in terms of formatting and layout of the questions and response options?

Question Design

_____ Have you carefully adapted measures usually presented in some other fashion?

_____ Have you carefully written any new questions needed?

_____ Have you reviewed questions for politeness?

_____ Are questions clear and appropriately precise?

_____ Are any questions or response options biased?

_____ Have you reviewed sensitive questions and considered alternatives?

_____ Have you had expert and novice respondents complete the survey and provide feedback?

_____ Are instructions on how to complete each task on an Internet survey provided at the point where they are needed?

Before You Duplicate or Post!

We have very rarely seen a survey that was completely error free! Errors range from a minor typographical error to disasters such as response-option scales reading from _Strongly Agree_ to _Strongly Agree_.

_____ Has the survey been thoroughly pretested?

_____ Have you, colleagues, and a proofreader or two carefully checked the survey? Again?

EXERCISES

[Note: Depending on the guidelines of your institutional human subjects review board, you may need to obtain approval to complete these exercises. Alternatively, you can complete every aspect of these exercises except for interviewing and data collection.]

Exercise 1

a. Think of a construct or variable that interests you. Try to keep your construct benign (or covering nonsensitive material) because you will eventually need to ask some of your friends or colleagues how they feel about your topic. Now write 5 to 10 items that you think are reflective of this construct. All of the items should tap the construct in some way, but don't worry if they are not all highly relevant to the construct.

For example, if I am interested in measuring *religious coping,* I may ask highly relevant questions such as (a) "When faced with a crisis in life, I often turn toward religion for comfort and support." (b) "When I feel stretched beyond my limits, I find prayer to be helpful in coping with it all."

I may also ask a question that seems only somewhat related to my construct such as, (c) "I often feel like a weight has been lifted after attending religious services." This item doesn't address coping with stressors by turning to religion per se, but it may tap religious sequelae that lead to more successful adjustment. The important point is to cover the breadth of the construct.

b. Once you have written your items, look them over to determine if you have violated any of the guidelines discussed under "Question Design" in this chapter. If you have, consider revising your items so that they are in line with these guidelines. For example, I may want to edit the following item to avoid the possibility of a double question.

Original item:

"When faced with a crisis in life, I often turn toward religion for comfort and support."

Revised items:

"When faced with a crisis in life, I often turn toward religion for comfort."

"When faced with a crisis in life, I often turn toward religion for support."

c. Now, find three volunteers to help you pilot test your items. These people should be conveniently chosen (e.g., friends, family, or colleagues) for this exercise. Ask them to read aloud each item that you have written. Ask them also to think aloud by verbalizing the thought processes they go through in deciding what their response will be. (You may want to take notes.)

The purpose of this step is to determine whether the meaning of the items is the same for all interviewees. You may want to revise your items if there were discrepancies between what you intended to ask and what your participants thought you were asking.

Exercise 2

In this exercise, you will be creating an e-mail survey and exploring some of the problems encountered with embedding a survey into an e-mail. You may use either the short survey that you created in Exercise 1 or an existing survey to complete the following steps.

a. If you have not already done so, type your survey items in a word processor such as Microsoft Word or WordPerfect. Now, save your word processing document as an HTML file. In Microsoft Word 2000 and XP, this is as simple as selecting the Save As Web Page option under the File menu.

b. Select three to five people (e.g., friends, family members, or colleagues) with access to e-mail. In selecting these individuals, be sure that most of them have different domain names (i.e., @xxxx.xxx) in their e-mail addresses. Open your e-mail software program and create a personalized message (e.g., use only one address per e-mail) that briefly explains the purpose of your survey, that participation is voluntary, that they are free to give *fake* answers, that regardless of the veracity of their responses they will be kept confidential, how to make their responses (i.e., hit Reply and then type answers in the appropriate location), and, *most important,* ask them to make comments on problems they encountered in responding to your e-mail survey (e.g., visual problems, incompatible software, wrapping response options). Place your cursor in the body of the e-mail where you want your survey to be placed and then add the HTML survey as an attachment. You may want to send the first e-mail to yourself to see how it turns out. If you are confident that the survey has been embedded, send it to your small sample and wait for the feedback.

Exercise 3

This exercise is designed to introduce you to Web surveying. If you do not have access to WebCT, you might try exploring one of the survey software demo programs listed at the end of this chapter.

a. Navigate your Internet browser to your WebCT home page. (If you do not have a WebCT homepage, consult your WebCT administrator to obtain a temporary homepage. Click on Add Page Or Tool and then Quizzes/Surveys under the heading Evaluation And Activity Tools. You will then be prompted to "Enter a title for this item." Type "Demo Survey," or choose another name for the introductory link to your survey. Also, click in the check box next to On An Organizer Page, and make sure that the drop-down box selection says Homepage. Then click Add.

b. You should now have a hyperlink (represented as a picture) on your WebCT home page titled "Demo Survey." Click on the hyperlink. Click on Create Survey under Options and enter the title of your survey (e.g., "Demo Survey"). Click on Create. Now, click on the hyperlink "Demo Survey."

c. Now you are ready to start adding questions to your survey. Unfortunately, WebCT does not allow users to upload and merge existing surveys. Instead, the questions and response options need to be reentered. Click Add Questions. Once the pop-up box comes up, select Question Type. For this example, choose Multiple Choice and then click on Create. Enter a title. This is the variable label associated with your question that will appear in the database. Type in your first question (e.g., "When faced with a crisis in life, I often turn toward religion for comfort."). Keep all of the default settings. Then enter the first response option in the text box for Answer 1. In our case, the first response option is *Almost never true.* Subsequent response options are entered in the same way (i.e., *Somewhat untrue* is entered in the text box for Answer 2, etc.). After you have entered all possible response options, click the Save button at the bottom of the window. Repeat this process until all of your survey items have been entered. When you have added and saved all of your items, be sure that the check boxes next to each new item are checked in the WebCT Question Browser. Then, click on the Add Selected box. You may want to preview your survey at this point and experiment with some of the design and format options that WebCT offers.

d. Before you can administer your survey, you will have to contact your WebCT administrator and request three to five temporary user IDs and passwords. You will also need to specify the date and time when the survey will become available. To do this, click on the box titled Edit Survey Settings on your survey-editing page. Under Availability click on Allow Access Now to unlock the survey for your participants. While you are in the Edit Survey Settings page, you may also wish to experiment with some of the other setting options (e.g., type a thank you or submission message).

e. Once you have allowed access and created temporary user IDs and passwords, you will need to e-mail three to five friends, family members, or colleagues and ask them to complete your survey. Include explanations in your e-mail regarding the purpose of your survey, that participation is voluntary, that they are free to give fake answers, that regardless of the veracity of their responses they will be kept confidential, and instructions on how to make their responses to the Web survey (i.e., how to gain access, navigate, and complete the survey). Make sure each personalized e-mail contains a hyperlink to the WebCT log-in Web page as well as the user ID and password information that each individual is to enter.

f. Once your participants have completed the Web survey, you can examine the responses in WebCT by clicking on the Detail box on your survey-editing page and then selecting Update Table. You can also download the data for further examination and analysis by clicking on Export Survey To Disk. Once you have downloaded the data file to your computer, you can open it using most spreadsheets or statistical programs.

RECOMMENDED READINGS

Crawford, S. (2002). Evaluation of Web survey data collection systems. *Field methods, 14*(3), 307–321.

Dillman, D. A. (2000). *Mail and Internet surveys: The tailored design method.* New York: Wiley.

Dillman, D. A., & Bowker, D. K. (2000). *The Web questionnaire challenge to survey methodologists.* Unpublished manuscript. Retrieved October 13, 2003, from http://survey.sesrc.wsu.edu/dillman/ Zuma_paper_dillman_bowker.pdf

Fienberg, S. E., & Tanur, J. M. (1989). Combining cognitive and statistical approaches to survey design. *Science, 243,* 1017–1022.

Fink, A., & Kosecoff, J. (1985). *How to conduct surveys.* Beverly Hills, CA: Sage.

Fowler, F. J. (2001). *Survey research methods* (3rd ed.). Thousand Oaks, CA: Sage.

Henry, G. T. (1990). *Practical sampling.* Newbury Park, CA: Sage.

King, K. A., Pealer, L. N., & Bernard, A. L. (2001). Increasing response rates to mail questionnaires: A review of inducement strategies. *American Journal of Health Education, 32*(1), 4–15.

Schaeffer, N. C., & Presser, S. (2003). The science of asking questions. *Annual Review of Sociology, 29,* 65–88.

Schwarz, N. (1999). Self-reports: How the questions shape the answers. *American Psychologist, 54*(2), 93–105.

Sudman, S., & Bradburn, N. M. (1982). *Asking questions: A practical guide to questionnaire design.* San Francisco: Jossey-Bass.

ANNOTATED KEY REFERENCES

Dillman, D. A. (2000). *Mail and Internet Surveys: The Tailored Design Method.* New York: Wiley.

Dillman (2000) is a must-read for the survey researcher. A significant update of his earlier classic text, this book seeks to provide practical advice—based on available research—about how to conduct self-administered mail and electronic surveys that will yield reliable and valid data and high response rates. It addresses issues common to all surveys (question design, survey structure, sampling, and enhancing response rates) but goes on to address issues arising from the many new survey options that technology has made possible.

Fowler, F. J. (2001). *Survey research methods* (3rd ed.). Thousand Oaks, CA: Sage.

Fowler (2001) provides a very readable overview of survey methods for the applied social researcher. It provides a good link between basic survey procedures and the quality of data they yield. It provides a useful guide to enhancing questions, interviewing, and obtaining good response rates.

Lohr, S. L. (1999). *Sampling: Design and analysis.* Pacific Grove, CA: Duxbury Press.

Lohr (1999) provides a thorough statistical and procedural review of sampling. She builds on a clear articulation of the requirements of a good sample and the benefits of probability sampling. She provides a thorough overview of major sampling strategies: simple random, systematic, stratified, and cluster sampling, as well as more complex strategies.

Schwarz, N. (1999). Self-reports: How the questions shape the answers. *American Psychologist, 54*(2), 93–105.

Schwarz (1999) uses cognitive theory and results from experimental studies to demonstrate the effects that various factors such as question wording, response alternatives, response scales, and context can have on the results that survey researchers obtain. He also discusses the implications of context effects and question wording on public attitudes. The theory and results provided throughout the article are striking and very informative. This is a must read for survey researchers, especially those who are developing or using new scales.

RECOMMENDED WEB SURVEY SOFTWARE

Twelve authors of Web survey articles referenced in this chapter were contacted and were asked for their recommendations regarding Web survey software. Three e-mail addresses were no longer in use. Six of the nine remaining authors responded within 1 day with their recommendations, and an additional researcher responded 4 days after the initial e-mail was sent. Their recommendations, along with the respective software URLs, are provided below. See Crawford (2002) for a more detailed examination of the important issues to consider when looking for Web survey software. Also, Dillman (personal communication, October 23, 2003) reminds us that the face of Web survey software may change very rapidly, thereby making older versions of software obsolete.

- Remark Web Survey 3 Professional (Principia Products)

    Product home page: www.principiaproducts.com/web/index.html
    Product demo and tour: www.principiaproducts.com/web/downloads.html

- Survey Solutions (Perseus Development Corporation)

    Product home page: www.perseus.com/
    Product trial: www.perseus.com/softwareprod/download.html

- Data Entry Enterprise Server and mrInterview (SPSS)

    DEES home page: www.spss.com/spssbi/data_entry_enterprise_server/
    mrInterview home page and product demos: www.spss.com/mrinterview/

- Marketing Survey Tool (Free)

    Product home page: www.surveyworld.org/

- MailWorkZ

    Product home page: www.mailworkz.com
    MailWorkZ demo: www.mailworkz.com/download.htm

- PHPSurveyor (Free)

    Product home page: http://phpsurveyor.sourceforge.net/
    Note: PHPSurveyor requires extensive script writing as a trade-off for flexibility.

- EZSurvey (Raosoft, Inc.)

  Product home page: www.raosoft.com/products/ezsurvey/
  Product demo: www.raosoft.com/downloads/demo.html

- Survey Said Survey Software

  Product home page: www.surveysaid.com/
  Product demo: www.surveysaid.com/survey-demo-download.html

NOTES

1. Instructions should be given to a respondent when answering a skip question that the respondent must first make a response and then click on the hyperlink. If the respondent doesn't make a selection first (e.g., *Yes* or *No*), the response may not be recorded.

2. Most commercial Web survey software programs also allow users to run basic descriptive analyses.

3. If both Internet and mail surveys are distributed, however, the two survey formats should be matched as closely as possible (Dillman, 2000).

4. Broadc@st is specifically designed for sending large numbers of e-mails—which may be personalized and contain an embedded survey—in a very short period of time. Broadc@st is not for developing e-mail or Web surveys, however.

REFERENCES

Adams, L. M., & Gale, D. (1982). Solving the quandary between questionnaire length and response rate in educational research. *Research in Higher Education, 17*(3), 231–240.

Altschuld, J. W., Thomas, P. M., McCloskey, W. H., Smith, D. W., Wiesmann, W. W., & Lower, M. A. (1992). Mailed evaluation questionnaires: Replication of a 96% return rate procedure. *Evaluation and Program Planning, 15,* 239–246.

American Psychological Association. (2002). Ethical principles of psychologists and code of conduct. *American Psychologist, 57,* 1060–1073.

Bachmann, D., Elfrink, J., & Vazzana, G. (1996). Tracking the progress of e-mail versus snail-mail. *Marketing Research, 8,* 31–35.

Bachmann, D., Elfrink, J., & Vazzana, G. (1999). E-mail and snail mail face off in rematch. *Marketing Research, 11*(4), 11–15.

Berge, Z. L., & Collins, M. P. (1996). IPCT journal readership survey. *Journal of the American Society for Information Science, 47*(9), 701–710.

Cochran, W. G. (1977). *Sampling techniques* (3rd ed.). New York: Wiley.

Cook, T. D., & Campbell, D. T. (1979). *Quasi-experimentation: Design and analysis issues for field settings.* Boston: Houghton Mifflin.

Crawford, S. D. (2002). Evaluation of Web survey data collection systems. *Field Methods, 14*(3), 307–321.

Crawford, S. D., Couper, M. P., & Lamias, M. J. (2001). Web surveys: Perceptions of burden. *Social Science Computer Review, 19,* 146–162.

Davis, J. A., & Smith, T. W. (1992). *The NORC General Social Survey: A user's guide.* Newbury Park, CA: Sage.

Dillman, D. A. (1978). *Mail and telephone surveys.* New York: Wiley.

Dillman, D. A. (2000). *Mail and Internet surveys: The Tailored Design Method.* New York: Wiley.

Dillman, D. A., & Bowker, D. K. (2000). *The Web questionnaire challenge to survey methodologists.* Unpublished manuscript. Retrieved October 13, 2003, from http://survey.sesrc.wsu.edu/dillman/Zuma_paper_dillman_bowker.pdf

Duffy, M. E. (2002). Methodological issues in Web-based research. *Journal of Nursing Scholarship, 34*(1), 83–88.

Fienberg, S. E., & Tanur, J. M. (1989). Combining cognitive and statistical approaches to survey design. *Science, 243,* 1017–1022.

Fink, A., & Kosecoff, J. (1985). *How to conduct surveys.* Beverly Hills, CA: Sage.

Fournier, L., & Kovess, V. (1993). A comparison of mail and telephone interview strategies for mental health surveys. *Canadian Journal of Psychiatry, 38,* 525–533.

Fowler, F. J. (2001). *Survey research methods* (3rd ed.). Thousand Oaks, CA: Sage.

Fox, R. J., Crask, M. R., & Kim, J. (1988). Mail survey response rate: A meta-analysis of selected techniques for inducing response. *Public Opinion Quarterly, 52,* 467–491.

Gitelson, R., & Drogin, E. B. (1992). An experiment on the efficacy of certified final mailing. *Journal of Leisure Research, 24,* 72–78.

Harewood, G. C., Yacavone, R. F., Locke, G. R., & Wiersema, M. J. (2001). Prospective comparison of endoscopy patient satisfaction surveys: E-mail versus standard mail versus telephone. *The American Journal of Gastroenterology, 96*(12), 3312–3317.

Heberlein, T. A., & Baumgartner, R. (1978). Factors affecting response rates to mailed surveys: A quantitative analysis of the published literature. *American Sociological Review, 43,* 447–462.

Heerwegh, D., & Loosveldt, G. (2002). Web surveys: The effect of controlling survey access using PIN numbers. *Social Science Computer Review, 20*(1), 10–21.

Henry, G. T. (1990). *Practical sampling.* Newbury Park, CA: Sage.

Hopkins, K. D., & Gullickson, A. R. (1992). Response rates in survey research: A meta-analysis of the effects of monetary gratuities. *Journal of Experimental Education, 6*(1), 52–62.

Jackson, R., Chambless, L. E., Yang, K., Byrne, T., Watson, R., Folsom, A., et al. (1996). Differences between respondents and nonrespondents in a multicenter community-based study vary by gender and ethnicity. *Journal of Clinical Epidemiology, 49*(12), 1441–1446.

Kaufman, J. S., Carlozzi, A. F., Boswell, D. L., Barnes, L. L. B., Wheeler-Scruggs, K., & Levy, P. A. (1997). Factors influencing therapist selection among gays, lesbians and bisexuals. *Counseling Psychology Quarterly, 10*(3), 287–297.

Kellerman, S. E., & Herold, J. (2001). Physician response to surveys: A review of the literature. *American Journal of Preventive Medicine, 20*(1), 61–67.

Kiesler, S., & Sproull, L. (1986). Response effects in the electronic survey. *Public Opinion Quarterly, 50*(3), 402–413.

King, K. A., Pealer, L. N., & Bernard, A. L. (2001). Increasing response rates to mail questionnaires: A review of inducement strategies. *American Journal of Health Education, 32*(1), 4–15.

Kittleson, M. J. (1995). An assessment of the response rate via the postal service and e-mail. *Health Values: The Journal of Health Behavior, Education and Promotion, 19,* 27–29.

Lohr, S. L. (1999). *Sampling: Design and analysis.* Pacific Grove, CA: Duxbury Press.

Matz, M. C. (1999). *Administration of Web versus paper surveys: Mode effects and response rates.* Unpublished master's thesis, University of North Carolina, Chapel Hill.

McHorney, C., Kosinski, M., & Ware, J. E. (1994). Comparison of the costs and quality of norms for the SF-36 Health Survey collected by mail versus telephone interview: Results from a national survey. *Medical Care, 32,* 551–567.

Meehan, M. L., & Burns, R. C. (1997, March). *E-mail survey of a listserv discussion group: Lessons learned from surveying an electronic network of learners* (ERIC Document Reproduction Service No. ED411292). Paper presented at the Annual Meeting of the American Educational Research Association, Chicago.

Mehta, R., & Sivadas, E. (1995). Comparing response rates and response content in mail versus electronic mail surveys. *Journal of the Market Research Society, 37*(4), 429–439.

Naglieri, J. A., Drasgow, F., Schmit, M., Handler, L., Prifitera, A., Margolis, A., et al. (2004). Psychological testing on the Internet: New problems, old issues. *American Psychologist, 59*(3), 150–162.

Nederhof, A. J. (1988). Effects of a final telephone reminder and questionnaire cover design in mail surveys. *Social Science Research, 17,* 353–361.

Paolo, A. M., Bonaminio, G. A., Gibson, C., Partridge, T., & Kallail, K. (2000). Response rate comparisons of e-mail and mail-distributed student evaluations. *Teaching and Learning in Medicine, 12*(2), 81–84.

Pitkow, J. E., & Kehoe, C. M. (1996). Emerging trends in the WWW user population. *Communications of the ACM, 39*(6), 106–108.

Pradhan, K. (1999). The Internet in Nepal: A survey report. *The International Information and Library Review, 31,* 41–47.

Rasinski, K. A., & Tourangeau, R. (1991). Psychological aspects of judgments about the economy. *Political Psychology, 12,* 27–40.

Roselle, A., & Neufeld, S. (1998). The utility of electronic mail follow-ups for library research. *Library and Information Science Research, 20*(2), 153–161.

Salant, P., & Dillman, D. A. (1994). *How to conduct your own survey*. New York: Wiley.

Schaeffer, D. R., & Dillman, D. A. (1998). Development of a standard e-mail methodology. *Public Opinion Quarterly, 62,* 378–397.

Schaeffer, N. C., & Presser, S. (2003). The science of asking questions. *Annual Review of Sociology, 29,* 65–88.

Schlegelmilch, B. D., & Diamantopoulos, A. (1991). Prenotification and mail survey response rates: A quantitative integration of the literature. *Journal of the Market Research Society, 33,* 243–255.

Schuldt, B. A., & Totten, J. W. (1994). Electronic mail vs. mail survey response rates. *Marketing Research, 6*(1), 36–39.

Schwarz, N. (1999). Self reports: How the questions shape the answers. *American Psychologist, 54*(2), 93–105.

Schwarz, N., Hippler, H. J., Deutsch, B., & Strack, F. (1985). Response categories: Effects on behavioral reports and comparative judgments. *Public Opinion Quarterly, 49,* 388–395.

Schwarz, N., Strack, F., & Mai, H. P. (1991). Assimilation and contrast effects in part-whole question sequences: A conversational logic analysis. *Public Opinion Quarterly, 55,* 3–23.

Shadish, W. R., Cook, T. D., & Campbell, D. T. (2002). *Experimental and quasi-experimental designs for generalized causal inference*. Boston: Houghton Mifflin.

Sheehan, K. (2001). E-mail survey response rates: A review. *Journal of Computer Mediated Communication, 6*(2), 1–16.

Sheehan, K. B., & McMillan, S. J. (1999). Response variation in e-mail surveys: An exploration. *Journal of Advertising Research, 39*(4), 45–54.

Sills, S. J., & Song, C. (2002). Innovations in survey research: An application of Web-based surveys. *Social Science Computer Review, 20*(1), 22–30.

Slevin, J. (1997, October). An integrated approach: Technology firm conducts worldwide satisfaction research survey via e-mail, Internet. *Quirk's Marketing Research Review.* Retrieved October 23, 2003, from www.quirks.com/articles/article.asp?arg_ArticleId=269

Sproull, L. S. (1986). Using electronic mail for data collection in organizational research. *Academy of Management Journal, 29*(1), 159–169.

Sudman, S., & Bradburn, N. M. (1982). *Asking questions: A practical guide to questionnaire design*. San Francisco: Jossey-Bass.

Swoboda, W. J., Muhlberger, N., Weitkunat, R., & Schneeweib, S. (1997). Internet surveys by direct mailing. *Social Science Computer Review, 15*(3), 242–255.

Tomaskovic-Devey, D., Leiter, J., & Thompson, S. (1994). Organizational survey non-response. *Administrative Science Quarterly, 39*(3), 439–457.

Tourangeau, R., & Rasinski, K. A. (1988). Cognitive processes underlying context effects in attitude measurement. *Psychological Bulletin, 103,* 299–314.

Tourangeau, R., Rasinski, K. A., Bradburn, N., & D'Andrade, R. (1989). Carryover effects in attitude surveys. *Public Opinion Quarterly, 53,* 495–524.

Tourangeau, R., Rasinski, K. A., & D'Andrade, R. (1991). Attitude structure and belief accessibility. *Journal of Experimental Social Psychology, 27,* 46–75.

Truell, A. D., Bartlett, J. E., & Alexander, M. W. (2002). Response rate, speed, and completeness: A comparison of Internet-based and mail surveys. *Behavior Research Methods, Instruments and Computers, 34*(1), 46–49.

Tse, A. C. B. (1998). Comparing the response rate, response speed, and response quality of two methods of sending questionnaires: E-mail vs. mail. *Journal of the Market Research Society, 40*(4), 353–361.

Tse, A., Tse, K. C., Yin, C. H., Ting, C. B., Yi, K. W., Yee, K. P., et al. (1995). Comparing two methods of sending out questionnaires: E-mail versus mail. *Journal of the Market Research Society, 37,* 441–445.

Walsh, J. P., Kiesler, S., Sproull, L. S., & Hesse, B. W. (1992). Self-selected and randomly selected respondents in a computer network survey. *Public Opinion Quarterly, 56,* 241–244.

Weible, R., & Wallace, J. (1998). The impact of the Internet on data collection. *Marketing Research, 10*(3), 19–23.

Yammarino, F. J., Skinner, S. J., & Childers, T. L. (1991). Understanding mail survey response behavior: A meta-analysis. *Public Opinion Quarterly, 55,* 613–639.

Yun, G. W., & Trumbo, C. W. (2000). Comparative response to a survey executed by post, e-mail, & Web form. *Journal of Computer Mediated Communication, 6*(1), 1–19.

14

CONDUCTING TELEPHONE SURVEYS

PETER Y. CHEN

YUENG-HSIANG HUANG

The telephone survey has become a widely used tactic in areas such as political polls or marketing. Prior to the 1970s, this method was criticized for its methodological weaknesses, particularly sampling bias due to high noncoverage rates (about 20% in 1963) in the United States (Thornberry & Massey, 1988). Over the years, this problem has been dramatically lessened, as estimated by Bourque and Fielder (2003; 97.25% in 2000) and the U.S. Census Bureau (2002; 94.49% in 2001). It is important to point out that the percentage of households with telephones in the United States differs by state, ranging from 87.83% in Mississippi to 98.10% in New Hampshire, based on U.S. Census Bureau data (2002). Overall, the percentages of telephone availability are likely to be higher than the above figures when both conventional phones and cellular phones are considered.

In this chapter, we will describe the process of conducting a telephone survey (see outline presented in Form 14.1; also refer to Dillman, 1978, 2000) in conjunction with a series of related hands-on exercises. The first section will focus on the advantages and disadvantages of using telephone surveys in comparison to mailed surveys and personal interviews. Because the sampling procedures employed in the telephone survey are quite different from those used in other survey methods, a portion of the chapter is devoted to its unique techniques for sampling among households and within households. Following that, we will elaborate on selection criteria, training, and supervision of interviewers, who play an extremely important role during the process of a telephone survey. Finally, we will give an overview of various uses of computers in the telephone survey (i.e., computer-assisted telephone interviewing, CATI; interactive voice response system, IVR). Other important topics, such as designing surveys, scale and test development, sampling (e.g., probability sampling, stratified random sampling, cluster random sampling), and statistical power are presented in Chapters 8, 9, 10, and 11 of this book. The principles presented in these chapters also apply to the telephone survey.

CRITERIA FOR CHOOSING THE TELEPHONE SURVEY

The choice of survey methods often depends on the goals of the research, available resources, characteristics of the sample, sample frame, and the strengths of the various methods. There have been studies (e.g., Groves & Kahn, 1979; Groves, Lyberg, & Massey, 1988; Mangione, Hingson, & Barrett, 1982; Siemiatycki, 1979) simultaneously comparing two or more survey methods (mainly telephone survey, personal

Form 14.1   An Outline for Conducting a Telephone Survey

- Define the goals and objectives of the survey.
- Choose the telephone survey over other modes of data collection.
  - Evaluate four aspects: administrative, sampling, measurement, and data quality.
  - Assess if the telephone survey is an appropriate choice.
- Select and generate sampling pools.
- Design and pretest the questionnaire, survey procedures, and rules book.
- Recruit interviewers; initially hire, train, and make final selection.
  - Recruit and select prospective interviewers who meet the initial standards.
  - Conduct orientation training, skill building, interviewer error training, feedback, and evaluation.
  - Select final candidates based on behavior criteria. If possible, assign other tasks to the remaining trainees who wish to stay in the project.
- Conduct pilot test, item analysis; revise the questionnaire and survey procedures.
- Print the questionnaire and other forms.
- Conduct the survey in a centralized setting.
  - Continue on-the-job training and daily briefing.
  - Provide on-site, taped monitoring or supervision.
  - Assess performance according to behavior criteria and give feedback promptly.
- Assemble results.
- Report findings.
- Evaluate results and costs; determine next steps.

interview, and mail survey) on limited evaluative criteria; however, no indisputable criteria or golden rules exist for such comparisons (Bourque & Fielder, 2003). In addition to the lack of golden rules, some extraneous variables, including sampling frame, training procedures, and wording in questionnaires that cannot be used identically across different methods, were not controlled in these studies. As a result, Biemer (1988) concluded that no definitive conclusion about "pure mode effect" can be made (i.e., comparisons between telephone surveys and other methods, given that extraneous variables are controlled in experiments). In the remainder of this section, we will summarize prior research pertaining to *relative* advantages and disadvantages of the telephone survey, along with a list of important criteria. A decision aid is then presented to facilitate decision making in weighing the potential benefits of choosing the telephone survey method. Tradeoffs on multiple study features, as you are learning, are key in making research decisions.

Critiques of the Telephone Survey

The unique characteristics of the telephone survey cannot be fully recognized without comparing it with other survey methods across multiple criteria. Two alternative methods, personal interview and mail survey, will be compared with the telephone survey because of their popularity as survey methods and the availability of empirical findings on the techniques. Although empirical data are somewhat limited at the time of writing this chapter, we will include a comparison between Internet (Web or e-mail) and phone surveys because of the increasing popularity of using the Internet survey (Gosling et al., 2004).

The criteria will be scrutinized on the basis of four aspects: administrative (e.g., cost, personnel, training), sampling (e.g., noncoverage, nonresponse), measurement process (e.g., length of data collection and questionnaire, type of questions), and data quality (e.g., response validity, social desirability). Comparative results between

Table 14.1   Comparisons Between Other Survey Modes and the Telephone Survey Based on Four Criteria

Data Collection	Administrative	Sampling	Measurement	Data Quality
Mail Survey	Less costly to implement, compared with telephone survey	Less problematic in coverage but lower response rates, compared with telephone survey	Less problematic in length of survey and easier to maintain anonymity, compared with telephone survey	One study showed more accurate recognition in mail survey than in telephone survey
Personal Interview	More costly to implement, compared with telephone survey	Less problematic in coverage and higher response rates, compared with telephone survey	Less problematic in length of survey, more difficult to control situational variables, and appropriate for more complex and sensitive questions, compared with telephone survey	Data quality of personal interview is likely similar to that in telephone survey
Internet Survey	More cost-effective than telephone survey	Likely more problematic in coverage and lower response rates, compared with telephone survey	Less problematic in length of survey and easier to maintain anonymity, compared with telephone survey	One study showed more accurate recognition in Internet survey than in telephone survey. Polling results are not always consistent with those reported in telephone survey

other survey modes and the telephone survey are summarized in Table 14.1.

The Administrative Aspect

Cost

Although a budget for the telephone survey is usually required in a research or grant proposal, little information pertaining to overhead, indirect costs, and unexpected expenses (e.g., three to six callbacks may be necessary) has been reported in the literature (Frey, 1989). Generally, the cost of the telephone survey rises when a large sample size or high response rate is planned. In order to achieve these goals, researchers must hire more personnel, make more callbacks (i.e., redial a telephone number at a different time or day in order to reach a selected respondent), spend more time in preparing the database, and so on.

If an initial screening, such as for 40- to 55-year-old females who work, or a long questionnaire is part of a telephone survey, more time and money will also be spent in identifying eligible respondents or completing the interviews. The cost of reaching respondents living in different geographical areas would also be greater; however, the use of a leased line, like a WATS line, can significantly reduce telephone charges because the line offers users low rates in calling anywhere throughout the country. If calls are to be made in one or more specific cities or locations, you might consider hiring on-site assistants to eliminate long-distance charges (although this may increase training and supervision costs).

Compared with the personal interview, the telephone survey can be less costly to implement due to reduced labor costs per interview. Generally, the cost of telephone surveys is less than the cost for personal interviews

(Miller & Salkind, 2002; Shuy, 2002) by about one third to two thirds (Lucas & Adams, 1977; Siemiatycki, 1979). Frey (1989) cited evidence that the cost of the telephone survey is about one sixth to one half more than the mail survey. Regarding the mail survey, cost generally does not rise considerably, even if a diverse sample or a lengthy questionnaire is planned; however, these factors would add to the administrative costs in the telephone survey. Finally, there seems a consensus among practitioners and researchers (Bandilla, Bosnjak, & Altdorfer, 2003; Dillman, 2000) that the Internet survey is the most cost-effective mode of data collection.

Personnel and Training

Compared with personal interviews, telephone surveys require a smaller staff for a given sample size. As a rule of thumb, approximately 10 interviewers, plus two to three supervisors, would be adequate for surveying 1000 interviewees by telephone. In practice, twice as many prospective interviewers may need to be recruited in the beginning because of attrition of interviewers due to inadequate skills or loss of interest. Fowler and Mangione (1990) estimated that it may take 20 to 30 hours to train an interviewer to perform at acceptable levels. In contrast, few personnel and little training or supervision are required in the mail survey or Internet survey (Sheehan & McMillan, 1999).

The Sampling Aspect

Noncoverage

Similar to the Internet survey (Best & Krueger, 2002; Dillman, 2000), a major limit of the telephone survey is that noncovered households have zero chance to be sampled, rendering the results invalid. Reasons for noncoverage include lack of telephone service and blocked, unlisted, new, or just-changed telephone numbers. With the advanced random-digit-dialing sampling technique (described later), unlisted, new, or just-changed numbers could still possibly be accessible to researchers; however, it is impossible to interview people by telephone if they do not have telephones at home. A 2002 official

report (U.S. Census Bureau) revealed that there are eight states (Mississippi, Arkansas, New Mexico, Illinois, Alabama, Florida, Tennessee, and Georgia) having household coverage of only between 88% and 92%. In general, noncoverage is higher for people who live in rural areas and inner cities, have low income or are unemployed, are young (less than 24), or are African American or Hispanic (Cannell, 1985b; Trewin & Lee, 1988). Hagan (1993) reported that coverage of Hispanics in the southwestern areas is as low as 65%. In addition, noncoverage is higher for very large (six or above) and single-person households. Thornberry and Massey (1988) report that race, marital status, geographical region, family size, and employment status do not explain significant variance of telephone coverage while family income, age, and education are held constant. If researchers wish to survey variables of interest (e.g., health) that are related to the above noncoverage characteristics, they would very likely run into under- or overestimation problems.

Nonresponse

Unlike noncoverage, nonresponse households are selected for a sample, but their responses are not assessed for either part or all of the survey questions. Failure to obtain measurement from the selected households may result from incapacity (e.g., selected respondents have physical and mental disability or language difficulty), noncontact (e.g., selected respondents cannot be reached by telephone after more than six attempts), or refusal (Groves & Lyberg, 1988). Generally, nonrespondents tend to be older and less educated (Weaver, Holmes, & Glenn, 1975). Nonresponse rates may also be affected by interviewer attributes, which will be discussed later in the training section.

The nonresponse rate is relatively higher in the mail and Internet survey than in the telephone survey, and the telephone survey nonresponse rate is higher than for personal interviews (Cho & LaRose, 1999; Miller & Salkind, 2002; Schaefer & Dillman, 1998). Most telephone surveys have difficulty reaching a 60% response rate, and most personal interviews have difficulty reaching a response rate higher than 70% (Brehm, 1993). Specifically, the cold telephone survey, in which no advance notice is sent before calling, has a lower response rate than does the face-to-face interview (Cannell, 1985b); however, this latter difference would likely disappear if the warm-call procedure (advance notice sent before calling) is used (Fowler, 2002).

High nonresponse rates may create potential difficulties in administration (e.g., multiple dialing, time used for persuasion, or monetary expenses) and threats to the validity of survey results (e.g., statistical conclusion validity, construct validity, or external validity). If nonrespondents are systematically different from the respondents on some individual characteristics, the survey results and conclusions could be distorted. Because all surveys are voluntary (or at least should be), it is very difficult for researchers to handle the aforementioned problems.

It should be noted that nonresponse rate is not a synonym of nonresponse error or bias (or degree of representativeness). The magnitude of nonresponse error varies as a function of both nonresponse rate and the size of the true difference between respondents and nonrespondents (Groves & Lyberg, 1988). High nonresponse rates, therefore, do not necessarily indicate the existence of nonresponse error if there is no difference between respondents and nonrespondents. Likewise, an extremely low nonresponse rate (say 5%) may be associated with a great amount of nonresponse error, should the nonrespondents be very different from the respondents. Visser, Krosnick, Marquette, and Curtin (1996) compared the prediction accuracy of election results over a 15-year period between mail surveys and telephone surveys. Although mail surveys tended to have lower response rates (about 20%) than telephone surveys (about 60%), the low response rates of the mail surveys (average error was about 1.6%), contrary to the conventional wisdom, have predicted the election outcomes more accurately than the high response rates of telephone interviews (average error was about 5.2%). This empirical finding led Krosnic (1999) to conclude that nonresponse error does not necessarily decrease monotonically with an increase of response rate, and a low response rate does not necessarily imply that a survey suffers from a large amount of nonresponse error.

Another confusion observed in the telephone survey is how to calculate the response rate. Unfortunately, there is no universal guideline. As suggested by Groves and Lyberg (1988), researchers should use different measures of response rate, rather than a single preferred calculation, to serve different purposes. An extensive list of response rate formulas is illustrated by Groves and Lyberg, including cooperation rate, contact rate, and refusal conversion rate. For example, the *cooperation rate* is calculated as a ratio of numbers of completed interviews over the sum of numbers of interviews (either completed or partial) and numbers of refusals.

The Measurement Aspect

Length of Data Collection and Interview

A strength of telephone surveys lies in the relatively short duration of the total interview period. A telephone survey can generally be completed within a short period of time (a few days to a few weeks); however, they have been criticized for the inability to conduct lengthy individual interviews longer than 30 minutes (Lucas & Adams, 1977). Providing evidence for this characteristic, Collins, Sykes, Wilson, and Blackshaw (1988) found long interview length to be associated with high refusal rate. Their finding, however, was contradictory to that of Frankel and Sharp (1981), who reported that the length of the interview was not related to the refusal rate. Frey (1989) also cited several successful examples of lengthy (an average of 50 minutes) telephone surveys. In general, research results are mixed on the effects of survey length on refusal rate (Sheehan, 2001). We suspect that the time limitation of the telephone survey would be contingent on the interest level of the topic, types of interviewees (e.g., younger or older people), experience of interviewers, the nature of the survey, and interview procedures.

Interviewing Process

In interview-related surveys, interviewers ask questions, probe short or incomplete answers, and record information provided by respondents. They have to read questions correctly with adequate tone of wording, probe incomplete answers without giving the respondents too much or too little feedback or instruction, and record information without subjective interpretation being involved. Lavrakas (1993) believed that phone interviewers experience more workload than personal interviewers. Personal interviewers have a disadvantage in that they may not safely meet respondents in certain places or at certain times (de Leeuw & van der Zouwen, 1988). Research has also shown that situational variables are easier to control in either mail or phone surveys than in personal interviews (Shuy, 2002). The statement is also likely applicable to Internet surveys. Nevertheless, the process of the phone survey is dynamic and situation-specific, and it is not uncommon for a well-trained interviewer to commit errors. The variation in interviewer performance (i.e., reliability) may be caused by interaction with respondents, supervisors, and coworkers, physical or emotional conditions of interviewers, and attributes of interviewers. Although it is virtually impossible to eliminate completely the problems occurring in the process, they may be reduced by standardization, close monitoring, immediate feedback, daily debriefing, and/or on-the-job training.

Anonymity or Confidentiality and Type of Questions

In most cases, respondents' names, telephone numbers, or even addresses are known in both the telephone survey and personal interview. Hence, it is virtually impossible to maintain anonymity in these types of methods. This would not be a problem, however, in most mail survey studies and Internet surveys (Andrews, Nonnecke, & Preece, 2003). With the nature of knowing the respondents' identification, distorted responses to sensitive, threatening, or embarrassing questions could very likely happen in interview-related surveys (Lucas & Adams, 1977). Even when confidentiality is assured to respondents in these surveys, data quality might suffer from their apprehensiveness (Frey, 1989).

Concerning the type of questions, the personal interview is more appropriate than the telephone survey and mail survey for more complex and sensitive questions (Miller & Salkind, 2002). Cannell (1985a) suggested that

researchers should make questions simple because respondents generally have difficulty understanding questions on the telephone. The use of less complex questions could also limit some interviewer errors resulting from inadequate probes. As will be discussed later, it usually takes a great deal of time to train interviewers to probe open-ended questions satisfactorily because (a) interviewers need to be able to detect inadequate responses, and (b) many probes may be required for the frequently shortened answers given in interview surveys (Frey, 1989). The use and merit of open-ended questions, however, should not be dismissed or discounted. Responses to open-ended questions often shed new light on research questions or generate research ideas.

The Data Quality Aspect

Criteria used to assess data quality include accuracy (or response validity), absence of social desirability, item nonresponse, amount of information given in an open-ended question, and similarity of response distribution obtained by different methods. De Leeuw and van der Zouwen (1988) meta-analyzed previous studies and concluded that the differences between the personal interview and the telephone survey on the above criteria are small but in favor of the personal interview; however, the authors speculated that the difference in data quality between these two modes has become minimal over time. This trend could possibly be attributed to increased experience with the telephone survey.

Other data quality indexes include response styles, including acquiescence, evasiveness, extremeness, and psychometric properties, including test-retest or internal consistency reliability estimates. For example, Jordan, Marcus, and Reeder (1980) found that more agreement, extremeness, and evasiveness were found in telephone surveys than in personal interviews. Some researchers concluded that there are no differences on psychometric properties between the two modes (Aneshensel, Frerichs, Clark, & Yokopenic, 1982; Herman, 1977), although Miller and Salkind (2002) judged that personal interviews showed overall better reliability and validity than mail surveys, followed by telephone surveys. Within limited research, Kellner

(2004) reported that there were more respondents in a mail survey and an Internet survey recognizing a false brand of bottled water than those in a telephone survey and personal interviews. He further showed that polling results of telephone surveys are not always consistent with those of Internet surveys. It seems that more often the results of telephone surveys do not share similar distributions with those of Internet surveys (Best & Krueger, 2002).

A Decision Aid for Choosing the Telephone Survey

If *only* one survey method is permissible in a research project, one needs to evaluate the strengths and weaknesses of each method. In most cases, there is no absolutely correct choice. It should be emphasized that the decision aid described below serves only as a guide, hence should not dictate the choice. While considering methods, first assess whether the mail survey or interview-related methods (e.g., telephone survey, personal interview, or Internet survey) have fewer constraints in achieving the goals of research. This decision may be reached by asking the following questions:

1. Do many questions to be asked depend on respondents' previous answers?

2. Must the survey be conducted at a specific time?

3. Are survey questions very complex?

4. Are accurate mailing lists of eligible and representative subjects available?

5. Are survey questions very sensitive, threatening, embarrassing, or personal?

6. Are numbers of the sample widely dispersed over a broad geographical area?

7. Does survey information need to be secured within a short period of time?

If responses to the above questions are affirmative, interview-related methods may be considered. Except for some cases (e.g., experience sampling methodology is applied to prompt the respondent by a pager or a timer), it would be very difficult to administer a mail survey at a specific time because researchers cannot control when survey questions are answered.

If interview-related surveys are considered to be a better choice than the mail survey, next determine which type of interview mode is desirable. The following questions may be helpful in making this decision:

1. Must data be collected at a special location such as a workplace, supermarket, or post office?

2. Must interviewers show something to respondents?

3. Must eligible respondents be selected on the basis of their behaviors or physical characteristics?

4. Are many questions employed in the interview?

5. Are certain types of people to be excluded?

6. Must data be collected within a very short period of time?

7. Do respondents reside in a broad geographical area?

8. Is it likely that respondents' companion(s) might influence their responses during the interviews?

The telephone survey would not be the right choice if prospective respondents must be interviewed at a special location or shown something (e.g., product packages or car colors). Neither is it appropriate if the eligibility of respondents is determined on the basis of their physical characteristics (e.g., blond hair) or behaviors (e.g., chewing tobacco) or if the questionnaire is lengthy (e.g., taking more than 60 minutes to complete the questionnaire). Telephones may not be available for certain geographical areas or types of people (e.g., homeless people). If these people represent an important part of the sample, the telephone survey should, at least, not be the sole mode of data collection.

The telephone interview is often the quickest. For example, suppose that you received an urgent request from the office of the president of your organization to find out within 10 days employees' opinions about a new parking permit system. You could probably spend 3 to 4 days to complete 300 interviews by telephone;

however, it would not be easy to complete the same task by using other methods such as the personal interview or mail survey. The telephone survey would also be the preferred choice if respondents live in a diverse area or if their companions might affect the respondents' answers because others present would not hear the questions being asked, thereby alleviating to some extent the respondent's needs for face saving. In addition to the above advantages of the telephone survey, it has a relatively high respondent rate, is easy to be monitored and recorded in the survey process, and can do complicated routing when combined with computer and other audio devices, which will be discussed later in the chapter.

Exercise 1 at the end of this chapter presents a hypothetical case study requiring consideration of the relative merits of the telephone survey.

GENERATING SAMPLING POOLS

Before conducting a telephone survey, the researcher needs to decide how many and what kind of people are to be sampled. The interest should not be primarily in the sample to be surveyed but in attempting to specify the population from which the sample is extracted. In other words, the goal is to understand the population through the selected sample. How well one can generalize from the sample to the population mainly depends on the sampling plan (i.e., sampling frame and sample size).

There are two distinctive but inseparable sampling plans employed in the telephone survey: sampling between and across households and sampling within households. The former is to sample representative households (i.e., telephone numbers) based on directories or other procedures, and the latter is to sample respondents within the selected households.

Sampling Between Households

Sampling between households is a procedure whereby researchers randomly generate telephone numbers by means of directories (e.g., telephone or membership directories), commercially available telephone numbers, random-digit

dialing (RDD), or Waksberg's (1978) two-stage RDD sampling. The numbers in directories are usually obtained from telephone companies, organizations (e.g., employee directories), associations (e.g., APA membership directories), or survey organizations (e.g., ASDE, Inc., 2004 or Survey Sampling International, 2004); however, directories other than telephone books are not easily accessible to the public. In addition to this obstacle, such directories generally contain duplicate or incorrect telephone numbers, cover ineligibles, and fail to cover eligible respondents (either new, unlisted, recently changed, or those without a telephone). Another challenge in using directories is that cellular phone numbers are not listed. Failure to cover eligible respondents presents a serious threat to statistical conclusion, as well as to external validities.

To generate sampling pools from one or more directories, randomly select numbers with the help of a computer or random-numbers table. The size of the sample pool depends on your resources and sampling errors you could tolerate. For stratified or area probability sampling, the telephone numbers could also be selected on the basis of geographical areas, prefix, or other characteristics of interest (e.g., size of companies, gender, job titles). Sampling pools can also be generated by the add-a-digit sampling method, which is a directory-assisted technique. This procedure requires researchers to add either one or two (can also be three) constant (or randomly assigned) digits to the last four digits of a selected telephone number. If the number 593–0822 is drawn, the actual number called is 593–0831 when number 9 is randomly assigned. In general, directory sampling will lead to biased samples because of incomplete records in directories, and even the add-a-digit sampling technique cannot eliminate the problem.

In order to reduce the bias resulting from noncoverage, random-digit dialing (RDD) and several modified versions were developed (Cooper, 1964; Waksberg, 1978). RDD is a method that creates a sampling frame of all working phones from which a sample can be randomly drawn. RDD has the major advantage of representing all phones in the selected geography. To understand how to use the RDD approach, we need to understand the structure of phone numbers. Any given telephone number, such as 555-491-2143, is construed as three parts: area code (i.e., AC, 555), prefix or central office codes (i.e., COC, 491), and suffix (2143). There are 640 3-digit COCs allotted to each AC, and there are 10,000 suffixes (from 0000 to 9999) assigned to each COC. No COC, however, is completely filled with all possible suffixes. Suffixes are generally assigned in bundles of 1000 or 100. For instance, a block of 1000 suffixes may be assigned to a university or a block of 100 suffixes may be assigned to a hotel. This information may be revealed from telephone directories or local telephone companies.

To conduct an RDD sampling, first determine the ACs from which part (or all) of the sample is to be extracted. Then COCs are randomly selected. Certain numbers of suffixes within each COC are also randomly selected. This random generation could be done by random-numbers tables or computers. Lavrakas (1993, pp. 44–46) provides computer programs (written in BASIC language) that can generate suffixes randomly. Other important information pertaining to the RDD sampling, such as identifying nonworking blocks of suffixes and determining the potential number of telephone access lines for each prefix, can also be found in Lavrakas. Waksberg (1978) has proposed a two-stage RDD sampling procedure, which has been continuously employed in telephone surveys. In stage 1, researchers randomly select small combinations (about 50 to 100) of AC and COC (AC-COC). Then, two random digits are added to each AC-COC combination. Thus, a series of the eight-digit combinations is compiled as the primary sampling units (PSUs), which serve as seeds to generate the final sampling pools. Each PSU provides a cluster of 100 numbers. For example, the possible 100 telephone numbers derived from the PSU of 555–491–21 start from 555–491–21–00 to 555–491–21–99. After two ending random numbers (e.g., 22) are added to the PSU, the final number called becomes 555–491–21–22. If this number is a residential number, the PSU will be retained for additional generation in stage 2. Otherwise, the PSU is discarded at this stage. In stage 2, additional two ending random digits are generated within each PSU until a certain number of respondents are reached. Overall, this sampling technique is efficient and cost-effective with such trade-offs

as an initial increase in clerical work and a small loss of precision on sampling (Frey, 1989; Groves, 1989). Exercises 2 and 3 at the end of this chapter present another hypothetical case study to practice how to generate sampling pools and maximize the response rate of a telephone survey.

Sampling Within Households

When an interviewer dials the generated telephone number, he or she may immediately face a dilemma: Who among the household members will be interviewed? The decision about choosing respondents can be made by one of the following procedures. The simplest way is to interview the first eligible person who picks up the telephone and also meets prior criteria (e.g., male over 21 years of age); however, this method creates underrepresentation of males because females tend to answer telephones first (Frey, 1989). Originally developed for personal interviews, Kish's (1949) procedure requires the person who answers the telephone to first name all members of the household and to list them by gender and age. Each member is then assigned a number by the interviewer according to the order of age and gender. According to the Kish tables, the candidate is then selected and interviewed. Examples of Kish's procedure and its modified versions are available in Lavrakas (1993) and Frey (1989), as well as Kish. Kish's procedure is considered to be a probability sampling method that attempts to eliminate the noncoverage error within households. Because all eligible respondents may not be enumerated in some households (e.g., refused or misreported by respondents, interviewers' clerical errors), a small amount of noncoverage error still occurs (e.g., underrepresentation of the youngest). Although minimizing noncoverage error, this procedure tends to suffer from high nonresponse rates resulting from the laborious and demanding sampling process. Frey concluded that Kish's procedure would be more suited to the personal interview than to the telephone survey.

Another technique of sampling respondents within households is called the last (or next) birthday method. This is also considered to be a probability sampling technique because the assignment of birth date is assumed to be random. Furthermore, because each household always has a person with a next or last birthday, the bias toward gender and age is eliminated. Less intrusive or demanding, and easy to use, this method has gained popularity in telephone surveying since the mid-1980s.

PERSONNEL

Telephone surveys can not be implemented successfully without adequate interviewer training and on-the-job supervision. Before discussing interviewer training and supervision, two critical but often ignored topics need to be addressed. First is the recruitment and initial selection of interviewers.

Recruitment and Initial Selection of Interviewers

Ten interviewers are generally needed for 1000 interviews, although the ratio may fluctuate depending on budget, sample size, time frame, available work space, and length of survey. Because of potential attrition, twice as many prospective interviewers as the number needed should be recruited. It is also advisable to provide the applicants with a realistic preview of their tasks. The content of the preview should consist of outcomes or rewards (e.g., pay, credit, grade, letter of recommendation, authorship), work hours and workload (e.g., 2 hours every night from 7 P.M. to 9 P.M., and numbers of interviewees who should be interviewed), selection criteria (e.g., prior experience, speech clarity, or training evaluation), responsibility (e.g., survey procedures or ethical principles), scope of the surveys, and other requirements (e.g., policies related to grooming, lateness, absence, smoking, food, drink). Both positive and negative features of the job preview could possibly prompt the applicants to reevaluate their own commitment. In addition, the preview would allow adjustment of unrealistic expectations before joining the training sessions. Any resulting self-selection would also make your task of selection easier.

If prospective interviewers decide to apply for the job, it is appropriate to evaluate the applicants' reading and writing (or typing) abilities by means of sample tasks or role plays. Demographic characteristics (e.g., ethnicity, gender, age, religion) should not be used as selection criteria unless there is evidence that these characteristics might influence interview results (Lavrakas, 1993). Fowler and Mangione (1990) suggested that selected interviewers should possess good reading and writing skills and have a reasonably *pleasant* personality. They further concluded that there appeared to be no other "credible selection criteria for distinguishing among potential interviewers" (p. 140). Other factors, however, may become relevant criteria. For instance, Groves and Fultz (1985) found that prior experience is an important factor in decreasing the refusal rate. Bourque and Fielder (2003) also presented a list of knowledge, skills, and abilities interviewers should possess in their jobs. Unfortunately, little job analytical and validation evidence has been reported regarding what specific skills (e.g., persuasive skill, communication skill), abilities (e.g., speech clarity, pitch), or personal characteristics (e.g., friendliness, tolerance for rejection) are essential to the interviewing job. As a result, selection criteria suggested by Fowler and Mangione or Bourque and Fielder should be applied with caution.

Training and Final Selection

Following the initial selection, a series of training sessions (about 20 to 30 hours) is required regardless of the prior experience of prospective interviewers. Contents of the training should cover how to contact interviewees and enlist their cooperation, build good rapport with the interviewees, interview the respondents in a structured manner, handle often occurring events during a telephone survey that deviate from the script (e.g., incomplete initial response from interviewees), and record the answers without personal opinions being involved. Contents of training should also contain critical events and challenges identified from the behavior-coding approach (Fowler & Cannell, 1996), in which observers monitor pretest phone surveys between interviewers and respondents and record any significant incident that interviewers would encounter. The training might include use of an interviewer manual, lectures or discussion, modeling, interactive computer-assisted programs, role playing, simulation, and supervised practice. A sample interviewer-training guideline is available in Frey (1989) and Bourque and Fielder (2003).

The training has a fourfold purpose: it orients the trainees about the scope of the survey, questionnaires, and survey procedures; it allows the trainees to sharpen their interview skills, to practice appropriate speech patterns, and to learn probing skills and feedback-seeking strategies; it reduces potential interviewer-related errors; and it evaluates the trainees' performance on which the final hiring decision will be based. The following sections describe how these purposes can be accomplished through the training.

Orientation Training

During the orientation, the trainees should learn the purpose of the survey, types of respondents they will interview, characteristics a good interviewer should have, ethical principles they are obliged to uphold, how telephone numbers are generated and processed, as well as other administrative policies. In addition, they will study and practice when and how to use properly the survey's call-sheet, introduction statements (e.g., who I am, how I got your telephone number, how long the survey will take, why we called you, who the principal investigator is), fallback statements, and refusal report form (sample forms are found in Bourque & Fielder, 2003; Lavrakas, 1993). The trainees should be given plenty of time to discuss and interpret questions in the questionnaire. It is not uncommon that interviewers do not understand some of the questions that they must ask, which can lead to confusion and errors.

Skill-Building Training

Interviewers will receive quite a few rejections per day while conducting the telephone survey. The trainees should learn how to enlist interviewees' cooperation, establish a good rapport, pace, and flow with the interviewees throughout the interview session. Furthermore, they need to understand the nature of refusal

(e.g., how many times should the same number be called), how to persuade the interviewees without being pushy, and how to deal with their own fear of rejection. Information about persuasion skills is available in Groves (1989). Table 14.2 gives some examples that are used to respond to a potential refusal. These responses were prepared based on a study for the National Center for the Study of Adult Learning and Literacy.

It should be noted that the telephone survey is not currently governed by the National Do Not Call Registry (2004). Nevertheless, people who request not to be called in prior surveys conducted by other survey organizations require special handling by interviewers. In practice, each survey organization maintains its own do-not-call list; however, people who were promised not to be called by an organization may be called again by another survey organization because of the nature of the random process. To avoid potential resentment and annoyance, and a potential regulatory system imposed from the outside, a do-not-call database has been created and updated, which is shared by some survey organizations (ASDE, Inc., 2004).

Besides the skills described earlier, trainees should practice improving their voice quality. The interviewers sometimes become sloppy with respect to speaking properly such that they do not move their lips fully (Strafford & Grant, 1993). Oksenberg and Cannell (1988) found that the refusal rate tends to decrease when interviewers are confident and competent in the interview or speak with a standard American accent, low pitch, loud voice, and relatively fast speaking rate. Strafford and Grant further suggested that interviewers should keep a *smile* in their voices (although interviewees cannot see them), which will lubricate communication smoothly.

Without visual cues during telephone surveys, interviewers usually attempt to seek out feedback in order to assure themselves that the communication is effective. The desire to seek feedback can be observed when the interviewers start to say more things than usual or say things they should not (Cannell, 1985b). During the training sessions, the trainees should learn that simple sentences such as "I understand" or

Table 14.2   Some Examples That Are Used to Respond to a Potential Refusal

Refusal reasons	Possible responses
I am very busy!	This survey will only take a few minutes. Sorry to have caught you at a bad time. When would be a good time for me to call you back in the next day or two?
I don't feel well right now!	I am sorry to hear that. I would be happy to call you back in a day or two. Would that be okay?
I am not interested in it!	It is very important that we get the opinions of everyone in the sample. Otherwise, the results won't be very useful. So, your participation is extremely important to us.
I am too young (or old).	Younger (older) persons' opinions are just as important in this survey as anyone else's. For the results to be representative, we have to be sure that younger (older) people have as much chance to give their opinions as anyone else does. So, your responses are so important to us.
I don't think I am capable of participating in the survey.	The survey questions are not at all difficult. There are no right or wrong answers. We are concerned about how you feel rather than how much you know about certain things. Some of the people we have already interviewed had the same concerns you have, but once we got started they didn't have any difficulty answering the questions. Maybe I could read just a few questions to you so you can see what they are like.

"I see" are sufficient to maintain the communication. Other feedback phrases such as "It is useful to get your ideas on this" or "I want to make sure I have that right" are also helpful.

Interviewer Error Training

Results of the telephone survey are obtained through the process in which interviewers read questions to interviewees, probe ambiguous or incomplete answers, and record the final answers. Distorted results can easily appear, even when the questionnaire is perfectly designed, because of one or more interviewer errors. For example, interviewers may fail to read questions exactly as worded or to use probe questions when necessary. Errors can also occur when the interviewers probe answers in a directive way (which may influence interviewees' clarifications or elaborations) or record answers with their own discretion. Other errors include inappropriate interpersonal behavior (e.g., aggression) and evaluative feedback to interviewees (e.g., "That's great" or "You're lucky"). These potential errors can be reduced in the telephone survey by interviewer error training; however, there is evidence that trainees without prior experience may need a great deal of time to master the probing skills, particularly for open-ended questions. Fowler and Mangione (1990) reported that only 47% of their trainees demonstrated excellent or satisfactory skills for probing open-ended questions after a 10-day training program.

Feedback and Evaluation

Throughout the training session, the trainees should have plenty of opportunities to practice the aforementioned skills by means of case studies, behavior modeling, role playing, discussion or critique, and so forth. After the training, the trainees should be instructed to make three to five interviews. For instance, the trainees interview confederate interviewees, each of whom answers questions on the basis of planned scripts. The trainees' performance then is evaluated along a list of critical behaviors. These behavioral criteria include, but are not limited to, speech clarity (timing between items, mispronunciation, poor inflection, or inadequate emphasis), number of questions read incorrectly, number of questions repeated unnecessarily or incorrectly, number of directive probes, frequency of skipping questions incorrectly, number of times the interviewer failed to probe incomplete answers, number of inaccurate recordings of answers, number of questions unnecessarily clarified, number of instances seeking or giving inappropriate feedback, number of instances of inappropriate interpersonal behavior, number of instances of laughing, and number of failures to follow instructions in the call-sheet form or other forms (Cannell, 1985a; Fowler & Mangione, 1990). It should be emphasized that these criteria should be reliably measured. By using these criteria, not only are qualified interviewers selected with much less subjective judgment, but also overall training quality (e.g., reliability of interviewer performance) is evaluated. Furthermore, these criteria in conjunction with others (e.g., nonresponse rate within interviewers; speed of processing records) can be used to monitor and evaluate interviewer performance after the formal survey starts. In an academic setting, the unsuitable trainees could still be assigned to do other tasks (e.g., printing, data entry) as long as they wish to stay in the project. Following the same scenarios described in the previous exercises, Exercises 4 and 5 at the end of this chapter require drafting an invitation statement and considering numbers of personnel needed in conducting the telephone survey.

ADVANCED TECHNOLOGIES IN TELEPHONE INTERVIEWS

Over the past decade, many large-scale surveys were conducted by computer-assisted telephone interviewing (CATI, Krosnick, 1999). CATI, first used in 1971, is a tool that standardizes the interviewing process. According to Nicholls (1988), the CATI approach facilitates telephone surveys (e.g., cost-effective), enhances and controls survey data quality and interviewer behaviors (e.g., reduction in various errors such as skip error), and allows flexible survey designs (e.g., randomization of questions, branching between questions). In a typical CATI program,

such as Survent® marketed by CfMC or SURVEYWin developed by Raosoft, a bank of phone numbers can be stored, randomly generated, and/or automatically dialed out. Users have the flexibility to store numerous questions (e.g., 15,000) in various forms (pictures, sounds, etc.). Each question is flashed on a monitor via a series of screens and can be answered by multiple response codes (e.g., 1,000). All information is keyed into the computer by the interviewers immediately after interviewees answer the questions, and the data will be automatically stored. Other features allow users to randomize question sequences and question wording, do a set of questions for each response, or choose the next questions to be asked (based on prior input), which would eliminate some interviewer errors. Furthermore, users may be able to use the program to track inconsistencies in responses, set up a maximum number of attempts to make a call based on specific time zone and time of day, record status codes (e.g., busy, no answer, callback), schedule calls and callbacks, or record interviewer performance. Other appealing features include monitoring interviewers for quality control, communicating between interviewers and supervisors, recording interviewing time, and exporting data to statistical software packages such as SPSS or SAS.

There is no doubt that CATI programs offer researchers great flexibility and convenience, given that users are trained adequately and the programs are bug-free; however, it should be emphasized that the CATI programs are not panaceas for problems caused by computer anxiety, poor questionnaire design, inadequate choice of sampling procedure, unstandardized interview processes, biased selection, sloppy interview training and monitoring, nonresponse and interviewer errors, or poor rapport with interviewees. These programs could also affect the way interviewers interact with interviewees because interviewers experience additional cognitive demands from the use of the computer, resulting in less attention paid to interviewees (Couper & Hansen, 2002).

In addition to CATI programs, some phone surveys have been conducted by using touch-tone data entry (TED) and interactive voice response systems (IVR). In a typical TED, selected respondents are invited (by phone, e-mail, mail, leaflet, sales slip, etc.) to partici- pate in the survey. The respondents first call a toll-free number anytime and listen to prere- corded voice instruction, questions, and response categories. After listening to each question, the respondents press keys on their touch-tone tele- phone to enter their responses. IVR systems such as TeleFlow or ASDE, a modern form of TED, are the culmination of computer hard- ware, voice hardware, and software program- ming to automate telephone surveys and gather data by touch-tone keypad and/or voice input. The survey is conducted either after respondents have dialed in or the system has reached the respondents (by using listed or RDD samples). The survey can also be conducted by live inter- viewers first, followed by the IVR. After listen- ing to a prerecorded interviewer's voice, respondents press the telephone keypad so that data are encoded directly into a database, such as an Excel or ASCII file for statistical analysis. For open-ended questions, respondents can pro- vide verbal inputs, which are recorded for later transcription. Although it is a cost-effective alternative, it does have some disadvantages compared with the traditional telephone survey. These disadvantages include that respondents are not able to ask interviewers questions, inter- viewers cannot control the speed of the survey, or respondents cannot answer questions easily via cellular phone or cordless phone (Dillman, 2000). It should also be noted that participation rates and optimal lengths of surveys are gener- ally lower (ranging from 15 to 40%) and shorter (about 4 to 8 minutes) for the IVR than for the conventional phone survey.

CONCLUSION

It should be noted that there is no single mode of data collection that can address all the issues of concern. Each method has its limitations; however, by employing more than one approach (i.e., triangulation), researchers will be able to examine questions from different perspectives.

EXERCISES

1. Background: As a researcher in a research institute, you are requested to find out, from the point of view of corporate safety directors, what is the greatest workplace safety concern they have in their organizations. Your plan is to use a telephone survey to collect the national representative data within a month.

List the reasons why the telephone survey is appropriate in this case. Please address this question by evaluat- ing the four criteria—administrative, sampling, measurement, and data quality—described in the section of the chapter entitled, "A Decision Aid for Choosing the Telephone Survey."

2. Following the same background scenario, where will you obtain the telephone numbers for these safety managers? How do you select and generate sampling pools?

How many participants do you plan to survey to have a margin error of ± 4 with 95% confidence? In order to address the question, please also refer to the sampling procedures described in Chapter 10.

3. What are the methods you plan to use in order to maximize the response rate?

4. Write a short paragraph that would be read to the participants regarding their privacy, confidentiality, and right to refuse, and which encourages their participation.

5. How many telephone callers will you hire for this project?

RECOMMENDED READINGS

There are four books that are recommended to readers for further study of the interview in general (Fowler, 2002, *Survey Research Methods;* Dillman, 2000, *Mail and Internet Surveys: The Tailored Design Method*) and telephone surveys in particular (Bourque & Fielder, 2003, *How to Conduct Telephone Surveys;* and Lavrakas, 1993, *Telephone Survey Methods).* The former two provide a theoretical background on developing and implementing surveys, whereas the latter two are written with the focus on telephone surveys. Important topics such as sampling, standardization, questionnaire development, persuasion skills, training, improving response rates, and use of the CATI are discussed in these books.

REFERENCES

Andrews, D., Nonnecke, B., & Preece, J. (2003). Electronic survey methodology: A case study in reaching hard-to-involve Internet users. *International Journal of Human-Computer Interaction, 16,* 185–210.

Aneshensel, C. S., Frerichs, R. R., Clark, V. A., & Yokopenic, P. A. (1982). Measuring depression in the community: A comparison of telephone and personal interviews. *Public Opinion Quarterly, 46,* 110–121.

ASDE, Inc. (2004). Retrieved April 26, 2005, from www.surveysampler.com/en/index.html

Bandilla, W., Bosnjak, M., & Altdorfer, P. (2003). Survey administration effects? *Social Science Computer Review, 21,* 235–243.

Best, S. J., & Krueger, B. (2002). New approaches to assessing opinion: The prospects for electronic mail surveys. *International Journal of Public Opinion Research, 14,* 73–92.

Biemer, P. P. (1988). Measuring data quality. In R. M. Groves, P. P. Biemer, L. E. Lyberg, J. T. Massey, W. L. Nicholls, II, & J. Waksberg (Eds.), *Telephone survey methodology* (pp. 273–282). New York: Wiley.

Bourque, L. B., & Fielder, E. P. (2003). *How to conduct telephone surveys* (2nd ed.). Thousand Oaks, CA: Sage.

Brehm, J. (1993). *The phantom respondents.* Ann Arbor: University of Michigan Press.

Cannell, C. F. (1985a). Experiments in the improvement of response accuracy. In T. W. Beed & R. J. Stimson (Eds.), *Survey interviewing: Theory and techniques* (pp. 24–62). Boston: George Allen & Unwin.

Cannell, C. F. (1985b). Interviewing in telephone surveys. In T. W. Beed & R. J. Stimson (Eds.). *Survey interviewing: Theory and techniques* (pp. 63–84). Boston: George Allen & Unwin.

Cho, H., & LaRose, R. (1999). Privacy issues in Internet surveys. *Social Science Computer Review, 17,* 421–434.

Collins, M., Sykes, W., Wilson, P., & Blackshaw, N. (1988). Nonresponse: The U.K. experience. In R. M. Groves, P. P. Biemer, L. E. Lyberg, J. T. Massey, W. L. Nicholls, II, & J. Waksberg (Eds.), *Telephone survey methodology* (pp. 213–231). New York: Wiley.

Cooper, S. L. (1964). Random sampling by telephone: An improved method. *Journal of Marketing Research, 1,* 45–48.

Couper, M. P., & Hansen, S. E. (2002). Computer-assisted interviewing. In J. F. Gubrium & J. A. Holstein (Eds.), *Handbook of interview research: Context and method* (pp. 557–575). Thousand Oaks, CA: Sage.

Dillman, D. A. (1978). *Mail and telephone surveys: The total design method.* New York: Wiley Interscience.

Dillman, D. A. (2000). *Mail and Internet surveys: The Tailored Design Method* (2nd ed.). New York: Wiley.

de Leeuw, E. D., & van der Zouwen, J. (1988). Data quality in telephone and face to face surveys: A comparative meta-analysis. In R. M. Groves, P. P. Biemer, L. E. Lyberg, J. T. Massey, W. L. Nicholls, II, & J. Waksberg (Eds.), *Telephone survey methodology* (pp. 283–299). New York: Wiley.

Fowler, F. J., Jr. (2002). *Survey research methods* (3rd ed.). Thousand Oaks, CA: Sage.

Fowler, F. J., Jr., & Cannell, C. F. (1996). Using behavioral coding to identify cognitive problems with survey questions. In N. Schwarz & S. Sudman (Eds.), *Answering questions: Methodology for determining cognitive and communicative processes in survey research* (pp. 15–36). San Francisco: Jossey-Bass.

Fowler, F. J., Jr., & Mangione, T. W. (1990). *Standardized survey interviewing: Minimizing interviewer-related error.* Newbury Park, CA: Sage.

Frankel, J., & Sharp, L. (1981, January). Measurement of respondent burden. *Statistical Reporter,* 105–111.

Frey, J. H. (1989). *Survey research by telephone* (2nd ed.). Newbury Park, CA: Sage.

Gosling, S. D., Vazire, S., Srivastava, S., & John, O. P. (2004). Should we trust Web-based studies? A comparative analysis of six preconceptions. *American Psychologist, 59,* 93–104.

Groves, R. M. (1989). *Survey errors and survey costs.* New York: Wiley.

Groves, R. M., Biemer, P. P., Lyberg, L. E., Massey, J. T., Nicholls, W. L., II, & Waksberg, J. (Eds.). (1988). *Telephone survey methodology.* New York: Wiley.

Groves, R. M., & Fultz, N. H. (1985). Gender effects among telephone interviewers in a survey of economic attitudes. *Sociological Methods and Research, 14,* 31–52.

Groves, R. M., & Kahn, R. L. (1979). *Surveys by telephone: A national comparison with personal interviews.* New York: Academic.

Groves, R. M., & Lyberg, L. E. (1988). An overview of nonresponse issues in telephone surveys. In R. M. Groves, P. P. Biemer, L. E. Lyberg, J. T. Massey, W. L. Nicholls, II, & J. Waksberg (Eds.), *Telephone survey methodology* (pp. 191–211). New York: Wiley.

Hagan, F. E. (1993). *Research methods in criminal justice and criminology* (3rd ed.). New York: Macmillan.

Herman, J. B. (1977). Mixed mode data collection: Telephone and personal interviewing. *Journal of Applied Psychology, 62,* 399–404.

Jordan, W. H., Marcus, A. C., & Reeder, L. G. (1980). Response styles in telephone and household interviewing: A field experiment. *Public Opinion Quarterly, 44,* 210–222.

Kellner, P. (2004). Can online polls produce accurate findings? *International Journal of Market Research, 46,* 3–21.

Kish, L. (1949). A procedure for objective respondent selection within the household. *American Statistical Association Journal, 44,* 380–387.

Krosnick, J. A. (1999). Survey research. *Annual Review of Psychology, 50,* 537–567.

Lavrakas, P. J. (1993). *Telephone survey methods: Sampling, selection, and supervision* (2nd ed.). Newbury Park, CA: Sage.

Lucas, W., & Adams, W. (1977). *An assessment of telephone survey methods.* Santa Monica, CA: Rand.

Mangione, T. W., Hingson, R., & Barrett, J. (1982). Collecting sensitive data: A comparison of three survey strategies. *Sociological Methods and Research, 10,* 337–346.

Miller, D. C., & Salkind, N. J. (2002). Handbook of research design and social measurement (6th ed.). Thousand Oaks, CA: Sage.

National Do Not Call Registry. (2004). Retrieved April 26, 2005, from www.donotcall.gov/default.aspx

Nicholls, W. L., II. (1988). Computer-assisted telephone interviewing: A general introduction. In R. M. Groves, P. P. Biemer, L. E. Lyberg, J. T. Massey, W. L. Nicholls, II, & J. Waksberg (Eds.), *Telephone survey methodology* (pp. 377–385). New York: Wiley.

Oksenberg, L., & Cannell, C. (1988). Effects of interviewer vocal characteristics on nonresponse. In R. M. Groves, P. P. Biemer, L. E. Lyberg, J. T. Massey, W. L. Nicholls, II, & J. Waksberg (Eds.), *Telephone survey methodology* (pp. 257–269). New York: Wiley.

Schaefer, D. R., & Dillman, D. A. (1998). Development of a standard e-mail methodology: Results of an experiment. *Public Opinion Quarterly, 62,* 378–397.

Sheehan, K. B. (2001). E-mail survey response rate: A review. *Journal of Computer-Mediated Communication, 6.* Retrieved April 26, 2005, from http://jcmc.indiana.edu/vol6/issue2/sheehan.html

Sheehan, K. B., & McMillan, S. J. (1999). Response variation in e-mail surveys: An exploration. *Journal of Advertising Research, 39,* 45–54.

Shuy, R. W. (2002). In-person versus telephone interviewing. In J. F. Gubrium & J. A Holstein (Eds.), *Handbook of interview research: Context and method* (pp. 537–555). Thousand Oaks, CA: Sage.

Siemiatycki, J. (1979). A comparison of mail, telephone and home interview strategies for household health surveys. *American Journal of Public Health, 69,* 238–245.

Strafford, J., & Grant, C. (1993). *Effective sales management* (2nd ed.). London: Butterworth-Heinemann Ltd.

Survey Sampling International. (2004). Retrieved April 26, 2005, from www.surveysampling.com/

Thornberry, O. T., Jr., & Massey, J. T. (1988). Trends in United States telephone coverage across time and subgroups. In R. M. Groves, P. P. Biemer, L. E. Lyberg, J. T. Massey, W. L. Nicholls, II, & J. Waksberg, (Eds.), *Telephone survey methodology* (pp. 25–49). New York: Wiley.

Trewin, D., & Lee, G. (1988). International comparisons of telephone coverage. In R. M. Groves, P. P. Biemer, L. E. Lyberg, J. T. Massey, W. L. Nicholls, II, & J. Waksberg (Eds.), *Telephone survey methodology* (pp. 9–24). New York: Wiley.

U.S. Census Bureau. (2002). Estimated percentages of households with and without telephones by state, 2001. Retrieved April 26, 2005, from www.cdc.gov/brfss/surveydata/2000/table3_00.htm

Visser, P. S., Krosnick, J. A., Marquette, J., & Curtin, M. (1996). Mail surveys for election forecasting? An evaluation of the *Columbus Dispatch* poll. *Public Opinion Quarterly, 37,* 373–387.

Waksberg, J. (1978). Sampling methods for random digit dialing. *Journal of the American Statistical Association, 73,* 40–46.

Weaver, C. N., Holmes, S. L., & Glenn, N. D. (1975). Some characteristics of inaccessible respondents in a telephone survey. *Journal of Applied Psychology, 60,* 260–262.

15

COLLECTING DATA IN GROUPS

STEPHEN J. ZACCARO

MEREDITH CRACRAFT

MICHELLE MARKS

Much human behavior occurs within a social context. People's actions are often influenced in some degree by the presence of other individuals. Such influence may be quite passive, in which case the mere presence of others affects the frequency, intensity, or appropriateness of behavioral responses (Zajonc, 1965). Alternatively, social influence may be integral to action, such that a person's response is entirely interdependent with the responses of other individuals (Orasanu & Salas, 1993). In either instance, or in any other that reflects social dynamics, behavior cannot be fully understood without considering the role of such dynamics. Recognition of this is the elemental raison d'être of most group research.

The differences between individual and group research are grounded primarily in the presence of interpersonal dynamics that characterize the latter. Conducting careful group research, therefore, requires a consideration of these dynamics, not only in the conceptualization of group phenomena but also in the design of studies, the collection of data from the group as a whole as well as from individual members, and the analysis of such data. In this chapter, we will offer prescriptions for conducting group research that proceed from this consideration. The major points that will be covered concern the selection of a research setting and relevant design issues, data collection procedures, including the selection or acquisition of groups and the measurement and coding of the group process, and the analysis of data from group research.

What are some fundamental differences between individual and group research? One is that because the latter often examines aggregations of individuals working in coaction or interaction, collective and interpersonal processes are likely to mediate subsequent individual and collective responses. This distinction is illustrated, for example, in individual versus group decision-making research. Individual decision making involves the use of cognitive processes to assess decision scenarios, organize information, define decision alternatives, and select the best-fitting alternative (Lipshitz, 1993; Montgomery & Svenson, 1989; Pennington & Hastie, 1986). The selection process may reflect the application of various decision heuristics that in turn may result in multiple biases (Cohen, 1993; Tversky & Kahneman, 1972, 1974). The primary emphasis is on the cognitive dynamics applied by the individual when making decisions.

Group decision making also includes these cognitive dynamics as critical antecedents

(Duffy, 1993); however, research on such decision making typically examines the group members' application of cognitive processes within the context of interpersonal dynamics (e.g., Gualtieri, Parker, & Zaccaro, 1995). For example, research on groupthink has demonstrated how collective norms that emphasize the paramount importance of group unanimity can create defective decision making by group members (Janis, 1982). Likewise, group polarization research has demonstrated that groups will make more polarizing decisions (i.e., more risky or more cautious) than individual members making decisions alone (Myers & Lamm, 1976; Wallach, Kogan, & Bem, 1962). Theorists explain groupthink and group polarization by focusing on the influences of interpersonal processes that cause individuals to act differently when in groups. As illustrated in several points in this chapter, the interpersonal quality of group research that distinguishes it from individual research affects how group studies are designed, the nature of variables chosen for study, and the statistical analyses required by such data.

The presence of interpersonal or collective processes leads to another characteristic of group research that becomes particularly critical when analyzing group data. When group members interact (even if such interaction is limited to nonverbal modes), their subsequent individual responses may be substantially influenced by the nature and content of these interactions. Kenny and La Voie (1985; see also Kenny & Judd, 1996) call this "non-independence," in that data from each individual cannot be considered as independent from the data of other individuals within the group. Because many statistical procedures require data independence (e.g., analysis of variance), this influence creates the need for different statistical treatments of the data (Anderson & Ager, 1978; Kenny & Judd, 1996; Kenny & La Voie, 1985).

Individual-level research allows a single unit of analysis—that of the individual providing the data. Alternatively, when group research includes the collection of data from individuals within groups, that is, when such research uses a "hierarchically-nested design" (Kenny & La Voie, 1985), then two levels of analysis, the individual level and the group level, are possible.

A common mistake in group research is to ignore one level or the other when conceptualizing about groups or when analyzing data from nested designs. Many collective phenomena are perhaps best understood by focusing both on the differences between aggregations (using group means, reflecting a group-level analysis) and differences within aggregations (using member scores, reflecting an individual-level analysis). This means that when framing hypotheses, the research ought to consider sources of variance at both levels. Also, when the data is collected from individuals nested within groups, then statistical analyses need to account for multiple levels of influence. Chan (Chapter 28 in this volume) speaks to issues regarding multiple levels of analysis (see also Chan, 1998).

This suggests another difference between individual and group research. Studies of individual behavior will often focus on the characteristics of the individual as sources of variance. In group research, sources of variance include not only the characteristics of individual group members but also qualities that emerge from the interaction of group members (e.g., group cohesion, normative pressures, role definition). Other group sources of variance include structural qualities of the group (group size, degree of hierarchical organization, communication structure, whether the group operates face-to-face or in a virtual technology environment). The design of group studies needs to account for these sources of variance, even if they are not the focal point of a study's hypotheses. For example, group size can influence the degree of cohesion in a group (Cartwright, 1968), the intensity of group conformity and obedience pressures (Asch, 1951, 1955; Milgram, 1963, 1965), and the amount of effort exerted by individual members on behalf of the group (Latane, Williams, & Harkins, 1979). Thus, when designing group research, researchers need to give considerable thought to the size of their sample groups.

SELECTING A GROUP RESEARCH SETTING AND DESIGN

The setting for group research has been a source of significant debate in the literature. Much of group research has been completed in laboratory settings using experimental methodologies. Such approaches provide control over proposed predictors of group actions and allow plausible inferences of causality. Further, an experimental methodology allows the researcher to create a number of situations and scenarios in the group that may occur infrequently in natural groups (e.g., stressors, crises). This tactic permits the investigation of rare but critical events that often determine subsequent group norms, culture, and long-term group action. The frequent use by researchers of ad hoc groups in experimental settings, however, has earned such research the criticism of artificiality and lack of external validity (Forsyth, 1990). Indeed, several group phenomena emerge only after group members have developed a significant set of shared experiences (e.g., group norms, cohesiveness). Because most laboratory groups meet for a short period of time and have no expectation of continued existence, an experimental investigation of these phenomena in such groups can become suspect.

Studying intact groups in their natural settings is an alternate and popular group research strategy. The most frequently used methodology in such studies is either *correlational,* in which surveys are given to group members, or *observational,* in which groups are observed for a period of time and their processes coded for significant events. Studying real groups has the advantage of greater generalizability and applicability than laboratory or ad hoc groups. Such research, however, can suffer from a number of other flaws. Correlational methodologies rarely provide the basis for causal inference regarding the key variables under study. This flaw significantly limits the ability of such approaches to assess hypotheses drawn from theories of group action. Further, if a survey is administered at a single point in the group's existence, key developmental issues such as the emergence of group norms or group cohesiveness cannot be investigated. Also, if the data consists solely of survey data collected from group members, then the results of correlational analyses may often be attributed to common method variance or other response biases. This situation is improved if (a) multiple surveys are administered over the history of the group, from its initial founding

through a number of significant events; and (b) survey data from group members are combined with data from other sources (e.g., group observers, archival records).

Observational methods provide an ongoing assessment of group processes; however, such methods can be criticized on two important grounds. First, the time of observation may not provide enough instances of critical group events or actions to fully assess hypothesized relationships among targeted variables. For example, if a researcher were interested in team responses to different kinds of stressors, an unrealistically long period of observation may be required to observe the full range of relevant stressors and the group's subsequent reactions to fully understand this phenomenon. Also, such methods may result in the Hawthorne effect (Roethlisberger & Dickson, 1939), in which group members' knowledge that they are being observed changes the quality and frequency of their behavior. Although one answer to this effect is covert observational strategies, this approach raises significant ethical concerns.

We (and other group researchers) suggest several responses to this dilemma of laboratory-experimental versus natural-correlational group research. One is that the methodological approach should be dictated by the primary purpose of the researcher. Driskell and Salas (1992) noted that laboratory settings allow researchers to test under controlled and strenuous conditions particular theories and hypotheses about real-world group phenomena. They argued that "it is theory that is applied to the real world" (p. 106), not the findings or setting of any particular experiment. Thus, if the purpose of the group research is to assess theories of group action, then controlled experimentation is the preferred approach. If the purpose is to understand specific real-world group settings or apply theory to such settings, then research with natural groups is more appropriate (Driskell & Salas, 1992).

Ad hoc groups do not necessarily have to be limited to artificial settings, nor are real groups excluded from experimental manipulations. Investigators can create groups for research purposes that operate in natural settings. Likewise, experimenters can manipulate conditions confronted by existing and ongoing groups.

Examples of such research include establishing project groups in classroom settings, having existing teams complete training simulations, and applying different work conditions to different organizational groups. Each of these strategies mitigates some (but not all) of the problems connected with exclusive laboratory-experimental or natural-correlational group research.

It is likely that a program of research on group phenomena will have multiple purposes. Accordingly, researchers are urged to consider a series of studies, some experimental with the intention of testing theories, others correlational with natural groups to examine the generalizability and applicability of experimental findings. Such a multistrategy approach will allow compensation for the flaws of separate methodologies (McGrath, 1984, 1991) and provide a basis for both the evaluation of theories of group behavior and their extension to real-world groups (Driskell & Salas, 1992).

Two basic approaches to data collection characterize group research. The first involves the collection of data entirely at the group level. Such a design would be used, for example, by a researcher who is interested in the relationship between group size or group structure and group coordination. The dependent variable in such a study is the product that emerges from the interaction of group members. Many decision-making studies in which the group is required to solve a problem collectively are examples of group level studies. The unit of statistical analysis in such studies would be the group as a whole. A second design is the collection of data from individuals within the group. Such a design is called a nested design (Kenny & La Voie, 1985). As illustrated by Kenny and La Voie (1985), the unit of analysis in these studies can be both the individual and the group. Group researchers often mistakenly analyze the data from such studies *only* at the individual level when multiple levels of analysis are more appropriate. As will be discussed later in this chapter, even if (a) the data are collected from individual group members, and (b) hypotheses postulate individual-level relationships, statistical analyses must still be used to evaluate the presence of group-level effects. Kashy and Kenny (2000) provide excellent guidance in this area.

DATA COLLECTION PROCEDURES

Other chapters in this book describe primarily procedures used to collect data from individuals, and Chan (Chapter 28) discusses multiple levels of analysis. There are some unique issues, however, that arise when collecting data from groups. These are related to subject acquisition and variable specification.

Subject Acquisition

The issues regarding subject acquisition in group research vary according to whether the setting is a laboratory-experimental one or a natural-correlational one. When conducting laboratory experiments, researchers will typically begin by soliciting volunteers. In many universities, subject pools from introductory psychology courses are often the source of such volunteers. A critical point for group researchers, though, is that the number of individuals required for each group of a given size sign up to participate for a particular time period. If an insufficient number of people show up, the experiment session cannot be completed and the researcher may lose the volunteers that did appear. One suggestion is that researchers sign up more subjects than needed for a particular experimental session. If more individuals appear than needed, the actual participants ought to be randomly selected, and the others can be given a choice to return to a later session or to participate in a concurrent unrelated research study.

Some experimental treatments may be confounded if individual members are friends or acquaintances before they meet in the experimental session. In such instances, investigators need to screen for such pairings either when soliciting volunteers or when assigning individuals to groups. For example, in a study of task-based and social-based group cohesion, Zaccaro and McCoy (1988) stipulated on a volunteer sign-up sheet that friends should not volunteer for the same experimental session. If friends did appear during the same session, they were assigned to different groups. In this way, the investigators minimized the chance that prior relationships would confound their manipulations of task and social cohesion.

A critical question for group researchers is the requisite size of their groups. If group size is to be manipulated, then this question is generally not applicable; however, most studies are likely to hold group size constant. What then should be that size? The larger the group, the more individual subjects that must be solicited as volunteers. This can be quite problematic for large research designs. For example, a $2 \times 2 \times 2$ factorial design that uses 5-person groups may require from 600 to 800 individual participants (i.e., 8 experimental cells with 15–20 groups per cell)! One might be tempted to use the smallest aggregation possible or "groups" of two persons. Some researchers, however, have argued for qualitative differences between dyads and groups of 3 or more individuals (Simmel, 1903/1950). Therefore, unless required by the study's purpose (e.g., Zaccaro, 1984), researchers should establish groups of no fewer than 3 individuals.

Another critical question is the number of groups that should be collected for each level of experimental treatments. Convention in individual research is that about 20 subjects per treatment level is sufficient to stabilize sampling error (although the number required for sufficient power may be more or less depending on anticipated effect sizes; Cohen, 1988). In group research, however, when groups are the unit of analysis, means are more stable than in individual-level research having the same number of data points. Although such convention has not emerged for group research, it is likely that fewer than 20 groups per treatment level are necessary for relative stability. Indeed, Hanges, Nelson, and Schneider (1990) completed a Monte Carlo simulation to compare the statistical power of the same number of individual- and group-level data points. They found that a group level of analysis had more power than an individual level of analysis when assessing the significance of regression coefficients. Thus, fewer groups are likely to be necessary to provide the same level of statistical power as a particular number of individual subjects.

Natural Settings

When collecting data from natural or existing groups, researchers need to consider issues of group composition and the likelihood of restriction of range in the nature of groups being studied. Unlike laboratory groups, in which members are randomly assigned to groups, natural groups typically contain members who have chosen to belong to them or to the organizations within which the groups are embedded. Such groups are likely to be more homogeneous and reflect characteristics that may need to be assessed as covariates for subsequent statistical control. Given the increasing use of technology and the ability of team members to be dispersed, a critical variable to consider is the extent to which real-world groups utilize different modes of communication and vary in the nature of their interactions. Also, the acquisition of a sample of natural groups typically requires permission from group leaders or from a governing organization. Leaders of successful and effective groups are more likely to grant permission to outside researchers than are leaders of poor or ineffective groups. Thus, researchers need to be sensitive to restriction-of-range issues when soliciting natural groups.

Preexisting groups will rarely be identical in terms of group size or group tenure. Yet, these and other related variables are likely to be critical determinants of most group phenomena. Accordingly, researchers need to identify the qualities and characteristics that vary from group to group in their sample and are likely to explain significant variance in their focal criteria. Measures of such characteristics can then be treated as covariates in subsequent statistical analyses.

The Measurement of Group Processes

The specification of key predictor and criterion variables to examine in a group study obviously proceeds from the conceptual basis of the research; however, because a key mediator of most relationships between independent (or input) variables and dependent (or output) variables is the process (throughput) or interpersonal dynamics in the group, most researchers will need to consider measures of such processes and the procedures to gather such data. Group processes can be assessed either through self-report measures completed by group members or through observational methods. In some circumstances, self-report measures can be notoriously unreliable and influenced significantly by the outcomes of group processes (e.g., group performance). Further, if measures of group inputs and outputs are also gathered from group members (e.g., measures of group cohesion, group norms), then any significant findings among input, process, and output variables could be attributed to common method biases. Thus, observational methods are generally more appropriate means of collecting group process data.

Some studies use coders who observe and record the ongoing processes of the group. A significant problem with such an approach is that unless the coder is highly trained and the coding scheme fairly simple, a significant amount of the group interaction is likely to be lost. This is because group interaction is often complex, can occur rapidly, and multiple behaviors may occur simultaneously. Thus, observational studies ought to utilize audio and visual recordings of group processes. This would provide a more permanent record of the group's entire process and allow a more careful analysis of such processes from multiple raters.

Four examples of observational systems that coders can use to analyze group interaction processes are the Bales interaction process analysis (IPA; Bales, 1950a, 1950b), SYMLOG (Bales & Cohen, 1979), TEMPO (Futoran, Kelly, & McGrath, 1989), and Targeted Acceptable Responses to Generated Events or Tasks (TARGETs) (Fowlkes, Lane, Salas, & Franz, 1994). Although differing in significant ways, these observational systems all provide a set of coding categories appropriate for a wide range of group performance situations. All four systems may present categories that allow task-related group interactions to be differentiated from social-related interactions. For example, the TEMPO system provides a categorical structure that includes production functions (task-related) and nonproduction functions (socially oriented statements). Within the production side, categories depict content- and process-related statements, and idea-proposing and idea evaluation statements.

TARGETs methodology is a recently developed technique that uses an event-based method of assessment. Events are built into exercises, allowing an observer to anticipate when an event is supposed to occur and what specific behaviors or processes a team should engage in to be effective. The rating system is specific to each individual event and requires the rater to check only whether or not a behavior occurred. Because the rating scales are very specific and do not require the rater to make judgments about the effectiveness of the behavior, there is less training required for observers (Dwyer, Fowlkes, Oser, & Salas, 1997). Performance can be assessed in terms of the extent to which effective behaviors were present overall, or behaviors can be categorized to determine if a team was weak in a given functional performance area (Dwyer et al., 1997).

Observational data can be collected through either covert or overt means. In laboratory settings, covert means may involve the use of one-way mirrors or hidden cameras. Although one-way mirrors have been common in group research, they rarely if ever fool group members who are the targets of observation. Such members may focus on the mirror to determine the presence of observers and confound measures of group process. Hidden cameras obviate this problem, but raise a number of ethical concerns. We have found in several studies that video cameras can be placed within the setting of the group without strong Hawthorne effects. Group members have indicated in debriefing sessions that after a relatively short time they did not attend to the camera, habituating to its presence. Thus, we suggest that researchers place cameras within sight of the group; such placement avoids significant ethical issues and provides a useable record of group process without necessarily constraining such processes. We should note that more than one camera is likely to be necessary to capture the interactions and reactions of *all* members of the group.

Studies involving virtual or dispersed teams may provide a new and interesting approach to observing and recording team processes and performance information. Typical modes of communication for these kinds of teams include instant messaging, electronic bulletin boards, e-mail, telephone, and file- or application-sharing (Martins, Gilson, & Maynard, 2004). The nature of this communication may allow a researcher to more readily record the exact content and sequence of communication without appearing obtrusive to the team members.

ANALYSIS OF DATA
FROM GROUP RESEARCH

Particular issues that must be attended to when analyzing data collected from groups depend on the basic design of the study. If the criteria or dependent variables are collected entirely at the group level (i.e., only group-level scores compose the data set), then the statistical procedures and assumptions are the same as those that apply to the analysis of individual-level data. For example, in a study of group performance in which the dependent variable is a solution generated by the entire group and the independent variables are task and social cohesion in which high and low levels of each type of cohesion are manipulated, then a conventional 2×2 analysis of variance is used to analyze the data (Zaccaro & McCoy, 1988). Note that a group-level analysis is still required when the predictor or independent variable is measured at the individual level but the dependent variable is still a group-level score. Thus, if in the previous study the predictor was perceived cohesiveness as reported by each group member instead of manipulated levels of cohesion types, the analysis would be correlational using group means of perceived cohesion and group performance scores as the data points.

When the data is collected from individual group members (i.e., in a hierarchical design, with individuals nested within groups), the appropriate unit of analysis needs to be determined before statistical tests of proposed effects are completed. That is, the researcher needs to determine if a *group effect* is present in the data. Such an effect means an individual's membership in a particular group was a source of influence on that person's responses. When individuals interact in a group, their subsequent responses are not likely to be independent from one another. Generally (although not always) these responses tend to become more homogeneous.

There are several statistical procedures for determining whether a group effect exists in the data. If the data is collected as part of an experiment in which subjects are randomly assigned to groups and other independent variables are manipulated, then the group an individual belongs to is entered as a random source of variance in a groups-nested-within-treatments analysis of variance (Anderson & Ager, 1978; Meyers, 1979). If the group effect is significant, then its means square is used as the error term to test treatment effects; if it is not, then a pooled error term can be used to test these effects. See Anderson and Ager (1978), George (1990), Meyers (1979), and Yammarino and Markham (1992) for additional information on these procedures.

Kenny and La Voie (1985) suggest that the presence of group effects in correlational data be assessed using the intraclass correlation. This statistic provides an index of how much variance in a measure exists at the group level by comparing within-group and between-group variance. Group effects are presumed to be present when within-group variance is significantly smaller than between-group variance. In such cases, Kenny and La Voie suggest that correlations be computed at both the group and individual level, with individual-level correlations being adjusted for group effects, and group-level correlations being adjusted for individual effects (see Kenny, 1985; Kenny & La Voie, 1986; and Kenny & Judd, 1996, for additional information on these procedures; also, see James, Demaree, & Wolf, 1984, for an alternate procedure to assess group effects).

Hierarchical linear modeling (HLM) strategies have also been used more recently to examine influences that cross different levels of analysis (i.e., individual, group, and organization). For example, research questions such as how group size or cohesion might influence individual member attitudes or how organizational structure, climate, or compensation policies might affect group cohesion and intergroup conflict would be approached using HLM. We refer the reader to Bryk and Raudenbush (1989) for a classic introduction and to Bleise (2000) and Hoffman (1997) for recent discussions of HLM.

When data are collected from individual group members, it is absolutely necessary to assess for the presence of group effects before proceeding to other statistical analyses. This assessment is required even if the study's hypotheses specify individual effects. In these instances, group membership may still be a significant source of variance that needs to be accounted for. Alternatively, if a researcher is interested in group phenomena but does not uncover a group effect in this initial assessment, careful consideration must be given to the meaning of the data. If the individual's own group is a meaningless influence on his or her behavior, the investigator has to wonder if the data has any relevance regarding group or collective behavior. We have noted instances in which group researchers tested for the presence of group effects and, finding none, proceeded to analyze the data at the individual level; however, their findings are then interpreted in terms of group influences! If group effects are not discerned in preliminary tests to determine appropriate levels of statistical analysis, then such interpretations are unwarranted. Thus, group researchers need to attend carefully to the presence or absence of group effects in their data and the meaning of such effects (or the lack thereof) for subsequent data analysis and interpretation.

CONCLUSION

We began this chapter by pointing out several differences between individual and group research. These differences are grounded in the interactions among individuals that characterize most group studies. A group researcher's interest is typically in the products of these interactions. Indeed, Lewin (1951, p. 192) described groups as "dynamic wholes" and noted that the "structural properties of a dynamic whole are different from the structural properties of subparts." Further, he noted that "structural properties are characterized by *relations* between parts rather than by the parts or elements themselves" (p. 192). These properties that emerge from the relations or interactions among individuals require some special attention from researchers. This chapter describes procedures that are unique to data collection and analysis in groups. We believe that adherence to such procedures can promote better group research and accordingly stronger theories of group phenomena.

EXERCISES

1. Pick a study done using individuals as the unit of analysis. Redesign it to take advantage of a group-level perspective. What are your key considerations?

2. First select an area of research, say social, counseling, or cognitive. Then formulate for your choice a list of several concepts that could be understood at a group level of analysis. How might a study be outlined for two of the concepts? As an example, in social psychology the concepts of performance and efficacy have been studied at an individual level. Is there any way to study these concepts at the group level?

3. Consider the following articles on group cohesion, which consist of meta-analyses and syntheses. Select any one, and examine the studies that are used in the meta-analysis. What are the features of the designs? What are the measures of independent and outcome variables? You may wish to consult Chapter 21 on meta-analysis by Cooper, Robinson, and Dorr in this handbook.

Beal, D. J., Cohen, R. R., Burke, M. J., & McLendon, C. L. (2003). Cohesion and performance in groups: A meta-analytic clarification of construct relations. *Journal of Applied Psychology, 88,* 984–1004.

Carron, A. V., Bray, S. R., & Eys, M. A. (2002). Team cohesion and team success in sport. *Journal of Sports Sciences, 20*(8), 119–126.

Evans, N. J., & Dion, K. L. (1991). Group cohesion and performance: A meta-analysis. *Small Group Research, 22,* 175–186.

Gully, S. M., Devine, D. J., & Whitney, D. J. (1995). A meta-analysis of cohesion and performance: Effects of levels of analysis and task interdependence. *Small Group Research, 26,* 497–520.

Mullen, B., & Copper, C. (1994). The relation between group cohesiveness and performance: An integration. *Psychological Bulletin, 115,* 210–227.

RECOMMENDED READINGS

We recommend that the reader consult the following sources for more in-depth information about the topic covered in this chapter: Driskell & Salas (1992), "Can You Study Real Teams in Contrived Settings? The Value of Small Group Research to Understanding Teams"; Forsyth's (1990), *Group Dynamics* (Chapter 2); Kenny and La Voie (1985); and McGrath's (1984) *Groups: Interaction and Performance* (Chapters 3 & 4). McGrath and Tschan (2004) provide a very recent book that shows the relevance of temporal matters for individuals, groups, and larger collectives. For the analysis of data from dyadic and group-level research, see Kashy and Kenny (2000). David Kenny's Web site, devoted to the social relation model, is at http://davidakenny.net/srm/srm.htm. Both this and his homepage at http://davidakenny.net/kenny.htm provide much useful information. Another interesting Web site at www.levelsofanalysis.com/compareapproaches.html offers comparisons between DETECT and alternative approaches to multilevel analysis. Note that the perspective taken is that of within-and-between analysis (WABA).

REFERENCES

Anderson, L. R., & Ager, J. W. (1978). Analysis of variance in small group research. *Personality and Social Psychology Bulletin, 4,* 341–345.

Asch, S. E. (1951). Effects of group pressure upon the modification and distortion of judgment. In H. Guetzkow (Ed.), *Groups, leadership, and men.* Pittsburgh, PA: Carnegie Press.

Asch, S. E. (1955). Opinions and social pressures. *Scientific American, 193*(5), 31–35.

Bales, R. F. (1950a). *Interaction process analysis: A method for the study of small groups.* Cambridge, MA: Addison-Wesley.

Bales, R. F. (1950b). A set of categories for the analysis of small group interaction. *American Sociological Review, 15,* 257–263.

Bales, R. F., & Cohen, J. S. P. (1979). *SYMLOG: A system for the multilevel observation of groups.* New York: Free Press.

Bliese, P. D. (2000). Within-group agreement, nonindependence, and reliability: Implications for data aggregation and analysis. In K. J. Klein & S. W. Kozlowski (Eds.), *Multilevel theory, research, and methods in organizations* (pp. 349–381). San Francisco: Jossey-Bass.

Bryk, A. S., & Raudenbush, S. W. (1989). Methodology for cross-level organizational research. *Research in the Sociology of Organizations, 7,* 233–273.

Cartwright, D. (1968). The nature of group cohesiveness. In D. Cartwright & A. Zander (Eds.), *Group dynamics: Research and theory.* New York: Harper & Row.

Chan, D. (1998). Functional relations among constructs in the same content domain of different levels of analysis: A typology of composition models. *Journal of Applied Psychology, 83,* 234–246.

Cohen, J. (1988). *Statistical power analysis for the behavioral sciences* (Rev. ed.). New York: Academic.

Cohen, M. (1993). The naturalistic basis of decision biases. In G. Klein, J. Orasanu, R. Calderwood, & C. E. Zsambok (Eds.), *Decision making in action: Models and methods* (pp. 51–99). Norwood, NJ: Ablex.

Driskell, J. E., & Salas, E. (1992). Can you study real teams in contrived settings? The value of small group research to understanding teams. In R. W. Swezey & E. Salas (Eds.), *Teams: Their training and performance* (pp. 101–124). Norwood, NJ: Ablex.

Duffy, L. (1993). Team decision-making biases: An information processing perspective. In G. Klein, J. Orasanu, R. Calderwood, & C. E. Zsambok (Eds.), *Decision making in action: Models and methods* (pp. 346–357). Norwood, NJ: Ablex.

Dwyer, D. J., Fowlkes, J. E., Oser, R. L., & Salas, E. (1997). Team performance measurement in distributed environments: The TARGETs methodology. In E. Salas (Ed.), *Team performance assessment and measurement: Theory, methods, and applications* (pp. 137–153). Mahwah, NJ: Lawrence Erlbaum.

Forsyth, D. R. (1990). *Group dynamics* (2nd ed.). Pacific Grove, CA: Brooks/Cole.

Fowlkes, J. E., Lane, N. E., Salas, E., & Franz, T. (1994). Improving the measurement of team performance: The TARGETs methodology. *Military Psychology, 6*(1), 47–61.

Futoran, G. C., Kelly, J. R., & McGrath, J. E. (1989). TEMPO: A time-based system for analysis of group interaction process. *Basic and Applied Social Psychology, 10,* 211–232.

George, J. M. (1990). Personality, affect, and behavior in groups. *Journal of Applied Psychology, 75,* 107–116.

Gualtieri, J., Parker, C., & Zaccaro, S. J. (1995). *Group decision making: An examination of decision processes and performance.* Manuscript submitted for publication.

Hanges, P. J., Nelson, G. L., & Schneider B. (1990, August). *Levels of analysis and statistical power.* Paper presented at the annual meeting of the American Psychological Association, Boston.

Hoffman, D. A. (1997). An overview of the logic and rationale of hierarchical linear models. *Journal of Management, 23,* 723–744.

James, L. R., Demaree, R. G., & Wolf, G. (1984). Estimating within-group interrater reliability with and without response bias. *Journal of Applied Psychology, 69,* 85–98.

Janis, I. L. (1982). *Victims of groupthink* (2nd ed.). Boston: Houghton Mifflin.

Kane, T. D., Zaccaro, S. J., Tremble, T. L., Jr., & Masuda, A. D. (2002). An examination of the leader's regulation of groups. *Small Group Research, 33,* 65–120.

Kashy, D. A., & Kenny, D. A. (2000). The analysis of data from dyads and groups. In H. T. Reis & C. M. Judd (Eds.), *Handbook of research methods in social and personality psychology* (pp. 469–475). New York: Cambridge University Press.

Kenny, D. A. (1985). The generalized group effect model. In J. Nesselroade & A. von Eye (Eds.), *Individual development and social change* (pp. 343–351). New York: Academic.

Kenny, D. A., & Judd, C. M. (1996). A general procedure for the estimation of interdependence. *Psychological Bulletin, 119*(1), 138–148.

Kenny, D. A., & La Voie, L. (1985). Separating individual and group effects. *Journal of Personality and Social Psychology, 4,* 339–348.

Latane, B., Williams, K., & Harkins, S. (1979). Many hands make light the work: The causes and consequences of social loafing. *Journal of Personality and Social Psychology, 37,* 823–832.

Lewin, K. (1951). *Field theory in social science.* New York: Harper & Bros.

Lipshitz, R. (1993). Converging themes in the study of decision making in realistic settings. In G. Klein, J. Orasanu, R. Calderwood, & C. E. Zsambok (Eds.), *Decision making in action: Models and methods* (pp. 103–137). Norwood, NJ: Ablex.

Martins, L. L., Gilson, L. L., & Maynard, M. T. (2004). Virtual teams: What do we know and where do we go from here? *Journal of Management, 30*(6), 805–835.

McGrath, J. E. (1984). *Groups: Interaction and performance.* Englewood Cliffs, NJ: Prentice-Hall.

McGrath, J. E. (1991). Time, interaction, and performance (TIP): A theory of groups. *Small Group Research, 22,* 147–174.

McGrath, J. E., & Tschan, F. (2004). *Temporal matters in social psychology: Examining the role of time in the lives of groups and individuals.* Washington, DC: APA.

Meyers, J. L. (1979). *Fundamentals of experimental design.* Boston: Allyn & Bacon.

Milgram, S. (1963). Behavioral study of obedience. *Journal of Abnormal and Social Psychology, 69,* 137–143.

Milgram, S. (1965). Some conditions of obedience and disobedience to authority. *Human Relations, 18,* 57–75.

Montgomery, H., & Svenson, O. (1989). *Process and structure in human decision making.* Chichester, UK: Wiley.

Myers, D. G., & Lamm, H. (1976). The polarizing effect of group discussion. *American Scientist, 63,* 297–303.

Orasanu, J., & Salas, E. (1993). Team decision making in complex environments. In G. A. Klein, J. Orasanu, R. Calderwood, & C. E. Zsambok (Eds.), *Decision making in action: Models and methods* (pp. 327–345). Norwood, NJ: Ablex.

Pennington, N., & Hastie, R. (1986). Evidence evaluation in complex decision making. *Journal of Personality and Social Psychology, 51,* 242–258.

Roethlisberger, F. J., & Dickson, W. J. (1939). *Management and the worker.* Cambridge, MA: Harvard University Press.

Simmel, G. (1950). The significance of numbers for social life. In K. H. Wolff (Trans.), *The sociology of Georg Simmel.* Glencoe, IL: Free Press. (Original work published in 1903)

Tversky, A., & Kahneman, D. (1972). Availability: A heuristic for judging frequency and probability. *Cognitive Psychology, 4,* 207–232.

Tversky, A., & Kahneman, D. (1974). Judgment under uncertainty: Heuristics and biases. *Science, 211,* 453–458.

Wallach, M. A., Kogan, N., & Bem D. J. (1962). Group influence on individual risk taking. *Journal of Abnormal and Social Psychology, 65,* 75–86.

Yammarino, F. J., & Markham, S. E. (1992). On the application of within and between analysis: Are absence and affect really group-based phenomena? *Journal of Applied Psychology, 77,* 168–176.

Zaccaro, S. J. (1984). Social loafing: The role of task attractiveness. *Personality and Social Psychology Bulletin, 10,* 99–106.

Zaccaro, S. J., & McCoy, M. C. (1988). The effects of task and interpersonal cohesiveness on performance of a disjunctive group task. *Journal of Applied Social Psychology, 18,* 837–851.

Zajonc, R. B. (1965). Social facilitation. *Science, 149,* 269–274.

PART IV

DATA ANALYSIS

16

Cleaning Up Data and Running Preliminary Analyses

David L. DiLalla

Stephen J. Dollinger

The literature has been reviewed; the study has been planned; the data have been carefully collected and entered. At this point, it's often tempting (for students as well as seasoned researchers) to dive into data analysis to see whether one's hypotheses have been supported. Tempering the temptation is the GIGO principle: Garbage In, Garbage Out. The integrity of a single scientific investigation, of a clinical case study, and of the entire field depends on data sets that are as internally valid and free of error as we can make them. Preliminary analyses serve this end by helping identify several sources of error. Of course, this effort to avoid error begins well before the data are ready to be analyzed. Clean data are more likely to emerge from well-conceived and carefully executed studies. Sample sizes must be sufficient to protect from Type II error (See Myors, Chapter 11, this handbook). Measures must be chosen with an eye toward reliability of observations and validity of those observations. Sampling and data collection must be conducted in a manner that reduces the effects of confounds and nonrandom error of measurement. Data entry must be double-checked to ensure the right data are being analyzed. And, analyses must be conducted that minimize the likelihood of Type I error.

The quest for clean data applies to all scientists. For psychologists, this is particularly salient because much of the data of psychology is collected and entered by research assistants, some of whom may not share the researcher's zeal for data hygiene. Moreover, the data collected by many psychologists offer myriad opportunities for introduction of error. Other authors in this volume address issues related to planning and execution of studies. We will venture into these areas briefly at the outset to discuss prevention of dirty data. Our principal focus will be on diagnostic and treatment strategies that researchers can use to ensure that their data are squeaky clean and ready for analysis. Many of the illustrations in this chapter focus on questionnaire or other self-report data. We recognize that other forms of data collection (e.g., psychophysiological measures, written or spoken narrative responses, direct behavioral observation) pose their own particular challenges. For example, electroencephalogram (EEG) researchers must be concerned with issues such as correct placement of electrodes, identification of artifacts (eye blinks, coughs, body movements) and reduction of raw EEG data into analysis-ready form. Researchers analyzing open-ended spoken or written responses must develop strategies for error-free transcription and entry of raw data in a form for analysis. Finally, behaviorally oriented investigations require reliable and valid coding systems and a mechanism for maintaining quality control though the study. Although we present some general strategies for data cleaning in this chapter, we recommend that newcomers to any research area investigate the accepted strategies for handling their data.

An Ounce of Prevention

Before the first research participant steps into the lab or puts pencil to scan sheet, there are several threats that must be addressed. One of the challenges of psychological research is selection of adequate measures to operationalize constructs of interest. In this regard, it pays to put on your psychometrician's hat and turn a critical eye on potential measures. It's tempting to follow the footsteps of other researchers and use measures that appear prominently in the literature. At the same time, it's possible that often used measures may not possess sufficient reliability and/or validity for the purpose at hand. Major psychological assessment instruments are routinely reviewed in the *Mental Measurements Yearbook* (*MMY,* Plake & Impara, 2001) by experts in the field. Reviews can also be purchased and downloaded from the Buros Center for Testing Web site (www.unl.edu/buros). For other measures, particularly unpublished instruments, you will need to evaluate the psychometric data that have been reported for the instrument. Constantine and Ponterotto (this handbook, Chapter 7) provide details pertinent to measure or scale selection, and Lounsbury and his colleagues (Chapter 9) address scale development.

It is also tempting in some instances to "extract" individual scales from a multiscale inventory when only a single scale is of interest for a study. Smith, Budzeika, Edwards, Johnson, and Bearse (1986), in an article aptly titled "Guidelines for Clean Data: Detection of Common Mistakes" suggested that standard scales should never be altered or embellished without clear statements of how and why changes were made. It cannot be assumed that an extracted scale will have the same psychometric properties as the same scale when it is embedded within a broader inventory. Moreover, the experience of taking the scale can be markedly different for participants, particularly if a group of like-items appears one after the other in the extracted scale.

Just as measures must be carefully chosen, researchers should keep in mind the constraints that the selected measures place on the ultimate methods of analysis. Doing so affords a more careful consideration of the possible outcomes of the study. (In one recent case in which this was not done sufficiently, the student realized that one hypothesis was untestable due to poor choice of measures, a problem not foreseen until the data were in hand and ready for analysis.) Although it is common for dissertation data to be reanalyzed (in new ways) before submission to a journal, it is always wise to plan study analyses before the data are collected. The message here is that once the data are collected, one has the wisdom of hindsight in how the study ought to have been designed. A priori planning for the analyses will help the researcher possess a bit of that wisdom.

It is also important to ensure that the response requirements for participants are unambiguous and straightforward. Researchers understandably acquire a certain degree of tunnel vision regarding their projects and, consequently, sometimes fail to detect problems that might arise when real participants respond to research instruments. An obvious place to start is careful proofreading of all measures so that typing, formatting, and item-numbering errors are avoided. We recommend, at minimum, that researchers engage the assistance of one or several dry-run consultants who are similar demographically to the proposed study population. In addition to screening for readability and clarity, such individuals might be instructed to fill out the measures while role-playing an uninterested, hostile, or careless participant. This may provide information about patterns of scores that may signify invalid responses. Time spent obtaining feedback from such individuals about the process of completing the research protocol is definitely worth a pound of the cure for bad data. Better yet, if time and resources permit, do a pilot study!

Experimenter Effects

A special class of error-inducing factors warrants its own discussion. Classic work by Orne

(1962) and Rosenthal (1966) demonstrated the social psychology of the psychological experiment and focused attention on potential biasing effects of experimenter behavior and expectancies, particularly as they relate to demand characteristics of participants. This work reminds researchers of the power that the act of participation in a research study may have on participants. Orne (1962) provided an amusing example:

> A number of casual acquaintances were asked whether they would do [me] a favor; on their acquiescence, they were asked to perform five push-ups. Their response tended to be amazement, incredulity and the question, "Why?"
>
> Another similar group of individuals were asked whether they would take part in an experiment of brief duration. When they agreed to do so, they too were asked to perform five push-ups. Their typical response was "Where?" (p. 777)

In a recent review, Rosenthal (2002) identified several types of experimenter bias. The most serious, of course, is intentional forgery or misrepresentation of data. If you are reading this chapter, we assume that you are a conscientious and honest investigator who knows that falsification or creation of data is an absolute wrong that undermines the entire enterprise of science and can end the career of a scholar or a scholar-in-training. (Note, however, that the discarding of data outliers is not an ethical issue and, in some research areas such as those involving reaction time, is routine if done in accord with accepted norms for the research topic.)

Less ethically serious, but of more pragmatic concern, Rosenthal (2002) described nonintentional, noninteractional biases (those residing within the experimenter alone), which include errors of observation, recording, and transcription of data. In terms of the scope of the problem, Rosenthal (1978) found an error rate of roughly 1% of observations. More troubling, errors do not appear to be random but tend to occur more often than chance would dictate in the direction of the hypotheses of the experimenter (Rosenthal, 2002). What is the message to take from this work? People err, and honest errors can be caught by double-checking. Taking a lesson from the methodology of applied behavior analysis, human data handlers

(like behavioral observers) are likely to be more accurate if they know that their reliability will be checked periodically throughout the study.

EXPECTANCY AND SOCIAL INTERACTION EFFECTS

Beyond characteristics of experimenters, the interaction of experimenter and participant can subtly influence research findings and introduce error into our work. Among the best known of these possibilities is the experimenter-expectancy effect. Recall, for example, the classic Pygmalion effect (Rosenthal & Jacobson, 1968) in which positive expectancies of classroom teachers led to increased IQ scores in children compared with the scores of children whose teachers did not have the experimentally induced positive expectancies. Bringing this matter closer to what graduate students in the clinical areas might experience, consider the biasing effects of one's expectancies while administering psychological tests, one area in which this effect is moderately large (Badad, Mann, & Mar-Hayim, 1975; Sattler, 2001; Sattler, Hillix, & Neher, 1970).

Rosenthal (2002) summarized even more insidious potential social interactional biases. Experimenters might respond differently to men as compared to women (and participants might respond differentially based on gender of the experimenter). More experienced experimenters might generate different responses as compared with their relatively less experienced peers. Even experimenter personality can play a role. Imagine yourself participating in a psychological study. What is your mood likely to be if you are greeted by a warm, friendly, smiling experimenter? How might your mood differ if you are greeted by a cold, indifferent, unsmiling experimenter?

Readers familiar with techniques for controlling confounds are no doubt shuddering at the thought of the methodological gymnastics required to address the problems noted above. Although some problems can be easily addressed (for example, deciding to use only experimenters of one gender, or to statistically evaluate gender-of-experimenter effects), it is surely not possible to control them all. One general strategy involves standardizing data collection procedures to reduce the introduction of inadvertent experimenter error. Time spent creating detailed research protocols (including scripts for experimenters) and then training research assistants to follow the protocols is time well spent in the prevention of error. Moreover, the principal investigator should be aware of the possibility of protocol drift and check on adherence to the procedures at various points in the project, retraining experimenters as needed. The ultimate goal is to have the experience of each research participant be as uniform as possible.

THE DATA ARE IN. NOW WHAT?

Prior to embarking on even preliminary analyses, several tasks must be accomplished: (a) screening of participant responses for obviously invalid data; (b) dealing with missing data; (c) computing the summary scores needed for analysis of the data. Smith et al. (1986) advised researchers to be thoroughly familiar with their measures, including scoring keys and scoring procedures for the survey instruments. As anyone who has collected data can attest, there will invariably be some participants who do not conscientiously engage in the research task and produce invalid data. Identifying such cases is the first order of business. A good starting point is a visual scan of each participant's responses. For those using Scantrons, this is the proverbial hunt for "Christmas treeing." Participants whose responses are clearly patterned should be dropped from the sample. The researcher should also ensure that the obtained item and values are consistent with the requirements of the measure. If possible responses range from 1 to 5, for example, and a respondent writes down or bubbles in a value of 6, this out of range value should attract attention. One option is to create a dummy variable that represents the number of out-of-range responses for each participant. Individuals high on this variable were likely either careless or confused and are likely candidates for removal from the sample. Frequency distributions and graphs are other useful tools for identifying out-of-range data. There are two strategies for dealing with such responses. The researcher might recode the offending values as *missing* and subject them to the missing values

screening process described below. A more conservative approach is to drop the participant's data entirely (at least for the measure where there were out-of-range responses).

MISSING DATA

Treatment of missing data requires you to make several a priori decisions. First, you must decide whether *any* amount of missing data is acceptable. Some might make the conservative argument that a participant's data should be dropped from the sample if any data points are missing. The risk, of course, is that such an approach overidentifies bad participants who could have remained in the sample. An alternative to zero tolerance is to specify a threshold for acceptable missing data, below which the participant stays in the sample. There is no universally accepted guideline for how much missing data is too much. In personality-oriented questionnaire research a common threshold is 5% missing for a given measure. For a 300-item multiscale questionnaire, this translates to up to 15 acceptable missing data points. Clearly, were all of these 15 items to congregate on a single scale, this would cause problems, so we recommend that the 5% rule also be applied to individual scales that constitute multiscale inventories. For some participants, then, it is conceivable that there would be valid data for some scales and not for others.

But the question remains, "What should be done with missing data when the number of data points does not reach the remove-from-sample criterion?" The goal is to substitute a value for each acceptable missing data point that will not bias the data as a whole. For true-false data, some researchers simply flip a coin and assign *true* or *false* randomly to the missing data point. Others suggest substitution of the samplewide median value for the variable in question. (For measures with known or suspected gender differences, the gender-specific sample median should be used.) For most purposes, we recommend the latter strategy. The most important issue is settling on your missing-data procedures before data collection begins and including a clear description of these procedures in your method section.

Bear in mind that missing data can be defined by statistical packages in a variety of ways. In general, if a data point is blank, the software package will define it "system missing" and assign some unique character to it (often a period). Additionally, researchers can define particular values of variables as "user missing." For example, data enterers might use a unique number not otherwise used (e.g., 9, 99 or 999) to represent missing data. Even better, choosing an impossible value (e.g.,–999) helps ensure that missing data are not mistaken for valid data and vice versa. An advantage of explicitly defining user-missing values is that it is clear to individuals perusing the data that a missing value was not simply a data point left out by the data entry person. For user missing values, it is crucial to tell the statistical software what values have been used (usually with a Missing Values command). If this is forgotten, two variables sharing numbers that signify missing data, 99s for example, will spuriously correlate as an artifact of this neglect (as happened with considerable embarrassment to one of the author's assistants). Similarly, one's means and other statistics can be corrupted by a missing value masquerading as a valid data point.

Computation of Summary Scores

Once missing data have been dealt with, it is time to compute the summary scores that will be used in your study. The first order of business often will be recoding (sometimes called reflecting) of reverse-scored items. Researchers who use questionnaires know that good measures generally have a mixture of positively and inversely keyed items. Failure to recode reversed items properly will transform potentially good data into garbage. A hint that this might have happened is the finding that one of your measures has extremely low (or negative) internal consistency as indexed by Cronbach's alpha. The recoding process is quite straightforward using the Recode or Compute command in SPSS. For example, to allow for spot checks later, it is useful to maintain the original (unreflected) variables and create new variables that correspond to reversed items. If Variable-1 has possible responses of 1, 2, 3, 4 & 5, Variable-1-Reflected would be created by Recoding 1 to 5, 2 to 4, 3 to 3, 4 to 2, and 5 to 1. Note that the "3 to 3" recode is critical when one variable is

being recoded into a new variable. Without it, the newly created reflected variable would be treated as missing when the original variable was 3. These should be reflected (e.g., by recoding each response category of the item or by subtracting the item—in this instance, from 6). Alternately, for the 5 categories above, Variable-1-Reflected can be computed by subtracting the value of the original Variable-1 from 6.

Smith et al. (1986) offered another suggestion, which is extremely useful for novice researchers: "Recode so that all items purporting to measure the same characteristic are scored in the same direction." For example, if test items were designed to measure anxiety and depression, interpretation would be easier and errors avoided if *high* scores meant *greater* negative affect for both items or scales. We would go one step further by suggesting that researchers routinely use higher numbers to signify more of the quantity in question (and to label the scale by its high end). Thus, if the researcher is measuring the trait of introversion-extraversion, the researcher's task, as well as that of his or her reader, is eased by consistent reference to the high-score endpoint.

Research projects often involve multiple measures and sometimes involve multiple data sets. This presents challenges in terms of keeping data files orderly and interpretable. Smith et al. (1986) offered two suggestions for the merging of several data sets. The order of data input is critical; if more than one logical record is planned per participant and if lines are omitted for some participants, the results will be uninterpretable (or worse, they may be interpretable but misleading). Similar problems occur when the input statement and data record are not in synchrony. Again, look for out-of-range scores in tables of descriptive statistics, or print a listing of selected participants' data for spot-check comparison with raw responses. When the data sets are combined into a larger sample, make certain that they are compatible and are sorted on the same variable (e.g., participant number). Also be certain that participant numbers are not used for more than one participant!

Alternatively, one can maintain separate raw data files (each with some common identification number) and create working analysis files (*data files* in SPSS terminology) and then merge these files into a main analysis file that includes the variables needed for the study. This obviates the need for literally merging all data records into one megafile. For example, in a large data set that one of us has used extensively, there are separate SPSS data files for diagnostic data, MMPI data, alcohol use data, personality trait data, and so on, each file with a common ID variable. To create a working data set, one simply chooses the variables of interest from the component files (matching by ID) and builds a new aggregate data file.

Smith et al. (1986) concluded with the recommendation to "label compulsively." This includes retention of duplicate copies of the instruments, scoring keys, and coding of variables (e.g., "Were control participants signified by 1 and experimental participants 2, or did we use 1 and 0 in this study?") Label as if you will hand the data over to a stranger. If you set the project aside for 1 month to complete other tasks, many aspects of the data set will have been forgotten. In addition to labeling of computer files, keeping an analysis log that documents what has been done to the data will refresh the researcher's memory if he or she is away from the data for a while and will provide a sense of order when more than one person is working on data analysis.

WHAT? STILL NOT READY TO ANALYZE?

So far, we've described procedures for identifying obviously bad data that must be purged. More insidious data-dirtying factors may also be afoot. Schultz (1969) noted that many participants in psychological studies attempt to be good or faithful participants who provide meaningful data or perhaps help out the experimenter. Our concern here is with participants who passively or actively sabotage a project with invalid data. Such persons may be motivated by testing conditions to fake good test profiles (or, sometimes to fake bad) or to respond carelessly (e.g., "to get out of this boring project quickly" by not reading instructions or items). In some cases, as described above, these bad data are easy to spot (e.g., strings of the same response or clear response patterns). In other cases, more stealth on the part of the researcher is called for.

Response Set Detection

Several strategies may be helpful for sniffing out invalid data. It may be useful to note *during data collection* the length of time that participants take to complete the study, with a possible exclusion rule for those who finish too quickly. If you are testing in a large group setting, another method is to assign an identification number that codes for order of completion and then determine whether this variable relates to the measures of interest. Just as time of participation in a semester can reflect personality and participant investment (Dollinger & Orf, 1991; Roman, Moskowitz, Stein, & Eisenberg, 1995), so completion time can be a sign of something meaningful that can affect a study's internal validity.

If you are using published self-report questionnaires, standardized response-set detection scales may be available. If this is the case, you should consult the research on the instrument and drop invalid data in accordance with prior work on the measure. If you are creating your own measure, or are using an instrument without validity scales, it might be worthwhile to build in infrequency items that might catch careless respondents (e.g., "I make my own clothes and shoes" (Jackson, 1984). It is conceivable, however, that the use of what could be viewed as outlandish items might have iatrogenic effects, prompting participants to take their participation as a matter of frivolity rather than seriousness. Various versions of the Big Five NEO inventories (Costa & McCrae, 1992) include the simple item, "I have tried to answer all of these questions honestly and accurately." If a participant endorses this item with a *neutral* or *disagree* response, it is likely that he or she either is not reading the item or has reversed the 5-point scale by giving higher ratings to the strongly disagree endpoint. Following this strategy, the junior author includes another item in long questionnaire sets but with the intent of identifying responses in the opposite direction; this involves an item such as, "I have had a hard time understanding many of the words in this questionnaire." An affirmative answer to this question (particularly a strong endorsement) may indicate that the participant is not reading the items or that, in fact, he or she has not understood much of what has been asked.

Classic "Lie Scale" items (e.g., "I always have told the truth") may be also useful in detecting invalid data. Or, you might administer a standalone social desirability inventory (such as the Balanced Inventory of Desirable Responding (BIDR, Paulhus, 1998) or the Marlowe-Crowne Social Desirability Scale (Crowne & Marlowe, 1960). In either case, a priori decisions must be made regarding the cutoff scores that will cause you to remove a participant's data from your study.

Outliers

All outliers will be extreme data points, but not all extreme data points need necessarily be outliers. Outliers are presumed to result from two factors: (a) measurement, observation, or coding error (including the sorts of invalid responses described above); (b) the presence of two distinct populations within the sample. In the former case, the data should be dropped from the sample as invalid; in the latter, it may be that the data must be analyzed separately by attempting to identify members of each population that was sampled (for example, one might expect that simultaneously sampling psychologically healthy individuals and individuals with known mental disorder could result in some data points that appear to be outliers).

Several methods may be used to evaluate possible outliers. Most are based on the idea (often referred to as Chebyshev's theorem, see Barnett & Lewis, 1994) that a particular proportion of valid data points will exist within a given number of standard deviations from the population mean. Chebyshev's theorem states that the proportion of good data points will equal $1-(1 / k^2)$ where k is the number of standard deviation units bracketing the mean. So, 75% of good data are expected to lie within two standard deviations of the mean, and 89% of good data are expected to lie within three standard deviations.

Some investigators set a threshold of three standard deviations above or below the mean to identify outliers; however, this might not be adequate when sample sizes are relatively small. Application of Grubb's test (Grubbs & Beck, 1972; see also Barnett & Lewis, 1994) accounts

for this problem. For each suspected outlier, a z score is computed:

$$z = \text{observed score} - \frac{\text{sample mean}}{\text{sample standard deviation}}$$

The suspected outlier is included in sample statistic calculations. Barnett & Lewis (1994) provide a table with critical values of z for various sample sizes. For Ns of 50, 100 and 140, the critical values of z are 3.13, 3.38, and 3.49, respectively. If the critical value is exceeded, the data point is considered a putative outlier.

Others have argued that outliers can be identified by using the first quartile (Q1) and third quartile (Q3) to create limits for valid data points. This is done by first calculating the interquartile range (IQR = Q3–Q1), then creating a series of "fences." Inner fences are set at Q1 – (1.5 * IQR) and Q3 + (1.5 * IQR). Outer fences are set at Q1 – (3 * IQR) and Q3 + (3 * IQR). Data points between the inner and outer fences are considered mild outliers, and points beyond the outer fences are considered extreme outliers. The SPSS Boxplot command will assist with application of this technique, with sample output illustrated below.

These data are for the personality trait Social Closeness, scaled as a T-score with mean = 50 and $SD = 10$. The top and bottom of the shaded box represent Q3 and Q1. The horizontal lines represent the fences at 1.5 * IQR above and below Q3 and Q1 (the fence at 3 * 1QR) is not shown). The value for case 127 is flagged as a potential outlier because it is more than 1.5 * IQR below Q1, but not so much as 3 * IQR below Q1 (see Figure 16.1).

The methods described above focus on individual variables in a data set. It is also possible to assess for globally outlying participants. This involves creating dummy variables that reflect a participant's overall response across all items in the data set (irrespective of the scales included). The first step is to create the new variables, say GRANDMEAN and GRANDSD, the participant's overall M and SD across all items. Next, identify those participants whose scores on GRANDMEAN and GRANDSD fall 3, 4, or more standard deviations above or below the GRANDMEAN and GRANDSD means. Like most of the strategies described here, it is important to identify your cutoff point a priori. In

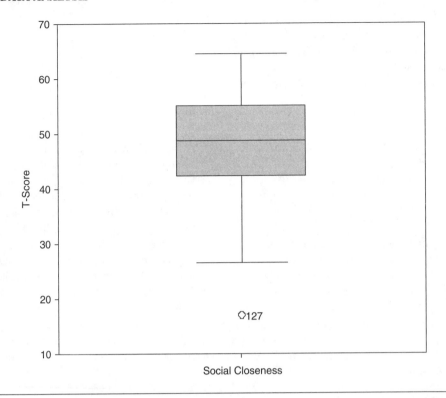

Figure 16.1   Sample Output From SPSS Boxplot Command Showing Data for the Personality Trait Alienation

analyzing several different data sets, we have found that lists of such participants will commonly identify individuals who too frequently use a string of consecutive high ratings, resulting in suspiciously high scores on GRANDMEAN and low scores on GRANDSD. Participants who employ the 1–2–3–4–5–4–3–2-1 pattern, even occasionally will obtain suspiciously high scores on GRANDSD.

What has been said thus far pertains to univariate outliers. With multivariate outliers, a variety of methods are needed, and several procedures may do a better job of jointly identifying problem cases (see Barnett & Lewis, 1994; Comrey, 1985; Hawkins, 1980). Comrey's method (1985) is based on the average squared deviation of a given participant's cross-product of standard score from the average overall correlations. Comrey noted that participants should not automatically be excluded as outliers just because a formula identifies them as such. Rather, these methods help identify cases that need scrutiny. On the basis of our use of the

GRANDMEAN/GRANDSD approach, we would agree. In this regard, a very useful step is to devise a series of preliminary graphs of the data, which can also help identify outliers (see Anscombe, 1973).

To bring the topic of outliers to a close, we note that the decision to remove a data point (or participant) from a sample should not be taken lightly and definitely should not be taken after undertaking substantive data analyses. An investigator who removes outliers after conducting substantive analyses can rightly be accused of data tampering. Our recommendation is to assess potential outliers a priori using a number of techniques and only to drop outliers when there is a confluence of evidence that the data points are bad.

Assessment of Normality

The data should now be fairly well scrubbed and ready for statistical analyses. At this point, it is important to recall the assumptions that most of our usual statistical tests demand.

Foremost among these is that the data to be analyzed are normally distributed. Distributions that are substantially positively skewed (bunched up at the low end) or negatively skewed (bunched up at the high end) violate this assumption and decrease the validity of our statistical tests. Statistical packages like SPSS and SAS provide information about each variable's distributional properties. A standardized test of skewness can be computed by dividing the skewness statistic (e.g., from the SPSS Descriptives command) by the standard error of the skewness. The result is distributed as a *z*, so that a test of significant skewness at the *p* < .05 level would require the *z* to exceed 1.96.

When the *z* value calculated above is below 1.96, you can be fairly comfortable that the level of skewness does not significantly violate the normality assumption. When significant skewness exists, the most likely culprit is out-of-range data or outliers; however, because you have so conscientiously applied the techniques described above, you should be fairly comfortable that outliers have already been sanitized. Consequently, you must make a decision regarding potential normalization of the data via a statistical transformation.

As a wise person once said, "There's no such thing as a free lunch" (and what would be tastier than a skewed distribution brought back to glorious normality?). Sadly, transformations come with a cost, the most serious of which is that the meaning of the original variable's metric is lost when the variable is transformed. This means that the newly transformed variable cannot be easily compared with prior work using the original metric. Velleman and Hoaglin (1981) provided some guidelines for transformations using the "ladder of powers," illustrated below.

X (in Table 16.1) refers to the untransformed value, x′ is the transformed variable, and Θ is the power applied to the observed data. For left-skewed distributions (values bunching at the right of the distribution), start by squaring the original values, then reassess the significance of skewness and proceed further up the ladder if needed. For left-skewed distributions, start with a square-root transformation and proceed down the ladder further if needed to bring the distribution into a reasonable degree of normality.

Table 16.1   Ladder of Powers for Transformations

Θ	x′	Transformation	Original Distribution
3	x3	Cube	Left Skew
2	x2	Square	Left Skew
1	x	None	Normal
1/2	$\sqrt{x}$	Square Root	Right Skew
1/3	$\sqrt[3]{x}$	Cube Root	Right Skew
0	log(x)	Log	Right Skew

PRELIMINARY ANALYSES

After the laborious process of checking and cleaning the data, it is time to turn attention to preliminary analyses. In fact, we generally recommend that the Results sections of theses and dissertations follow the simple outline of Preliminary Results, Main Results, and Supplementary Results. Preliminary analyses help the researcher decide how best to proceed with telling the story of the data. The first matter for preliminary analyses is to consider whether the sample behaved—that is, whether the descriptive statistics *(M, SD)* and reliability (e.g., alpha coefficient) for the measures were comparable to those reported by other researchers. As noted above, if data transformations were required to normalize the distribution, this step will not be possible. Obviously, the concern here is with standard or control conditions of test administration rather than with experimental effects. If your basic descriptive statistics are off in some manner (e.g., your average IQ for a college student sample is 85), your participants may be atypical, they may have misunderstood your instructions, or you may have erred in your reduction of the data into numerical form.

There may be several variables you wish to ignore beyond the preliminary stage, and your goal here is to show that the main results are not limited by age, gender, year in school, or other demographic characteristics. Thus you may wish to test for dependent variable differences by gender, interactions of other variables with gender, or a differential correlational pattern by gender. If using a true experiment rather than correlational design, you also may have built in several manipulation-check questionnaire items to document the internal validity of the treatment manipulation. In addition to these examples, there are some particular preliminary analyses that pertain to studies that will use factor analysis, and we turn to these next.

Factor Analysis

It is our observation that too often researchers are tempted to throw in factor analyses of their data as part of a broad exploratory approach to data analysis. To the degree that factor analysis programs will happily attempt to extract factors from almost any unsuspecting data, it is important to recognize some limitations of data that could lead to erroneous interpretations if not detected.

The first step in appropriately using factor analysis is visual inspection of the relevant correlation matrix. If correlations among variables are generally quite small, it is unlikely that the matrix will give rise to sensible common factors. Following this initial check, it is useful to evaluate two basic diagnostic statistics that are provided by most factor analysis programs. These give information about whether it is appropriate to subject data to factor analysis.

Bartlett's Test of Sphericity

Bartlett's test of sphericity (1950) affords a statistical test of the visual inspection recommended above. It assesses whether the correlation matrix of the variables to be factor-analyzed is actually an identity matrix (value of 1 for all diagonal elements of the matrix, with all off-diagonal elements equal to 0). The test statistic is distributed as a chi-square. When the value of the test statistic is sufficiently high, the probability level reaches statistical significance, and the researcher can comfortably reject the null hypothesis that the correlation matrix is an identity matrix. Generally, this appears to be a rather liberal test, and a significant value for the sphericity statistic is necessary but not sufficient for continuing with further factor analysis.

Kaiser-Meyer-Olkin (KMO) Measure of Sampling Adequacy

In addition to Bartlett's test, one should also evaluate the KMO measure of sampling adequacy (Kaiser, 1974). This statistic reflects the degree to which it is likely that common factors explain the observed correlations among the variables and is calculated as the sum of the squared simple correlations between pairs of variables divided by the sum of squared simple correlations plus the sum of squared partial correlations. To the degree that partial correlations approach zero as common factors account for increasing variance among the variables, the KMO statistic will be higher when a common-factor model is appropriate for the data. Small values for the KMO statistic indicate that correlations between pairs of variables cannot be accounted for by common factors. The KMO statistic can range from 0 to 1. Kaiser (1974) described KMOs in the .90s as "marvelous," in the .80s as "meritorious," in the .70s as "middling," in the .60s as "mediocre," in the .50s as "miserable," and below .50 as "unacceptable." If the value of the statistic is below .50, the researcher should seriously reconsider the appropriateness of a factor model, given the observed correlations. It should be noted that even in cases in which the KMO statistic indicates inappropriateness of a factor model, the factor analysis program will doggedly extract and rotate what it believes to be the best factor solution.

After determining that one's data are well suited for factor analysis, a researcher is faced with myriad choices regarding type of factor extraction, number of factors to extract, whether to rotate the factors and, if so, what type of rotation strategy to use. All of these decisions should be guided by the goals of the research project.

How Many Factors?

Although a detailed discussion of factor extraction strategies is beyond our scope here (see Harman, 1967, and Kim & Mueller, 1978, for additional information), a few general points can be made. When the goal of analysis is reduction of a large number of variables to a more manageable (and analyzable) number, principal components analysis (PCA) is likely to be the extraction of choice. Formally, PCA is not factor analysis but a close statistical cousin that is often the default option for statistical packages such as SPSS. PCA extracts principal components that are linear combinations of observed variables to account for shared variance among the variables being analyzed. The first principal component explains the most variance among the observed variables, the second principal component the next largest amount of variance, and so forth. The end result is the transformation of correlated variables into uncorrelated principal components. The first principal component is often used by researchers as a general index of a construct represented by shared variance among related variables. For example, if one had administered five tests of specific cognitive abilities, the first unrotated principal component extracted from intercorrelations among the five individual ability measures could be viewed as a measure of general ability. Among true factor analysis algorithms, principal axis factoring is probably the most common. This technique is quite similar to the linear strategy employed by PCA but uses an iterative procedure whereby estimates of communalities (amount of a variable's variance that is accounted for by common factors) are inserted into the diagonals of the correlation matrix being analyzed.

One of the challenges of factor analysis is determining the most appropriate number of factors to extract and rotate. Statistical programs can sometimes trip the unwary factor analyst by choosing a number of factors to extract based on an arbitrary default setting. The most commonly used default criterion is selecting the number of factors that have eigenvalues (an index of variance accounted for by the factor) exceeding 1.0. Researchers should also evaluate a full plot of eigenvalues for all potentially extracted factors. This so-called scree plot will show a decrease in the amount of variance accounted for by the addition of each new factor, and it has been argued (Cattell, 1966) that at the point when the plot breaks substantially and tails off, no further factors should be extracted. For exploratory factor analyses, it is recommended that the researcher extract one or more factors *above* and *below* the number of factors suggested by the

statistical program's default options. This allows for assessment of which extraction appears to provide a clearer simple structure (small number of variables with high loadings, relatively few variables with split loadings across factors).

To Rotate or Not to Rotate?

If the goal of the researcher is pure data reduction of the sort described above, then an unrotated first principal component will do the job nicely. It is often the case, however, that researchers are interested in identifying the most interpretable and meaningful structure of a group of variables, perhaps in an attempt to understand better the construct validity of a particular measure. In this case, a variety of factor rotation strategies assist in interpretation of the initially unrotated factor solution. Rotation basically reflects mathematical alignment of a reference axis through points in "factor space" that are held by the variables in the factor model. Variables that cluster closely together on some axis are presumably related to each other. The two principal forms of rotation are orthogonal and oblique. An *orthogonal* rotation creates factors that are independent of each other (the reference axes are at right angles to each other), whereas an *oblique* rotation allows for the rotated factors to correlate with each other (reference angles may be at oblique angles). In some cases, there may be a theoretically important reason for picking either a correlated or an uncorrelated factor solution. When there is no such rationale, it may be most prudent to proceed with an oblique solution, given that the constructs encountered most often by behavioral researchers are not independent. It may also be useful in exploratory analyses to use both oblique and orthogonal rotations to explore various ways of bringing meaning to the factors extracted from the observed data.

CONCLUSION: CLEANING UP THE DATA REQUIRES GETTING A LITTLE DIRTY

One memorable teacher in the junior author's graduate education, a teacher of statistics, was fond of reminding her class, "Don't be afraid to get your nose dirty in the data." It may seem ironic, but a dirty nose may be the best way to ensure clean data. In general, preliminary analyses are the most legitimate times to commit the statistical sin of data snooping. As much as you may want to quickly check out whether your hypotheses were supported, it is important to remember that the first analyses done on a new data set (or an old one being reanalyzed) should be considered preliminary. By becoming intimately acquainted with such trivial details as the number of participants on different variables or sets of items, you will be better able to spot problems or discrepancies in the data set and ultimately ensure a study with greater integrity.

EXERCISES

1. Consider a potential research project in an area of interest. What steps would you take in the planning stages of your project to ensure that your data will be as clean as they can be when they are collected? Think in terms of specific strategies that will be well suited for your area of research interest.

2. Imagine that you are a teaching assistant who is charged with teaching an undergraduate discussion section about data-cleaning strategies. Outline the points that you would make and consider how to communicate your points in a way that a relatively methodology-naive undergraduate psychology student would understand.

3. Choose a published research article in an area of interest to you. Read and critique the article in terms of the techniques used by the researchers to ensure that the data were clean. Are there additional steps that the researcher(s) should have taken?

Exercises 4 and 5 require some supervised assistance and support, as well as some real data.

4. Approach a faculty member with whom you are working and ask whether it would be possible to use a portion of an uncleaned data set to hone your data-cleaning skills (taking precautions to preserve confidentiality of the data). Identify a data-cleaning strategy suitable for the data and use SPSS or another statistical package to assist with the data-cleaning process. To what degree does your clean version of the data file compare with the official cleaned version of the data file? If there are differences between the two files, it may be instructive to use the differences as an opportunity to discuss different strategies for data cleaning.

5. Ask a supervising faculty member to assist you by planting bad data points in a copy of an already cleaned data file. These might be out-of-range data, response sets, and so forth. How successful are you at identifying the dirty data?

RECOMMENDED READINGS

Readers interested in more detail on the topics of clean data and preliminary analyses should consider the works by Anscombe (1973), Kim and Mueller (1978), and Smith et al. (1986).

REFERENCES

Anscombe, E J. (1973). Graphs in statistical analysis. *American Statistician, 27,* 17–21.

Badad, E. Y, Mann, M., & Mar-Hayim, M. (1975). Bias in scoring the WISC subtests. *Journal of Consulting and Clinical Psychology, 43,* 268.

Barnett, V., & Lewis, T. (1994). *Outliers in statistical data.* New York: Wiley.

Bartlett, M. S. (1950). Tests of significance in factor analysis. *British Journal of Psychology, 3,* 77–85.

Cattell, R. B. (1966). The scree test for the number of factors. *Multivariate Behavior Research, 1,* 245–276.

Comrey, A. L. (1985). A method for removing outliers to improve factor analytic results. *Multivariate Behavioral Research, 20,* 273–281.

Costa, P. T., & McCrae, R. R. (1992). *The Revised NEO Personality Inventory (NEO-PI-R) and NEO Five-Factor Inventory (NEO-FFi) professional manual.* Odessa, FL: Psychological Assessment Resources.

Crowne, D. P., & Marlowe, D. (1960). A new scale of social desirability independent of psychopathology. *Journal of Consulting Psychology, 24,* 349–354.

Dollinger, S. J., & Orf, L. A. (1991). Personality and performance in "personality": Conscientiousness and openness. *Journal of Research in Personality, 25,* 276–284.

Grubbs, F. E., & Beck, G. (1972). Extension of sample sizes and percentage points for significance tests of outlying observations. *Technometrics 14,* 847–854.

Harman, H. H. (1967). *Modern factor analysis* (2nd ed.). Chicago: University of Chicago Press.

Hawkins, D. M. (1980). *Identification of outliers.* New York: Chapman & Hall.

Jackson, D. N. (1984). *Personality research form manual* (3rd ed.). Port Huron, MI: Research Psychologists Press.

Kaiser, H. F. (1974). An index of factorial simplicity. *Psychometrica, 39,* 31–36.

Kim, J. O., & Mueller, C. W. (1978). *Introduction to factor analysis.* Beverly Hills, CA: Sage.

Orne, M. (1962). On the social psychology of the psychological experiment: With particular reference to demand characteristics and their implications. *American Psychologist, 17,* 776–783.

Paulhus, D. L. (1998). Manual for the Balanced Inventory of Desirable Responding: Version 7. Toronto/Buffalo: Multi-Health Systems.

Plake, B. S., & Impara J. C. (Eds.). (2001). *The fourteenth mental measurements yearbook.* Lincoln, NE: Buros Institute of Mental Measurements.

Roman, R. J., Moskowitz, G. D., Stein, M. I., & Eisenberg, R. F. (1995). Individual differences in experiment participation: Structure, autonomy, and time of the semester. *Journal of Personality, 63,* 113–138.

Rosenthal, R. (1966). *Experimenter effects in behavioral research.* New York: Appleton-Century-Crofts.

Rosenthal, R. (1978). How often are our numbers wrong? *American Psychologist, 33,* 1005–1008.

Rosenthal, R. (2002). Experimenter and clinician effects in scientific inquiry and clinical practice. *Prevention and Treatment, 5,* Article # 38. Retrieved on April 3, 2004, from http://journals.apa.org/prevention/volume5/pre0050038c.html

Rosenthal, R., & Jacobson, L. (1968). Pygmalion in the classroom: Teacher expectation and pupils' intellectual development. New York: Rinehart and Winston.

Sattler, J. M. (2001). *Assessment of children: Cognitive applications* (4th ed.). San Diego, CA: Author.

Sattler, J. M., Hillix, W. A., & Neher, L. A. (1970). Halo effect in examiner scoring of intelligence test responses. *Journal of Consulting and Clinical Psychology, 34,* 172–176.

Schultz, D. P. (1969). The human subject in psychological research. *Psychological Bulletin, 72,* 214–228.

Smith, P. C., Budzeika, K. A., Edwards, N. A., Johnson, S. M., & Bearse, L. N. (1986). Guidelines for clean data: Detection of common mistakes. *Journal of Applied Psychology, 71,* 457–460.

Velleman, P. F., & Hoaglin, D. C. (1981). *Applications, basics, and computing of exploratory data analysis.* Boston: Duxbury Press.

17

QUALITATIVE METHODS

HOWARD R. POLLIO

T. R. GRAVES

MICHAEL ARFKEN

In 1959, the English physicist and novelist C. P. Snow wrote a small book titled *The Two Cultures and the Scientific Revolution.* The basic premise of this book was that science and humanities represent two different ways of understanding the world and that the two different cultures, as he termed them, were in danger of becoming so estranged as to speak different languages, engage different values, and attract different audiences. This state of affairs, he felt, could only lead to a breach in contemporary thought, and for this reason he suggested that universities seek ways of bridging the gap between the sciences and the humanities. He further argued that if we continued to pursue science without reference to literature and literature without reference to science, we would only exacerbate the major problems of his/our age: nuclear destruction, overpopulation, and the disparity between rich and poor nations.

A similar situation seems to apply, in miniature, in psychology. Some of our best thinkers and researchers came to psychology from chemistry and physiology, but others came from literature and art. The usual way of dealing with this issue has been for psychology to disregard its literary and artistic roots and to see itself primarily in terms of procedures defined by the scientific method. Under this approach, some topics are moved to the periphery and others are moved center stage, not because they are uniquely significant but because they are methodologically pure: human beings remembering nonsense syllables or rats learning a T-maze.

In the early part of the 20th century, a new philosophy associated with the names of Husserl, Heidegger, and Merleau-Ponty proposed that the proper study of human (and animal) life should concern phenomena that were characteristic of the organism, not whether they could be turned into quantifiable behavior, reliably recorded by an unbiased observer. In place of an emphasis on scientific method, Husserl suggested that philosophy—and psychology—should be concerned with direct experience. Philosophically, this meant that even the activities of the scientist must be construed as beginning in experience. Psychologically it meant that we must first experience and know phenomena such as sleep or hunger before we can study them on the basis of scientific procedures such as measuring eye movements or stomach contractions. It also meant that every analysis invariably requires human interpretation, whether such interpretation concerns statistical significance levels or the conceptual meaning of experimental results considered in terms of some theory. The activities of the psychologist, like those of the nonscientist, begin in experience and end in interpretation; a new method, phenomenological analysis, was required both at a foundational level for understanding psychological research and at a more empirical level for deciding on the subject matter of psychology.

When a description of personal experience is at issue, methods are required that are both appropriate to the topic and rigorous in application. Because experience is not often transparent to itself, the problem of describing it requires the help of some other person whose own experience is not now at issue. One method natural to this task is that of dialogue in which an interviewer takes a respectful stance toward the real expert, the interviewee. If we view psychology in this way, it can no longer be seen solely as a third-person discipline in which facts depend on an observation of strangers. Nor can it be considered as a first-person discipline in which information derives from the self-reports of solitary individuals. Rather we must come to consider it as a discipline of the second person, in which interview methods encourage a participant and an investigator to clarify for each other the meaning of an experience as it unfolds between them in dialogue.

A QUALITATIVE RESEARCH SCRIPT:
PHENOMENOLOGICAL INTERVIEWING
AND INTERPRETATION

The most direct application of phenomenological philosophy to psychology concerns the development of phenomenological interviewing and interpretation. Because this approach concerns issues likely to arise in other qualitative procedures, it offers a research script for approaching other possibilities and problems. As a general overview of interview research, consider the chart presented as Figure 17.1. At the right, six different focal points are noted, each defining different phases of the research process. In the first phase, the investigator is at issue because it is he or she who chooses the topic. Because the researcher is one of the major participants in a dialogical study, it is important to know how he or she personally feels about the

topic and what assumptions he or she brings to the interview. Learning about these assumptions does not rid the investigator of presuppositions or biases; it only serves to make him or her aware of them.

The Bracketing Interview

To help an investigator become aware of presuppositions, a specific procedure—the bracketing interview—is used in interview studies. The term *bracketing* was used by Husserl to describe the (philosophical) need to suspend the ordinary attitude of daily life toward the nature of reality. As such, it was meant to function in the same way as Descartes's "methodological doubt" was supposed to work some 350 years earlier: to help the thinker understand a phenomenon without presuppositions or biases to cloud the mind. Although Husserl and Descartes came to different conclusions, we should not be surprised if we accept the idea that human understanding always depends on a fusing of perspectives. When we engage in a phenomenological interview, for example, there are always two people and two histories, and communication takes place only when this fact is considered. We cannot lose ourselves and become the other person. We are who we are, just as the person being interviewed is who he or she is, and the best we can do is mediate between us in meaningful conversation.

Bracketing is accomplished by having the researcher interviewed about the topic of study. Although this procedure is meant to help the investigator become aware of presuppositions, it also allows him or her to have experience with what it is like to be interviewed. To be useful, the interview must be interpreted, and what the phenomenon means to the researcher must be described before beginning the study. This understanding then becomes part of the study, because it will help the reader locate the researcher's presuppositions and provide an intellectual context for any interpretations that follow.

The Participants

The second focal point is the participant; here there are two principal criteria for eligibility: The

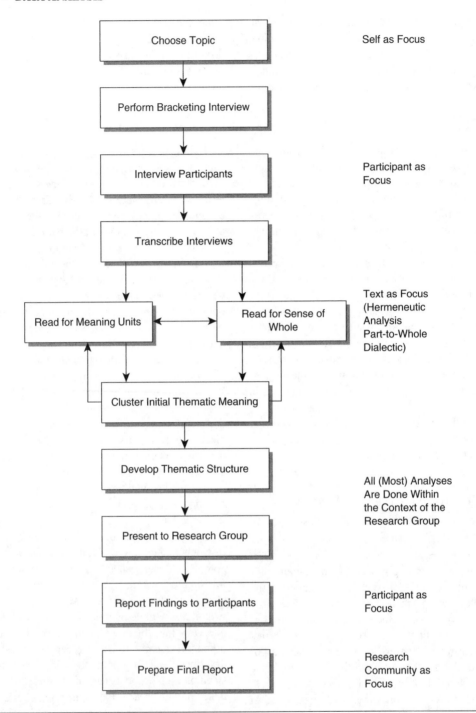

Figure 17.1 Summary of Steps in Conducting an Existential-Phenomenological Study.

SOURCE: Adapted from Pollio, H. R., Henley, T., Thompson, C. B. (1997). *The Phenomenology of Everyday Life.* New York: Cambridge University Press. Reprinted by Permission.

participant needs to (a) have experienced the phenomenon of interest and (b) be willing to talk about it in an interview. Among the recruitment procedures that have been used are newspaper articles, posters and flyers, professional and community intermediaries (such as psychologists in a clinic or presidents of civic clubs), and word of mouth (snowball sampling in which one interviewee tells the researcher of other individuals and identifies customary gathering places). An appropriate sample size ranges from 6 to 12 persons and is sometimes adjusted as the study proceeds. If redundancy is evident after talking with six participants, the researcher may decide it is unnecessary to interview additional participants.

Dealing with vulnerable populations such as homeless persons or abused women presents unique challenges. Not only is it difficult to locate participants, it is also necessary to ensure their safety. For example, in a study of homeless women, Anderson (1996) found participants at a local cafe that served as a safe place. After describing her study, she waited for interested individuals to approach and make an appointment. Anderson was clear in describing her study to potential interviewees and gave them time to evaluate her proposal in a safe environment. Special arrangements also must be made when working with these populations: Rather than obtain written consent, leaving the participant with a piece of paper that could be discovered by an abusive husband or the police, the researcher should obtain verbal consent while taping the interview.

The Phenomenological Interview

Once participants agree to be interviewed, a critical issue is the specific question to be asked. Although some interviewers prefer a general question such as "Please tell me about your experience of X," a more useful question is one that focuses on specific experiences: "Please tell me about some specific situations in which you experienced X." This question not only gives the participant a possibility of talking about significant issues, it also allows him or her to select the incidents to be discussed.

During a phenomenological interview, it is important to create an atmosphere in which the participant feels comfortable. Unlike a structured interview, the flow of dialogue is controlled by the participant, and the interviewer's role is to ensure that each experience is discussed in detail. The give and take that defines a good interview is helped along by a stance of respect and openness to the participant's report. The reciprocal influence that is necessarily present, and considered a source of error in other contexts, thus becomes an area of connection and possibility.

Although the researcher does not control the interview, he or she may be directive at times because participants sometimes need help focusing on unfolding themes and details. To this end, the researcher seeks to cover each incident described at the beginning of the interview and may even ask for comparisons and contrasts. For example, a researcher asking men about anger may initially hear stories about malfunctioning cars, boats, or computers (Thomas, 2003) and may wonder about anger in intimate relationships. Although it is not appropriate to ask, "What about anger at your wife?" the researcher could ask, "Can you think of another situation in which you became angry?" To ensure that the participant has nothing to add, the researcher asks just before the interview ends, "It is there anything else you would like to say?" (By the way, if a participant never mentions his wife, the researcher never does either.)

The Text

The next phase concerns the text of an interview and the activities of a special research team known as the interpretive research group. Because members of this group have thematized the researcher's bracketing interview, it is possible for them to point out whenever the researcher's assumptions surface in an interview, usually in the form of leading questions that deal with the interviewer's personal presuppositions. Members of the group are not only concerned with noting overly leading questions, they actively seek counterexamples and contradictions. All proposed thematic interpretations are continuously challenged until all members of the group agree that an interpretation is supported by the text. Interpretations that seem theoretical are put aside in favor of meanings that are more descriptive. Although this process may sound argumentative, its tone is respectful but critical. Everyone is vitally involved in producing the best thematic description of the interview, and this communal purpose makes every comment an attempt to help, not to put down, the person proposing the interpretation.

The Interpretive Process

Interpretation depends on a continuous process of relating a part of some text to the whole of that text. This part-to-whole process takes place in two phases. First, the interpretive group works toward a thematic description of each interview, which consists of reading the transcript and noting specific parts that stand out as significant. These parts are sometimes referred to as *meaning units* and serve as the basis for themes. In discussing how the process works, Thomas and Pollio (2002) describe the operation of an interpretive group they lead at the University of Tennessee. This group, which meets weekly, usually is able to analyze only one transcript during a single 2-hour meeting. During this time, each group member is provided with the text of a transcribed interview. The transcript is read aloud by two members of the group—one serving as interviewer, the other as participant—and an attempt is made to summarize meanings as the reading proceeds. Reading is stopped anytime someone is struck by something in the text, even if initially unsure what it means. For example, someone might say, "I want us to talk about the word *received* in line 5." In this interview with a hospitalized patient, the word *received* was used in a very embodied way in the sense of being comforted. The patient also experienced the staff as holding her, as one might hold an infant in a receiving blanket. The word *received* thus became a metaphor for her hospital experience. In deciding what is thematic, the group not only considers specific words but the meaning of these words in conjunction with the text as a whole.

A second phase of interpretation takes place after all transcripts have been thematized. At this point the task expands to include commonalities across interviews. Once global themes are noted, the interpretive group considers whether they are supported by individual texts and whether they offer a clear description of the phenomenon. The rationale for looking across interviews is not to produce generalizability but to improve interpretive vision. By looking both within and across interviews, the group is able to consider diverse experiences and to recognize how one situation resembles another. Although some researchers name themes in theoretical terms, others describe them in words and phrases actually used by participants.

Developing and Refining Thematic Structure

The structure of a phenomenon is "the commonality (of meaning) running through the many diverse appearances of the phenomenon" (Valle, King, & Halling, 1989, p. 14). This meaning must be agreed on by the researcher and the interpretive group. After completing an overall thematization of various texts, the researcher brings a list of proposed themes to the interpretive group. This list not only names the themes, it also supplies specific textual support: page numbers, line numbers, quoted words and phrases, and so forth. The group then considers these excerpts and helps to choose the most apt descriptive term for each one. The final thematic structure is sometimes (but not always) presented in the form of a diagram that depicts interrelationships among themes.

Return to Participants

When thematizing is complete, the research focus returns to the participant. During this phase, the newly developed thematic structure is presented to each participant, who is asked to judge whether it captures his or her personal experience. There is usually a supportive response; if disagreement occurs, participants are asked to suggest an alternate wording or interpretation, and the process continues until participants and researcher are comfortable with the new structure. Researchers would do well to remember, however, that participants sometimes have difficulty in seeing their own experiences as part of a larger pattern. For this reason, the participant's evaluation is not the final word. If significant differences remain between a participant and the researcher, it may be necessary to engage in a new dialogue to attain a structure that can be agreed on by both. These interviews must involve the same considerations as before: The researcher must remain open to new descriptions and seek to create an air of equal participation between the participant and him or her.

Communicating Results

The final phase of a phenomenological investigation is the same as for any other study: to communicate with the larger research community. The same attention to detail that prevailed during the interview and its interpretation must now be observed at this stage. The researcher is obliged to share the themes identified in his or her bracketing interview; although extensive disclosure is not necessary, the reader does have a right to know the researcher's perspective. Beyond discussing one's own presuppositions, Polkinghorne also notes, "It is important to include . . . an implications section where the significance of the findings for practice and policy is spelled out" (1989, p. 58). Throughout the written report, the researcher must follow the ordinary amenities of clear writing and compelling example.

Addressing the Literature

For any qualitative study, a question often arises as to what role knowledge of the prior research literature should play in the development of a study. One radical position holds that a review of the relevant literature must always follow an analysis of current data so as not to unduly influence present results (Carpenter, 1999). A different position assumes that prior to undertaking any research project, qualitative or otherwise, the researcher should be aware of what is already known—and not yet known—about the phenomenon of interest (Thomas & Pollio, 2002). Although phenomenological research does not require a theoretical framework, investigators should be familiar with theoretical positions used by previous researchers to think about the phenomenon. A general familiarity with prior research is also necessary in evaluating possible contributions of the present study to the ongoing stream of discoveries about the overall phenomenon. One way in which to develop an initial overview of the

literature is to identify significant studies by using a citation index such as Web of Science. Having an initial command of the pertinent literature does not mean that the researcher will be profoundly influenced by what is already known, provided that he or she brackets, and continually rebrackets, prior knowledge while interacting with participants and analyzing data.

There is an additional reason for learning about the existing research literature: The researcher may only know after completing a study which research community will be most interested in what has been learned. The "who" of one's audience also has implications for the final literature review in terms of both content and style of exposition. Often in qualitative studies, findings are relevant to many different disciplines, and the researcher must be attentive to discipline-specific theories and concepts and seek to present them in an accessible way. This means the researcher should write in a less discipline-specific style and try to explain what often are taken-for-granted concepts and methods in his or her home discipline. Qualitative research requires the investigator to move in and across disciplines because the audience for qualitative studies is often interdisciplinary.

Focus Groups

Research methods deriving from a phenomenological perspective are time- and labor-intensive. The initial interview often takes over an hour to conduct and about 4–5 hours to transcribe. Group interpretation may take 3–4 hours to complete, making a total of over 8 hours for each participant. Although not intended to deal with this issue, focus groups offer one way to reduce the workload by talking with many participants at once. In general, *focus groups* consist of 4–10 participants who engage in a conversation designed to discuss the complexities and subtleties of first-person experiences concerning some topic. In this context, participants emphasize things that stand out to them and build on one another's comments to provide an overall picture of the phenomenon.

Focus groups had their beginnings in World War II (Krueger & Casey, 2000; Stewart & Shamdasani, 1990). Sociologists given the task of assessing how people reacted to propaganda films were able to learn how various parts of the films made people think and feel about the war. After the war, focus groups caught on with political pollsters and consumer researchers and, by 1994, 70% of all consumer research dollars were allocated for such research (Luntz, 1994). This brief historical overview suggests that focus groups derive largely from applied settings and continue to function in such settings. Within these settings, they are usually conducted for a brief period and analyzed on the basis of impressions offered by the moderator or by an outside analyst observing the group on video or through a one-way mirror.

Applied focus groups have one characteristic that leads to their name: They are *focused* on a single issue. This means that the job of the moderator is to encourage participants to discuss the topic freely and openly. To accomplish this, researchers develop a questioning path that consists of a series of questions serving to direct the group's conversation (Krueger & Casey, 2000). Useful questions are defined by the following criteria: They sound conversational, use ordinary words, are easy to say, and provide clear direction. Such questions are most useful when they move the group from general to specific issues and are mindful of the total time available. The skills of the moderator are crucial; not only must he or she be able to provide a feeling of freedom and a sensitive ear, he or she must also move the group (gently) along the questioning path. Although open, applied focus groups have a strong element of direction, and both aspects determine its power (and limitations) in learning how participants experience the topic under consideration.

Focus groups can also be used for pure research. In this context, a few changes are made in certain aspects of the process. For one, participants are now given less direction as to what to talk about, aside from an initial question. The atmosphere is more open and the moderator functions as a phenomenological interviewer rather than as someone directly concerned with a commercial product. Interpretation, or analysis, is also different: no longer does it depend on the impressions of a moderator or outside observer; now transcripts provide for more rigorous methods of analysis, such as content analysis or thematic interpretation.

Loosening the connection between focus groups and targeted commercial interests enables them to become more like phenomenological interviews. Unlike a phenomenological interview, however, a group now provides the text, and this difference affords possibilities and problems. On the positive side, Madriz (2000) notes that "focus groups allow access to . . . participants who may find one-on-one, face-to-face interactions 'scary' or 'intimidating' [and offer] a safe environment where [they] can share ideas, in the company of people from the same backgrounds." From her perspective as a Latina feminist researcher, Madriz feels that the voices of minority group members—those out of the cultural power structure—have not often been heard because of the unique nature of social science research. When participants are allowed to become part of a focus group, their voices combine and rise above a threshold that cannot be overlooked.

One issue in focus group research concerns the ordinary properties of group interaction. Here it is useful to consider Yalom's (1980) description of the way group process and individual style come together: What a person does in everyday life tends to show up in a group setting. This means that a dominant person may monopolize group discussion, whereas a shy person may not be able to contribute his or her insights. A further problem concerns the quality of the conversation: Some groups are lively and articulate, others are tongue-tied; and there seems to be no way to predict what the present group will be like.

These concerns relate to group members; what about the moderator? Although the researcher may try to be open to different points of view, it is unlikely that he or she will be aware of personal presuppositions brought to the research setting. Although it is possible to do a bracketing interview, few focus groups, even those of the research variety, require this step of the moderator. Most training manuals do offer helpful advice to prevent the leader from monopolizing and/or overcontrolling the flow of dialogue. In the former case, such advice suggests asking nondirective questions that help maintain an open stance toward participants. In the latter case, different advice is offered to applied and pure research groups. For applied groups, the moderator is advised to develop a series of questions capable of eliciting the maximum amount of information. For pure research groups, the moderator is advised to ask more open-ended questions. Such questions allow the interview to be controlled largely by participants, and the moderator now either simply reflects back what has been said or asks for clarification. The latter strategy should be used sparingly because other group members may understand what is being said and discuss issues not yet understood by the moderator.

Although the leader should try to keep participants on track, he or she should never ask a question that moves the group in a direction different from the one presently being pursued. No matter how much the moderator may want to have a certain issue discussed, the most that he or she should ever ask is "Do you want to add anything?" If the moderator makes a strong request for changing group focus, he or she has made a bracketing error, and it will not be possible, during the interpretive phase of analysis, to determine what members of the group might have said if such a redirecting question had not been asked.

The final output of a focus group is a thematic description. The transformation that leads from text to theme is not easy to describe, although it usually involves an "insight-like" process that comes from a complete immersion in the interview text. In developing thematic descriptions, the researcher should not try to thematize using formal or abstract principles but should focus instead on what the experience was like for participants using their own words. What is sought is an "experience-near" description, not an empirical confirmation of abstract theoretical principles.

NARRATIVE ANALYSIS

Narrative analysis begins on the assumption that one way to learn something about a person, group, or culture is to consider the stories they tell. For example, when we meet new people, we often begin by saying "Tell me about yourself," or "What do you do?" We sometimes miss the point that their answers frequently take the form of a story, that we expect a particular structure to the stories we are told (and tell), and that we use such expectations to derive meaning from these stories. Narrative analysis addresses how stories guide personal and social meanings and views human life as a text that can be analyzed much as literary critics or biblical scholars analyze their texts.

The Nature of Narrative Understanding

Riessman (1993) has developed a model for dealing with narrative meanings that assumes that everyday narratives provide a reconfigured version of human experience using structures available in language. A narrative is defined by its temporal structure and depends on shared cultural understandings of order and causality, much like the concept of a research script articulated by Hershey, Jacobs-Lawson, and Wilson in the opening chapter of this volume. Although our immediate experience of the world may not necessarily unfold as a narrative, when we reflect on it and tell it to others, it usually does assume this form. Narrative structure can thus become a topic of research in its own right and provide insight into how people go about reflecting on and structuring activities and meanings in their everyday and professional lives.

The first level of narrative development takes place when personal experience is reconfigured as we emphasize certain aspects of our first-person world and allow others to become context. Language is significant to this process because it provides words that direct us to some things and allow us to ignore others. Although it is clear that we also choose what we attend to, the language we speak often influences such choices even to the point of sometimes making it seem not at all like a choice. It is at this point in the narrative cycle that we *identify and isolate* aspects of our experience and begin to represent it as a cluster of observations to which words can be applied.

At the next level, a story formulated as experience is shaped into an account that can be told to someone else. The narrative—what you can know of my world—is different from the world as I live it, and you and I are negotiating the meaning of my story as I tell it to you. It is not just the two of us, however, who are involved. As every sentence requires an understanding of grammar, so every story requires an understanding of *narrative grammar.* Such grammars are social and historical phenomena—what is coherent and understandable depends on accepted and socially shared beliefs about what is considered a story. As cultural and historical events shape the acceptable forms of a coherent sentence, they similarly shape the acceptable forms of a coherent narrative (Bruner, 1991). For both written and spoken narratives, the narrator and the listener are part of a specific social and historical context, and narrative research is frequently designed to determine how such contexts affect narrative understanding. As an example, Hershey, Jacobs-Lawson, and Wilson (Chapter 1, this volume) define *research expertise* in terms of a person having a highly articulated research script; from a narrative perspective, the very idea of an expert research script must be situated in a historical and cultural context that values facility with scientific thinking and method.

Sociohistorical constraints also shape our understanding of acceptable narrative form—*how one orders the events of experience into a story*—and of acceptable narrative content—*what gets included and what does not.* Questions of narrative form deal with what is lifelike and believable, not what is true and factual, as in narratives of courtroom testimony or in scripts of scientific research. A researcher may, in fact, attempt to learn about the various ways in which context contributes to how we create a story from significant life events. Within the research literature, such stories often deal with situations such as illness (Good, 1994; Kleinman, 1988), religious transformation and spiritual healing (Csordas, 1997), personal histories (Creswell, 1998), and even stories told about us by other family members (Beier, 1994).

Methodological Issues: Transcription

A number of factors must be kept in mind when transcribing spoken narratives. How the words of participants are transcribed may influence what can and cannot be said about the narrative. For example, do you want to record every pause in speech or note that your participant whispered or that he or she spoke in a monotone? Sometimes carefully attending to the nuances of the spoken narrative is useful, sometimes not. Riessman (1993) characterizes transcription as "taking a snapshot of reality," and just as photographers make decisions about what they wish to portray, so too transcriptionists make decisions as to how to represent a spoken narrative as text.

Methodological Issues: Analysis and Interpretation

There are many ways to analyze a transcribed narrative. Sometimes it is analyzed in terms of cognitive script structures (a psychological approach); at other times, it may involve an evaluation of figurative language (a more humanistic, literary approach). The analyst also may look at character, setting, plot sequence, themes, repeated words, and other structural elements that participants draw on in telling their stories. Once analytic units have been identified, the researcher will often combine the narratives of individual participants into a *metastory.* This process is similar to the one described in dealing with the way in which phenomenological interviews are thematized, although the emphasis here is on story structure, not thematic meanings. Although narrative analysis does not use an interpretive research group, there is no reason why it could not make use of this technique.

Stories of Illness: An Example of Narrative Research

Researchers often study narratives of illness as a way of understanding how people deal with chronic conditions. In one study (Steffen, 1997), stories told as part of an Alcoholics Anonymous (AA) treatment program were analyzed for narrative structure and for how AA group members shaped the narratives of new participants to fit a preexisting structure of understanding. Because in the culture of AA members believe that individuals are only able to come to terms with alcoholism when they are open about their illness, new participants are encouraged to tell their life stories. Each particular story is then slowly (and implicitly) shaped to fit the preexisting alcoholic narrative held by AA group members. According to Steffen, the AA metanarrative typically includes the following features:

1. My life was going well.

2. It then became more stressful.

3. I began drinking more and more.

4. I became distant from family, friends, and work.

5. My life fell apart and I "bottomed out."

6. I realized I am an alcoholic.

7. I had a turning point.

8. I started to work toward recovery.

9. I must always remember that I am an alcoholic.

This structure can be recognized as it is frequently described in discussions of alcoholism in psychology, sociology, and medicine. AA members understand each other's personal stories with respect to this narrative because it is shared by most members of the group. Steffen further points out that the AA narrative may be related to broader cultural narratives of religious transformation, such that the newly recovering AA member is viewed as a "type of sinner" who is "transformed" and "healed" by sharing in "sacred" testimony with other members of AA.

Narrative Analysis and Psychology

Narrative methods are not new to psychological research. Case studies have long been used in clinical contexts to provide a richness of detail not available in other approaches. Narrative analysis allows the researcher to capture a similar richness, thus developing a more nuanced understanding of what individual stories have in common. It also allows the researcher to address socially shared beliefs that take a narrative form. For example, one narrative that captures a significant set of American values is that of the self-made person, someone who rises from poverty and a harsh childhood and who, against all odds, becomes extraordinarily successful. This narrative gained cultural currency during the 19th century in the more literary form of a bildungsroman (a novel or story concerning the development of a person's character).

The general structure, or script, of culturally shared stories is of interest to cognitive and social psychology because they frame individual and cultural meanings of specific human experiences. Sontag (1989), for example, traced the development of a social narrative of tuberculosis in the 19th century and paralleled it with a 20th century narrative of cancer. Both diseases have a clear medical origin and, as Sontag points out, share metaphoric meanings that make attributions about their sufferers that may lead to additional problems. Tuberculosis was initially viewed as a disease of the artist—primarily afflicting a person of sensitive and sad temperament—and later as a product of urban moral decay and sexual excess. Cancer is still sometimes viewed as a disease of suppressed or concealed emotions that must be fought, defeated, and removed. Both social narratives affected the experiences of those unfortunate enough to have contracted these diseases and sometimes even led to treatment regimens not altogether helpful to the healing process.

ETHNOGRAPHY

But what about behavior? Is there no role in qualitative research for carefully observed and interpreted activities other than those of speaking? What is important to remember here is that speech is a behavior—a public doing in the world—and that certain methods of linguistic analysis are extremely behavioral, particularly those used to identify the sound patterns of language. In this context, it is possible to describe the sounds of language in two different ways: phonetically and phonemically. In the *phonetic* case, such description provides an objective rendering of all of the differences detected by a trained observer in the stream of sound regardless of language. *Phonemic* description, on the other hand, requires the participation of a native speaker or listener to help the linguist determine the minimal set of sounds making a difference to speakers of some specific language.

It is possible to generalize this usage, as cultural anthropology does in its distinction between *emic* and *etic* descriptions of culture. This analogy—which derives from the terms, *phonemic* and *phonetic*—suggests that an observer is free to describe the meanings of objects, words, and actions from the first-person perspective of individuals in the culture or from the third-person perspective of an external observer. In both the cultural and linguistic case, it is clear that although inquiry starts with etic description, emic description is a second, more significant, moment in the anthropologist's understanding of the culture.

Observing Situated Behavior

The term *ethnography* derives from two Greek words, *ethnikos* (meaning a nation, or people) and *graphe* (meaning to write or to draw); thus, ethnography cast in terms of its etymology is the "writing or drawing of a nation or people." Although ethnography can be described in this way, social scientists have applied ethnographic methods in far more particular contexts. In fact, ethnography offers a useful method for any social scientist interested in observing how people behave—and in finding out what these behaviors mean—within a bounded social or geographic situation. Bounded situations of this type are called *field sites* and may be as vast as a city or village or as particular as an organization, neighborhood, or street corner. Ethnographic methods emphasize the situated study of people and can be used to provide insights into what life is like for specific people living in specific situations.

The Relativistic Attitude

To perform ethnographic analysis, we first need to understand certain past problems current thinking seeks to redress. Many of these problems derive from the fact that ethnographic research began under a pall of moral ambiguity defined by the literature of Western imperialism, a literature used to justify religious conversion, racism, and the denigration of indigenous peoples (Jahoda, 1998). In response to this view, early 20th century American anthropology began to develop a different attitude toward non-Western cultures known as cultural relativism, which sought to describe cultures as internally coherent entities having unique social beliefs and practices that could not be judged by Western standards. The intent of ethnographic research thus became one of describing, not evaluating, cultures. A side purpose of this approach was to have as little effect as possible on the culture being studied, not only out of respect for the culture but also in terms of the rigor of ethnographic description.

Current ethnography is less a specific method than an attitude of openness in bounded social settings. This attitude requires total immersion in a situation different from one's own combined with a willingness to have one's current social world cease to make sense as one comes to inhabit a new one. In contemporary ethnography, the general attitude is relativistic, with an emphasis on emic practices and meanings. In a half-jesting way, ethnography could be described as *deep hanging out* in hopes of producing a thick, rich description of the meanings, structures, and ways of life of settings and cultures vastly different from our own (Geertz, 2000).

Ethnographic research can also be viewed in terms of dialogue. This means that what we know about a culture and its rituals often derives from a unique conversational situation involving an ethnographer and an informant. In this context, the informant gains a new understanding of his or her culture and its rituals as the ethnographer gains a new understanding of the informant's culture and rituals, not to mention his or her own culture and rituals. Both individuals alternate in the roles of researcher and informant, and the understanding reached is often new to both participants.

Why might a psychologist be interested in ethnographic methods? Too often Western psychology views its constructs and theories as transcultural and ahistorical. Psychology seeks to talk about universal mechanisms and behaviors and to deemphasize those that are culturally specific. Ethnographic research often challenges this assumption because in a cross-cultural context one soon discovers that each culture has its own unique beliefs about what makes us human and what counts as a viable explanation for our thoughts and behaviors.

Cultural Context and Meaning

Despite its emphasis on cultural uniqueness, ethnography also recognizes that all human beings share a similar existential situation: We are born, we grow up, and, eventually, we die (Shweder, 1990). What ethnography allows us to study are the unique ways in which cultural worlds offer a trajectory for human life and provide ways of making it comprehensible to us and to others. For instance, the image of the newly divorced, middle-aged man, driving an aubergine Lotus Elise and hanging out with women 15 to 20 years his junior is an image we understand, if not condone. We say he is having a "midlife crisis," that he feels there is less life ahead than behind, and that he has not yet *really* lived. Such an image would make little sense to the Hindu Brahman, who sees midlife as a time to deepen his spirituality through isolation, reading, and meditation. Both men may be seeking to make sense of their lives in the face of death, although each culture provides them with different ways of going about this most significant task (Shweder, 1998). A cultural world creates the possibilities for a meaningful life by providing human beings with symbolic universes and ritual practices. It is through inheriting, maintaining, and transmitting these symbolic universes and ritual practices that individuals experience personal and social meanings for their lives. Viewing culture in this way presupposes a particular relationship between human beings and their social worlds, a relationship in which culture becomes a text of symbols and practices, "an acted document" that can be read from everyday actions and language (Geertz, 1973, p. 10).

Interpretive Ethnography: Criticism and Response

One criticism often leveled at ethnographic research is that aspects of social life defined by ritual performances are rare and not necessarily the best way to understand everyday life. This criticism seems to misunderstand the intent of ethnographic analysis in which all of social life is viewed as a ritual performance that exhibits particular beliefs, expectations, and symbols. Because informants are not always able to articulate the traditional meaning of a ritual does not mean they do not understand how it is relevant to their current lives or that everyday activities, such as teaching a class or driving a car, do not also have ritual aspects. The significance of ethnographic methods for psychology is that they enable the researcher to observe everyday situations in which behaviors and meanings become manifest and to discuss these behaviors and meanings with those who live them. In this way, ethnographic research is able to provide a detailed first-, second-, and/or third-person description of behaviors and meanings shared by a group of people without slighting the role of culture, situation, or place in contextualizing them.

GROUNDED THEORY

Although the methods of grounded theory are qualitative in nature, their purpose goes beyond that of description. Whereas phenomenology, focus groups, narrative analysis, and ethnography all seek a rigorous description of various aspects of human life, grounded theory ultimately seeks a theoretical understanding of these phenomena. The basic tenets of grounded theory were first introduced by Glaser and Strauss in their book, *The Discovery of Grounded Theory* (1967). Initially grounded theory was viewed as a starting place for quantitative research; however, it soon came to occupy its own niche largely because it took exception to traditional preoccupations with testing hypotheses derived from abstract theories (Pidgeon, 1996). Although a clear theory may help organize research, it can also restrict observation. Instead of seeking information to confirm or refute an existing theory, grounded theory sought to derive its explanations from the *ground* (i.e., the data) of the phenomenon itself.

Using this as its starting point, grounded theory made four innovations in thinking about qualitative research:

1. It gave a voice to researchers who sought to break from the view that research should only proceed on the basis of quantitative testing of theoretical predictions.

2. It pointed the way to more discovery-based research by highlighting the role of qualitative analysis in generating new ideas.

3. It demonstrated how qualitative research could be systematic and simultaneously stimulate innovative empirical work and theory.

4. It made the case for valuing detailed, contextually sensitive, interpretive research, thereby counteracting the view that such research could only serve as an exploratory investigation or pilot study (Pidgeon, 1996).

Glaser and Strauss sought to distinguish their methods from those of more traditional social science. For these researchers, theory should emerge during, rather than prior to, exploring phenomena. Whereas traditional researchers seek to verify a particular theory through hypothesis testing, grounded theory emphasizes ongoing theory development as part of the research process. Because theories constructed on the basis of grounded methods derive from a continuous focus on relevant data, they are thought to be more sensitive than other methods to critical aspects of their phenomena (Strauss & Corbin, 1998).

To assist a researcher in developing meaningful theory, grounded theorists suggest that research include the following steps:

1. *Data selection.* It is important to begin any research project with a rich source of data. For grounded-theory projects, data have been derived from archived material, participant observation, or, most commonly, from semi-structured interviews (Pidgeon, 1996). In the case of interviews, grounded theorists attempt to balance the openness of an unstructured interview with the focus provided by an unfolding conceptual understanding of the topic. After initial data have been collected, it is important to organize them in a clear way. For interviews, this takes the form of transcribed texts, which the researcher then inductively divides into emergent units that can be used for further analysis (Pidgeon & Henwood, 1996).

2. *Constant comparison.* In this phase of the process, the researcher compares current ideas regarding the phenomenon with current data in order to ensure a fit between all available data and the developing theory (Pidgeon, 1996). This process not only ensures that novel approaches will be explored, it also serves to prevent existing data from being squeezed or stretched to fit theoretical presuppositions. By remaining continuously aware of the emerging properties of their data, grounded-theory researchers are able to avoid implicitly distorting their findings by only considering them from a single (theoretical) point of view.

3. *Theoretical sampling.* Whereas constant comparison involves an open posture toward emerging phenomena, theoretical sampling is meant to ensure that the researcher will encounter new data. As research proceeds, data are sought specifically to challenge the present ideas of the researcher. For example, in the initial stages of a grounded-theory analysis, it is important to be open to a variety of new and creative interpretations of the data. Although grounded theorists hope to gain fruitful insights from what was once a corpus of scattered data, such insights do not necessarily follow a linear path and often are recursive, with various stages of the process influencing one another.

By continually encountering (and seeking) new data, the researcher ultimately comes to a point of *saturation* when new results are not significantly different from existing ones. Grounded theorists advise researchers to continue past this point to confirm that any further data will be congruent with those previously gathered. Once a researcher is confident the saturation point has been reached, he or she can continue to the next stage of research.

4. *Coding.* During this stage, the researcher seeks to identify categories or themes that have emerged while reading and rereading the data. Initially, it may be possible to identify discrete sections of the data defining a similar theme. This is referred to as *open coding* and involves a provisional identification of concepts noted in the data. During this stage, the researcher carefully examines a particular portion of the data until its meaning is transparent. This often involves a line-by-line process, in which it is assumed that approaching the data in this way will lead, in the initial stages of a project, to maximize potential interpretations for different sections of the overall data set (Charmaz, 2000).

Once potential themes or categories have been identified, the researcher's attention shifts to clarifying relationships among them. Whereas open coding is concerned with describing the meaning of elements in isolation, *axial coding* focuses on the way individual elements relate to one another (Strauss & Corbin, 1998). As coding progresses, researchers usually develop particular methods of coding with which they feel most comfortable. It is important to remember that coding does not signal the end of data collection and that open and axial coding often occur simultaneously.

5. *Memo writing.* When coding data, it is often helpful to keep a journal of any thoughts that emerge during the process. By reflecting on how data fit (or do not fit) the existing schema, the researcher may discover ways of organizing the data not envisioned in the initial stages of coding. Any ideas regarding data collection and analysis

should be written down as soon as they occur. Fresh notes are seen as an essential tool for generating a new focus as well as for facilitating subsequent theorizing (Pidgeon & Henwood, 1996).

6. *Categorizing*. Throughout the research process, data tend to migrate from one category to another as different categories become salient. An ability to modify ideas about the particular categories used to code data is one hallmark of a grounded-theory approach. Despite being open to emerging data, it is also necessary to settle on some clearly defined coding system. Once this has been accomplished, it is then necessary to articulate the conditions for each of the categories. By referring to notes taken during data analysis, researchers should be able to specify why certain portions of the data are subsumed under particular categories. Categories derived from various stages of grounded-theory research are next organized and presented to support a particular conceptual understanding of the phenomenon. The final presentation may be in the form of a hypothesis, a narrative, or some sort of visual model. By remaining open to a variety of interpretations throughout the study, researchers hope to ensure that their understanding of the data will maintain fidelity to the phenomenon of interest.

Morrow and Smith's (1995) study of the survival and coping styles of sexually abused women offers a good example of grounded-theory research. Rather than appropriating theoretical constructs traditionally used to understand the experiences of such victims, Morrow and Smith sought to generate a theory congruent with the lived experience of their participants. In other words, the categories, themes, and concepts used to understand sexual abuse were arrived at on the basis of an inductive analysis of the experiences of victims and not on the basis of a priori theoretical categories. The authors specifically describe the aim of their study as seeking to "understand the lived experiences of women who had been sexually abused as children and to generate a theoretical model for the ways in which they survived and coped with their abuse" (Morrow & Smith, 1995, p. 24).

To accomplish this task, data were derived from semistructured interviews, videotaped recordings of a 10-week group exercise exploring the various meanings of coping and survival, participant journals, and from the field notes of one of the researchers (Morrow & Smith, 1995). Rather than using preexisting theoretical principles to guide them, their analysis depended on a willingness to see alternative ways of categorizing the data throughout the research project. The results of this process uncovered a variety of factors that contribute to specific ways of coping with childhood sexual abuse. One such factor was the cultural context in which the abuse occurred. Focusing on social context was thought to help victims recognize the contribution of social factors while simultaneously minimizing the amount of blame they directed toward themselves. Another factor contributing to particular coping styles centered on experiences of powerlessness, which tended to facilitate emotion-focused rather than problem-focused coping strategies. These findings tend to support prior research (Long & Jackson, 1993) in suggesting that problem-focused strategies are used to combat the abuse directly, whereas emotion-focused strategies are used to combat the stress endemic to such situations.

The results of this research were useful in a number of ways. Some participants described their experience of the research project as "empowering," others noted that insights gained from the project were beneficial to relationships with spouses and other family members. The researchers concluded that "presenting this model to clients and significant others has potential, as a psychoeducational tool, to ease the difficult and perilous journey that individuals must travel as they work through abuse trauma and its consequences" (Morrow & Smith, 1995, p. 32). Finally, the theoretical model that emerged provides a useful framework for understanding how particular coping styles enable particular individuals to come to terms with experiences of childhood sexual abuse.

CRITICAL THEORY

Like grounded theory, critical theory is concerned with more than simple description. In this case, rigorous description is sought only to the degree that it is capable of leading to some change in the status quo. The term *critical theory* is associated with social philosophers such as Adorno and Marcuse, who developed it as a form of social criticism directed primarily at attitudes fostered by capitalistic economics and positivistic science. Critical theory, however, is not a single approach but an attitude adopted by the researcher to significant social issues such as gender, sexuality, education, race, poverty and so on (Guba, 1990). Critical theory has long embraced an interdisciplinary approach to understanding social phenomena, and although its initial impetus derived from Marxist philosophy, it has become increasingly critical of any wholehearted adoption of such principles (Morrow, 1994).

Today, critical theory represents a neo-Marxist critique of capitalist societies combined with a metatheory of scientific research. For a given piece of research to be considered an example of critical theory, it must meet the following criteria:

1. The topic of the research must deal with a *crisis* in some current social system.

2. The crisis must be understood as emanating from the belief by those experiencing the crisis that their present circumstances are inevitable and not a consequence of existing power dynamics.

3. The debilitating beliefs manifest in crisis situations (what is called *false consciousness* by critical theorists) must be amenable to a process of change known as *enlightenment*.

4. The experience of enlightenment must lead to social *emancipation*, in which a group, empowered by its new-found self-understanding, radically alters the social situation, thereby alleviating its suffering (Fay, 1987).

Critical theorists are particularly hesitant to adopt a position of value neutrality in their research. Whereas traditional researchers emphasize the need for neutrality, critical theorists feel such an aspiration only creates an illusion of impartiality, which then becomes almost impervious to scrutiny (Agger, 1998). By noting that a value-free position is impossible, critical theorists maintain that all inquiry invariably derives from a particular perspective, defined by particular prejudices. The problem with emphasizing value neutrality in research is that it assumes a positivistic view of reality is more accurate than any other way of understanding human life and that science simply uncovers things "as they are." Critical theorists view claims of value neutrality as legitimizing oppressive forms of social control and seek to uncover the implicit biases of researchers claiming to know "the truth" about significant social issues.

Critical social scientists also question the wisdom of basing social policy on the presuppositions of natural science. One area saturated with implicit values concerns the way our society has come to rely on a biomedical model for psychological diagnosis and treatment. For this model, undesirable behavior is often diagnosed and treated without taking into account the social context in which the behavior occurs. What constitutes pathological behavior for one group may, to another, be an authentic reaction to a coercive situation. Because the homeostatic model of mental health locates disorder within the neurochemistry of an individual, it precludes the possibility that abnormal behavior may be the result of legitimate grievances. Instead of affirming an individual's reaction to a coercive situation, using medication to limit undesirable behavior would seem to ensure that certain segments of society will never be able to realize the extent of their subjugation. By uncovering implicit value concerns of this type, critical theorists hope to empower oppressed groups to change their present circumstances.

Emancipation

If one word may be used to clarify the aims of critical social science, it would be *emancipation*. Intending their research to have an emancipatory effect, critical researchers are avowedly political. They maintain that traditional social scientists promote a "false consciousness" in which individuals are led to believe their present situation is the result of immutable laws and not under their control (Agger, 1998). Critical theorists strive to point out alternatives to present understandings and, in so doing, to facilitate more authentic and less oppressive forms of social engagement (Fay, 1987).

Critical theory systematically explores how human experience is influenced by dominant ideologies (Schwandt, 1990). By detailing various means of exploitation in contemporary society, critical theorists hope to empower those exploited by the elite of the society. Empowerment through understanding is seen as a step toward promoting a radical transformation of society and the liberation of groups oppressed by dominant ideologies. One way to accomplish these goals is to enable individuals to see themselves in a radically new way. By viewing themselves in this way, they may be motivated to engage in behavior that will improve their current circumstances and help them overcome their present oppressive situation.

Dialogical Approach

Critical social scientists are particularly disparaging of the traditional roles of subject and experimenter. They call into question situations in which the researcher's perspective is privileged over that of the participant and endeavor to maintain an egalitarian stance in their research (Schwandt, 1990). In this way, they hope to emphasize the collaborative nature of the research process and to combine research and practice. Dissolving the distinction between researcher and subject is thought to encourage those engaged in the research project to identify other oppressive aspects of current social conditions.

Participatory Action Research

In an attempt to remove conditions contributing to the oppression of a specific group, critical theorists often engage in participatory action research (PAR). Rather than accept a passive role (as in standard research), participants are encouraged to contribute actively to the research process by collecting, analyzing, and interpreting data. Encouraging members of the disadvantaged community to participate in research, creates a sense of ownership is created.

According to Brydon-Miller (1997), participatory action research can be understood as adhering to the following general guidelines:

1. The research originates in communities that have traditionally been exploited or oppressed. Work with groups of indigenous peoples, immigrant groups, labor organizations, and women's groups offer a few examples of the communities in which PAR has been employed.

2. PAR works to address the specific concerns of the community as well as the fundamental causes of their oppression, with the goal of achieving social change.

3. PAR is at once a process of research, a mode of education, and a call to action in which all participants contribute their unique skills and knowledge and through which they learn and are transformed (Hall, 1981).

Although traditional researchers may define an oppressed community as a "population to be studied," action researchers seek to liberate the oppressed community from the constraints of their situation. By identifying specific reasons for a community's exploitation, action researchers hope to empower those within the community to initiate radical changes in their circumstances.

Much action research has been influenced by Freire's classic book, *Pedagogy of the Oppressed* (1970). In this work, Freire brings a critical perspective to bear on traditional approaches to education while seeking to uncover the ways in which education legitimizes current power structures. He stresses that critical pedagogy should not aim at placing the oppressed in positions previously held by the oppressors but at considering novel relationships between oppressor and oppressed. Through a reformulation of such relationships, teachers and students can bring about a radical transformation of existing power structures. For Freire, when one group dominates another, neither the oppressor nor the oppressed is completely human; and only by radically restructuring their relationship can both become more fully alive (Freire, 1970). Renegotiating traditional roles—such as those of teacher and student, subject and experimenter—will cause a new understanding to emerge that may come to serve as a model for transforming other social inequities.

QUALITATIVE DATA ANALYSIS (QDA) SOFTWARE

It should be clear that what counts as data in a qualitative study is often different from what

Table 17.1   Types of Qualitative Data Analysis (QDA) Software

Type	Description	Software
Text retrievers	Locate instances of words or phrases intext; count and display key words; generate concordances	Sonar Professional; the Text Collector
Textbase managers	Database programs; store text for later sorting and analysis	askSam; Folio Views; Idealist
Code-and-retrieve	Code passages of text and retrieve according to coding; ability to search for words and phrases	Hyperqual2, Kwalitan; the Data Collector
Code-based theory builders	Share code-and-retrieve features but allow user to represent relations among codes; link segments of text together	NUD-IST QDA; Nvivo
Conceptual network builders	Creation and analysis of network displays; graphic representations of relationships	Inspiration; MetaDesign; Visio

SOURCE: Derived from Weitzman (2000).

counts as data in a quantitative study. Although there is no single way to do qualitative research, most researchers are interested in exploring various relationships among themes, categories, and units of meaning relevant to a particular phenomenon. Because this type of research involves keeping track of a large number of different units and/or observations, data management becomes an extremely important aspect of the process. For this reason an increasing number of software options have been developed to aid the qualitative researcher in this task.

Software appropriate to qualitative data analysis (QDA) provide a variety of features specifically tailored to the needs of qualitative researchers. As noted, qualitative analysis can be extremely time-consuming and QDA software is designed to allow the researcher to code, organize, and access large amounts of data in a relatively short period of time. Weitzman (2000) observes that this increased efficiency is in many ways similar to the impact of computers in quantitative research:

In the days of slide rules . . . before statistical software was available, doing factor analysis was a months-long enterprise. Now a factor analysis can be run in minutes . . . on a desktop computer. As a result, researchers can run factor analyses much more often, as part of other analyses rather than only as major undertakings of their own, and on multiple sets of scores in the same project. The speed of the computer alone can change what researchers even contemplate undertaking. (p. 807)

Although computational efficiency in qualitative analysis is nowhere near as complete as in the case of quantitative analysis, it does afford the researcher a number of new possibilities. These include searching for particular words or phrases within a text, searching for similarities between multiple themes and categories, and hyperlinking memos relevant to a particular analysis. Qualitative researchers are now able to choose from a variety of software options based on the particular needs of their project. Table 17.1, adapted from Weitzman (2000), provides a useful collection of software options presently available for a variety of projects.

QUALITATIVE RESEARCH IN PSYCHOLOGY

As contemporary researchers, we have more methodological and technological options at our disposal than ever before, and both quantitative and qualitative methods have led to significant breakthroughs in social science. Even so, we still sometimes find mutual resistance and even more overt hostility between researchers working in different empirical traditions. Although it is tempting to draw a line and view quantitative and qualitative approaches in opposition to one another, it may be more appropriate to view these approaches as complementary, with each allowing us to understand different aspects of the same phenomenon (Creswell, 2003).

In doing research, it always seems reasonable to ask two questions: (a) "What is it that I am studying?" (b) "What is the most reasonable way of studying it?" Adopting this perspective encourages researchers to confront epistemological differences between methods and to make sure that the choice of method makes sense in terms of the proposed project. For example, if one wants to make statements about a generalizable causal law or covarying relationships between independent factors, the researcher would be wise to stick to quantitative methods. If, on the other hand, the researcher wants to offer a detailed description as to what people experience and/or how they act, he or she would be wise to use phenomenological, focus group, narrative, or ethnographic approaches. Finally, if the researcher wants to develop a

theory or challenge a social practice, he or she would be well advised to use grounded- or critical-theory approaches. All of these methods involve a different stance toward what is being studied and how one ought to go about studying it.

From emphasizing personal experience to calling for radical social transformation, qualitative methods provide an array of perspectives and approaches bound together under a single heading, yet holding to different points of emphasis and intended outcomes. Although each serves as an alternative to the quantitative mainstream and provides a way of addressing the estrangement articulated in Snow's small book, such methods have only begun to be used in psychology. Other social sciences, such as cultural anthropology, sociology, and cultural studies, have embraced qualitative methods and organized their disciplines around them. Despite acceptance by these disciplines, psychology still seems wedded to a view of humankind as a behaving machine whose functions are largely unaffected in moving between everyday life and laboratory settings. Qualitative methods offer an alternative research script in which the investigator and the participant jointly take up significant human phenomena and together articulate the meanings of these phenomena for the discipline and for themselves.

EXERCISES

1. Interviewing and Being Interviewed

   Develop an open-ended interview question about a particular life experience. Pair with a colleague and have him or her interview you for about 15 minutes about this experience, making sure to take notes or tape-record the interview. Ask your interviewer to be careful to ask only follow-up questions using your own words and not elicit any information that you do not bring up yourself. Reverse roles and interview a colleague about a particular life experience following the same set of rules. Afterward, respond to the following questions:

   A. Describe your experience of being interviewed or interviewing.

   B. What do you feel went well in the interview? What could have been better?

2. Transcribing and Interpreting Texts

   Tape record an interview and transcribe a 10-minute portion of the tape. What issues came up in transcribing the interview? What decisions did you have to make when transcribing?

   Describe the general sets of topics and themes that came up in the interview. Provide a description of these topics and themes and give supporting evidence in the form of quotations from the transcribed interview text.

3. Practicing With Group Interpretation and Focus Group Research

Bring to class a picture of a piece of art that you find interesting. Have your colleagues respond to and interpret the picture or artwork. Practice applying different theoretical perspectives and then try putting these perspectives aside to talk about the artwork based on your own life experiences. Now discuss the following questions:

A. What was this activity like for you?

B. What issues or concerns came up when interpreting the picture or artwork?

C. How does cultural or historical context contribute to the interpretations you and your colleagues made?

RECOMMENDED READINGS

Phenomenology

Polkinghorne, D. E. (1989). Phenomenological research methods. In R. Valle & S. Halling (Eds.), *Existential-phenomenological perspectives in psychology: Exploring the breadth of human experience* (pp. 41–60). New York: Plenum.

Thomas, S. P., & Pollio, H. R. (2002). *Listening to patients: A phenomenological approach to nursing research and practice.* New York: Springer.

Valle, R., & Halling, S. (1989). *Existential-phenomenological perspectives in psychology: Exploring the breadth of human experience.* New York: Plenum.

Focus Groups

Krueger, R. A., & Casey, M. A. (2000). *Focus groups: A practical guide for applied research* (3rd ed.). Thousand Oaks, CA: Sage.

Stewart, D. W., & Shamdasani, P. N. (1990). *Focus groups: Theory and practice.* Newbury Park, CA: Sage.

Narrative Analysis

Kleinman, A. (1988). *The illness narratives: Suffering, healing, and the human condition.* New York: Basic Books.

Polkinghorne, D. E. (1988). *Narrative knowing and the human sciences.* Albany: State University of New York Press.

Riessman, C. K. (1993). *Narrative analysis.* Newbury Park, CA: Sage.

Ethnography

Geertz, C. (1973). *The interpretation of cultures.* New York: Basic Books.

Shweder, R. A. (1990). Cultural psychology: What is it? In J. W. Stigler, R. A. Shweder, & G. Herdt (Eds.), *Cultural psychology: Essays on comparative human development.* Cambridge, UK: Cambridge University Press.

Grounded Theory

Glaser, B. (Ed.). (1994). *More grounded theory: A reader.* Mill Valley, CA: Sociology Press.

Glaser, B., & Strauss, A. (1967). *Discovery of grounded theory.* Chicago: Aldine.

Strauss, A., & Corbin, J. (1998). *Basics of qualitative research: Techniques and procedures for developing grounded theory* (2nd ed.). Thousand Oaks, CA: Sage.

Critical Theory

Agger, B. (1998). *Critical social theories: An introduction.* Boulder, CO: HarperCollins.

Fay, B. (1987). *Critical social science: Liberation and its limits.* Ithaca, NY: Cornell University Press.

Freire, P. (1970). *Pedagogy of the oppressed.* New York: Continuum.

REFERENCES

Agger, B. (1998). *Critical social theories: An introduction.* Boulder, CO: HarperCollins.

Anderson, D. G. (1996). Homeless women's perceptions about their families of origin. *Western Journal of Nursing Practice, 18*(1), 29–42.

Beier, B. F. (1994). *A phenomenological study of the experience of having family stories told about oneself.* Unpublished doctoral dissertation, University of Tennessee, Knoxville.

Bruner, J. (1991). The narrative construction of reality. *Critical Inquiry, 18,* 1–21.

Brydon-Miller, M. (1997). Participatory action research: Psychology and social change. *Journal of Social Issues, 53,* 657–667.

Carpenter, D. R. (1999). Phenomenology as method. In H. J. Streubert & D. R. Carpenter (Eds.), *Qualitative research in nursing: Advancing the humanistic imperative* (pp. 43–63). Philadelphia: Lippincott.

Charmaz, K. (2000). Grounded theory: Objectivist and constructivist methods. In N. K. Denzin & Y. S. Lincoln (Eds.), *Handbook of qualitative research* (2nd ed., pp. 509–535). Thousand Oaks, CA: Sage.

Creswell, J. (1998). *Qualitative inquiry and research design: Choosing among five traditions.* Thousand Oaks, CA: Sage.

Creswell, J. (2003). *Research design: Qualitative, quantitative, and mixed methods approaches* (2nd ed.). Thousand Oaks, CA: Sage.

Csordas, T. J. (1997). *The sacred self: A cultural phenomenology of charismatic healing.* Berkeley: University of California Press.

Fay, B. (1987). *Critical social science: Liberation and its limits.* Ithaca, NY: Cornell University Press.

Freire, P. (1970). *Pedagogy of the oppressed.* New York: Continuum.

Geertz, C. (1973). *The interpretation of cultures.* New York: Basic Books.

Geertz, C. (2000). *Available light: Anthropological reflections on philosophical topics.* Princeton, NJ: Princeton University Press.

Glaser, B., & Strauss, A. (1967). *Discovery of grounded theory.* Chicago: Aldine.

Good, B. J. (1994). Illness representations in medical anthropology: A reading of the field. In B. J. Good (Ed.), *Medicine, rationality, and experience: An anthropological perspective* (pp. 25–64). New York: Cambridge University Press.

Guba, E. (1990). The alternative paradigm dialog. In E. Guba (Ed.), *Paradigm dialog* (pp. 17–27). Newbury Park, CA: Sage.

Hall, B. (1981). Participatory research, popular knowledge and power: A personal reflection. *Convergence, 14,* 6–17.

Jahoda, G. (1998). *Crossroads between culture and mind: Continuities and change in theories of human nature.* Cambridge, MA: Harvard University Press.

Kleinman, A. (1988). *The illness narratives: Suffering, healing, and the human condition.* New York: Basic Books.

Krueger, R. A., & Casey, M. A. (2000). *Focus groups: A practical guide for applied research* (3rd ed.). Thousand Oaks, CA: Sage.

Long, P. J., & Jackson, J. L. (1993). Childhood coping strategies and the adult adjustment of female sexual abuse victims. *Journal of Child Sexual Abuse, 1*(1), 81–102.

Luntz, F. I. (1994). Focus group research in American politics. *The polling report.* Retrieved June 1, 2004, from www.pollingreport.com/focus.htm

Madriz, E. (2000). Focus groups in feminist research. In N. K. Denzin & Y. S. Lincoln (Eds.), *Handbook of qualitative research* (2nd ed., pp. 835–850). Thousand Oaks, CA: Sage.

Morrow, R. (1994). *Critical theory and methodology.* Thousand Oaks, CA: Sage.

Morrow, S. L., & Smith, M. L. (1995). Constructions of survival and coping by women who have survived childhood sexual abuse. *Journal of Counseling Psychology, 42,* 24–33.

Pidgeon, N. (1996) Grounded theory: Theoretical background. In J. Richardson (Ed.), *Handbook of qualitative research methods for psychology and the social sciences* (pp. 75–85). Leicester, UK: BPS Books.

Pidgeon, N., & Henwood, K. (1996) Grounded theory: Practical implementation. In J. Richardson (Ed.), *Handbook of qualitative research methods for psychology and the social sciences* (pp. 86–101). Leicester, UK: BPS Books.

Pollio, H. R., Henley, T., & Thompson, C. (1997). *The phenomenology of everyday life.* New York: Cambridge University Press.

Polkinghorne, D. E. (1989). Phenomenological research methods. In R. Valle & S. Halling (Eds.), *Existential-phenomenological perspectives in psychology: Exploring the breadth of human experience* (pp. 41–60). New York: Plenum.

Riessman, C. K. (1993). *Narrative analysis.* Newbury Park, CA: Sage.

Schwandt, T. (1990). Paths to inquiry in the social disciplines: Scientific, constructivist, and critical theory methodologies. In E. Guba (Ed.), *Paradigm dialog* (pp. 258–276). Newbury Park, CA: Sage.

Shweder, R. A. (1990). Cultural psychology: What is it? In J. W. Stigler, R. A. Shweder, & G. Herdt (Eds.), *Cultural psychology: Essays on comparative human development.* Cambridge, UK: Cambridge University Press.

Shweder, R. A. (1998). *Welcome to middle-age! (and other cultural fictions).* Chicago: University of Chicago Press.

Snow, C. P. (1961). *The two cultures and the scientific revolution.* Cambridge, UK: Cambridge University Press. (Originally published in 1959)

Sontag, S. (1989). *Illness as metaphor; and, AIDS and its metaphors.* New York: Anchor.

Steffen, V. (1997). Life stories and shared experience. *Social Science and Medicine, 45,* 99–111.

Stewart, D. W., & Shamdasani, P. N. (1990). *Focus groups: Theory and practice.* Newbury Park, CA: Sage.

Strauss, A., & Corbin, J. (1998). *Basics of qualitative research: Techniques and procedures for developing grounded theory.* Thousand Oaks, CA: Sage.

Thomas, S. P. (2003). Men's anger: A phenomenological exploration of its meaning in a middle-class sample of American men. *Psychology of Men and Masculinity, 4*(2), 163–175.

Thomas, S. P., & Pollio, H. R. (2002). *Listening to patients: A phenomenological approach to nursing research and practice.* New York: Springer.

Valle, R. S., King, M., & Halling, S. (1989). An introduction to existential-phenomenological thought in psychology. In R. Valle & S. Halling (Eds.), *Existential-phenomenological perspectives in psychology: Exploring the breadth of human experience* (pp. 3–16). New York: Plenum.

Weitzman, E. (2000). Software and qualitative research. In N. Denzin & Y. Lincoln (Eds.), *Handbook of qualitative research* (2nd ed., pp. 803–820). Thousand Oaks, CA: Sage.

Yalom, I. (1980). *Existential psychotherapy.* New York: Basic Books.

18

A Basic Guide to Statistical Research and Discovery

Planning and Selecting Statistical Analyses

Charles A. Scherbaum

Statistics have revolutionized modern science (Salsburg, 2002). They have provided the modern researcher with a set of tools to deal with the uncertainty inherent in scientific inquiry (Loftus & Loftus, 1988). The development and proliferation of statistics, however, has also presented researchers with a formidable challenge. That is, "Which analyses are the most appropriate?" Ultimately, the choice of appropriate statistical analyses will be based on the purpose of the research (i.e., exploratory or confirmatory), the research questions being asked (i.e., hypotheses), and the nature of the data (i.e., scale of measurement, shape of the distribution; Yaffee, 1996). Yet, determining the specific analyses can still be exceedingly difficult because of the unwieldy array of options that must be weighed in choosing statistical analyses.

The challenge, especially for students, also stems from the difficulty associated with developing a framework or mental model for understanding statistics. Statistics is not simply a set of techniques to be applied to data. Rather, it is a way of systematically thinking about research questions and the observed patterns in the data. One could even consider statistics a language that allows researchers to communicate using an agreed on vocabulary. It is a mental model of statistics that serves as an invaluable aid in making choices about appropriate statistical analyses.

This chapter covers some of the options available when using statistics to answer research questions. It is not intended to provide a rule-bound system for choosing appropriate statistical analyses. As Abelson (1995) argues, there is rarely only one *correct* choice or rule. The purpose is to provide undergraduate and graduate students with an initial framework for understanding and navigating the options and choices involved in statistical discovery. It is beyond the scope of this chapter to describe every statistical procedure mentioned in detail. This chapter may, however, serve as a starting point in making decisions about statistical analyses that can be built on using the other chapters in this book

AUTHOR'S NOTE: I would like to thank Jim Austin, Kira Barden, Jennifer Ferreter, Michael Kern, Aaron Reid, and Karen Scherbaum for their insightful comments on earlier versions of this chapter.

Table 18.1 Overview of Common Statistics Software

Program	Description
SPSS	Performs the majority of statistical analyses covered in this chapter. Analyses are conducted using pull-down menus or the SPSS programming syntax. Descriptions of any option or procedure can be found by clicking the text in the program with the right mouse button. Extensive help menus are available. Student versions of SPSS can be purchased.
SAS	Performs the majority of statistical analyses covered in this chapter and many advanced analyses. Analyses are performed using the SAS programming syntax. Extensive help menus are available.
SYSTAT	Performs all basic statistical analyses and many advanced analyses. Analyses are conducted using pull-down menus or the SYSTAT programming syntax. SYSTAT has extensive graphic capabilities. Extensive help menus are available.
JMP	Performs basic statistical analyses and links these analyses to the program's extensive graphing capabilities. Analyses are conducted using pull-down menus. Extensive help menus are available.
MINITAB	Performs basic statistical analyses and many advanced analyses. Analyses are conducted using pull-down menus. MINITAB has a wide range of graphic capabilities. Extensive help menus are available.
S-Plus	Performs all basic statistical analyses and some advanced analyses. Analyses are conducted using pull-down menus. The graphic capabilities are very flexible. Extensive help menus are available.
Excel	Performs many basic statistical operations. Analyses are performed using predefined functions inside the cells in a worksheet. Extensive help menus are available.

(e.g., Dickter, Chapter 19; Steelman & Levy, Chapter 20) and the sources listed in the recommended readings section at the end of the chapter. An overview of the statistical methods that are covered in this chapter is presented in the appendix.

One of the forces behind the statistical revolution in science has been technology. Throughout this chapter, the statistical software available to perform the various statistical analyses is noted. An emphasis is placed on conducting analyses using SAS and SPSS, as these are the most commonly used and available statistics programs in the social sciences. A list of additional statistics programs is presented in Table 18.1. Reviews of these programs and others regularly appear in statistics journals such as the *American Statistician* and *Journal of Mathematical & Statistical Psychology*. Additionally, the Internet provides a wealth of free statistical resources and software. In any discussion of statistical software, it is important to keep in mind that being able to run an analysis and being able to understand or select an analysis are not the same thing. Most students will find the running of the analyses much easier than the selection and interpretation of statistical analyses. Thus, the treatment of technology is restricted to what software (i.e., SPSS, SAS) is available to perform the analyses discussed rather than how to use the software to perform the analyses. Several sources are listed in the recommended readings that provide assistance with how to use specific statistical software programs.

This chapter is organized into three sections that will provide an introduction to the statistical analyses that must be considered at several points in the research process. First, the analyses performed before data collection and in the planning stages of research are considered. Next, the analyses performed to describe and understand the data are discussed. This discussion will include some of the preliminary analyses one conducts in preparation for the tests of the

Table 18.2   Chapter Overview

Section	Topics covered
Analyses Conducted Before Data Collection	Sample Size Requirements and Statistical Power
	Determining Effect Sizes
Analyses Performed to Describe and Understand the Data	Data Preparation
	Creating Composites and Scales
	Measures of Association
	Describing the Distribution of the Data
	Examining the Underlying Properties of the Data
Analyses Performed to Test Hypotheses	Univariate Analyses
	Analyses With a Single Group
	Analyses With Multiple Groups
	General Linear Model
	ANOVA
	Regression
	Multivariate Analyses

hypotheses. The third section of the chapter will cover the statistical analyses performed to test hypotheses. I will begin with *univariate* statistical analyses (i.e., one dependent variable), including analyses that can be used with a single group and analyses that can be used with multiple groups. Next, I will consider the *general linear model*. Last, *multivariate* statistical analyses (i.e., multiple dependent variables) are reviewed. The assumptions underlying univariate and multivariate statistical analyses will be discussed in each section. An overview of the structure of the chapter is presented in Table 18.2.

ANALYSES CONDUCTED BEFORE DATA COLLECTION

In the planning stages of research and before data collection, one needs to make choices concerning the necessary sample size and statistical power. These statistical choices are highly intertwined with methodological design choices (Austin, Boyle, & Lualhati, 1998). In this chapter, we will only cover statistical aspects of these choices. Hershey, Wilson, and Jacobs-Lawson consider many of the methodological aspects in Chapter 1. As several authors have noted (e.g., Austin, Scherbaum, & Mahlman, 2002; Cohen, 1992; Mone, Mueller, & Mauland, 1996), researchers

often pay little attention to statistical power. Power, however, is an essential and highly beneficial part of the research planning process (e.g., Murphy, 2002). Students are well advised to incorporate considerations of statistical power into their mental model of the research process (Cohen, 1990). Myors, in Chapter 11, discusses power extensively.

Sample Size Requirements and Statistical Power

When planning a research study, one of the first decisions is the determination of the necessary sample size. Namely, a researcher must estimate the sample size needed to achieve an acceptable level of statistical power. *Statistical power* is the probability of correctly rejecting a false null hypothesis. In other words, power is the likelihood of finding an effect if an effect actually does exist. For example, if power is equal to 0.50, the researcher has a 50% chance of rejecting the null hypothesis when it should be rejected. Ideally, one would like power to be close to 1.0, but a general rule of thumb is that the estimated level of power should be greater than 0.80 (Cohen, 1988).

Each statistical test has a unique formula to estimate power. In general, however, these formulas consist of four elements. The first element is power. The second element is *alpha* (α), or the probability of a Type I error. A *Type I error* is the probability of incorrectly rejecting a true null hypothesis. That is, it is the likelihood of finding an effect when the effect *does not* actually exist. Alpha is also used in significance testing, as is discussed below. The third element is the effect size (*ES*). The *effect size* is a measure of the magnitude of the effect or the degree to which the effect exists. Effect sizes are often standardized so that they can be interpreted as standard deviations or the percentage of the total variance explained by the effect. Last, the fourth element is *sample size* (*N*), that is, how many individuals are needed to participate in the research. If the values for three of the elements are held constant (e.g., *N*, α, and *ES*), one can estimate the value of the fourth element (e.g., power).

The specific formulas for combining these elements to estimate power or required sample sizes for a variety of statistical techniques can be found in Cohen (1988) or Murphy and Myors (1998). In many cases, these formulas can be used to estimate power and required sample sizes using a calculator or a spreadsheet program (e.g., Microsoft Excel). There are over 30 different commercial software packages (e.g., SamplePower, PASS, StatPower), shareware programs (e.g., G*Power), and Web sites that are available for estimating statistical power (Thomas & Krebs, 1997). Goldstein (1989) and Thomas and Krebs (1997) provide reviews and comparisons of the various statistical power software programs.

It is important to keep in mind that the sample size requirements and power are simply estimates. These estimates are based on assumptions (e.g., population parameters) that may or may not hold true (Parker & Berman, 2003). Therefore, the actual statistical power may be higher or lower than the estimated value, and more or fewer participants may be needed when the study is carried out. A more detailed treatment of power, required sample sizes, and the issues involved in estimating these values is provided by Myors in Chapter 11.

Determining Effect Sizes

One difficulty in estimating power or required sample sizes is determining the value of the other three elements (e.g., α, *N*, *ES*, Power). By convention, the level of α is usually set to 0.05 or 0.01 (Cohen, 1994). When estimating the level of power, the sample size is often determined by practical considerations (e.g., time, available resources, size of the population of interest). When estimating the required sample size, power is initially set to a value between 0.80 and 0.99. The level of power is then adjusted (upward or downward) until one finds the highest level of power that is possible given the practical constraints on the sample size.

Effect sizes can be determined using a number of different strategies. First, the simplest strategy is to use rules of thumb about the values for small, medium, and large effects (e.g., Cohen, 1988, 1992). Second, one can estimate the smallest value of the effect that would be of interest. Third, one can review the literature for the size of the effects that have been found in previous research. Particularly useful are the results of studies using meta-analysis. Cooper, Robinson, and Dorr discuss meta-analysis in Chapter 21. If the effect sizes are not reported, a variety of formulas can be used to transform commonly reported statistics (e.g., means and standard deviations) into effect sizes (see Cohen, 1988, for the formulas). Last, one can use empirical strategies, such as pilot studies or Monte Carlo studies (i.e., computer simulations). The choice of strategy will, in part, be determined by the degree of precision needed for the estimate of effect size. Myors provides mention of issues related to estimating effect sizes in Chapter 11.

ANALYSES PERFORMED TO DESCRIBE AND UNDERSTAND THE DATA

Once the data have been collected and before the hypotheses are tested, one should perform a series of statistical analyses to understand the nature of the data. This process involves describing the distribution of your data, cleaning the data, transforming the data for use in the tests of the hypotheses, exploring the relationship between the variables, and examining the underlying properties of the data. It also involves testing the assumptions required for the intended statistical analyses. The results of these analyses can determine the types of conclusions that can be made from the subsequent hypothesis tests. Furthermore, these analyses can determine if the planned statistical analyses will be appropriate. DiLalla and Dollinger discuss a number of these issues in greater detail in Chapter 16.

Data Preparation

First, the data should be screened for missing data and data entry errors. The screening can be performed using a frequency analysis. A *frequency analysis* provides information about the number of observations at each observed value of the variables. If missing data is found, it can be left as missing or a replacement value can be used. There are a variety of strategies for replacing missing data (Switzer & Roth, 2002). DiLalla and Dollinger discuss some of these strategies in Chapter 16.

Often psychological research includes measures that are scored in different directions. On an inventory of personality, for example, responses at the lower end of the response scale may indicate high levels of the personality trait on some items, but it may indicate low levels of the trait on different items (i.e., reverse scoring or keying). The data may need to be recoded such that the responses are in the same direction. Typically, this type of transformation is easily performed in most statistical software packages (e.g., the Recode command in SPSS; if-then statements in SAS).

Creating Composites and Scales

Many psychological measures utilize multiple items to assess a single construct (e.g., intelligence, personality). These individual items are combined (i.e., aggregated) into composite scores or scales. For example, the 10 items on a personality inventory that assess extroversion could be summed to create an extroversion score for each respondent. In some instances, the data are aggregated across individuals into a higher level of analysis. For example, the responses to items about job satisfaction from each individual on a work team could be summed or averaged to create a variable that represents the work team's job satisfaction. This type of aggregation is done as a part of multilevel research. *Multilevel* research utilizes multiple levels of analysis

(e.g., individuals and teams) to answer the research questions. Chan describes multilevel research in Chapter 28.

When aggregating variables into composites or scales, a researcher needs to examine the resulting composite or scale in terms of the relationships between the items that constitute the composite or scale. This can be done using measures of association. These are typically referred to as *correlational analyses.* Correlations and measures of association are a family of statistical techniques that assess the direction and strength of the association between two or more variables. The choice of the specific correlation coefficient or association measure depends on the measurement properties of the variables to be examined.

Measures of Association

Prior to computing any correlation or measure of association, a scatterplot of the relationship between the variables should be constructed. A *scatterplot* displays the relationship between two variables in a two-dimensional plane. This is often referred to as the *bivariate* relationship. When examining these plots, one should consider (1) the direction of the points (i.e., pointing to the upper right or lower right corner), (2) the cluster of the points in the plot (i.e., tightly or loosely clustered), and (3) whether the plot is best described by a straight line (i.e., is it linear?). If the plot clearly indicates that the points are not linear, transformations (e.g., a log transform) or nonlinear statistical techniques may be necessary. These plots can be easily constructed using the graphing options in most statistical software (e.g., SPSS, SAS).

When both variables are continuous and on at least an interval scale of measurement, the Pearson product-moment correlation can be used. All major statistical software packages include the Pearson correlation, and the Pearson formula can be found in Cohen and Cohen (1983), Cohen, Cohen, Aiken and West (2001), or Chen and Popovich (2002). The value of the Pearson correlation can range from 1.0 to +1.0. It is important to remember that correlations, like the Pearson correlation, are typically symmetric when the variables are on the same scale of measurement. Therefore, which variable is labeled the independent and dependent variable does not matter mathematically. When the variables are not on the same scale of measurement, however, the correlations may not be symmetric. In these situations, the results of the analysis will depend on which variable is labeled the independent and dependent variable.

If both of the variables are not continuous and on at least an interval scale, a number of possibilities exist depending on the scale of measurement. If both variables are dichotomous (e.g., yes/no), the phi (ϕ) coefficient may be used. The ϕ coefficient can be thought of as a Pearson correlation. In some cases, the dichotomy in the data is artificial, and the distribution underlying the data is actually continuous. For example, age and income are continuous variables but may be collected by asking if someone is older or younger than 18 and if they make more or less than $25,000. When this is the case, the relationship between the variables (if they were continuous) can be estimated using a tetrachoric correlation. Although the ϕ coefficient is fairly simple to compute, the tetrachoric correlation is difficult to compute and can only be done using special programs in the major statistical software (e.g., SPSS, SAS) or using specialty software (e.g., LISREL). Additionally, one can use Yule's Q when both the independent and dependent variable are dichotomous. *Yule's Q* is a measure of association between consistent (e.g., high, high) and inconsistent (e.g., high, low) data pairs in a 2 × 2 contingency table. The values for all three measures can range from 1.0 to +1.0.

If the independent variable is dichotomous and the dependent variable is nominal, three measures of association are possible. The first is the *contingency coefficient (CC)*. The *CC* is based on the chi-square (i.e., χ^2) statistic and the sample size. It ranges between 0.0 and 1.0, though attaining 1.0 is not possible. The number of rows and columns in the contingency table determines the maximum value of the *CC*. The second possible choice is *Cramer's V*. This technique is an extension of ϕ, and, in most instances, it is a better choice than the *CC*. *V* ranges from 0.0 to 1.0 and attaining 1.0 is possible. When there are only two rows and columns in a contingency table, *V* and ϕ will be equal. The third choice is the *Goodman-Kruskal lambda* (λ). This technique assesses the proportionate reduction in error in predictions about the

dependent variable when the values of the independent variable are known. There are symmetric and asymmetric versions of λ. Thus, for any two variables there are two asymmetric λs. The symmetric λ can be thought of as the average of the asymmetric values. The λ coefficient ranges from 0.0 to 1.0 and can equal 1.0.

If the independent variable is dichotomous and the dependent variable is ordinal, the *rank-biserial* correlation may be chosen. This coefficient is essentially a Pearson correlation. If the independent variable is dichotomous and the dependent variable is interval or ratio, the *point-biserial* correlation may be chosen. This coefficient is also basically a Pearson correlation. The point biserial typically ranges from 0.8 to +0.8. If the dichotomous variable used in the point biserial actually represents a continuous distribution, the biserial correlation can be computed. The *biserial* correlation estimates the strength of the relationship if both of the variables were continuous. The biserial correlation can range from 1.0 to +1.0, and may be larger than 1.0 if the distribution of the data takes certain shapes (e.g., bimodal; Chen & Popovich, 2002). Special routines in the major statistical software (e.g., SPSS, SAS) can be used to compute the biserial correlation.

If the independent and dependent variables are nominal, the contingency coefficient, Cramer's *V,* or Goodman-Kruskal's λ may be chosen. If the independent variable is nominal and the dependent variable is on an interval or ratio scale of measurement, *eta* (η), *omega* (ω), or *epsilon* (ε) may be selected. Each can range from 0.0 to 1.0. These measures are typically squared and interpreted as the percentage of variance that one variable accounts for in the other variable. It is important to note that these are not measures of linear association.

If both the independent and dependent variables are ordinal, one can choose Spearman's rho (ρ), Goodman-Kruskal's gamma (γ), the tau coefficients (τ), or the Somer's *d* coefficients. *Spearman's* ρ is essentially a Pearson correlation between ranked data. Spearman's ρ does not account for potential ties in the rankings. Like ρ, *Goodman-Kruskal's* γ assesses the direction and strength of the relationship between two ordinal variables. There are three tau coefficients (Kendall's τ_a, Kendall's τ_b, and Stewart's τ_c). *Kendall's* τ_a is similar to

Spearman's ρ (Chen & Popovich, 2002). Like ρ, τ_a does not account for ties in the rankings. Ties in the ranks are corrected in Kendall's τ_b and Stewart's τ_c; but because of differences in the corrections, the value of τ_b will be larger than τ_c. Each of the measures of association described above can range from 1.0 to +1.0. When the number of ties in the rankings is large, γ is a better choice than the ρ or τ coefficients.

Somer's d includes both a symmetric and asymmetric measure of association. Somer's *d* can be considered an asymmetric modification of γ. As is the case for the λ coefficient described above, there will be two asymmetric values for *d*. The symmetric *d* can be thought of as the average of the asymmetric values. Somer's *d* can take values ranging from 1.0 to +1.0. If the independent variable is ordinal and the dependent variable is interval or ratio, eta (η), omega (ω), or epsilon (ε) may be selected. The measures of association discussed above are summarized in Table 18.3.

Most the measures of association described above are available in the major statistical software (e.g., Crosstabs command under Descriptive Statistics in SPSS; PROC CORR or PROC FREQ in SAS). The various correlational analyses described above are often also used to test research questions. The considerations about choosing a measure of association also apply in these situations.

Describing the Distribution of the Data

Once the data are prepared, the shape of the distribution of the data should be examined. Many of the statistical procedures used to test hypotheses make assumptions about the shape of the distribution that need to be considered. A reasonable first step is to examine the frequency distribution of the data. This will provide a first indication of the shape (e.g., symmetric, positive skew, negative skew) and any potentially extreme data points. Extreme data points are called *outliers.* The distribution can be displayed using frequency tables, or it can be presented graphically using a histogram. There are a variety of additional graphical procedures under the label of exploratory data analysis (e.g., boxplots, normal probability plots, stem and leaf plots; Tukey, 1977) that can be utilized to describe a distribution. Many of these procedures can be performed

Table 18.3 Summary of the Measures of Association

		Independent Variable			
		Dichotomous	Nominal	Ordinal	Interval/Ratio
Dependent Variable	Dichotomous	Phi* Yule's *Q*			
	Nominal	Contingency coefficient Cramer's *V* Lambda	Contingency coefficient Cramer's *V* Lambda		
	Ordinal	Rank-biserial		Spearman's rho Gamma Tau Somer's *d*	
	Interval/Ratio	Point-biserial**	Eta Omega Epsilon	Eta Omega Epsilon	Pearson correlation

NOTE: *Phi can be corrected to the tetrachoric correlation
**Point-biserial can be corrected to the biserial correlation

using the major statistical software (e.g., Explore command under Descriptive Statistics in SPSS; PROC UNIVARIATE in SAS).

Next, the measures of central tendency, variability, and skew should be examined. In terms of central tendency, the mean, median, and mode should be inspected. If potential outliers are present, trimmed measures of central tendency can be used. *Trimmed* measures of central tendency drop a certain percentage (e.g., 5%) of the data at the ends of the distribution. In terms of variability, the range, the interquartile range, the variance, and the standard deviation should be examined.

To examine the shape of the data, the kurtosis and skewness should be inspected. *Skewness* is a statistic that reflects the degree to which the distribution is symmetric. Symmetry exists when the right and left sides of a distribution are mirror images of one another. Often, distributions are not symmetric. Distributions can be positively skewed (i.e., tail of the distribution points to the right). In these cases, the skewness statistic will be positive. Distributions can be negatively skewed (i.e., tail of the distribution points to the left). In these cases, the skewness statistic will be negative. Larger values indicate a greater degree of skewness. *Kurtosis* reflects the "peakedness" of a distribution—that is, how pointed or flat a given distribution is relative to a symmetric unimodal distribution. Positive values of kurtosis indicate that a distribution is peaked and possesses thick tails (i.e., a *leptokurtic* distribution). Negative values of kurtosis indicate that a distribution is flat and possesses thin tails (i.e., a *platykurtic* distribution). The measures of the shape of a distribution are not well understood and are often not reported, but they provide useful information about a distribution (DeCarlo, 1997). The interpretation and usefulness of any of the above measures will depend on the scale of measurement of the variables examined. The techniques described above should be performed for each item and for the composite or scale scores. These procedures can be performed using the major statistical software (e.g., Descriptive or Frequency command under Descriptive Statistics in SPSS; PROC MEANS, PROC FREQ, or PROC UNIVARIATE in SAS).

Many of the statistic procedures discussed below require specific assumptions about the shape of the distribution of sample data. To test if the distribution of the data takes a particular distributional shape (e.g., normal), the Kolmogorov-Smirnov test or Shapiro-Wilk test can be used. The Shapiro-Wilk test is particularly useful when sample sizes are small. Additionally, if one needs to examine if there are undesirable response patterns in the data (e.g., only selecting options 1 or 5), the "runs test" can be used. These techniques are available in many of the statistical software packages (e.g., Explore command under Descriptive Statistics and Non-parametric command in SPSS; PROC SPECTRA in SAS). DiLalla and Dollinger provide a detailed discussion of describing the distribution of a data set in Chapter 16.

Examining the Underlying Properties of the Data

Once a scale or composite has been created and relationships between the items have been examined, the scale or composite should be evaluated in terms of its consistency, accuracy, and underlying structure. The *consistency* of a scale or composite is its reliability. *Reliability* is a property of the responses to the items in a composite. Thus, it is assessed using the responses to the items in the scale, not the composite or scale scores. Reliability coefficients can range from 0.0 to 1.0 with 1.0 indicating perfect consistency. Although there is no definitive standard for reliability (Pedhazur & Schmelkin, 1991), many researchers follow Nunnally's (1978) recommendation that reliability should be at least 0.70. Demonstrating satisfactory reliability is essential. Scales for which the responses demonstrate low levels of reliability are of little value for evaluating research questions.

There are several types of reliability coefficients. First, there are coefficients that evaluate the stability of the responses over time. These are often called *test-retest* or *stability* coefficients. Correlations between the responses at the two different points in time are used to compute this reliability coefficient. Second, there are coefficients that evaluate the equivalence of different items or forms measuring the same construct. These are called *equivalence* coefficients. Correlations between the different sets of items or forms are used to compute this reliability coefficient. Last, there are coefficients that assess internal consistency. *Internal consistency* can be thought of as the homogeneity of the responses to the items. If the responses to the items are on a continuous scale, Cronbach's alpha (i.e., α) can be used. Kuder-Richardson's KR-20 or KR-21 can be used when the responses are dichotomous. Internal consistency reliability estimates are available in most statistical software (e.g., Reliability command under Scale in SPSS; PROC CORR in SAS).

The accuracy of a composite or scale in terms of measuring the intended construct is its *validity*. There are a variety of ways to establish validity evidence (Cook & Campbell, 1979; Messick, 1989). A researcher can begin by examining the underlying structure of the data using factor analysis. *Factor analysis* is a set of procedures that can be used to extract the factors or dimensions underlying the data. For example, an attitude questionnaire may include 90 items about beliefs, affective reactions, and behavioral intentions. The factor analysis can reduce the data to these three underlying dimensions. The results of a factor analysis can be used to determine the number of dimensions present and the loadings of each item on the dimensions. An exploratory or confirmatory approach to factor analysis can be taken.

In exploratory factor analysis (EFA), the number of dimensions and the pattern of factor loadings are determined from the data. The results of EFA will provide information about the underlying dimensions in the data and the loadings of each item on those dimensions, but the researcher will need to interpret how many factors actually exist in the data. This interpretation is typically done using eigenvalues or a scree plot, but techniques such as parallel analysis (Horn, 1965; Kauffman & Dunlap, 2000) or minimum average partial correlations (Velicer, Eaton, & Fava, 2000) are preferable. If the structure (i.e., number of factors and pattern of loadings) is consistent with what could be expected based on theory or the design of the measurement device, there is some evidence for the validity of the scale or composite. Additionally, a factor score for each individual can be computed and used in subsequent analyses. There are a number of specific choices involved in EFA (e.g., extraction method, rotation methods) that are beyond the scope of this chapter. Thompson (2004) or Pedhazur and Schmelkin (1991) provide additional information on these specific choices. EFA is available in the majority of statistical software (e.g., Factor command under Data Reduction in SPSS; PROC FACTOR in SAS). Parallel analysis and the minimum average partial correlation techniques require special software that is available on the Internet or from the authors of the programs.

When the factor structure can be derived a priori from theory or previous research, confirmatory factor analysis (CFA) is preferable. In CFA, the factor structure is specified and the researcher examines the fit of the hypothesized factor structure to the data. If there is good fit between the factor structure and the data, then there is some evidence for the validity of the measure. CFA is much more technically complex than EFA, and it requires the researcher to have a specific factor structure to test. CFA can be performed using specialty statistical software (e.g., Amos, EQS, LISREL).

A researcher can also support the validity of a scale or composite by examining the relationships of a given scale with other conceptually similar and dissimilar scales. For example, one could examine the correlation between conceptually similar scales, such as self-esteem and self-worth. In this case, one would expect the correlations to be positive and moderate in size. This is an example of *convergent* validity evidence. Alternatively, one could examine the correlation between conceptually dissimilar scales, such as self-esteem and attitudes toward the government. One would expect the correlations to be small in this case. This is an example of *divergent* validity evidence. Ideally, one could also examine the relationships between different measurement techniques that assess the same construct and similar measurement techniques that assess different constructs. This allows the researcher to separate out the variability that is due to the measurement technique from the variance due to the construct. The researcher can then rule out obtained relationships that are an artifact of similar or identical measurement methods. Taken together, this forms a *multitrait-multimethod matrix* (Campbell & Fiske, 1959). Additionally, a researcher can examine the correlations between the measures of the construct and external indicators. For example, a researcher could examine the correlation between attitudes toward voting and actual voting behavior. This is an example of *criterion-related* validity evidence. Constantine and Ponterotto discuss several of the issues involved in evaluating scales or composites in more detail in Chapter 7.

ANALYSES PERFORMED TO TEST HYPOTHESES

After the data have been collected and the distribution of the data has been examined, a researcher can perform statistical analyses to test the primary hypotheses and research questions. The results of statistical analyses are usually evaluated using *null hypothesis significance testing* (NHST). NHST involves the specification of a hypothesis of no effect or relationship that the researcher attempts to disprove. The determination of whether the null hypotheses should be rejected is made using the probability of a Type I error (α). Typically, it is set to 0.05 or 0.01 (Cohen, 1994). If the probability of obtaining the particular value or a more extreme value of the test statistic under the null hypothesis is less than 0.05 or 0.01, a researcher can reject the null hypothesis and conclude that an effect or relationship is not due to chance. The use of NHST has been criticized (e.g., Schmidt & Hunter, 2002) and has clearly been abused (e.g., Frick, 1996). A researcher is well advised to incorporate the use of multiple pieces of information (e.g., effect sizes, confidence intervals) into his or her mental model of evaluating the results of statistical analyses. Many psychology journals now require the reporting of effect sizes, as well as significance tests (Wilkinson & Task Force, 1999).

In this section, we will consider univariate analyses (i.e., one dependent variable), including analyses using a single group and analyses using multiple groups. Next, we will consider the general linear model. Finally, we will consider multivariate analyses (i.e., multiple dependent variables). Many of the issues involved in using basic and advanced statistical analyses are given detailed treatment by Dickter in Chapter 19 and Steelman and Levy in Chapter 20.

Univariate Analyses

Analyses With a Single Group

Some research questions involve only a single group of participants. In these cases, the researcher is typically asking if a sample comes from a particular population. For example, a teacher must often determine if a group of students belongs to a population of gifted individuals who are capable of advanced course work or some other population (e.g., remedial student population). If the population parameters (i.e., means and standard deviation) are known and the dependent variable is continuous, the single sample *z-test* may be chosen. If the population parameters are unknown, the single sample *t-test* may be chosen.

When the dependent variable is not continuous, several options are available. If the dependent variable is nominal, the χ^2 goodness-of-fit test may be used. This χ^2 test compares the observed frequencies in the data with the expected frequencies. If the dependent variable is dichotomous, the binomial test can be selected to determine the probability of the possible outcomes. These procedures are available in many statistical software packages (e.g., One-sample *t*-test command under Compare Means and Nonparametric tests in SPSS; PROC TTEST and PROC FREQ in SAS).

Analyses With Multiple Groups

For some research questions, a researcher may need to compare two different groups on a particular variable. For example, a researcher could examine potential differences between men and women in their attitudes toward presidential candidates. These procedures require several assumptions. We will cover two of these assumptions: (1) the sampling distribution is normally distributed and (2) homogeneity of variance (HOV). The first assumption states the distribution of the sample statistic (e.g., *t*-statistic) should take the shape of a normal distribution. If the data come from populations that are normally distributed or if sample sizes are large enough (i.e., $n > 30$) to invoke the central limit theorem, the assumption is usually satisfied. The second assumption states that the population variances of the different groups are equal. Tests for HOV are included in the statistical software (e.g., Levine's test for equality of variances in SPSS).

If the HOV assumption is not satisfied, corrections to the degrees of freedom of the statistical test are made (e.g., Geisser-Greenhouse correction; see Tabachnick & Fidell, 2000). If the normality assumption cannot be satisfied, a class of statistical techniques called *nonparametric* statistics should be used. These techniques make few or no assumptions about the shape of the sampling distribution. When the sampling distribution is normal, nonparametric techniques are less powerful than the corresponding parametric procedure. The statistical power of different tests is compared by dividing the sample size required for a particular level of power for the most powerful test into the required sample size of the less powerful test for the same level of power. This quotient is called the *power efficiency*. As the sampling distribution becomes less normal, the efficiency of nonparametric procedures typically increases, but the change in efficiency will depend on the shape of the distribution. When appropriate, the maximum power efficiency is noted for these analyses. Although nonparametric statistics are not often used, they are valuable statistical tools that should be incorporated into one's mental model of statistics (Wilcox, 1998). All of the procedures discussed below are available in commercial statistical software (e.g., Nonparametric tests command in SPSS; PROC UNIVARIATE, PROC NPAR1WAY, or PROC FREQ in SAS).

If the data come from different groups of individuals (e.g., men and women) and the normality assumption is satisfied, the *independent samples t-test* can be chosen. This *t*-test examines difference in the means for the two groups. The corresponding nonparametric test is the *Mann-Whitney test*. This test uses the median to examine the difference in the rank order of the data for the two groups. The Mann-Whitney test is 95.5% as powerful as the *t*-test (Gibbons, 1993). In situations where multiple measurements

on the same variable are taken, repeated measures tests should be used. If the normality assumption is satisfied, the *paired samples t-test* can be chosen. When the normality assumption is violated, there are several nonparametric tests that can be selected.

The first is the *Wilcoxian signed-rank test*. This test examines differences in the ranks of paired variables. The resulting test statistic is compared to a *z*-distribution. The Wilcoxian signed rank test is 95.5% as powerful as the repeated measures *t*-test. The second nonparametric test is the *sign test*. This test utilizes the sign (i.e., + or −) of the difference between a pair of variables (e.g., pretest and posttest). The resulting test statistic is compared to a *z*-distribution for large samples or a binomial distribution for small samples. The sign test is 67% as powerful as the repeated measures *t*-test (Gibbons, 1993). The third is the *McNemar test*, which is best used with experimental research designs. The McNemar test examines the differences in the observed and expected change resulting from the experimental manipulation. The resulting test statistic is compared to a χ^2 distribution. The McNemar test is 95.5% as powerful as the *t*-test (Gibbons, 1993). *Cochran's Q* is the fourth test, which is useful when the dependent variable is a proportion. The resulting test statistic is compared to a χ^2 distribution. *Kendall's coefficient of concordance* is useful for comparing the agreement between pairs of measures. The resulting test statistic is compared to a χ^2 distribution, as well. Last, when the dependent variable is a count or frequency, the χ^2 *test of independence* may be used.

General Linear Model

The general linear model (GLM) is the most frequently used statistical analysis (DeShon & Morris, 2002). All of the subsequent analyses that will be discussed in this chapter are special cases of the GLM. The GLM is based on the assumption that the relationship between pairs of variables is linear and that a linear, additive equation (e.g., $y = ax + b$) can describe the relationship (Tabachnick & Fidell, 2000). Additionally, the parametric methods require the assumption of normality and homogeneity of variance. As with the tests described above, the analysis chosen will also depend on the independence of the data (i.e., nonrepeated measures).

Analysis of Variance

If a researcher is interested is testing the differences between three or more groups and the dependent variable is continuous, analysis of variance (ANOVA) procedures can be used. If there is only one independent variable, a *one-way* ANOVA is appropriate. If the independent variables represent repeated measures, *repeated measures* ANOVA can be used. If there are multiple independent variables, *factorial* ANOVA is appropriate. Factorial ANOVA is much more complex because the analysis involves examining the effects of each independent variable and the interaction between the independent variables. If a continuous control variable is available, analysis of covariance (ANCOVA) can be used. The test statistics of these procedures are compared to an *F*-distribution to determine if the null hypothesis should be rejected.

The ANOVA procedures provide an omnibus test. That is, the results of these tests indicate that a difference exists between the groups but do not indicate where the difference exists. To determine which specific groups are different, either planned contrasts or posttests are used. *Planned contrasts* specify in advance which group means will differ. When possible, planned contrasts should be used. Theory and previous research can serve as the basis for specifying group differences for planned comparisons. There are several different posttests (also called post hoc tests) that a researcher can select to examine group mean differences. Posttests assist the researcher in controlling the Type I error rate when conducting multiple comparisons and should only be used when the omnibus *F*-test from the ANOVA is significant. One of the most versatile and conservative posttests is the Scheffé test. Two of the most liberal posttests are Tukey's honest significant difference (HSD) test and Fisher's least significant difference (LSD) test. Turner and Thayer (2001) provide a detailed discussion of posttests. All of the procedures discussed above are available in commercial statistical software (e.g., One-way ANOVA command under Compare Means or Univariate command under General Linear Model in SPSS; PROC ANOVA or PROC UNIVARIATE in SAS).

If assumptions of the ANOVA (e.g., normality, HOV, linearity) are seriously violated, nonparametric procedures should be used. If there is a single independent variable, the *Kruskal Wallace test* can be used. This test uses the median to examine the differences between groups in the ranks on the dependent variable. The Kruskal Wallace test is 95.5% as powerful as the one-way ANOVA (Gibbons, 1993). If there is a single independent variable that represents a repeated measure, the *Friedman test* can be used. This test also uses the median to examine the differences in the ranks between the groups. The Friedman test is 95.5% as powerful as a repeated-measures ANOVA (Gibbons, 1993). Posttests are available for both the Kruskal Wallace and Friedman test. The procedures for conducting these posttests can be found in Gibbons (1993) or Siegel and Castellan (1998). These nonparametric procedures are available in the major statistical software (Nonparametric tests in SPSS; PROC NPAR1WAY or PROC FREQ in SAS).

Regression

The most basic form of the GLM is regression (Cohen et al., 2002). *Regression* is a set of procedures that can be used to estimate the linear equation for predicting the value of the dependent variable from one or more independent variables. Regression and correlation are closely related. *Correlation* assesses the strength and direction of the relationship between a set of points. Regression produces the equation for the best fitting (straight) line though that set of points. The fit of a regression line is determined by the degree to which it minimizes the squared distance between the data points and the regression line. There are a variety of minimization strategies, but the ordinary least squares (OLS) strategy is the most common. The use of regression requires several assumptions. These include (1) uncorrelated residuals (i.e., the distance between the line and the points), (2) normality of the residuals, (3) homoscedasticity (i.e., constant error variance of the DV at each level of the IV), and (4) the independent variables are not substantially correlated. Additionally, it is assumed that a linear relationship best describes the data.

The order and criteria by which the independent variables are entered into a regression model can be specified. The independent variables can be entered in a single step or in multiple steps. When the variables are entered in multiple steps, it is call *hierarchical regression*. Within each step there are several criteria that can be used to determine which independent variables are entered (or not entered) into the regression model. These include stepwise, forward, backward, and forced entry. The forced-entry procedure uses theoretical criteria and the judgment of the researcher to determine which independent variables are entered into a regression equation. The other procedures only use statistical criteria for entering independent variables into a regression model. Thus, the resulting equation may not be interpretable or generalizable beyond the immediate sample.

If the dependent variable is continuous, simple linear regression is appropriate. The overall regression model is evaluated using an *F*-test and each independent variable is evaluated using a *t*-test. Regression analyses should also be evaluated using the multiple correlation (*R*). The *multiple correlation* is the relationship between the dependent variable and the set of independent variables. The square of the multiple correlation can be used to determine the percentage of variance that the set of independent variables account for in the dependent variable. If the dependent variable is not continuous, there are several different regression models that can be selected. If the dependent variable is dichotomous, logistic regression, logit regression, or probit regression procedures can be appropriate choices. If the dependent variable is categorical, multinomial or ordinal regression can be chosen. Interpreting the results of these models is much more complex than simple linear regression. The regression procedures described above are available in virtually all statistical software (e.g., Regression command in SPSS; PROC REG in SAS). If the assumptions of regression cannot be met, there is variety of nonparametric and nonlinear regression procedures that are available (see Agresti, 1997, or Fox, 1997, for a description of these procedures).

Multivariate Analyses

When the research question requires that more than one dependent variable is included in the analysis, multivariate statistical analyses should be used. When a researcher needs to examine group differences on multiple dependent variables, multivariate analysis of variance (MANOVA) is appropriate. When there are multiple repeated measures (e.g., pretest, posttest, and 6-month follow-up), *repeated measures MANOVA* should be used. When a continuous control variable is available, MANCOVA can be used. The MANOVA procedures provide an omnibus multivariate test. Subsequent univariate posttest or planned contrasts need to be performed to discover the source of the effect. The MANOVA procedures share the same assumptions as the univariate GLM analyses. Additionally, these analyses assume multivariate homogeneity of variance. Tabachnick and Fidell (2000) provide an excellent treatment of the issues involved in using MANOVA. The MANOVA procedures are incorporated in most statistical software programs (e.g., Multivariate command under General Linear Model in SPSS; PROC GLM or PROC MIXED in SAS).

There are several additional multivariate procedures available to researchers. *Canonical correlation* is a procedure that can be used to examine the association between a set of independent variables and a set of dependent variables. *Multiway frequency analyses* examine the relationships between three or more nominal variables. *Discriminant analysis* is similar to MANOVA, but flipped around so that the values of multiple dependent variables are used to predict membership in a group on the independent variable (Tabachnick & Fidell, 2000). A summary of the preceding univariate, general linear model, and multivariate analysis can be found in Table 18.4. In the table, the type of data that is appropriate for the analysis and the major assumptions are listed.

Table 18.4   Summary of Univariate, General Linear Model, and Multivariate Analyses

Analysis	Data for the Dependent Variable	Major Assumptions
Univariate		
Single sample z-test	Interval	Normality
Single sample t-test	Interval	Normality
Independent samples t-test	Interval	Normality, HOV
Repeated measure t-test	Interval	Normality, HOV
Binomial test	Dichotomous	
χ^2 goodness-of-fit-test	Nominal	
χ^2 test of independence	Nominal	
Mann-Whitney test	Ordinal	
Sign test	Ordinal	
Wilcoxian signed-rank test	Ordinal	
McNemar test	Ordinal	
Kendall's coefficient of concordance	Ordinal	
Cochran's Q	Proportion	
General Linear Model		
ANOVA	Interval	Normality, HOV
ANCOVA	Interval	Normality, HOV
Kruskal Wallace test	Ordinal	
Friedman test	Ordinal	
Ordinary least squares regression	Interval	Uncorrelated residuals,
Logistic regression	Dichotomous	Normality of the residuals,
Logit and probit regression	Dichotomous	Homoscedasticity, Linearity
Multinomial regression	Nominal	
Ordinal regression	Ordinal	
Multivariate Analyses		
MANOVA	Interval or Ratio	Normality, Multivariate HOV
MANCOVA	Interval or Ratio	Normality, Multivariate HOV
Canonical correlation	Interval or Ratio	Normality, Homoscedasticity, Linearity
Multiway frequency analyses	Nominal	
Discriminant analysis	Nominal	Normality, Multivariate HOV, Linearity

CONCLUSIONS

Once the analyses have been performed and evaluated, the researcher is able to make conclusions about the research questions. The validity of these conclusions rests on the appropriateness of the statistical analyses chosen, the degree to which the assumptions of the statistical analyses are satisfied, and statistical power. A well-developed mental model of statistical discovery will direct a researcher to consider these issues in advance and incorporate them into the analysis plan. Diligence in this regard can often make the difference between successful and unsuccessful research. It is hoped that this chapter can serve as a starting point in the process of developing a mental model about statistical discovery and aid researchers in choosing appropriate statistical analyses.

EXERCISES

1. A researcher is interested in examining the relationship between life satisfaction and job satisfaction. Life satisfaction is measured using the "Life-Is-Good Scale" and job satisfaction is measured using the "Happy-Employee Scale." Each measure is on an interval scale of measurement. What steps should be taken to prepare the data and examine the properties of the responses to these measures? This researcher is particularly concerned that the data will not be normally distributed. What techniques could he or she use to examine this? To examine the relationship between these variables, which statistical analyses could be used? Now assume that the job satisfaction scale is not on an interval scale of measurement. In this case, what analyses could the researcher use? Before the researcher starts this study, what should he or she do to enhance the likelihood of finding a relationship using the analyses you have selected? Outline all of the steps you would take to answer these questions.

2. As part of a research assistantship, your advisor gives you a data set to examine how the dosage level of a psychoactive drug affects cardiovascular reactivity. In the study, patients were given 0 mg, 250 mg, 500 mg, or 1000 mg of a psychoactive drug. Cardiovascular reactivity was measured using physiological measures, as well as a self-report measure. Before conducting the analyses, you want to examine the convergent validity of the cardiovascular reactivity measures. What analyses could be used to do this? You are interested in examining potential differences in reactivity as a function of the dosage level of the drug. Which analyses are appropriate to answer this question? How could you compare differences between the specific dosage levels? What assumption do you need to examine? Outline all of the steps you would take to answer these questions.

3. As a developmental psychologist, you are interested in the effects of parental style on students' academic self-confidence. To study this question, you needed to develop a new measure of academic self-confidence that contains 12 items. What analyses could you use to demonstrate that your new measure meets the minimum standards for use in research? You want to show that parents with an involved style have children with greater academic self-confidence than the parents with an uninvolved style. Which types of univariate and multivariate techniques are appropriate? How could you predict the level of academic self-confidence from the parental style? Outline all of the steps you would take to answer these questions.

4. Previous research has indicated that individuals are more likely to receive help when the number of bystanders is small rather than large. As part of your dissertation, you would like to replicate this effect. You have operationalized receiving help as the amount of time it takes for a bystander to help you. You will count the number of bystanders present. You decide that you will use the actual number of bystanders and a new variable that groups the number of bystanders into clusters (e.g., 1–4, 5–8, etc.). What types of analyses could you perform to examine the relationship between the bystander variables and the amount of time it takes to obtain help? How could you analyze the data to examine the effect of bystanders on receiving help? You now decide that you will also create a variable that indicates if help was received at all (e.g., yes/no). How can you now analyze the relationship and group differences using this data? Outline all of the steps you would take to answer these questions.

RECOMMENDED READINGS

In this section, several sources of additional information are recommended. For a conceptual overview of statistical discovery, Abelson (1995), Good and Hardin (2003), and van Belle (2002) are invaluable resources. Wainer and Velleman (2001) provide an insightful discussion of the role of statistical graphics in statistical discovery. An entertaining overview of the history of statistics can be found in Salsburg (2002). Texts by Kirk (1995); Shadish, Cook, and Campbell (2001); and Whitley (1996) are recommended for basic and advanced research design. For basic statistics, refer to Howell (2003), Kranzler and Moursund (1999), or Larson and Farber (2000). Gonick and Smith's (1994) *Cartoon Guide to Statistics* is an amusing introduction to statistics. For an intermediate treatment of statistics, consult Agresti and Finlay (1997) or Hays (1994). In addition, Wilcox (2001) provides an excellent treatment of modern statistical developments.

For multivariate statistics, consult Grim and Yarnold (1995), Pedhazur and Schmelkin (1991), or Tabachnick and Fidell (2000). For regression and correlation, consult Aiken and West (1996), Chen and Popovich (2002), Cohen and Cohen (1983), or Cohen et al. (2002). For exploratory or confirmatory factor analysis consult Conway and Huffcutt (2003), Loehlin (2004), or Thompson (2004). For nonparametric statistics consult Conover (1998), Gibbons (1993), or Siegel and Castellan (1998). For statistical power, consult Cohen (1988) or Murphy and Myors (1998). For recent and advanced information, the articles in statistically oriented journals, such as *Psychological Methods, Applied Psychological Measurement, Organizational Research Methods*, and *Educational and Psychological Measurement,* can be consulted. The *Annual Review of Psychology* regularly publishes reviews of particular statistical topics.

For hands-on exercises and assistance using SAS, consult Cody and Smith (1997) or Spector (2001). For SPSS, consult Morgan, Griego, and Gloeckner (2003) or Zagumny (2001). SAS and SPSS provide many publications and additional assistance through their Web sites (www.spss.com; www.sas.com). Additionally, the Internet is home to a wealth of information and exercises. Particularly useful are the statistics consulting Web site at UCLA (www.ats.ucla .edu/stat) and Rice University's Virtual Lab in Statistics (www.ruf.rice.edu/~lane/rvls.html). There are several e-mail discussion lists, such as APA's Division 5 list or the SAS list (www.sas.com), where an individual can pose statistical questions to an audience composed of many experts in statistics.

REFERENCES

Abelson, R. P. (1995). *Statistics as principled argument.* Hillsdale, NJ: Lawrence Erlbaum.

Agresti, A. (1997). *Categorical data analysis.* New York: Wiley.

Agresti, A., & Finlay, B. (1997). *Statistical methods for the social sciences* (3rd ed.). Upper Saddle River, NJ: Prentice Hall.

Aiken, L. S., & West, S. G. (1996). *Multiple regression: Testing and interpreting interactions.* Thousand Oaks, CA: Sage.

Austin, J. T., Boyle, K. A., & Lualhati, J. C. (1998). Statistical conclusion validity for organizational science researchers: A review. *Organizational Research Methods, 1,* 164–208.

Austin, J. T., Scherbaum, C. A., & Mahlman, R. A. (2002). History of research methods in industrial and organizational psychology: Measurement, design, analysis. In S. G. Rogelberg (Ed.), *Handbook of research methods in industrial and organizational psychology* (pp. 3–33). Malden, MA: Blackwell.

Campbell, D. T., & Fiske, D. W. (1959). Convergent and discriminant validation by the multitrait-multimethod matrix. *Psychological Bulletin, 56,* 81–105.

Chen, P. Y., & Popovich, P. M. (2002). *Correlation.* Thousand Oaks, CA: Sage.

Cody, R. P., & Smith, J. K. (1997). *Applied statistics and the SAS programming language.* Upper Saddle River, NJ: Prentice Hall.

Cohen, J. (1988). *Statistical power for the behavioral sciences* (2nd ed.). Hillsdale, NJ: Lawrence Erlbaum.

Cohen, J. (1990). Things I have learned (so far). *American Psychologist, 45,* 1304–1312.

Cohen, J. (1992). A power primer. *Psychological Bulletin, 112,* 155–159.

Cohen, J. (1994). The earth is round (p < .05). *American Psychologist, 49,* 997–1003.

Cohen, J., & Cohen, P. (1983). *Applied multiple regression/correlation analysis for the behavioral sciences* (2nd ed.). Hillsdale, NJ: Lawrence Erlbaum.

Cohen, J., Cohen, P., Aiken, L. S., & West, S. G. (2002). *Applied multiple regression-correlation analysis for the behavioral sciences* (3rd ed.). Mahwah, NJ: Lawrence Erlbaum.

Conover, W. J. (1998). *Practical nonparametric statistics* (3rd ed.). New York: Wiley.

Conway, J., & Huffcutt, A. I. (2003). A review and evaluation of exploratory factor analysis practices in organizational research. *Organizational Research Methods, 6,* 147–168.

Cook, T. D., & Campbell, D. T. (1979). *Quasi-experimentation: Design and analysis for field settings.* Chicago: Rand McNally.

DeCarlo, L. T. (1997). On the meaning and use of kurtosis. *Psychological Methods, 2,* 292–307.

DeShon, R. P., & Morris, S. B. (2002). Modeling complex data structures: The general linear model and beyond. In S. G. Rogelberg (Ed.), *Handbook of research methods in industrial and organizational psychology* (pp. 390–411). Malden, MA: Blackwell.

Fox, J. (1997). *Applied regression analysis, linear models, and related methods.* Thousand Oaks, CA: Sage.

Frick, R. W. (1996). The appropriate use of null hypothesis testing. *Psychological Methods, 1,* 379–390.

Gibbons, J. D. (1993). *Nonparametric statistics: An introduction.* Thousand Oaks, CA: Sage.

Goldstein, R. (1989). Power and sample size via MS/PC-DOS computers. *American Statistician, 43,* 253.

Gonick, L., & Smith, W. (1994) *The cartoon guide to statistics.* New York: Harper.

Good, P., & Hardin, J. (2003). *Common errors in statistics: (and how to avoid them).* New York: Wiley-Interscience.

Grim, L. G., & Yarnold, P. R. (1995). *Reading and understanding multivariate statistics.* Washington, DC: APA.

Hays, W. L. (1994). *Statistics.* Fort Worth, TX: Harcourt Brace.

Horn, J. L. (1965). A rationale and test for the number of factors in factor analysis. *Psychometrika, 30,* 179–185.

Howell, D. (2003). *Fundamental statistics for the behavioral sciences* (5th ed.). Pacific Grove, CA: Duxbury.

Kaufman, J. D., & Dunlap, W. P. (2000). Determining the number of factors to retain: A Windows-based FORTRAN-IMSL program for parallel analysis. *Behavioral Research Methods, Instruments & Computers, 32,* 389–395.

Kirk, R. E. (1995). *Experimental design: Procedures for the behavioral sciences.* Pacific Grove, CA: Brooks/Cole.

Kranzler, G., & Moursund, J. (1999). *Statistics for the terrified* (2nd ed.). Upper Saddle River, NJ: Prentice Hall.

Larson, R., & Farber, B. (2000). *Elementary statistics: Picturing the world.* Upper Saddle River, NJ: Prentice Hall.

Loehlin, J. C. (2004). *Latent variable models: An introduction to factor, path, and structural analysis* (4th ed.). Mahwah, NJ: Lawrence Erlbaum.

Loftus, G., & Loftus, E. (1988). *Essence of statistics* (2nd ed.). New York: McGraw-Hill.

Messick, S. (1989). Validity. In R. L. Linn (Ed.), *Educational measurement* (3rd ed., pp. 221–262). Washington, DC: American Council on Education.

Mone, M. A., Mueller, G. C., & Mauland, W. (1996). The perceptions and usage of statistical power in applied psychology and management research. *Personnel Psychology, 49,* 103–120.

Morgan, G., Griego, O., Gloeckner, G. (2003). *SPSS for Windows: An introduction to use and interpretation in research.* Mahwah, NJ: Lawrence Erlbaum.

Murphy, K. (2002). Using power analysis to evaluate and improve research. In S. G. Rogelberg (Ed.), *Handbook of research methods in industrial and organizational psychology* (pp. 119–137). Malden, MA: Blackwell.

Murphy, K., & Myors, B. (1998). *Statistical power analysis: A simple and general model for traditional and modern hypothesis tests.* Mahwah, NJ: Erlbaum.

Nunnally, J. (1978). *Psychometric theory* (2nd ed.). New York: McGraw-Hill.

Parker, R. A., & Berman, N. G. (2003). Sample size: More than calculations. *American Statistician, 57,* 166.

Pedhazur, E., & Schmelkin, L. (1991). *Measurement, design, and analysis: An integrated approach.* Mahwah, NJ: Lawrence Erlbaum.

Salsburg, D. (2002). *The lady tasting tea: How statistics revolutionized science in the twentieth century.* New York: Owl Books.

Schmidt, F., & Hunter, J. (2002). Are there benefits from NHST? *American Psychologist, 57,* 65–66.

Shadish, W. R., Cook, T. D., & Campbell, D. T. (2001). *Experimental and quasi-experimental designs for generalized causal inference.* Boston: Houghton Mifflin.

Siegel, S., & Castellan, N. (1998). *Nonparametric statistics for the behavioral sciences* (2nd ed.). New York: McGraw-Hill.

Spector, P. (2001). *SAS programming for researchers and social scientists.* Thousand Oaks, CA: Sage.

Switzer, F. S., & Roth, P. L. (2002). Coping with missing data. In S. G. Rogelberg (Ed.),

Handbook of research methods in industrial and organizational psychology (pp. 310–323). Malden, MA: Blackwell.

Tabachnick, B., & Fidell, L. (2000). *Using multivariate statistics* (4th ed.). New York: HarperCollins.

Thomas, L., & Krebs, C. (1997). A review of statistical power analysis software. *Bulletin of the Ecological Society of America, 78,* 126–139.

Thompson, B. (2004). *Exploratory and confirmatory factor analysis.* Washington, DC: APA.

Tukey, J. (1977). *Exploratory data analysis.* Reading, MA: Addison-Wesley.

Turner, R., & Thayer, J. (2001). *Introduction to analysis of variance: Design, analysis and interpretation.* Thousand Oaks, CA: Sage.

van Belle, G. (2002). *Statistical rules of thumb.* New York: Wiley-Interscience.

Velicer, W., Eaton, C., & Fava, J. (2000). Construct explication through factor or component analysis: A review and evaluation of alternative procedures for determining the number of factors or components. In R. Goffin & E. Helmes (Eds.), *Problems and solutions in human assessment: Honoring Douglas N. Jackson at seventy* (pp. 41–71). Norwell, MA: Kluwer Academic.

Wainer, H., & Velleman, P. F. (2001). Statistical graphics: Mapping the pathways of science. *Annual Review of Psychology, 52,* 305–335.

Whitley, B. (1996). *Principles of research in behavioral science.* Mountain View, CA: Mayfield.

Wilcox, R. (2001). *Fundamentals of modern statistical methods: Substantially improving power and accuracy.* Chicago: Springer-Verlag.

Wilcox, R. R. (1998). How many discoveries have been lost by ignoring modern statistical methods? *American Psychologist, 53,* 300–314.

Wilkinson, L., & Task Force on Statistical Inference. (1999). Statistical methods in psychology journals: Guidelines and explanations. *American Psychologist, 54,* 594–604.

Yaffee, R. A. (1996). A basic guide to statistical research and discovery. In F. Leong & J. Austin (Eds.), *The psychology research handbook* (pp. 193–207). Thousand Oaks, CA: Sage.

Zagumny, M. J. (2001). *The SPSS book: A student guide to the statistical package for the social sciences.* Lincoln, NE: iUniverse.

APPENDIX: STATISTICAL PROCEDURES COVERED IN THE CHAPTER

Descriptive Statistics	Univariate Analyses
Mean	Single sample z-test
Median	Single sample t-test
Mode	Independent samples t-test
Kurtosis	Repeated measure t-test
Skewness	Binomial test
Variance	χ^2 goodness-of-fit test
Standard deviation	χ^2 test of independence
Range	Mann-Whitney test
Interquartile range	Sign test
Kolmogorov-Smirnov test	Wilcoxian signed-rank test
Shapiro-Wilk test	McNemar test
Runs test	Kendall's coefficient of concordance
Exploratory data analysis	Cochran's Q

Measures of Association	General Linear Model
Phi	ANOVA
Tetrachoric correlation	ANCOVA
Yule's Q	Kruskal Wallace test
Contingency coefficient	Friedman test
Cramer's V	Ordinary least squares regression
Lambda	Logistic regression
Rank-biserial	Logit and probit regression
Point-biserial	Multinomial and ordinal regression
Biserial	
Spearman's rho	**Multivariate Analyses**
Gamma	MANOVA
Tau	MANCOVA
Somer's d	Canonical correlation
Eta	Multiway frequency analyses
Omega	Discriminant analysis
Epsilon	Exploratory factor analysis
Pearson correlation	Confirmatory factor analysis

19

BASIC STATISTICAL ANALYSIS

DAVID N. DICKTER

Generally, it is impossible to sample an entire population for a study. Psychologists obtain data from a sample instead and make conclusions about the population based on these data (see McCready, Chapter 10 in this handbook). It is always possible, however, that the study's results occurred solely by chance, and it is incumbent on the researcher to provide statistical evidence to the contrary. Thus, statistical analysis is indispensable in psychological research.

Basic statistical analysis is a broad topic, a thorough explanation of which requires more space than is available in this chapter. This chapter offers helpful highlights and procedural suggestions for the novice who is developing or building on his or her skills and scripts for research and analysis. (See Hershey, Jacobs-Lawson, and Wilson, Chapter 1 in this volume for more details on research as a script). The primary topics covered in this chapter are shown in Table 19.1. The reader is also urged to explore the topic of basic statistical analysis further, both in useful texts and online. For more information about the statistical theory behind the methods described here, readers should consult texts such as Hays (1994) or Runyon, Coleman, and Pittenger (1999). A few very helpful Web sites are also listed at the end of the chapter.

Table 19.1   Primary Chapter 19 Topics

Getting Started

Choosing Statistical Software

Working With Data Files

Descriptive Statistics

    Getting a Summary Picture of Your Data

Inferential Statistics

Issues in Statistical Significance Testing

t-Tests

Analysis of Variance (ANOVA)

Correlations and Regression

Chi-Square Analysis

Recommended Reading

Exercises

This chapter gives readers a good start at data analysis and covers several inferential statistics that psychologists use often, from *t*-tests and analysis of variance (ANOVA) to correlations and regression. In addition, the chapter addresses the use of chi-square analysis for frequency data. All of the approaches to analysis discussed will be univariate; the analysis of multiple dependent variables and multiple levels is covered in other

AUTHOR'S NOTE: This revision from the first edition is dedicated to first edition coauthor Mary Roznowski—researcher, adviser, mentor, and teacher—who passed away in 2002.

chapters in this volume (Steelman & Levy, Chapter 20; Chan, Chapter 28).

GETTING STARTED

Before conducting any analyses, researchers will need to prepare their data files and to select statistical software. A variety of options exist, including using Microsoft Excel for simple analyses, SYSTAT, Minitab, and others, though arguably the most flexible and most frequently used are the SAS and SPSS statistical packages. SAS and SPSS use similar logic, and both offer user-friendly interfaces with drop-down menus and data exchanges with other applications such as Microsoft Excel. Although white papers and other online documents and assistance are available (especially for registered users of SAS and SPSS) and both packages have PC-based tutorial software, researchers frequently will need to refer to manuals in order to understand the analysis procedures they are using. The primary manuals (and those most likely to be on professors' bookshelves) are voluminous tomes that often prove daunting to the new researcher looking for a straightforward overview and step-by-step process or a clear description of how to work with data files. For good references on basic statistical analysis using SAS, see *The Little SAS Book: A Primer* (Delwiche & Slaughter, 2003) and *SAS System for Elementary Statistical Analysis* (Schlotzhauer & Littell, 1997). For SPSS, see Pallant (2001) and Kinnear (2000) for useful beginners' references.

Although an analysis should begin with a careful research design and with thoughts about potentially appropriate analyses (see Scherbaum, Chapter 18 in this volume), often the research assistant will join the project after data have been collected and will be responsible for deciding the next steps. Frequently the data are on paper or in scattered computer files and must be organized into a data file that the statistical package can recognize. A data file is simply a collection of numbers, and researchers can create or organize the file in a variety of ways. The statistics package can be used for file creation and organization, though it may be just as efficient to use any word processor. Spreadsheet software such as Microsoft Excel is also useful for moving data around.

Typically, each subject in the data file has one or more rows of data, beginning with a subject number and followed by that subject's scores on each variable. Categorical data are often given codes in order to save space. For instance, the data file might look like the lines of data in Figure 19.1.

The experimenter should keep a list of the values represented by the codes. In this example, the first three characters are the experimental participant number. Always have a number for each participant or unit on whom the data are kept. The number is an important piece of reference information with many uses, including identifying errors or anomalies and merging two or more data sets. The second entry indicates home state (1 = Michigan, 2 = California); the third entry is age; and the remaining numbers are responses to a questionnaire that uses a Likert-type rating scale that ranges from 1 to 7, where 1 = *Strongly Disagree,* and 7 = *Strongly Agree.* (You may also notice one or more "errors" in the data set, for use in Exercise 1 at the end of this chapter.)

When creating a data file, make the structure as simple and consistent as possible. Enter each subject or participant's data in its own row, and use the same column for every piece of data (e.g., age is always in columns 7 and 8). If you receive the data in column format, use Excel or other spreadsheet software to transpose it to rows. If the data appear in different columns for different subjects and it is not difficult to edit the spacing with a word processor to make the columns consistent, then do so. If there are missing data, indicate it in the file with some code, such as 999. For researchers who are new to data entry, it is inadvisable to leave a blank space when there are missing data because the computer will ignore the blank (unless informed otherwise) and will mistake the next number down the line for the missing one. As a result, the computer will be one column off after that point, like a student who forgets to fill in an answer for one question on an exam and answers the rest of the items incorrectly. If using a word processor to create the file, be sure to save it as "text only" (also known as DOS text, or ASCII). Otherwise, the file will contain extraneous icons that are invisible on screen but cause statistical packages to reject the data file. If Excel is used to create the data file, the data can be saved as text also or can be pasted into memory while SAS or SPSS

001	2	23	40	7	4	5	5	3	3	1	5	4	5	6	5	4	4	4	3	2	7
002	1	22	40	7	4	5	5	2	3	1	5	6	5	6	5	4	3	4	3	2	1
003	2	25	35	5	6	3	5	5	4	3	2	2	5	4	3	2	2	4	1	1	2
004	1	24	42	3	4	5	4	2	3	7	5	2	3	7	2	6	5	3	2	3	4
005	2	28	33	5	5	3	7	2	3	2	2	3	5	6	3	7	2	4	3	6	3
006	1	25	44	5	4	3	5	6	7	3	6	3	5	3	3	2	2	1	3	3	5
007	2	26	36	2	6	3	5	2	4	3	2	3	5	7	3	3	3	4	5	2	2
008	1	24	43	5	4	2	5	5	2	3	2	2	5	4	3	2	2	1	7	1	4
009	1	27	45	7	6	3	5	2	4	3	2	6	8	5	3	7	3	4	7	3	6
010	2	23	33	6	7	4	5	4	4	3	4	3	5	5	4	5	6	5	7	5	2
011	2	25	32	4	5	3	3	4	6	5	3	2	3	4	5	5	4	2	2	1	3
012	1	24	50	4	4	2	5	3	5	3	2	3	5	1	3	2	2	3	3	4	2
013	2	24	35	4	3	4	2	3	5	5	2	5	5	2	4	1	2	6	2	5	1
014	1	23	46	7	7	3	4	2	5	3	2	5	5	3	5	1	2	5	4	1	5
015	2	24	50	3	5	4	4	6	5	4	2	4	5	2	3	2	2	4	2	1	3
016	1	25	47	2	2	3	5	3	5	3	2	3	5	3	4	3	2	3	4	4	7
017	1	23	47	3	1	5	3	2	4	4	2	4	5	4	5	2	2	4	3	1	2
018	1	24	48	6	6	5	6	3	2	3	2	4	5	3	5	4	2	2	2	3	3
019	2	27	35	5	6	3	7	3	4	3	2	3	5	1	3	4	2	4	2	1	6
020	2	30	34	4	6	2	5	3	5	3	2	5	5	3	2	2	2	2	3	2	1

Figure 19.1   Survey and Personality Test Data From Ten People

are running (see the SAS and SPSS manuals and guides for more details).

Once the researcher has created the data file, he or she will need to use a statistical package to tell the computer what the numbers in the files mean (i.e., assign variable names to the numbers) before running the analyses. This stage involves stating a command that specifies where each of the data points is located. If any of the variables have been entered without spaces in between (e.g., if subject 001's data reads, 0012274235372335576334251), then it will be necessary to specify a *fixed* format, indicating which variable is found in which column. Alternatively, if one uses the format given in the earlier example, *free* format, this is not necessary. For more advanced users, SPSS and SAS permit a variety of more complex data structures; the manuals provide adequate guidance for appropriate data preparation.

DESCRIPTIVE STATISTICS

Once the computer or statistical package has read in the data file, read the output to make sure that there are no data entry mistakes and that any inappropriate values have been changed

(e.g., using the program or a word processor to recode variable values; see DiLalla & Dollinger, Chapter 16 in this volume for guidance on cleaning the data). One can use descriptive statistics for this purpose as well as to summarize the data and to check statistical assumptions (described later).

Means and standard deviations provide important information about representative scores and the amount of variation in the data, respectively. In addition, the researcher can use descriptive statistics and graphics to check for several potentially problematic characteristics of the data set. These include *nonnormality,* that is, a distribution of scores that departs substantially from a bell-shaped curve, and *outliers,* scores that are highly discrepant from most other scores. A good starting point is a data plot, such as a *frequency chart* or *normal plot,* graphically depicting the distribution of scores in the sample. The former illustrates the frequency distribution and identifies outliers and can be done perhaps as easily with Excel as with a statistical package. The latter is a graph provided on statistical packages, which is a straight line when the data are normally distributed but which becomes curved when there is nonnormality. Skewness and kurtosis provide further information about the shape of the data, indicating whether values are clustered in particular patterns that may depart from normality. A *skewed distribution* is asymmetric, with higher frequencies on one side and a long tail of low frequencies on the other; and a *kurtotic distribution* has a high peak and long tails on both sides. Most statistical packages provide simple commands that yield information about a variety of characteristics of the data set (e.g., the Descriptive procedure in SPSS and Univariate procedure in SAS).

INFERENTIAL STATISTICS

It is informative to plot the data and to use other descriptive statistics in order to get a good sense of what the data distribution looks like; however, the demands of a research assistantship rarely end with descriptive statistics. Researchers need to make inferences about the population from which the sample was drawn. The chapter addresses several types of inferential statistics. First, however, a discussion of statistical significance testing is in order.

The Significance Test

This chapter discusses each type of statistical analysis in a consistent format. First, the purpose and underlying assumptions of each test are covered, followed by a brief discussion of one or more statistics calculated for each test and how the statistics are used to decide whether or not to reject the null hypothesis.

Before discussing basic analysis, it is important to devote some space to several issues about significance tests, as outlined by Cohen (1990, 1994) and others.

Statistical significance tests begin with the supposition that the null hypothesis is true (e.g., that there is no treatment effect, or that the difference between two sample population means is zero) and asks how likely it would be to obtain the observed data, given the truth of this supposition. If assuming that the null hypothesis is true makes the results seem unlikely (customarily, less than a 5% p value, or probability of occurring), then the researcher rejects the null hypothesis and concludes that there is support for the alternative, that a treatment effect exists.

This notion is simple enough, but unfortunately it is subject to serious misinterpretations. Cohen (1994) pointed out two misconceptions that researchers exhibit about hypothesis testing and p values that should be mentioned here. One misconception is that the p of .05 is the probability that the null hypothesis is true and that its complement, .95, indicates the chance that the research hypothesis is "true." On the contrary, the 5% probability refers to the likelihood of obtaining the observed *results* if the null hypothesis is true and does not provide proof of the "truth" or falsity of the null hypothesis or research hypothesis. A second misconception outlined by Cohen (1994) and termed the "replication fallacy" by Rosenthal (1993) is that if a study with results that were significant at $p < .05$ were replicated numerous times, researchers would find a significant result most of the time (in particular, 95%). Unfortunately, the p value says nothing about the chance of replicating the results. Instead, the level of statistical power, or the ability to detect an effect when it exists (see Cohen, 1988, and Myors, Chapter 11 in this handbook) provides a better estimate.

Cohen (1990, 1994) and others have also emphasized the importance of extending research beyond the significant-nonsignificant dichotomy that characterizes much of the literature in psychology (see also Wilkinson & Statistical Task Force on Statistical Inference, 1999). First, it is important not to limit all research to studies whose results will hinge on a significance test. Valuable contributions to theory should not be hindered by the pervading acceptance of the $p < .05$ requirement. Strict adherence to the .05 value makes an arbitrary cutoff that categorizes potentially important findings as nonsignificant, and therefore, nonfindings. In numerous publications, Cohen and other methodologists have argued that researchers should pay attention to the size of an effect or result, not just whether or not a result is significant. Cohen (1994) bemoaned the small effect sizes in many studies. Other researchers (e.g., Hunter & Schmidt, 1991, 2004; Schmidt, 1992) have focused on this issue in their work on meta-analysis, a statistical method that involves aggregating the results of multiple studies and calculating an overall effect size. Researchers must bear in mind that statistical significance and effect size are distinct (Rosenthal, 1993). Results that are significant at $p < .05$ are not necessarily "large"; similarly, researchers should avoid the temptation to proclaim that an effect that is significant at a smaller probability (e.g., $p < .001$) is "very large" (Cohen, 1994).

When a significance test is reported, it is most informative to report the confidence interval, which shows the range of values for which the null hypothesis would be retained. A large range may indicate sampling error, such as an inadequate sample size or poor variability in scores, and indicates that it would be difficult to reject the null hypothesis even if it were false, that is, that there is a substantial Type II error.

In summary, researchers can obtain important information about their data by doing more than simply conducting a hypothesis test. Moreover, by being aware of common misconceptions and misstatements about hypothesis tests, they can avoid common pitfalls in their conclusions.

Format of Statistical Tests

Statistical tests follow a consistent sequence. A statistical indicator is calculated from the study results and is used to test the null hypothesis that there is no treatment effect. This *test statistic* must meet or exceed some threshold value, known as a critical value, ideally determined prior to the study. The *critical value* is a number taken from a table of statistical distributions. Its magnitude depends on the sample size, the value of p the researcher chooses, and may depend on other characteristics as well. The p value is selected depending on the experimenter's tolerance of Type I error, the probability that the observed data will lead the researcher to reject the null hypothesis falsely. If the statistic is equal to or exceeds the critical value, then the researcher rejects the null hypothesis, concluding that there is a treatment effect.

t-Tests

One elementary statistical test, with several variants, is the analysis of the difference between means. This section will focus on the two-sample *t*-test. Suppose that a graduate student collects test scores for a treatment group and a control group. A good way to compare the groups is to find the average test score for each group and to judge whether they are significantly different. Suppose that on a 40-point scale, the treatment group has a score of 20, and the control group has a score of 25. Is this a trivial difference that probably occurred by chance, or is there a treatment effect? Another way of stating this question is, "Do the two sample means come from the same population distribution or two different ones?" By conducting a *t*-test, we can answer this question, judging whether there is a significant difference between these scores. The answer will depend not only on the size of the effect but on the sample size and level of tolerance for Type I error (the *alpha* level).

The *t*-test assumes certain things about the data that researchers should verify before conducting the test. First, do the data in each group follow a normal distribution? If the sample is small, the test may be incorrect because the test statistic calculated from the data may not have the normal distribution that is assumed for the statistical test. If the sample size is moderate or large (e.g., 40–100 or more), however, the distribution of the test should closely approximate a normal distribution and the test will be accurate (Hays, 1994). Second, the *t*-test assumes that the variance for the two groups is about the same. Researchers should check this *homogeneity of variance* assumption. This assumption is more important and can lead to inaccurate results, particularly for small groups with unequal sample sizes. Third, observations are assumed to be independent, such that one subject does not influence another subject's score (e.g., copying a test answer). Researchers should check to be sure that these assumptions are met when conducting a *t*-test.

The *t*-test uses a statistic calculated from the sample means divided by a variance estimate. This obtained *t*-statistic is compared to the critical value obtained from a probability table at the selected p value (usually .05, but may be .01 or .001). If the *t*-statistic is equal to or exceeds the critical value, then the difference between the group means is significant at the chosen level of alpha. Note that the significance test can be *one-sided* or *two-sided* (also called *one-tailed* or *two-tailed,* respectively). The former is used when the mean for a particular group is hypothesized to be higher than the mean for the other group. The latter is used when the means are expected to be different, but there is no a priori hypothesis that a particular mean will be higher. For the two-sided test, the alpha level (and therefore, the p value) is halved in order to guard against the increase in Type I error that would accompany such a general hypothesis. As a result, a larger t-statistic is necessary if the null hypothesis is to be rejected.

A similar type of t-test is the *paired-differences test.* For instance, suppose that a researcher wants to compare the job performance of a group of employees who receive a 1-week job-training course with the performance of a control group that receives no training. The performance of each employee is rated prior to training and several weeks later. For this test, it is assumed that each pair (pre, post) of observations is independent from other pairs. In order to examine whether the performance ratings of the treatment group improve more than those of the control group, the researcher may perform a one-sided t-test on the means of the pre and post difference scores for the two groups.

Analysis of Variance (ANOVA)

The t-test is useful for determining whether two means are significantly different; however, there is a Type I error associated with each test that increases as the number of group means being compared increases. For instance, if a researcher conducts five t-tests and permits the usual .05 Type I error on each, the error rate would be 1−.955, or nearly a 23% chance of falsely rejecting the null hypothesis. An alternative to conducting multiple t-tests when there are more than a few groups is ANOVA. Like the t-test, ANOVA involves a comparison of group means. Unlike the t-test, however, there need be no limitation on the number of group comparisons a researcher may make. (Of course, group comparisons should be made on the basis of theoretical predictions rather than by random fishing for differences among the groups.) Researchers use ANOVA in order to examine the variability of scores within and between groups. Subjects' scores within the same group will vary due to individual differences and random error. If there is a treatment effect, however, there will be more variance between groups than there is within groups. When there are only two groups, using ANOVA and a t-test will produce identical results.

As with the t-test, ANOVA assumes that observations are independent, the data are normal, and group variances are equal. A violation of the homogeneity of variance assumption can undermine the results, particularly when group sample sizes are unequal. Therefore, one should be especially vigilant in spotting this violation.

The first step in conducting an ANOVA is to determine if any group mean is significantly different from any other group mean. This is called an overall F-test. If there are no differences (i.e., if the F-test is not significant), then there is no point in comparing any of the groups. The results have indicated that the researcher should retain the null hypothesis that all group means are equal. On the other hand, if the overall F is significant, the researcher may then make *post hoc* comparisons between group means. A significant F indicates that at least one group mean is significantly different from one other group mean. The researcher should then investigate his or her hypotheses about the groups. For instance, the researcher might have hypothesized that the mean of group A is significantly different from the means of groups B, C, and D, or that the means of groups A and B are significantly different from the means of groups C and D. It is important to emphasize that these statistical tests must be based on the study hypotheses (e.g., that groups A and B will have higher exam scores than C and D, because A and B received a new type of tutoring and groups C and D did not.) Clearly, the tests must not be conducted after looking at all of the group means, taking note of the ones that differ markedly, and conducting statistical comparisons between these groups in order to find a significant result. Researchers must decide on meaningful group comparisons before they see the data rather than hypothesize after viewing the results and claim that the results are what they predicted all along.

Researchers can use a variety of statistical tests to compare group means after finding a significant overall F. With each test, the researcher runs some risk of making a Type I error. This is least likely for the Tukey and

Scheffe tests, and more likely with the Fisher and Newman-Keuls tests. With the Tukey and Scheffe tests, however, the reduction of Type I error comes at some expense: increased Type II error, failing to find a treatment effect that is present. Nevertheless, the Tukey test is generally the best choice (Keppel, 1991).

Conducting ANOVA can involve higher levels of complexity. The reader should consult additional sources (e.g., Keppel, 1991) in order to find out more about when it is appropriate to conduct various kinds of ANOVA. Factorial ANOVA, which includes two or more independent variables, may involve interaction effects. An interaction occurs when the effect of an independent variable on the dependent variable depends on the level of another independent variable. For instance, if students in an experiment who set high goals for themselves can solve more physics problems than students who set low goals, but this difference is observed only for individuals with high cognitive ability, then there is a goal setting X ability interaction. An interaction indicates that one cannot generalize about physics problem solving that occurs when high and low goal levels are set, for instance, without specifying whether the students have high cognitive ability. The main effects of goal level and ability depend on the category of the other variable to which the students belong.

Due to the brevity of this chapter, the reader is urged to consult additional sources of information about ANOVA (and, for that matter, about all of the analyses described in this chapter). For instance, ANOVA permits analysis of repeated-measures designs in which subjects receive more than one treatment, and effects within a group of subjects are examined. Keppel's (1991) handbook provides a wealth of information on the use of ANOVA for repeated measures and other experimental designs.

CORRELATIONS

Before discussing regression, it will be useful to devote some attention to correlations. A correlation is an association between two variables that takes on a value between +1.0 and −1.0. If two variables are positively correlated, then as one increases, the other increases. If they are negatively correlated, then as one variable increases, the other decreases. If they are not associated at all, the correlation is zero. If each subject's scores on the two variables were plotted as a point on an x-y axis (i.e., in a *scatterplot*), a zero correlation would appear as a roughly circular field of points with no clear relationship between x and y. A positive correlation would appear approximately linear (somewhat cigar-shaped, but heading in a straight line) and increasing, and a negative correlation would appear approximately linear and decreasing. Correlations can be used to make inferences about the associations between two variables in a population, such as by testing the null hypothesis that two variables are unrelated. When such inferences are made, the data are assumed to be normally distributed.

Although it is customary to test the null hypothesis that the population correlation is 0.0, in practice it is somewhat unusual to see many sample correlations that are 0.0; however, even tiny correlations may be statistically significant because the significance of a correlation depends partly on the sample size. Indeed, given a large sample size, one can expect correlations of .001 between theoretically unrelated variables to achieve significance, a phenomenon contemptuously named the "crud factor" (Meehl, 1990, cited in Cohen, 1994). Psychologists typically attach more importance to correlations that are plus or minus .3 or greater. By squaring the correlation between two variables, A and B, one can find how much of the variance in A can be explained (accounted for) by knowing the value of B (and vice versa). Thus, a correlation between A and B of .3 means that A explains 9% of the variance in B.

It is important not to make causal statements about the relation between two variables based solely on the correlation between them. People often fall prey to this mistake, proclaiming, for instance, that an observed decline in SAT scores in the United States was due to an increase in the number of hours American youth spent watching television. Just because an association is observed does not mean that there is a causal relationship. All that a correlation tells is that there is some association, positive or negative, and not that A causes B or B causes A.

REGRESSION

The concept of variance explained or accounted for, as discussed above, is an important concept for regression analysis, as will be discussed shortly. Researchers can use regression to do everything ANOVA does, and more. ANOVA analyzes mean differences between groups satisfactorily, but what if, instead of discrete groups, there is a continuous variable, such as age? The researcher could divide the sample into two discrete groups, such as those over or under 40 years of age, and compare the two, but to do so would place 5-year-olds in the same category as 37-year-olds. The best thing to do would be not to use two, three, ten, or any number of categories, but to make use of the continuous nature of the age variable. Regression can do this; ANOVA cannot. Regression typically involves creating a linear equation to predict scores in a dependent variable. The equation represents a line that best fits through a scatterplot of points describing the relationship between the dependent variable and one or more independent variables. The beta weights, or coefficients on the independent variables in the equation, provide information about the relationships between the independent variables and the dependent variable. For instance, the beta weight for a regression equation with one independent variable can be understood as follows: Imagine an x-y coordinate axis that plots each subject's score on the independent variable versus his score on the dependent variable. If one draws a single line to best fit the data, the slope of that line will be the *beta weight* and will represent the changes in the value of the dependent variable that are associated with each change of one unit in the independent variable.

Like *t*-tests and ANOVA, regression analysis assumes independence, normality, and constant variance. In addition, linear relationships between the independent variables and dependent variable are typically assumed. Researchers may wish to test for nonlinear trends in the data in order to create a regression equation with a better fit to the data (e.g., see Cohen, Cohen, West, & Aiken, 2002; Pedhazur, 1997).

Simple linear regression involves a single independent variable that is used to estimate scores in the dependent variable. Regression is used to determine whether the variance accounted for by the continuous independent variable (e.g., GRE score) in the dependent variable (e.g., first-year grade point average in graduate school) is significant. To do this, one finds the square of the correlation between them (the R^2) and tests whether it is significantly different from zero. If so, then one can make a statement such as the following: "GRE score accounts for 16% of the variance in first-year grades" (if the R^2 were .16). Thus, regression analysis provides some index of the magnitude of the association between the independent and dependent variables. Another way of testing the significance of the independent variable is to perform a *t*-test on the estimated value of its beta weight (also known as its *parameter estimate*) to determine if it is significantly different from zero.

Multiple linear regression can be used to determine if the amount of variance a set of independent variables explains in the dependent variable is significantly different from zero. As with factorial ANOVA, interactions are possible because there is more than one independent variable. In addition, one may also want to ask more complex questions, such as what percentage of unique variance an independent variable explains in the dependent variable. That is, what explanatory value does the independent variable add over and above the others? This statistic is known as a *squared semipartial correlation*. Note that entering variables into the regression equation in different orderings produces different results. Readers should consult an additional resource such as Cohen et al. (2002) for information about partialling out variance and the use of regression procedures, such as *forward selection, backward elimination,* and *stepwise regression* to evaluate the predictive contributions of particular variables and sets of variables.

Chi-Square Tests

A different type of study might involve analyzing frequencies to see if they differ across some category. For instance, one might want to study whether males and females hold different opinions about a political issue, such as whether or not smoking should be banned in restaurants. None of the statistical tests discussed above are appropriate because the data are categorical.

Moreover, this type of study examines the shape of the entire frequency distributions for each group (e.g., the proportion of people who answer *always, sometimes, never*) rather than some summary statistics, such as means or variances. In this example, chi-square analysis can be used to ask the question, "Do men and women hold different opinions on this political issue?" The null hypothesis that there is no difference of opinion will be rejected if the proportion of men who believe that smoking should be banned in restaurants is significantly different from the proportion of women who hold this belief.

As with the other statistical tests, several assumptions are made when conducting a chi-square analysis. One assumption is that the observations are independent. That is, one person's response to the smoking ban question should not be influenced by another respondent. In addition, observations must fall into mutually exclusive categories (e.g., smoker vs. nonsmoker) rather than count toward more than one frequency tabulation. Finally, the expected frequency for a given category (discussed below) should generally not be lower than 5 (see Hays, 1994).

Chi-square analysis uses observed and expected frequencies to test the null hypothesis. Under the null hypothesis, the same proportion of men and women would be in favor (or against) the smoking ban. The expected frequencies of favorable (or unfavorable) responses for men and women are those that would make these proportions the same. To the extent that the observed (actual) frequencies differ from the expected frequencies, the results provide evidence for rejecting the null hypothesis.

The chi-square test follows the same format as other statistical significance tests: If the chi-square value exceeds a threshold, then the researcher rejects the null hypothesis that the groups are the same. In this case, that would mean that men and women hold different opinions about the smoking ban. Chi-square analysis is particularly useful for survey research, which generally involves frequency data that are not appropriate for the other types of basic analysis discussed in this chapter.

CONCLUSION

This basic statistics chapter and its coverage of chi-square analysis, *t*-tests, ANOVA, and correlation and regression should answer some of the reader's questions as well as serve as a source of useful references. Try the approaches and examples described in this chapter, consult the texts and online resources, and confer with your colleagues, professors, and research supervisors. Mastery of basic statistical analysis is an invaluable skill that you will be able to draw on every day in your research.

EXERCISES

Try these exercises to build your comfort level with basic statistical procedures and analyses. All are based on the made-up survey data in Figure 19.1. The questions are arranged in increasing order of difficulty.

Create a data file from the data in Figure 19.1, using any method or software you wish. Refer to any of the references listed earlier if you need help.

- Make the first 3 columns the Survey Respondent Number.
- Make the Columns 4–5 the Home State (1 = Michigan, 2 = California). (Or you can just use Column 5, because Column 4 is always blank in this data set. Either way will work.)
- Column 6 is just blank; no need to do anything with it.
- Make Columns 7–8 the Age.
- Make columns 10–11 the score on an Openness-Candidness personality test.
- Make the Column 13 the answer to the first survey question, Column 15 for the second survey question, and so on. Column 47 is the answer to the 18th question. (Remember that blank spaces count toward the

number of columns.) Note that the survey questions are on a rating scale that ranges from 1 to 7, where 1 = *Strongly Disagree,* and 7 = *Strongly Agree.* Each of the 18 questions asks about how much the person agrees he or she likes to eat a particular healthy vegetable (such as broccoli, spinach, etc.).

- Submit the data to a statistical program and print out the values. Compare them with Figure 19.1 and correct any data entry mistakes.
- Run a statistical procedure that gives you frequencies, mean averages, and the minimum and maximum values of each variable (i.e., all of the elements in the data set: the subject number, home state, age, and survey questions 1 through 18). Also find the standard deviation of each answer to each survey question. Note that for question 1F you will need to create a new variable by performing computations on variables in the data set.

1. Then answer these questions using your data printout:

A. At least one of the people has a mistake in the original data in Figure 19.1: one or more numbers are out of the permitted range for one or more variables. Reading from your frequency printout, which subject number(s) have a mistake? (Leave the mistake in.) *Remember that though you can probably tell from scanning the data on the page, you will soon be working with data sets that are far too large to "eyeball" statistical results. You **will** need a statistical program to read in your data and do your analyses!*

B. What is the percentage of people in the data set from Michigan?

C. What is the average age? What age is the youngest person? What age is the oldest?

D. What is the standard deviation of survey question 18? Is this the survey question with the most variation in responses?

E. Are scores on the Openness personality test approximately normally distributed? How can you tell?

F. For each person in the data set, add the 18 survey questions to get a total for the survey. Which person had the highest total—that is, likes eating healthy vegetables the most? (Consult one of the statistical package reference books for instructions.)

G. Find the mean average of the total from F for Michigan and California people separately. (Consult the references for methods of averaging by gender or any other grouping variable.)

2. Although the data set is small (so that readers do not have to type in a large file of numbers), test the hypothesis that people from Michigan are more candid about their opinions than people from California, using a one-tailed *t*-test. (No offense to Californians is intended!)

A. Assume that the assumption of independent observations—one of several required for a *t*-test—is met. Aside from the small sample size, what other reasons for caution should one have, if any, about conducting a *t*-test?

B. Are we able to reject the null hypothesis that people hailing from Michigan and from California are equally open? Compare the means for the two home states statistically and explain what the results indicate.

3. Conduct an analysis of variance (ANOVA) to test the same hypothesis in Question 2.

A. What is the result? Should you expect a different result than was obtained in 2B?

B. Add the data below to the data set:

```
021 3 21 21 4 5 3 3 4 6 5 3 2 3 4 5 5 4 2 2 1 3
022 3 21 27 4 4 2 5 3 5 3 2 3 5 1 3 2 2 3 3 4 2
023 3 25 30 4 3 4 2 3 5 5 2 5 5 2 4 1 2 6 2 5 1
024 3 23 35 7 7 3 4 2 5 3 2 5 5 3 5 1 2 5 4 1 5
025 3 27 23 3 5 4 4 6 5 4 2 4 5 2 3 2 2 4 2 1 3
026 3 27 21 2 2 3 5 3 5 3 2 3 5 3 4 3 2 3 4 4 7
```

027 3 24 19 3 1 5 3 2 4 4 2 4 5 4 5 2 2 4 3 1 2
028 3 28 27 6 6 5 6 3 2 3 2 4 5 3 5 4 2 2 2 3 3
029 3 24 26 5 6 3 7 3 4 3 2 3 5 1 3 4 2 4 2 1 6
030 3 35 24 4 6 2 5 3 5 3 2 5 5 3 2 2 2 2 3 2 1

With the 30 observations now in the data set, test the hypothesis that there are differences in Openness depending on whether the person's home state is Michigan, California, or North Dakota (Home State = 3; see Column 5 above). Are people from Michigan more open than those from North Dakota? What about Californians versus North Dakotans?

4. Using your statistical package, merge these data with the data set of 20 people (shown below). Use the Subject number in columns 1–3 to match the data.

    Columns 1–3 below contain the Survey Respondent Number. Column 4 is blank. Column 5 is Home State. Columns 7–9 indicate whether or not the respondent reports that at least once within the last year, he or she complained to the staff at a restaurant about the food or service. (You can either change *yes* and *no* to numbers, or consult your statistical package instructions about reading in character or *string* (nonnumeric) values.)

001	1	Yes
002	1	No
003	2	No
004	1	Yes
005	2	Yes
006	2	No
007	1	Yes
008	2	No
009	1	Yes
010	2	No
011	2	No
012	1	Yes
013	1	Yes
014	2	No
015	2	No
016	1	Yes
017	1	Yes
018	2	No
019	1	Yes
020	2	No

A. What type of analysis discussed in this chapter would be most appropriate for comparing the percentage of people from Michigan versus California who reported complaining, and why?

B. Although the sample size is small in this exercise, conduct the analysis and determine the results and *p* value.

5. Add all of the 18 survey answers together (as you did for Question 1F) to get a total score indicating how much each person enjoys eating healthy vegetables.

A. Determine, by calculating a correlation, whether the data suggest that more open-candid people were also less likely to say that they like to eat healthy vegetables. Is the correlation statistically significant?

B. Using regression analysis, predict how well people will like to eat healthy vegetables (the dependent variable—use the sum of the 18 survey questions for this analysis). As your predictors (independent variables), use both age and openness-candidness. What do the results mean?

Answers:

1.A. Subject number 9 has a value of 8 on survey question 10. This is not possible because the survey only has possible answers of 1 to 7, and is therefore a mistake. If you made a data entry mistake typing in the numbers, there may be more than one error! **B.** 50%. **C.** 24.8. Youngest is 22, oldest is 30. **D.** 1.96. Yes, survey question #18 has the highest standard deviation and therefore the most variability. **E.** Yes. If you do a normal plot, you will see that it is fairly straight. You can also test for normality using a hypothesis test and will find that the null hypothesis (that the data set is normal) is retained. **F.** There is a tie for subjects #9 and #10, both having survey totals of 84. **G.** Means are 66.3 for Michigan and 66.2 for California.

2.A. Other assumptions for t-tests include normality and homogeneity of variance. We can assume from 1E that the test is normally distributed. Comparing the variances on Openness for the two states statistically, we retain the null hypothesis that they are the same. **B.** Yes. People from Michigan have an Openness score of 45.2, versus a score for California of 36.3. Using a one-tailed t-test, this difference is statistically significant at $p < .05$ (and $p < .001$, in fact). Remember the cautions discussed in this chapter about significance testing and the value of a confidence interval.

3.A. An ANOVA test is the same as a t-test when there are only two groups (e.g., Michigan vs. California). Therefore we expect to come to the same conclusion (null hypothesis rejected), and we do. **B.** The overall F-test is significant. When we go looking for where the differences are with a Tukey test, we find that "Michiganders" (or "Michiganians"?) are the most candid, followed by Californians and then North Dakotans.

4.A. A chi-square analysis is appropriate because the data are categorical. Let us assume here that the assumptions underlying this statistical test are met. **B.** The test is significant at $p < .001$. Therefore, there is evidence that people from Michigan are more likely to speak up about being dissatisfied with the food or service at a restaurant. (Could it be because they're more open about their opinions, or is there a difference by state in the quality of food or service? This analysis does not address that question.) Note that North Dakota was not included in the analysis.

5.A. The correlation is slightly negative ($-.15$), but with just 20 people it is not statistically significant (p is .515, well over .05). If it had been, it would have indicated that people who are more candid are less likely to say they like to eat healthy vegetables. (Please, no letters from the broccoli industry.) **B.** The test is not significant ($F = .55$, $p > .05$). A statistical model that includes age and openness does not account for significant variance in liking for healthy vegetables. Note that the t-tests of the beta weights of each predictor are also nonsignificant ($t = -.81$ and $-.93$ for age and openness, respectively, resulting in p values well over .05).

Recommended Readings

Books

Readers are urged to examine one or more texts for each of the main statistics topics discussed in this chapter (e.g., Bobko, 2001, and Cohen et al., 2002, for correlation/regression; Hays, 1994, for chi-square tests and hypothesis tests in general; Keppel, 1991, for ANOVA; and Runyon, Coleman, & Pittenger, 1999, for t-tests and other topics in statistics). SPSS users may find it helpful as well to examine a text that introduces both statistics and the use of SPSS (e.g., Bryman & Cramer, 1999). As described earlier, SAS and SPSS publish large volumes describing the available procedures (e.g., Schlotzhauer & Littell, 1997; SPSS, Inc., 2001) that can be ordered through a college or university bookstore. Manuals are also available on distribution CDs. More concise supplements are recommended, such as Delwiche & Slaughter (2003) for SAS and Pallant (2001) for SPSS.

Online Resources

- www.ruf.rice.edu/~lane/rvls.html - Rice University's virtual lab in statistics. Includes an online statistics book, statistical simulations, and case studies.
- www.statpages.net - A long list of statistical calculation Web pages maintained by John C. Pezzullo, an emeritus professor of pharmacology and biostatistics at Georgetown University. (Be sure to use more than one source to verify the information.)
- www.forrest.psych.unc.edu/research - Readers may wish to explore ViSta, a free, open-source statistics software package that provides interactive, visual display of data and statistical analysis procedures.

REFERENCES

Bobko, P. (2001). *Correlation and regression: Applications for industrial-organizational psychology and management.* Thousand Oaks, CA: Sage.

Bryman, A., & Cramer, D. (1999). *Quantitative data analysis with SPSS Release 8 for Windows: A guide for social scientists.* London: Routledge.

Cohen, J. (1988). *Statistical power analysis for the behavioral sciences* (2nd ed.). Hillsdale, NJ: Lawrence Erlbaum.

Cohen, J. (1990). Things I have learned (so far). *American Psychologist, 45,* 1304–1312.

Cohen, J. (1994). The earth is round (p < .05). *American Psychologist, 49,* 997–1003.

Cohen, P., Cohen, J., West, S. G., & Aiken, L. S. (2002). *Applied multiple regression/correlation analysis for the behavioral sciences* (3rd ed.). Mahwah, NJ: Lawrence Erlbaum.

Delwiche, L. D., & Slaughter, S. J. (2003). *The little SAS book: A primer* (3rd ed.). Cary, NC: SAS.

Hays, W. L. (1994). *Statistics* (5th ed.). Orlando, FL: Harcourt Brace.

Hunter, J. E., & Schmidt, F. L. (1991). Meta-analysis. In R. K. Hambleton & J. N. Zaal (Eds.), *Advances in educational and psychological testing: Theory and applications.* Boston: Kluwer.

Hunter, J. E., & Schmidt, F. L. (2004). *Methods of meta-analysis: Correcting error and bias in research findings* (2nd ed.). Thousand Oaks, CA: Sage.

Keppel, G. (1991). *Design and analysis: A researcher's handbook* (3rd ed.). Englewood Cliffs, NJ: Prentice Hall.

Kinnear, P. R. (2000). *SPSS for Windows made simple: Release 10.* Hove, UK: Taylor & Francis Group.

Meehl, P. E. (1990). Why summaries of research on psychological theories are often uninterpretable. *Psychological Reports, 66* (Monograph Suppl. 1-V66), 195–244.

Pallant, J. (2001). *SPSS survival manual: A step by step guide to data analysis using SPSS for Windows (Version 10).* Chicago: Open University Press.

Pedhazur, E. (1997). *Multiple regression in behavioral research* (3rd ed.). Orlando, FL: Harcourt Brace.

Rosenthal, R. (1993). Cumulating evidence. In G. Keren & C. Lewis (Eds.), *A handbook for data analysis in the behavioral sciences: Methodological issues* (pp. 519–559). Hillsdale, NJ: Lawrence Erlbaum.

Runyon, R. P., Coleman, K. A., & Pittenger, D. (1999). *Fundamentals of behavioral statistics* (9th ed.). New York: McGraw-Hill.

Schlotzhauer, S. D., & Littell, R. C. (1997), *SAS system for elementary statistical analysis* (2nd ed.). Cary, NC: SAS Institute.

Schmidt, F. L. (1992). What do data really mean? Research findings, meta-analysis, and cumulative knowledge in psychology. *American Psychologist, 47,* 1173–1181.

Spector, P. E. (1993). *SAS programming for researchers and social scientists.* Newbury Park, CA: Sage.

SPSS, Inc. (2001). *SPSS Base 11.0 for Windows user's guide.* Englewood Cliffs, NJ: Prentice Hall.

Wilkinson, L., & Statistical Task Force on Statistical Inference (1999). Statistical methods in psychology journals: Guidelines and explanations. *American Psychologist, 54,* 594–604.

20

USING ADVANCED STATISTICS

LISA A. STEELMAN
PAUL E. LEVY

One's research questions or specific hypotheses should be the key in determining what statistical analyses will be employed in a particular study. In general, research questions may be broken into four categories: degree of relationship among variables, significance of group differences, prediction of group membership, and finally structure (Tabachnick & Fidell, 2001). In this chapter, we discuss each of these four categories of analysis, as well as the types of research questions associated with each (see Table 20.1). Before pursuing these advanced statistical techniques, we will begin with the notion of statistical power because this is one of the most important issues in research design and analysis, yet one of the most neglected. A full treatment of power analysis can be found in Chapter 11.

Table 20.1 Advanced Statistics Discussed in This Chapter

Type of Analysis	Advanced Statistic Example
Degree of relationship	canonical correlation
Significance of group differences	Hotelling's T^2
	MANOVA
	MANCOVA
Prediction of group membership	discriminant analysis
Structure	principal components analysis
	factor analysis
	path analysis
	structural equation modeling

POWER

The *power* of a research design or statistical analysis is the ability to detect a significant difference when one exists. If a study has low power, the researcher could derive erroneous conclusions from the statistical analysis. Just as a microscope with low power may not illuminate the true nature of the item we are looking at, a study with low power will not have enough magnification to detect the effect. The power of a statistical test, then, is defined as the probability of rejecting a null hypothesis when it is false (i.e., the likelihood of correctly rejecting the null hypothesis of no difference between experimental groups when there is in fact a true population difference).

There are four major factors that affect the power of a statistical test: (a) the statistical test itself, (b) alpha level, (c) sample size, and (d) effect size. First, in any data analytic procedure, we want to select the most sensitive statistical test for which the assumptions of that particular test can be met. Different statistical tests have different levels of power when applied to the same data. For example, nonparametric tests (e.g., Mann-Whitney *U,* Kruskal-Wallis) are generally less powerful than are parametric tests (*t*-test, ANOVA) when the assumptions of the latter are met. Thus, researchers must choose their statistical tests carefully.

The second determinant of power is alpha level (α). Alpha level indicates the percentage of time we are willing to reject a true null hypothesis or make a Type I error. If, for instance, we choose a very small α such as .001, this will protect us from making Type I errors (i.e., rejecting a true null hypothesis) but will inflate beta (β) and increase the likelihood of making a Type II error (i.e., accepting a false null hypothesis). By setting α, we decide what kind of ratio is acceptable for our research. In behavioral research, we are usually more concerned with Type I errors and therefore keep α very low (i.e., .01 or .05). Power is defined as $1 - \beta$ and is thus directly and inversely related to Type II error; it is the probability of avoiding a Type II error. Because power is the probability of rejecting a false null hypothesis, any increase in Type II error rate consequently lowers power, whereas increasing Type I error rate increases power. This suggests that small α levels reduce power. One way to increase power is to be willing to accept a larger Type I error rate by increasing a priori the α level.

Sample size is also a critical factor in determining the power of a statistical test. The larger the sample size, the more likely our statistical test will be able to detect a real treatment effect. This occurs because larger sample sizes, if drawn appropriately, are more likely to be representative of the population and thus associated with smaller sampling error. A common misconception is that any increase in sample size provides a corresponding increase in power. Schmidt, Hunter, and Urry (1976) empirically demonstrated that the sample size needed to attain adequate power in validation research is substantially greater than most people believe.

Therefore, one limitation of using sample size to increase power is that we will often need a substantial increase in sample size to achieve the desired increase in power. Further, this substantial increase in sample size is generally costly and time-consuming for the researcher.

Finally, power is determined by effect size. Effect size is a standardized indication of the impact of the treatment effect. The effect size, for experimental two-group designs, indicates the difference between the treatment and control groups and depends on the means and variances of the two groups. The larger the effect size between the two experimental groups, the greater the power. Effect size is related to experimental design because the more error introduced into the experimental design (e.g., sampling error, measurement error, and the quality of the manipulation itself), the smaller the effect size and, therefore, the lower the power. Thus, the clever experimenter initially designs research to minimize as much extraneous error as possible, which will consequently improve power through its impact on effect size.

An understanding of power analysis will facilitate a researcher both in the study development phase and in the analysis and conclusions phase. In planning a study, a power analysis can be conducted a priori to determine the sample size needed to detect a given effect size. For instance, if we by convention set alpha equal to .05 and power equal to .80 (a guideline suggested by Cohen, 1988) and estimate a medium effect size, we can determine the sample size needed to meet those criteria. We can also conduct a post hoc power analysis to determine how powerful the study was (what level of confidence we can have in our results) or what minimum effect size could have been detected with a sample of the given size.

The reader is referred to Cohen (1988), Lipsey (1990), and Murphy and Myors (1998) for detailed discussions of power issues and instructions on conducting power analyses. There are also several power analysis software packages that can be purchased (e.g., Power and Precision and PASS 2002 are popular). Alternatively, a free power analysis Web site might suit your needs just fine. Check out

PC-Size (ftp://ftp.simtel.net/pub/simtelnet/msdos/ statstcs/size102.zip) and G*Power (www.psycho .uni-duesseldorf.de/aap/projects/gpower/index .html) or the UCLA power calculator (www.stat .ucla.edu/).

DEGREE OF RELATIONSHIP AMONG VARIABLES

The first category of research questions concerns degree of relationship. This refers to the association among variables and suggests some form of correlation or regression. For instance, a researcher might be interested in whether or not people who are satisfied with their jobs are also satisfied with their lives in general. This question would be analyzed with a correlation between measures of job satisfaction and life satisfaction. Other common analyses in this category include regression and chi-square contingency analysis, which were examined in Chapter 19 of the present volume. A useful extension of the basic linear regression approach is *canonical correlation,* which examines the relationship between multiple independent variables and multiple dependent variables. For instance, we might study the relationship between social economic status indicators (e.g., income, job level, occupational prestige, assets) and measures of perceived quality of life (e.g., job satisfaction, family satisfaction, contentment, feelings of generativity). The canonical correlation tells the researcher if there is a statistically significant relationship between the two sets of variables and what the nature of that relationship is. This is called a *canonical variate.* In bivariate or multiple correlation, there is one index of the particular relationship. In the canonical correlation extension, there may be multiple pairs of canonical variates indicating a more complex relationship among the numerous variables being studied. Bobko (1990), in his chapter on multivariate correlational analysis, covers canonical correlation in more detail and is a very readable resource. He notes that canonical correlation is actually the grandparent of most of the basic statistical tools with which you are familiar, such as simple and multiple correlation and regression; these are just special cases of canonical correlation.

Other useful resources include Stevens (2002) and Tabachnick and Fidell (2001). These sources provide both a conceptual understanding and the technical details of this analytic tool.

SIGNIFICANCE OF GROUP DIFFERENCES

Most experimental research is interested in the differences on some dependent variables (DVs) among individuals assigned to different conditions. Group differences, which form the second category of question, are also the focus of a great deal of field research, which often involves naturally occurring groups. In fact, the significance of group differences is one of the most frequent research questions. Dickter (Chapter 19) discusses some of the basic tests for mean differences between groups, such as *t*-tests, one-way ANOVAs and ANCOVAs, and factorial ANOVAs and ANCOVAs. A major focus of the current chapter is the multivariate extensions of these analytic strategies. By multivariate extensions, we are referring to studies that are interested in group differences on *multiple dependent variables.*

Hotelling's T^2

A developmental psychologist might be interested in comparing 10-year-old and 12-year-old children on multiple measures of cognitive functioning (e.g., an IQ test, a reading ability test, a series of Piagetian tasks, practical knowledge). These data could be analyzed by using *Hotelling's T^2,* which is the multivariate analogue of a *t*-test. Hotelling's T^2 tells the researcher whether the two groups differ on the DVs combined. These data could be analyzed by four separate *t*-tests, but the problem of *experimentwise error rate* would strongly suggest that this approach not be used. The error rate problem is simply that multiple tests inflate the Type I error rate. The DVs are likely to be related, which further exacerbates the Type I error rate problem. In other words, although the individual differences (i.e., the separate *t*-tests) were tested with an $\alpha = .05$, the experimentwise error rate as a result of the multiple tests might be .20 (see Keppel, 1991, for a detailed discussion of this issue). The researcher might think the α level is .05, but it has really been inflated to .20. Hotelling's T^2 avoids this problem by doing only one *t*-test on the combined DVs.

One-Way MANOVA

An industrial-organizational psychologist might be interested in how different leadership styles (transformational, transactional, or authoritarian) might influence multiple measures of performance (absence rates, coworker ratings of employee performance, quantity or quality of output). Because we have three groups in this example rather than two, Hotelling's T^2 is inappropriate. In the univariate sense, these data would be analyzed using ANOVA (rather than *t*-tests); but with multiple DVs, the analogue is MANOVA (multivariate analysis of variance). In particular, if we were only interested in the effect of leadership style on quality of performance, our knowledge gleaned from Chapter 19 would lead us to use a one-way ANOVA. Because we have multiple DVs, however, the analysis of choice here would likely be a one-way MANOVA.

MANOVA examines differences between two or more groups on two or more DVs combined. As in the previous example, in which we noted the problem of doing multiple *t*-tests and inflating our Type I error rate, the same problem would arise if we chose to do an ANOVA on each DV. Rather than taking this approach, the astute researcher avoids the problem of inflated Type I error rates and chooses the more appropriate analytic strategy MANOVA. There are other benefits of this approach. First, using multiple measures increases the scope of a research project (Spector, 1977) and allows the researcher to look at the *set* of measures as they represent an underlying construct, such as, in our example, performance (Bray & Maxwell, 1982). Second, using multiple measures allows the researcher to examine the relationships among the DVs and to determine how the independent variable relates differentially to those DVs.

MANOVA is a two-step process with the first step often called the *omnibus test,* meaning that it focuses on testing whether, overall, there are differences between groups on the combined DVs. This is analogous to the overall *F*-test in ANOVA. In our example, the omnibus test tells

us whether leadership style has an effect on performance. An answer in the affirmative to this question (i.e., we reject the null hypothesis of no difference) only provides a partial answer to the researcher. Usually, we want to know where those differences lie. This simple statement—where the differences lie—is typically the focus of the analytic approach, as well as the real crux of the researcher's interest. Therefore, the second step in the process is to conduct follow-up tests to examine these differences.

After finding a significant MANOVA result, there are a number of ways in which the researcher can examine where the differences lie. First, perhaps the most frequent approach used by researchers is to follow-up a significant MANOVA with univariate ANOVAs. For instance, we could conduct four separate ANOVAs to reveal the DVs on which the groups differ. Perhaps, the multivariate effect identified by the MANOVA is driven by group differences on absence rates and performance quantity only. This would be revealed by significant ANOVAs on these two DVs and nonsignificant ANOVAs on the other two DVs. The ANOVA tells us on what variables the groups differ, but it does not tell us which groups differ on these variables. If we only had two groups, this would not be an issue because the differences could only be between those two groups; however, because we have three groups, the researcher must further explore these differences with one of the available post hoc tests (see Keppel, 1991, for a comprehensive discussion of these tests) to determine which groups (1 vs. 2, 1 vs. 3, and 2 vs. 3) differ on absence rates, for example. Our choice of follow-up tests to a significant MANOVA should again be based on our research question (Spector, 1977). If the question has to do with testing a hypothesis or a theory regarding on which DVs the experimental groups differ, univariate ANOVA is the best approach.

A second common approach to following-up MANOVAs is to use *discriminant analysis* (DA), which specifies a linear combination of the DVs, which maximizes the separation between groups (Spector, 1977). Mathematically, it is helpful to conceive of DA as a special type of regression with group membership being the criterion variable. In this way, DA tells the researcher how well the data predict group membership. In our leadership example, we could examine how well the performance measures predict which leadership style individuals experienced. The discriminant coefficients are analogous to regression weights and reveal the relative contributions of the DVs to the maximum differentiating function. Spector (1977) suggests that using DA as a follow-up is appropriate if the researcher is interested in prediction and classification. Let us assume that our MANOVA was significant and, therefore, we conclude that leadership style affects performance. If we were interested in determining which DVs or what linear combination of the DVs differentiates among group members best, then DA would be a logical approach to answering this question. Although in this chapter we are viewing DA as a follow-up tool to MANOVA, we want to emphasize that DA is a major analytic tool that can also stand alone.

A MANOVA Example

We will present one example from the applied psychology literature to illustrate this approach. Abelson (1987) was interested in determining what variables could predict employee termination—turnover. He argued that individuals might leave for various reasons, which can be categorized in at least two ways. First, there are those who leave for reasons that the organization could not control (e.g., spouse gets another job in another location)—*unavoidable leavers.* Second, there are those who leave for reasons that the organization could control (e.g., employee finds a new job with better working conditions and better pay)—*avoidable leavers.* Finally, there are those individuals who do not leave—*stayers.* Abelson's hypothesis was that stayers would be very much like unavoidable leavers and that these two groups would differ significantly from the avoidable leavers. The rationale was that neither stayers nor unavoidable leavers really wanted to leave their jobs and certainly not because of anything about the organization. The avoidable leavers, however, were motivated by different issues to leave the organization.

Abelson (1987) conducted a study in an organization using nursing personnel. Among the variables of interest were age, marital status, job satisfaction, organizational commitment, job

tension, and perceptions of leaders' sensitivity. The MANOVA revealed a significant effect indicating that, as expected, the groups differed on the combined DV. Univariate ANOVAs were conducted to examine where the differences lie. In other words, on what variables did the groups differ? The univariates were significant for about half of the variables, including job satisfaction and organizational commitment. This indicates that the groups differed on these variables, but we do not know at this point which groups differ. The prediction was that unavoidable leavers would be similar to stayers, and these two groups would differ from avoidable leavers. Post hoc tests were used to uncover which groups differed. As predicted, for both job satisfaction and organizational commitment (as well as other variables), unavoidable leavers and stayers did not differ from each other, but both differed significantly from avoidable leavers, who were less satisfied and committed.

In addition to employing the univariate ANOVA approach, Abelson (1987) also employed DA to follow up the significant MANOVA in an attempt to "determine which of the variables best predict(s) membership in the stayers, unavoidable leavers, and avoidable leavers groups (p. 383)." The DA revealed that six of the variables were the best discriminators among the groups and that the analysis discriminated avoidable leavers from both stayers and unavoidable leavers. The DA had a hit rate of 80%, which means that the discriminant function (i.e., individuals' scores on the significant variables) classified 80% of the subjects into their correct groups. The results of the MANOVA, univariate ANOVAs, post hoc tests, and DA supported the researcher's a priori predictions. Results such as these can be used to identify the characteristics that separate (discriminate) the avoidable leavers from the other two groups. Organizational retention programs can then be targeted to address issues associated with turnover in the avoidable leavers group and thus have a positive impact on a costly organizational problem.

Other Extensions

We should point out that we have really only opened the door slightly to the world of analyses with multiple DVs. As with ANOVA, MANOVA can be extended to factorial designs with multiple independent variables. Similarly, MANCOVA is the multivariate analogue of ANCOVA and looks at the effect of an independent variable(s) on multiple DVs while controlling for other variables that are predicted to be related to the DVs. For instance, in our leadership example, tenure working for a particular leader could have served as a covariate in our one-way MANOVA design turning it into a one-way MANCOVA. Keep in mind that the primary objective of covariate designs is to reduce the error term by controlling for the relationship between the covariate and the DV (see Pedhazur & Schmelkin, 1991, for more discussion on the use and misuse of covariate analyses).

There are a great variety of statistics texts and quantitative journal articles that provide thorough treatments of the MANOVA and discriminant analysis techniques, including their advantages, disadvantages, and the procedures involved. The interested reader is referred to Bray and Maxwell (1982, 1985), Grimm and Yarnold (1995, 2000), Spector (1977), Stevens (2002), and Tabachnick and Fidell (2001) for more detailed information.

STRUCTURE

The last research question we cover in this chapter is that of the latent structure underlying a set of variables. Common analytic tools include *principal components analysis* and *factor analysis.* These approaches are often used for variable reduction purposes or to determine an underlying latent structure that defines the multiple variables. For instance, principal components analysis may be used to reduce subjects' responses to 100 items, assessing what they like about their jobs into a more workable number of dimensions, such as characteristics related to their supervisor, the work environment, their coworkers, what they do on their job, and the pay and benefits. These five dependent variable composites could then be used in various analyses in a much more useful and manageable way than the 100 original variables. Factor analysis may be used to examine whether a researcher's 10-item scale designed to measure

one construct—let's say self-esteem—really measures one construct or more than one. In other words, factor analysis might be used to demonstrate the validity of a particular scale, as well as the extent to which a particular construct is uni- versus multidimensional.

Path analysis is an extension of multiple regression that also deals with the structure of one's data. Path analysis is useful when researchers want to analyze certain causal structures among variables. For instance, Levy (1993) used path analysis to examine an a priori model that predicted relationships among self-esteem, locus of control, self-assessment, and attributions. The analysis is a straightforward extension of multiple regression with a few extra considerations. In general, each DV is regressed on every independent variable that is predicted to affect it. For instance, Levy (1993) predicted that self-assessment would be affected by self-esteem and locus of control, whereas attributions would be affected by self-assessment and locus of control. One multiple regression was conducted for each of these DVs. The resulting regression weights indicate the strength and direction of the relationships among the hypothesized variables. The predicted model can be examined for fit by recomputing the correlations among the variables and by using Q, a conventional fit index (see Pedhazur, 1982). If the model seems to fit the data well, the researcher can conclude that the data are consistent with the a priori causal model. Please note that this is not the same as saying that the path analysis *proves* causality (see Bobko, 1990). This latter statement cannot be made with any degree of certainty. The reader is referred to Pedhazur (1982) and Grimm and Yarnold (1995) for detailed discussions of the analytic procedures involved in path analysis.

One of the fastest growing analytic strategies in the social sciences is *structural equation modeling* (SEM). Pedhazur (1982, ch. 16) in his excellent introduction to SEM refers to this as a generic term for the various approaches to the analysis of causality (note that path analysis is one of these approaches). He also notes that more powerful approaches than path analysis such as LISREL (linear structural relations) have been developed. It is based on maximum-likelihood statistical theory rather than the more typical least-squares statistical theory, which is the foundation for simple and multiple regression.

Bobko (1990) provides one of the better summaries of LISREL when he notes that LISREL is a general combination and extension of path analysis—the structural aspect—and confirmatory factor analysis—the measurement aspect. In fact, in a frequently cited paper, Anderson and Gerbing (1988) suggested that LISREL analyses proceed via a two-step process. The first step is similar to factor analysis and is commonly referred to as testing the *measurement model.* After determining the latent constructs, the second step deals with the structural aspect as in path analysis and is referred to as testing the *structural model.* LISREL models deal with *latent variables,* or hypothetical constructs, and *manifest variables,* or indicators of the hypothetical constructs. For instance, an educational psychologist may be interested in the relationships among the following latent variables: social economic background, academic achievement, and career success. Let's assume that social economic background is measured by family income during formative years, per pupil expenditure in elementary school district, and occupational prestige of parents. Academic achievement could be measured by highest level of schooling completed, GPA, honors and awards, and rank in school. Finally, career success could be measured by income, occupational prestige, job level within organization, and peer ratings of individual's success. All of these specific measures represent indicators of the construct of interest. The extent to which these measures do represent the hypothesized constructs in the way predicted is a test of the measurement model. The structural part of the analysis tests whether the latent variables (as measured by the manifest variables) are related in the way predicted by the researcher. For instance, we might predict that social economic background is causally related to academic achievement and that both of these variables have direct effects on career success.

In summary, LISREL estimates the loadings of each indicator on its respective latent variable to provide information about the measurement model. In other words, are these good measures of each construct? If not, then the measurement model requires more work before testing the structural model. If the data indicate support for the measurement model, then the researcher proceeds to examine the structural model. LISREL then tests for the causal relations among the latent variables. Both the measurement model and the structural model should be tested for goodness of fit using one or more of the many fit indexes available. Again, this is a thumbnail sketch of this very complex and potentially useful procedure. In addition to Pedhazur (1982) and Joreskog and Sorbom (1993), for other good discussions of the general approach, the reader is directed to Bobko (1990), Byrne (2001), Hoyle (1995), Hu and Bentler, (1998, 1999), Kline (1998), Long (1983), and Pedhazur and Schmelkin (1991).

USING COMPUTERS IN ADVANCED STATISTICS

Using computer software programs to conduct data analysis has become the most convenient and prevalent approach in psychological research. There are myriad software programs available, as well as freeware that can be found on the Internet. Some of the more popular general packages include SPSS, SAS, SYSTAT, and MYSTAT. Each of these is very comprehensive, and you will probably find that one or more are available at your university under a site-licensing system. Check with the computer support staff at your university to get more information on the applications available. One freeware package called VISta allows you to import your data and view visual, graphic representations of your data. You can find VISta at http://forrest.psych .unc.edu/research/index.html. There are also several Internet sites where you can submit your data set and receive the statistical output of your choice. One example is NetMul, an online multivariate analysis system at http://pbil.univ-lyon1 .fr/ADE-4/NetMul.html.

EXERCISES

1. In 2004, the national average for the verbal subtest of the Scholastic Aptitude Test (SAT-V) was 508, with a standard deviation of 100. Imagine you are going to conduct a study looking at the effects of a preparation course on SAT scores and hypothesize that SAT scores of students taking the preparation course will be higher than average SAT scores. What is the minimum number of students you need in your study to have adequate power for this study? There are many Web sites on the Internet that will calculate sample size for the particular study characteristics specified in our example. To try it yourself, point your browser to www.stat.uiowa.edu/~rlenth/ Power/.Select "One Sample t test" from the options. "Sigma" is the standard deviation; enter 100. Let's suppose you predict the preparation course will increase SAT-V scores by 10% or 50 points. "True [mu-m0]" is the difference you are expecting; enter 50. Slide the power bar to .80 to indicate you want average power. What is the required sample size (n)? Click to delete the check mark in the two-tailed box, indicating a one-tailed test. What does this do to your required sample size? Change the alpha level to .01 instead of .05. What does this do to your required sample size?

2. Test your multivariate IQ. What statistical test would you use to analyze your data in each of the following studies?

A. In a study examining the impact of parent characteristics on childhood attachment style, children are classified into one of Ainsworth's (1978) three levels of attachment style: secure, ambivalent, and avoidant. Parent characteristics measured are ambient stress level, amount of social support, education level, and socioeconomic status.

B. In a follow-up study, researchers seek to classify children into one of the three attachment style categories (above) based on children's behavioral characteristics: amount of separation anxiety, attention-seeking behavior, temperament, and independent play.

C. A researcher wishes to test a model in which she expects certain triggers (unfair treatment, inequitable pay) will cause angry feelings in employees, and these feelings of anger will in turn cause angry behaviors and thoughts (yelling, rumination).

RECOMMENDED READINGS

We hope that this chapter has met our goal: to provide an overview of some of the common advanced statistical techniques used in the analysis of data, as well as some suggestions as to where to go next for additional useful information. Our discussion is certainly not exhaustive with respect to the different approaches available nor with respect to the statistical and conceptual details associated with the procedures covered. Throughout the text, we have referred the reader to other sources, some of which are advanced technical discussions and others which are more basic introductory discussions focusing on conceptual understanding. Some excellent sources to begin with are Grimm and Yarnold (1995, 2000) and Pedhazur and Schmelkin (1991). Grimm and Yarnold, for instance, provide chapters covering all of the techniques that we've described in this chapter and additional topics as well (cluster analysis, psychometrics). More advanced multivariate textbooks include Stevens (2002) and Tabachnick and Fidell (2001). These references are not exhaustive but should be an excellent way for students to take the next step in their attempt to familiarize themselves with these various techniques.

REFERENCES

Abelson, M. A. (1987). Examination of avoidable and unavoidable turnover. *Journal of Applied Psychology, 72,* 382–386.

Anderson, J., & Gerbing, D. (1988). Structural equation modeling in practice: A review and recommended two-step practice. *Psychological Bulletin, 103,* 411–423.

Bobko, P. (1990). Multivariate correlational analysis. In M. D. Dunnette & L. M. Hough (Eds.), *Handbook of industrial and organizational psychology* (Vol. 1, pp. 637–686). Palo Alto, CA: Consulting Psychologists Press.

Bray, J. H., & Maxwell, S. E. (1982). Analyzing and interpreting significant MANOVAs. *Review of Educational Research, 52,* 340–367.

Bray, J. H., & Maxwell, S. E. (1985). *Multivariate analysis of variance.* Beverly Hills, CA: Sage.

Byrne, B. M. (2001). *Structural equation modeling with AMOS: Basic concepts, applications, and programming.* Mahwah, NJ: Lawrence Erlbaum.

Cohen, J. (1988). *Statistical power analysis for the behavioral sciences* (2nd ed.). Hillsdale, NJ: Lawrence Erlbaum.

Grimm, L. G., & Yarnold, P. R. (Eds.). (1995). *Reading and understanding multivariate statistics.* Washington, DC: APA.

Grimm, L. G., & Yarnold, P. R. (Eds.). (2000). *Reading and understanding more multivariate statistics.* Washington, DC: APA.

Hoyle, R. H. (1995). *Structural equation modeling: Concepts, issues, and applications.* Thousand Oaks, CA: Sage.

Hu, L., & Bentler, P. M. (1998). Fit indices in covariance structure modeling: Sensitivity to underparameterized model misspecification. *Psychological Methods, 3*(4), 424–453.

Hu, L. & Bentler, P. M. (1999). Cutoff criteria for fit indexes in covariance structure analysis: Conventional criteria versus new alternatives. *Structural Equation Modeling, 6*(1), 1–55.

Joreskog, K., & Sorbom, D. (1993*). LISREL8: Structural equation modeling with the SIMPLIS command language.* Hillsdale, NJ: Lawrence Erlbaum.

Keppel, G. (1991). *Design and analysis: A researcher's handbook* (3rd ed.). Englewood Cliffs, NJ: Prentice Hall.

Kline, R. B. (1998). *Principles and practice of structural equation modeling.* New York: Guilford Press.

Levy, P. E. (1993). Self-appraisal and attributions: A test of a model. *Journal of Management, 19,* 51–62.

Lipsey, M. W. (1990). *Design sensitivity: Statistical power for experimental research.* Newbury Park, CA: Sage.

Long, J. S. (1983). *Covariance structure models: An introduction to LISREL.* Beverly Hills, CA: Sage.

Murphy, K. R., & Myors, B. (1998). *Statistical power analysis: A simple and general model for traditional and modern hypothesis tests.* Mahwah, NJ: Lawrence Erlbaum.

Pedhazur, E. (1982). *Multiple regression in behavioral research* (2nd ed.). New York: Holt, Rinehart & Winston.

Pedhazur, E., & Schmelkin, L. (1991). *Measurement, design, and analysis.* Hillsdale, NJ: Lawrence Erlbaum.

Schmidt, F. L., Hunter, J. E., & Urry, V. W. (1976). Statistical power in criterion-related validation studies. *Journal of Applied Psychology, 61,* 473–485.

Spector, P. E. (1977). What to do with significant multivariate effects in multivariate analyses of variance. *Journal of Applied Psychology, 62,* 158–163.

Stevens, J. (2002). *Applied multivariate statistics for the social sciences* (4th ed.). Mahwah, NJ: Lawrence Erlbaum.

Tabachnick, B. G., & Fidell, L. S. (2001). *Using multivariate statistics* (4th ed.). New York: HarperCollins.

21

CONDUCTING A META-ANALYSIS

HARRIS COOPER
JORGIANNE CIVEY ROBINSON
NANCY DORR

Literature reviews typically serve to summarize results of past studies, suggest potential reasons for inconsistencies in past research findings, and direct future investigations. There are two ways a review of a literature can be conducted: in the traditional narrative manner or by meta-analysis. The traditional narrative reviewer identifies articles relevant to the topic of interest, examines the results of each article to see whether the hypothesis was supported, and provides overall conclusions. Conclusions are typically left up to the individual reviewer. Traditional narrative reviews have been criticized because they easily allow the reviewer's biases to enter into the conclusions and because information in the original studies can be discarded unconsciously or inconsistently.

A meta-analysis has the same goals as the traditional review. A meta-analysis uses statistical procedures to combine the results of previous studies. One positive aspect of meta-analysis is its specific and transparent procedures for how the results of relevant studies are combined and how conclusions will be drawn.

The implications of quantitatively combining the results of studies rather than qualitatively drawing conclusions were explored in a study conducted by Cooper and Rosenthal (1980). They asked university professors and graduate students to examine seven studies that tested

whether females showed more persistence at tasks than males. Participants were randomly assigned to one of two conditions: (a) a traditional narrative review condition, in which participants "were asked to employ whatever criteria they would normally use" in drawing conclusions about the results of the seven studies (p. 443), or (b) a statistical review condition, in which participants were taught how to combine the results of the null hypothesis significance tests and effect sizes from the same seven studies. Statistical reviewers concluded that there was more support for the notion that females were more persistent than males and perceived a larger difference between females and males than did traditional narrative reviewers.

With the advent of meta-analysis and the rigorous standards for how literature is to be synthesized, literature reviewing has been elevated to a respected scientific endeavor in its own right. This chapter first explores the history of meta-analysis, focusing on the need for its development. Then the major meta-analytic procedures are described.

A BRIEF HISTORY OF META-ANALYSIS

The year 1904 witnessed the earliest known application of what today we call meta-analysis.

Karl Pearson (1904), having been asked to review the evidence on a vaccine against typhoid, gathered data from 11 relevant studies. For each study, Pearson calculated a recently developed statistic called the correlation coefficient. He averaged these measures of the treatment's effect across two groups of studies distinguished by the nature of their dependent variable. On the basis of the average correlations, Pearson concluded that other vaccines were more effective and, with political sagaciousness that transcends a century, counseled that "improvement of the serum and method of dosing, with a view to a far higher correlation, should be attempted" (Pearson, 1904, p. 1245).

In the decades following Pearson's original application of meta-analysis, the utility of combining results from primary studies became increasingly evident. As interest grew, meta-analysts developed more sophisticated techniques for analyzing and presenting data. For example, Ronald Fisher, an agricultural researcher, presented in his classic 1932 text, *Statistical Methods for Research Workers,* a test for combining *p*-values from statistically independent tests of the same hypothesis.

Although statistical techniques for meta-analysis had been developed, they were not widely implemented until the 1960s. This decade heralded increased interest in social issues and a proliferation of social scientific research (Chalmers, Hedges, & Cooper, 2002).

It was not until 1976, however, that Gene Glass coined the term *meta-analysis.* Interestingly, introduction of the term was accompanied by some of the most significant contributions to the field. In Cambridge, Massachusetts, Rosenthal and Rubin (1978) undertook a review of research studying the effects of interpersonal expectations on behavior in laboratories, classrooms, and the workplace. They found not 11 but 345 studies that pertained to their hypothesis. In Boulder, Colorado, Glass and Smith (1979) conducted a review of the relation between class size and academic achievement. They found not 345 but 725 estimates of the relation based on data from nearly 900,000 students. The same authors also gathered assessments of the effectiveness of psychotherapy. This literature revealed 833 tests of the treatment (Smith & Glass, 1977). Hunter, Schmidt,

and Hunter (1979), at Michigan State University and the U.S. Office of Personnel Management, uncovered 866 comparisons of the differential validity of employment tests for Black and White workers.

Each of these research teams drew the inescapable conclusion that the days of the traditional research review were over. They realized that the influx of personnel into the social and behavioral sciences at midcentury had had its intended effect. For some topic areas, prodigious amounts of empirical evidence had been amassed on why people act, feel, and think the way they do and on the effectiveness of psychological, social, educational, and medical interventions meant to help people act, feel, and think better. These researchers concluded that the traditional narrative review, involving the selective search for studies, the use of post hoc criteria to exclude studies from consideration, and the application of faulty cognitive algebra, simply would not suffice.

Largely independently, the three research teams rediscovered and reinvented Pearson's and Fisher's solutions to their problem. They were quickly joined by others. Among these were Richard Light and David Pillemer (1984), who prepared a text that focused on the use of research reviews in the social policy domain. Larry Hedges and Ingram Olkin (1985) provided the rigorous statistical proofs that established quantitative synthesis as an independent specialty within the statistical sciences. Robert Rosenthal presented an early catalog of meta-analytic techniques in 1984.

Cooper (1982) proposed that the research synthesis process be conceptualized in the same manner as original data collections. He presented a five-stage model for the integrative research review that paralleled primary research (see Table 21.1). This model presents research questions applicable to each stage of the process and can be used as a guide for both novice and experienced meta-analysts.

The stages include problem formulation, data collection or the literature search, data evaluation, analysis and interpretation, and public presentation. For each stage, Cooper codified the research question asked, its primary function in the review, and the procedural differences that might cause variation in synthesis conclusions.

Table 21.1 The Integrative Review Conceptualized as a Research Project

	Stage of Research				
Stage Characteristics	*Problem Formulation*	*Data Collection*	*Data Evaluation*	*Analysis and Interpretation*	*Public Presentation*
Research question asked	What evidence should be included in the review?	What procedures should be used to find relevant evidence?	What retrieved evidence should be included in the review?	What procedures should be used to make inferences about the literature as a whole?	What information should be included in the review report?
Primary function in review	Constructing definitions that distinguish relevant from irrelevant studies	Determining which sources of potentially relevant studies to examine	Applying criteria to separate "valid" from "invalid" studies	Synthesizing valid retrieved studies	Applying editorial criteria to separate important from unimportant information
Procedural differences that create variation in review conclusions	1. Differences in included operational definitions 2. Differences in operational detail	Differences in the research contained in sources of information	1. Differences in quality criteria 2. Differences in the influence of nonquality criteria	Differences in rules of inference	Differences in guidelines for editorial judgment
Sources of potential invalidity in review conclusions	1. Narrow concepts might make review conclusions less definitive and robust 2. Superficial operational detail might obscure interacting variables	1. Accessed studies might be qualitatively different from the target population of studies 2. People sampled in accessible studies might be different from target population of people	1. Nonquality factors might cause improper weighting of study information 2. Omissions in study reports might make conclusions unreliable	1. Rules for distinguishing patterns from noise might be inappropriate 2. Review-based evidence might be used to infer causality	1. Omission of review procedures might make conclusions irreproducible 2. Omission of review findings and study procedures might make conclusions obsolete

SOURCE: Cooper, H. (1982). Scientific guidelines for conducting integrative research reviews. *Review of Educational Research, 52,* 291–302. Copyright 1982. American Educational Research Association, Washington, DC. Reprinted by permission.

In addition, Cooper suggested that the notion of threats to inferential validity (such as internal and external validity), introduced by Campbell and Stanley (1966), expanded by Cook and Campbell (1979), and further refined in Shadish, Cook, and Campbell (2002), be applied to the evaluation of research synthesis. Cooper also stated the supposition underlying the efforts of all the research synthesis methodologists: that the second, and later, users of data must be as accountable for the validity of their methods as the original data gatherers.

Meta-analysts' ability to synthesize and draw causal inferences from large and unwieldy areas of primary research did not go unnoticed by policy makers and practitioners. By the late 1980s, meta-analysis had become a needed tool for making sense of massive amounts of data from individual studies (Chalmers et al., 2002). Perhaps for this reason, meta-analytic strategies have garnered wide interdisciplinary appeal. The use of the technique spread from psychology and education to medicine and public policy. Today, meta-analysis is an accepted and respected technique in the behavioral and social sciences, both theoretical and applied.

Procedures of Meta-Analysis

Searching the Literature and Coding Studies

Let us turn now to the more mundane issue of the procedures that constitute a present-day research synthesis. Suppose we enter the office of Dr. Polly C. Analyst, about to undertake a review of research assessing the effects of remedial education on the self-esteem of adolescents. In addition, suppose that Dr. Analyst has already completed her search for relevant studies. Her search strategy employed computer reference databases (e.g., PsycINFO), convention programs, the reference lists of reports, a search of related journals, inquiries to government agencies, and letters to active researchers (see Chapter 3 of this volume). Notice that in conducting her search for relevant studies, Polly attempted to uncover both published and unpublished reports. This is important because although there are many reasons for a report not to be published,

one reason is that the study failed to reject the null hypothesis (that is, the study did not find a statistically significant difference in self-esteem between participants who received remedial education and those who did not). If Polly did not include unpublished research in her meta-analysis, she would be likely to conclude that remedial education has a greater effect on self-esteem than if she included unpublished research. Thus, taking the results of unpublished research into account allows for a more accurate assessment of the relation between education and self-esteem.

Suppose further that Polly's search uncovered 20 reports that included relevant data testing the hypothesis that remedial education increases self-esteem. In glancing at the results of the 20 studies, Dr. Analyst notices that some studies suggested that individuals who received remedial education had higher self-esteem than individuals who did not, some studies showed no difference in self-esteem between individuals who received education and those who did not, and a few studies showed that individuals who received education had lower self-esteem than individuals who did not. Quite appropriately, she decides that she would like to explore potential reasons that the studies have different results. Polly further notes that the 20 studies use a variety of methods. She thinks about which characteristics of the 20 reports might affect the results of the study. She may wonder, for example, whether remedial education will affect the self-esteem of females and males differently, whether remedial education will affect students of varying ages differently, and whether the type or length of the educational program will affect self-esteem. Thus, Polly systematically extracts from the Method and Results sections of the reports information on each of the study characteristics she wants to include in the analysis. Polly also has another individual extract information from a sample of the 20 studies to determine the extent to which she accurately and reliably coded the information from the reports.

Vote Counting

Dr. Analyst's data collection is now complete. Next she must decide how to combine the results of the 20 studies to draw overall conclusions about remedial education's effectiveness. First, she could cull through the 20 reports, isolate those studies that present results counter to her own position, discard these disconfirming studies due to methodological limitations (e.g., no random assignment of participants to educational conditions), and present the remaining supportive studies as representing the truth of the matter. Such a research synthesis is not unheard of. Its conclusions, however, would be viewed with extreme skepticism. It would contribute little to the public debate.

As an alternative procedure, Polly could take each report and place it into one of three piles: statistically significant findings indicating that education is effective in improving self-esteem, statistically significant findings indicating that education is counterproductive, and nonsignificant finds that do not permit Polly to reject the hypothesis that education has no effect. She could then declare the largest pile the winner.

This vote-counting strategy has much intuitive appeal and has been used quite often; however, the strategy is unacceptably conservative. In research, it is typically accepted that the results of a study are statistically significant when the difference between conditions could have occurred purely by chance only 5% of the time or less (i.e., $p < .05$; see Chapter 11 of this volume on statistical power). In Dr. Analyst's review, if the null hypothesis is true and remedial education has no effect on self-esteem, then chance alone should produce, out of the 20 studies, only about one (5%) study falsely indicating that remedial education is effective; however, by dividing the 20 reports into three piles, the vote-counting strategy requires that a minimum 34% of findings (seven studies) be positive and statistically significant before the program is ruled the winner. Thus the vote-counting strategy could, and often does, lead to the suggested abandonment of effective programs and to the implication that resources have been wasted when, in fact, such waste has not occurred. In addition, the vote-counting strategy does not differentially weight studies on the basis of sample size: A study with 100 adolescents is given weight equal to that of a study with 1,000 adolescents. This is a potential problem because large samples are more likely to estimate the precise population value. Therefore, effect sizes from larger samples should be given more weight. Another problem with the vote-counting strategy is that the revealed impact of the treatment in each study is not considered: A study showing a slightly lower mean for the students who received remedial education as compared with students who did not is given weight equal to that of a study showing a much higher mean for students who received education as compared with students who did not. For these reasons, Polly may report in her meta-analysis the number of studies that fall into each pile, but she decides not to base her conclusions on these data alone.

Combining Probabilities

Trying to take these shortcomings into account, Polly next considers combining the precise probabilities of results in each study. Each of the 20 studies tested the null hypothesis (i.e., adolescents receiving education and not receiving education do not differ in self-esteem) by conducting a statistical test and examining its associated probability. To combine the probabilities of results for each study, Dr. Analyst would locate each test of the null hypothesis and extract the probability associated with it. She would then use one of several statistical formulas to generate a single probability that relates to the likelihood of obtaining a run of studies with these results, given that the null hypothesis is true. For example, Polly's results might show that the combined probability of obtaining the results of the 20 studies, assuming that education has no effect on self-esteem, is $p < .03$. Thus she could conclude that remedial education is related to higher self-esteem. Alternatively, if the combined probability of obtaining the results of the 20 studies was $p < .19$, Polly would conclude that there was not evidence to suggest that education is related to self-esteem.

The combining-probabilities procedure overcomes the improper weighting problems of the vote count. It has severe limitations of its own, however. First, whereas the vote-count procedure is overly conservative, the combining-probabilities procedure is extremely powerful. In fact, for treatments that have generated a large number of studies, rejecting the null hypothesis is so likely that testing it becomes a rather uninformative exercise; it is very rare that this procedure does not allow the meta-analyst to reject the null hypothesis and conclude that the treatment had an effect. For Polly, this means that if this were the only meta-analytic procedure she used, she would be very likely to conclude that education is related to self-esteem.

Effect Size Estimation

The combined probability addresses the question of whether an effect exists; it gives no information on whether that effect is large or small, important or trivial. Therefore, Polly decides "Does remedial education influence self-esteem?" is not really the question she needs to ask. Instead, she chooses to reframe her question as, "How much does remedial education influence self-esteem?" Polly's answer might be zero, or it might be either a positive or a negative value. Positive values typically indicate that the effect size is consistent with the meta-analyst's hypothesis. For example, if Polly's effect size was positive, this would mean that students receiving remedial education had higher self-esteem than those who did not. Alternatively, if her effect size was negative, this would mean that students receiving education had lower self-esteem than those who did not. Dr. Analyst can then use this effect size to assess whether education's benefits justify its costs. Further, she can ask, "What factors influence the effect of remedial education?" She realizes that the answer to this question could help her make sound recommendations about how to improve and target educational interventions.

Given her new questions, Polly decides to base her conclusions on the calculation of average effect sizes, such as Pearson's correlation coefficient. Because her research involves comparing a treatment group with a control group— that is, adolescents receiving and not receiving remedial education—she is likely to describe the magnitude of effect by calculating what is called a d index, or standardized mean difference (Cohen, 1988). The d index is a scale-free measure of the separation between two group means. It describes the difference between two group means as a function of their standard deviations. Figure 21.1 presents the results of three hypothetical studies in Polly's review.

In Figure 21.1A, education has no effect on adolescents' reported self-esteem; thus $d = 0$. In Figure 21.1B, the average adolescent receiving education has a self-esteem score that is four tenths of a standard deviation above that of the average adolescent not receiving education. Here $d = .40$. In Figure 21.1C, $d = .85$, indicating an even greater separation between the two group means.

Suppose for a moment that Polly's research did not compare two group means but instead explored the relationship between two continuous variables (e.g., suppose Polly wanted to investigate the relationship between high school grade point average and self-esteem). Instead of calculating a d index, she would use Pearson's product-moment correlation coefficient (i.e., r; see Chapter 19 of this volume). Unlike the d index, the r index is typically reported in the primary research report, and additional computation is not required to obtain effect sizes.

Once Polly has calculated a d index for each outcome in each study, she might next average all the d indexes, weighting them by sample size. This would tell her how big of a difference between the education and control condition exists for all 20 studies, on average. This average effect size ignores the characteristics of the studies, such as the sex makeup of the sample and the length of education program.

As a modern-day meta-analyst, Polly has access to many good software programs that will both calculate and combine effect sizes across studies. The use of such programs decreases both errors in effect size computation and time spent on the meta-analytic portion of research syntheses (Cooper, 1998). Both SPSS and SAS can be used to perform meta-analytic calculations. (The interested reader should refer to Lipsey and Wilson (2001) for helpful SPSS and SAS code.) Moreover, several statistical packages have recently been developed specifically for meta-analysis (e.g., Comprehensive Meta-Analysis, Borenstein, Hedges, Higgins, & Rothstein, 2005). Many of these programs can be downloaded from the Internet at no cost or up to several hundred dollars. The interested researcher need only enter the keywords "effect size" into any popular Web browser to view these options.

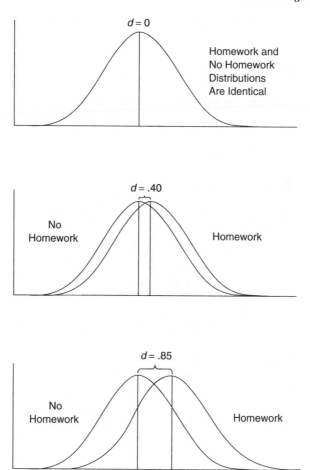

Figure 21.1   Three Hypothetical Relations Between Education and Control Groups in Self-Esteem
Experiments

Influences on Effect Sizes

Polly next may decide that she wants different estimates of the effect of education on self-
esteem based on certain characteristics of the
data. Recall that as Polly was glancing through
the results of the studies, she noticed they have
varying methodological characteristics. She can
test whether some of the differences in study
outcomes are due to different characteristics and
procedures of the original studies. To do this,
she calculates average *d* indexes for subsets
of studies that have characteristics in common.
For example, she might wish to compare the
average effect sizes for different educational
formats, distinguishing treatments that used
classrooms of students who needed remediation
from treatments that used one-on-one instruction.
Polly might also want to look at whether education is differentially effective for different types
of adolescents, say males and females. Her ability to broach these questions about whether such
variables are related to the size of education's
effect reveals one of the major contributions of
meta-analysis. Specifically, even if no individual study has compared different educational
formats or sex of adolescents, by comparing
results across studies, Polly's synthesis can give
a first hint about whether these factors would
be important to look at as guides to theory and
policy.

Next, Polly will statistically test whether
these factors are reliably associated with different
magnitudes of effect—that is, different average

d indexes (Cooper & Hedges, 1994; Hedges & Olkin, 1985). This is sometimes called a *homogeneity analysis,* and it is likely to provide the most interesting results of Polly's synthesis. Because effect sizes are imprecise, they will vary somewhat, even if they all estimate the same underlying population value. Homogeneity analysis allows Polly to test whether sampling error alone accounts for this variation or whether features of studies, samples, treatment designs, or outcome measures also play a role. Polly will group studies according to potentially important characteristics and test for between-group differences. If she finds that differences exist, her average effect sizes corresponding to these differences will take on added meaning and will help her make recommendations concerning whether, and especially which, educational programs should be continued for whom, when, and for how long. For example, Polly could conduct a homogeneity analysis to test whether studies with a 1-month educational program produced a larger effect of remedial education on self-esteem than studies with a 1-week program.

If the homogeneity analysis was significant, Polly could suggest that the differences in effect sizes between studies employing 1-month or 1-week programs were not due to sampling error alone. Polly then might calculate the average effect size (weighted by sample size) for 1-month programs to be higher than the average effect size for 1-week programs (e.g., $d = .55$ vs. $d = .05$, respectively). This would provide an initial hint that the length of the educational program is related to self-esteem and that perhaps longer programs are more beneficial.

The results of Polly's homogeneity analysis, however, do not permit her to make causal statements. That is, Polly cannot conclude that longer programs cause an increase in self-esteem. The reasoning behind this lies in random assignment: A meta-analyst cannot randomly assign studies to procedures. In research, unless the investigator randomly assigns participants to conditions (e.g., 1-week vs. 1-month programs), causality is very difficult to assess. Without random assignment, the possibility that a third variable is the true cause is always present. Nevertheless, Dr. Analyst's homogeneity analyses are still beneficial in summarizing past research and directing future research, especially if none of the original 20 studies examined the impact of program length.

Sensitivity Analysis

Before Dr. Analyst draws any conclusions from her meta-analysis, she should conduct a *sensitivity analysis.* A sensitivity analysis will enable Polly to answer the question, "What happens if some aspect of the data or the analysis is changed?" (Greenhouse & Iyengar, 1994). Polly realizes that her data and, as a result, the inferences that she will draw from them may be influenced by a host of factors including publication biases, data points that are statistical outliers, and other idiosyncratic characteristics of the data and assumptions she has made about them.

Testing for publication bias provides a good example of a sensitivity analysis. Although Polly has taken care to collect data from both published and unpublished sources, she most likely still does not have in her database the entire population of studies on her topic. The problem is that published studies are likely to have larger effect sizes than are unpublished studies (Lipsey & Wilson, 1993). In order to evaluate how such biases affect her distribution of effect sizes, Polly could create a *funnel plot* (Light & Pillemer, 1984). A funnel plot graphically depicts the sample size of studies versus the estimated effect size for the group of studies (Greenhouse & Iyengar, 1994). Funnel plots should ideally approximate the shape of the normal distribution; however, publication biases will restrict the range of the distribution, resulting in overrepresentation of studies in one tail of the distribution. Recently, researchers have developed a *trim and fill* statistical method that, through an iterative process, "fills-in" effect sizes from studies that were not represented in the data set (Duval & Tweedie, 2000). The trim and fill method is a nonparametric method that estimates missing effect sizes based on the normal distribution, expressed in the funnel plot. As such, it is relatively easy to understand and conduct. Knowing this, Polly could use the trim and fill method to correct her data for publication biases.

Polly could continue her sensitivity analysis by examining her distribution of effect sizes in different forms than the funnel plot. Specifically, she could prepare *stem-and-leaf plots* and *boxplots* to examine the distribution of standardized mean differences. Dr. Analyst could examine the *robustness* of her overall effect through removing any outlying effect size and comparing the result to the total effect with all studies included (Cooper, 1998).

CONCLUSION

In describing Dr. Analyst's pursuit of the perfect research synthesis, we have made her task appear simpler than it is. Polly will encounter missing information, coding ambiguities, correlated data points, and a host of other problems. How she chooses to handle these problems will influence the trustworthiness of her results and the value that others place on her conclusions. If, however, social science research is to contribute to rational decision making, then research synthesis is a most critical component in our methodological toolbox, and it needs to be held to the same standards of rigor and systematicity as the primary research on which it is based. Meta-analysis helps us meet these standards.

EXERCISES

Exercise 1. Vote Counting Scenario

When Polly was in graduate school, she began to work on a meta-analysis examining the influence of peer-mentoring programs on academic achievement for high school students. She searched all published issues of the major journals in education and was disappointed to find that 12 of the 20 studies that she retrieved reported that participation in peer-mentoring programs did not result in increased achievement. As a result, she abandoned the project.

Do you think that Polly made a wise decision? What, if any, mistakes did she make during her attempt to synthesize the relevant literature? What would you recommend that she do to improve her techniques?

Answer to Exercise 1.

Polly probably didn't make the best decision when she abandoned her project. First of all, her search strategy was not very broad. By only considering published studies in major journals in education, Polly greatly limited the scope and generalizability of her search. Secondly, Polly made her decision concerning the influence of peer-mentoring on achievement based on a vote-counting technique. She could improve her research synthesis by searching both published and unpublished studies. Moreover, she could improve her meta-analytic technique by calculating effect sizes for each study. Then, she could examine the difference between mean effect sizes across studies for the different peer-mentoring conditions.

Exercise 2. Calculation of the Standardized Mean Difference, *d*

Homework (Treatment group grades)	No homework (Control group grades)
97	88
88	90
92	91
89	80
78	78
98	92
94	95
79	80
80	95
92	78

Calculation of the d index is straightforward. The formula is

$$d = \frac{x_1 - x_2}{\dfrac{SD_1 - SD_2}{2}}$$

where x_1 and x_2 = the treatment and control group means; and

SD_1 and SD_2 = the average standard deviations of the two groups.

Using the data for the treatment and control groups presented in the table above, calculate the effect size for the influence of homework (treatment vs. control) on participants' class grades. Interpret this effect size.

Answer to Exercise 2.

Homework (Treatment group grades)	No homework (Control group grades)
97	88
88	90
92	91
89	80
78	78
98	92
94	95
79	80
80	95
92	78
$M = 88.70$	$M = 86.70$
$SD = 7.380$	$SD = 6.980$

$$d = \frac{88.7 - 86.7}{\dfrac{7.38 + 6.98}{2}} = \frac{2}{7.18} = .28$$

The effect size is $d = .28$. That is, on average, the mean homework grade for students in the treatment group lies .28 standard deviation above the mean of the control group.

RECOMMENDED READINGS

For more information on conducting a meta-analysis, we recommend starting with Cooper's *Integrating Research: A Guide for Literature Reviews* (1998). This text provides an overview of each step in the research synthesis process in addition to presentation of more general issues surrounding the use of meta-analysis. Additionally, we recommend Lipsey and Wilson's *Practical Meta-Analysis* (2001). This book presents helpful coding guide templates, formulae, and programming code for SPSS and SAS. For further information on more advanced meta-analytic issues, we recommend consulting Cooper and Hedges's *Handbook of Research Synthesis* (1994) and Hunter and Schmidt's *Methods of Meta-Analysis: Correcting Error and Bias in Research Findings* (2004). These texts offer detailed chapters on many issues central to modern meta-analytic theory, methodology, and practice.

REFERENCES

Borenstein, M., Hedges, L., Higgins, J., & Rothstein, H. (2005). Comprehensive meta-analysis (Version 2.1) [Computer software]. Englewood, NJ: BioStat.

Campbell, D. T., & Stanley, J. C. (1966). *Experimental and quasi-experimental designs for research.* Chicago: Rand McNally.

Chalmers, I., Hedges, L. V., & Cooper, H. (2002). A brief history of research synthesis. *Evaluation and the Health Professions, 25,* 12–37.

Cohen, J. (1988). *Statistical power analysis for the behavioral sciences* (2nd ed.). Hillsdale, NJ: Lawrence Erlbaum.

Cook, T. D., & Campbell, D. T. (1979). *Quasi-experimentation: Design and analysis issues for field setting.* Chicago: Rand McNally.

Cooper, H. (1982). Scientific guidelines for conducting integrative research reviews. *Review of Educational Research, 52,* 291–302.

Cooper, H. (1998). *Integrating research: A guide for literature reviews* (3rd ed.). Thousand Oaks, CA: Sage.

Cooper, H. (1998). *Synthesizing research* (3rd ed.). Thousand Oaks, CA: Sage.

Cooper, H., & Hedges, L. B. (Eds.). (1994). *Handbook of research synthesis.* New York: Russell Sage.

Cooper, H. M., & Rosenthal, R. (1980). Statistical versus traditional procedures for summarizing research findings. *Psychological Bulletin, 87,* 442–449.

Duval, S., & Tweedie, R. (2000). A nonparametric "trim and fill" method of accounting for publication bias in meta-analysis. *Journal of the American Statistical Association, 95,* 89–98.

Fisher, R. A. (1932). *Statistical methods for research workers* (4th ed.). London: Oliver and Boyd.

Glass, G. V., & Smith, M. L. (1979). Meta-analysis of research on class size and achievement. *Educational Evaluation and Policy Analysis, 1,* 2–16.

Greenhouse, J. B., & Iyengar, S. (1994). Sensitivity analysis and diagnostics. In H. Cooper & L. V. Hedges (Eds.), *The Handbook of research synthesis* (pp. 383–398). New York: Russell Sage.

Hedges, L. V., & Olkin, I. (1985). *Statistical methods for meta-analysis.* Orlando, FL: Academic.

Hunter, J. E., & Schmidt, F. L. (2004). *Methods of meta-analysis: Correcting error and bias in research findings* (2nd ed.). Thousand Oaks, CA: Sage.

Hunter, J. E., Schmidt, F. L., & Hunter, R. (1979). Differential validity of employment tests by race: A comprehensive review and analysis. *Psychological Bulletin, 86,* 721–735.

Light, R. J., & Pillemer, D. B. (1984). *Summing up: The science of reviewing research.* Cambridge, MA: Harvard University Press.

Lipsey, M. W., & Wilson, D. B. (1993). The efficacy of psychological, educational, and behavioral treatment. Confirmation from meta-analysis. *American Psychologist, 48,* 1181–1209.

Lipsey, M. W., & Wilson, D. B. (2001). *Practical meta-analysis.* Thousand Oaks, CA: Sage.

Pearson, K. (1904). Report on certain enteric fever inoculation statistics. *British Medical Journal, 2,* 1243–1246.

Rosenthal, R. (1984). *Meta-analytic procedures for social research.* Beverly Hills, CA: Sage.

Rosenthal, R., & Rubin, D. B. (1978). Interpersonal expectancy effects: The first 345 studies. *Behavioral and Brain Sciences, 3,* 377–386.

Shadish, W. R., Cook, T. D., & Campbell, D. T. (2002). *Experimental and quasi-experimental designs for generalized causal inference.* Boston: Houghton Mifflin.

Smith, M. L., & Glass, G. V. (1977). Meta-analysis of psychotherapy outcome studies. *American Psychologist, 32,* 752–760.

22

ARCHIVAL DATA SETS

Revisiting Issues and Considerations

BARBARA H. ZAITZOW
CHARLES B. FIELDS

WHAT ARE ARCHIVAL DATA SETS?

As different as experiments, surveys, and field studies may seem, they do have one common feature that distinguishes them from the methodological approach described in this chapter: Each involves the firsthand collection of data. Doing any of these three kinds of research entails gathering information, either by questioning or direct observation, from the people and groups who are the objects of study. Thus, the data originate with the research; they are not there before the research is undertaken.

By contrast, the fourth general strategy for doing social research is to make use of available data. Often, a social scientist can answer pressing research questions through the analysis of *secondary or archival data sets,* which are "published information . . . that were collected for some general information need or as a part of a research effort designed to answer a specific question" (Stewart & Kamins, 1993, p. 2). Two broad categories of existing records are (a) those collected as part of an agency's normal process of implementing a program (sometimes called agency records and/or utilization data) and (b) existing data such as surveys or reports completed by outside sources. Existing records may include information on number of program participants, participant characteristics, vital statistics, spending levels, income and poverty levels, resources acquired and spent, productivity, school dropout rates, test scores, divorce proceedings, and recidivism rates (Hatry, 1994).

Sources of this information can include governmental agencies at local, state, national, or international levels and nongovernmental organizations. Some governmental agencies gather data regularly (McKenzie & Smeltzer, 1997). Certain data collection is required by law (e.g., census, births, deaths, notifiable diseases), whereas other collection methods are voluntary (e.g., use of seat belts). Additionally, most programs are required to keep records on their participants and the resources expended (Rossi & Freeman, 1993). Various types of existing data can be obtained from published reports on the World Wide Web or from the actual agency records.

Archival data is considered a nonreactive data collection method, as the researcher does not come into contact with the subjects under investigation; thus, the potential error that may result from a researcher's activities on those studied is eliminated (Webb, Campbell, Schwartz, Sechrest, & Grove, 1981). Only through the efforts of primary data collection, however, do secondary data sets exist. Thus, the extent to which secondary data sets are affected by the methodology employed by the initial investigator is one of several issues to be addressed in this chapter. The purpose of this chapter is to provide an overview on the use of archival data sets for social science research.

CLASSIC STUDIES THAT UTILIZED ARCHIVAL DATA

Every literate community generates a considerable amount of statistical data on the behavior of its members. Although these data have been accumulated primarily for purposes of administration and historical description, social science researchers can make good use of them. The variety of such data is tremendous; it is limited only by the researchers' imagination. That imagination has found sources of data in letters and diaries, government and court records, and newspapers and magazines. Even tombstones and graffiti have been used as the raw material for social research.

One of the earliest studies to make use of official records—in this case, death records—was Emile Durkheim's classic work entitled *Suicide* (1897/1966). Durkheim, a founder of the sociological discipline, used existing records of approximately 26,000 reports from various countries to examine variation in rates of suicide between mechanical (small, rural) and anomic (large, urban) societies. Using statistics from official publications in several European countries, Durkheim related suicide rates to such variables as religion, season of the year, gender, and marital status. With these data, he rejected several hypotheses popular at the time, such as the notion that suicide was the result of mental illness and that suicide increased with the temperature. Ultimately, he arrived at his influential theory that a lack of social integration contributes to suicides. Supporting his theory were data showing that suicide rates were lowest when social ties were strong (as among persons who were married and members of religions that emphasize social cohesion) and highest when social ties were weak (as among the divorced and members of religions that emphasize individualism). Today, we may draw on the materials published by the U.S. Bureau of the Census in order to talk about trends in population growth and decline, or we may use world statistics gathered by the United Nations to study patterns in world economic change and development.

We may also study novels, songs, television programs, and other mass-media productions in order to better understand our society. We can delve into the past, using records kept by historical societies or the diaries and letters of pioneer mothers and fathers to ask questions about the differences between today's families and those of the last century. The path-breaking work of Terman's (1925) *Genetic Studies of Genius* at Stanford University—which followed some 1,600 gifted California children from 1922 to the present, in concert with several well-known longitudinal studies at the Institute of Human Development at the University of California, Berkeley—launched a life study approach to data archives that has enabled researchers to examine historical influences on the lives of people from different birth cohorts.

Data from available records were used in a series of studies by Ted Gurr in his attempts to explain the incidence and magnitude of violence in modern societies. Gurr (1968) systematically searched a number of sources such as the *New York Times* and *Africa Digest* for "strife events" in 114 nations and colonies during the period 1961–1965. These events were supplemented by reports of incidents of strife in the *Annual Registrar of Events in Africa* and *Hispanic-American Report,* as well as country and case studies. All of these are publicly available reports. Based on Gurr's analysis, support was found for the hypothesis that the greater the difference between value expectations and value capabilities (what people are actually able to receive), the greater the magnitude of civil strife. Relative deprivation was found to increase as the state of the economy declined or as restrictions on political liberties increased. Part of the ingenuity of this study stemmed from the imaginative use of aggregate data to test a hypothesis on a cross-national basis. Today, with more data being collected on an international basis, comparative research on a variety of topics is possible.

WHEN SHOULD YOU CONSIDER USING ARCHIVAL DATA?

Archival data sets are, for the most part, longitudinal data. There are many methods that can be used to collect longitudinal data, which means there are also many types of research, including trend studies, panel studies, and vent history or duration data (Bijleveld, Mooijaart, van der Kamp, & van der Kloot, 1998; Buck, Gershuny, Rose, & Scott, 1994; Davies & Dale, 1994; Ruspini, 2000; Taris, 2000). The benefit of using archival data is that it can be used in a multitude of ways and for a variety of research questions. Sharing of research data is an important part of the scientific method because it reinforces open scientific inquiry; allows for verification, refutation, and refinement of original findings; and ensures more efficient use of financial and other research resources. Although open access to all kinds of social and behavioral science data is important, sharing data from longitudinal studies is especially valuable and necessary for addressing many research questions. Sequences of events and patterns of change that occur within the individual, the family, or some other unit can be studied most effectively through the use of longitudinal data.

Long-term longitudinal data of substantial duration are difficult, if not impossible, for researchers to collect during their own lifetimes. Few individual investigators are able to make the kind of time investment that is required and still meet their career goals. By making the data available and accessible to others, the process of data sharing allows individuals to conduct longitudinal studies in a few years that would otherwise require prohibitive time commitment.

There are several reasons why a researcher may want to analyze someone else's data. One is a desire to check on the accuracy of another's results, either by directly replicating the analyses or by using somewhat different analytic techniques that may, for example, statistically control for a confounding variable not accounted for in the original analyses. Sharing data for this kind of re-analysis is required by scientific conventions that promote objectivity in research.

Another reason for using existing data is to address original research questions without collecting new data. Often this involves analyzing data that were collected but never analyzed by the original investigators. The economics of doing research are improved in this case, both for the original investigator (because information is not wasted) and for the secondary analyst (because the costs of data collection are decreased or avoided).

Finally, and perhaps most important, a researcher may have questions that are very difficult to answer adequately without using existing data. These questions include the effects of social change or historical events on the lives of the people who experience them, the relationships between very early development and outcomes in middle and late adulthood, and the early causal factors that explain the development of relatively rare outcomes, such as alcoholism or extraordinary achievement in adulthood.

Aggregate data can be used to focus on the social forces that affect crime. For example, to study the relationship between crime and poverty, criminologists make use of Census Bureau data on income and the number of people on welfare and single-parent families in an urban area and then cross-reference this information with official crime statistics from the same locality (Blau & Blau, 1982; Currie, 1998; Reiman, 1998). The use of these two sources of archival data provides enhanced understanding about the effect of overall social trends and patterns on the crime rate. Archival data may also be used to compare socioeconomic characteristics of different ethnic or racial groups over 10-year intervals to determine if gaps in their socioeconomic status are widening or declining; or one may examine the suburbanization of industrial activity since World War II and analyze its impact on minority unemployment in the central cities.

Social scientists have at their disposal data from public opinion polls, which are conducted and disseminated on a regular basis. Many survey organizations, such as the American Institute for Public Opinion (which conducts the Gallup polls), the Roper Organization, and Louis Harris and Associates, have conducted literally hundreds of polls over the past few decades. Data from these and similar polls are particularly useful for studying social change and habits. So extensive are the data provided in the various censuses that opportunities for secondary analysis seem to be limited only by the imagination of the researcher.

Disadvantages

Secondary analysis is very closely related to survey analysis (see Goddard & Villanova, "Designing Surveys and Questionnaires for Research," Chapter 8). The basic difference between survey research and secondary analysis is that, in the latter, the data have been collected by someone else for some other purpose. This means that the researcher has little control over the nature of the data or the data collection process. As a result, it is sometimes difficult to formulate appropriate operational definitions because the data have not been collected in the appropriate form. Emile Durkheim's 19th-century study of suicide illustrates some of the dangers of this approach. He relied on official death records to investigate suicide rates among various types of people, but he had no way to check how many accidents were incorrectly classified as suicides or what numbers of suicides were recorded as accidents or deaths due to some other cause. Thus, let the researcher beware of distortions.

Questions may have been phrased and presented to respondents in a way not exactly suited to the current researcher's goals, or the subjects who responded may not have been the ones the researcher would have chosen. "Careful attention must be given to what information actually was obtained in a particular study" (Stewart & Kamins, 1993, p. 23). Knowledge of the methodology employed during the data collection procedure (e.g., sample characteristics, response rates, interview or survey protocol, measurement instrument, coding forms) is necessary to ensure the validity and generalizability of conclusions based on the use of secondary data sources.

Depending on the source, existing data may not be in the format you require. For example, it may not be specific to your geographic location (e.g., the data was collected in New York City, but you are conducting a study in a small Kansas community) or it may be in an overly aggregated form (e.g., you want to break participants out by their specific grade level, but the statistics you are utilizing only report information for elementary students, middle school students, and high school students) (Hatry, 1994; Kettner, Moroney, & Martin, 1990).

Perhaps the major shortcoming of census data in particular for social science research is that many variables of interest to social scientists are not reported in the censuses. For example, no information is collected about sentiments, attitudes, values, or beliefs. Missing or incomplete data will affect the overall accuracy of the information (Hatry, 1994). Researchers interested in social-psychological studies must, therefore, look elsewhere for secondary sources of data or conduct their own field studies or experiments.

"Secondary data are, by definition, old data" (Stewart & Kamins, 1993, p. 6). Census publication delays, for example, will affect the temporal boundaries from which measurements are taken, results are obtained, and generalizations put forth. Concepts may not have been defined and measured in the same way over time or across sources (Hatry, 1994). This will affect the reliability and comparability of the information (O'Sullivan & Rassel, 1995; Rossi & Freeman, 1993). One common example is the use of race or ethnic categories. Some studies may describe only ethnicity, whereas others may mix race and ethnicity. Similarly, if you are using archival data to study changes in Americans' premarital sexual behavior, results will have to be interpreted in light of several sociohistorical events. Clearly, the reasons for older Americans waiting until marriage are qualitatively distinct from more recent respondents' concerns that "the first time may result in a death sentence via HIV/ AIDs." In both scenarios, the responses may appear quite celibate in nature yet for very different reasons! Again, one must be alert to these sociohistorical issues when using archival data sets (Gergen, 1973). Obviously, we are dealing with a trade-off here; the usefulness of the data must be balanced against the ease with which they can be obtained. Therefore, whenever researchers use information collected by others, they must interpret the data with care and in a way suitable to their goals.

Advantages

On the other hand, it can be argued that secondary analysis frees researchers from the responsibility and the time and expense of collecting and coding their own data. The use of archival data sets enables social scientists with low budgets to undertake research that might otherwise be impossible (O'Sullivan & Rassel, 1995). Furthermore, sampling and measurement error in U.S. censuses, for example, are among the lowest of all sources of survey data. To mitigate these errors, Bureau of Census personnel review enumerators' work, verify the manual coding and editing, check the tabulated figures, and utilize statistical techniques, such as ratio estimation of sample data, to control totals in the complete count. Through such efforts, errors in the printed reports are usually kept at an acceptably low level so that secondary analysis of these data will not generally yield misleading results.

What makes archival data particularly useful for secondary analysis is that most variables are available, not only cross-sectionally (at one point in time) but also on a longitudinal basis (at a number of different occasions). Thus, the researcher is able to focus on research outcomes rather than collection activity. This also enables researchers to measure particular social relationships and examine their historical trends. For example, criminologists make extensive use of official statistics— especially the Uniform Crime Reports prepared and distributed by the Federal Bureau of Investigation—concerning the frequency of various crimes in the United States, yet they are always on guard against distortions in these statistics. We know, for example, that many crimes are not reported to the police (e.g., illegal drug use); and to make this problem more complex, the rate of reporting varies according to the type of crime. Homicides are very likely to come to the attention of police, whereas rapes have traditionally been underreported. One attempt to correct for this discrepancy entails researchers collecting their own data to check the accuracy of official crime statistics. The value of available data is clearly enhanced if we have some idea of how accurate they are. Moreover, the use of multiple sources of information may be the best strategy to overcome some of the problems that may be present in secondary data.

ARCHIVAL DATA ACCESSIBILITY ISSUES

On a more practical or applied level, additional considerations must be weighed in your decision to use archival data: (a) Will the data be transferable to your computer system? (b) Will the documentation, that may(not) be provided, be sufficient to carry out the analyses? (c) Do you have the expertise and patience to deal with conflicts arising from differing levels of aggregation, classification schemata, and appropriate software to facilitate analyses?

In their work with archival data, Elder, Pavalko, and Clipp (1993), see the following themes recurring:

1. Archival data are never precisely what one wants or expects. Given this, the investigator is challenged to do what is possible, given time and resources, in shaping the data according to needs.

2. The data at hand often reflect the perspectives of the original investigators, as expressed in research questions, data collection procedures, and analytic techniques.

3. Longitudinal data archives do not guarantee life-record or longitudinal data analysis. Cross-sectional data entries and storage are far more common than temporal records of information on people's lives, and often these cross-sectional records have to be converted to a life-record format.

4. [These] studies can draw on quantitative and qualitative data and analysis. Effective use of both kinds of data requires careful planning to permit their application to identical topics or problems.

5. The rationale for using archival data should be based on strengths of the data. It should not be defended through attempts to disarm or ignore the weaknesses. (p. 11)

Careful consideration of these points is necessary to determine the usefulness of archival data for your particular research question. In order for the data to be usable, you must know exactly what you are dealing with.

It is no trivial matter to access and link data from large complex databases. Often the researcher has to make assumptions about what data to combine and which variables are appropriately aggregated into indexes. Perhaps more important, when you use data collected by others, you often don't know what problems occurred in the original data collection. Large, well-financed national studies are usually documented quite thoroughly, but even detailed documentation of procedures is often no substitute for direct experience collecting data. Moreover, additional challenges exist.

As noted by Silver (2000), although the introduction of advanced information and communication technologies has allowed researchers to understand the physical and natural worlds, further understanding of the social, economic, and political world will be driven by the ability to gather and analyze more data and information, particularly longitudinal in character, and to connect that data together in multidisciplinary, cross-national, and sophisticated ways. Here, barriers still remain. These barriers can be categorized around the issues of access, linkage, confidentiality and nonresponses, missing topics, and funding.

Access

Despite electronic access to archives, many researchers still have difficulty getting the data they need. One problem is that electronic data dissemination is still in its early stage of life, and there are many kinks to work out. We have all experienced frustrations with the Web and its quirkiness. Licensing costs and intellectual property considerations continue to constrain accessibility. Lag times in data depositing in archives are another problem. Data documentation is sometimes not what it should be.

Governments are also reluctant to divulge their data to researchers. Restrictions are placed on access to many countries' administrative data, particularly microdata at the individual level. Often, they are restricted to officials of statistical offices, or if they are available, they must be used within a statistical office (Silver, 2000).

Linkage and Comparability

Although there are enormous amounts of data, the difficulty has been linking them together in such a way that meaningful statistical analysis of particular phenomena can be conducted.

The comparability problem is acute, especially with international data sets. Most databases are written in the language of the data owner, especially in the case of social survey outputs. Translation programs may eventually solve this problem, but reading election polls in Danish remains a barrier for most people. Data may simply be incompatible because variables are examined in slightly different ways. Different surveys ask dissimilar questions to get at the same issues. The Survey of Income and Program Participation (SIPP) asks questions somewhat differently from the Current Population Survey and also somewhat differently from the Panel Study on Income Dynamics. If information is not being categorized in the same way in different countries, then researchers may be comparing apples and oranges (Silver, 2000).

Confidentiality and Nonresponses

Social science research often requires obtaining extensive, sensitive data on individuals and organizations. As such, social scientists need to protect their subjects against privacy invasions and to inform them about what is going to happen to the information they provide. Those who collect and/or use archival data sets must be attentive to issues related to informed consent of subjects, identifiers, and protecting confidentiality at the individual as well as institutional level (Silver 2000). These topics have been the subject of much debate and judicial intervention.

We also know that the number of people refusing to respond to survey questionnaires is climbing (Groves & Couper, 1998). A good survey researcher now has to budget sufficiently for a larger number of call-backs to reach the desired response rate. Yet, at the same time, people are allowing the government to draw blood from them in government health surveys. Is it the impersonal phone call that sounds too much like another telemarketing spiel versus the friendly government worker assuring you of confidentiality that makes the difference here?

Missing Topics

There is clear agreement that more longitudinal studies are the key to answering important questions for social policy. The capability to have data across a person's life cycle, as they do in Denmark for twins, would be immensely valuable. As the population ages, how children learn and how people use their time are areas for deeper exploration. Current plans and studies—along with new tools to study subjects (e.g., Geographic Information Systems (GIS) and remote sensing)—will add more improved data to examine and evaluate social phenomena, along with more confidentiality considerations (Silver, 2000).

Funding

Finally, it must be acknowledged that funding of social science research is a political venture, and funding has been withheld for various data collection agencies in the past. The question arises, where does the funding come from to support all these great plans for improved data collection and dissemination? Although government funding for the social and behavioral sciences has remained fairly steady, funding may be suddenly cut or reduced so that research dependent on future series may have to be dropped (Silver, 2000).

SOURCES OF ARCHIVAL DATA

As you are probably aware, thousands of surveys have been conducted in recent decades by college- and university-based researchers, private organizations and corporations, and various government agencies. Most of these surveys have resulted in computerized data archives, many of which are available to researchers. Access to information collected by the government is free. Reports can be obtained from the agency that collects the data, from a library that is a U.S. government depository for government documents (e.g., many college and university libraries and large public libraries), or on the World Wide Web.

There are currently three main sources of existing data: (a) various public and private data archives, (b) the U.S. Census and related sources, and (c) published or broadcast media suitable for content analysis. The following discussion(s) will focus on the first category, as it encompasses numerous data sources that typify already collected data.

PUBLIC AND PRIVATE DATA ARCHIVES

Many college professors conducting research are willing to share their data with others whose research interests are slightly different from their own. In fact, some do this on a regular basis through organizations such as the Henry A. Murray Research Center of Radcliffe College, which serves as a "national repository for data in the fields of psychology, psychiatry, sociology, anthropology, economics, political science, and education" and contains much useful information for secondary analysis (Elder et al., 1993, p. 83). Similarly, the Inter-university Consortium for Political and Social Research (ICPSR) is a national organization in which most major universities participate.

Murray Research Center

Founded in 1976, the Murray Research Center: A Center for the Study of Lives is a national repository for social and behavioral science data on human development and social change, with special emphasis on the lives of American women. Data housed at the Murray Center are made available to qualified scholars and researchers for secondary analysis, replication, and sometimes follow-up studies. Many of these studies include in-depth interviews or, at the very least, some open-ended survey questions. The research center makes it a priority to acquire data for their collection that have not been exhaustively analyzed, that contain qualitative or interview data, or that are longitudinal in design. Although the sharing of qualitative data is more unusual and in many ways more complicated than the sharing of quantitative data, qualitative data permit researchers to look at the data in innovative ways and allow for restructuring old data for new questions. Perhaps a few examples will ignite the reader's imagination to think outside the box.

Roberto (1993; Roberto & Stansis, 1994) conducted a follow-up study of the participants in Traupmann's McBeath Institute Aging Women Project. The original study, conducted in 1978–1979, examined many aspects of the lives of older women. Interview questions covered family status, health, work history, relationship equity, major life changes, life satisfaction, organizational affiliations, and more specific topics such as "winter as a life stress" and "the meaning of aging." In the follow-up study, Roberto recontacted 109 of the original participants to examine stability and change in interaction patterns between older women and their close friends over time. Using telephone interviews and a mailed questionnaire, she also examined the extent to which the life situations of older women (income, health, psychological well-being) influence their relationships with close friends. Data were gathered on 78 friendships mentioned in the 1978–1979 data and still in existence in 1992. The follow-up resulted in the finding of a pattern of stability in emotional qualities of the friendships from 1978–1992 but change with respect to other aspects of the relationships in terms of recreational activities, lifestyles, and ways to connect. Health changes proved to have a significant impact on changes in relationships. Without the open-ended material in the original study, Roberto would not have been able to examine such personal data (1993; Roberto & Stansis, 1994).

In another example, Parker and Aldwin (1997) used two longitudinal data sets, both of which included multiple cohorts, to study the extent to which personality change is developmental (age related) or cohort specific. They examined age, cohort, and period effects in both personality (gender identity) and values. The data sets were chosen on the basis of the variety of comparisons they permitted and the availability of relevant measures and open-ended material for content coding. Their analyses provided consistent support for differential impacts of age, cohort, and period on personality and values. "Whereas personality change (in this case 'masculinity' and 'femininity') is clearly an effect of developmental processes, changes in value orientation are clearly the result of changing socio-historical norms and opportunities"

(p. 102). Although this study made use mostly of precoded computer data, some content coding was made possible by open-ended questions about life values.

These are but a few examples of possibilities for research using data that already exist. These examples show the importance of preserving and making available qualitative as well as quantitative data. Archival qualitative data afford the possibility of creating new prospective studies from old without having to wait for the issue of interest to emerge as the data are collected over many years. This approach also makes it possible to study topics that might not have been brought to the attention of researchers and/or policymakers when the original study was initiated. Moreover, the value of adding new waves of data to existing longitudinal data or making a cross-sectional study into a longitudinal one while adding new findings and new causal inferences also renders the data more useful for new research. Finally, although there are few good examples, the value of using multicohort designs for illuminating developmental patterns related to age, period, and cohort effects cannot be underestimated.

Inter-university Consortium for Political and Social Research

Founded in 1962 as a partnership between the University of Michigan's Survey Research Center and 21 research universities around the country, the Inter-university Consortium for Political and Social Research (ICPSR) currently has a membership of 500 colleges and universities in the United States and Canada and several hundred additional institutions around the world. Thousands of data sets are available to researchers and students at ICPSR member institutions. The ICPSR archive receives, processes, and distributes computer-readable data on phenomena occurring in over 130 countries. The content of the archive extends across economic, sociological, historical, organizational, social, psychological, and political concerns. Further, ICPSR offers training in quantitative methods to facilitate effective data use. To ensure that data resources are available to future generations of scholars, ICPSR preserves data, migrating them to new storage media as changes in technology warrant. In addition, ICPSR provides user support to assist researchers in identifying relevant data for analysis and in conducting their research projects. Data and supporting documentation are available at no (or nominal) cost through member institutions; nonmembers may also obtain ICPSR data, but it can be more expensive.

The ICPSR also provides various kinds of assistance in using their data sets effectively. For example, assistance in selecting equipment and data storage media, identification of appropriate software, and utilization of computer networking technology are available to members through written materials, special workshops and seminars, and telephone consultation. A major concern is to assist in the use of new technologies that "are radically changing the potentialities for social science instruction and research (Interuniversity Consortium for Political and Social Research [ICPSR], 1994, p. viii).

A few of the many data sets available from the ICPSR that may be of interest to psychology students include the following:

Americans View Their Mental Health, 1957 and 1976 (ICPSR 7949)

Containing the data from a nationwide survey sponsored by the National Institute of Mental Health, the survey ($N = 4,724$; 262 variables) focused on the areas of marriage, parenthood, employment, leisure time, motives for achievement and power, and general social relationships. In addition, extensive information was collected in the areas of help seeking, the readiness of people to use professional help, referral mechanisms, and evaluation of help received.

Marital Instability Over the Life Course (U.S) (ICPSR 3812)

A six-wave panel study (1980, 1983, 1988, 1992–1994, 1997, 2000), this data collection attempts to identify the causes of marital instability throughout the life course. A national sample ($N = 2,033$; 5,057 variables) of married individuals 55 or younger were interviewed by telephone in 1980, 1983, 1988, 1992–1994 (adult offspring included), 1997 (adult offspring included), and 2000 (adults and adult offspring). Questions dealing with economic resources, employment, children, and life goals were asked to determine links that tend to cause divorce.

Survey of Parents and Children, 1990 (ICPSR 9595)

Conducted by the National Commission on Children, this collection was designed to assess the attitudes, well-being, and life circumstances of American families. The sample consisted of 1,738 parents and 929 children aged 10–17, and households with Black and Hispanic children were oversampled.

Project TALENT Public Use File, 1960–1976 (ICPSR 7823)

This project was a longitudinal survey assessing the personal and educational factors promoting or inhibiting the development of human talents. In 1960, 400,000 (subsample of 4,000 included here) students in grades 9–12 were surveyed on interests, plans, family background, cognitive skills, and so forth. Follow-up surveys conducted 1 year, 5 years, and 11 years after graduation produced information regarding post–high school education, family development, plans and aspirations, and life satisfaction.

Other Government Existing Data Sources

Peterson (2005) provides an excellent overview of the federal agencies from which data may be obtained:

Some of the major statistical agencies of the federal government who collect, compile, analyze, and publish data for general use that may be of interest to you include (a) the National Center for Health Statistics, (b) the National Institutes of Health, (c) the Bureau of the Census, (d) the Bureau of Labor Statistics, (e) the National Center for Education Statistics, and (f) the Bureau of Justice Statistics. Statistics from these federal sources can be applied to your own geographic location. For example, if you know the prevalence of a problem is 2.5 per 100, and there are 26,000 individuals in your area, you can compute that the prevalence in your area is 600 (26,000 × .025).

Below is a description of information available from the federal government. Similar information is available from state and local governments.

The National Center for Health Statistics (NCHS, www.cdc.gov/nchs/) is one of the seven divisions of the Centers for Disease Control and Prevention (CDC; O'Sullivan & Rassel, 1995). This agency obtains vital statistics and collects information through a variety of national surveys, including the National Health Interview Survey (NHIS), the National Health and Examination Survey (NHANES), the Youth Risk Behavior Surveillance System (YRBSS), and the Health Records Survey. Basic vital statistics are published in the Monthly Vital Statistics Report: Provisional Data and in annual volumes of the Vital Statistics of the United States (www.cdc .gov/nchs/products/pubs/pubd/vsus/vsus.htm). Data from the NHIS and NHANES are published in the Vital and Health Statistics series (http://www.cdc.gov/nchs/nvss.htm). Information from the YRBSS appeared in the Morbidity and Mortality Weekly Report in 1995.

The National Institutes of Health (NIH, www.nih.gov) is the "flagship of federal government health websites, and the gateway for many other public health websites" (www.nih.gov). NIH includes 24 separate institutes, centers, and divisions, including the National Institute on Aging, the National Institute on Alcohol Abuse and Alcoholism, the National Institute of Child Health and Human Development, the National Institute on Drug Abuse, and the National Institute of Mental Health. Although a great deal of public health information can be accessed from this site, it is important to point out that much of the material is quite technical.

The Bureau of the Census (www.census.gov) is part of the U.S. Department of Commerce. Information collected by this agency is typically an excellent source of demographic information because the bureau is concerned with producing high-quality data that can be compared across time (O'Sullivan & Rassel, 1995). The Statistical Abstract of the United States has been published since 1878 and provides a summary of statistics on the social, political, and economic organization of the United States. A new edition is published in January and includes data for up to 2 years prior to the current data. Information from several surveys is included in this publication. A brief description

of various surveys conducted by the Census Bureau follows (McKenzie & Smeltzer, 1997):

- The Decennial Census of Population and Housing. The Bureau takes a census of the United States every 10 years to obtain information on population, income, employment, family size, education, type of dwelling, and other social indicators.

- The Current Population Survey. This is a monthly survey of households conducted by the Bureau of Labor Statistics and the Bureau of the Census to gather population and labor force information. The Census Bureau examines only the population data and produces the Current Population Reports. The data usually represent approximately 60,000 households.

- The Survey of Income and Program Participation. The Census Bureau and the Social Services Administration created the SIPP to collect monthly information on income, employment, and receipt of government assistance. This shows the effect of federal assistance on recipients and on the level of federal spending. Approximately 30,000 households are included. Each household participates for 2.5 years, with data being collected once every 4 months, thus only 25% of the households are contacted every month.

The Bureau of Labor Statistics (BLS, http://stats.bls.gov/) is an independent national agency that collects, analyzes, and disseminates statistical data on employment and unemployment, prices and living conditions, compensation and working conditions, and productivity and technology. The BLS releases information on labor force participation from the Current Population Survey in its monthly report on the nation's employment and unemployment rates.

The National Center for Education Statistics (NCES, http://nces.ed.gov/) is part of the U.S. Department of Education. The purpose of this agency is to collect and report "statistics and information showing the condition and progress of education in the United States and other nations in order to promote and accelerate the improvement of American education" (http://nces.ed.gov/). Some of the major surveys conducted by NCES are Early Childhood Longitudinal Study, High School and Beyond, National Adult Literacy Survey, National Household Education Survey,

Private School Survey, and Schools and Staffing Survey.

The Bureau of Justice Statistics (BJS, www .ojp.usdoj.gov/bjs) is part of the U.S. Department of Justice. This agency collects information on crimes reported to the police, including juvenile justice statistics. The Web site contains links to statistics from the FBI and other federal agencies, to international crime and justice statistics, to other crime statistics Web sites, and to the Office of Juvenile Justice and Delinquency Prevention. (Peterson, 2005, Obtaining Existing Data From Outside Sources, ¶ 1–6)

STEPS IN THE RESEARCH PROCESS

The procedure for using existing records will vary somewhat depending on the type and source of the information. In looking for an optimum fit between your research questions and the archival data, the following steps are suggested:

Step 1: Problem Specification

When conducting secondary analysis, research questions are often less specific than when conducting research in the more traditional methods. Often the data themselves dictate what questions can be asked and how to ask them. The first thing to do is to identify what you know about your topic, as well as what you want to know.

Step 2: Search for Appropriate Data

Always keep in mind that not all information collected from secondary sources is equally reliable or valid. You must evaluate the data carefully to see if it is indeed appropriate for your needs. Stewart and Kamins (1993, p. 17–30) identify six questions that should be asked when evaluating the data you want to use:

1. What was the purpose of the study?

2. Who collected the information?

3. What information was actually collected?

4. When was the information collected?

5. How was the information collected?

6. How consistent is the information with other sources?

Remember that these may not be the only questions that will come up when searching for the data for your study. The authors suggest keeping an attitude of "healthy skepticism" (p. 31) when using secondary sources; other constraints may exist as well. Access to the data may be limited, for example. Sometimes the original collector (or owner) may require approval before allowing use of data. Hence, some general guidelines for working with agency records and existing data may prove helpful (Hatry, 1994, as cited in Peterson, 2005):

Before actual data collection begins:

(a) Make friends with staff who collected the data. If you are asking for information from people you do not know, getting to know these individuals early can be beneficial throughout the process.

(b) Try to work with the staff most familiar with the records. Ask about possible problems, such as changes in the way concepts were defined, problems in getting the information, and reliability and validity problems. This will tell you what information you will be able to obtain and will help you decide how to handle problems that may arise.

(c) If you ask the agency to provide information instead of requesting access to their files, you can make the task easier for staff by providing advance notice, putting your request in writing, providing clear descriptions of the information you need, and indicating why the information is needed; however, remain open to alternatives that may be suggested.

(d) Obtain samples of the data formats and definitions before you actually compile your data to see what information is available. This will help you decide whether to sacrifice some of the desired information, to obtain information not currently in the desired form, or to accept the data as it is. (Peterson, 2005, Obtaining Data From Agency Records, ¶ 1–4)

Step 3: Preparation of Research Proposal

Preparation of the research proposal for secondary analysis is very similar to that of other types of research. Organization of research proposals or reports will vary by the specifications of the audience (e.g. university professor vs. professional journal). A comprehensive literature review of existing theoretical and empirical work that is of relevance to the research problem at hand will result in criticisms of past efforts as well as the discovery of new frontiers that beckon for inquiry. It is during the preparation of the research proposal that the information provided by others will assist you in selecting a research methodology (i.e., developing measurement techniques, deciding on relevant samples, analytic strategies) and avoiding pitfalls noted in previous efforts. As with any research methodology, the advantages of the data collection strategy are weighed against the disadvantages.

Step 4: Initial Analysis of Archival Data; Recasting Data

Once you decide on what data to use, then you must determine how to use it. More often than not, the data as it was originally measured will not be entirely suitable for the researcher's current needs; it sometimes must be reformulated for your specific purposes. This reformulation, sometimes called recasting, is a process in which some variables may be recategorized and those with inadequate data may be eliminated altogether (McCall & Appelbaum, 1991).

The following are advisable during this data collection phase (Hatry, 1994, as cited in Peterson, 2005):

> Identify the periods of time and geographical areas that apply to each piece of information collected. This information may be necessary if adjustments need to be made or if discrepancies need to be explained when writing your report.
>
> (a) Decide how to handle missing or incomplete information for each item of interest.
>
> (b) Check for illogical and inconsistent data and try to obtain the correct information.
>
> (c) Have staff who initially collected the data verify it, if they are able and willing.
>
> (d) Thank the staff for assisting.
>
> (e) Provide necessary cautions in your report. Be sure to indicate how any problems with the data may have affected your findings. (Peterson, 2005, Obtaining Data From Agency Records, ¶ 6–10)

Step 5: Analysis

Obviously, the methods used to analyze data must fit the question(s), the measures, and the characteristics of the original sample. But many times, questions do not get asked unless the researcher knows how to answer them statistically (McCall & Appelbaum, 1991, p. 916).

CONCLUSION

Social science, in all its guises, is practical knowledge for society's sake. The disciplines that constitute the social sciences seek to provide answers to questions of pressing concern, or questions that we think should be of pressing concern, to the general public—issues related to, perhaps, democracy, equality, justice, physical and/or psychological health, life satisfaction, peace, prosperity, violence, or virtue. The trick is to make social science speak to problems that we care about without sacrificing the rigor that qualifies it as a science.

Although one can list the ideals of research, real-life situations often force social scientists to settle for something that falls short of the ideal. Consequently, the typical dilemma that social researchers confront is either not to study what they want to study or to do so under less than ideal conditions. Researchers' choice of methodology is dependent on available resources. For example, although they prefer to conduct a survey, they may find that finances will not permit it and instead turn to the study of documents or utilize an already collected data archive. Each method is better for answering some questions than for others. If you wish to study the causes of revolution in an underdeveloped country, you don't necessarily need to become a participant observer among the guerillas. You might be able, instead, to use existing documents and records to relate revolution to such factors as poverty.

Archival data provide an efficient, cost-effective, and timely way for researchers to pursue important theoretical and policy-related questions about a variety of issues. Perhaps the greatest scientific value of archival data lies in the potential for replication by other researchers. Confidence in the validity of a relationship increases as it can be reproduced in a variety of settings. And, as Traugott (1990) notes,

The resulting data may lend themselves to other analyses that were never anticipated by the original researchers. A secondary analysis effort may arise because a researcher has a different set of theoretical interests or reconceptualizes the problem. Or it may result from the accumulation of data in an archive. Multiple data sets, each originally collected for a different purpose, may take on new analytical utility based upon their possible combinations or a series of complementary analyses which none of the principal investigators could have contemplated. (p. 146)

More researchers are working with better data than would be available if they had to organize and administer their own data collection projects. And they are devoting more of their effort to analysis than to the necessarily time-consuming administrative tasks associated with managing large-scale data collection projects. Although care must be taken in reviewing the principal investigator's decisions about conceptualization and operationalization, secondary analysis has increased research opportunities and, hence, has resulted in an extension of our understanding of a multitude of topics and issues. And that is exactly what science needs more of—imaginative, and sometimes daring, research conducted in an imperfect world under less than ideal conditions. This is what it is all about. The application of research methods takes us beyond common sense and allows us to penetrate surface realities so that we can better understand social life.

ADDITIONAL SOURCES OF STATISTICS ON THE INTERNET

- The U.S. Department of Education's Educational Resources Information Center (ERIC) has links to sources of demographic data on educational achievement, general demographic data, and school demographic data. (www.accesseric.org/)
- The University of Michigan Documents Center has information on agriculture, business and industry, consumers, cost of living, demographics, economics, education, energy, environment, finance and currency, foreign economics, foreign governments, foreign trade, government finances, health, housing, labor, military, politics, science, sociology, transportation, and weather. (www.lib.umich.edu/govdocs/)
- CYFERNet (www.fedstats.gov), the Cooperative Extension System's Children, Youth and Family Information Service, also has links to various children, youth, and family statistics and demographics.
- FedStats (www.fedstats.gov) is known as a one-stop-shopping site for federal statistics. Although over 70 agencies in the U.S. federal government produce statistics of interest to the public, visitors to this site currently have access to statistics from 14 of these agencies. Other agencies will be added as the site develops; however, a list of all agencies is accessible to help point you toward additional sources of information.
- The Centers for Disease Control and Prevention (www.cdc.gov) Web site contains links to scientific data, studies, laboratory information, health statistics, and to the CDC's individual centers, institutes, and offices.
- The Institute for Research on Poverty (IRP) (www.ssc.wisc.edu/irp/) at the University of Wisconsin-Madison publishes a newsletter three times per year called *Focus*. This newsletter includes articles on poverty-related research and issues. Although the publication can be ordered (free of charge) in print form, articles are also available at IRP's Web site.
- The Children's Defense Fund (www.childrens-defense.org) is a private, nonprofit organization supported by foundations, corporation grants, and individual donations. The Web site includes state-by-state data on key indicators that measure aspects of children's lives.

ANNOTATED BIBLIOGRAPHY

Peterson (2005) provides a comprehensive listing of eight useful resources:

1. Baj, J. and colleagues. (1991). *A feasibility study of the use of unemployment insurance wage-record data as an evaluation tool for JTPA. Report on project's phase 1 activities.* (Research Report Number 90-02).

This is a feasibility study of the use of unemployment insurance wage-record data as an evaluation tool for JTPA (available from EDRS). This report discusses the use of state unemployment insurance wage-record data to assess the effectiveness of Job Training Partnership Act (JTPA) programs. It discusses several issues associated with the use of existing records: coverage, accuracy, timeliness, and confidentiality.

2. Federal Interagency Forum on Child and Family Statistics (1997). *America's children: Key national indicators of well-being.* Available on the Web at www.childstats.gov/ac2000/ac00.asp

This report is the result of collaboration by several government agencies that collect and report data on children. It describes population and family characteristics and contains information on key indicators of children's well-being: economic security (poverty and income, food security, housing problems, parental employment, and health insurance), health (prenatal care, infant mortality, low birth weight, immunizations, activity limitation, child mortality, adolescent mortality, teen births, and a summary health measure), behavior and social environment (cigarette smoking, alcohol use, substance abuse, and victims of violent crime), education (difficulty speaking English, family reading to children, early childhood education, math and reading proficiency, high school completion, detached youth, and higher education), and child abuse and neglect. There is also a discussion of the sources and limitations of the data presented.

3. Hernandez, D. J. (1995). Changing demographics: Past and future demands for early childhood programs. *The Future of Children, 5*(3).

This article describes how demographic changes among American families from the mid-1800s to the present have influenced the demand for early childhood care and educational programs.

4. Hernandez, D. J. (1997). Child development and the social demography of childhood. *Child Development, 68,* 149–169.

This article describes historic and current trends and statistics regarding the demographic characteristics and environments of children. The information can be used by individuals to compare their study populations to the general population of children. It also includes an appendix with questions to measure the demographic characteristics and environments of children.

5. National Commission for Employment Policy. (1992). Using unemployment insurance wage-record data for JTPA performance management (available from EDRS, ERIC Document Reproduction Service No. 347296).

This report discusses the potential use of unemployment insurance wage records to track the employment and earnings experiences of participants in programs of the Job Training Partnership Act (JTPA). It is an example of how to use existing records or share data. One section of the report describes the data itself, the data-sharing experience, confidentiality issues, and issues involved in data sharing, such as costs and data accuracy.

6. O'Sullivan, E., & Rassel, G. R. (1995). *Research methods for public administrators* (2nd ed.). White Plains, NY: Longman.

Chapter 9 in this book ("Secondary Data Analysis: Finding and Analyzing Existing Data") provides a very detailed description of the use of secondary data. It discusses strategies for identifying, accessing, and evaluating the quality of existing data and describes the general content of major U.S. Census Bureau population surveys and vital records.

7. Record exchange process: A set of records for handicapped students in vocational education (available from EDRS, ERIC Document Reproduction Service No. 231961).

This article describes a process for the sharing of records by agencies.

8. Soriano, F. I. (1995). *Conducting needs assessments: A multidisciplinary approach.* Thousand Oaks, CA: Sage.

This book discusses needs assessments from the initial stages of planning and developing (methods and measures) to evaluating and reporting findings. Examples and exercises are included. (Peterson 2005, Annotated Bibliography, ¶ 1–8)

EXERCISES

1. List (at least 3 each) the advantages and disadvantages of secondary data analysis in social research. Continue by identifying a problem that would be helpful to the field of psychology that you could possibly investigate through an established database. State how you would find and access the needed data.

2. Describe an example of a research project that would combine archival data with some other method of collecting data. Continue by stating how you would use these different approaches to augment one another. Discuss how this might this combined approach bolster your findings and conclusions.

3. Using the internet, search for articles dealing with archival research and use these resources identified to prepare a powerpoint presentation on the major strengths and weaknesses of archival data sources when conducting social research.

4. Reliability and validity problems often emerge when using agency records for a research project. Using the problem identified in 1. above, list reliability and validity (at least 5 each) problems that a research could possibly encounter.

5. Maxfield and Babbie explain that criminal justice record keeping is a social process. Explain what they mean by this and how it influences the production of agency records. Illustrate your answer with a criminal justice example.

RECOMMENDED READINGS

Barrett, R. E. (1994). *Using the 1990 U.S. Census for Research.* Thousand Oaks, CA: Sage.

Brooks-Gunn, J., Phelps, E., & Elder, G. H., Jr. (1991). Studying lives through time: Secondary data analyses in developmental psychology. *Developmental Psychology, 27,* 899–910.

Davis, J. A., & Smith, T. W. (1991). *The NORC General Social Survey.* Newbury Park, CA: Sage.

Elder, G. H., Jr. (1992). Studying women's lives: Research questions, strategies and lessons. In S. Powers (Ed.), *Studying women's lives: The use of archival data.* New Haven, CT: Yale University Press.

Hedrick, T. E., Bickman, L., & Rog, D. (1993). *Planning applied research.* Newbury Park, CA: Sage.

Jacob, H. (1984). *Using published data: Errors and remedies.* Newbury Park, CA: Sage.

Terman, L. M. (1925). *Genetic studies of genius* (Mental and Physical Traits of a Thousand Gifted Children, Vol. 1). Stanford, CA: Stanford University Press.

Terman, L. M., & Oden, M. H. (1959). *Genetic studies of genius* (The Gifted Group at Mid-Life: Thirty-Five Years of Follow-Up of the Superior Child, Vol. 5). Stanford, CA: Stanford University Press.

Young, C. H., Savela, K. L., & Phelps, E. (1991). *Inventory of longitudinal studies in the social sciences.* Newbury Park, CA: Sage.

REFERENCES

Bijleveld, C. C. J. H., Mooijaart, A., van der Kamp, L. J. Th., & van der Kloot, W. A. (1998). Structural equation models for longitudinal data. In C. C. J. H. Bijleveld et al. (Eds.), *Longitudinal data analysis: Designs, models and methods* (pp. 207–268). London: Sage.

Blau, J., & Blau P. (1982). The cost of inequality: Metropolitan structure and violent crime. *American Sociological Review, 47,* 114–129.

Buck, N., Gershuny, J., Rose, D., & Scott, J. (Eds.). (1994). *Changing households: The BHPS 1990 to 1992.* Colchester, UK: ESRC Research Centre on Micro-Social Change, University of Essex.

Currie, E. (1998). *Crime and punishment in America.* New York: Henry Holt.

Davies, R. B., & Dale, A. (1994). Introduction. In A. Dale & R. B. Davies (Eds.), *Analyzing social and political change: A casebook of methods.* London: Sage.

Durkheim, E. (1966). *Suicide.* New York: Free Press. (Original work published in 1897)

Elder, G. H., Jr., Pavalko E. K., & Clipp E. C. (1993). *Working with archival data.* Newbury Park, CA: Sage.

Gergen, K. (1973). Social psychology as history. *Journal of Personality and Social Psychology, 26,* 309–320.

Groves, R., & Couper, M. (1998). *Non-response in household interview surveys.* New York: Wiley.

Gurr, T. R. (1968). A causal model of civil strife: A comparative analysis using new indices. *American Political Science Review 62,* 1104–1124.

Hatry, H. P. (1994). Collecting data from agency records. In J. S. Wholey, H. P. Hatry, & K. E. Newcomer (Eds.), *Handbook of practical program evaluation* (pp. 374–385). San Francisco: Jossey-Bass.

Inter-university Consortium for Political and Social Research (1994). *Guide to resources and services, 1994–1995.* Ann Arbor, MI: Author.

Kettner, P. M., Moroney, R. M., & Martin, L. L. (1990). *Designing and managing programs: An effectiveness-based approach.* Newbury Park, CA: Sage.

McCall, R. B., & Appelbaum M. I. (1991). Some issues of conducting secondary analysis. *Developmental Psychology 27*(6), 911–917.

McKenzie, J. F., & Smeltzer, J. L. (1997). *Planning, implementing, and evaluating health promotion programs: A primer* (2nd ed.). Boston: Allyn&Bacon.

O'Sullivan, E., & Rassel, G. R. (1995). *Research methods for public administrators* (2nd ed.). White Plains, NY: Longman.

Parker, R., & Aldwin, C. (1997). Do aspects of gender identity change from early to middle adulthood? Disentangling age, cohort, and period effects. In M. Lachman & J. James (Eds.), *Multiple paths of midlife development* (pp. 67–107). Chicago: University of Chicago Press.

Peterson, D. (2005) CYFERNet Evaluation (University of Arizona). Retrieved May 31, 2005, from http://ag.arizona.edu/fcs/cyfernet/cyfar/Exisrec5.htm

Reiman, J. (1998). *The rich get richer and the poor get prison* (5th ed.). Boston: Allyn&Bacon.

Roberto, K. A. (1993). Friendships of older women: Changes over time. (Final Report to the Henry A. Murray Research Center at the Institute for Advanced Study, Harvard University). Greeley: Gerontology Program, University of Colorado.

Roberto, K. A., & Stansis, P. I. (1994). Reactions of older women to the death of their close friends. *Omega, 29*(1), 17–27.

Rossi, P. H., & Freeman, H. E. (1993). *Evaluation: A systematic approach* (5th ed.). Newbury Park, CA: Sage.

Ruspini, E. (2000, Spring). Longitudinal research in the social sciences. *Social Research Update, 20.* Retrieved May 2, 2005, from www.soc.surrey.ac.uk/sru/SRU28.html

Silver, H. J. (2000, March). *Data needs in the social sciences* [keynote address]. Presented at the Columbia University Conference on Information and Democratic Society: How to Represent and Convey Quantitative Data, New York.

Stewart, D. W., & Kamins M. A. (1993). *Secondary research: Information sources and methods.* Newbury Park, CA: Sage.

Taris, T. W. (2000). *A primer in longitudinal data analysis.* London: Sage.

Terman, L. M. (1925). *Genetic studies of genius* (Mental and Physical Traits of a Thousand Gifted Children, Vol. 1). Stanford, CA: Stanford University Press.

Traugott, M. W. (1990). Using archival data for the secondary analysis of criminal justice issues. In D. L. MacKenzie, P. J. Baunach, & R. R. Roberg (Eds.), *Measuring crime: Large-scale, long-range efforts.* Albany: State University of New York Press.

Webb, E. T., Campbell, D. T., Schwartz, R. D., Sechrest L., & Grove, J. B. (1981). *Nonreactive measures in the social sciences.* Boston: Houghton Mifflin.

PART V

RESEARCH WRITING

23

WRITING IN APA STYLE

Why and How

ROBERT F. CALDERÓN

JAMES T. AUSTIN

The importance of communicating research findings through publication cannot be overemphasized within science. Valuable research findings, if not communicated, may fail to influence science and society. Scholarly communication (Hills, 1983) ensures that the results of research are not isolated from other researchers and information users. The functions served by the review-publication process include conveying information, defining the field, setting quality standards, certifying individual merit, storing information, contributing to intellectual life, and protecting the public. Undergraduate and graduate students are often asked to prepare lab and research reports. Writing graduate and undergraduate research (theses and dissertations) is an early step in learning to communicate research findings. Thus, writing is a component of a researcher's higher-order repertoire at all career stages!

Writing for scientific audiences differs from other writing styles taught in schools (Lannon, 1988; Sides, 1989; Woodford, 1967). Therefore, students of psychology can have difficulties in acquiring this skill. Realizing this difficulty and wishing to standardize communication within the psychological research community, the American Psychological Association, or APA, requires a specific format and style for researchers to follow in preparing research reports, grants, or other communications (APA, 2001). This style has been evolving for over 60 years (Anderson & Valentine, 1944). Although this style may seem alien as you start to learn it, it is a standard format that helps to transmit conceptual arguments and empirical results in a logical and concise manner (Budge & Katz, 1995). Additionally, it is a format that has been adopted in areas outside of psychological research (e.g., education, military research), so it is all the more important for you to become familiar with it. At the same time, though, there have been critiques of scientific writing (Blakeslee, 2003; Richardson, 1994). Proper scientific writing is critical to ensuring your research findings are adequately communicated to your target audience.

This chapter addresses basic requirements for format and style defined by the latest edition of the APA *Publication Manual* (2001). We begin by discussing the different parts of the empirical research report. APA format and word processing technology are then integrated into the chapter, given the increasing importance of the computer in publication (APA, 2001; Standera, 1987; Wright, 1987). Last, an appendix is included that provides a meta-template for preparing and evaluating draft manuscripts with respect to their match to the *Publication Manual*. Note that in this chapter we are treating writing stylistically rather than substantively. Other chapters in this handbook cover the topics of preparing drafts (Peterson, Chapter 24), revising manuscripts (Nagata & Trierweiler, Chapter 25), and interactions during the editorial process. In addition, Becker (1986), Runkel and Runkel (1984), and Jones (1976) focus on scientific and technical writing.

Writing in APA style and format is not equal to writing well, although both share elements of self-discipline. The *Publication Manual* provides advice within a dual framework of specificity and sensitivity (APA, 2001, p. xxvi). *Specificity* is the standard that research be described in sufficient detail to permit replication. *Sensitivity* is the standard that language be free from bias against societal groups. Specific recommendations for reducing language bias include choosing an appropriate level of specificity, being sensitive to labels and labeling processes, and acknowledging the contributions of all participants (APA, 2001). Additionally, the choice of precise words, avoidance of ambiguity, order and sequence of ideas, and consideration of the reader are additional guidelines. Although these are useful global recommendations, writing and how to do it better are best treated by other sources, listed near the end of this chapter. One tested method for improving writing style and substance is to practice. For example, when considering a research topic as a novice researcher, you might prepare miniproposals (2–3 pages) to help automate the components of this skill. These types of skills, in turn, can assist in such activities as winning research-related grants and contracts (Borkowski & Howard, Chapter 30 of this handbook).

A researcher may be interested in producing several types of documents. The *Publication Manual* identifies empirical, literature review, theoretical, methodological, and case study categories of manuscripts. It is unlikely that you, as a research assistant, would be asked to prepare the latter two types of manuscripts. These are typically prepared by more experienced researchers who have been studying a certain topic area over time. Therefore, the empirical manuscript, which describes a study or set of studies, is the primary focus of this chapter.

COMPONENTS OF THE EMPIRICAL MANUSCRIPT

Manuscripts generally consist of three parts: front matter, body, back matter. *Front matter* consists of the title page and abstract. The *body* of the empirical manuscript consists of the Introduction and the Method, Results, and Discussion sections. *Back matter* includes supporting material, such as the references, notes, tables and figures, and appendixes. Not all of these back matter elements will be required for every manuscript, but it is useful to have a working knowledge of each part and to refer to the *Publication Manual* for more detailed descriptions. Additionally, there may be subsections within the four major parts of the body (e.g., the Method section may have subsections for participants, apparatus/measures, and procedures). Although all three parts are necessary to ensure your research findings are adequately presented, the bulk of your research report will be contained within the body. Therefore, we describe each of the components within the body in greater detail below.

Introduction

The introduction informs the reader of the specific problem under study and how that problem is related to prior research. In writing the introduction, you should attempt to answer four questions for the reader: (a) What is the point of the study? (b) What is the relation of the study to previous work? (c) What is the rationale that links the study and the research design? and (d) What are the theoretical limitations of the study? The most difficult part of writing the introduction is to develop explicitly the logical connection between your research question(s), the work in the literature, and your research design. You need to clarify these matters for the reader as you write.

The introduction section typically begins with a short summary of the research to be discussed. This describes why the research is important and focuses on what specifically you intend to examine. This is then followed by a concise, yet thorough review of the relevant research. The thing to realize in this section is that an exhaustive review of the literature is not necessary. Rather the review should contain enough information (both seminal and current research) to provide a framework for your research and a rationale for why you are studying what you are studying.

Writers should list hypotheses or research questions at or near the end of their introductory section. Hypotheses are *specific* predictions about expected results, whereas research *questions* are general and indicate an exploratory focus. A separate heading might be used for this section of the introduction, and justification for each hypothesis might be placed in the text immediately before or after the statement of hypothesis. Each hypothesis should contain enough detail to explain the specifics about what you are attempting to discuss via the study. The hypotheses should be tied to previous research yet contain enough original thought in order to further research.

In sum, the introduction gives readers a method of judging whether the purposes of the study are related to the empirical literature. It sets the stage for the rest of the body, consisting of the Method, Results, and Discussion sections. If this section is poorly written, readers may lose interest or develop a negative perception of the research. Because the initial readers of a manuscript are often editors and reviewers, it is wise to avoid such negative perceptions.

Method

The Method section of an empirical manuscript details what was done to collect the data to be analyzed. It has several subsections, with the exact number depending on the complexity of the study. In general it informs the reader about the participants (also called subjects), any apparatus or equipment that was used, and what procedures were followed, along with the design of the study. A competent researcher should be able to evaluate the quality of the research and replicate the study after reading this section alone. Moreover, you can and should apply this test yourself when reading an article's Method section.

The Participant subsection should provide clear answers to three questions: (a) Who took part in the study? (b) How many participants were there? (c) How were the participants selected (i.e., are they representative of a defined population?)? Additionally, you may provide major demographic characteristics of the sample and the number of participants assigned to the experimental groups or condition(s). Last, always report any incentives for participation (monetary, extra credit).

In the Apparatus subsection, you should describe the major devices or materials that were used in the study. If you constructed the apparatus (e.g., questionnaires, rating scales, activities) yourself, you may have to provide greater detail so that a reader can comprehend exactly what the device was. Appendixes or a separate technical report may be required to provide a detailed description of the apparatus. Any questionnaire measures should be referenced here and deviations from the original scales or instructions should be described. At a minimum, a representative item from each questionnaire should be included to ensure that the reader understands what a typical item is measuring (and what form each item takes). Some writers provide the psychometric characteristics (e.g., reliability estimates, standard errors of measurement) in this section, whereas others provide such details in the Results section. Either of these options is adequate, but these characteristics should be included to demonstrate the psychometric properties of your measure(s). Furthermore, these should represent the psychometric properties based on your sample, not the published properties. Although these are often the same, there may be instances when discrepancies exist. These discrepancies need to be presented so as to try and justify the gaps.

A Procedures subsection presents the steps in the actual running of the study. It may include instructions to participants, formation of groups, and any specific experimental manipulations. The researcher should describe the subject assignment, any counterbalancing that was completed, and other control features. This section should inform the reader of what was done, how it was done, and in what order. Again, it needs to do so in sufficient detail to permit replication.

Last, the informed consent, debriefing, and other ethical requirements must be mentioned in this section.

In summary, then, the Method section details the participants, apparatus and measures, and the procedures used to present stimuli and measure responses. Again, this section should be written in enough detail to allow another researcher to replicate the study.

Results

The Results section summarizes the collected data and their statistical treatment. The researcher should briefly state the main types of analyses to begin. Detail is needed only for the more esoteric of statistical tests. In these instances, you should report those analyses in detail so that you can justify conclusions you intend to make in later sections. One thing to remember is that you should only state the results and not discuss their implications or make inferences until the discussion section. Last, you should make sure to report all relevant results, including those that counter your hypotheses (this is important!). Every researcher should be aware that often results that are counter to your hypotheses are just as valuable as those that support your hypotheses.

In this section, you may choose to present results using graphs or tables, but consider the value of this mode of presentation carefully, as tables and figures are expensive to typeset (figures are more difficult to typeset than tables). On the other hand, the saying, "One picture is worth a thousand words" is also applicable. If you do use tables or figures, refer to graphs, pictures, or drawings as *Figures* and to tabular matter (with columns and headings) as *Tables*. For example, you could say in the text, "Figure 1 depicts the goal acceptance levels for each of the experimental groups." If you include tables and figures, they are placed together at the end of the manuscript (after the references). Tables should have the running head and page number, whereas figures do not. On the other hand, figures do require a caption on a separate page immediately preceding the figure (which does have the running head). The *Publication Manual* gives additional details on tables and figures ("Table Checklist," Section 3.74, pp. 175–176; "Figure Checklist," Section 3.86, pp. 201). Nicol and Pexman (1999, 2003) also provide details for both tables and figures.

The statistical presentation of data should include sufficient information so that the reader can confirm that appropriate analyses were conducted. Therefore, all inferential statistics (e.g., t-tests, F-tests, chi-square tests, etc.) *must* include information concerning the means, variability measures (e.g., variance, standard deviation), obtained magnitude of the test statistic, the degrees of freedom, the probability of observing such a test statistic given a true null hypothesis, and the direction of the effect (Wilkinson & APA Task Force on Statistical Inference, 1999). Here are examples: "As predicted, females ($M = 9.55$, $SD = 1.67$) reported greater liking for school than did the males ($M = 7.62$, $SD = 1.22$), $t(22) = 2.62$, $p < .01$," and "The ANOVA indicated significant differences in latency of response for participants not provided with training, $F(1,34) = 123.78$, $p < .001$." However, if exact probabilities are presented, then an a priori probability level (i.e., alpha level) must be stated before specific results are reported. Here are examples: "An alpha level of .01 was used for all statistical analyses" and "With an alpha level of .01, the effect of gender was statistically significant $t(22) = 2.62$, $p = .006$." Furthermore, if descriptive statistics are provided in a table or figure, they do not need to be repeated in the text unless they are supporting or rejecting a hypothesis or research question. The *Publication Manual* gives additional details on sufficient statistics and statistical presentation (Section 1.10, pp. 20–26; Sections 3.55–3.61, pp. 137–147), as does Capraro and Capraro's (2003) examination of analytical preferences of journal editorial board members.

Increasingly, statistical power associated with the tests of hypotheses is also included in this section (Scherbaum, Chapter 18). Statistical power pertains to the likelihood of correctly rejecting the hypotheses of interest and is dependent on the chosen alpha level, effect size, and sample size (all of these values should also be reported in a summary of research). Further, statistical power should be considered during the design phase of a study so that necessary changes (e.g., larger N, increased number of trials) can be made to ensure that sufficient power will be obtained in the study. Without sufficient power, it will be difficult to ascertain whether the results were due to the experimental manipulation or due to some other factors. Methods for calculating both statistical power and effect size are presented in various statistics classes and in articles (Cohen, 1987; Cohen, 1992).

At the novice researcher level, common analyses include *t*-tests on means for two groups, one-way analysis of variance for three or more groups, and simple regression or multiple regression to study interrelationships among larger sets of measures (Dickter, Chapter 19). Complex and more sophisticated techniques, including multivariate ones, become common with greater exposure to research or in graduate education (Steelman & Levy, Chapter 20). It should be noted, though, that more complex statistics should not be used just for the sake of using them. Such complexity can hinder the message that a researcher wishes to convey to the audience. A researcher should use the *necessary* statistics in order to adequately answer the question at hand. In summary, then, the Results section includes summary statistics and statistical significance tests of a priori hypotheses and any hypotheses that may emerge from your planned analyses.

Discussion

The Discussion section is where authors elaborate their results. One way to begin the discussion is to open with a statement about the support of your original hypotheses or research questions. In addition, you may examine, interpret, and qualify your results, as well as advance generalizations. The researcher should be guided by questions such as (a) What is the contribution of this research? (b) How has this study helped to resolve issues in this content area? (c) Can a clear conclusion be drawn from this study? (d) What further research could be done in this specific topic area? Some attention to the soundness of the results, perhaps by applying Cook and Campbell's (1979) validity taxonomy of internal, external, statistical conclusion, and construct types, is often a useful self-evaluation technique. In summary, the Discussion section includes a synopsis of the results, their significance, and self-criticism. When a researcher attempts to get research published, he or she must realize that the study will be greatly scrutinized. Therefore, the researcher may want to use the Discussion section to identify areas that are problematic or that may be questioned. He or she will then have the first chance at addressing these issues and proposing ways to remedy these concerns (possibly via future research).

WORD PROCESSING AND APA STYLE

Because of the widespread and increasing usage of computerized text or word processing, we offer comments on establishing default formatting. Smith (1992), for example, provided commands for users of WordPerfect 5.1 (note that this software package is now in the 12th version, as of 2004). Although the commands may vary from program to program (e.g., WP to MS Word), several major program features to consider are line spacing, page margins, running headers, justification and hyphenation, and spell-checking. First, manuscripts should always be entirely double-spaced, even the references and tables, to permit comments from editors and reviewers or copy editors. Page margins should be set at least 1.0 inch all around, with one exception being the top margin. This exception occurs because the margin should be 1.0 inch from the top to the first line, not to the running head. Therefore, a top margin of approximately .50 or .60 inches works best. Running headers are usually set up in the formatting section of the word processing program. There are two requirements for the running head: top flush right placement and a page number (now placed on the same line as the short title). Manuscripts should be left justified only, meaning that the right edges should be ragged, not straight. Further, hyphenation should be turned off from the beginning of the manuscript.

Last, using the set of writing tools provided by computer packages is highly recommended. Primarily, spell-checking a document during its preparation and definitely before sending it out for comments or review is mandatory. Remember that it is not necessarily your spelling that is problematic but rather your psychomotor (typing) skills. The thesaurus is useful when trying to avoid the overuse of certain words. An additional feature is a grammar checker, which yields valuable information on such common errors as the overuse of passive voice. Last, helpful statistics—such as reading ease formulas and the number of characters, words, and paragraphs contained within the document—are available within the writing tools. Our advice is to learn APA format from the beginning of your word processing days and to practice until it becomes automatic. As was mentioned earlier, APA format is prevalent outside of psychological research, so it is very likely you will need to use APA format, even if you decide to pursue a career outside of psychology.

Several commercial programs offer more specialized writing functions. Some maintain a bibliography and provide references in correct APA style (e.g., EndNote Plus by Niles & Associates, 1993; WPCitation by Oberon/askSam Systems, 2003), whereas another provides a shell for the entire document (e.g., Manuscript Manager by Pergamon, 1988). The integration of technology into the entire writing process has developed tremendously over the past 20 years, from the basic use of computers in writing to the complex manner in which technology now shapes the manner and style in which researchers report on their findings (Haas, 1996).

Name of Software	Vendor	Year
EndNote Plus	Niles & Associates	1988–1993
WPCitation	Oberon/askSam Systems	2003
Manuscript Manager	Pergamon	1988

SUMMARY

In summary, APA style or format is easy to learn and follow with the proper effort. Automating this format endears you to teachers and fellow researchers alike. Following this style also demonstrates your professional self-discipline. This chapter provided a basic discussion of some elements of the fifth edition of the APA *Publication Manual.* Specific examples of some of the key points discussed in this chapter are located in the appendix. This job aid should be used as a template to ensure the primary elements that define APA format are adhered to. There is no substitute for the careful examination of the *Publication Manual* and related materials (e.g., writing style guides). Repetition will enhance anyone's style of writing; therefore, every researcher should get used to iterating or cycling as they write (e.g., for class, for your groups). Specifically, you should rewrite your papers for classes, prepare miniproposals, and of course practice, practice, practice!

EXERCISES

1. Although practicing writing in APA format will definitely help you to hone your skills, there are several additional exercises that may be useful as you attempt to become more familiar with this format. The first is to examine a published journal article to determine where discrepancies with proper APA format exist. We suggest you examine a journal that is not affiliated with APA (a list of APA journals is available on their Web site) and preferably one that is not refereed (i.e., does not go through a peer review process). Remember to pay particular attention to both the specific formatting issues (e.g., running head, types of headings, references), as well as the information contained within the article (e.g., how extensive is the literature review that is contained within the introduction).

2. A second exercise, similar to the first, is to examine a dissertation to determine where discrepancies with proper APA format exist. You may use a search engine such as PsycINFO to search on Dissertation Abstracts.

You can then search for topics of interest and select a dissertation to review. The dissertation should contain all the subtleties associated with APA format (including the front matter and back matter in APA format). As suggested above, you should pay particular attention to both the specific formatting issues and the information contained within the dissertation. One note is that in some instances, the university may have a select format that is slightly different from APA format. You should consider this when reviewing the dissertation to determine where this format differs.

3. A final exercise is to download a trial version of bibliographic software (e.g., EndNote Plus, WPCitation) and then conduct a literature search using a search engine such as PsychInfo on a topic area of interest to you. You should then enter the references of interest into the software, paying particular attention to the information being entered and the type of reference you are examining (e.g., journal article, book chapter). As many researchers will attest, writing references accurately is often just as difficult as writing the actual paper! This exercise will allow you to practice referencing different materials and provide you with an overview of some of the bibliographic software tools that exist.

RECOMMENDED READINGS

This section provides recommended sources for following up on this chapter. First and foremost is the *Publication Manual* itself, which is easily the most important and final arbiter (Knapp, Storandt, & Jackson, 1995). Additionally, Hummel and Kaeck (1995) provide a short treatment of the essentials of APA format that, for the most part, conforms to the *Publication Manual*. Chapell (1995), however, critiqued the format for references presented by Hummel and Kaeck (1995) noting that it was incorrect because of the use of the 3rd edition. You need to be aware that the *Publication Manual* is currently in the fifth edition, so there are certain styles (e.g., how references are written) that may have changed over time. From a more general writing sense, three classic sources of information on writing style include *The Elements of Style* (4th ed., Strunk & White, 1999), *The Chicago Manual of Style* (15th edition, University of Chicago Press, 2004), and *The Manual of Style* (U.S. Government Printing Office, 1986). Other book-length treatments for the social sciences include *Writing for Social Scientists* (Becker, 1986); *Writing Scientific Papers and Reports* (Jones, 1976); *A Guide to Usage for Writers and Students in the Social Sciences* (Runkel & Runkel, 1984); and *The Psychologist's Companion* (Sternberg, 1993). Rubens (1991) presents a manual of style specifically for scientific-technical writing. Sternberg's (1992) article develops a framework about writing for psychological journals. His complete organization scheme includes (a) what you say, (b) how you say it, (c) what to do with what you say, and (d) what to do with what others say (e.g., colleagues, reviewers). Although these will not guarantee that you will write flawlessly and correctly apply APA format, they will provide helpful hints on how to write in a professional manner that allows the reader to completely comprehend the message that you, as a researcher, are trying to get across. Last, there is excellent guidance about writing literature reviews in articles by Bem (1995) and Baumeister and Leary (1997). Because literature reviews are a component of every empirical article, this skill is important for novice researchers.

REFERENCES

American Psychological Association. (2001). *Publication manual of the American Psychological Association* (5th ed.). Washington, DC: Author.

Anderson, J. E., & Valentine, W. L. (1944). The preparation of articles for publication in the journals of the American Psychological Association. *Psychological Bulletin, 41,* 345–376.

Baumeister, R. F., & Leary, M. R. (1997). Writing narrative literature reviews. *Review of General Psychology, 1,* 311–320.

Becker, H. S. (1986). *Writing for social scientists.* Chicago: University of Chicago Press.

Bem, D. J. (1995). Writing a review article for *Psychological Bulletin. Psychological Bulletin, 118,* 172–177.

Blakeslee, A. M. (2003). Interacting with audiences: Social influences on the production of scientific writing. *American Journal of Psychology, 116*(1), 123–128.

Budge, G., & Katz, B. (1995). Constructing psychological knowledge: Reflections on science, scientists, and epistemology in the *APA Publication Manual. Theory & Psychology, 5,* 217–231.

Capraro, M. M., & Capraro, R. M. (2003). Exploring the APA fifth edition *Publication Manual's* impact on the analytic preferences of journal editorial board members. *Educational and Psychological Measurement, 63,* 554–565.

Chapell, M. S. (1995). Correction to APA style. *American Psychological Society Observer, 8*(6), 33.

Cohen, J. (1987). *Statistical power analysis for the behavioral sciences* (2nd ed.). Hillsdale, NJ: Lawrence Erlbaum.

Cohen, J. (1992). A power primer. *Psychological Bulletin, 112*(1), 155–159.

Cook, T. D., & Campbell, D. T. (1979). *Quasi-experimentation: Design and analysis issues for field settings.* Boston: Houghton Mifflin.

Haas, C. (1996). *Writing technology: Studies on the materiality of literacy.* Mahwah, NJ: Lawrence Erlbaum.

Hills, P. J. (1983). The scholarly communication process. *Annual Review of Information Science and Technology, 8,* 99–125.

Hummel, J. H., & Kaeck, D. J. (1995). How to use the '94 APA style guide. *American Psychological Society Observer, 8*(4), 16–22.

Knapp, S., Storandt, M., & Jackson, D. (1995). Fourth edition of the *Publication Manual. American Psychologist, 50,* 581–583.

Jones, W. P. (1976). *Writing scientific papers and reports* (7th ed.). Dubuque, IA: W. C. Brown.

Lannon, J. M. (1988). *Technical writing* (4th ed.). Glenview, IL: Scott, Foresman.

Nicol, A. A. M., & Pexman, P. M. (1999). *Presenting your findings: A practical guide for creating tables.* Washington, DC: APA.

Nicol, A. A. M., & Pexman, P. M. (2003). *Displaying your findings: A practical guide for creating figures, posters, and presentations.* Washington, DC: APA.

Niles & Associates, Inc. (1993). EndNote Plus [Computer software]. Berkeley, CA: Author.

Oberon/askSam Systems, Inc. (2003). WPCitation [Computer software]. Perry, FL: Author.

Pergamon Press, Inc. (1988). Manuscript Manager [Computer software]. Elmsford, NY: Author.

Richardson, L. (1994). Writing: A method of inquiry. In N. K. Denzin & Y. S. Lincoln (Eds.), *Handbook of qualitative research* (pp. 516–529). Thousand Oaks, CA: Sage.

Rubens, P. (Ed.). (1991). *Science and technical writing: A manual of style.* New York: Holt.

Runkel, P. J., & Runkel, M. (1984). *A guide to usage for writers and students in the social sciences.* Totowa, NJ: Rowan & Allanheld.

Sides, C. H. (Ed.). (1989). *Technical and business communication: Bibliographic essays for teachers and corporate trainers.* Urbana, IL: National Council of Teachers of English, Society for Technical Communication.

Smith, R. (1992). Formatting APA pages in WordPerfect 5.1. *Teaching of Psychology, 19,* 190–191.

Standera, O. (1987). *The electronic era of publishing.* New York: Elsevier.

Sternberg, R. J. (1992, September). How to win acceptances by psychology journals: 21 tips for better writing. *American Psychological Society Observer,* 12 ff.

Sternberg, R. J. (1993). *The psychologist's companion* (3rd ed.). New York: Cambridge University Press.

Strunk, W., & White, E. B. (1999). *The elements of style* (4th ed.). Upper Saddle River, NJ: Pearson Education.

U.S. Government Printing Office. (1986). *Manual of style.* Washington, DC: Author.

University of Chicago Press. (1993). *The Chicago manual of style* (14th ed.). Chicago: Author.

Wilkinson, L., & APA Task Force on Statistical Inference. (1999). Statistical methods in psychology journals: Guidelines and explanations. *American Psychologist, 54,* 594–604.

Woodford, F. P. (1967). Sounder thinking through clearer writing. *Science, 156,* 743–745.

Wright, P. (1987). Reading and writing for electronic journals. In B. K. Britton & S. M. Glynn (Eds.), *Executive control processes in reading* (pp. 107–144). Hillsdale, NJ: Lawrence Erlbaum.

Annotated Bibliography

In addition to the traditional references we just listed, often an author may use an annotated bibliography like the one shown below. This type of reference includes a brief description of what is contained within each book or journal article. This information may be useful to the reader in determining whether to further examine a particular reference. For example, the annotated references below refer to different means of presenting data, and both describe the information that is contained within their respective books on this topic.

Nicol, A. A. M., & Pexman, P. M. (1999). *Presenting your findings: A practical guide for creating tables*. Washington, DC: APA.

> This book provides advice on how to create many types of tables in keeping with APA style. The organization is by chapter for different statistical techniques. Included for each is a "Play It Safe." Multiple examples, however, demonstrate a range of presentation options for each statistical technique.

Nicol, A. A. M., & Pexman, P. M. (2003). *Displaying your findings: A practical guide for creating figures, posters, and presentations*. Washington, DC: APA.

> This book provides advice on how to create many types of visual displays in keeping with APA style. It accomplishes for graphics what the Nicol and Pexman (1999) accomplished for tables.

Often a researcher may include both a traditional reference section and an annotated bibliography to provide the reader with additional information. Typically the ordering of the two reference sections is the same as provided here. That is, the traditional reference section is listed first followed by the annotated bibliography. The researcher needs to consider whether the additional information will be needed to enable the reader to better understand the current study (and potentially replicate the study or expand on the existing research).

A final reference is the APA Style Web site (www.apastyle.org/). This site presents a large amount of information, organized by the fifth edition of the *Publication Manual* (2001) and various other topics (e.g., electronic reference citations, software). In the current technology age, more and more information can now be found via the Internet.

Appendix: A Job Aid for Writing in APA Format

The following pages present a two-level template for writing in APA style, compiled from earlier versions prepared by Dr. Evan Mendes (George Mason University) and Dr. Peter Villanova (Appalachian State University). This appendix template works at two levels. The first level, which focuses on physical or surface features, shows the actual layout of a manuscript written in current APA format (2001). Thus, the document in this appendix is set up in the format of the empirical research report. You could, therefore, use this (along with the 2001 *Publication Manual,* Appendix A) as a template as you set up your own research report. The second level, which pertains to the cognitive features, elaborates on the physical features. For example, the abstract contained in the template provides a rationale for any abstract and also provides details of its preparation. Thus, the document in this appendix both discusses APA format and serves as a model of correct APA format. Please note two things about this appendix. First, all possible features of an empirical manuscript could not be incorporated, so the current *Publication Manual* is still the final and best arbiter. Second, the page numbering begins at 1 for correctness.

Running head: SHORT TITLE OF YOUR CHOICE (all caps)

Title of Your Manuscript
(Typed in Mixed Case and
Centered on the Page)
Your Name
Organizational Affiliation
(Compiled by James T. Austin)

Correspondence:
Name
Address
Phone and E-mail Address
(optional but helpful)

ABSTRACT

This job aid teaches you American Psychological Association (APA) style in two ways. The text explains the elements and organization of a typical empirical research report, and the text is also formatted in proper APA style. The section you are reading, the *abstract,* is written on a separate page immediately after the title page. This page must have the running head in the upper right corner of the page, with the page number following it (e.g., page 2), and the word *Abstract* centered on the page. The abstract is written in block form (i.e., single paragraph with no indentation). The abstract contains a brief summary of the article, and it should inform intelligent readers so that they can decide whether the article is relevant to their interests. In many cases, the abstract determines whether or not the article will be read in its entirety. Thus, it should present information about the problem, the method, the results, as well as implications and conclusions. Typically, the length of the abstract for an empirical article is 100–150 words and should not exceed 960 characters (this specific abstract has 231 words and is thus slightly long). In summary, the abstract should be short and informative.

TITLE OF YOUR MANUSCRIPT

(Typed in Mixed Case and Centered on the Page)

The introduction starts on a fresh page after the title and abstract pages. Note that the running head and the full title are on the top of the first page of the introduction, but there is no subheading. Also, note that the entire text is typed without right justification and hyphenation. Other information about manuscript preparation can be obtained by consulting the American Psychological Association *Publication Manual* (5th ed., 2001). Other specific treatments of social science writing may be found in Sternberg (1993) and Becker (1986). Last, a useful source of general style information is *The Elements of Style* by Strunk and White (1999). All of these writing sources were cited in the main reference section of this chapter.

Because the function of the introduction is obvious, a heading is not needed. Specifically, the introduction informs the reader of the specific problem under study and how that problem is related to prior scientific work. In writing the introduction, keep these four questions in mind: (a) What is the point of the study? (b) What is the relation of the study to previous work in the area? (c) What is the rationale or logical link between the study and the research design? (d) What are the theoretical limitations of the study? The most difficult part of writing the introduction is to develop explicitly the logical connection between your research question(s), the work in the literature, and your research design. It is your responsibility to clarify these matters as you write a manuscript.

The introduction does discuss the literature, but it need not be an exhaustive review. If you have completed an exhaustive review, consider writing it as a review or theoretical article, a quantitative review (or meta-analysis), an annotated bibliography, or perhaps a technical report. When writing an empirical report, try to cite only those studies pertinent to specific issues under investigation. When selecting studies for your literature review, include recent literature as well as any classic citations (i.e., seminal works), the former to ensure that you are not reinventing the wheel and the latter to demonstrate your grasp of the history of the phenomenon. Consider including meta-analyses (quantitative reviews) of the research domain if they are available (and they usually are). Do not completely describe the studies you cite; often all that is needed is a brief description of the variables, procedures, analyses and findings, and conclusions. Finally, avoid tangential or general references unless they buttress your arguments.

In the body of the paper, articles and books are cited by the last name(s) of the author(s) and the year of publication. This form of citation is termed "scientific" in order to distinguish it from citations in literary writing, which follow the style guide of the Modern Language Association (MLA). For example, you might say, "Distinctions between operant and classical conditioning, originally stated by Skinner (1938), have recently been challenged (Rescorla & Wagner, 1969)." Notice that when a citation is enclosed completely within parentheses, the ampersand (&) is used instead of the word *and.* However, *and* is used outside of parentheses. In citing more than one work by the same author(s) in one year, the suffixes a, b, c, and so forth are added after the year. These suffixes are also used in the reference section. For instance, you might say, "Recent studies by Smith (1965, 1975, 1978a, 1978b) have shown support for the expectancy interpretation." If different authors are cited simultaneously at the same point in the text, the citations are always arranged *alphabetically* by the author's surnames, separated by semicolons, and enclosed in parentheses. An example of this would be "Recent studies dispute the behaviorist position (Smith, 1983; Smith & Jones, 1984; Toffler, 1979)."

Although you are trying to communicate the importance and relevance of literature you are reviewing, you should put forth every effort to avoid footnotes and quotations. The literature you cite should be from original work and should be your interpretation of it. Plagiarism is extremely dishonest and is severely punished by most schools and professions. Sometimes, however, you have no choice but to rely on secondary sources, which are someone else's interpretation of a study. You should then cite the secondary source in the text. For example, you would place the source in the text as " . . . Heider (1958) reported that Asch observed . . . ." You would then list Heider, not Asch, in the reference section, in spite of the fact that it is the work of Asch that is of interest.

Last, you should try to write with clarity and avoid using flowery language. For example, "The eminent American clinical psychologist, Dr. George Kelly, is credited with the first portrayal of individuals as naive scientists" could be better stated as "Kelly (1955) was the first to portray persons as naive scientists." Three simple principles are to know your audience, know your communication goals, and be simple, brief, and concise. Outlines can help clarify your thinking and can be constructed either after you finish writing (a reverse outline) or before you start.

Hypotheses

Authors should list hypotheses or research questions at the end of the introductory section. Hypotheses are specific predictions about expected results; research questions are general and indicate an exploratory study. The hypotheses should provide enough detail so that the reader will understand what specific questions are being asked by the study. Furthermore, each hypothesis should be adequately justified by the literature contained in the introduction (e.g., what relationships are expected, how variables are being operationalized). A third-level heading might be used for this section of the introduction.

In summary, the introduction tells readers, within the framework of the existing research, why this study is being conducted. It sets the stage for the rest of the manuscript, which consists of the Method, Results, Discussion, and Reference sections.

METHOD

The Method section is headed with the word *Method*—in mixed case and centered. This is an example of a first-level heading, and it immediately follows the introduction section and any hypotheses or research questions. The Method section generally has several subsections, with the exact number depending on the complexity of the study. Its purpose is to inform readers about the participants, what apparatus and/or measures were used, and what procedures were followed so that competent researchers can evaluate the quality of the research and could replicate the study.

Participants

Note that the subsections of the Method section, such as *Participants,* have capitalized headings, are italicized, and are flush left. These are called third-level headings in the American Psychological Association's style guide. The Participant subsection should provide clear answers to three questions: (a) Who participated in the study? (b) How many participants were there? (c) How were the participants selected (i.e., are they representative of a defined population?)? Additionally, you should give the major demographic characteristics and the number of participants assigned to each experimental group or condition. Report any incentives, whether monetary or otherwise, that were offered for participation. Finally, the word *subjects* is sometimes considered to be derogatory, so the word *participants* is typically used to define the individuals participating in the study.

Apparatus and Measures

In this subsection, give brief descriptions of the major apparatus or materials used in the study and their functions. If you constructed the apparatus yourself, you may have to go into greater detail so that readers can comprehend exactly what the apparatus was. Perhaps an appendix or a separate technical report will be required. Questionnaire measures, whether homemade or off the shelf, should also be referenced here, and all deviations from the original scales or instructions should be described. You may want to include a representative item from each questionnaire so that the reader can understand what a typical item is measuring.

Procedure

This subsection should present each step in the actual execution of the study. It should include initial instructions to participants (informed consent), formation of the groups, and the specific experimental manipulations, if any. This subsection should also describe the randomization, counterbalancing, and other control features of the research design. Last, you should state how the participants were debriefed to ensure the study adheres to the APA ethical guidelines. In general, this section informs the reader what was done, how it was done, and in what order, in sufficient detail to permit replication.

RESULTS

The Results section immediately follows the Method section. The word *Results* is centered and in mixed case as a first-level heading. The purpose of this section is to summarize the collected data and the statistical treatment of those data. First, you should briefly state the main thrust of your results or findings. Second, you

should report the analyses in detail so that you can justify the conclusions you intend to make in later sections. You need to bear in mind that you should state the results only and not discuss implications or make inferences until the discussion section. Last, remember to report *all* relevant results, even any that may be counter to your hypotheses (this is important!).

Once you have analyzed the data, you may choose to present data or results in the form of graphs or tables. Although these means of presenting data are often expensive to typeset, they provide a pictorial representation of the data that may allow the reader to more fully grasp the results of your study. If you decide to use these representations, you should label graphs, pictures, or drawings as *Figures* and tables as *Tables*. For example, you could say, "Figure 1 presents the proportion of participants in each group who recalled the target in the team list." Both figures and graphs are placed at the end of the manuscript and figures require a short, descriptive caption on the page immediately preceding the figure. Last, although the figures and tables are placed at the end of the document, you should indicate where the table or figure should fit within the text as follows.

Insert Table (or Figure) 1 about here

When you report the results of a test of statistical significance, you must include information concerning the means, measures of variability (e.g., variance, standard deviation), obtained magnitude of the test statistic, the degrees of freedom, the probability of observing such a test ratio given a true null hypothesis, and the direction of the effect. Here are several examples: "Employees who received immediate feedback from their supervisors were more satisfied with the appraisal process ($M = 4.2$, $SD = 0.67$) than those who did not receive any feedback ($M = 2.8$, $SD = 0.78$), $t(22) = 6.39$, $p < .01$," and "The analysis of variance indicated that children displayed significantly more positive affect after receiving desirable gifts than after receiving undesirable gifts, $F(1,61) = 42.62$, $p < .01$." Some of the conventions for reporting statistical significance and the effect size are presented in statistics and research methods classes.

Further, tables are often used to present the results of complex analyses such as factor analysis, multiple regression, or factorial analysis of variance.

At the undergraduate level, the most common statistical analyses to be reported include *t*-tests on dependent variable means for two groups, one-way analysis of variance to compare the means of three or more groups on a single manipulated factor, simple correlation and regression to relate two measured variables, and multiple regression to examine interrelationships among multiple measured variables. More sophisticated techniques are typically used at later stages of exposure to psychological research.

DISCUSSION

The Discussion section follows immediately after the Results section. Note the mixed case and the centering of the section heading. One way to begin the discussion is to open with a statement on the support of your original hypotheses or research questions. In addition, you may examine, interpret, and qualify your results, as well as advance generalizations. When writing up the Discussion section, you should be guided by questions such as the following: (a) What have I contributed in this research? (b) How has my study helped to resolve issues in this content area? (c) Can I draw a clear conclusion from this study? (d) What further research could be done in this specific topic area?

In sum, note that the research report is a logical flow of information from how the problem was stated, how the problem was conceptualized, how the problem was researched, how the data were analyzed, what the findings were, how the findings were interpreted, and some suggestions for new studies. Last, the best way to improve your writing is to practice, practice, practice!

REFERENCES

Psychological writing places references in one place at the end of the text so that they do not interfere with the reading of the manuscript. There is generally little use of notes in the text (they too are placed in the reference section immediately before the references). The reference section starts on a new page immediately after the discussion section. The purpose of references is to enable a reader to obtain the sources used in the writing of an article. Every article mentioned in the text should be included in the reference section (and vice versa). The listing of the references should be done alphabetically by the first author's last name. The heading *References* is typed in mixed case and centered. Below are examples of the format required for common manuscript references. Further information and examples pertaining to references can be obtained by consulting the APA *Publication Manual* (2001, Section 4.16, pp. 231–281). Additional material on citing legal materials is provided in the latest revision (Appendix D, pp. 397–410).

Adams, J. E., & Aronfreed, J. L. (1971). Group dynamics in the prison community. *Journal of Experimental Social Psychology, 42,* 17–21. (example of an article)

American Psychological Association. (2001). *Publication manual of the American Psychological Association* (5th ed.). Washington, DC: Author. (APA Style Guide—the "Bible")

Riesen, A. H. (1966). Sensory deprivation. In E. Stellar & J. M. Sprague (Eds.), *Progress in physiological psychology* (Vol. 1, pp. xxx–xxx). New York: Academic Press. (example of a book chapter)

Stogdill, R. M. (1974). *Handbook of leadership.* New York: Free Press. (example of a book)

APPENDIX A

Informative Title of Your Choice
(Centered, Mixed Case)

An appendix presents additional material of interest to the reviewer or reader. The material may not fit conveniently into the body of the paper but is important in reading or reviewing the manuscript. Examples of such material include questionnaires developed by the author specifically for the research project (e.g., for a senior honors thesis), computer program listings, a list of stimulus materials (e.g., for verbal learning experiments), or a complicated mathematical proof. It should be double-spaced and begin on a new page following the references. Letters are used to identify each appendix. If only one appendix is used, no identifying letter is required.

AUTHOR NOTES

In a typical empirical paper, there are three components of author notes. The first provides the departmental affiliations of the authors. The first paragraph of the author notes should identify each author's affiliation at the time of the study. A second paragraph should then be used to identify any changes to an author's affiliation since the time of the study (if applicable). The second component of the author notes acknowledges help or assistance the author has received, whether from colleagues, from external funding sources, or from research assistants. This information would be included in the third paragraph of the author notes and would also contain any information about whether the study was based on an earlier study, if it is a doctoral dissertation or master's thesis, or if additional publications have (or will be) based on the same data set. This paragraph would also state any disclaimers desired by an employer or funding agent (e.g., the findings stated in this report do not reflect opinions of the funding organization). The final part indicates where the author may be contacted for reprints, including standard and electronic addresses. This information is located in the fourth and final paragraph of the author notes. Author notes are not numbered and should be listed on their own page.

Table 1 (Left Justified, Mixed Case)

Average Maze Performance for Prenatal Malnourished and Control Rats

	Prenatal Malnourished Rats		Control Rats	
	Sample Size	Average Time	Sample Size	Average Time
Trial 1	12	75 sec	12	54 sec
Trial 2	11	77 sec	11	55 sec
Trial 3	12	72 sec	12	53 sec

Table notes go here

As was mentioned in the body of the text, a table is often used to elaborate on the results. It allows the reader to view larger amounts of data in a relatively small space. It may also provide data that can be used by researchers to perform follow-on studies. Each table is presented on a separate page. A short title is placed above the table to describe the information contained within the table. Although the table is offered in conjunction with the description in the text, the researcher should provide enough information here to allow the table to stand alone. Therefore, the title should provide enough information to accurately describe the data contained in the table. The table then follows with the variables of importance and their respective values. Last, the table notes go immediately below the table. These notes may include general notes meant to explain the table as a whole, specific notes, which may call attention to a specific column or row of data (or even a single data point), and probability notes, which indicate the p values being used to indicate significance. Specific examples of what types of tables to include or suggestions on how to set up tables are provided in the APA *Publication Manual* (2001, section 3.62, pp. 147–176) as well as in Nicol and Pexman (1999).

Figure Caption
(Centered, Mixed Case)

Figure 1. Mean body weight for rats in the prenatal malnourished (X——X) and control groups (O——O) from birth through 200 days of age.

Figures, like tables, are meant to provide additional information to what is discussed in the body of the text. However, unlike tables, which provide specific quantitative data, figures provide a graphical representation of the data (i.e., a quick glance at the results). Figures are located after the tables in the research paper. A separate page is used to describe what is located in the figure. Specifically, the figure caption page includes the figure number and a short yet informative description of what is found within the figure (as in the example above). The page immediately after the figure caption contains the figure itself. Because the goal of the figure is to provide a graphical representation of the data, you need to ensure that the figure is readable (e.g., large enough to read and containing a manageable amount of data). Also, make sure to include a legend if it will help the reader distinguish between data points or experimental conditions.

Figures may include charts, graphs, photographs, drawings, or other graphical illustrations. They are particularly useful when describing interactions and nonlinear relationships, as these are often easier to understand when viewed graphically. Specific examples of what types of figures to include or suggestions on how to set up figures are provided in the *APA Publication Manual* (2001, section 3.77, pp. 178–201) as well as in Nicol and Pexman (2003).

The fifth edition of the *APA Publication Manual* has been revised and updated to include the latest guidelines for referencing electronic and online sources, guidelines for transmitting papers electronically, improved guidelines for avoiding plagiarism, simplified formatting, guidelines for writers using up-to-date word-processing software, all new guidelines for presenting case studies, improved guidelines for the construction of tables, updates on copyright and permissions issues for writers, new reference examples for audiovisual media and patents, new guidelines on how to choose text, tables, or figures to present data, guidelines for writing cover letters for submitting articles for publications, plus a sample letter, expanded guidelines on the retention of raw data, new advice on establishing writing agreements for the use of shared data, and new information on the responsibilities of coauthors.

24

WRITING ROUGH DRAFTS

CHRISTOPHER PETERSON

All who give advice to would-be writers stress that final products are impossible to create without going through a series of drafts. Despite the universality of this advice, drafting imperfect versions of a final product is *not* part of the writing repertoire of many undergraduate and graduate students. My purpose in this chapter is not to extol the value of rough drafts. I take that as a given. Rather, I provide some concrete steps involved in writing drafts.

MAGICAL THINKING

Like many self-defeating behaviors, not being able to write is caused in part by deeply held but poorly examined beliefs (Beck, 1976). Individuals can be tyrannized by *automatic thoughts,* rigid and overly simple beliefs that come unbidden to mind, producing emotional and behavioral difficulties. These thoughts are maintained by *magical thinking* that keeps them immune to reality testing. In terms of writing, a magical belief system interferes with the business of beginning and finishing because it leaves no room for what happens in between. Writing is often spoken of in terms of art, inspiration, genius, and the like. Writing in actuality is a mundane activity taking place over time. Repetitive actions are the essence of writing.

Let me be concrete. An aspiring writer may believe, for example, that writing should be effortless. When it proves otherwise, the conclusion might follow that he or she is incapable of writing. Not helpful here is the way that students are socialized early in their school careers (Nicholls, 1978, 1984). We somehow learn that good students do not sweat, that effort trades off with ability, that *quick* is a synonym for *smart,* that things come easily or not at all, and so on. None of these notions has anything to do with actual writing.

Or a writer might believe that there is a perfect way to phrase sentences. Again, when sentences do not take immediate and immortal form, the conclusion may follow that one is not ready to begin writing. Perhaps one never will be ready until one knows exactly what is to be said. How can this be accomplished? One strategy is to read everything ever written on a given topic. The student disappears to the library or the Internet and postpones writing indefinitely (see Chapter 3, "Bibliographic Research").

AUTHOR'S NOTE: I thank James T. Austin and Lisa M. Bossio for their comments on rough drafts of this chapter. Address correspondence to chrispet@umich.edu or Christopher Peterson, Department of Psychology, University of Michigan, 530 Church Street, Ann Arbor, MI 48109–1043.

I often ask would-be writers who sits on their shoulders while they write. Sometimes it is a critical parent. Sometimes it is a seventh-grade teacher who presented writing solely in terms of participles, pluperfect tenses, and diagrammed sentences. Sometimes it is an admired figure who has unwittingly mystified the process of writing. And most commonly, it is an unidentified yet omniscient "they" passing harsh judgment on one's intelligence and ability.

Most students eventually do write, but because writing is fraught with supposed implications for self-esteem and competence, their final product is far from satisfactory. Getting in the way of writing are rituals and superstitions that students believe are necessary for the process to occur (Becker, 1986). I am not ranting against routines in writing because they are obviously needed. But I am criticizing magical routines because they prevent the would-be writer from beginning to work.

Perhaps the most critical determinant of whether one can write a useful rough draft is the belief that this can be done. Several influences on this belief in one's own efficacy with regard to drafts can be specified, notably prior success in producing rough drafts, available examples by others that this can be done, and verbal persuasion that drafts are possible (cf. Bandura, 1986). Teachers in psychology could break down a required manuscript into its components (title page, abstract, and so on) and ask that each component be produced in sequence over an academic term through revisions and resubmissions. This process would allow self-efficacy to be built through the accumulation of small successes. The present chapter is a finished product, but the reader should know as well that what appears here is the tenth draft of what began in rough form.

Taking Ownership

Students often have a confused view of why they are writing. On one level, of course, a person writes for an audience and usually because of an external demand. Teachers assign essays. Graduate school admission committees ask for personal statements. Research supervisors request proposals. The academic profession requires published journal articles and books. But the most immediate reason for writing must be located within one's self, and the would-be writer has to think in these terms.

I try to encourage the student to take ownership of what he or she is doing. The most important part of taking ownership of a written product is to take responsibility for doing it. Writing is a verb, and it refers to something that a specific person does. If it is your paper, then you are that person. This reframing becomes increasingly necessary as the eventual written product becomes lengthy or important.

My doctoral students almost always fall into a way of speaking about their dissertations as THE DISSERTATION. Those influenced by the hip-hop generation sometimes call it THE DISS or even THE BIG D. Goodness. It is one thing to speak about THE WEATHER or THE GOVERNMENT because these are matters over which we expect no control and assume no ownership. But to move one's writing into this category is to undercut any role of personal agency in the process.

I insist that my doctoral students stop referring to their dissertations with definite articles and instead start using personal pronouns. I even tell them not to use the word dissertation at all because it sounds so imposing. One does not really write a dissertation per se. One writes words and sentences and chapters; when a student presents these in an appropriate fashion, then we call it a dissertation. When my students start to talk about writing up their research, I know the process has begun. When they start to talk about writing up their hypotheses, their methods, and their results, I know the process is all but over.

There is a myth that some academics write only outstanding papers. A corollary of this myth is that some of the very best academics write just a handful of influential articles and books. The evidence does not bear this out. Those who write frequently cited papers are those who write lots of papers (Merton, 1968). Some prove influential and some not. Consider Freud, Lewin, and Skinner—among the most important figures in psychology. Some of their papers are awkward, incoherent, and inconsequential. But we honor their good papers. I am sure that none of these individuals set out to write classic papers. They simply wrote.

My point is that the writer should not simultaneously take on the role of critic or historian. Yes, the writer should try to do a good job while writing, but this means putting in time and effort, not trying to match some abstract template of profundity and impact. There are limits to what the writer should attempt to own.

SPEWING IT OUT

The most obvious thing about a rough draft is that it is rough; it should be rough: preliminary, incomplete, even stupid and contradictory. Yet many students do not want to write a rough draft because *rough* has such negative connotations. As a result, when a writer starts a paper, he or she may try to begin with a finished product. Every sentence must be grammatical, every example apt, and every transition seamless. These are daunting goals, and the writer who tries to write perfect prose from the start ends up editing as he or she goes along and may never get as far as the second sentence.

The more realistic alternative is to separate writing from rewriting. Writers should adopt the *spew method,* letting their words and sentences tumble out in a first draft. The only rule governing the spew method is not to rewrite as one goes along. Some common sense must be employed, of course, because the writer has to stay within the demands of the given product, but otherwise, anything goes.

Said another way, a writer starting a rough draft needs to have only an approximate idea of what is to be written. I think the notion of planning out one's writing before one starts has been given too much emphasis. To be sure, a *general* outline is a good idea, and I use one when I write. But if a writer tries to create too detailed an outline before actually writing, then the tendencies to perfectionism that handicap writing drafts are displaced to writing outlines, and the writer is another step farther from being done.

Much of what we write in psychology has an accepted format. A research report, for example, consists of an Introduction, Method, Results, and Discussion (see Chapter 23, "Writing in APA Style: Why and How"). There is a prescribed way of organizing ideas within each of these sections. Once a writer has this general organization in mind, how much of a further outline is really needed before he or she begins?

With regard to writing a literature review, I often advise my students to alternate between reading and writing. They must have some familiarity with a topic before they begin to write about it, but they need not have read everything before writing. A strong argument can be made in favor of *not* reading everything, just enough to get started with the writing. In the course of writing, it becomes evident where more information is needed, and these places can be marked with an asterisk or parenthetical comment. But writers should keep spewing and only later track down needed details.

As part of my background research for something I am writing, I often take notes. And I invariably have a pile of pertinent articles and books on the floor next to my desk. When spewing out a rough draft, however, I do not consult these sources unless the essential meaning of what I want to say is in doubt. They come into play when I rewrite and polish the rough draft.

One need not spew in any particular order. Final versions of an article or book may be read from start to finish, but they do not have to be written this way. I often begin by writing sections with which I am most familiar and comfortable. Getting something on a page, wherever that particular page will eventually appear, is a good way to begin a rough draft.

For example, it is often easiest to write the Methods section of a research article first. I usually do this because it is the most formulaic. Then I jump to the end of the Introduction and specify my hypotheses. Next it is time—at least for me—to draft the Results section, and I usually do this before I have completed the data analyses. I find this efficient because as I try to describe what a study showed, I am reminded of just which empirical details are needed. These may not be immediately evident if one tries to do all the analyses before writing about them. Often what happens is that the data are overanalyzed, which wastes a lot of time, not to mention computer funds and paper.

There are many ways to put the spew method into action. In the 1970s, I put aside pens and pencils and wrote first drafts on a typewriter.

Even though I am a two-finger typist, I could type more quickly than I could write, and I made a deliberate effort to avoid x-ing out words and sentences while spewing. A decade later, with the advent of word processors, spewing became even easier for me, although word processors bring with them an even stronger temptation to fiddle with spelling and phrasing instead of writing.

If a writer cannot resist the temptation of rewriting, one extreme measure is to spew into a computer after turning off the video monitor. What you cannot see, you cannot rewrite. Needless to say, make sure your word processing program is not set on its overwriting option. Another extreme technique of spewing is to dictate your ideas into a tape recorder for later transcription. This is time-consuming, but it can be a useful short-term solution if you have inordinate trouble writing a first draft.

Some teachers react negatively when students ask how long a paper should be. I find this misguided. Writing in the real world needs to fit within a page limit, and nothing could be more reasonable than knowing how long a written product should be. Although the exact content of what I write may not be clear when I begin a draft, the intended length is never a mystery to me. The same is true for the sections of what I plan to write. Word processing programs can be helpful here in keeping track of written volume, because they typically provide a character, word, or page count.

A related issue is knowing when the final draft is due. For class assignments, there is no doubt, but ambitious writing projects like theses or dissertations are much more open-ended, which may explain why they can stretch infinitely to meet their nonexistent deadlines. Or consider a research report to be submitted for presentation at a conference. It is not enough to know when the conference is to be held; one must also know the submission deadline, and it is always months prior to the conference.

Most people are terrible at estimating how long it takes to do something, and their estimates invariably err on the side of optimism. I remember a few years ago planning my first automobile trip from Ann Arbor to Washington, DC. I did not know how long the trip would take, so I asked a friend who had lived in both cities. He told me with confidence that I could do it in 5 or 6 hours. As it turns out, the distance between these two cities is about 500 miles, and short of finding an interstate wormhole, no one—not him and certainly not me—could ever make the drive that quickly.

Even simple actions we have done many times—like washing, drying, and folding our laundry—take much longer than we estimate, and we rarely benefit from experience and budget enough time. And when what we are called on to do is something we have never done before—like writing a thesis or dissertation—estimates are footless and thus apt to be unrealistic. It is essential to talk to other people with more experience to arrive at a feasible deadline. But even when you do this, you need to take what they say with a huge grain of salt because advisors also are vulnerable to unrealistic optimism. Tack on lots of extra time to what they say, and start early. The same advice holds for what seem to be minor aspects of writing, like tracking down a few stray references or drafting a succinct abstract.

LETTING IT SIT

Once a rough draft has been written, it needs to be rewritten. But there is an important step in between: doing nothing with it. Letting it sit for a day or two or even longer allows the writer to approach his or her work with a fresh eye. Sometimes ideas and their expression need to incubate (cf. Poincaré, 1913). In my own writing, I have had the frequent experience of coming back to a draft and not knowing why I said certain things or why I failed to say others.

Another benefit of letting a draft sit is that a writer may realize when returning to it that it is more complete than it originally seemed. I have problems with introductions, particularly those that begin lengthy literature reviews (see Chapter 3, "Bibliographic Research"). I try to foreshadow what will follow, but I often overdo it. One solution I have devised is to write a very brief introduction with the intent to expand on it when I am rewriting. More often than not, though, I end up deciding that the brief introduction is sufficient.

Time constraints dictate the length of the period between successive drafts, and here I am again reminded of the maxim about starting projects early and the threat posed by procrastination. A discussion of procrastination is beyond my scope here (see Silver & Sabini, 1981), but one way to get started early enough to allow the rough draft time to sit is to plan to show it to one or more people. The writer should establish a deadline by which to show the draft to them, and this deadline should be taken as seriously as the final deadline for the written product.

REWRITING

Time has presumably passed, and the writer returns to his or her rough draft to rewrite it. There should be a plan about what to do with the next draft. Perhaps more material should be spewed out. Perhaps gaps need to be filled and missing information provided. Perhaps grammar, punctuation, and spelling should be checked. A given draft may be too rough to do all of these things at the same time, and if the writer attempts to turn a very rough draft into a final product in one swoop, he or she will probably become bogged down.

As people write more and more, they usually become aware of their idiosyncratic foibles, and these should receive special attention while rewriting. For example, while spewing, I often write passive sentences, and I look for these when I rewrite, turning them into active ones. I also start lots of sentences with *thus* and *indeed,* and at least in my usage, these words usually occupy empty space. When I rewrite, I search for these words and delete most of them.

Other foibles are more structural in nature but should be treated in the same way. Writers may consistently write too much or too little in a rough draft. They may neglect to use examples or transitions. They might fail to be explicit about the import of conclusions. Writers should make a list of such common problems and put extra effort into correcting these flaws when they are rewriting drafts. In many cases, through this application of multilevel, meta-cognitive

oversight, the process will eventually become automatic and part of how one spews.

Although I have de-emphasized the importance of outlines for first drafts, they can prove quite helpful for subsequent drafts (see Chapter 25, "Revising a Research Manuscript"). In a strategy called *reverse outlining,* the writer outlines what he or she has already written. Reverse outlining allows misplaced paragraphs and sections to be identified and uneven coverage to be corrected.

Let me comment here on the need to strike a balance between holding onto copies of early drafts and getting rid of them. Some writers who use a word processor end up with dozens of versions of the same paper on a disk and then get mixed up about what is what. Students with some frequency have given me the wrong draft of a paper. Sometimes they save an early draft over a later draft. And sometimes different versions of the same paper become jumbled together.

My own style of writing is *not* to keep copies of drafts that I have rewritten because I have learned that I never go back to them. To be sure, if there is a paragraph or page that I think might someday be useful but does not fit in the current draft, I keep it at the end of my manuscript, in a separate section. But I see no reason to keep a copy of a draft filled with awkwardness once I have smoothed it out. If you wish not to follow my lead, at least be sure to keep successive drafts clearly identified, perhaps labeling them with the draft number or the date they were completed.

RECEIVING (AND FOLLOWING) ADVICE

Writing is not as solitary an endeavor as popular stereotypes suggest. Someone will read most of what is written, and perhaps the best way to satisfy the eventual audience is to involve other people while working on a manuscript. Many resist this because drafts seem embarrassing, and we hesitate to reveal ourselves to others. But receiving (and following) useful advice from another person is a critical step in writing.

The would-be writer must struggle with fear of feedback, realizing that it is much preferable to be criticized at a time when change is possible than when it is too late. Most teachers would rather teach than assign grades, and they are usually happy to comment on a draft. So too are research supervisors, and I have on occasion had success running early versions of what I have written past journal editors. Fellow students and researchers may often be the most suitable individuals for advice. I regularly rely on several colleagues to advise me on what I have written, and I reciprocate the favor. To repeat: I think every would-be writer should solicit advice on rough drafts.

Not all to whom you show your drafts are helpful; they may be too late, too critical, or too cursory in their suggestions. Critics might advise you that a sentence is awkward or unclear but not explain why. A would-be writer might have to shop around a bit for a good critic and to take responsibility by being explicit about the sort of advice that is needed. And beware the overly positive reader; unconditional praise makes a writer feel good, but it does not improve his or her writing.

Once you find someone who will read and comment on your drafts, what can you do to make the process palatable to your advisor? To begin with, do not rely on someone else to do what you can do for yourself. For example, it is insulting and wasteful to use another person as a spell-check program. She may spend a lot of time correcting your spelling errors at the expense of more substantive advice.

Students sometimes give me a rough draft and ask for advice, but the manuscript they hand over is single-spaced and printed with a condensed typeface and minimal margins. Not only do I have trouble reading it, I have no room to note suggested changes. On purely physical grounds, drafts vary in how amenable they are to advice. Similarly, do not hand a potential advisor a computer disk containing your draft or send it as an e-mail attachment and expect him or her to print it before making comments, unless the two of you have agreed that this is how to proceed. Again, this can be time-consuming for your advisor if not impossible, granted the variety of operating systems and word-processing programs, not to mention the ever-present danger of computer viruses. A related problem—at least for me—is when someone commenting on an electronic draft I have written uses a sophisticated word-processing option unknown to me to track changes or reformat the draft. Then I need to spend time undoing their well-intended damage. Again, the point is to be explicit about *how* advice should be conveyed.

Although drafts are not expected to be complete, too preliminary a draft does not lend itself to comments. It must have at least some content. Students sometimes show me a bare-bones outline of what they wish to write—that is, (i) beginning, (ii) middle, and (iii) ending—and I am at a loss to say anything. If a writer wants substantive comments on the Results section of a potential journal article, tables and figures need to be included. I rarely find an abstract included as part of a rough draft given to me for comments, but an abstract is as helpful to the reader of a preliminary draft as it is to the reader of a final product, perhaps even more so.

As mentioned earlier, tell the person the sort of advice you most need. The more specific you can be, the better. A deadline for returning comments should be agreed on. You may not be able to control your advisor's end of the agreement, but do not ask for comments to be left for you on Monday and then not pick them up until Friday.

When advice is given to you about your draft, be sure to abstract the gist of the suggestion and follow it, not just where it is indicated on your manuscript but elsewhere as appropriate. I remember suggesting the identical word change 20 times in someone's dissertation. The student diligently made the suggested changes in the given 20 locations and not at all anyplace else. In other words, think about the advice, and if it is useful, learn a general lesson from it that you can apply broadly.

You of course should thank the person who gives you advice, and perhaps the best way to express gratitude is by offering to review your critic's own drafts and then following through if your offer is accepted. And speaking of following through, it is imperative that you take advice seriously. This need not mean doing everything that is suggested, but neither does it mean finding reasons not to do so (see Chapter 26, "Dealing With Journal Editors and Reviewers"). At the very least, if someone suggests that a draft be changed in a given way, the writer should usually change it in some way. There must have been something amiss to elicit criticism in the first place.

I ask those who read my drafts to make as many changes as they can in the text: reorganization, word choice, punctuation, and the like. I almost always incorporate these changes, but when I do not, I ponder the material in question and figure out how to revise it. If somebody does not like a word I chose, and I do not like his or her suggested word, then I find a third word. The recipient of advice is not a participant in a debate, and the writer who fails to follow sincere suggestions is not triumphing over an opponent.

If you are fortunate, you have several people on whom to rely for advice about your writing. Time permitting, the best way to make use of multiple sources of suggestions is successively. Simultaneous advice can be contradictory and overwhelming. Like writing and rewriting, responding to suggestions is most likely to be successful when it can be spread out over time.

Conclusions

In sum, I have described writing rough drafts as a process that necessarily extends over time. Several steps in writing a rough draft need to be distinguished and enacted (see Exercises). First, the writer must take ownership of what is to be written, assuming responsibility for what follows. Second, the writer needs to get his or her preliminary ideas on paper or disk. Third, the writer should, if possible, let the rough draft sit for a period of time. Fourth, the draft must be rewritten, perhaps several times if revisions are extensive. Fifth, the writer should solicit (and follow) advice from others.

The writing of rough drafts needs to be separated from their polishing at a later date. Counterproductive assumptions and habits can inhibit the writing of rough drafts, and these should be monitored and challenged on an ongoing basis. But with this all said and done, the fact remains that the final step in writing anything is deciding that it is done.

A writer should not become so smitten with writing and revising drafts that a product is never deemed complete. One must be willing to recognize that a written product cannot be perfect, that "good enough" is indeed good (cf. Schwartz, 2004). A paper or book that no one ever reads is a wasted opportunity to participate in one's chosen field. Get it out the door!

EXERCISES

This entire chapter is a "how-to" formula, but simply reading it will not make you a good writer any more than reading a cookbook will make you a gourmet chef. You need to put the advice into practice with a concrete writing project. What do you need to write in the next few weeks or months? Make this the focus of your exercise.

It can be a research proposal, a research report, or an essay for a class. (At the risk of being paranoid, I suggest that you consult with your teacher if you plan to solicit advice from others about a draft of a paper you will turn in for a grade; be sure that your plan will not be construed as a form of plagiarism.) If it is currently late fall, you might even choose as your writing project the yearly update that many include in holiday greeting cards. How wonderful it would be to send (or receive) a well-written update, as opposed to something that reads like an annotated appointment book.

Figure 24.1 is a flow chart that you should tailor to your specific writing project.

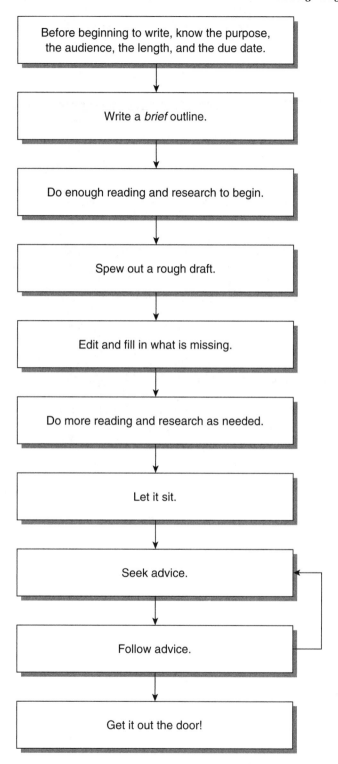

Figure 24.1   Writing Flowchart

RECOMMENDED READINGS

Consistent disagreement between you and someone who reads your drafts may mean that there is a technical misunderstanding about the right way to describe, for example, complex data analyses. It might also mean that you have different writing styles, although this should not be offered glibly as a reason not to follow suggestions. The *APA Publication Manual* (American Psychological Association, 2001) and *Elements of Style* (Strunk & White, 1959/1984) are explicit in many cases about correct and incorrect ways of writing. These should be consulted when the two of you begin to butt heads about style.

Other useful sources on writing include Gelfand and Walker's (2002) *Mastering APA Style,* Runkel and Runkel's (1984) *Guide to Usage for Writers and Students in the Social Sciences,* and—my personal favorite—Becker's (1986) *Writing for Social Scientists.* Yet another good source is *The Craft of Research* by Booth, Colomb, and Williams (1995). Swan and Gopen (1990) discussed the "science" of scientific writing, and Sternberg (1992) offered a brief set of tips about how to write better papers, which are elaborated in *The Psychologist's Companion* (Sternberg, 2003). Bem's (1995) terse discussion of how to write literature reviews probably deserves your attention, as does his longer essay on writing research reports (Bem, 1987). Nicol and Pexman (1999, 2003) provide solid advice about how to create tables and figures, respectively, for research reports. Peters (1997), Bolker (1998), and Zerubavel (1999) specifically addressed how to write a dissertation, but their books are filled as well with practical advice about writing per se. Most generally, I recommend that aspiring writers read a variety of well-written articles and books—not just by psychologists—with the goal of abstracting effective strategies.

The abundance of articles and books on writing deserves comment. Like the "how-to-diet" genre in the contemporary United States, the "how-to-write" genre flourishes because it meets a desperate need. Writing is difficult, and there is no magic formula for accomplishing it. I hope you consult several of the sources I have mentioned, but I implore you not to study all of them. The only way to learn how to write is to write, and reading extensively about writing postpones the hard work.

REFERENCES

American Psychological Association. (2001). *Publication manual of the American Psychological Association* (5th ed.). Washington, DC: Author.

Bandura, A. (1986). *The social foundations of thought and action: A social cognitive theory.* Englewood Cliffs, NJ: Prentice Hall.

Beck, A. T. (1976). *Cognitive therapy and the emotional disorders.* New York: Harper & Row.

Becker, H. S. (1986). *Writing for social scientists: How to start and finish your thesis, book, or article.* Chicago: University of Chicago Press.

Bem, D. J. (1987). Writing the empirical journal article. In M. P. Zanna & J. M. Darley (Eds.), *The compleat academic: A guide for the beginning social scientist* (pp. 171–201). Mahwah, NJ: Lawrence Erlbaum.

Bem, D. J. (1995). Writing a review article for *Psychological Bulletin. Psychological Bulletin, 118,* 172–177.

Bolker, J. (1998). *Writing your dissertation in fifteen minutes a day: A guide to starting, revising, and finishing your doctoral thesis.* New York: Owl Books.

Booth, W. C., Colomb, G. G., & Williams, J. M. (1995). *The craft of research.* Chicago: University of Chicago Press.

Gelfand, H., & Walker, C. R. (2002). *Mastering APA style: Student's workbook and training guide* (2nd ed.). Washington, DC: APA.

Merton, R. K. (1968). The Matthew effect in science: The reward and communication systems of science are considered. *Science, 159,* 56–63.

Nicholls, J. G. (1978). The development of the concepts of effort and ability, perception of academic attainment, and the understanding that difficult tasks require more ability. *Child Development, 49,* 800–814.

Nicholls, J. G. (1984). Achievement motivation: Conceptions of ability, subjective experience, task choice, and performance. *Psychological Review, 91,* 328–346.

Nicol, A. A. M., & Pexman, P. M., (1999). *Presenting your findings: A practical guide for creating tables.* Washington, DC: APA.

Nicol, A. A. M., & Pexman, P. M. (2003). *Displaying your findings: A practical guide for creating figures, posters, and presentations.* Washington, DC: APA.

Peters, R. L. (1997). *Getting what you came for: The smart student's guide to earning a master's or Ph.D.* (2nd ed.). New York: Noonday Press.

Poincaré, H. (1913). *The foundations of science.* New York: Science Press.

Runkel, P. J., & Runkel, M. (1984). *Guide to usage for writers and students in the social sciences.* Totowa, NJ: Rowman & Allanheld.

Schwartz, B. (2004). *The paradox of choice: Why more is less.* New York: HarperCollins.

Silver, M., & Sabini, J. (1981). Procrastinating. *Journal for the Theory of Social Behaviour, 11,* 207–221.

Sternberg, R. J. (1992, September). How to win acceptance by psychology journals: 21 tips for better writing. *American Psychological Society Observer,* 12.

Sternberg, R. J. (2003). *The psychologist's companion: A guide to scientific writing for students and researchers* (4th ed.). New York: Cambridge University Press.

Strunk, W., & White, E. B. (1984). *Elements of style* (3rd ed.). New York: Macmillan. (Originally published in 1959)

Swan, J. A., & Gopen, G. D. (1990). The science of scientific writing. *American Scientist, 78,* 550–558.

Zerubavel, E. (1999). *The clockwork muse: A practical guide to writing theses, dissertations, and books.* Cambridge, MA: Harvard University Press.

25

REVISING A RESEARCH MANUSCRIPT

DONNA K. NAGATA
STEVEN J. TRIERWEILER

Most authors would agree that there is a great feeling of relief and satisfaction after sending your final manuscript off to the journal editor. By that point, you have expended considerable energy into the paper's conceptualization, analyses, and write-up. (See Chapters 2, 23, 24, and Section IV of this text for guidelines in each of these areas respectively.) Now the manuscript moves into the review process. The American Psychological Association (APA) *Publication Manual* (APA, 2001) describes this process and includes a useful flowchart (p. 359) of the general publication process, which begins with an editor's acknowledgment that your manuscript has been received. Several months after submission, you will receive feedback from the editor about the acceptance or rejection of the paper as well as reviewer comments about your work.

This chapter describes how one goes about revising a research manuscript once it has been submitted for publication. In line with the notion of the "research method script" presented in Chapter 1, the chapter describes a series of steps that are relevant to the revision. It begins with a discussion of journal reviewer comments and how an author might respond to such comments. Next, the chapter illustrates various decision points in the rewriting process. Finally, concrete suggestions are made for resubmitting the paper for further review. Although the focus is on authors who decide to revise and resubmit their research manuscript to the same journal, one should keep in mind that this is not the only option. After carefully reading the review comments and suggestions, you may feel that the requested changes are not appropriate and decide not to resubmit your paper. The fit between your manuscript and the journal may be too discrepant, and you may wish to submit your work to another journal. (It should be noted, however, that such a decision might also require substantial revision of the manuscript.) Therefore, issues relevant to evaluating the fit between a paper and journal will also be discussed. Figure 25.1 provides a summary flowchart of these various stages in the revision process that will be covered.

WHO ARE THE REVIEWERS?

Peer review is a major mechanism for establishing the legitimacy of a research finding and the overall acceptability of an author's interpretation and conclusions. Several works discuss and critique aspects of the editorial and review process

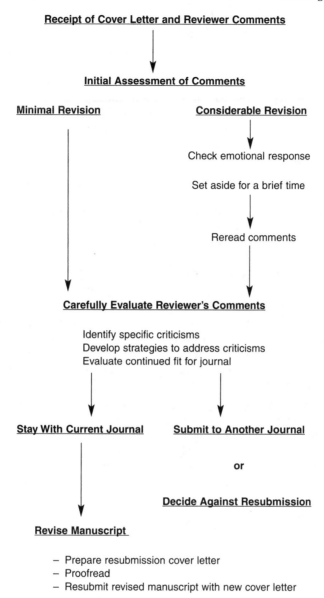

Figure 25.1   Summary Flowchart of Stages in the Revision Process

(e.g., APA, 2001; Ceci & Peters, 1984; Cofer, 1985; Daft, 1995; Finke, 1990; Harcum & Rosen, 1993; Peters & Ceci, 1985; Roediger, 1987). Chapter 26 offers specific suggestions concerning how to deal with journal editors and reviewers. The review process is a critical part of academic scholarship because the quality of a science depends as much on the rigor and accuracy of reviewer scrutiny as it does on the scientific method. Typically, reviewers are researchers and scholars whom editors have identified as experts in the area of research addressed in your manuscript. In all the effort that is required to prepare a manuscript, it is easy to forget that the individuals reading and evaluating your work are highly accomplished individuals in their own right and may be the foremost experts available anywhere in the country or even in the world. Their work usually is anonymous and completely voluntary. Rarely do such individuals treat their responsibility lightly, although the effort they give the task of reviewing may vary considerably from time to time. When functioning properly, there is a tradition and integrity in this system that merits respect. One can refer to the *Journals in Psychology: A Resource Listing for Authors* (APA, 1997) to obtain information on the editorial policies of specific journals as well as the number of published pages per year for each of those journals. The high ratio of submissions relative to the low rate of published articles means that if you get a thorough review, whether it is positive or negative, someone has put a good deal of effort into looking at your paper.

Throughout your work with the publication process, keep in mind that editors and reviewers operate from a systems-level perspective, whereas you will generally be completely wrapped up in your own research. This means that those evaluating the manuscript will be exposed to and affected by comparative information—such as other manuscripts in related areas and their overall sense of the field—to which you will have no access. This is particularly an issue for beginning authors. As part of the general consensus-building process of science, authors must understand how their work fits into this system. The better you become at managing your relationship to the system, the broader will be your opportunities to communicate with others through publication of your work.

Receiving Review Comments

Notification from a journal editor will typically include a cover letter from the editor summarizing the editor's recommendation for acceptance, rejection, or suggestion for revision of your paper based on a summary of reviewer's comments. The length and level of detail in editors' letters vary a great deal, although the majority will provide a restatement of reviewer comments (Fiske & Fogg, 1990). (In some cases, the editor also serves as a reviewer; see Fiske & Fogg, 1990.) Copies of comments from two or more reviewers who have read your manuscript are also typically included. The editor's cover letter

is important. It should give you a sense as to whether a manuscript revision and resubmission to the journal are encouraged or feasible. It can also highlight the most major concerns that would need to be addressed in such a rewrite. Some journals also provide an indication as to whether the manuscript requires major versus minor revisions prior to reconsideration. This, in turn, can help you determine the amount of work that you would need to do to resubmit.

There is understandably a level of apprehension regarding rejection of a manuscript. Similarly, researchers may have concern regarding critical comments from the individual reviewers (Fiske & Fogg, 1990). Such comments play an important role in a decision about resubmitting an article or about submitting it elsewhere. They also provide the author with guidelines for revising the manuscript because in most cases revisions are requested by the editor before a final decision to accept an article is made. First readings of review comments can be emotional: As an author, you may feel that criticisms from a reviewer are misdirected, unhelpful, or incorrect from your perspective. Critiques of your work may feel like a personal insult, especially at the early stages of your career (Sternberg, 2004).

Alternatively, comments may seem helpful and justified, spurring you to notice aspects of the paper that slipped your attention before. For example, a reviewer might provide specific references that expand your thinking on a particular analysis, conceptualization, or interpretation. Two points should be noted here. First, reviewers vary in the tone of their feedback. Some may be bluntly critical, whereas others may raise the same concerns in a more positive manner. Reviewers also vary in the length and detail of their reviews. Second, the typical reviewer spends little time providing positive feedback (Fiske & Fogg, 1990), so authors should be prepared for this. There can be an initial reaction of frustration and disappointment on first reading of the criticisms raised in one's reviews. This response is understandable because you have no way of immediately responding to or rebutting the reviewers' remarks. Still, an emotional response need not be negative: It can bolster a sense of commitment to refining the paper and addressing the questions raised. The goal of any revision should be a stronger presentation of one's work.

One strategy for dealing with the initial receipt of reviews is to read through them and then put them aside for a period of time before rewriting. This can be helpful in allowing you to step back from a potentially emotional first response. How long should you set aside your revision? This, of course, depends in part on other demands on your schedule. Generally, a week or two should help provide some distance from initial emotional reactions. After that time, you can reexamine your comments without experiencing the emotions elicited during a first reading. Try not to leave the task of rereading reviews for too long. Robert Sternberg (2004), a well-known academic psychologist and former president of the APA, noted that one's first reaction to reviews can make the task of revision seem larger than it actually is and lead to procrastination. Setting a time period within which to reread your reviews will prevent you from relying on first reactions to determine the nature of what work you might have ahead of you. In rereading a review, focus on the substance, and you will often find comments to be less negative than initially felt. You may also come to realize that positive indications in the review have been overlooked. These realizations can help you achieve the sense of confidence and efficacy required to approach the task of rewriting.

Applying a step-by-step, problem-focused strategy can also help you manage the emotion associated with evaluation and increase a sense of efficacy. Priority tasks should include the following: (a) evaluate how serious the questions raised by reviewers are; (b) weigh how adequately they can be addressed by revision; (c) determine if revision seems an appropriate course of action; and, if so, (d) develop a plan for revision, including a time frame for its execution.

If there are multiple criticisms to be addressed in a rewrite, it can be helpful for the author to simply begin by listing reactions to those criticisms on one side of a paper and tentative strategies for addressing them on the other side of the paper. In so doing, carefully consider the following questions and strategies. Is something basic to the major message of the study being questioned? If so, can it be addressed?

Alternatively, has the reviewer somehow misunderstood something? If so, how might that have happened? Never assume that your writing is as clear as it can be; sometimes relatively minor changes in writing can get a message across that reviewers could not discern during their examination of the manuscript. Consider carefully your message at each point in the manuscript receiving commentary from the reviewers. Because the reviews you receive will raise different points and suggestions, it can be difficult to track all of these in relation to your manuscript. As an alternative to writing columns of criticisms and strategies, you can also use software tools as an aid to determining the scope of changes to consider. For example, the Tools menu in Microsoft Word offers a Track Changes option. This function allows you to highlight changes and insert text and commentary while still reviewing the original text. You might insert reviewer comments alongside the areas of text requiring attention.

Just because reviewers do not comment on particular sections does not mean that those sections cannot be improved. Imagine a conversation with the reviewer, responding to what she or he seems to be saying and anticipating what the response might be if she or he were to react to your revision. Address each reviewer point, one at a time. Do not ignore or take lightly any comment, however off the mark it may seem from your perspective. Because of time and communication constraints, reviewers will not always be able to articulate thoroughly what is troubling them. Some will tell you this directly; others may express their concern by concentrating on relatively minor specifics, but in a tone that sounds more condemnatory than the crime. Try to read past this to discern the source of the reviewer's concern. In some ways, you are more the expert on your paper than the reviewers can ever be because you have the clearest sense of your intentions and goals. If there is a point of disagreement, then it must be addressed directly if the revision is to succeed. Recognize that ultimately the task is to convince reviewers, and particularly the editor, that their concerns have been adequately addressed. Always operate from a position of balance and clarity; the reviewers are windows to your audience, and heeding their feedback, even when it is vague and uncertain, can greatly improve the presentation of your research.

Do not expect multiple reviewers to provide consensus in their comments. Fiske and Fogg (1990) noted that agreement between reviewer general recommendations typically correlates about .30. In their study of over 400 "free response" comments of reviewers for 153 papers submitted to 12 editors of journals published by the APA, they found that "rarely did one reviewer make the same point as any other reviewer of that paper" (p. 593). This means that you should carefully consider the full range of issues raised before attempting to rewrite your paper.

Despite the lack of consensus about particular events, certain areas of weakness appear in reviewer comments frequently. Fiske and Fogg (1990) examined the distribution of manuscript weaknesses reported by their sample of reviewers across 10 categories: presentation of conceptual work prior to execution; linkage of conceptual work to execution, design, procedures, measurement, statistical analyses, results, interpretations and conclusions, editorial and writing, and general weaknesses. Of these 10, the most frequently cited locus was "interpretations and conclusions," followed by, in order, presentation of conceptual work prior to execution, results, procedures, and design. One can also refer to Daft's (1995) chapter titled, "Why I Recommended That Your Manuscript Be Rejected and What You Can Do About It," in which he identified frequent problems encountered in over 100 of his own reviews. An additional resource cited by Fiske and Fogg (1990) is Smigel and Ross's (1970) presentation of reasons for acceptance and rejection from the perspective of associate editors.

COMMON AREAS FOR REVISION OF A RESEARCH MANUSCRIPT

The particular areas requiring revision for a given paper will, of course, vary. Reviewers may urge an author to expand the coverage of literature in the introductory portion of the paper or in the Interpretations and Conclusions, or both. The editor or reviewers may also suggest the need for additional or different statistical analyses in the

study. In that case, the revision requires not only the running of more analyses but also changing the Results and Interpretation/Conclusion sections to reflect those findings. Consistent with the 10 categories of manuscript weakness used by Fiske and Fogg (1990), we can divide reviewer comments into five overarching areas of concern: (a) substantive or theoretical, (b) methodological, (c) data analytic, (d) interpretive, and (e) publication fit. In this section, we provide an overview of some common ways these areas of critique interact with the structure of the research report and discuss their implications for revising the manuscript. When reviewer comments are nonspecific, it is especially important for authors to consider the possibility that portions of the manuscript other than those discussed by reviewers might be strengthened, thereby reducing the probability of additional questions down the line.

Revising the Front Matter

The front matter of a manuscript will set the reviewers' expectations for the article and the research it describes. Even a small oversight or lack of clarity here can make a huge difference in reviewer response to your article. By the same token, a small change can sometimes completely eliminate reviewers' concerns. Never underestimate the possibility that your title and abstract have led reviewers to expect something you have not delivered in the body of your manuscript. Does your title contain words and phrases that link directly to the central themes of your report? Does the abstract tell the story in a way that is logically consistent with your more detailed development in the body of the article? If not, then consider changing them or rewriting parts of the manuscript so as to strengthen the logical ties between the front matter and the body of the article.

Revising the Introduction

The Introduction consists of three major components: a statement of the research problem, a literature review, and an elaboration of a basic theoretical framework. Fiske and Fogg (1990), consistent with our own experience as reviewers and authors, suggested that any one or all of these can be a source of reviewer concern.

These different elements are usually strongly linked. As with the front matter, the statement of the problem will lead reviewers to have expectations about what follows. The literature discussed should be directly focused on the research problem and provide the reader with a sense of the state of the field with respect to the problem. Reviewers, as experts in relevant areas, may notice problems in the completeness, appropriateness, and accuracy of your presentation of the literature. Sometimes, these concerns can be handled by adding, or even eliminating, references. Usually, however, they revolve around the more central issue of elaborating a theoretical framework: Too often this is left implicit in the presentation as authors pay too much attention to what others have said and shy away from the problem of justifying and rendering comprehensible their own research. Good literature reviews for research reports stay strongly focused on the problem at hand and provide only enough detail to inform the current study. Theoretical frameworks guiding the research should be as specific as possible, given the area of research. They are evaluated in terms of appropriateness, adequacy, the extent to which they justify the Method and Results to follow, and the clarity and logic with which they link what is known in the literature to the findings of your study. A well-designed figure provides an excellent visual presentation of a theory's key constructs and their interrelationships. Because of their great power in summarizing complex information, we recommend that authors include such displays whenever feasible, for both qualitative and quantitative information (Tufte, 1990).

Revising the Method Section

If reviewers find something basic to be wrong with the design or execution of the study, such as a confound, additional data collection may be the only way to correct it. Less severe reviewer concerns about the method usually will involve questions about clarity. The focus will be on matters such as the participant sample, study design, measures, and procedures. In a well-designed study and successful research report, these elements will be clear and obviously linked to the overall goals of the research. The aim is to get the reviewers nodding as they read so that all makes sense and there are few or no surprises. Good reviewers and good readers will notice if you fail to report material like relevant reliability coefficients, so a policy of full and unabashed disclosure is a must. Even problematic research situations play well with reviewers when handled appropriately by authors. On revision, attend to and correct any situation that may have led the reviewer to doubt that the manuscript is a complete account of what was done—such doubts can quickly generalize to other aspects of the manuscript and can greatly impede the success of the report. Of course, it is possible that reviewers will identify design flaws or weaknesses in the study that are insurmountable in a revision. If so, one should look again at the study trying to establish the level of conclusion that is supported in the work. It still may be possible to publish the results if the interpretation and conclusions are developed at a level consistent with the strengths and weaknesses of the study. Alternatively, reviewers may have given a clear indication of what additional work is needed to achieve a publishable product.

Revising the Results Section

For many studies, results are altogether harder to report than scientists care to admit. Beginning authors often miss the subtlety of a good presentation of research findings, particularly the subtlety of balancing everything one looked at with the practical matter of making a focused and compelling case for what your study reveals about the research problem. The trick is to find the proper level of focus in the Results—neither too detailed nor too general—and to organize the presentation in such a way that the reader is taken to ground level in your research and back up again so as to be ready for the conclusions to be drawn in the Discussion. The logical ties between the research question, the design of the study, and the major results to be considered should be carried in both the way the results are presented and in the order of the presentation. Secondary but important matters are held apart from the central development and presented as such with the promise of later interpretation in the Discussion section. Again, thoroughness is extremely important, but reviewers will not appreciate unnecessary and distracting detail. It is also extremely important to be accurate and thorough in presenting statistical findings, but do not succumb to the trap of depending too heavily on statistical sophistication to impress reviewers. Studies need to be up to date and sophisticated, but ultimately reviewers want to know how the data from this study inform the research question. Consider that statistical tests address the probability that differences observed in your results might occur by chance; once dealt with, this problem is of little substantive significance to your presentation (see Cohen, 1994). The essence of your study is in the structure of the data, as in the size of mean differences observed between groups in your design. You will never be faulted for presenting basic descriptive and summary information along with the higher-level statistical analyses—these can easily be removed if not required, but you may well be faulted if you do not. If the Results section requires revision, efforts designed to make clear the interesting and informative aspects of your data, including addition of or editing of tables and figures, are the most likely to be successful. The APA *Publication Manual* (2001) devotes specific sections to data presentation and Nichol and Pexman (2003) have also written a practical guide to displaying research findings. As you rewrite your results, be sure there is a logical order in the presentation that helps the reader quickly grasp what is being examined and how. The tighter this organization, the less likely that reviewers will be led to questions they might not have otherwise considered.

Revising the Discussion

Discussion sections can also be difficult to write, and it is here that reviewers often find inadequacies in first submissions. The objectives of a good discussion are to unravel the major themes of the research, drawing out their implications for theory and research, and to elaborate conclusions that are appropriately sensitive to the strengths and limitations of the study. Reviewers are looking for it all to come together in the Discussion, and they are not expecting to have to expend much effort to understand how it comes together. That is the job of the author. Unfortunately, in our experience as reviewers, too often one finds that the

Discussion trails off inconclusively or the theoretical implications of the work are minimally dealt with, even in otherwise strong research projects. One often gets the impression that authors have not really thought seriously about the larger implications of their work. Or worse, it can seem as though they are waiting to see what reviewers say before committing themselves. Although this seems like a good—albeit Machiavellian—strategy for getting a paper published, it is extremely bad form to leave it to reviewers to figure out how to explain what they believe the paper needs. Thus, revisions of Discussion sections are typically oriented toward broadening the interpretation of the results to place them in the context of the larger theoretical problems addressed by the project, to correct any tendencies to draw conclusions that are too strong or too weak, given the limitations for the study design, and to link the results to other areas that are theoretically or empirically related to the study. Because discussions are interpretive, there are no simple rules governing their production and revision. It is useful, however, to keep in mind a goal of striking a balance between staying close to the data in your interpretations, and fairly discussing the broader implications of the work.

Important future research can emerge from a well constructed Discussion section, so carefully consider what you would like your reader audience left with as you paper comes to a conclusion. The more explicitly and incisively you can articulate these thoughts, the more affirmative will be reviewer response. Alternatively, if reviewers find points for disagreement, your clarity will have established the basis for productive dialogue with reviewers in defense (or modification) of your position that can greatly improve both your paper and your understanding of your research area. Remember, a major ideal in science is to establish a consensus around an area of study and to establish unequivocally the empirical basis for that consensus. In working toward this goal, you will note that some concrete ways of interpreting your results are fairly noncontroversial. The problem, however, comes in linking these basics to higher-level theoretical interpretations (e.g., Cronbach & Meehl, 1955). This is an art form that is often best learned and exercised in revision of a scientific report based on reviewer response.

EVALUATING JOURNAL FIT

In many cases, it is clear that the journal to which you have chosen to submit your work is the right one for its ultimate publication. Nonetheless, it is important to be aware that the fit of a manuscript with the journal's usual type and quality of article is regularly assessed by reviewers. The APA *Publication Manual* (APA, 2001) lists summaries of policy statements on its journals and descriptions of the kinds of articles they publish. Many of the descriptions indicate the major criteria for acceptance as well as the content areas deemed appropriate. Authors may also consult the *Journals in Psychology: A Resource Listing for Authors* (APA, 1997), and the *Author's Guide to Journals in Behavioral Sciences* (Wang, 1989). The APA *Publication Manual* (APA, 2001), however, and the organization Web site (www.apa.org) suggest that authors always refer to the policy statements published in the most recent edition of the particular journal to which they are submitting because that is where changes in current editorial policies will be documented.

Reviewers will be judging the extent to which your research is of interest to the journal's readership and the overall importance of the work in advancing knowledge in your area. These are obviously comparative judgments depending as much on the pool of submissions to a journal as on the merits of any given manuscript—this is true of publishing in general. Journals will vary in the extent to which they seek only the most advanced level of research product. Depending on the type of feedback you get from reviewers, you might use the opportunity to revise to reassess whether you have submitted your manuscript to the best journal. What constitutes the *best* journal? Many feel publication is most desirable in an APA journal; however, whether an APA journal provides the best outlet and readership for your particular work is a personal decision. Therefore, you may wish to examine other journals as well, although there is

general agreement that you should, if at all possible, keep to a peer-reviewed journal rather than a journal that does not apply review standards.

In their letter of response, editors will be tentative about the extent to which a revision will be successful: After all, they cannot know how effectively you will be able to handle the revision. Generally, however, the suggestion that an author "revise and resubmit" is positive feedback, suggesting at least the possibility that an article appropriate for the journal can be produced from your research. In all this, keep in mind that once you have produced a successful manuscript, your interest will immediately transform to a focus on whether or not the work is getting adequate exposure in the journal. Use the revision time to carefully reconsider this issue, but be mindful not to delay resubmission of your paper too long. As Sternberg (2004) points out, "Scientific products, like refrigerator products in a supermarket, have a shelf life (p. 145)," and procrastination can delay getting one's work out and diminish the timeliness of its impact.

ADDITIONAL POINTS TO CONSIDER IN EXECUTING THE REVISION

So far we have focused largely on the feedback from journal editors and reviewers as key in revising a research manuscript. Attention to such feedback is essential if one wishes to have work published in a refereed journal; however, the revision process is much broader than this. To revise is to, quite literally, *re-see* one's work. An author may, on the basis of feedback from the reviewers and his or her own rereading of the paper, wish to incorporate additional new material. In this sense, a reviewer's comments can offer the author an outside view of his or her paper. As reviewer criticisms are addressed, authors gain a new perspective on their work. Similarly, it is useful to have revisions read by colleagues before resubmission to the journal because authors can become so involved in the rewrite that it becomes difficult to identify flaws in the paper.

In fact, one challenge in rewriting a research manuscript stems from the incorporation of changes while maintaining a coherent, logical writing style. Although the cut-and-paste functions of word processing are enormously helpful, they can lead to choppy manuscripts. Authors should carefully review their own papers during the revision process, paying attention to their writing, grammar, and punctuation. Fiske and Fogg (1990) noted that "it is impressive that the reviewers saw as many problems in the presentation—exposition and description—as in the actual research activities" (p. 592) of the papers reviewed in their study. Clearly, editors and reviewers would pay equal or perhaps even more attention to this issue when reviewing a resubmitted manuscript.

In writing your manuscript, and once again in preparing your revision, pay special attention to the overall unity and tightness of the writing. These qualities of good writing can be difficult to achieve, but they will become increasingly apparent as your revision develops. Basically, they give readers a sense of everything fitting together in a lucid and seamless manner; readers are effectively pulled along by the writing, with relative ease, through even the most complicated sections. This does not mean that you cannot write about complicated topics but rather that effort is made to anticipate where readers are as they enter a section and that provision is made to help them move quickly through it. Economy is of the essence. A few well-chosen transitions or subheadings can work wonders in this regard, and authors revising wisely are ever on the lookout to improve this aspect of a manuscript. It is a virtual certainty that reviewers will respond positively to their efforts.

Once you feel your revised manuscript is ready for resubmission, you should prepare a cover letter to accompany the rewritten paper when it is sent to the journal editor. In addition to specifying the paper as a resubmission, it is often helpful to describe how the various points raised in the editor's feedback and reviewer comments have been addressed in the revision. If there are points that you decided not to change or address, you should articulate your reasons for doing so. This alerts the editor to the fact that you have not missed a reviewer's suggestion and provides a rationale for the decisions in the rewrite. Overall, such a letter clarifies in summary form the significant ways in which the revised manuscript has taken into account previous concerns. (See Chapter 26 for additional information on dealing with editors and reviewers.)

In closing, here are two final thoughts: First, if reviewers have worked for you, whether their work has seemed easy or difficult, fair or misguided, it is likely your manuscript is better at resubmission than before. Although the APA *Publication Manual* (2001) discourages the acknowledgment of peer reviewers or editors, associate editors, and consulting editors in the author's notes of a paper, they do state that authors may acknowledge a specific idea raised by a reviewer in the text where that idea is addressed. Second, we have presented revision as a common and workable step in the process of publishing research findings. Nonetheless, it is not without its pitfalls: For example, the added clarity of a revision can, on occasion, raise new, unanticipated questions for reviewers. Editors are generally not inclined to put authors in double jeopardy, but neither will they ignore serious doubts legitimately raised in the review process. It is important for authors to recognize that this is simply a part of the consensus-generating system, however arduous it may seem. It is useful to always consider yourself in a learning process, learning new things about how your research might be conceptualized, perhaps about how to communicate in the peer review system, perhaps about yourself and your work. Such attitudes may help you accept the discipline and humility required to publish your work and, perhaps, will make the problem of manuscript revision a bit more palatable. In any case, standing with your conclusions in the presence of your peers is a big part of what science is all about, and few aspects of the process will put you there quite like revising your work. As with the initial submission, there is relief again when the revision is complete and comfort in the sense that the manuscript has improved. It should be remembered, however, that revision does not guarantee acceptance, although the probability of acceptance can improve with revision. Fiske and Fogg (1990) pointed out that whereas only 2% of initial submissions are accepted (Eichorn & VandenBos, 1985), between 20% and 40% of revised manuscripts are accepted. The process of review and publication is an imperfect art form (Kupfersmid, 1988; Sussman, 1993), and the reliability between reviewers has been questioned (Peters & Ceci; 1982; Spencer, Hartnett, & Mahoney, 1986). Nonetheless, peer review remains the standard in science, and this is unlikely to change anytime soon. With luck and diligence, the effort will pay off, and you will see work you can be proud of go to print.

EXERCISES

1. Find a peer with whom you can share a paper you have written in psychology. Have that person write a critical review of your paper. Once you have read your review, try to follow the suggestions in this chapter in responding to it. Next, write a revision, including the cover letter, outlining how you have addressed various points raised by your reviewer. Finally, meet with your peer reviewer to discuss the revision process. Repeat these steps, but this time you take on the role of the reviewer who evaluates and comments on a peer's paper. This exercise allows you to get an idea of both sides of the process: receiving and responding to a reviewer's comments and taking the perspective of a reviewer. The exercise also includes the added benefit of allowing you to talk with your reviewer to get an inside perspective on how he or she came to write their review comments. This step does not occur in the actual reviewing process but serves here as an added way to deconstruct the commentary process.

2. Select a published paper and carefully evaluate it. Identify what makes this paper successful. What sections are especially clear? Next, consider what areas could be improved. (Note: even published papers that have successfully passed through the review process can have areas for improvement.) Finally, consider your own writing and assess the degree to which your writing reflects these strengths and weaknesses. This exercise will help you to identify models of effective writing and pinpoint potential areas of your own writing where revision may be most challenging.

RECOMMENDED READINGS

The APA *Publication Manual* (2001) provides an excellent overview of many of the issues covered in this chapter, including specifics on manuscript preparation, an overview of the editorial and review process, and general writing guidelines. Additional readings that cover more specific issues related to editorial and review procedures include Cummings and Frost's *Publishing in the Organizational Sciences* (1995), Jackson and Rushton's *Scientific Excellence: Origins and Assessment* (1987), and DeBakey's *The Scientific Journal: Editorial Policies and Practices* (1976). Another perspective on these issues can be found in Sussman's (1993) article, "The Charybdis of Publishing in Academia." There are also several excellent books that discuss the construction of figures, graphs, and visual displays of information. These include two volumes by Tufte, *Envisioning Information* (1990) and *The Visual Display of Quantitative Information* (1983) and Nichol & Pexman's *Displaying Your Research Findings: A Practical Guide for Creating Figures, Posters, and Presentations* (2003). Additional sources are Kosslyn's *Elements of Graph Design* (1994) and Wilkinson, Hill, and Vang's *Graphics* (1992).

REFERENCES

American Psychological Association. (1997). *Journals in psychology: A resource listing for authors.* Washington, DC: Author.

American Psychological Association. (2001). *Publication manual of the American Psychological Association* (5th ed.). Washington, DC: Author.

Ceci, S. J., & Peters, D. (1984). How blind is blind review? *American Psychologist, 39,* 1491–1494.

Cofer, C. N. (1985). Some reactions to manuscript review from a questionnaire study. *Behavioral and Brain Sciences, 8,* 745–746.

Cohen, J. (1994). The earth is round ($p < .05$). *American Psychologist, 49,* 997–1003.

Cronbach, L. J., & Meehl, P. E. (1955). Construct validity in psychological tests. *Psychological Bulletin, 52,* 281–302.

Cummings, L. L., & Frost, P. J. (Eds.). (1995). *Publishing in the organizational sciences* (2nd ed.). Homewood, IL: Richard D. Irwin.

Daft, R. L. (1995). Why I recommended that your manuscript be rejected and what you can do about it. In L. L. Cummings & P. J. Frost (Eds.), *Publishing in the organizational sciences* (2nd ed., pp. 193–204). Homewood, IL: Richard D. Irwin.

DeBakey, L. (1976). *The scientific journal: Editorial policies and practices.* St. Louis, MO: C. V. Mosby.

Eichorn, D. H., & VandenBos, G. R. (1985). Dissemination of scientific and professional knowledge: Journal publication within the APA. *American Psychologist, 40,* 1309–1316.

Finke, R. A. (1990). Recommendations for contemporary editorial practices. *American Psychologist, 45,* 669–670.

Fiske, D. W., & Fogg, L. (1990). But the reviewers are making different criticisms of my paper! Diversity and uniqueness in reviewer comments. *American Psychologist, 45,* 591–598.

Harcum, E. R., & Rosen, E. F. (1993). *The gatekeepers of psychology: Evaluation of peer review by case history.* Westport, CT: Praeger.

Jackson, D. N., & Rushton, J. P. (Eds.). (1987). *Scientific excellence: Origins and assessment.* Newbury Park, CA: Sage.

Kosslyn, S. M. (1994). *Elements of graph design.* New York: W. H. Freeman.

Kupfersmid, J. (1988). Improving what is published: A model in search of an editor. *American Psychologist, 43,* 635–642.

Nichol, A. A. M., & Pexman, P. M. (2003). *Displaying your research findings: A practical guide for creating figures, posters, and presentations.* Washington, DC: APA.

Peters, D., & Ceci, S. J. (1982). Peer-review practices of psychological journals: The fate of published articles submitted again. *Behavioral and Brain Sciences, 5,* 187–255.

Peters, D., & Ceci, S. J. (1985). Peer review: Beauty is in the eye of the beholder. *Behavioral and Brain Sciences, 8,* 747–750.

Roediger, H. L., III. (1987). The role of journal editors in the scientific process. In D. N. Jackson & J. P. Rushton (Eds.), *Scientific excellence: Origins and assessment* (pp. 222–252). Newbury Park, CA: Sage.

Smigel, E. D., & Ross, H. L. (1970). Factors in the editorial decision. *American Sociologist, 5,* 19–21.

Spencer, N. J., Hartnett, J., & Mahoney, J. (1986). Problems with review in the standard editorial practice. *Journal of Social Behavior and Personality, 1,* 21–36.

Sternberg, R. J. (2004). Psychology 101-1/2: *The unspoken rules for success in academia.* Washington, DC: APA.

Sussman, M. B. (1993). The Charybdis of publishing in academia. *Marriage and Family Review, 18,* 161–169.

Tufte, E. R. (1983). *The visual display of quantitative information.* Cheshire, CT: Graphics Press.

Tufte, E. R. (1990). *Envisioning information.* Cheshire, CT: Graphics Press.

Wang, A. Y. (1989). *Author's guide to journals in the behavioral sciences.* Hillsdale, NJ: Lawrence Erlbaum.

Wilkinson, L., Hill, M., & Vang, E. (1992). *Graphics.* Evanston, IL: Systat.

26

DEALING WITH JOURNAL EDITORS AND REVIEWERS

SAMUEL H. OSIPOW

A fter all the work on a research project has been completed, it is logical to pursue publication. After all, part of the scientist's obligation is to share results with a wide audience. But many potential barriers exist to thwart reaching this objective, not the least of which are those thrown up by the editor and reviewers of periodicals to which one submits the work. In what follows, I will present some fundamental procedures that may reduce the frustration that attempts to publish may cause and possibly even enhance the success of the publication effort.

PREPARING THE MANUSCRIPT

The first step starts long before the research has been completed. It is imperative to begin with a good (read "important and interesting to your field") research idea and a sound research design (see Wampold, Chapter 6 of this volume). Next, the data must be based on a sample that is appropriate and large enough to test the hypotheses. These hypotheses, in turn, should be clearly stated, and their source—that is, the theory or empirical findings of others—should be identified and illustrated. A thorough literature review should be conducted to enable the author to be satisfied that the study is either

sufficiently different from those that have gone before or an accurate replication. (See Reed and Baxter, Chapter 3 of this volume.) Last, in this early state, is the adequate analysis of the data, using appropriate statistics interpreted properly. In other words, there is no substitute for good work in enhancing the probability of successful publication in journals. (See DiLalla & Dollinger, Chapter 16, and Steelman & Levy, Chapter 20 of this volume.)

SELECTING AN OUTLET

Good work alone, however, though necessary, is not sufficient to achieve publication. With your research results in hand and your research report in front of you, the next task is to identify the appropriate outlets for your work. The easiest way to accomplish this is to read or skim several issues of the journals that you think might be appropriate outlets. Most periodicals have a statement of goals and definitions as part of their masthead. Read these statements carefully to satisfy yourself, at least at a preliminary level, that the journal has possibilities as an outlet for your research. You should also look at the table of contents of several recent issues to see what has recently been judged to be appropriate. If you are still uncertain, drafting a letter of inquiry to the editor briefly summarizing your study (in a page) and asking for an opinion of the appropriateness of its submission may be helpful. Most editors will respond to such an inquiry because it can save hours of wasted editorial and reviewer time. One of the more annoying things that editors experience is receiving a manuscript from someone who obviously has never seen the periodical, because anyone who had would have known better than to submit it.

Also be sure that you look at the most recent issues in considering topical appropriateness. Although the mission statement on the masthead may be constant over several years, there is often a drift of topical importance as various interests under the general topic of the journal wax and wane. It is also important to send the manuscript to the current editor, so check carefully the name and address to which it should be sent.

While reading the masthead statement, determine several other important mechanical pieces of information that can cost you time (and the good will of the editor) if not followed. Make yourself aware of such simple things as how many copies to submit, whether the manuscript should be prepared to expedite blind review, manuscript style and format requirements, and if a disc must be submitted. *Blind review* permits the author to be anonymous to the reviewers. To a young investigator, this has the advantage of permitting the manuscript to be judged on its merits, not on the author's reputation (or lack thereof).

At this state, prepare your manuscript in the proper format. Important here is the need to avoid falling in love with your words. Often manuscripts submitted for publication are based on master's thesis or doctoral dissertation research. An editor can almost always tell if that is so, partly because the manuscript is probably too long, provides a more comprehensive literature than is necessary or appropriate, and goes into more detail in the presentation of results and discussion than is necessary in journal publication. You must learn to take a heavy hand with the blue pencil, cutting down your paper to journal length while maintaining the important methodological details and results so that the article is comprehensible to a reader who

is relatively unfamiliar with your topic. You have probably grown so familiar with your study that you cannot always see where holes may exist in your presentation. You may want to consult with experienced colleagues about these gaps. The question of length is another good reason to become familiar with the journal you are considering. You can get some idea of the typical paper length by examining several recent issues.

A word about the presentation of tables and figures is in order. Detailed instructions in the American Psychological Association (APA) *Publication Manual* (2001) describe the format of tables and figures and should be carefully followed. It is important, however, to emphasize that the author must use good judgment in deciding what is appropriately presented in a tabular or pictorial manner. If the information is readily presented in the text, a table or figure is probably unnecessary.

After you have produced a draft that you think is reasonably good, turn it over to a colleague or professor and ask for critical comment. The pain of receiving criticism is more than offset by the value such feedback provides. A naive (to your paper, anyway) reader can perceive flaws that you, as the author, will gloss over because of your familiarity with the topic and paper. Thus, such outside friendly readers may find poor sentence structure, vague antecedents, poor organization, sentences that are not clear, gaps in information provided, confusing tables and figures, and many other shortcomings. Remember that it is far better to get this critique from a sympathetic reader than from an editor or reviewer, whose critical words may be far harsher.

SOME TYPICAL EDITORIAL RESPONSES

After you are sure that the manuscript is typed accurately and attractively and that the tables and figures are properly presented, you are ready to mail your manuscript to the editor for review. Then the long wait for word of the outcome begins. Most psychology journals hope to have the reviews back to authors in about 2 months, but sometimes it takes far longer because of tardy reviewers or editorial workload. Most editors will acknowledge the receipt of a manuscript and at the same time provide some idea of the length of time the review might take. If you have received no word after more than 3 months, it is reasonable to inquire about the status of the manuscript.

When you finally get the editorial response, it may take various forms, each of which stimulates its own distinctive author reaction. By far the best outcome is for the editor to say the paper is wonderful and is accepted as submitted. To give the reader an idea how rare that outcome is, in my experience as a journal editor (during which I have made editorial decisions on close to 3,000 manuscripts), I can remember only three times that I accepted a paper as it was submitted originally, and two of those times the paper was by the same author.

The worst outcome, of course, is outright rejection. Your feelings as an author will be hurt. There is a predictable sequence of emotions that authors experience after a paper is summarily rejected. First is shock: How could this happen after all my hard work? Then, anger: Those readers and the editor are fools, or they are prejudiced against me or my topic, or both. These stages last different lengths of time in different people. An experienced author, full of confidence, will experience less extreme reactions of shorter duration because such an author has a context within which to evaluate the decision and more self-confidence in his or her ability to write for professional publication. During the anger stage, it is important to do nothing: Don't change the manuscript and don't write or call the editor (lest your emotions lead to statements that make the matter worse).

There is another type of rejection, which, though inconvenient, is less painful. That is when the editor suggests that you submit your paper to another periodical for which your topic may be more relevant. Often the editor will even make suggestions about where to submit.

After the first two stages have passed, a more rational reaction begins to emerge. The author can read the comments and evaluate them with better judgment. Sometimes it becomes clear that the paper would go better elsewhere. Other times, the comments will lead the author either to develop alternative ways of presentation that might be more publishable or to identify flaws in the study or analysis that can be corrected through conducting another study. Sometimes an author will gradually get to the point of wanting to thank the editor and reviewers for rejecting the paper because it has spared the author the embarrassment of publishing something with serious defects for the entire world to see.

Whatever the outcome, remember that many journals in psychology reject 85–90% of the manuscripts submitted, so don't overreact to a rejection. If you believe that your paper fundamentally has merit despite the rejection, think of ways to revise and new places to submit the paper. A persistent author is usually successful in achieving publication, although perhaps not in the outlet of first choice.

Two other editorial decisions frequently occur. The editor may write, "This manuscript is not publishable as submitted, but if you are willing to make the changes suggested by the reviewers (see enclosed), we will be willing to consider a revised manuscript." Here, you must realize, the editor is not making a commitment to publish if you change the paper, only a commitment to re-review, something not ordinarily done by editors. This type of decision can be discouraging and contains certain pitfalls. An author may spend a great deal of time reworking the manuscript, only to find that on resubmission the editor sends the manuscript to one or more new reviewers, who then find different flaws. Even worse, a new editor might have been appointed since the invitation to revise, opening up the possibility for even further suggestions for change. Following this scenario, revision can proceed ad infinitum without reaching closure. If this happens to you, you would be wise to impose a limit on the number of times you will revise the paper.

A better outcome is when the editor tells you that the paper is publishable, provided you are willing to make certain specific changes in the presentation, and then tells you what must be changed or where the shortcomings of the paper lie. Here it is important for the author to understand clearly the changes desired before proceeding. If the changes are not clear to you, feel free to ask the editor for clarification.

Revising the Manuscript

Ordinarily, when the accept-with-revision option is offered, the author has a limited amount of time to make the changes. (See Nagata & Trierweiler, Chapter 25 of this volume.) If you do not think the editor has given you enough time, either because the changes will take more time and effort than the editor estimates or because your own schedule is very hectic and will delay your ability to pay prompt attention to the manuscript, then write or call the editor and ask for more time, explaining your reasons and indicating how much more time you will need. Most editors will grant such extensions if the request is made in a timely fashion and seems reasonable.

Another point to remember is that editorial feedback can and should be educational. If it is possible for you, assume the attitude that the editor and the reviewers are trying to help you and are on your side, or at least are not against you. Many, if not all, editors perceive part of their job as editor is to teach neophytes how to publish.

Regardless of which of the above-described outcomes occurs, there should be detailed and substantive feedback from which the author can learn more about conducting research and writing about its results. Of course, this educational phase cannot occur until the shock and anger have passed.

Dealing With Critical Feedback

One of the most difficult features of reading feedback about a manuscript is the tone of the reviewer's comments. Very often the editor encloses uncut copies of the criticisms made by the reviewers. As an author, you may sometimes get the feeling that the review and editorial process is adversarial in nature. Unfortunately, the comments are often extremely hostile and derogatory. All too often, they pass beyond the realm of genuine constructive criticism and enter into the realm of ad hominem attacks. Usually, the editor is more tactful in giving feedback, but sometimes editors, too, slip into that angry and demeaning style. In the periodicals I have edited, the reviewers are instructed to avoid taking an adversarial approach and instead view their role as helping to make the manuscript the best it can be, or at least provide feedback that the author can use to improve later manuscripts. Experience with that approach has shown not only that the authors appreciate that style but that the reviewers do as well. It would be well for authors to remember that principle when they become reviewers.

One might think that such angry, hostile comments would be connected exclusively with manuscripts that are rejected; however, one is likely to find them in connection with manuscripts that are accepted with revision or invited for a resubmission. This factor makes it all the more difficult for the author to pass through the angry reactive stage and into the constructive stage necessary for writing a revision. The best thing an author can do is put the manuscript aside for a day or two. The comments will still look bad in a few days, but usually the author is calmer. Then abstract the main features of the needed revisions so that it will not be necessary to keep rereading the irritating comments, which will only rekindle the unconstructive, angry feelings.

Disagreeing With Editorial Recommendations

At this point, the author can set about the task of revising the manuscript on the merits of the comments. As noted earlier, after a short time has passed, the comments are likely to look less intimidating and the author's emotion about them has probably drained away to a manageable level. It is likely that the author will have some good arguments to use in rebuttal about one or more of the suggested changes. These counterarguments can be made in a cover letter with the resubmitted manuscript.

In fact, it is useful, and may be mandatory, to write a letter with an explanation about how each of the editorial concerns raised was resolved. Some editors actually require authors to write a letter detailing their treatment of each of the needed changes. Such a letter serves the purposes of both the editor and the author. For the editor, the letter serves as a quick summary of changes needed and made, enabling the editor to make a faster decision about whether the new version is now satisfactory. For the author, the letter can serve a similar purpose. It can serve as a checklist that the author can use to see whether all the required changes have been made. This is when it is appropriate to make your counterpoints because they can be made in a naturally flowing manner.

When the editorial recommendations seem patently incorrect to you, it may be tempting to argue with the editor. This option should be approached with caution because such behavior could antagonize an editor and could also be a waste of your own time. If, however, you cannot accept a major recommended change and your arguments cannot be easily incorporated into the cover letter, the most likely way to present an effective rebuttal is to use the literature, existing data as well as your own, and, above all, logic in attempting to persuade the editor to your point of view.

A related issue is when, if ever, it is appropriate to challenge the rejection of a manuscript. My personal opinion is never, but many authors have had success with their challenges. To challenge, use the same points mentioned (literature, data, and logic) to make your case. It is likely that the best outcome you will achieve is a fresh review by two different editorial consultants, a not altogether trivial result. In fact, that might be the specific request to make when petitioning the editor.

The checklist below summarizes the points made in this chapter about how to deal with editors and reviewers:

1. Thoroughly review the related literature.

2. If possible, start with a theoretical underpinning.

3. Ensure the importance of your research.

4. Prepare a sound research design and use appropriate statistical analyses.

5. Identify appropriate publication outlets.

6. Prepare the manuscript using the proper format for the publication you chose.

7. Upon return from review, do not react emotionally to editorial feedback or decisions.

8. If suggestions about revisions are made, be sure you clearly understand the revisions that the editor requires.

9. Write an explanatory cover letter about the changes you have made.

I have left unsaid the importance of learning the skills involved in effective writing. These skills are necessary before even the first step in publishing your research can be taken. You might consider the usefulness of having someone help with the editorial aspects of your writing before the original submission.

EXERCISES

Exercise 1: Volunteering

Volunteering to do proposal reviews for conferences at the regional and national level helps with gaining practice in looking at research projects in a critical way, especially with regard to attaining particular standards. This exposure not only helps students practice critical inspection of research by recognizing what one needs to look out for but also exposes one to current quality research in the field. Besides, these conference committees often look for student volunteers, and this is a good way to get involved in organizations that match one's interests.

Exercise 2: Journal Reviews

It would be beneficial for students or novice researchers to go to their local library and look up journals that match their research interests or projects. It would be advisable then to list and summarize themes, requirements, and contact information of the potential journals, keeping in mind that this information changes and thus needs to be updated on a regular basis. This activity will help familiarize students with the quality and requirements of published articles in the journals of interest. This will also save time in the long run, as students can adapt their research to meet those standards and can keep them in mind as they develop their research projects with the goal of publishing in those journals of interest.

Exercise 3: Practicing

Novice researchers or students can write class papers and conduct class research projects with these standards and expectations in mind. Friends and faculty can be enlisted to review them as if they were being sent to editors of journals. It is advisable to approach faculty whose research interests and specialty areas match those of the project at hand, as this increases the probability that they will have a vested interest in helping you publish as well. Faculty will also be able to advise one about the process of publishing. This exercise will provide experience with feedback, revising work, and basically being open to this process of conducting publishable research.

RECOMMENDED READINGS

We recommend that the reader consult the following sources for more in-depth information about the topics covered in this chapter: Daft (1985), Cummings and Frost (1985), Weick (1985), and Dorn's *Publishing for Professional Development* (1985), especially the chapter by Gelso and Osipow (1985).

REFERENCES

American Psychological Association. (2001). *Publication manual of the American Psychological Association* (5th ed.). Washington, DC: Author.

Cummings, L. L., & Frost, P. J. (Eds.). (1985). *Publishing in the organizational sciences*. Homewood, IL; Richard D. Irwin.

Daft, R. L. (1985). Why I recommended that your manuscript be rejected and what you can do about it. In L. L. Cummings & P. J. Frost (Eds.), *Publishing in the organizational sciences* (pp. 193–204). Homewood, IL; Richard D. Irwin.

Dorn, F. J. (Ed.). (1985). *Publishing for professional development*. Muncie, IN: Accelerated Development.

Gelso, C. J., & Osipow, S. H. (1985). Guidelines for effective manuscript evaluation. In F. J. Dorn (Ed.), *Publishing for professional development* (pp. 68–69). Muncie, IN: Accelerated Development.

Weick, K. E. (1985). Editing a rejection: A case study. In L. L. Cummings & P. J. Frost (Eds.), *Publishing in the organizational sciences* (pp. 774–780). Homewood, IL: Richard D. Irwin.

PART VI

SPECIAL TOPICS

27

COORDINATING A RESEARCH TEAM

Maintaining and Developing a Good Working Laboratory

DENNIS L. MOLFESE

ALEXANDRA P. FONARYOVA KEY

MANDY J. MAQUIRE

GUY O. DOVE

KELLEY R. PEACH

MELISSA C. FERGUSON

SHARON STRAUB

MARY ANNE MOSELY

CHRISTINE WETTIG

EVA J. RATAJCZAK

In today's complex world of science, research is becoming increasingly interconnected and multifaceted. As a result, it is almost impossible for a single individual to possess all of the expertise and wide range of skills needed to carry out a relevant research program and to keep up with the continuing developments within and across fields. Consequently, more and more investigators find themselves working in research teams to pool resources, training, and talent.

For the purpose of this chapter, a large research team, or laboratory, can be defined as four or more students working with the same faculty mentor. Most likely, these students will vary in their experience (e.g., first-year students vs. senior students), interests (e.g., students from various departmental programs), and projects (different students may work on different sections of the same large project or on separate smaller projects). Joining such a research team may be intimidating to a graduate student just

AUTHORS' NOTE: This work was supported in part by grants from the National Institute of Child Health and Human Development (R01-HD17860) and the U.S. Department of Education (R215K000023, R215R990011).

starting out in a program because a lot of work is being done at the same time, many tasks are in various stages of completion, there are numerous people to fit in and interact with, and there are fewer chances for personal attention from the faculty mentor. The same aspects, however, can also be viewed as very stimulating and encouraging: the number of research questions to choose from, the opportunities for experience with various aspects of research, the availability of more people to learn from. The final decision on how to view a research team will depend mostly on one's personality and expectations about his or her graduate training. The most important things that a beginning student can bring into a large team are a fervent desire to learn and a confidence in one's own abilities. Any research team works in two directions: On the one hand, many individuals working together complete more projects and achieve greater success; even the newest member of the research team can make valuable contributions to the team. On the other hand, a good research team enables its members to reach their own goals and prepares them for an independent career.

In the sections below, we discuss the features we believe characterize a good research team, as well as the qualities that make a student succeed in such a setting.

Choosing the Best Research Team

During the process of evaluating applicants, many graduate schools require interviews with some or all faculty of the department. For some students, the interview for acceptance to graduate school is also the interview for assignment to a particular lab for training. Once accepted into a graduate program, students may be assigned to a research lab or have an opportunity to choose their placement. In either case, a formal or informal interview will most likely be a key step in determining your graduate school placement. These interviews serve two purposes: to determine whether a student is a good fit for the team and to find out whether the particular team is a good fit for the student.

From the team perspective, a faculty mentor, often together with the lab director or senior research staff, will interview students to determine if they fit with a particular research lab

team. The evaluation criteria usually include how well individuals' research interests match the lab focus, the strength of their academic background, prior research experience, their personal goals and expectations, availability and time commitment to research activities, their compatibility and temperament, and any unique perspectives these individuals might bring to the research lab team. Based on the information gathered from the interview, the principal researcher decides if students have the potential to be successful members of the research team.

From the student's perspective, joining a research team is a serious commitment of time and energy. Given the extent of this commitment, one should carefully examine the overall effectiveness and productivity of the team. Many factors are important to the success of a large research team, such as a set of specific research goals with clearly defined expectations for the members of the team, open and continuous communication within the team, and grant history. Below we mention a few characteristics that are worth considering before making the decision to join the team.

Team Goals

A large research team should be organized around a clearly defined set of goals. If the project is funded by a grant, then its goals, at least in part, should be in line with those outlined in the grant. These goals should break down into more specific targets and be presented in a concrete manner to the team. For example, if one of the project goals is to test a particular number of subjects within a specified period of time, a realistic and detailed testing schedule indicating how many individuals are to be tested each week should be available. A well-run research team also provides each member with a clear set of individual expectations. These expectations encompass such factors as how the team members should approach their assignments, their level of professionalism in carrying out experiments, and so forth.

Team Communication

Good communication is vital to the success of a large research team. It should flow in all directions. Not only should the team director or directors communicate effectively and readily with team members, but the team members themselves should be able to communicate readily with each other and the team director. If, for whatever reason, this communication is stymied or if communication occurs only in one direction, the effectiveness of the team will likely be compromised. Multidirectional communication is especially important in long-term projects because without it, experimental drift and potentially devastating alterations in procedures can occur. There are several ways in which large research teams can establish successful lines of communication among its members and leaders. One way is through frequent and regular lab meetings with all the team members. Such meetings help the team maintain consistent goals and address practical (e.g., equipment breakdowns) or interpersonal (e.g., distribution of workloads) problems early. Another way to encourage healthy communication is to have weekly supervisory sessions for those who are new to the team with more experienced members, the lab director, or both. These supervisory sessions are best conducted on an individual basis. This format allows each member to deal directly and privately with the supervisor and can facilitate problem solving in a nonthreatening manner. These sessions can be an important means of providing feedback to new members concerning their individual progress in terms of experimental procedures and their developing role within the lab. Because senior graduate students may be in the position to run these meetings, they also allow for experience in training, mentoring, and improving one's own research skills.

Individuals need to be aware of their own communication skills. Efficient and clear communication involves listening and being aware of nonverbal characteristics of the speaker, as well as clearly stating one's own perspective. The ability to put oneself in another's shoes is very helpful for understanding why some individuals may respond as they do. Each person comes from a different background and likely has a different approach to planning and carrying out his or her goals. One of the major ways to accomplish this understanding is to *listen* and not pass judgment on what the speaker is saying or interrupt with advice.

Nonverbal characteristics, particularly facial expression and tone of voice, can also help each lab member receive the message from the speaker. For example, someone who seems to be uninterested in participating in a new project (as demonstrated by lack of eye contact, use of a quiet or whiney voice, etc.) already may be overwhelmed with projects. These nonverbal characteristics provide additional information on what a speaker is trying to communicate. On occasion when we feel a bit confused about what someone is saying, we are likely responding to nonverbal characteristics that are discrepant from the verbal; these nonverbal characteristics outweigh the verbal information when a listener is attempting to understand a message. Likewise, we may be unaware of how our own nonverbal signs may affect the message we are sending.

All of the above affect the functioning of a team in a research lab. Many times we perceive good communication as the ability to clearly define the content, but the process of communicating that content is also extremely important. Developing an open and accepting emotional climate for discussions and problem solving is imperative for the smooth functioning of a team. Disagreements, lack of participation, or attempts by an individual to dominate the conversation are common problems that occur in a group discussion. Being aware of these communication characteristics, along with trust, openness, and respect for each other, will facilitate the process of communication and result in a well-functioning team.

Grant History

In the last decade, grant support for research has become increasingly common, so there is high probability that a large research team will have at least one grant-funded project. When choosing a team to work with, it may be important to consider its grant history, that is, the number of grants the team has been awarded, how long the team has had grant support, whether the grants are intramural (from the same university) or extramural (from funding agencies outside of the university), and the scope (e.g., range of issues studied, duration) of the grant projects.

Having continuous funding from single or multiple grants is beneficial for everyone in the team. Grants provide support for graduate students in the form of assistantships and tuition, as well as potential funds for travel to conferences or for short-term training in other labs. Having assistantships paid for through a grant may allow students more time to do research, as opposed to earning their stipends through other work outside of the lab, like teaching or work-study jobs. This holds true for both summer and school-year appointments. The last two options allow the students to meet other researchers in the field and establish professional connections beyond their immediate contacts within their own graduate programs. Another great benefit from joining a team with grant support is the opportunity to assist in the preparation of grant applications and gain first-hand knowledge about the grant process and the features of successful applications.

Higher grant activity is usually linked to a higher publication rate because most grants expect high levels of publications in peer-reviewed journals. Higher publication rates for the lab team are a good indicator of whether members of the team are likely to have some publications on their vitae by the end of the graduate program. The rate and number of publications are increasingly important to one's market value or competitiveness for a desired job upon graduation.

Collaborations

Most large research teams conduct multiple projects at the same time. Some of these projects are likely to occur in collaboration with other researchers from the same department, other divisions at the university, or even with colleagues from other universities. Most breakthroughs in any area of modern science come from such collaborative efforts. Participation in collaborative projects is another effective way of creating a professional network of contacts to rely on after completing one's PhD and starting an independent career.

Collaborations also allow the persons involved to get a taste of related fields and potentially extend the skills and/or understanding of the topic in question. A collaborative project may be a good way to start one's interaction with a large research team while working in a different laboratory. Furthermore, working as part of a large research team does not necessarily limit your contact with other labs. If there is an interesting project underway in a different lab, an opportunity to participate may be worked out with the directors of both labs.

Lab Manuals

Another important feature of a well-run research team is a lab manual. Lab manuals communicate structure, goals, and expectations of the research team. They provide a written record that can be readily referenced and accessed by everyone in the lab. A well-conceived manual should include detailed information concerning lab philosophy, test objectives, testing priorities, experiment and analysis protocols (including copies of all test instruments), as well as comments on research ethics and acceptable behavior, demeanor, and dress.

The manual can serve two main purposes: as a training tool and as a reference source. As a training tool, a manual is a textbook for a student just joining the team. By reading the manual, students can better understand the overall lab functions and procedures. It also provides an authority for students when they have questions and the lab director or senior lab members are not available. The manual can also benefit the more experienced students by preventing experimental drift. If procedures outlined in a manual are available to all lab staff, everyone can refer to the manual to check about situations or procedures that appear ambiguous.

The lab manual is usually written by students or the lab director (or both working together) in collaboration with the faculty mentor. The process of writing and regularly updating the manual is also beneficial in that it can help to better organize duties, responsibilities, and procedures. Developing and maintaining a lab manual is a continuous and time-consuming affair: The manual will need to be updated every time a new testing procedure or piece of equipment is introduced or removed. The time demands of this task can be reduced, however, if certain students assume responsibilities for developing and updating different sections that then are reviewed by the entire research team prior to inclusion in the manual. A joint effort in keeping the lab manual up to date also gives all involved in the process a sense of ownership over the document and further encourages participants to rely on the manual in daily activities. The newest members of the lab, with their fresh perspective on the lab, can make a valuable contribution to the development of the lab manual by identifying areas that are unclear or missing.

Lab Coordinator

In a large research team, the primary investigator may not always be in the lab every hour of every day. In such cases, many large teams have a lab coordinator, an experienced graduate student or a full-time researcher who serves as the team manager and facilitates communication between the research team and the primary investigator. The lab coordinator's main responsibilities are to ensure that the lab is functioning smoothly and efficiently and to oversee all technical aspects of the ongoing projects. The lab coordinator usually handles most of the administrative aspects: testing schedules and task assignments for lab personnel and training of new lab members, as well as maintaining subject and test databases, tracking lab supplies and information (i.e., human subjects review board certifications, research protocol forms, consent forms, etc.), and recruiting and scheduling of subjects. The lab coordinator plays a vital role in the communication within the lab and between the team members and the faculty supervisor. Team members often report any individual problems or team needs (e.g., running low on supplies) first to the lab coordinator, who can either handle the problem alone or relay the information to the primary investigator.

Essential skills that make a lab coordinator successful include good organization and management abilities (organizing tasks, distributing workload), mastery of computer skills (maintaining schedules, databases, paperwork), and effective communication (ensure information flow throughout the lab). Overall, the lab coordinator must be familiar with all aspects of lab functioning and be comfortable interacting with all members of the team, regardless of level of research experience.

For a graduate student just joining a research team, the lab coordinator can be a good source of answers to many questions about the group and projects.

Research Ethics

There are a number of ethical issues that should be kept in mind when choosing a large research team. First and foremost is the question of the ethical character of the research itself. Before joining a team, the student should learn about the ongoing research carried out by the team. This is clearly important for both human and animal research.

It is useful to consider the research ethics training and guidelines of the research team. Research in the lab should be carried out under specific and clear directives that fit with nationally recognized standards. The relevant guidelines are different for human and animal subjects. Research involving human subjects should conform to the Code of Federal Regulations Part 46 on the Protection of Human Subjects published by the Department of Health and Human Services (DHHS), as well as to the individual institution's standards. If the research involves collecting the medical history of human subjects, this training should include the relevant Health Insurance Portability and Accountability Act (HIPAA) regulations. Animal research should conform to the guidelines for the ethical care and use of animals developed by American Psychology Association's Committee on Animal Research Ethics (CARE). In order to assure that these ethical standards of conduct are upheld, the members of the team should receive explicit ethics training.

On a more practical level, a large research team must have an excellent relationship with its institutional review board (or IRB). If this relationship is at all contentious, this could delay research and diminish the overall productivity of the team. Any ethical lapses in the past by members of the team could damage this very important relationship.

One final point to keep in mind is the ethical culture of the team itself. One should consider, for instance, how the team handles mistakes by trainees. The director and the more established members of a well-run research team should make it clear that, although mistakes are undesirable, they are a natural part of the process of learning. Teams that mete out heavy punishment or use public shaming as an "instructive" tool are often divisive and create a less supportive atmosphere for students. A successful team will often have an established protocol for dealing with this issue. The need to catch mistakes early should be combined with a respect for the individual members of the team. In general, there should be an open atmosphere in which students feel free to discuss both the positive and negative aspects of the research process.

What to Expect After Joining a Research Team

Lab Meetings

Weekly lab meetings provide an additional place to communicate about the lab and about each person's involvement in the lab. Participation in these meetings helps maintain consistent goals over time and provides opportunities for the lab team to systematically solve problems confronting the lab. Such problems may be practical ones, such as equipment breakdowns, or more interpersonal ones, such as the distribution of workloads. Each lab member should communicate with the supervisor about issues needing resolution at the lab meetings. Efficient recognition of problems and discussion of these problems prevent them from becoming larger and potentially damaging to the research enterprise. These lab meetings also provide an opportunity for each individual to discuss her or his own goals and progress. Many of the individual's lab goals can interact with other members' progress and goals. Consequently, clearly defined and regular discussions are important to everyone's success.

Training

When a new member joins the research team, there will be a period of training. The faculty supervisor and senior lab members are responsible for teaching the student the protocols for all lab activities. This may include training on data collection techniques, behavioral assessments, data analysis procedures, participant recruitment and follow-ups, as well as manuscript development and the grant-writing process. The training

period is a crucial time for the student to become a competent, effective, and experienced member of the research team. Depending on the type of research lab, the time it takes to become fully trained will vary greatly and will most likely involve multiple stages of increasing complexity. Training in the best of circumstances will continue throughout graduate school and likely throughout a professional career. Most likely, a student will be trained in data collection and participant recruitment before mastering specific data analyses techniques.

The goal in nearly all laboratories is to help every new member acquire specific skills as quickly as possible. Therefore, in the beginning, training may be quite intense and take most of the student's lab time. The purpose of the training process is to ensure that a student knows not only *how* to perform various tasks but also *why* they are performed in certain ways. As a result, an important part of training often includes a large amount of reading to fully understand the theoretical background and methodological procedures that are important to how the lab is run. At the end of each training section, a student is often tested by the faculty mentor, the lab director, or both to verify mastery of the skills before he or she is allowed to assume a more independent and active role in the lab.

For the student, training provides additional opportunities to ask questions concerning specific aspects of the team's procedures. The senior lab members expect questions or concerns about procedures. Making appropriate inquiries demonstrates critical thinking skills and dedication to the thorough understanding of material. Students should not be afraid to ask questions; they facilitate training and lead to developing into a successful research team member.

Reliability and Data Checks

When multiple people are working on a project together, reliability becomes an important and critical issue that must be considered. The integrity of the laboratory depends on the accuracy of the data that is collected. Reliability and data checks safeguard against shifts in data collection among laboratory members. Although data checks may be time-consuming and may appear to interrupt the process of the laboratory, they are necessary to ensure the collection of high-quality data. New members and senior members alike will be required to participate in periodic data checks to ensure consistency and uniformity in data collection.

Reliability checks may be conducted on data collected in the form of the scoring of behavioral testing protocols, questionnaires, experimenter ratings of participants' behavior, computer collection of participant responses, and data analyses. Data checks can include verifying participant records, checking the recorded data for accuracy, and ensuring that the data are entered in a timely and accurate fashion. In this way, the laboratory can maintain consistency in the collection of data. Reliability checks ensure that every member's work is consistent with the methods that are used by others in the laboratory.

Inconsistencies can occur at any point in the data collection process. Without ongoing data reviews, data quality can suffer. It is possible for even skilled lab members to display some variations in the methods they use to collect data. Over time, these variations can grow, producing some experimental drift that is inconsistent with the methods outlined in the lab manual. Such shifts away from accepted laboratory practices can adversely affect data quality, ultimately endangering the overall research project.

Procedures for checking data are often outlined in the lab manual and routinely discussed at lab meetings to ensure that all members understand the process. One useful procedure for checking data accuracy uses an individual who was not involved in the original data collection to check the stored data. This rechecking process can help to identify data inconsistencies. Another method uses double data entry programs that require the entry of data twice before it is saved into the master data set. Such programs highlight inconsistencies that are apparent across the two entries and allow correction of errors made in the initial data entry process.

Data checks may initially occur with somewhat higher frequency for a new member of the laboratory staff to ensure that he or she meets the standards of reliability. It is imperative not to take this personally and to remember that these checks are a key component of the success of the entire laboratory. Also, mistakes occasionally are made during the data collection process.

They are a part of the learning process that contributes to one's growth and development as a skilled researcher. One of the benefits of data checks is learning to identify errors and inconsistencies, correct them, and find effective means to avoid the reccurrence of such errors in the future. The chapter in this handbook by DiLalla and Dollinger presents data cleanup and checking in great detail.

Recruitment and Training of Undergraduate Research Assistants

Graduate assistants may find themselves in the position of recruiting new lab members, including undergraduate students. In this case, they interview undergraduate students interested in joining the lab team and later oversee their research activities in the lab. Most undergraduates will probably not have extensive research experience, so other evaluative criteria are used. Many undergraduates plan to apply to graduate school and need the research experience; lab members should discuss these future academic plans and research interests. Some undergraduates, however, may be uncertain about their interests and are exploring different options. Because their interests may not be well defined at this time, one needs to examine other qualities (e.g., find out what courses they have taken and what classes most appealed to them). It is imperative to assess their commitment to lab research activities and their expectations for the research experience. Students joining your lab team must have a high level of intellectual integrity, so their academic record must be evaluated. A set criterion for grade point average, such as 3.5, is generally a basic requirement for lab assistants. Thus, three important qualities to consider are reliability, commitment, and attention to detail. This will help the lab member who is interviewing a potential candidate to determine if the lab can provide the appropriate learning experience to facilitate the new student's intellectual academic pursuits and whether the student will be a successful addition to the lab.

In most cases, the undergraduate students are assigned to an individual graduate member of the team, who is responsible for mentoring and training them. Such assignments provide an excellent opportunity for mentoring and teaching experience without the stress of a classroom. Explaining it to others can improve one's own understanding and mastery of the material. The main goal of training undergraduate assistants is to provide thorough information that is consistent with the training given to all new lab members. Graduate mentors should hold their students to the same standards as other lab members and not assume that undergraduates cannot be as competent just because they are not in graduate school. At first, undergraduates may feel intimidated by the lab; therefore, it is important to keep communication open so that they feel comfortable asking questions. Treating them with the same respect and courtesy as other lab members will encourage everyone to be successful in lab. Undergraduate students can be a significant asset to the research team. The experience is enriching and beneficial for their academic careers as well as for the professional development of the graduate student serving as their mentor.

Stress in the Lab

Regardless of how smoothly the research team operates and interacts, tensions are bound to arise. Research teams have a variety of stressors—conference presentations, grant applications, and manuscript deadlines—that can all occur at the same time. These demands can interfere with the daily research activities and ultimately jeopardize the quality of the data and the effectiveness of the lab. High levels of stress often occur at certain times during the year, such as final exams or in the weeks before a large conference; however, preventive measures can be taken to reduce the pressures that contribute to lab stress. Such measures may include temporarily shifting the lab's priorities (e.g., suspend data collection in favor of data analysis). It is more important to produce quality work than to inadequately meet a large number of demands. By maintaining lab calendars that list subject test dates and times, conference or grant application deadlines, and exam and paper deadline dates, the entire lab has the opportunity to discuss work schedules and personal needs to meet the host of deadlines that may come at otherwise inopportune times. Discussions of these

potential conflicts at lab meetings, preferably before they occur, should produce strategies that reduce stress.

In addition to the stressors due to professional responsibilities, members of the research team inevitably experience individual pressures of exams, term papers, and project deadlines. With many different research projects conducted in the lab, a student may be involved in some studies that are not related to the topic he or she finds interesting; however, most research fields are becoming increasingly multidisciplinary, and learning new skills is a definite advantage. At times, an individual's own project(s) may start to lag behind because of the overall team demands. If a student believes that the work given him or her can't be handled effectively, a meeting with the lab director or the faculty mentor is definitely needed. Clarifying goals and expectations usually leads to a beneficial solution for all involved.

Another source of stress can come from interpersonal conflicts. People from differing backgrounds can, at times, find it difficult to work together. Also, in an attempt to produce innovative high-quality research, people can become quite protective of their own projects and ideas. Negotiating different personality types and personal goals can often be a difficult task. Nevertheless, for the scientific process to move forward, the lab members must work efficiently and professionally with each other. Infighting and squabbling between lab members detracts from the daily process and affects the quality of the team's research, as well as individual progress.

Strategies to reduce individual conflicts include helping people understand their roles in the lab and their individual work expectations. When serious disputes occur between students, they need to work out their disagreements; however, there are situations when the director must step in, for the sake of the students' development and the quality of the research experience. When such conflicts arise, the lab director should deal with the concerned individuals expeditiously, professionally, and in private. It is important that the director set clear-cut guidelines for discussion and resolution of the problems. Such an approach offers an opportunity for students to learn to handle similar situations professionally. Airing problem issues at a public forum, such as the lab meeting, invariably produces unwanted results, such as more intransigence and discord. Finally, the director should make it very clear at the outset of the training experience that any discrimination based on sex, age, or race is unacceptable. Having explicitly stated codes of behavior can often reduce the likelihood of conflicts related to these issues.

How to Maximize Your Experiences in a Large Research Team

Read Widely

One never knows in advance how little or how much information is necessary to accomplish a goal. Consequently, one should never limit oneself to studying only a narrow topic. This can be avoided in a number of ways: First, ask the research director for additional readings beyond those normally assigned. Also, once a topic for the next meeting has been decided, search for review articles on the topic. Last, research is a fast-paced field, so it is important to keep up on the newest findings. Scan the new editions of relevant, widely respected journals and attend conferences to stay on top of the latest work. Conferences also allow the opportunity to discuss and obtain feedback on current work with leaders in the field. Consider purchasing a student subscription to one or two professional journals most directly related to your lab work and interests. Many publishers also offer significant, unadvertised book discounts to students if the student submits the request on department letterhead.

Learn More

Large research labs generally have multiple ongoing research projects that cover a wide variety of topics. Although becoming involved in multiple projects at once can be time-consuming, the benefits generally outweigh the drawbacks. Some of these advantages include a larger number of possible publications, generally more funds to pay for travel to conferences, and an opportunity to get to know and learn from a large variety of people from different backgrounds. Also, multiple projects give a student the chance to learn new techniques and areas.

Do It Now

When assigned a project or activity, focus on that work and complete it expeditiously. The old adage, "Never put off until tomorrow what you can do today," is the sine qua non of a successful graduate research assistant, teaching assistant, student, scholar, teacher, and scientist.

Speak Up

It can be easy to get lost in a large research lab, but every member was brought in because he or she has something to offer to the group. It is important to make everyone's voice heard. The lab meetings are an obvious place to do so, but there are other ways as well. A student who has ideas for new studies may need to take some initiative to get the project started. The best way to do this is to research the project enough to explain why it is important and what it will take to complete, then talk to the research director about how to get it started. One goal of graduate school is to become an independent researcher. It can sometimes be hard to get your own projects running in a large research lab, but this should remain a priority.

Listen

The advantage of a large research lab is that there are many people from many different backgrounds. Everyone, from undergraduates to faculty mentors, has different experiences that can be helpful to a graduate education. Give everyone an opportunity to voice his or her concerns about projects and practices in the lab. It is easy to become very involved in one's own work. As a result, a student may overlook something important that an outside observer or someone from a different area may see. Do not become defensive when someone suggests or notices something that might have been overlooked. Learning from constructive criticism is a talent that many never fully develop, yet it is essential to future success. A large research team is an excellent place to develop these skills.

Time Management

Time management is one of the hardest aspects of graduate school. Often students receive multiple assignments from different sources (classes, teaching, research) and different instructions as to which has the highest priority. The most important tasks necessary for completing your degree and for future employment are completing the dissertation and publishing research articles. These end goals, however, do not have the immediate deadlines of class assignments. Therefore, prioritizing becomes essential. This is especially important when working in a research team.

When joining a team, it is necessary to specify the duties and the time requirements for working in the lab so that everyone is in agreement about how many hours per week it should normally take. These types of time requirements may vary from one institution to another, and personal availability may also vary from student to student and from semester to semester based on class schedules and other commitments. Throughout most of the graduate school career, students will work more hours than formally required. This is especially true for those working in a research lab with many different projects. Thus, time is an important factor to consider when deciding where to work in graduate school.

In addition to balancing lab and classes, a student must allow time to work on personal research and develop one's own ideas. Research team activities should not interfere with one's own goals or stifle one's growth and development. If time issues arise and force a student to completely set aside his or her own research, the best solution is to communicate with the faculty mentor. It may be an issue that is easily resolved, or it may turn out that a different lab would be a better fit. Either way, it is important to deal with this type of situation so that the lab as a whole and the individual students benefit from the experience.

A graduate student is the person most invested in the completion of his or her thesis or dissertation. It is therefore the student's job to set reasonable deadlines and make sure that these deadlines are met. Theses and dissertations are more than just large research papers; no one can write them without feedback and guidance. Begin thinking about possible ideas early in graduate school and set up meetings with the advisor to discuss them. Large research teams can be a great place to start looking for that individual topic. Finding the right size topic can also be difficult. It may not be necessary to change the world all at once in a single study. The thesis or dissertation should be completed in a reasonable amount of time; however, the work needs to be significant and carefully executed in order to be published. Working in a research team provides students with first-hand knowledge of the time typically required for various stages of research projects, thereby better preparing students for planning their own thesis or dissertation.

Once a topic is selected, it is important to set up regular meetings with the faculty advisor (in addition to the lab meetings) to track individual progress, get feedback, and discuss papers. The frequency of these meetings may vary based on the advisor's availability and the project stage. At times, ongoing research or class work can make a student want to delay or skip these meetings. Because it is the student's responsibility to complete the thesis or dissertation, he or she should make every effort to continue to progress and report it to their advisor. To graduate, the student must complete all course work, research lab work, *and* the thesis or dissertation. This fact seems so basic, but it can be extremely easy to lose sight of it in graduate school.

A personal calendar or planner can be very helpful in organizing one's time and reminding one of coursework, research, and personal deadlines, especially when paired with the lab calendar. Some labs have their schedules and deadlines posted online and can be accessed with a password. It is imperative for a student to know the times for lab meetings and other functions (training, data collection, etc.) so that one does not miss any. The planner also helps to track the number of hours worked in the lab and the tasks performed in case any discrepancies arise. During finals or conferences, students may not be able to put in the required number of hours. The documentation of excess hours worked at other times may be important to indicate that the student is meeting the overall lab time commitments.

CONCLUSION

We believe that a large research team must, by necessity and choice, view science as a collaborative effort involving all those who are part of the lab, from the newest undergraduate or graduate student to the most senior postdoctoral fellow or research director or mentor. This chapter has outlined elements that we deal with on a day-to-day basis in our own laboratory and includes contributions from all of us. Generally, it all seems to work, but it is a process that requires, like the research itself, continuous attention to details.

As noted above, lab members will vary in their prior work and educational experience, interests, current training level, and the projects on which they work. Although joining such a research team can be expected to appear intimidating at first to those just beginning their graduate programs, the support system within the lab that moves the research forward successfully must invest time and energy in successfully mentoring the new additions. As long as they succeed, the lab succeeds. When a project is successfully completed or a paper published or a grant obtained, all benefit and the reputations of all are advanced. When errors occur or individuals fail, the members of the lab feel some of that pain as well.

There is no question that participating as a member of a large research group can be very stimulating and exciting. There is almost always something going on and someone available to talk with about the science, as well as one's own progress in the lab or even in the graduate program. It is not uncommon for members of the lab enrolled in the same class to study together for exams. As a member of a research group, you may find yourself part of a built-in study group. As we noted, the final decision on how to view a research team will depend on a number of factors such as the mentor's personality, lab philosophy and work ethic, and one's own personality and expectations about graduate training. A strong desire to learn, a work ethic that says, "Do it now," openness to ideas, and a confidence in one's own abilities are all traits that can make one's experience in such labs rewarding and productive. Even the newest member of the research team can make valuable contributions, and, in return, a good research team supports its members' efforts to reach their own goals and eventually become independent and successful.

EXERCISES

1. Your advisor asks you to draw up plans for recruiting, selecting, and managing undergraduate students into the laboratory group at a large university. What features of the group would you use in advertising? How would you select new members for the group? How would you measure and manage performance of lab group members?

2. Conduct a self-generated training needs assessment with a focus on becoming a valuable member of a research group as (a) undergraduate student, (b) graduate student, and (c) postgraduate student. In particular, what are your levels of the skills and attributes mentioned in this chapter in comparison with what you believe are the desired levels? Develop a list of the skills and attributes with two columns to the right: *current level* and *desired level*. Feel free to use a combination of personal characteristics that include dependability, communication skills, word processing skills, spreadsheet or database skills, programming skills, statistical analysis skills, and literature searching. After you complete your needs assessment, think about how to address any deficiencies you identify. Reading books suggested by more experienced colleagues, asking for tutorials, and requesting a mentor are some strategies that you might deploy to increase your value for a research group.

3. Your task for the lab group's annual self-improvement conference is to develop a training plan for ensuring that all lab group members have appropriate skills for their present roles and for future roles with increased responsibility (a mini career path). How would you review the literature? What would you propose?

RECOMMENDED READINGS

There is little that can be recommended—due to the specialized nature of the topic—in the way of additional reading. Books on teamwork and group performance might have some relevance. Recent work on the structure of collaboration networks in science by M. E. J. Newman (2000) and K. W. Boyack (2004) show some promise from a statistical perspective. The references cited are the best that can be located (Carley & Wendt, 1991; Kraut, Egido, & Galegher, 1990).

REFERENCES

Boyack, K. W. (2004). Mapping knowledge domains: Characterizing PNAS. *Proceedings of the National Academy of Sciences, 101*(Suppl), 5192–5199.

Carley, K., & Wendt, K. (1991). Electronic mail and scientific communication: A study of the Soar extended research group. *Knowledge: Creation, Diffusion, Utilization, 12,* 406–440.

Kraut, R., Egido, C., & Galegher, J. (1990) Patterns of contact and communication in scientific research collaborations. In J. Galegher, R. Kraut, & C. Egido (Eds.), *Intellectual teamwork: Social and technological foundations of cooperative work.* Hillsdale, NJ: Lawrence Erlbaum.

Newman, M. E. J. (2001). The structure of scientific collaboration networks. *Proceedings of the National Academy of Sciences, 98,* 404–409.

28

MULTILEVEL RESEARCH

DAVID CHAN

M any studies in psychology are concerned with phenomena and theories that are multilevel in nature. The central defining feature of multilevel research is that the data is hierarchically structured or nested, that is, the units of observation at one level of analysis are nested (meaning grouped) within units at a high level of analysis. In psychology, the most common examples of hierarchically structured data may be found in organizational and educational research. For instance, a study may consist of employees nested within work teams resulting in a two-level research with the individual employees at the lower level (Level 1) and teams at the higher level (Level 2). As another example, a study consisting of students nested within classes and classes in turn nested within schools would result in a three-level research with individual students at Level 1, classes at Level 2, and schools at Level 3. Many constructs and situations of interest to psychologists can be conceptualized and studied from a multilevel perspective.

From the perspective of multilevel research, the phenomenon under study is characterized as part of a dynamic system, with critical antecedents, processes, and outcomes conceptualized and measured at multiple levels of analysis (Chan, 1998b). For example, employee job satisfaction (Level 1) may be affected by variables at the same level, such as employee personality traits, or variables at the work team

level (Level 2)—which is a higher level—such as team size, averaged tenure of the employees in the team, and the within-team variation in employee intelligence levels. Employee job satisfaction may also affect outcome variables at multiple levels, such as intent to quit (Level 1) and team performance (Level 2). More complex relationships, such as the interaction effect of a Level 1 variable and a Level 2 variable on a Level 1 (or Level 2) variable, may also exist. As explained later in this chapter, to the extent that multilevel effects exist, conceptualizations, measurement, analyses, and inferences that adopt a single-level approach and disregard the hierarchical nested structure of multilevel data are problematic.

Although the multilevel nature of much psychological research has been acknowledged for a long time (e.g., Fleishman, 1953), it is only in the last decade that more researchers have begun to systematically explicate the many complexities inherent in multilevel research and apply multilevel approaches and analyses to empirical studies in substantive areas, particularly those in educational and organizational psychology. Complexities in multilevel research involve problems in validation of multilevel constructs, decomposition of sources of variance in responses, and the associated issues of multilevel measurement and data analysis. One major reason for the recent increase in attention to multilevel research is that recent significant

Table 28.1   Basic Questions on Multilevel Research

Question 1: Why do we need a multilevel approach to multilevel data?
Question 2: How do we conceptualize and measure similar constructs at different levels?
Question 3: How do we analyze multilevel data?
Question 4: What are the pitfalls to avoid when implementing and making inferences in multilevel research?

advances in data analytic techniques and development of statistical software have markedly increased our ability to model and empirically test complex multilevel relationships that were previously restricted to the conceptualization stage. Unfortunately, the majority of methodological work on multilevel research, particularly those addressing data analytic issues, are highly technical and not easily understood by beginning researchers or researchers who may not be methodological experts. Hence, the purpose of this chapter is to provide a nontechnical introduction to the major issues in multilevel research.

This chapter addresses the basic issues of conceptualization, measurement, data analysis, and inference in multilevel research by responding to the four general questions shown in Table 28.1. The chapter will go beyond a cookbook description of multilevel issues to explicate the underlying conceptual bases and rationale to guide decisions concerning construct definition, construct measurement, choice of analytic technique, and interpretations of results. The ultimate aim is to introduce the reader to the basic issues in multilevel research and provide a road map for the reader to acquire the necessary knowledge and technical skills for designing or understanding adequate multilevel research and making valid multilevel inferences. At the end of the chapter, advanced issues will be briefly mentioned and recommended readings provided for the interested reader who wishes to gain a deeper understanding of multilevel issues and design and to implement more complex multilevel research.

WHY DO WE NEED A MULTILEVEL APPROACH TO MULTILEVEL DATA?

The simple answer to the question of why we need a multilevel approach to multilevel data is

that the phenomena of interest operationalized by the multilevel data do, in fact, occur at multiple levels. Hence, to accurately represent the phenomena of interest, we need multilevel models (both conceptual and statistical) that appropriately focus on the respective levels and provide linkages across the levels. Single-level approaches to multilevel data, such as the traditional regression model, are inadequate due to conceptual and statistical problems associated with the failure to attend to the hierarchical nested structure of multilevel data. The conceptual problems are best understood in terms of fallacies that occur as a result of misspecification of the level of analysis, given the focal level of the theory or inference. Many of these conceptual problems, which will be explicated later in the chapter, are related to statistical problems that arise from the violation of a major assumption of traditional single-level regression models. This is the assumption that the observations are randomly sampled from a homogeneous population and therefore statistically independent. The violation of this assumption leads to wrong sample sizes in statistical computations and wrong standard errors, which in turn lead to misestimated precision and ultimately inaccuracy of substantive inferences drawn from the data.

Before we consider an illustration of the problems associated with the violation of the statistical independency assumption, we need to define several multilevel terms (first discussed in a typology of relationships between types of variables developed by Lazarsfeld & Menzel, 1961). *Global* variables refer to variables measured at their natural level. For example, class size is a global variable at the class level and student intelligence and gender are global variables at the student level. Variables measured at a level may be "moved" upwards to a higher level or downwards to a lower level by aggregation and disaggregation, respectively. In *aggregation,* which involves moving a variable from

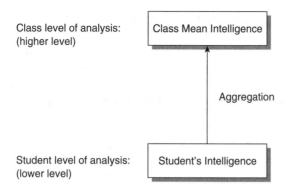

Figure 28.1   Example of Aggregation of a Variable (Intelligence) From a Lower Level (Student) to a Higher Level (Class)

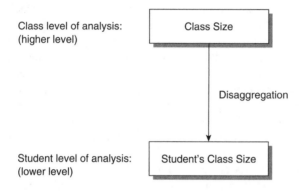

Figure 28.2   Example of Disaggregation of a Variable (Class Size) From a Higher Level (Class) to a Lower Level (Student)

the lower level to a higher level, the lower-level units are grouped to form a smaller (by necessity due to grouping) number of higher-level units. For example, as shown in Figure 28.1, student intelligence scores may be aggregated (moved to the higher level) by computing the mean of the intelligence scores within the class to form class mean intelligence. Such new variables at the higher level, which are composed or aggregated from the variables at the lower level, are referred to as *analytical* variables. As explained later in this chapter, aggregation can proceed in several different forms; and ideally, a composition model, which explicitly describes the aggregation process, should be formulated for each form (Chan, 1998b). Both global and analytical variables may be disaggregated. In *disaggregation,* which involves moving a

variable from the higher level to a lower level, the variable or data at the higher level (e.g., class size, class mean intelligence) is decomposed into a larger (by necessity due to distribution) number of lower-level units. For example, in the disaggregation of class size to the student level, each individual student within the same class will be assigned the same value of class size (as shown in Figure 28.2). In the disaggregation of class mean intelligence to the student level, each individual student within the same class will be assigned the same value of intelligence (i.e., the class mean score and not the student's individual score). Note that in disaggregation, the resulting new variable at the lower level provides information on the higher-level context (class) of the lower-level units (students). Hence, such new variables at the lower level, which are decomposed or disaggregated from the variables at the higher level, are referred to as *contextual* variables.

Now that we are clear with these various terms, we can proceed to explicate an illustration of the dependency problem in multilevel data, which violates the independency assumption of single-level regression models. Consider a multilevel data set of students nested within classes. For various reasons (e.g., classroom learning environment, allocation of students to classes based on prior academic achievement), students in the same class are more similar than students from different classes. Applying the single-level regression model to this data set is problematic because the model ignores the grouping effects (i.e., class effects) associated with the nested structure of the data. Suppose we have a data set of 50 classes with varying class size giving a total sample size of 2000 students, and we are interested in predicting student examination scores from student intelligence and class size. In the single-level regression analysis, this prediction analysis will be accomplished by first performing a disaggregation of class size to the student level and then running a "typical" regression analysis at the individual level of analysis by regressing student examination scores on student intelligence and class size (class size is used here as a contextual variable). This procedure is problematic for various reasons. First, there are only 50 classes and therefore the "true" sample size (independent observations) for the class size variable is in fact 50. The disaggregation, however, has inflated the sample size from 50 to 2000, and the regression analysis treats the 2000 disaggregated values on the contextual variable (i.e., class size) as 2000 independent observations. Using this grossly inflated sample size to compute statistical significance tests in the regression analysis is likely to lead to spurious inferences because the large sample size increases the probability of a Type I error (i.e., rejecting the null hypothesis when it is in fact true). The inflated sample size also leads to an artificial reduction of standard errors (because standard error decreases as sample size increases) resulting in an overestimation of the precision of the respective parameters. The reduction of standard errors, which amounts to a misestimated

precision, also occurs because the standard error estimates fail to take into account the variance and covariance components associated with the effects of grouping (i.e., the nested-structure effects) of the data (for an example, see Aitkin, Anderson, & Hinde, 1981).

The converse problem exists if we apply the single-level regression analysis to aggregated data. Suppose now we are interested in predicting examination scores from class size. A single-level analysis might compose or aggregate the student examination scores data to the class level so that the two variables are on a single and same level of analysis. For example, the mean of the examination scores all the students within a class can be computed to form class mean examination scores, which is an analytical variable aggregated from the lower-level units. A single-level regression is then performed by regressing class mean examination scores on class size. If the research question is whether student examination scores are affected by the size of the class they are in, then the regression analysis is problematic. Specifically, in aggregating student examination scores within each class to form the analytical variable, information on the lower-level units (i.e., the different values of student intelligence within each class) is lost and the sample size is reduced. The consequences are increased standard errors and reduced statistical power (i.e., a higher probability of committing a Type II error).

In addition to the above statistical problems, the single-level model approach to multilevel data has conceptual problems that often lead to inadequate or misleading inferences. Many of these problems are often described as the fallacy of the wrong level. In general, this fallacy refers to a mismatch or disconnect between the level of data analysis and the level of substantive conclusion. In other words, data is analyzed at one level, but the conclusion is made at another (wrong) level. This general fallacy may take different forms, and they are, historically, given different names to reflect the specific nature of the problematic conclusion. The two most well known are the ecological fallacy and the atomistic fallacy.

The *ecological fallacy* refers to making substantive conclusions at the lower level from aggregated data analyzed at the higher level. In other words, conclusions are made about the lower-level variables based on the results of the analysis on the aggregated variables instead of the lower-level units. For example, it is a fallacious inference to conclude about the relationship between global variables at the lower level based on results of the single-level analysis of the corresponding aggregated variables at the higher level (i.e., the level to which the lower-level units are aggregated). The fallacy is evident from the fact that the correlation or regression coefficients from the data at the aggregated level can be very different in magnitude from the corresponding correlation or regression coefficients from the data at the lower level. The correlations at the aggregated level are often referred to as ecological correlations, a term made popular by Robinson's (1950) study. Robinson found that the correlation between percentage of Blacks and illiteracy level in several geographic regions ($r = .95$), computed based on the two aggregated variables that were at the region level (i.e., the ecological correlation), is very much higher than the corresponding correlation computed based on the two global variables at the individual level ($r = .20$). This disparity in the magnitude of correlation clearly shows that it is erroneous to make substantive conclusions about the global variables at the individual level based on the results of analysis of aggregated variables. To conclude that there is a very strong relationship between being Black and being illiterate at the individual level based on the ecological correlation of .95 is to commit an ecological fallacy (also known as the *Robinson effect*) because the adequate conclusion should be based on the individual-level correlation of .20, which is likely to be a conclusion that only a small or trivial relationship exists.

The ecological fallacy occurs because of a failure to take into account the aggregation problem. A disaggregation problem can also exist, and the failure to take it into account leads to the *atomistic fallacy*. This fallacy refers to making substantive conclusions at the higher level from data analyzed at the lower level. In other words, conclusions are made about the higher-level variables based on the results of the analysis on the lower-level variables instead of the higher-level units. For example, consider the case of disaggregating class size and class mean examination scores, both of which are variables at the class level, to the individual student level by assigning all students within the same class the same mean examination score and same class size value. The individual-level correlation between the two disaggregated variables will be different in magnitude (probably much larger) than the corresponding higher-level correlation. Using the lower-level correlation as an index of, and to make conclusions about, the relationship between class size and class mean examination scores will be committing an atomistic fallacy.

Readers interested in the details of the statistical explanations for the differences in magnitude of correlations between levels of analysis can refer to Robinson (1950). A more recent account is provided by Kreft and de Leeuw (1987, 1998). But note that both the ecological and atomistic fallacies are fallacies of *inference*. In other words, the underlying problem in the commitment of these fallacies is a conceptual one, one that consists of making inferences at the wrong level. For example, when a lower-level variable is aggregated to form a variable at the higher level, we cannot assume that the two variables at different levels of analysis are representing the same construct. If the construct has changed when we move from one level to another, then it is not surprising that the corresponding correlations differ in magnitude across levels. Using a correlation between variables at one level to make inferences about the relationship between variables at another level is not simply a statistical problem of inaccurate or misestimated precision. More fundamentally, it is a conceptual problem of flawed inferences due to mismatch between analysis and interpretation, analogous to making interpretations about apples based on analysis of oranges. When multilevel models, as opposed to single-level models, of analysis are appropriately employed to multilevel data, the hierarchical nested structure is directly attended to and the respective level-specific sources of variance can be isolated and estimated. In so doing, analysis and interpretations can be aligned to avoid the conceptual problem of making inferences at the wrong level. In short, when we have multilevel data, multilevel modeling is necessary, not just because it provides more accurate results in terms of precision of estimates but also (and more fundamentally) because it is conceptually more adequate than single-level modeling.

How Do We Conceptualize and Measure Similar Constructs at Different Levels?

Multilevel models of data analysis are very flexible in terms of testing a variety of hypotheses concerning variables and relationships at multiple levels, as well as cross-levels relationships; however, the flexibility of multilevel models also brings with it a higher potential for misuse, thereby leading to misleading inferences. The dangers of misuse and misleading inferences are real. For example, after acquiring the technical competence in multilevel techniques, it is tempting for the researcher to "freely" compose a new construct at the higher level by aggregating the lower-level units representing an established construct in one of several ways and then subject the resulting multilevel data to multilevel analyses. Because conceptualization should drive statistical application, it is critical that we are clear, or at least clarify, how similar constructs are conceptualized and decide how they should be measured at different levels of analysis (e.g., self-efficacy at the individual level and collective efficacy at the team level).

To clarify conceptualizations and decide on measurements or operationalizations of similar constructs at multiple levels, we need to formulate and apply appropriate composition models in a given multilevel study. Composition models specify the functional relationships among phenomena or constructs at different levels of analysis that reference essentially the same content but that are qualitatively different at different levels (Hannan, 1971; Roberts, Hulin, & Rousseau, 1978; Rousseau, 1985). As noted in Chan (1998b), specifying functional relationships between constructs at different levels provides a systematic framework for mapping the transformation across levels. The explicit transformation relationships provide conceptual precision in the target construct, which in turn aids in the derivation of test implications for hypothesis testing. Accompanying the increased interest in multilevel research is an increased proliferation

of new constructs at multiple levels. Unless we have explicit composition models to guide the development and validation of newly proposed constructs in multilevel research, we could easily end up with a multitude of labels, all of which purportedly refer to scientific constructs but in reality have no incremental explanatory value.

Chan (1998b) provided one of the first systematic frameworks for organizing, evaluating, and developing constructs and theories in multilevel research. The framework consists of a typology of composition models that specify functional relationships between constructs at different levels. The typology is briefly summarized here, and the reader should refer to Chan (1998b) for more details.

Chan's composition models are relevant for most elemental composition in multilevel research. Elemental composition is essentially aggregation that refers to situations in which data from a lower level are used to establish the higher-level construct. In other words, the higher-level construct has an aggregate nature and is construed as some form of combination of the lower-level units (i.e., an analytical variable). The use of data from the lower level to establish the higher-level construct does not imply that it is necessary to begin conceptualization at a level lower than the level of the target or composed construct. The starting level of conceptualization is dependent on the research question. For example, a researcher may start at the group level with the established construct of group norms and then move down to the individual level to collect perceptual data for subsequent aggregation to the group level to establish the construct of group norms. It is important to focus on elemental composition (aggregation) because of the actual constraints and practice in empirical multilevel research. As noted by several researchers (e.g., Ostroff, 1993; Roberts et al., 1978), we often do not have global indexes of the higher-level (organizational or group) variables of interest and hence have to rely on aggregated data from the lower level (individuals) to represent the higher-level variable.

Chan's typology described five different basic forms that composition models can take. These are (a) *additive,* (b) *direct consensus,* (c) *referent-shift consensus,* (d) *dispersion,* and

(e) *process* composition. A theory of the focal construct in a multilevel study may contain one or more of the five composition forms. In Chan's typology, each composition model is defined by a particular form of functional relationship specified between constructs at different levels. Corresponding to each form of functional relationship is a typical operational process by which the lower-level construct is combined to form a higher-level construct. The operational combination process is the typical form, as opposed to a necessary consequence of the functional relationship specified. Chan also gave several suggestions on what constitute the forms of evidence needed to support the relevant functional relationships and to establish that appropriate combination rules are applied (see Chan, 1998b, table 1).

A description of all the composition models is beyond the scope of this chapter, and the reader is referred to Chan (1998b) for details. The central point to note here is that the researcher should not uncritically assume construct validity for a "new" higher-level construct aggregated from the lower-level units. Instead, an adequate composition model should be explicated. For example, a composition model of work group climate for justice would specify how the group-level construct of justice climate is derived from the established individual-level construct of justice perceptions and how this new group-level construct can be empirically validated. The nature of the aggregated construct can be very different, depending on the specific composition used. Different composition models, when applied to the same individual-level construct of justice perceptions, would result in different group-level climate constructs with different measurement implications.

To illustrate how composition models drive conceptualizations and measurement of constructs, let us consider the aggregation of justice perceptions at the individual level to a group-level construct using a direct consensus composition versus using a dispersion composition. In a *direct consensus composition,* which is the most familiar and popular form of composition among multilevel researchers, "within-group consensus of the lower-level units" is used as the functional relationship for specifying how the construct conceptualized and measured at the lower level is

functionally isomorphic to another form of the construct at the higher level (i.e., the analytical construct). Based on this composition model, the researcher may construe psychological climate for justice as an individual's perception of fairness in the work environment in terms of the psychological meaning and significance to the individual (James, 1982). The researcher may then derive a conceptual definition for a group-level construct called *group climate for justice,* which refers to the shared assignment of meanings among individuals within the work group. In this conceptualization, within-group agreement among individual climate perceptions indicates shared assignment of psychological meaning. It is this "sharedness" that constitutes functional equivalence between the climate constructs at the two levels. Hence, the definition of *group* climate for justice is essentially the same as psychological climate for justice, except that the former refers to the *shared* perceptions among the individuals. The conceptual relationship between the two forms of the construct at different levels then drives the manner in which the lower-level construct composes to the higher-level construct. In terms of the operational combination process, the conceptual relationship would specify the manner of, and precondition(s) for, combining the individual lower-level measurements to represent the higher-level measurement. For example, within-group agreement indexes such as the r_{wg} index (James, Demaree, & Wolf, 1984) may be calculated, and some cutoff level of within-group agreement of psychological climate responses is used to justify aggregation of the individual-level responses to form the group-level construct of group climate for justice. High within-group agreement indicates consensus and justifies aggregation of individual climate responses to represent scores on the group climate variable. Typically, in direct consensus composition, the mean of the individual-level responses within a group is used to represent the group's value on the group-level construct after passing the selected cutoff for within-group agreement. In this example, the aggregation procedure and preconditions, together with the conceptual definition of group climate for justice (i.e., the group-level construct) determine the meaningfulness and validity of the operationalization of the group-level construct.

If we apply a *dispersion composition* model to the aggregation of individual-level justice climate perceptions to the group level, then we could derive a group-level construct called *justice climate strength,* which is distinct from the group-level construct called *justice climate level,* which is derived from a direct consensus composition. The following paragraphs describe how a dispersion construct at the group level could be composed.

Recall that in direct consensus composition, within-group agreement of scores from the lower-level units or attributes is used to index consensus. The researcher hopes to achieve a high agreement at the lower level in order to justify aggregation to represent variables at the higher level. In this composition model, consensus is a necessary condition for construct validity at the higher level, and high within-group agreement constitutes an empirical or statistical precondition to be fulfilled for the operational combination process to be legitimate. In contrast, dispersion composition would, based on some theory, conceptualize the degree of within-group agreement of scores from the lower-level units or attributes as a focal construct, as opposed to a statistical prerequisite for aggregation. That is, instead of treating within-group variance as error variance (which is what the direct consensus composition model does), within-group variance (i.e., the within-group dispersion of scores) could serve as an operationalization of a focal construct. In essence, the dispersion composition model focuses on the use of within-group dispersion (i.e., variance or agreement) to specify the functional relationship in composition of a dispersion construct.

Continuing with our climate example, the researcher may propose the construct of climate strength conceptualized as the degree of within-group consensus of individual climate perceptions and index the construct using within-group variance or some dispersion measure of individual climate responses. The dispersion measure then is correlated with some criterion variable such as a measure of group cohesion to test the researcher's hypothesis (e.g., that group climate strength is associated positively with group cohesion).

To summarize, the above examples show that the two aggregated constructs, namely group justice climate level and group justice climate strength, although aggregated from the same individual-level climate construct, are distinct constructs with different conceptual definitions and measurement implications driven accordingly by their respective composition model. For example, in the aggregation to form values for the group-level construct of justice climate level, the direct consensus composition model would treat within-group agreement of individual-level climate responses as a statistical hurdle to be cleared in order to justify an aggregation method that would use the group's mean to represent the group's value on the aggregated construct. On the other hand, in the aggregation to form values for the group-level construct of justice climate strength, the dispersion composition model would use each group's within-group agreement of individual-level climate responses to represent the group's value on the aggregated construct.

Because group climate level and group climate strength are distinct constructs, they are likely to have different antecedents, correlates, and outcomes. They may also interact to affect an outcome variable. For example, the magnitude of the relationship between group climate level and a criterion variable (e.g., group performance) may be dependent on the values of group climate strength. Applying the appropriate composition models (multiple models can be applied in the same study) would clarify the conceptualization and measurement of the focal variables in a multilevel study. Recently, several researchers, particularly those in climate research, have employed various composition models to formulate and test interesting multilevel and cross-levels hypotheses, and they have produced results that significantly advanced the field (e.g., Klein, Conn, Smith, & Sorra, 2001; Schneider, Salvaggio, & Subirats, 2002).

Chan (1998b) noted that an adequate typology of composition models could contribute to multilevel research in at least two important ways. First, it provides an organizing framework for existing focal constructs, facilitating scientific communication in multilevel research. Researchers can be more confident that they are referring to the same construct when it is explicated according to the same form of composition. Meaningful replications and extensions of current findings then are possible. Apparent contradictory findings may be reconciled, and debates may be clarified. For example, many so-called inconsistent findings simply could be a result of confusion of terminology (i.e., comparing apples and oranges), and the confusion may become apparent when each study locates its construct in the typology corresponding to the composition model. Organizing existing constructs also aids cumulation of research findings by providing a framework for performing meaningful meta-analytic studies in multilevel research. Second, the typology provides a conceptual framework for developing and validating new focal constructs and multilevel theories. It could help compose new explanatory constructs from established ones. In addition, being cognizant of different models allows the researcher to consider alternative designs, measurements, and data analyses for testing competing hypotheses, modifying existing theories or developing new ones, or performing a more rigorous test of the original hypothesis. In short, an adequate typology of composition models is important because it helps clarify conceptualizations and measurement of similar constructs at different levels of analysis.

How Do We Analyze Multilevel Data?

Assuming that we have formulated and applied adequate composition models to obtain reliable and valid measures of the relevant aggregated group-level constructs, the next class of important issues concerns how the data should be analyzed so that the hierarchical nested structure of the multilevel data is taken into account. The two major types of established techniques are multilevel regression models and multilevel latent variable models. These techniques are more appropriate than single-level analyses of multilevel data. Specifically, the techniques incorporate simultaneously into the analysis two or more levels, thereby addressing the problems associated with single-level analyses of multilevel data as described earlier, such as biases in estimation of standard errors and the various inferential fallacies due to mismatch of levels. These multilevel techniques are relatively recent

developments. Understanding multilevel regression models requires basic knowledge of multiple regression. Understanding multilevel latent variable models requires basic knowledge of latent variable (i.e., covariance structures) analyses. Multilevel latent variable models will be mentioned only briefly, and further readings on these techniques are provided later in the chapter. The discussion on data analysis will focus on multilevel regression models because these models constitute the most common class of multilevel techniques used in multilevel research. The purpose is to provide an overview and nontechnical introduction to the logic of multilevel regression models. The reader should refer to the recommended readings at the end of the chapter in order to acquire the expertise in application of these techniques.

Conceptually, multilevel regression models may be viewed as traditional regression models (as in single-level regression) with additional variance terms to represent variables specifically associated with the hierarchical nature of the multilevel data. To understand the importance of these additional terms, we first need to examine the single-level regression model that does not contain these terms. Consider the traditional ordinary least squares (OLS) simple regression model for predicting y from x:

$$y_i = b_0 + b_1 x_i + e_i \qquad (28.1)$$

in which b_1 is the slope or regression coefficient for x, b_0 is the intercept, and e_i is the error (or residual) term. As long as the prediction of y from x is imperfect (i.e., the value on the actual y is not the same as the value on the predicted y), which is almost always the case in psychological research, e_i is non-zero. In OLS regression, we make three assumptions about e_i. First, e_i is assumed to be normally distributed with a mean of zero (this is called the *normality assumption*). Second, it is assumed that the variances of e_i are constant across different values of x (this is called the *homoscedasticity assumption*). Finally, it is assumed that the e_i from each observation is not correlated with (i.e., independent of) the e_i's from the other observations in the sample (this is called the *independence assumption*). Although some scholars have shown that violations of the normality and homoscedasticity assumptions in OLS regression analyses tend to have little impact, it is well established that the violation of the independence assumption can have serious impact and could lead to inaccurate or incorrect inferences.

Recall that in multilevel data, the lower-level observations within the group (i.e., within the higher-level unit) are typically not independent insofar as they tend to share some similar characteristics or are exposed to the same effects by virtue of being in the same group. When the within-group observations are not independent, the errors from these within-group observations are more similar to one another than would be expected by chance. In other words, the errors from the observations in the sample will be correlated with group membership. That is, the e_i's are correlated (dependent), and the independence assumption of OLS regression is violated. When the observations are not independent (and therefore the e_i's are correlated), the line of best fit defined by the regression equation no longer represents the sources of variance in y adequately. Specifically, two sources of variance are not represented. First, the source of variance from group membership (i.e., there are between-group differences in mean y values) is not represented by the regression equation. In other words, the group differences in the b_0 parameter estimate are not represented. Second, the source of variance from between-group differences in the x-y relationship (i.e., the different groups have different x-y relationships) is not represented by the regression equation, which specifies only a single x-y relationship. In other words, the group differences in the b_1 parameter estimate are not represented. Therefore, the traditional single-level regression model is inadequate for analyzing multilevel data because there are no additional variance terms in the regression equation to represent these two between-group sources of variance. Multilevel regression models solve these problems by including these additional (multilevel) variance terms.

To illustrate a multilevel regression model, consider a two-level data set in which j refers to the group membership (e.g., class) to which the lower-level units i (e.g., students) belong. We are interested in predicting or explaining the lower-level variable y (e.g., math performance) from a lower-level variable x (e.g., gender of student) and a higher-level variable z (e.g., teacher experience). Considering first only the lower-level variables, we can now rewrite equation (28.1) as follows so that each observation's (i) group membership is represented:

$$y_{ij} = b_{0j} + b_{1j} x_{ij} + e_{ij} \qquad (28.2)$$

The "first-order" multilevel questions of interest here are whether the intercepts (b_0) will differ across the j groups and whether the slopes (b_1) will differ across the j groups. In other words, do classes differ in mean math performance (i.e., differences in intercepts), and does gender predict math performance differently across classes (i.e., differences in slopes)? The "second-order" multilevel questions of interest are, given that they exist, whether we can predict these group differences in parameter estimates. For example, can we predict class differences in mean math performance and class differences in the gender-math performance relationship using teacher experience?

To examine the first-order questions, the multilevel model will allow the intercepts as well as the slopes to vary randomly across groups. This is why multilevel regression models are often referred to as *random coefficient models*. Equation (28.2) is known as the Level 1 regression representing the prediction of the lower-level y variable (i.e., student math performance) from another lower-level predictor variable x (i.e., student gender). In this model, across all j classes, the intercepts have a distribution with some mean and variance. Similarly, across all j classes, the slopes have a distribution with some mean and variance. As mentioned above, the first questions of interest are establishing that intercept variance, as well as the slope variance, is significantly different from zero. The next step in the multilevel modeling procedure is to address second-order questions, namely to predict or explain these coefficient variances by introducing some variable at the higher level. In the math performance example, this refers to introducing teacher experience (z), a class-level variable, to predict or explain the class differences in mean math performance (i.e., variance in intercepts) and the class differences in gender-math performance relationship (i.e., variance in slopes). This is done by estimating Level 2 regressions as follows:

$$b_{0j} = \gamma_{00} + \gamma_{01} z_j + \mu_{0j} \qquad (28.3)$$

$$b_{1j} = \gamma_{10} + \gamma_{11} z_j + \mu_{1j} \qquad (28.4)$$

Equation (28.3) predicts class differences in mean math performance (b_{0j}) from teacher experience (z). A significant and positive γ_{01} indicates that classes with more experienced teachers tend to have higher mean math performance. Conversely, a significant and negative γ_{01} indicates that classes with more experienced teachers tend to have lower mean math performance. Equation (28.4) states that the relationship between student gender and student math performance (i.e., the gender effect on math performance) is dependent on teacher experience. A significant and positive γ_{11} indicates that the gender effect on math performance is larger in classes with more experienced teachers. Conversely, a significant and negative γ_{11} indicates that the gender effect on math performance is smaller in classes with more experienced teachers. That is, γ_{11} indexes the moderator relationship in which teacher experience moderates the relationship between student gender and student math performance.

Unlike b_{0j} and b_{1j} in equation (28.2), which are random coefficients that vary across groups (classes), the regression coefficients γ_{00}, γ_{01}, γ_{10}, and γ_{11} in equations (28.3) and (28.4) do not have the subscript j to indicate group membership. These coefficients are fixed coefficients (as opposed to random coefficients), which are not assumed to vary across groups (classes). The remaining between-group variance in the b coefficients after accounting for the effect of the group-level variable z is the residual error variance at the group level. As shown in equations (28.3) and (28.4), these group-level residual errors are represented by the μ terms. These errors are assumed to have a mean of zero and to be independent of the errors (e_{ij}) at the individual (student) level; however, the covariance between the two higher-level error terms is typically not assumed to be zero.

Substituting equations (28.3) and (28.4) into equation (28.2) and rearranging terms, we obtain the following regression equation:

$$y_{ij} = \gamma_{00} + \gamma_{10} x_{ij} + \gamma_{01} z_j + \gamma_{11} x_{ij} z_j$$
$$+ \mu_{1j} x_{ij} + \mu_{0j} + e_{ij} \qquad (28.5)$$

Equation (28.5) represents a basic multilevel regression model involving two levels (student level and class level). To better understand this equation, we can replace the abstract variable notations with the variable labels as follows:

Math Performance$_{ij} = \gamma_{00} + \gamma_{10}$Gender$_{ij}$
$+ \gamma_{01}$Teacher Experience$_j$
$+ \gamma_{11}$ Gender$_{ij}$ Teacher
Experience$_j$
$+ \mu_{1j}$ Gender$_{ij} + \mu_{0j}$
$+ e_{ij} \qquad (28.6)$

There are three noteworthy points about the multilevel regression equation (28.5). First, the component, $[\gamma_{00} + \gamma_{10} x_{ij} + \gamma_{01} z_j + \gamma_{11} x_{ij} z_j]$, of the equation has all the fixed coefficients and this constitutes the fixed part of the regression model. The other component, $[\mu_{1j} x_{ij} + \mu_{0j} + e_{ij}]$, which has the error terms, is the random part of the regression model. Typically, the substantive interest is to maximize the fixed part and minimize the random part. Second, note that the $\gamma_{01} z_j$ represents the effect of teacher experience, which is a higher-level variable, on math performance, which is a lower-level variable, and is therefore referred to as a *cross-levels* effect. In addition, the interaction term $\gamma_{11} x_{ij} z_j$ represents the interaction effect of a lower-level variable (i.e., student gender) and a higher-level variable (i.e., teacher experience) on a lower-level variable (i.e., student math performance). Therefore, this interaction effect is referred to as a *cross-levels interaction* effect. Third, note that the error term μ_{1j} is associated with x_{ij}. This indicates that the errors will be different for different values of x_{ij}. In other words, there is heteroscedasticity of errors and this heteroscedasticity characteristic of multilevel data is explicitly taken into account in the multilevel regression model. In contrast, recall that the traditional single-level regression model assumes homoscedasticity of errors, an assumption that is typically violated in multilevel data.

At this point, the reader who is familiar with OLS regression may wonder why it is worth going through all the above complicated equations when we can simply analyze multilevel data using a "contextual analysis" through an OLS regression. In other words, why not simply disaggregate the group-level variable z (e.g., teacher experience) to the lower-level units (students) and perform an OLS regression of student math performance on student gender and the disaggregated contextual variable teacher experience? That is, why not simply run the following OLS regression equation?

$$y_{ij} = b_0 + b_{1j} x_{ij} + b_2 z_j + e_{ij} \qquad (28.7)$$

The answer is that this contextual analysis via OLS regression is problematic because, unlike multilevel regression models, it fails to take into account the critical characteristics of the hierarchical nature of multilevel data. First, the errors e_{ij} in the OLS regression equation (28.7) are assumed to be independent. As explained above, this independence assumption is almost always violated in multilevel data. Second, the sample size for determining the statistical significance of b_2 in equation (28.7) is the number of lower-level observations (i.e., students), which is incorrect, instead of the number of classes, which is the correct sample size for the group-level variable z (i.e., teacher experience). Hence, using the wrong (inflated) sample size, yields the wrong standard errors (misestimated precision), and it is easier to obtain statistical significance for the effect of z (increasing Type I error). In contrast, multilevel regression models evaluate the effect of z using the correct sample size (i.e., number of classes), resulting in correct standard errors.

What Are the Pitfalls to Avoid When Implementing and Making Inferences in Multilevel Research?

The various "fallacies of the wrong level" have been explicated earlier in this chapter. This section focuses on some common pitfalls to avoid when implementing multilevel research and making multilevel inferences.

The most common and perhaps most severe pitfall is to let multilevel statistical techniques drive the substantive research. Statistical sophistication does not replace need for construct-oriented approach and theory-driven research. No amount of sophistication in an analytic model can turn invalid inferences resulting from inadequate design, measurement, or data into valid inferences (Chan, 1998a). Like any other analytic models, multilevel data analytic techniques have no magical solutions if there is poor study design and instrument development or if the researcher selected constructs, measurements, and groupings that fail to capture the "true" multilevel relationships and effects underlying the phenomenon of interest. Multilevel regression models are statistical techniques for data analyses, and their use should be driven by theory, the nature of the constructs, and their measurement in the substantive research in question. The appropriate application of multilevel regression models to data provides accurate multilevel inferences only if the constructs are appropriately specified and measured at the different levels of analysis. Appropriate specification and measurement of multilevel constructs requires the formulation and application of appropriate composition models as described in the previous section.

Another related pitfall concerns the introduction of "new" multilevel constructs. Specifically, this relates to the failure to employ adequate theory to guide the formulation and application of composition models or, worse still, the failure to specify any composition models. For example, in the case of proposing a dispersion construct at the group level of analysis, we cannot simply assume that within-group variance represents a true value on some group-level construct. Dispersion is by definition a group-level characteristic (but not necessarily a group-level construct) because it refers to the variability within a group and a variance statistic is indexing an attribute of a group as opposed to an attribute of any individual-level response (Roberts et al., 1978). In Chan's (1998b) dispersion composition model, within-group variance (or some derivative) is used as the operationalization of the purported group-level construct; however, an adequate dispersion model always must give primacy to the construct as opposed to the variance index. Statistically, within-group dispersion is simply a result of individual differences within the group. Interindividual variability is ubiquitous for the kinds of individual-level data collected by organizational researchers. This variability could result from true differences on some construct, random error, or both. Without a conceptual definition of the group-level construct (purportedly indexed by within-group dispersion) and a theory of its substantive meaning (e.g., how it relates to other related established constructs in a nomological network), the researcher may not be measuring what he or she intends to measure. By proceeding in a totally empirical fashion (i.e., atheoretical), one is not likely to replicate results. In short, the essence of dispersion composition is in specifying the nature of the higher-level construct represented by dispersion along some lower-level variable.

Assuming that we already have an adequate conceptual definition of the group-level dispersion construct that may be empirically translated into group differences in within-group variance, one way to help justify a dispersion composition (i.e., establish construct validity for the dispersion construct) is to test for an empirical prerequisite for dispersion composition. This prerequisite is the absence of multimodality in the within-group distributions of lower-level scores (Chan, 1998b). Multimodality in the distribution of scores within a group indicates that substantively meaningful subgroups may exist within the group, with low individual differences within each subgroup (i.e., high within-subgroup agreement) and high individual differences across subgroups (i.e., low intersubgroup agreement). When there is multimodality, it is possible that the variance or dispersion along the original grouping variable does not represent a meaningful dispersion construct. One may have to move downward from the group level to the subgroup level to identify any potentially meaningful subgrouping variable corresponding to the multimodal responses. In exploratory situations, simply graphing the group distribution could help identify the appropriate subgrouping level by matching distributional modality to potential grouping boundaries. Of course, matching modality to grouping boundaries is not sufficient evidence for a dispersion construct. A theory of the dispersion construct should be formulated, and further construct validity evidence, including establishing the validity of the dispersion variable, is required. For example, when exploring the possibility of a dispersion construct of climate strength, multimodality at the division level suggests that the construct of climate strength is probably inappropriate at that level. The modality may correspond to a subgroup level, such as the level of the department. The individual-level data then could be regrouped, and a dispersion measure of departmental climate strength could be validated by correlating it with external criterion variables.

Some important conceptual and methodological issues in change analysis are especially relevant to dispersion composition, and the complexity of these issues illustrates the potential pitfalls in implementing dispersion composition models in multilevel research and, more generally, in making multilevel inferences. For example, when groups differ in variances, the heteroscedasticity of variances does not necessarily reflect direct absolute differences on the dispersion construct purportedly measured by the grouping variable. *Beta* or *gamma changes* in individual responses across groups (Golembiewski, Billingsley, & Yeager, 1976) also could result in differences in within-group variances. A beta change occurs when there is a change in the subjective metric, resulting in a recalibration of the measuring instrument, given a constant conceptual domain. For example, given the same justice climate item, individuals from two different cultures may differ in the psychological metric that the rating scale represents to them. The difference in the subjective metric will result in variance differences. That is, when there is beta change, some or all of the variance difference across the two cultures no longer reflects true differences in climate strength but rather differences in calibration of the measuring instrument. A gamma change occurs when there is a shift in the meaning or conceptualization of the construct being measured. For example, the same justice climate item may in fact be measuring the climate for justice in one group but measuring the respect for authority in another. When there is gamma change, comparisons of variances across groups are no longer meaningful. Thus, before using within-group variances as values on the dispersion construct, the researcher should, whenever possible, test for scalar and factorial invariance of individual responses across groups. Methods for testing invariance are provided in Chan (1998a); Chan and Schmitt (1997); Drasgow (1984); Reise, Widaman, and Pugh (1993); and Schmitt, Pulakos, and Lieblein (1984) among others. For a more detailed discussion of the various measurement and statistical issues involved in the formulation and application of a dispersion composition model, see Chan (1998b).

One important pitfall is the failure to attend to the number of higher-level units. It is important not to confuse the number of high-level units with the total sample size in the study, which refers to the total number of lower-level observations. Although the power of the tests of significance of the lower-level coefficients is dependent on the total sample size, the power of the tests of significance of the higher-level and cross-level interaction effects is dependent on the number of higher-level units. Because multilevel regression models and other multilevel techniques (e.g., multilevel latent variable models) are asymptotic (i.e., they assume large sample sizes), it is important that researchers ensure the presence of a sufficient number of groups before attempting to test and interpret effects in multilevel research. A simulation study by Maas and Hox (2001) showed that if this number is small (i.e., less than 50), then the standard errors for the fixed parameters in multilevel regression models are slightly biased downward.

EXERCISES

1. Think of a phenomenon in a research area that you are familiar with. How would you represent this phenomenon from a multilevel perspective using data that is hierarchically structured (i.e., nested)? For this multilevel phenomenon, define the units of observation at one level of analysis and say how these units are nested (meaning grouped) within units at a high level of analysis. For examples, see the first paragraph of this chapter.

2. Using the same phenomenon that you have selected above, describe how researchers may commit (a) the ecological fallacy and (b) the atomistic fallacy when making substantive inferences from correlations observed from the multilevel data set.

3. In your field of research, think of an established relationship between two variables at the same level of analysis (e.g., a personality trait positively predicts individual task performance). For each variable, describe how you could aggregate it to compose a construct at the higher level of analysis. Now, consider the relationship between these two aggregated variables. Is this relationship meaningful in your field of research? Does the relationship tell you anything new beyond what you already know from the relationship between the two original variables (prior to aggregation) at the lower level of analysis? Can you think of situations in which the original relationship at the lower level of analysis holds but the relationship linking the aggregated variables at the higher level of analysis does not hold, and vice versa? Based on your knowledge of the field of research, what are some of the similarities and differences that you think exist between the two relationships? This exercise is complex and in some ways goes beyond the basic issues discussed in this chapter. Hence, I suggest you perform this exercise one more time after you have read about some of the advanced issues pertaining to composition models in multilevel research (see Chan, 1998b; Hofmann, 2002; Kozlowski & Klein, 2000).

4. Go to the Internet discussion list www.jiscmail.ac.uk/lists/multilevel.html. Select an issue that is of interest to you, follow the discussion thread, and summarize the discussion.

RECOMMENDED READINGS

ADVANCED ISSUES AND FURTHER READINGS

This chapter has provided only an overview and nontechnical introduction to the major conceptual and statistical issues involved in multilevel research. Before embarking on the first multilevel research, the reader would need to acquire more technical knowledge as well as be familiar with some of the more advanced and complex issues associated with the implementation of multilevel studies. This section highlights some of these issues and recommends references for further reading.

Formulating and applying appropriate composition models in multilevel research is one of the most important problems that needs to be addressed. This chapter elaborated only two of the five composition models described in Chan's (1998b) typology. The reader could refer to Chan (1998b) for a detailed discussion of the five models. Note that Chan's typology is one of several existing frameworks for conceptualization and validation of constructs at multiple levels. Examples of other frameworks, some of which are extensions of Chan's typology, include Hofmann (2002) and Kozlowski and Klein (2000).

As mentioned earlier, multilevel analyses can be performed using multilevel latent variable models instead of multilevel regression models. The major conceptual difference between the two types of models is that, unlike multilevel regression models, multilevel latent variable models do not assume perfect measurement of constructs, and they explicitly take measurement error into account when estimating parameters. Another advantage of multilevel latent variable models over multilevel regression models is that it is possible in the former to perform multivariate analyses and specify all the hypothesized relationships among the focal constructs in the substantive research in a single model. For example, when there are multiple dependent or criterion variables, multiple regression models would require estimating separate multilevel regression equations for separate dependent or criterion variables. Multilevel latent variable models, on the other hand, can specify all the dependent or criterion and independent or predictor variables and estimate their relationships in a single model. It is also possible to specify direct and indirect effects in the model; however, in practice, these models may not be easy to implement, as they often involve complexities associated with the need to have separate covariance structure matrices for each higher-level unit. Hence, various ways of simplifying the analyses have been proposed, but there is currently little research to examine the effects these simplifying procedures have on the accuracy of parameter estimates. Excellent introductions to multilevel latent variable models are available in Heck and Thomas (2000) and Hox (2002).

This chapter has focused on the "traditional" type of multilevel data in which individuals are nested within groups. There are two other types of multilevel data in which the multilevel structure is less obvious. Although there are some additional complexities involved in data analyses, the basic logical structure of both types of data is similar to the conventional multilevel data mentioned above. The first type is what I would call one-to-many repeated measures data and the second type is longitudinal data. An example of a *one-to-many repeated measures data* is performance appraisal data in which several direct reports (Level 1) are nested within supervisors (Level 2). In this example, each supervisor evaluates several direct reports. Although the direct reports nested under a supervisor are distinct individuals, they are all evaluated by the same supervisor, and the data are repeated (i.e., multiple evaluations from the same supervisor) in this sense. In longitudinal data obtained from measurements repeated on the same individuals over time, a multilevel structure is established with the repeated observations over time (Level 1) nested within individuals (Level 2).

Unlike the traditional multilevel analysis of hierarchical data in which the concern is with interindividual differences associated with group membership, multilevel analysis of longitudinal data is concerned with modeling intraindividual change over time. Multilevel regression models can also be used to analyze these changes over time (see Bryk & Raudenbush, 1992; Hofmann, Jacobs, & Baratta, 1993); however, the issues of changes over time are often very complex and may involve facets of change over time (e.g., conceptual changes in the constructs, changes in calibration of measurement, various types of time-related error-covariance structures) that are not readily handled by multilevel regression models. In modeling change over time, the primary purposes are describing the nature of the trajectory of change and attempting to account for the interindividual differences in the functional forms or parameters of the trajectories by relating them to explanatory variables that may be in the form of experimentally manipulated or naturally occurring groups, time-invariant predictors, time-varying correlates, or the trajectories of a different variable. Latent growth modeling and its extensions are well suited to address these issues. For a review of these issues and the application of latent growth modeling techniques, as well as an overview comparison between latent variable models and multilevel regression models, see Chan (1998a).

SOFTWARE FOR MULTILEVEL ANALYSES AND INTERNET RESOURCES

It is possible to perform multilevel regression analyses using widely available and established multipurpose statistical packages such as SAS, SPSS, and S-PLUS. For example, multilevel analyses can be performed using the PROC MIXED procedure in SAS and the commands in the Advanced Models module in SPSS. Although many of the conceptual and statistical problems associated with single-level analyses of multilevel data have been known to many researchers since more than two decades ago, appropriate multilevel analyses are rare due to the practical difficulties in implementing the complex statistical procedures involved. In the last decade, several computer programs have been specifically developed for multilevel analyses. These programs addressed many implementation problems and made multilevel analyses widely available to researchers in substantive research. Examples of programs developed for multilevel regression analyses include HLM (Bryk, Raudenbush, & Congdon, 1996), MIXOR/MIXREG (Hedeker & Gibbons, 1994), and VARCL (Longford, 1987). Probably the most commonly used program for multilevel regression analysis in substantive psychological research is HLM (for examples of substantive application of HLM, see Hofmann, Griffin, & Gavin, 2000).

Multilevel latent variable models can be specified and tested using any of the widely available structural equation modeling programs such as AMOS (Arbuckle, 1999), EQS (Bentler, 2004), and LISREL (Joreskog & Sorbom, 2002), although the procedures are somewhat difficult to implement at times because the programs were not specifically written for multilevel analyses. MPLUS (Muthen & Muthen, 2004) is a structural equation modeling program that has specifically incorporated features for estimating multilevel models and is well suited to specify and test a variety of different multilevel latent variable models.

There are several useful Internet resources on multilevel research. A good way to begin is to go to comprehensive Web sites that give a variety of information on multilevel research including publications, newsletters, workshops, multilevel data sets, software reviews, and useful links to other Web sites. Examples include the UCLA Multilevel Modeling Portal (www.ats.ucla.edu/stat/mlm/) and the Web site of the Center for Multilevel Modeling (http://multilevel.ioe.ac.uk/index.html). The latter Web site provides a comprehensive list of references on multilevel modeling, an excellent set of reviews of computer software for performing multilevel analyses, and a library containing multilevel data sets that you can download for purposes of teaching and training in the application of multilevel models. There is also an active Internet discussion list where subscribers discuss conceptual and statistical problems in multilevel modeling ranging from elementary to advanced issues (www.jiscmail.ac.uk/lists/multilevel.html).

REFERENCES

Aitkin, M. A, Anderson, D., & Hinde, J. (1981). Statistical modeling of data on teaching styles. *Journal of the Royal Statistical Society, Series A,* 144, 419–461.

Arbuckle, J. L. (1999). AMOS (Version 4.0) [Computer software]. Chicago: Smallwaters.

Bentler, P. M. (2004). *EQS structural equations program manual* [Computer software manual]. Encino, CA: Multivariate Software.

Bryk, A., & Raudenbush, S. W. (1992). *Hierarchical linear models.* Newbury Park, CA: Sage.

Bryk, A., Raudenbush, S. W., & Condon, R. (1996). *HLM: Hierarchical linear and nonlinear modeling with HLM/2L and HLM/3L programs.* Chicago: Scientific Software.

Chan, D. (1998a). The conceptualization of change over time: An integrative approach incorporating longitudinal means and covariance structures analysis (LMACS) and multiple indicator latent growth modeling (MLGM). *Organizational Research Methods, 1,* 421–483.

Chan, D. (1998b). Functional relations among constructs in the same content domain at different levels of analysis: A typology of composition models. *Journal of Applied Psychology, 83,* 234–246.

Chan, D., & Schmitt, N. (1997). Video-based versus paper-and-pencil method of assessment in situational judgment tests. *Journal of Applied Psychology, 82,* 143–159.

Drasgow, F. (1984). Scrutinizing psychological tests: Measurement equivalence and equivalent relations with external variables are central issues. *Psychological Bulletin, 95,* 134–135.

Fleishman, E. A. (1953). The description of supervisory behavior. *Personnel Psychology, 37,* 1–6.

Golembiewski, R. T., Billingsley, K., & Yeager, S. (1976). Measuring change and persistence in human affairs: Types of change generated by OD designs. *Journal of Applied Behavioral Science, 12,* 133–157.

Hannan, M. T. (1971). *Aggregation and disaggregation in sociology.* Lexington, MA: Heath.

Heck, R. H., & Thomas, S. L. (2000). *An introduction to multilevel modeling techniques.* Mahwah, NJ: Lawrence Erlbaum.

Hedeker, D., & Gibbons, R. D. (1994). A random effects ordinal regression model for multilevel analysis. *Biometrics, 50,* 933–944.

Hofmann, D. A. (2002). Issues in multilevel research: Theory development, measurement, and analysis. In S. Rogelberg, *Handbook of research methods in industrial and organizational psychology* (pp. 247–274). Oxford, UK: Blackwell.

Hofmann, D. A., Griffin, M. A., & Gavin, M. B. (2000). The application of hierarchical linear modeling to organizational research. In K. J. Klein & S. W. J. Kozlowski (Eds.), *Multilevel theory, research, and methods in organizations* (pp. 467–511). San Francisco: Jossey-Bass.

Hofmann, D. A., Jacobs, R., & Baratta, J. (1993). Dynamic criteria and the measurement of change. *Journal of Applied Psychology, 78,* 194–204.

Hox, J. (2002). *Multilevel analysis: Techniques and applications.* Mahwah, NJ: Lawrence Erlbaum,

James, L. R. (1982). Aggregation bias in estimates of perceptual agreement. *Journal of Applied Psychology, 67,* 219–229.

James, L. R., Demaree, R. G., & Wolf, G. (1984). Estimating within-group interrater reliability with and without response bias. *Journal of Applied Psychology, 69,* 85–98.

Joreskog, K., & Sorbom, D. (1996). *LISREL 8 user's reference guide* [Software manual]. Chicago: Scientific Software.

Klein, K. J., Conn, A. B., Smith, D. B., & Sorra, J. S. (2001). Is everyone in agreement? An exploration of within-group agreement in employee perceptions of the work environment. *Journal of Applied Psychology, 86,* 3–16.

Kozlowski, S. W. J., & Klein, K. J. (2000). A multilevel approach to theory and research in organizations: Contextual, temporal, and emergent processes. In K. J. Klein & S. W. J. Kozlowski (Eds.), *Multilevel theory, research, and methods in organizations* (pp. 3–90). San Francisco: Jossey-Bass.

Kreft, I. G. G., & de Leeuw, J. (1987). Model-based ranking of schools. *International Journal of Education, 15,* 45–59.

Kreft, I. G. G., & de Leeuw, J. (1998). *Introducing multilevel modeling.* London: Sage.

Longford, N. T. (1987). *VARCL: Software for variance component analysis of data with hierarchically nested random effects (maximum likelihood).* Princeton, NJ: Educational Testing Service.

Maas, C. J. M., & Hox, J. J. (2001). Robustness of multilevel parameter estimates against non-normality and small sample sizes. In J. Blasius, J. Hox, E. de Leeuw, & P. Schmidt (Eds.), *Social science methodology in the new millennium: Proceedings of the Fifth International Conference on Logic and Methodology.* Opladen, FRG: Leske & Budrich.

Muthen, B. O., & Muthen, L. (2004). *Mplus user's guide* [Software manual]. Los Angeles: Muthen & Muthen.

Ostroff, C. (1993). Comparing correlations based on individual level and aggregated data. *Journal of Applied Psychology, 78,* 569–582.

Reise, S. P., Widaman, K. F., & Pugh, R. H. (1993). Confirmatory factor analysis and item response theory: Two approaches for exploring measurement invariance. *Psychological Bulletin, 114,* 552–566.

Roberts, K. H., Hulin, C. L., & Rousseau, D. M. (1978). *Developing an interdisciplinary science of organizations.* San Francisco: Jossey-Bass.

Robinson, W. S. (1950). Ecological correlations and the behavior of individuals. *American Sociological Review, 15,* 351–357.

Rousseau, D. M. (1985). Issues of level in organizational research: Multi-level and cross-level perspectives. In B. M. Staw & L. L. Cummings (Eds.), *Research in organizational behavior* (pp. 1–7). Greenwich, CT: JAI.

Schmitt, N., Pulakos, E. D., & Lieblein, A. (1984). Comparison of three techniques to assess group-level beta and gamma change. *Applied Psychological Measurement, 8,* 249–260.

Schneider, B., Salvaggio, A. N., & Subirats, M. (2002). Climate strength: A new direction for climate research. *Journal of Applied Psychology, 87,* 220–229.

29

COMPUTATIONAL MODELING

MICHAEL J. ZICKAR

The foundation of traditional research methods in psychology involves collecting data from human participants or animal subjects through various observational and experimental methods. In fact, Cronbach (1957) called experimental and observational (correlational) research designs the two scientific disciplines of psychology. Ilgen and Hulin (2000) proposed that computational modeling be thought of as a third scientific discipline that could complement the tools and findings of the first two disciplines. Although correlational and experimental designs dominate the knowledge base in psychology, in some situations it may be important and necessary to study simulations of human and animal thoughts and behavior due to various ethical, epistemological, or practical challenges.

In recent years, the price of computers has been going down even as computing power has risen significantly. Zimmerman and Dorn (2002) claimed that "the $700 computer under the average desk is at least as powerful as the supercomputers of the late 1980s" (p. 2). The increased accessibility of high-powered computing devices will make it easier for those who are considering modeling research as an option in their research investigations. In this chapter, I first define what I mean by computational modeling, and then I review the history of computational modeling in psychology. Then I will present the modeling work of Hanisch, Hulin,

and Seitz (e.g., Hanisch, Hulin, & Seitz, 1996) on organizational withdrawal as an exemplar that can be used to better understand the concepts and research process of modeling. Finally, I outline various aspects of the computational modeling process and highlight several key considerations for implementing and evaluating this type of research.

WHAT IS COMPUTATIONAL MODELING?

There is a plethora of terminology that relates to simulating human and animal behavior. In this chapter, I refer to a *simulation* as an operation that approximates some of the essential aspects of a particular phenomenon. Some simulations concentrate on generating the output of a particular process without being concerned with modeling the particular mechanisms that are used to generate the outcome in real life. This type of simulation could be thought of as a *black box* simulation. Other simulations, for example in the human memory domain, attempt to mimic the exact processes used in the phenomena of interest. In this chapter, I will be discussing simulations that use a computer (usually in conjunction with a statistical or mathematical procedure and quite often a random-number generator) to generate the outcomes of the simulation.

A key aspect of the computer simulation is the model. In this context, a *model* is a set of formal propositions that are used to simulate behavior and other relevant phenomena. The formal propositions can be based on mathematical formulae, statistical techniques, or logical propositions. These formal propositions should be derived from psychological theory and prior research. In many cases, the model will be based on a formal statistical framework such as structural equation modeling or item response theory or exploratory factor analysis. Other frameworks could include fuzzy logic, genetic learning algorithms, or Bayesian logic. *Computational modeling* is a phrase that has been used to describe this body of research; this name acknowledges explicitly the importance of a computing machine in conducting the simulation. Taber and Timpone (1996) succinctly define computational models as "theories rendered as computer programs" (p. 3).

Monte Carlo (MC) simulations are a specific type of simulation that involves a systematic varying of different levels of input conditions to test the effects of a particular variable set on the dependent variable(s). In MC simulations, a stochastic process is used in which a statistical distribution along with a random-number generator is used in conjunction with a mathematical formula to simulate behavior. Monte Carlo simulations are quite popular in statistical and psychometric research to determine the effects of varying important study factors such as sample size, number of items, and the discriminating power of each item on the statistical properties of statistical estimates (see Harwell, Stone, Hsu, & Kirisci, 1996, and Tucker, Koopman, & Lim, 1969, for excellent discussions of Monte Carlo simulations). In addition, industrial-organizational psychologists have used Monte Carlo simulations to test the effects of selection testing on minority hiring (see Sackett & Roth, 1996). MC simulations are usually designed to test various statistical and methodological procedures (e.g., are parametric or nonparametric methods better at identifying biased test items? Bolt, 2002).

HISTORY OF COMPUTATIONAL MODELING

Computational modeling has had a rich history in many of the social sciences, especially the ones that deal with large social systems that are difficult to directly manipulate. Researchers in fields like political science and economics have used modeling to test the effects of various nuclear disarmament policies (Zimmerman & Dorn, 2002), the growth of AIDS (Seitz & Mueller, 1994), and even how computer "shopbots" that search the Internet for best prices affect pricing of goods (Kephart, Hanson, & Greenwald, 2000). In addition, applied domains such as public health and urban planning have used computational modeling to help solve complex problems such as housing segregation (Schelling, 1971) and traffic flow (Arnott & Small, 1994).

The first example of computational modeling is generally acknowledged to have been conducted by John Von Neumann and Stanislaw Ulam to research neutron diffusion during World War II (see Neelamkavil, 1987). In psychology, cognitive psychologists were among the first to see the benefits of computational modeling. Artificial intelligence researchers used the developing computer technology as an analogy for the mind and particularly the memory system (see Simon, 1979). In 1968, Robert Abelson wrote a chapter in the second edition of the *Handbook of Social Psychology* that showed the value of using modeling to represent social phenomena such as teams and interpersonal interaction (Abelson, 1968). These were some of the first usages of computer simulations to understand human behavior.

In recent years, computational modeling has been used frequently to study important elements in cognition and neuroscience (O'Reilly & Munakata, 2000). In addition, industrial-organizational psychologists have begun to realize the opportunities that modeling provides in studying the effects of interventions on large-scale organizations (see Ilgen & Hulin, 2000). Other areas such as developmental psychology (Shultz, 2003) and clinical psychology (Lambert, 1989) have also begun to use modeling techniques.

As computer software (and hardware) becomes more user-friendly and more accessible, the number of simulation applications continues to increase. In fact, the amount of simulation research in psychology (as identified in PsycINFO) has nearly doubled every 10 years for the past three decades from 397 references in the 1970s, to 746 in the 1980s, and 1,510 in the 1990s. All indications suggest a similar increase in the future. Simulation applications have penetrated most areas of psychology. Increasingly, simulations have become more complex including dynamic elements and extensive nonlinear relations between incorporated variables. As simulations become more complex and nonlinear, predictions from the simulation model can provide surprising results that would be difficult to discern using other methodologies (Woolfson & Pert, 1999).

EXEMPLAR OF MODELING

Hanisch, Hulin, and Seitz (Hanisch, 2000; Hanisch, Hulin, & Seitz, 1996, 2000, 2001; Seitz, Hanisch, & Hulin, 1997) created a virtual organization simulation and computer simulation tool called WORKER that allows researchers to examine the effects of environmental-, organizational-, and individual-related factors on different organizational withdrawal behaviors (e.g., quitting, showing up late to work). Hanisch and colleagues' program of research is a useful example in highlighting the potential of simulation research both to advance theory development and evaluate possible consequences of expensive organizational interventions. Like many modeling research projects, this simulation helps advance basic and applied research. For example, the simulation can help untangle the consequences of various theories of organizational withdrawal as well as provide guidance on how to develop interventions to address withdrawal.

The user of the WORKER program can specify a variety of environmental, organizational, and individual conditions that may affect withdrawal behaviors. For example, the mean and standard deviation of simulated employees' ages can be specified, as well as the distributions of tenure in the organization and gender ratios. With regard to environmental conditions, the user can specify the unemployment rate; this factor is relevant because propensity to leave an organization has been linked to the external job market (e.g., Carsten & Spector, 1987). The user can also manipulate features of the "virtual organization," such as organization size, base rates of specific withdrawal behaviors, and organizational sanctions and incentives for specific withdrawal behaviors. WORKER is flexible in that it allows the user to specify the withdrawal behaviors included in the simulation; past withdrawal behaviors specified by Hanisch and colleagues include absenteeism, tardiness, surfing the Web for pleasure, tampering with equipment, daydreaming at work, personal use of equipment, missing meetings, postwork impairment, and turnover (see Munson & Hulin, 2000). Finally, different theoretical models that have been used to explain the relations between different withdrawal behaviors can be specified as the underlying mechanisms that people use to deal with job dissatisfaction. Models that can be tested include the independent-forms model (March & Simon, 1958), the compensatory behaviors model (Hill & Trist, 1955), the spillover model (Beehr & Gupta, 1978), and the progression-of-withdrawal model (Baruch, 1944). See Table 29.1 for a brief summary of each of these theories. In short, WORKER has a built-in level of flexibility that allows individual researchers to explore various environment, individual, and organizational factors and to specify the theoretical mechanism that is thought to explain organizational withdrawal.

The WORKER program uses the principles of fuzzy logic and fuzzy calculus along with information theory to generate data from the user-specified conditions (Seitz, 2000). With these principles, random-number generators are used, along with thresholds that are generated based on the user specifications and dynamic feedback loops, which are used to model the interrelations between different withdrawal behaviors. These latter feedback loops are also used to model how different behaviors may change over time. For example, heightened withdrawal behaviors at Time 1 may lead to a change in organizational interventions at Time 2.

As an example of WORKER research results, Hanisch (2000) created a large number of virtual organizations with the same characteristics: 300 employees, equal proportions of men and women, a normal distribution of age that centered on 38 ($SD = 4.2$), and tenure in the organization from 0 to 20 with all values equally

Table 29.1   Organizational Withdrawal Theories

Theory	Authors	Summary
Independent forms	March & Simon (1958)	The sources of various withdrawal behaviors are unrelated. There should be no correlation between the varieties of behaviors.
Compensatory behaviors	Hill & Trist (1955)	All withdrawal behaviors should reduce dissatisfaction. Therefore, engaging in one withdrawal behavior means that individuals are less likely to engage in other withdrawal behaviors.
Spillover	Beehr & Gupta (1978)	Dissatisfaction is likely to result in multiple types of withdrawal behaviors. There should be positive correlations between the various behaviors.
Progression of withdrawal	Baruch (1944)	Withdrawal behaviors vary in severity. People try to relieve dissatisfaction by engaging in less severe behaviors (e.g., tardiness). If dissatisfaction persists, more severe behaviors (e.g., turnover) are used.

likely (i.e., a uniform distribution); the job market was characterized by a fixed unemployment rate of 6.0%. She simulated four withdrawal behaviors: turnover, early retirement, absenteeism, and tardiness. A prespecified vector dictates the relationship between the attitude of job dissatisfaction and each of those withdrawal behaviors. For example, Hanisch used values of .50 for tardiness and .85 for early retirement. These values suggest that early retirement is more directly related to job dissatisfaction than tardiness. In addition, each withdrawal behavior is given a threshold. This threshold determines the amount of job dissatisfaction that somebody needs to engage in a particular withdrawal behavior. Less severe behaviors, such as tardiness, have lower thresholds (.15 in Hanisch's case) than more severe withdrawal behaviors, such as turnover (.75).

Hanisch simulated withdrawal behaviors over a period of 20 years under three theoretical models (spillover, compensation behaviors, and progression of withdrawal). These runs were designed to ask the question, "Suppose this theoretical model is really the way the world works. What would the long-term consequences be?" By running three separate models, Hanisch was able to compare the results of each model. She found little differences between the spillover

model and the compensation model. Withdrawal behaviors were high in the early years and then stabilized at a lower rate in later years; however, for the progression-of-withdrawal model, Hanisch found that withdrawal behaviors fluctuated between years. In some years, there was little withdrawal; however, in the following years, withdrawal would be higher. Hanisch also studied the effects of hypothetical organizational interventions designed to reduce absenteeism and to reduce turnover. In these simulations, she found several important differences across the three models. For example, interventions designed to reduce absenteeism showed larger drops in absenteeism rates under the progression-of-withdrawal models.

Two key strengths of this program of research relate to theory exploration and the built-in longitudinal capabilities. Many of the theories that were used in the WORKER program were vaguely specified in their original source materials. The translation of vague verbal statements into specific mathematical formulations was one of the most challenging tasks for Hanisch and colleagues. For example, theorists who only claim there is a relation between job dissatisfaction and turnover might fail to specify the mathematical form (linear, exponential, polynomial) of that relation. Through carefully reading the source texts of these theorists, Hanisch and colleagues might have had a better grasp of the original theories than was originally communicated by the theorists themselves! (See Gelso, this book, Chapter 32, for additional discussion on the interplay of theory and research).

In addition to the clarification of the vague verbal theories, the capability of WORKER to generate predictions of different theories allows for model testing. Munson and Hulin (2000) used WORKER to compare predictions generated from the different theories with work withdrawal data from a sample of female members of a large university. Data were collected across eight time periods for these workers. A correlation matrix of withdrawal behavior measures (e.g., missed meetings and absenteeism) was computed for the actual data and also from data generated by WORKER. They concluded that the independent-forms model fit the real data best, in that the correlation matrix generated by the independent-forms model was closest (had the lowest root mean square residual) to the actual correlation matrix. In this case, the computer simulation allowed Munson and Hulin to generate specific predictions of what the correlation matrix should be under various conditions.

As mentioned, the other major benefit of WORKER is its dynamic modeling capabilities. Most work environments have dynamic feedback loops, in that behavior engaged in at Time 1 may directly influence the probability of another type of behavior being enacted at Time 2. In the work withdrawal context, a worker who is dissatisfied may choose to be absent from work during a particular time period. If that absenteeism relieves some of the pent-up frustration and dissatisfaction, that worker may be less likely to engage in withdrawal behaviors during the subsequent time period. In addition, worker behavior at Time 1 may influence organizational policy at later time periods. Despite the clarion calls for longitudinal data collections, this type of data is infrequently collected. WORKER, by having built-in feedback loops, is able to model directly the behavioral implications of different organizational interventions, changes in economic conditions, and characteristics of individuals.

Hanisch and colleagues' modeling research is an exemplar in the use of computational modeling to study real-world events. The flexibility of the WORKER program allows for theoretical and applied questions to be asked, allows for dynamic modeling of behavior over time, and provides a framework in which modeling research helps spur additional real-world empirical research. I hope that this review provides some insight into the capabilities of modeling research and into the process behind the design of modeling research. Next, I will highlight several of the steps involved in modeling research.

THE PROCESS OF COMPUTATIONAL MODELING

There are several steps that should be considered in modeling research: developing a computational model, conducting the modeling research, examining the validity of the model, and refining the model. Ideally, computational modeling is an iterative process that involves validation and revision. I will discuss each of these stages and discuss relevant material from the work of Hanisch and colleagues when appropriate. See Figure 29.1 for an overview of the process.

Development of a Computational Model

One of the reasons that computational modeling has been limited to a small cadre of researchers is that conducting modeling research often requires programming skills and mathematical knowledge that is beyond that of many in psychology. Fortunately, there are more and more computer programs available that make modeling research accessible to those of us who do not have extensive training in mathematics and computer programming.

A statistical or mathematical framework is necessary for beginning a computational model project. For example, Zickar (2000) used the statistical framework of item response theory (IRT) to model the response process that individuals use when faking personality test items (Zickar, 2000). IRT provides a framework that relates characteristics about individuals (e.g., the level of someone's personality trait of

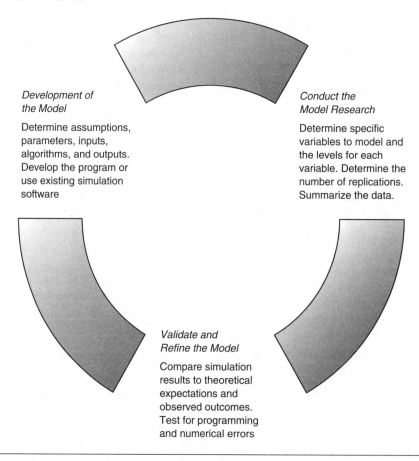

*Development of
the Model*

Determine assumptions,
parameters, inputs,
algorithms, and outputs.
Develop the program or
use existing simulation
software

*Conduct the
Model Research*

Determine specific
variables to model and
the levels for each
variable. Determine the
number of replications.
Summarize the data.

*Validate and
Refine the Model*

Compare simulation
results to theoretical
expectations and
observed outcomes.
Test for programming
and numerical errors

Figure 29.1   Summary of the Modeling Research Process

conscientiousness) and properties of items with
the probability that an individual answers the item
in a positive direction. A random-number generator was used in conjunction with IRT models to
test the effects of faking. Hanisch and her colleagues used principles of fuzzy logic to develop
their simulation. In their fuzzy logic analysis, a
degree of randomness is built into the simulation;
this randomness acknowledges that the simulation
model is only a rough approximation to the way
that the system works (see Hanisch, 2000).

When creating a model, Whicker and Sigelman
(1991) stress that you need to consider assumptions, parameters, inputs, algorithms, and outputs. Perhaps the first step is to decide the
algorithm that will be used to generate the model.
Contemporary modeling researchers have many
options to consider when choosing a simulation
algorithm. Preprogrammed software is available
to generate simulation data under a variety of

simulation frameworks. For example, PARDSIM
(PARameter And Response Data SIMulation)
uses a random-number generator to generate
hypothetical responses according to specified
item response theory models (Yoes, 1997). In the
structural-equations modeling domain, the EQS
software allows for simulations to be conducted
using models generated by the user (Bentler,
1995), as does AMOS (Arbuckle, 1997; see also
Paxton, Curran, Bollen, & Kirby, 2001, for general discussion). Other types of simulation software packages such as ProcessModel focus on
developing simulations of business processes
using flowcharts (ProcessModel, 2004). Even
general multipurpose software packages are
developing simulation and bootstrapping capabilities (SYSTAT 11, 2004).

Other modeling approaches use custom-
written software. Zickar (2000) used Turbo
Pascal to generate the algorithms to simulate

faking on personality tests. Other simulation software has been written using Visual Basic (Brown, 1999), which seems to be a currently popular language for writing simulation software because of its ease of use. The advantage to written custom software is customization; the downside, of course, is that the time and difficulty in programming the software may be prohibitive to many psychologists.

Once the software is chosen (or written), decisions need to be made on inputs, outputs, algorithms, and assumptions. Input parameters are the variables that the researcher believes are important in modeling the output process. For example, in the WORKER program, the input conditions would be the individual (e.g., sample distributions of age and sex), organizational (e.g., types of management interventions), and environmental (e.g., external unemployment rate) factors that are believed to influence withdrawal behaviors. The output variables can be thought of as traditional dependent variables. In WORKER, output variables include the prevalence of withdrawal rates such as absenteeism and turnover. The algorithms are the specific mechanisms used to relate the input variables to the output variables. Assumptions are made about the variables considered for inputs and outputs, as well as about the specific algorithms used to relate the two. One of the dangers of using off-the-shelf simulation software is that you are often limited by the software's assumptions. For example, if you are interested in studying how variable x relates to the output variable y, the simulation software may be constrained to use linear relationships when, in fact, you would like to use a curvilinear relationship.

Conducting the Modeling Research

Once the infrastructure has been created, input parameters need to be determined. Two decisions need to be made: (a) Which variables should be manipulated in a particular simulation? (b) Which values should be used as input parameters? In any particular study, there may be a large number of variables that could be studied. Researchers need to make decisions on which variables to include in the simulation model and which factors should be held constant. For example, in the WORKER software, there are a variety of variables that can be manipulated as input variables. If all possible input variables are allowed to vary, however, it may be difficult to make interpretations about the effects of any particular variable on the output variable(s).

In addition to deciding which factors to vary, decisions should be made on the input values used for the simulation. Values can be chosen based on correspondence with observed values from known data sets. For example, with WORKER it may be useful to consider recent historical data on local unemployment rates to determine the span of rates used in a particular study. Limiting the number of factors to vary (and the number of levels considered for each factor) is important because the number of simulation runs can quickly become difficult to manage if too many factors are considered.

If a stochastic or probabilistic process is used in the simulation (as is the case in Monte Carlo studies), a number of replications should be conducted. Replications allow for an assessment of the role of sampling error to be assessed, in addition to making sure that outliers do not bias conclusions. Just like in traditional empirical research, outliers are possible in modeling research. For example, consider a coin toss; although rare, it is possible to have 10 heads in a row. Occasionally in simulation research with stochastic algorithms, extreme outputs are possible.

Summarizing the output of computer simulation studies can also be complex. Given the ease in drawing large numbers of samples and data points, it is easy to generate a large number of cases that can be difficult to manage. Many simulations run several replications for a particular configuration of input conditions in order to reduce sampling error. In fact, simulation studies that are done to test the effects of sampling error replicate identical runs of the same experiment (varying only the input conditions of the random-number generator); in such an experiment, the variation across identical replications can only be attributed to sampling error. By running a large enough number of simulations, it is possible to determine the sampling distribution for a particular statistic.

Validating and Refining the Model

Just as one would assess the validity of a theory, the validity of the model should be assessed. Computational models can be evaluated using criteria similar to those used to evaluate other types of theories. Validity and parsimony are two key considerations. Taber and Timpone (1996) present several types of evidence that can be used to support a model's claim to validity: outcome validity, process validity, and internal validity.

Outcome validity measures the correspondence of simulation outcomes with events that have been observed in the real world. Computational models can be run under known conditions that have been well understood from previous research. For example, Munson and Hulin (2000) tested the validity of the WORKER program by examining the fit between the simulation model and data that had been obtained from an actual organization. They collected data on a work withdrawal scale and perceived sanctions (e.g., what would the punishment be) for various work withdrawal behaviors. They compared the correlation matrix from the actual data set with a correlation matrix generated from WORKER, run under separate theoretical conditions. Munson and Hulin concluded that the data generated by WORKER using the independent forms of withdrawal theory were more consistent with the actual data compared with data generated under theories. Therefore, they concluded, at least in the organization that they studied, the independent-forms theory was a more descriptive theory of work withdrawal. Munson and Hulin (2000) found more outcome validity for the WORKER model when it used the independent-forms model compared with other models.

In cases when outcome validity is not found, there are three major explanations of the mismatch between the model and the real-world outcomes (Woolfson & Pert, 1999). *Programming errors* occur when the computer program fails to run in the intended way due to miscoding. Initial checking of the programming logic along with feeding the program a range of values allows one to rule out programming errors. In addition, most computer language programs now include extensive debugging features that allow one to monitor the values of program variables. *Numerical errors* refer to errors caused by rounding and truncation of variables. Finally, *modeling errors* refer to mismatches between the simulation model and the real-world process. Although programming and numerical errors should be checked for, it is often this latter type of error that is most vexing (and most illuminating) for the researcher. Of course, an additional problem when lack of outcome validity is found would be with the real-world data used for validation. One should conduct the traditional data investigations of the real-world data to make sure that it is sufficient.

Internal validity relates to the correspondence of the simulation model to the theory that it was based on. This might best be checked by having independent researchers, knowledgeable with the basic theory, examine the correspondence of the simulation to the theory. For example, Hanisch and colleagues could have had the original withdrawal behavior theorists examine the logic and algorithms of the WORKER program to see if there was correspondence between the two. In addition, Woflson and Pert (1999) mention how internal validity can be tested using sensitivity analysis. In this type of internal validity check, systematic changes are made in the input parameters to determine how the model output is changed. Relations between variables should be consistent with theory; however, as mentioned previously, when models include complex interaction variables, it may be difficult to determine a priori how changes in input variables should result in changes in outputs.

Process validity relates to the correspondence of the mechanisms used to generate the simulation outcomes with the actual processes used to generate the real-world outcomes. As mentioned before, process validity is a desirable quality of computational models; however, models that do not possess process validity (i.e., black-box models) may still be useful in generating predictions. In general, though, the higher the amount of process validity that a model possesses, the more useful a model is in helping understand the phenomena being studied. The best way of determining process validity would be to have content experts study the model and its relevant output to determine whether there is correspondence between the modeler's contrived system and the way that the real world operates.

Besides validating the model, it is important to refine the model. All models are approximations. Model research should be considered a process and not a single study that resolves questions. After a current model has been understood, with the relationships of the studied variables and the outcome variables well understood, additional levels of complexity can be added to simulations to make them more realistic. In addition, a wider range of input variable conditions can be considered so that results become more generalizable. For example, the WORKER program could be expanded to include additional input variables.

ADVANTAGES OF COMPUTATIONAL MODELING

The methods discussed in this chapter have several key strengths compared with traditional research methods.

Testing Situations That Cannot Be Tested in Real Life

Simulation research can be important for investigating phenomena that cannot be tested for various ethical, logistic, or practical reasons (see Dell, Schmidt, & Meara, Chapter 12, this book, for discussion of ethical issues in research). Correlational research is constrained in examining how conditions as they exist in the real world covary with other conditions of interest. Given this, researchers may be interested in testing the ramifications of certain conditions of interest that have not been observed yet. For example, in studying the effects of unemployment on turnover, it may be important to test how an unemployment rate of 25% would influence turnover, although unemployment has not reached those levels in the past 60 years in the United States economy.

Ethical reasons may also preclude studying other phenomena. In ecological research, computer simulations are conducted to test the effects of proposed policies on important irrevocable outcomes, such as elimination of endangered species (Gilpin & Soule, 1986). Modeling in epidemiological research is important to test the effects of public policies that might result in saved lives or might actually exacerbate a particular disease (Seitz & Mueller, 1994). In addition, simulation research may be important for

practical reasons. It is extremely costly (and often risky) for organizations to implement large-scale interventions. By modeling the possible outcomes of those interventions, it may be possible to get a good idea of what will work and what would be risky under different scenarios.

Simulation Demands Rigor

A side advantage of modeling research is that it demands that theoretical propositions be made formal. Many theories in psychology are based on vague statements of association between variables of interest. A common theme of different researchers who have attempted formal modeling of theoretical phenomena is that the whole process helped them understand the theory better (see Fiorina, 1975). For example, many theories will state that behavior x is related to outcome y. To translate that vague statement of relationship into a simulation requires consideration of the nature of the relationship. Is that relationship linear or nonlinear? What is the degree of association? Are there any boundary conditions that may exaggerate or ameliorate the relationship? Developing a computational model demands consideration of all of these questions.

Supreme Control

Computational modeling is unique compared with all other research methods in that it permits the researcher *total control* of the research environment. In correlational research, the researcher attempts to measure every possible variable that may affect the phenomena of interest. Variables that go unmeasured (either for lack of time or foresight) can influence the relationships of measured variables in unpredictable ways. In the experimental paradigm, the researcher manipulates one or more variables of interest and then relies on random assignment to minimize the effects of unmanipulated variables. Also, in experiments, the effects of the manipulation on participants are often unknown and variable. In both experimental and correlational research paradigms, control depends on a combination of foresight, luck, and large sample sizes. With computational modeling, the experimenter designs the world in which the phenomena exist;

in a sense, the researcher plays the omnipotent figure who determines which variables have an impact and which are irrelevant.

Dynamic Simulations

Pleas and demands for longitudinal research conclude many research articles in psychology. The advantages to empirical longitudinal research are more confidence in determining causality, a better understanding of the interconnectedness of variables assessed in a model, and an understanding of the role of time on psychological processes (e.g., Rosnow, 2000). Unfortunately, collecting longitudinal data is often impractical or impossible for many types of research questions. Computational modeling provides a nice alternative, in that it is possible to simulate the effects of time on variables and relationships of interest. In dynamic simulations, outputs from one stage become inputs for the next stage. For example, Hanisch (2000) was able to simulate 20 years of a virtual organization and to test the effects of organizational interventions on reducing turnover over time. This might be particularly important in the withdrawal literature because it may be possible that reducing one form of withdrawal might result in an increase in another form in the long term. For example, if an organization penalizes strongly employees who show up to work late, they may decrease tardiness, but in the long term they may increase absenteeism, turnover, or both. This represents a powerful and pragmatic application of computational modeling.

Pedagogical Reasons

Computer simulations are also an excellent way to supplement instruction with concrete, interactive technology that simulates processes that might be difficult or costly to replicate in the classroom laboratory. Chemists have been using computer simulations of the molecule for a long time to illustrate chemical reactions that are difficult (and occasionally dangerous) to observe and costly to replicate. Brown cites the unpredictability of student experiments and the lack of control as reasons for using a computer simulation of an experiment (Brown, 1999). He cites increased control, reduced

required class time, and elimination of concerns about human subjects–review issues as reasons for using computer simulations. In other areas of psychology in which actual replication of behavior may be difficult to do, simulations provide a nice alternative. For example, computer simulations of the transmission process of a neuron may be the only option for providing a somewhat hands-on learning experience for students.

DISADVANTAGES OF MODELING

Simulated Behavior Is Not Behavior

In many fields, modeling research is difficult to publish in mainstream journals. One criticism that modeling researchers report hearing is that simulation research is less valued because simulation data are the result of the model, not actual behavior observed in the real world. This criticism does have some merit. The veracity of the simulation model is paramount in simulation research. To address this complaint, exemplary programs of modeling research use a combination of modeling along with experimental and correlational studies that rely on actual behavior to better understand the phenomena being modeled. Nobel Prize–winning economist Wassily Leontief stated,

> True advance can be achieved only through an iterative process in which improved theoretical formulation raises new empirical questions and the answers to these questions in their turn, lead to new theoretical insights. The "givens" of today become the "unknowns" that will have to be explained tomorrow. (Leontief, 1985, p. 278)

The interplay between computational modeling and real-world studies can be quite productive. Real-world studies can be used to form the basis of the model used to conduct the simulation research. Modeling research can then be used to explore anomalous findings from experimental and correlational data sets. Without that interplay between model and real-world data, however, computational models can digress into mere intellectual exercises, into a hypothetical fantasy world.

Garbage In, Garbage Out

The output and results of computational modeling rely on the fidelity of the simulation to actual behavior. Even if a model is faithful to the actual process, it is important that input values that are used to guide the simulation reflect realistic values that could potentially be observed in real life. In some cases, it may be important to consider unrealistic values to determine boundary conditions. For example, it may be important to determine how withdrawal behavior would be affected by an unrealistically high or unrealistically low unemployment rate. In general, though, values for input parameters should be chosen to mimic values observed in real-data situations. These values could be obtained from archival sources (e.g., census data; see Zaitzow & Fields, Chapter 22, this book), individual studies, or even meta-analyses (see Cooper, Robinson, & Dorr, Chapter 21, this book).

Models Must Be Reductionist

Computational models often make simplifying assumptions about the phenomena they attempt to model. Many times the software, mathematics, and statistical frameworks force decisions to be made that oversimplify the phenomena being studied. For example, in Costa and De Matos's (2002) computational model of attitude change within organizations, their model assumes that attitudes are binary entities that are either negative or positive. This assumption is inconsistent with a long line of research that shows that individual attitudes vary in valence and intensity. The findings of their simulation might or might not have been influenced by their decision to simplify the phenomena. To check this, it would be necessary, however, to compare results from a more complex simulation.

Simulation research should be thought of as a process. Simple models are used to establish the utility of a simulation tool and to identify the effects of basic factors thought to influence the phenomena of interest. As simulations are established, they should be made more complex; additional relevant factors should be included and modeled. Simplifying assumptions are relaxed to be more consistent with the precise psychological processes that they are attempting to model. The criticism of reductionism is not unique to computational modeling. It is the natural process of theory development (see Gelso, Chapter 32, this book).

CONCLUSIONS

In this chapter, the basic components of computational modeling research were presented, along with an exemplar of how modeling research can be used in psychological research. Computational modeling is not for everyone. In fact, given that good computational modeling research is based on the foundation of previous empirical research, modeling research should not replace empirical research based on human participants and animal subjects. The methodological tool bag of research psychologists, however, should be vast and provide many choices. The strengths of computational modeling complement many of the other research strategies presented in this book. The first two scientific disciplines of psychology as envisioned by Cronbach—correlational and experimental research—are not all-exclusive. Computational modeling, the new third scientific discipline of psychology, provides a nice complement to existing methodologies.

EXERCISES

1. Think of a real-world phenomenon for which you would like to develop a computational model.

   A. Decide on the relevant input and output variables that would be important to model this phenomenon.

   B. Determine the type of mathematical or statistical framework you would use to model the relationships between the input variables and the outcome variables.

   C. What criteria would you use to judge the validity of your model?

2. Consider an article on simulation research conducted on a research topic in which you are interested. Read that article and then answer the following questions:

A. What types of predictive and process validity evidence did the author(s) use to evaluate the simulation model?

B. What types of assumptions were made about the model? Are those assumptions viable?

C. What could be done to make the simulation model more realistic? Are there more input variables that could be added? Are there other outcome variables that could be added?

D. Was simulation research a good methodological choice for this particular research area?

Recommended Readings

You may wish to consult further material to increase your understanding of computational- or simulation-based research. An excellent source, within the organizational science tradition, is Ilgen and Hulin's (2000) work titled *Computational Modeling of Behavior in Organizations: The Third Scientific Discipline.* This set of chapters includes material by those who have been investigating substantive phenomena (withdrawal, faking on personality inventories, performance) using a third paradigm. Work by Seitz and by Hanisch illustrates the application of computational modeling to worker absenteeism and spread of viral infections such as AIDS.

Four Key References

Hanisch, K. A., Hulin, C. L., & Seitz, S. T. (1996). Mathematical/computational modeling of organizational withdrawal processes: Benefits, methods, and results. In G. Ferris (Ed.), *Research in personnel and human resources management* (Vol. 14, pp. 91–142). Greenwich, CT: JAI.

This chapter provides the most detailed summary of the WORKER research presented throughout this chapter. I recommend this chapter for an in-depth presentation of one modeling research example.

Ilgen, D. R., & Hulin, C. L. (2000). *Computational modeling of behavior in organizations: The third scientific discipline.* Washington, DC: APA.

This edited volume provides ten examples of modeling research from industrial-organizational psychology, as well as discussion on the value of modeling. This is a good volume for interested readers to investigate the range of modeling options in one content area of psychology.

Neelamkavil, F. (1987). *Computer simulation and modeling.* Chichester, UK: Wiley.

This textbook approaches modeling research, not from a social science perspective but from a general research perspective. This book is highly technical and will be challenging to most psychology graduate students; however, it provides a detailed overview of modeling research and many mathematical examples.

Taber, C. S., & Timpone, R. J. (1996). *Computational modeling.* Thousand Oaks, CA: Sage.

This primer on computational modeling provides both background and rationale for modeling research, as well as practical advice on how to conduct modeling research. This would perhaps be the book I would recommend that graduate students read first before considering modeling research.

REFERENCES

Abelson, R. P. (1968). Simulation of social behavior. In G. Lindzey & E. Aronson (Eds.), *Handbook of social psychology* (Vol. 2, pp. 274–356). Reading, MA: Addison-Wesley.

Arbuckle, J. L. (1997). *Amos users' guide version 3.6.* Chicago: SmallWaters.

Arnott, R., & Small, K. (1994). The economics of traffic congestion. *American Scientist, 82,* 446–455.

Baruch, D. W. (1944). Why they terminate. *Journal of Consulting Psychology, 8,* 35–46.

Beehr, T. A., & Gupta, N. (1978). A note on the structure of employee withdrawal. *Organizational Behavior and Human Performance, 21,* 73–79.

Bentler, P. M. (1995). *EQS program manual.* Encino, CA: Multivariate Software.

Bolt, D. M. (2002). A Monte Carlo comparison of parametric and nonparametric polytomous DIF detection methods. *Applied Measurement in Education, 15,* 113–141.

Brown, M. F. (1999). Wildcat World: Simulation programs for teaching basic concepts in psychological science. *Behavior Research Methods, Instruments, & Computers, 31,* 14–18.

Carsten, J. M., & Spector, P. E. (1987). Unemployment, job satisfaction, and employee turnover: A meta-analytic test of the Muchinsky model. *Journal of Applied Psychology, 72,* 374–381.

Costa, L. A., & De Matos, J. A. (2002). Towards an organizational model of attitude change. *Computational and Mathematical Organization Theory, 8,* 315–335.

Cronbach, L. J. (1957). The two disciplines of scientific psychology. *American Psychologist, 12,* 671–684.

Fiorina, P. (1975). Formal models in political science. *American Journal of Political Science, 19,* 133–159.

Gilpin, M. E., & Soule, M. E. (1986). Minimum viable populations: Processes of species extinction. In M. E. Soule (Ed.), *Conservation biology: The science of scarcity and diversity* (pp. 19–34). Sunderland, MA: Sinauer.

Hanisch, K. A. (2000). The impact of organizational interventions on behaviors: An examination of different models of withdrawal. In D. Ilgen & C. L. Hulin (Eds.), *Computational modeling of behavior in organizations* (pp. 33–60). Washington, DC: APA.

Hanisch, K. A., Hulin, C. L., & Seitz, S. T. (1996). Mathematical/computational modeling of organizational withdrawal processes: Benefits, methods, and results. In G. Ferris (Ed.), *Research in personnel and human resources management* (Vol. 14, pp. 91–142). Greenwich, CT: JAI.

Hanisch, K. A., Hulin, C. L., & Seitz, S. (2000). Simulating withdrawal behaviors in work organizations: An example of a virtual society. *Nonlinear Dynamics, Psychology, and Life Sciences, 4,* 33–65.

Hanisch, K. A., Hulin, C. L., & Seitz, S. (2001). Temporal dynamics and emergent properties of organizational withdrawal models. In M. Erez & E. Kleinbeck (Eds.), *Work motivation in the context of a globalizing economy* (pp. 293–312). Mahwah, NJ: Lawrence Erlbaum.

Harwell, M., Stone, C. A., Hsu, T. C., & Kirisci, L. (1996). Monte Carlo studies in item response theory. *Applied Psychological Measurement, 20,* 101–125.

Hill, J. M., & Trist, E. L. (1955). Changes in accidents and other absences with length of service: A further study of their incidence and relation to each other in an iron and steel works. *Human Relations, 8,* 121–152.

Ilgen, D. R., & Hulin, C. L. (2000). *Computational modeling of behavior in organizations: The third scientific discipline.* Washington, DC: APA.

Kephart, J. O., Hanson, J. E., & Greenwald, A. R. (2000). Dynamic pricing by software agents. *Computer Networks, 32,* 731–752.

Lambert, M. E. (1989). Using computer simulations in behavior therapy training. *Computers in Human Services, 5,* 1–12.

Leontief, W. (1985). Theoretical assumptions and nonobserved facts. In W. Leontief (Ed.), *Essays in economics: Theories, theorizing, facts, and policies* (pp. 272–282). New Burnswick, NJ: Transaction Books.

March, J. G., & Simon, H. A. (1958). *Organizations.* New York: Wiley.

Munson, L. J., & Hulin, C. L. (2000). Examining the fit between empirical data and theoretical simulations. In D. R. Ilgen & C. L. Hulin (Eds.), *Computational modeling of behavior in organizations: The third scientific discipline* (pp. 69–83). Washington, DC: APA.

Neelamkavil, F. (1987). *Computer simulation and modeling.* Chichester, UK: Wiley.

O'Reilly, R. C., & Munakata, Y. (2000). *Computational explorations in cognitive neuroscience: Understanding the mind by simulating the brain.* Cambridge: MIT Press.

ProcessModel. (2004). ProcessModel [Computer software]. Provo, UT: Author.

Rosnow, R. L. (2000). Longitudinal research. In A. E. Kazdin (Ed.), *Encyclopedia of psychology* (Vol. 5, pp. 76–77). Washington, DC: APA.

Sackett, P. R., & Roth, L. (1996). Multi-stage selection strategies: A Monte Carlo investigation of effects on performance and minority hiring. *Personnel Psychology, 49,* 549–572.

Schelling, T. C. (1971). Dynamic models of housing segregation. *Journal of Mathematical Sociology, 1,* 143.

Schultz, T. R. (2003). *Computational developmental psychology.* Cambridge: MIT Press.

Seitz, S. T. (2000). Virtual organizations. In D. Ilgen & C. L. Hulin (Eds.), *Computational modeling of behavior in organizations* (pp. 19–32). Washington, DC: APA.

Seitz, S. T., Hanisch, K. A., & Hulin, C. L. (1997). *WORKER: A computer program to simulate employee organizational withdrawal behaviors.* University of Illinois at Urbana-Champaign and Iowa State University.

Seitz, S. T., & Mueller, G. E. (1994). Viral load and sexual risk. Epidemiologic and policy implications for HIV/AIDS. In E. H. Kaplan & M. L. Brandeau (Eds.), *Modeling the AIDS epidemic: Planning, policy, and prediction* (pp. 461–480). New York: Raven Press.

Simon, H. A. (1979). Information-processing models of cognition. *Annual Review of Psychology, 30,* 363–396.

SYSTAT. (2004). SYSTAT 11.0. [Computer software]. Point Richmond, CA: Systat Software.

Taber, C. S., & Timpone, R. J. (1996). *Computational modeling.* Thousand Oaks, CA: Sage.

Tucker, L. R., Koopman, R. F., & Linn, R. (1969). Evaluation of factor analytic research procedures by means of simulated correlation matrices. *Psychometrika, 34,* 421–459.

Whicker, M. L., & Sigelman, L. (1991). *Computer simulation applications: An introduction.* Newbury Park, CA: Sage.

Woolfson, M. M., & Pert, G. J. (1999). *An introduction to computer simulation.* Oxford, UK: Oxford University Press.

Yoes, M. (1997). *User's manual for the PARDSIM Parameter and Response Data Simulation Program.* St. Paul, MN: Assessment Systems.

Zickar, M. J. (2000). Modeling faking on personality tests. In D. R. Ilgen & C. L. Hulin (Eds.), *Computational modeling of behavior in organizations: The third scientific discipline* (pp. 95–108). Washington, DC: APA.

Zimmerman, P. D., & Dorn, D. W. (2002). *Computer simulation and the Comprehensive Test Ban Treaty.* Fort McNair, Washington, DC: Center for Technology and National Security Policy, National Defense University.

30

APPLYING FOR RESEARCH GRANTS

JOHN G. BORKOWSKI

KIMBERLY S. HOWARD

It's easy to win research grants. Simply form a good idea, develop a plan of action, be willing to expend highly focused effort, find several appropriate funding agencies, be willing to tolerate initial setbacks, and then persevere until you receive an award.

Despite the ease of winning grants, most young scholars fail to seek research grants primarily because they fear failure, not because of the quality of their ideas. Those who seek grant support but don't succeed usually lack perseverance in the face of their initial failure. From this perspective, the major reason for not winning the grantsmanship game is rooted in the personal-motivational aspects of scholarship, not the conceptual or intellectual.

This chapter provides suggestions about applying for research grants, with a special focus on creating the motivation necessary to follow through the long process until an award is received. First, we develop a rationale for submitting research grants and then present a mental model of grant writing, and finally offer practical suggestions that provide some direction in writing your first grant or doing a better job the second time around.

WHY WRITE A RESEARCH GRANT?

I doubt if there will be a single PhD in the United States in the decade ahead, aspiring to succeed in academia or professional life, whose career won't be significantly advanced by writing, and winning, a research grant. The case in the academy is straightforward: Tenure committees are impressed by assistant professors who have developed a solid track record in grantsmanship. Some senior faculty and most administrators maintain that a successful grant record is as important as the record of research publications, including the dean whose financial flexibility is enhanced by the return of indirect costs associated with grants and the vice president for research, whose research portfolio will bulge a bit more if it contains your award.

The important reason, however, for developing and submitting research grants is the unique framework they provide for carrying out a long-term research plan that is more integral, thoughtful, and systematic than would otherwise be the case. With a grant, you'll find that you're more invested in research and devote more time to it; your research will reflect your higher level of commitment and competence gained from the months of grant preparation because of your increased intellectual investment.

For instance, you might choose to "buy off" a course each semester for three consecutive years, thus providing more time and energy for research. Certainly, you'll benefit from hiring more helping hands. The additional graduate and undergraduate students budgeted in your grant will provide new talent, not only for carrying out the research plan but, more important, for revising, rethinking, and charting new research directions. You'll also have additional flexibility and control of your professional life, in that you'll no longer need to ask your department chair for funds for computers, supplies, and travel costs. But most important of all, you'll gain the additional self-confidence necessary to enter the "invisible college of scholars" in your area of expertise. Your sense of self-efficacy will increase. Entrance into this select group will build, or strengthen, your scholarly networks and enhance collaborative possibilities. All of these positive offshoots from your first research grant should strengthen the quality of your research program as well as contribute significantly to the success of your long-term scholarship.

A final reason for applying for a research grant is related to the quality and scope of your ideas. There are very few simple ideas left to pursue in most areas of contemporary psychology. More than likely your model idea will be theoretically complex, multifaceted, process-oriented, and perhaps longitudinal in nature. If this is the case, its corresponding research program will require a large undertaking, with many component parts and several collaborators involved. It may become an undertaking so large in scope that it necessitates grant support for successful completion. Although in some areas of psychology it is still possible to mount a sustained research campaign without external grant support, there is no doubt that the energy and competence you bring to your project will be enhanced through grant support.

Many young, aspiring clinicians and counselors believe that knowledge of grant writing is irrelevant for their future careers. I tend to disagree, in large part because I've seen so many professionals move rapidly up the administrative ladder in mental health organizations when they have the skills necessary to obtain grant support for their organization's demonstration, planning, and evaluation programs. Every new idea for treating patients or preventing problems in homes, schools, or clinics needs careful documentation, in terms of implementation, accuracy, and the range of resulting outcomes.

Possessing the skills (and the will) necessary to write a research grant is a major advantage

for almost all professional psychologists. It would not be surprising to learn that we always recommend that talented students in graduate training to become counselors and clinicians take the full complement of statistics and research methods courses (not the bare minimum as is sometimes the case) and that they learn the art of grant writing. Forewarned is forearmed: It is often too late to return to graduate school to pick up missing computer, quantitative, and research methods courses. For most aspiring professionals as well as scholars, this knowledge base and requisite research skills, together with an understanding of the grant-writing process, will be useful, perhaps essential, for career advancement.

Most people form mental models of the world around them to understand and interpret reality. For instance, expert teachers often form models of what constitutes good teaching, including knowledge about best instructional practices and effective disciplinary techniques. These models not only summarize what a teacher knows about classroom practice but also guide future practice, which can, in turn, reshape the original model. In this sense, mental models are dynamic. Similar mental models can be formed about the process of grant development and can be useful in several respects: They succinctly summarize the most important steps in successful grant writing; they simplify the writing process; they serve to energize the writer; and they can be easily revised and updated as new, relevant strategies about grant development are learned.

A GRANT-WRITING MODEL

In a model of grant writing, there are at least five major ingredients: First, form an idea about which you are proud and excited. Of necessity, this means that you've developed an innovative idea that will require testing in multiple ways. It probably is a complex idea that will challenge you in its implementation at multiple levels of your proposed studies. But through it all, your commitment to the idea energizes and guides the writing process. Second, find an appropriate audience: You'll need to match your idea to an appropriate funding agency. In other words, your research goals require a proper home, and finding the right home for your grant proposal requires both advanced planning and creative exploration. Reviewers in the wrong home may fail to recognize the merits and significance of your idea. Third, frame the research plan so that, if at all possible, it has both theoretical and applied significance. Of the two kinds of significance, the former is the more important because it means that you hope to advance the state of knowledge in an important domain of inquiry. Fourth, do your homework thoroughly so that you have a set of refereed papers published (or in press) in respected journals. These papers lead up to the idea that is at the heart of your grant proposal. At the very least, you'll need to have conducted a major pilot project that demonstrates the methodological feasibility of your design. Finally, you must persevere until an award is received. Hardly anyone is successful with an initial submission. The trick is to return immediately to the funding agency with an improved, revised submission that is responsive to the reviewers' feedback. If you respond to all of the reviewers' comments, you'll be in good position to obtain a positive review the second time around.

Seek and You Shall Find

Creating Good Ideas

If we could tell you how to develop an interesting and theoretically important idea, we would probably be millionaires, or at least have formulated a few more good ideas during our own research careers. The problem is, of course, that good research ideas emerge through a somewhat mysterious integration of existing knowledge within a domain, knowledge in adjacent domains, and technical skills—welded together by inspiration, imagination, and good timing. How these ingredients, which are all necessary to form an important and researchable idea, come together in each scientist's mind is something you may have experienced, or will experience, first-hand. We do know, however, that a sincere commitment to expanding your field, a willingness to explore the forefronts of its boundaries for its sake (not yours), a determined

sense of perseverance, and a recognition that the game of science is fun and challenging will put you in good position for preparation and inspiration to unite with luck in creating an original, significant research idea.

Remember that raw ideas need to be sharpened and reshaped in order to transform them into researchable hypotheses. All too often, young scholars outline premature ideas in their grants, not theoretically refined ideas supported by the pilot data that demonstrate their plausibility. Chapter 24 of this handbook by Peterson on writing drafts is relevant. Don't be afraid to let your ideas ferment, to share them with others, and to test them in preliminary studies. Sometimes you need to admit, perhaps grudgingly, that what you first thought was a great idea isn't a researchable idea, or perhaps not a significant one. Continue to struggle over time to come up with your best, sharpest idea, and then pursue its implementation with vigor and determination in a series of studies designed to test interrelated hypotheses.

The Audience and the Idea

Rarely will you develop a research grant, whether designed to test a theory or conduct intervention program, without a specific granting agency in mind. You should match your idea, not only to a specific funding agency but also to potential reviewers. That is, you should ascertain with some certainty that your proposal falls within the objectives of a targeted foundation or granting agency, and if possible you should attempt to discover who will review, and ultimately judge, your grant: *Write with a specific audience in mind, if at all possible.*

If your project falls within the auspices of a major federal agency such as the National Science Foundation (NSF), the National Institutes of Health (NIH), or the Office of Education, then existing brochures, program officers, or both will be available to provide their mission statements and current research priorities. These agencies also have extensive Internet resources, which allow for easy access to all the information you'll need to write your proposal. For example, the National Science Foundation (NSF, 2005) has a link, "Funding—Preparing Proposals" on its main page, and the

National Institutes of Health grants page (NIH, 2005) includes everything from funding opportunities to forms and application guidelines. If you are responding to a special initiative called a request for proposals (RFP), then the Federal Register will likely provide detailed information; your institution's grants office likely subscribes to the Federal Register service, or you can also access the information using search features of the Federal Register Web site (Government Printing Office, 2004). Your grants officer will also have available a volume describing the range of private foundations that have interests similar to yours.

There are also several Web-based search engines that are designed to locate a variety of funding opportunities (from both federal and private agencies) to match your particular interests. It is often helpful to develop a list of key words to use in your search that includes some very general words (i.e., *psychology*) as well as words that are more specific to your topic. The Illinois Researcher Information Service (IRIS; 2003) is hosted by the University of Illinois at Urbana-Champaign, and the Community of Science (COS, 2003) is a private resource for subscribers only (though it is likely that your university will have a subscription to COS). Both search engines allow you to choose the type of award you want to search for, as well as keywords to describe your areas of interest. They both have funding alert features that enable you to set up an automatic alert every time a new funding opportunity arises that meets the specifications of your search.

If your proposal is headed to a private foundation, you should take several preliminary steps: Ensure that their priorities match your research interests by reviewing the annual report for the foundation's most recent funding decisions; develop a short two- or three-page abstract that outlines your proposal in relation to the foundation's objectives; and most important of all, try to get your foot in the door: Initiate phone contact with the relevant program officer to whet the foundation's appetite prior to the arrival of your abstract (do it yourself or enlist a well-chosen colleague). *It is rare that unsolicited grants, presented without prior personal contact, are awarded by a foundation.* If you have no direct connection to the foundation, it may be worth paying an in-person visit so that

officers can get to know you and hear the enthusiasm you have for your idea.

The point of this discussion is to make you aware of the need to shape your general idea in such a way as to make it appealing to potential reviewers. Your proposal ought to reflect your excitement and enthusiasm for you research. You also need to follow the agency or foundation's guidelines without deviation (e.g., do not exceed page limits for any section; do not burden reviewers with excessive materials in an appendix). Remember to present your ideas in accord with the unique goals and specific format of the granting agency.

Framing the Research Plan

Generally, research plans evolve in your mind over time. Start with a tentative outline of the body of the proposal early in the game. Modify it frequently as you churn the idea and its ramifications over and over in your mind. Be flexible in your attempts to locate your project in terms of a narrow context (e.g., testing a specific theory), as well as a context that reveals its long-term applied, or practical, significance. As socially oriented priorities emerge from federal agencies as well as private foundations that formerly funded only basic research, the day may come when it is simply impossible to fund theoretically oriented research ideas without their potential long-term, applied significance being adequately addressed.

Of the two goals in your research plan—*theoretical importance* and *potential significance*—the former should be of greater concern. You simply must convince the reviewers that your research will advance the current state of knowledge and understanding in an important domain of inquiry. You do this in at least three ways: (a) Present a logical and coherent argument for your theoretical position, showing clearly how it differs from the prevailing view(s); (b) Discuss your aims, objectives, and general hypotheses in sufficient detail and with a clear sense of how they interrelate; (c) Present the background literature, especially your own recent work in this area.

The final step—showing your research competence—is essential, because you must present convincing evidence of the quality of your own scholarship (e.g., recent, relevant publications) or at least strong pilot data showing your experimental savvy and the feasibility of the methodological approach. In the case of a large-scale clinical demonstration or intervention project, the documentation of your scholarship might consist of a pilot study dealing with a mini version of the proposed intervention or individual case studies demonstrating that the full program can indeed be implemented, with reasonable potential for changing deviant or delayed behaviors. As you end this initial section of the proposal, be sure to outline specific hypotheses (although only the major ones), as well as corresponding predictions about major outcomes that are expected to result from your studies or intervention.

The Research Specifics

The second major section of most grants deals with Proposed Research. This section mirrors, in many respects, the Methods section of a journal article and is made up of the following subsections: Participants, Design, Materials, Procedures, and Proposed Statistical Analyses. If the proposal contains multiple experiments (as is usually the case), you'll need to repeat similar procedural and analytic information for each study, unless there is redundancy across the series of studies. A table can demonstrate such redundancy and reinforce the interrelated network of your hypotheses.

Participants

The number of participants and their most important characteristics need to be described, often in considerable detail. For instance, if the population under study is composed of juniors and seniors from a particular college, then little additional information will be needed except the number of subjects, gender distribution, and any special considerations about their abilities or academic achievements. On the other hand, if you are studying children with disabilities, then you would likely include the number of participants, their sex, age, mental age (or IQ), types of disabilities, relevant motor or visual disabilities, grade level or reading capacity, medication history, and other essential characteristics.

Remember to describe participant characteristics in detail sufficient to enable the reviewer to generalize from your sample to the appropriate population. Often the method of obtaining participants—whether they are volunteers or paid, of normal intelligence or from a clinically defined population—will affect the experimental outcomes; hence, such information should be provided in detail in the proposal. Also, whether the subjects are highly trained for the task, have previous experimental participation in similar tasks, or are naive are important considerations that should be included in this section. Consideration of statistical power at this point is important (See Myors, Chapter 11, on that topic).

Design

If your study includes a number of independent variables, some being given on repeated occasions, it is wise to refer the reviewer to the entire set of variables that make up the design in a table. This table will make it easier for the reviewers to understand the measures you're taking and when (and how often) they'll be collected. Mention in the text proper, not only a description of your variables but also whether they represent within- or between-subjects manipulations. It will usually be the case in a grant proposal that you've developed a novel and complex design, and this section should be highlighted as a major component of your proposal.

Methods and/or Materials

The Methods section should describe either the type of testing instrument and/or apparatus (brand name) or, if it isn't commercially available, its essential features and dimensions. The description of apparatus should tell what the equipment does rather than how it was put together. Include key dimensions and functional operations instead of a picture or diagram. If the to-be-presented materials are complex—such as the number and size of categorically related words in a free recall list of 30 items—then their specifications should be presented in detail so as to allow for replication. For commonly used tests (e.g., Stanford-Binet test of intelligence or the Beck Depression Inventory) less detail about reliability and validity is needed than for questionnaires and tests you have developed; in these cases, considerable detail about reliability and validity is required.

Procedures

The best way to handle the Procedures section is to place the reader in the position of the participant. Treat first things first, proceeding from the point when the participant begins the experiment to the point of the final to-be-recorded behavior. The Procedures section should describe exactly what the subject will be shown and what he or she will be asked to do. Generally, it is best to focus on the participant's activities rather than on the movements of the experimenter. For instance, in a reaction time study, assume that the experimenter will need to reset the clock after each trial. Critical details necessary for replication, like the order of events, their timing, the instructions to subjects (paraphrased rather than reported verbatim, unless the instructions represent one of the manipulated variables), the type of response measurements, and the controlled events, should all be reported in the Procedures section. Remember, however, to report only those details essential for replication. Avoid redundancies in the Procedure section, as well as redundancies across studies in your overall project.

Data Analyses

Remember that this section is a statement of the expected outcomes backed up by the statistics you need in order to analyze the data. Use statistical techniques that are state-of-the-art, but at the lowest level of complexity necessary to analyze your data set. In other words, don't try to be too sophisticated, unless such treatment is called for by your design and hypotheses. Be sure to focus on the key comparisons among treatment means, as well as on individual difference analyses (where theoretically appropriate). Individual difference analyses often provide secondary support for a major hypothesis that itself centers on comparisons among group means. Power calculations, which reveal the number of subjects needed to detect reasonable effects, will also strengthen this section of the proposal. Because many review panels will have a sophisticated statistician on board, it is important for this section to be reviewed by your in-house statistician.

Additional Points to Include

The final part of the Proposed Research section will likely contain a statement about the use of human subjects (including a reference to consent forms that can be found in an appendix and the appropriate inclusion of women and minorities as participants; the latter is required by agencies such as NIH).

The final subsection in the body of the proposal is likely to be titled, "Research Significance." It represents your last chance to show the potential long-range impact of your work on the field and why it would be a wise decision to fund your project in order to benefit science, society, or both. Of course, the Reference section will conclude the body of your grant proposal. This section should be complete, accurate, and faithful to current APA style (APA, 2001). A sloppy bibliography may be viewed as an indication of a potentially sloppy researcher.

The Most Important Part of the Grant: The Summary or Abstract

The Abstract represents the initial section of the research proposal. It should summarize the major manipulated or measured variables, tasks, key procedural features, theoretical relevance, and potential significance. I intentionally saved the discussion of this first section of the grant until last in order to emphasize that, in practice, the writing of the Abstract is the final order of business in grant writing, but one of its most important. Also, it is easier to write the Abstract after all else is completed.

Conciseness, precision, and theoretical significance are the chief ingredients that characterize a successful Abstract. Of all the information contained in a well-written Abstract, the main hypotheses and how they are to be addressed are the most critical. It is difficult to accomplish this goal and simultaneously to include the essential features of the design, the major variables, and their significance in a limited space (often no more than 250 words).

Finally, don't overlook the fact that a good Abstract, much like the title of the proposal itself, is likely to induce the reader to peruse your proposal in greater depth, and with greater seriousness of purpose. Hence, you should construct the Abstract with carefully chosen words, sentences, and transitional phrases. It should be the most interesting section of the grant proposal. Remember that some reviewers on your panel won't be directly assigned your proposal; they'll likely read only your Abstract in detail. Don't miss the chance to impress them with the importance and scope of your project.

Preparing a Budget

Most young investigators spend an unduly large amount of time in budget preparation. Budgets should be adequate but not excessive: Your salary (for both the academic year and the summer), staff or graduate student salaries, equipment, supplies, travel, and participant costs are typical items in the direct costs portion of the budget; a reasonable increase due to inflation (e.g., 2% per year) is often used to form the budgets for additional years. Indirect costs, as determined by your university or agency, are added to the direct cost to form the total cost of the grant for each year. Indirect costs for projects funded by foundations are often negotiable with your office of grants and contracts but are usually never more than 10%. Any unusual item in the budget (such as the amount of assistance needed for collecting data) needs to be justified fully. If in doubt, spend extra time justifying budget items rather than leaving the reviewers with possible unanswered budgetary questions.

USEFUL TIPS IN THE ART OF GRANTSMANSHIP

How to Get Started

Grant preparation should be a constant part of your daily professional life. Keep a notebook on your desk where new ideas can be recorded for posterity and old entries reshaped and expanded. Begin modestly—with your first grant being submitted to an internal unit of your university or to a local agency. Many universities and foundations have seed grants for junior researchers that are designed to provide start-up money. A quick reading of Sternberg's (1992) comments on winning acceptance by a psychological journal will be helpful at this point in the process. Your first grant should not be unduly time-consuming and should have a high probability of funding.

Build on your first award by publishing two or three research papers in respected journals.

You'll then be in a good position to seek your first major external award. My advice is to write this first grant proposal very quickly (e.g., in 2 or 3 weeks). First of all, you'll be building from an existing base of scholarship that is both theoretical and empirical. Hence, the first half of the grant (Rationale, Significance, Literature Review and Background Research, and Hypotheses) will flow fast, given you have preexisting written materials to draw from. More time, perhaps, will be required for the Proposed Research section, although I suspect most of the individual studies will have already been outlined in your little black book. The reason that you should complete this first grant proposal quickly, but competently, is that you most likely won't be funded in this first attempt at securing external funding for your research.

The Need for Perseverance

Roughly 80% of reasonably good grants are initially rejected—at both federal agencies and private foundations. Hence, rejection is a fact of life in grant development that you must learn to expect, accept, and tolerate. To paint an even bleaker picture, consider this fact: Of the 20% of grants approved by most agencies, relatively few will have been approved on the occasion of their initial submission. That is, most funded proposals are resubmissions. For instance, within NIH about 75% of funded grants occur in the second or third rounds of the submissions process. This means that although you will, in some sense, fail in your initial submission, you'll receive valuable feedback necessary to correct and strengthen your to-be-revised proposal. If you address these criticisms earnestly and thoroughly, your chances of success will improve dramatically the second time around. If not, the third time might be your charm. Hence, a major secret—often kept hushed among successful grant-getters—is that failure breeds success. But perseverance is required! Start rewriting your grant for resubmission as soon as you receive the reviewers' summary statement from your initial submission.

Locating Multiple Funding Sources

Although journal articles are submitted to only one journal at a time, grants can and should be submitted simultaneously to multiple funding sources. For instance, it wouldn't be unusual for the same grant (with minor modifications to meet specific formatting requirements) to be under review at the same time at NSF, NIH, and a private foundation. Of course, if a positive decision is received from one agency, the grant should be withdrawn immediately from further consideration at the other agencies. It may be helpful to conduct ongoing searches, either through the grants pages of federal agencies or through one of the search engines mentioned previously. Such ongoing searches can help you to assess how your research interests square with the current priorities of various agencies and organizations, thus helping to narrow your focus. Current research agendas are explained in great detail on the aforementioned Web sites.

On the Importance of Writing Style

A research grant should enable the reader to comprehend and evaluate your ideas, without requiring a monumental struggle. In order to understand the project, the reviewer must be led through the initial comments on the general hypothesis to the final statements about research significance. If you are genuinely concerned with making the task of reading your proposal more manageable, you must interest and motivate the reviewer. Initially, a reader's attention is drawn to your project because of its title and then by its Abstract. Your reviewer may be doing similar research or perhaps may find your title and general idea intriguing, although he or she may know absolutely nothing about the specific background literature or proposed methodology.

You can make the reader's job easier by writing the proposal for the person who is not well informed about your topic, rather than for the most knowledgeable person in your research area. You must lead the reviewer from a general statement of the idea to the relevant issues and literature, the specific research hypothesis, the design and procedures, and finally to the proposed analyses and the long-range significance of the data. Good grammar, an interesting style, and neither too much nor too little detail will likely result in a high level of readability. A readable proposal will interest and attract your audience, whereas a dull or unintelligible proposal might well result in a negative judgment. A member of the National Academy of Science, chemist Ernest Ebel, who was one of the most published scientists in America, once said, "It's not so much that I'm a better scientist than the rest, it's just that I'm a better writer." Your grant proposal must be readable if it is to attract and influence its target audience, the panel of reviewers.

Skills in communication, both oral and written, usually are not developed simply within the confines of your scientific training but rather are acquired and refined during the early years of your liberal education—in grade school, high school, college composition classes, or journalism activities. I find it surprising that so many aspiring young psychologists are not informed about, or do not avail themselves of, opportunities to develop general writing skills, both prior to and during graduate training. These skills are essential for winning research grants, which after all must be accurate, informative, and interesting to read in order to be successful.

In the end, the entire process of successful grant writing boils down to three simple rules: (a) Form an idea you're proud of; (b) make a concentrated effort to write about your idea and its research implications; and (c) persevere until others see its full merits. At that point, you'll experience a great personal satisfaction: winning your first research grant.

EXERCISES

As you consider beginning the process of applying for a research grant, here are a few exercises that can get you moving in the right direction.

1. Once you've decided from which agency or organization you'll seek funding, construct a checklist of the specific requirements for that agency. This will not only ensure that you assemble a complete proposal but will also help to familiarize you with the policies of the granting agency.

2. Another task that may prove helpful in your writing is to begin with the introductory sections from two or more of your recent publications and outline the additional steps you would need to take in order to transform them into a 9- to 12-page introduction to a grant proposal. Your outlined proposal would need to include at least four sections: Rationale, Significance, Background Research (including your own work), and Research Hypotheses. This will help you start thinking about what it will take to transform your existing ideas into a complete research proposal.

3. Finally, once you've written your proposal, seek constructive criticism from mentors and peers. The questions they have will likely be similar to those of some of your reviewers. Being able to accept and integrate constructive criticism will generally result in a more solid proposal, with a better chance of its being funded in rounds one or two of the review process.

Recommended Readings

This chapter has laid out some tips about grant writing. A more complete description of the grant-writing process can be obtained in excellent texts titled *Research Proposals: A Guide to Success* by Ogden and Goldberg (2002); *Proposals That Work* by Locke, Spirduso, and Silverman (1999); and Lauffer's (1997) *Grants, Etc.* These books elaborate on themes only briefly sketched in this chapter: how to get the process started, what and when to write, checking for infractions, specific contents, and the decision-making process. Many parts of the Ogden and Goldberg (2002) text will be helpful to you, particularly for preparation and development of NIH grant proposals. Even if you are not applying for an NIH grant, it may still be good practice to review their guidelines and procedures, as most agencies have similar policies. Peterson (2000) provides a companion for using the Internet to find grants and funding, and Kraicer (1997) provides a totally Web-based approach to teaching grantsmanship. Useful Web sites are operated by libraries of the University of Wisconsin (http://grants.library.wisc.edu/ organizations/proposalwebsites.html) and Baylor University (www3. baylor.edu/Library/LookingForInfo/grantbibl.html). The Corporation for Public Broadcasting operates a Web site that features a basic approach to grant writing at www.cpb.org/grants/grantwriting.html. Non-profit Guides (www.npguides.org/links.htm) offers a listing of links to different grant-writing Web sites, thus operating as a portal to information.

References

American Psychological Association. (2001). *Publication manual of the American Psychological Association* (5th ed.). Washington, DC: Author.

Community of Science. (2003). COS funding opportunities. Retrieved April 26, 2005, from www.osu-ours.okstate.edu/Pages/cos.html

Government Printing Office. (2004, December 21). *The Federal Register (FR)*. Retrieved April 26, 2005, from www.gpoaccess.gov/fr/

Kraicer, J. (1997, May 5). The art of grantsmanship. Retrieved March 6, 2005, from www.hfsp.org/how/ArtOfGrants.htm

Lauffer, A. (1997). *Grants, etc.* Thousand Oaks, CA: Sage.

Locke, L. F., Spirduso, W. W., & Silverman, S. J. (1999). *Proposals that work* (4th ed.). Thousand Oaks, CA: Sage.

National Institutes of Health. (2005). National Institutes of Health Office of Extramural Research. Accessed April 26, 2005, from http://grants1.nih.gov/grants/oer.htm

National Science Foundation. (2005). National Science Foundation: Where Discoveries Begin. Accessed April 26, 2005, from www.nsf.gov

Ogden, T. E., & Goldberg, I. A. (Eds.). (2002). *Research proposals: A guide to success* (3rd ed.). San Diego, CA: Academic.

Peterson, S. (2000). *The grantwriter's Internet companion: A resource for educators and others seeking grants and funding.* Thousand Oaks, CA: Sage.

Sternberg, R. J. (1992, September). How to win acceptance by psychology journals: 21 tips for better writing. *APS Observer,* 12–14.

University of Illinois at Urbana-Champaign. (2005*).* Illinois Researcher Information Service (IRIS). Accessed April 26, 2005, from www.library.uiuc .edu/iris/

31

CROSS-CULTURAL RESEARCH METHODOLOGY

KWOK LEUNG

FONS J. R. VAN DE VIJVER

The world is becoming a truly global village. Globalization of businesses has often resulted in people of different nationalities working under the same roof. Migration patterns have rapidly changed the ethnic composition of once relatively homogenous societies. For instance, Hispanics in the United States are forecast to be the largest minority group in the near future, and a large increase in the Muslim populations of western European countries is also predicted. Furthermore, challenges of humankind such as global warming, terrorism, and arms control require the cooperation of many nations.

The globalization trend has led to a vast increase in intercultural contact. As a consequence, there is a pressing need to understand similarities and differences across cultures and to distinguish cultural stereotypes from real cross-cultural differences. Psychological research can provide us with these insights. The goal of this chapter is to provide a comprehensive overview of issues in cross-cultural research methodology.

CHARACTERISTICS OF CROSS-CULTURAL RESEARCH

In "true" experiments, participants are randomly assigned to different experimental conditions, such as the experimental and control groups. The most typical independent variable in cross-cultural research is culture, but we cannot randomly assign participants to different cultures. We cannot assign, say, a Japanese to assume an American identity. In other words, culture is a variable that is beyond the experimental control of a researcher. This inherent difficulty makes it hard to evaluate causal relationships in cross-cultural studies. When we discover a difference between two cultural groups, it is hard to conclude that a proposed factor is the actual cause of the observed cultural difference. For instance, if we discover that American college students score higher than farmers from Vietnam on reasoning tests, there may be numerous explanations for this difference. The Vietnamese farmers may be less educated or less familiar with such tests, which causes them to perform poorly. If test familiarity causes the difference, an instrument that uses questions less foreign to the Vietnamese farmers may result in higher scores for this group. It is a major challenge for cross-cultural researchers to identify the most plausible explanation for cross-cultural differences observed.

Another challenge of cross-cultural research is that the concept of culture is global and hard to define. When we observe that Chinese regard effort as more important for educational achievement than do Americans (Hess, Chang, & McDevitt, 1987), we may be tempted to attribute the difference to culture. But culture includes so many elements that the use of culture as an explanation is almost meaningless. The difference may be caused by, among other things, socialization, parental styles, and educational systems. We need to "unpackage" culture into a set of elements and verify which particular element is responsible for the cultural differences observed (Whiting, 1976).

CROSS-CULTURAL EQUIVALENCE

Most cross-cultural studies involve at least two cultural groups, but some studies are monocultural and rely on results from previous studies for cross-cultural comparisons. When we try to compare two or more cultures, the comparison may take two forms: structure-oriented or level-oriented. *Structure-oriented* studies examine relationships among variables and attempt to identify similarities and differences in these relationships across cultures. For example, Schwartz and his associates (e.g., Schwartz, 1992; Schwartz et al., 2001) have gathered data to support a universal value structure that comprises 10 value types. In other words, values are related to each other in a similar fashion across a diverse group of cultures. In a similar vein, Leung and Bond (2004) have confirmed a five-dimensional structure of general beliefs, or social axioms, across a wide range of cultural groups. The five-factor model of personality is also identifiable in many cultural groups (Allik & McCrae, 2002).

Level-oriented studies, on the other hand, focus on differences in the magnitude of variables across cultures. For example, Heine, Lehman, Markus, and Kitayama (1999) have argued that self-enhancement, the tendency to evaluate oneself positively, is absent among Japanese. Choi and Nisbett (2000) found that Koreans showed less surprise than did Americans when someone's behavior contradicted their expectations.

In both types of studies, equivalence provides the basis for cross-cultural comparisons, because we cannot compare apples with oranges.

Similarity of meaning is called *conceptual* or *structural equivalence,* which is typically assessed in structure-oriented studies. Some concepts may have different meanings in different cultures. For instance, Chinese tend to describe psychological problems in terms of physical symptoms, a process called *somatization* (Cheung, 1996). Thus, the concept of depression may have different meanings in China and in the United States. Although depression is mostly concerned with psychological problems in the United States, the concept of depression among Chinese may include somatic complaints.

There are a number of ways to ascertain conceptual equivalence. We may examine the psychometric properties of the instrument used to measure a concept. Assume that we measure depression with a scale in China and the United States. Conceptual equivalence is supported if the scale has similar internal psychometric properties, such as similar levels of internal consistency in the two cultures as measured by Cronbach's alpha or similar factor structures based on factor analysis. Conceptual equivalence is also supported if similar relationships between depression and other variables can be demonstrated in the two cultures. For instance, if depression is correlated with adverse life events in the two cultures, we can be fairly confident that depression has a similar meaning in the two cultures. More generally, conceptual equivalence is supported if our measure of depression shows an expected pattern of correlations with other measures. Various statistical techniques are commonly employed to study conceptual equivalence, such as regression analysis, multidimensional scaling, exploratory factor analysis, and structural equation modeling.

In level-oriented studies, we want to go beyond conceptual equivalence and find out whether cultural groups studied differ in their average scores on a target variable. Unfortunately, even if conceptual equivalence is established, we still cannot be sure that scores derived from an instrument can be directly compared across cultures. When we measure body length in inches in one group and in centimeters in another group, the same concept is measured in the two groups, but the scores cannot be directly compared. For instance, although Japanese typically report a lower level of self-esteem than do

Americans (Heine et al., 1999), we cannot take this difference as real without further evidence (e.g., Brown & Kobayashi, 2003). Many explanations may account for the observed differences. Response sets may bias the responses of Japanese, who may tend to use the middle of a rating scale. Japanese may report a lower level of self-esteem because of a humility norm, which discourages people from bragging about their ability. We will explore this controversy in detail in a subsequent section.

We need to establish *scalar equivalence* or *full score comparability* before we can compare scores obtained from different cultures. Physical measures such as weight and height are typical examples of variables that show scalar equivalence. Unfortunately, it is often difficult to establish scalar equivalence for psychological constructs, because unlike physical measures, they are usually based on scales without an absolute zero. We can claim that one cultural group is higher than another group on a given variable only when we are able to demonstrate a reasonably high level of scalar equivalence. In a subsequent section, we will discuss some procedures and strategies commonly used for establishing scalar equivalence.

DESIGN OF A CROSS-CULTURAL STUDY

The identification of significant cultural differences is often much easier than their interpretation. Cultural groups differ in many respects, which may be construed as plausible explanations for any cultural difference observed. In the design of cross-cultural studies, it is important to rule out alternative explanations and enhance the interpretability of cultural differences that emerge. For instance, the interpretability of cross-cultural studies can be enhanced by including covariates, which refer to unintended variables that may produce cultural differences, such as educational level or income level. The inclusion of covariates can help evaluate the proposed explanation for the observed cross-cultural differences and rule out alternative explanations. A good example is Earley's (1989) study on social loafing, which refers to the phenomenon that people work less when they are in a group than when they do the same task

individually. Americans were found to show a higher level of social loafing than Chinese participants. A measure of the individualism-collectivism of participants was used as a covariate. Individualism refers to a weaker emphasis on one's in-groups, such as one's family, whereas collectivism refers to a stronger emphasis (Hofstede, 1980). After controlling for cross-cultural differences in individualism-collectivism with the use of hierarchical regression analysis, the cross-cultural differences in social loafing disappeared. The covariance analysis provided good evidence for individualism-collectivism as the explanation for the observed cross-cultural difference in social loafing.

Leung and Zhang (1996) argued that many studies have been exported from the West to non-Western countries, and some of the issues examined in these studies are of little relevance to the local culture. It is also possible that results obtained in some of these studies are influenced by the cultural background of the researchers. Different results may be obtained if these studies are designed by researchers from different cultural backgrounds. Two approaches can be adopted to avoid the possibility that one single culture will dominate the research questions explored and bias the results obtained. First, in the *decentered* approach, a culturally diverse perspective is taken in the conceptualization and design of a study. For instance, Schwartz (1992) encouraged researchers from different cultures to add culture-specific value items to his pancultural set when examining the structure of values. In a global project on leadership behaviors, input from diverse cultures was integrated to arrive at a culture-general set of leadership behaviors (House, Hanges, Javidan, Dorfman, & Gupta, 2004).

In the *convergence* approach, the basic idea is to design a study that is as culturally distant as possible from existing studies and to see if the results obtained converge with existing results. If convergence is obtained, the cultural origin of existing studies is unlikely to have exerted a biasing influence. If different results are obtained, however, the cultural origin of existing studies cannot be ignored. A good example to illustrate this approach is provided by Bond and his colleagues, who designed a value survey based entirely on Chinese values and administered it in 22 countries (Chinese Culture Connection, 1987). It was found that three factors overlapped with factors identified by Hofstede (1980), whose results were based on a Western instrument. A new factor was also found, termed *Confucian Work Dynamism,* which correlated highly with economic growth of a nation. A more recent example is provided by Cheung and her associates, who have identified basic dimensions of personality based on Chinese notions of personality (Cheung et al., 1996). It is interesting to note that when the Chinese personality dimensions were compared with the five-factor model of personality from the West, Openness was missing in the Chinese personality dimensions, whereas Interpersonal Relatedness, a Chinese dimension that is concerned with interpersonal issues, was missing in the five-factor model (Cheung et al., 2001).

Cross-Cultural Experimentation

Experimental designs have been used in many cross-cultural studies, but the focus is to compare experimental findings obtained in each culture and see if the results are different (Leung & Su, 2004). For instance, Gelfand and Realo (1999) conducted a negotiation experiment involving collectivists and individualists and found that accountability led to negotiation behaviors that were consistent with cultural norms. Accountability led to more competitive judgments and behaviors among individualists but more cooperative judgments and behaviors among collectivists. In this type of experiment, however, culture is not a manipulated variable, and its causal effect cannot be firmly established. In some recent work, researchers have tried to manipulate some cultural elements to see if the manipulation shows the intended effects, an approach termed the *cultural manipulation approach* by Leung and Su (2004). A good example is provided by Hong, Morris, Chiu, and Benet-Martinez (2000). It is well documented that compared with Americans, Chinese show a stronger tendency of external attribution (to attribute the behavior of a person to external causes such as social demand) (Choi & Nisbett, 1999). Hong Kong Chinese were randomly exposed to a set of American icons, such as Superman, or a set of Chinese icons

(this procedure is known as priming); and as expected, their tendency to make external attribution was higher in the Chinese icons than in the American icons conditions. This finding provides some causal evidence that American culture (individualism in this case) causes the tendency for making internal attribution. The experimental manipulation of cultural elements can take other forms. Trafimow, Triandis, and Goto (1991) asked respondents to think about either what they had in common with, or what made them different from, their family and friends. They found that for University of Illinois students with Chinese or European names, the percentage of social self-description (e.g., I am a Roman Catholic; I am from a certain city) increased when they were asked to think about what they had in common with their family and friends. This experiment showed that the focus on interdependence led to more social self-descriptions, which is consistent with the cross-cultural finding that East Asians, who are oriented toward interdependent self-construal, tend to report more social self-descriptions than North Americans. More important, this experiment provides some causal evidence for the role of independent-interdependent self-construal in influencing the nature of self-description.

Sampling of Cultures

The selection of cultures is often essential in evaluating the cross-cultural hypotheses proposed. *Systematic sampling,* in which cultures are selected in a theory-guided fashion, is a frequently adopted strategy. In the classic study by Berry (1967), two groups were studied, one agricultural and one hunting. It was hypothesized that agricultural societies impose stronger pressure on conformity and hence will lead to *field dependence,* which refers to the tendency to be more influenced by the background of an object when perceiving this object. Hunting societies encourage their members to be autonomous and hence are conducive to a lower level of field dependence. These two types of societies were selected systematically to evaluate this hypothesis. More recent examples include the many studies that are guided by the individualism-collectivism framework, in which participants sampled from individualistic and collectivistic societies are contrasted (e.g., Chirkov, Ryan, Kim, & Kaplan, 2003).

In *random sampling,* a large number of cultures are randomly sampled, usually for evaluating the universal structure of a construct or a pan-cultural theory. It is almost impossible to obtain a truly random sample, but the sampling procedure of large-scale studies may have approximated a random sampling procedure. For instance, Schwartz (1992) has initially sampled 20 cultures to evaluate the structure of human values, but the current number of cultures included is more than 60 (Schwartz et al., 2001). Leung and Bond (2004) have included participants from 40 cultural groups to evaluate the structure of social axioms.

Sampling of Participants

In order to make valid cross-cultural comparisons, the participants from different cultural groups must be similar in their background characteristics. Otherwise, it is hard to conclude whether the cultural differences observed are due to real cultural differences or sample-specific differences. For instance, if we compare illiterate participants from one culture with highly educated participants from another culture, the differences observed are likely to be explainable by educational differences rather than differences in other aspects of their cultures. One approach to overcome this problem is to match the samples in terms of demographic characteristics so that sample differences can be ruled out as alternative explanations. College students from different cultures are often compared, and it is usually assumed that they have similar demographic characteristics. In a similar vein, Hofstede (1980) attempted to reduce the influence of presumably relevant individual and organizational background variables by studying respondents from a single multinational firm from 40 countries.

It is sometimes impossible to match samples from different cultures because of practical reasons or because there are sharp cross-cultural differences in their demographic profiles. One solution is to measure the relevant demographic variables as covariates. For instance, in a study comparing the delinquent behaviors of adolescents in the United States, Australia, and Hong Kong, it was found that the educational standing of the fathers of the Hong Kong participants was significantly lower than that of the fathers of the Australian and American participants (Feldman, Rosenthal, Mont-Reynaud, Leung, & Lau, 1991). To overcome this problem, an analysis of covariance was carried out to compare the three cultural groups, with the father's educational standing equated statistically.

Data Collection

Before gathering cross-cultural data with an instrument, we need to decide whether the instrument is applicable to all cultural groups involved. Items of the instrument may not make sense in some cultures. When the Minnesota Multiphasic Personality Inventory (MMPI) was applied in China, some items were found to be meaningless in the Chinese context and had to be modified (Cheung, 1989). When too many items are inappropriate, an entirely new instrument may need to be constructed. Church (1987) argued that Western personality instruments are unable to capture many of the indigenous personality constructs of the Filipino culture. The development of the Chinese Personality Assessment Inventory is another example of the need for locally validated instruments (Cheung et al., 1996; Cheung et al., 2001).

We may also need to translate an instrument in a cross-cultural study (Beling & Law, 2000; Hambleton, Merenda, & Spielberger, 2004; Harkness, 2003; Van de Vijver & Hambleton, 1996; see also the Web site of the International Test Commission at www.intestcom.org). The *back translation method* is probably the most widely adopted procedure (Brislin, 1980). An instrument is translated from one language to another and then back translated to the original language by a different translator. This method is usually adequate; back translation can provide researchers who lack proficiency in the target language control of the adequacy of the translation. But the method has a drawback: it may produce a stilted language that reproduces the original language well but is unnatural and not easily comprehensible. This problem is particularly serious when test items contain idioms that are difficult to translate.

Werner and Campbell (1970) have proposed a *decentering* process in translating instruments to adjust both the original and the translated versions simultaneously. The aim of decentering is not the mechanical reproduction of the original instrument in a different language but the enhancement of the convergence and readability of the versions in all target languages simultaneously.

When we administer an instrument to participants from different cultures, we need to pay attention to the personal characteristics of the experimenter or interviewer. The presence of an experimenter or interviewer may affect the responses of the participants (e.g., *deference*— the participants' tendency to provide answers that they think are expected by the experimenter or interviewer), particularly when the experimenter and the participants come from different cultural backgrounds. In intelligence testing, the influence of racial differences between the tester and the examinee has been studied systematically, and the way they interact with each other may also be a source of bias. The experimenter may inadvertently affect the responses of participants by unintended signals or cues, such as his or her appearance and demeanor. Finally, the stimuli and response procedures involved may be a source of bias. For instance, participants who are not familiar with questionnaires may take them as an examination with true and false answers. A study by Deregowski and Serpell (1971) illustrates the importance of stimulus familiarity. Scottish and Zambian children were asked to sort miniature models of animals and motor vehicles in one experimental condition and their photographs in another one. No cultural differences were found when models were sorted, but the Scottish children obtained higher scores than the Zambian children when photos were sorted.

FOUR COMMON TYPES OF CROSS-CULTURAL STUDIES

Four types of cross-cultural studies can be distinguished, depending on whether the orientation is exploratory or hypothesis testing and on whether or not contextual or cultural factors are considered (Van de Vijver, 2002). The first two types emphasize hypothesis testing. *Generalizability studies* attempt to establish the generalizability of research findings obtained in one typically Western group to other Western or non-Western groups. In general, these studies make little or no reference to local cultural elements. For instance, Schwartz (1992) has collected data from various countries to evaluate the universality of a structure of human values. Leung and Bond (2004) have evaluated a structure of social axioms across 40 cultural groups.

In contextual theory studies, cultural factors constitute the core of the theoretical framework. *Contextual theory studies* test the predictions about a particular relationship between cultural variables and a psychological outcome. This approach involves the sampling of various cultures that differ on some focal dimension and the confirmation of expected cultural differences derived from the theoretical framework. The study by Berry (1967) on field dependence described earlier, which involves the means of subsistence as a contextual factor, is a good example of this approach. Leung (1987) predicted that cultural collectivism should be associated with the use of mediation in conflict resolution, and collectivism constitutes the contextual factor in this study. Chinese and Americans were sampled to represent two levels of collectivism, and the expected cultural difference in the preference for mediation was found. The more current work on culture and cognition has linked differences in cognitive styles to differences in cultural characteristics (e.g., Nisbett, Peng, Choi, & Norenzayan, 2001).

Hypothesis testing is deemphasized in the following two types of cross-cultural research. In *psychological differences studies,* some measures are taken in at least two cultures, usually by the administration of assessment instruments, and the focus is on whether there are any differences in the averages, standard deviations, reliability coefficients, or other psychometric properties of the measures across cultural groups. There is often no compelling theory about the nature of the cross-cultural differences to be expected. Contextual factors are typically not included in the design, and post hoc explanations are invoked to interpret the cross-cultural differences observed. For instance, Guida and Ludlow (1989) compared the test anxiety of American and Chilean school children and found that for upper- and middle-class participants, Americans reported a lower level of test anxiety than did Chileans. As commonly done in this type of research, post hoc explanations were given to explain this finding.

The last type of cross-cultural research, *ecological linkage studies,* attempts to explore the meaning and causes of cross-cultural differences with the aid of contextual factors. In these types of studies, however, specific a priori hypotheses are absent and a large set of contextual variables that may be able to explain an observed cultural difference is included in an exploratory manner. This type of exploration does not target at conceptual or scalar equivalence but seeks an empirically derived interpretation of observed cross-cultural differences. For instance, Bond (1991) examined the relationships between the values endorsed by various national groups and a variety of health-related measures and found that values are related to some specific health-related variables. Leung and Bond (2004) have examined the correlations of social axioms with a wide range of variables to confirm the validity of the axiom dimensions.

The examples of the four designs described before focus either on individual- or country-level variations. In cross-cultural psychology, it is often necessary to compare findings at the individual as well as the cultural levels (Leung, 1989; Leung & Bond, 1989). Since the last decade, there has been increasing interest in multilevel studies (e.g., Raudenbush & Bryk, 2002; also see Chan, Chapter 28 of this volume), in which both individual and cultural factors are examined in a single study. Two kinds of multilevel studies are relevant for cross-cultural psychology. The first kind addresses cultural differences in mean levels. Suppose we are interested in explaining cultural differences in performance on an achievement test, as was done in the Programme for International Student Assessment (the PISA project, www.pisa.oecd.org). Achievement tests were administered to 15-year-old students in 32 countries. The performance of a student can be seen as a function of factors at the individual level (e.g., intelligence and motivation), school level (e.g., teachers' education and quality of learning materials), and country level (e.g., educational expenditure per capita of a country). In multilevel modeling, variation of the predictor variables at these three levels is examined in a single analysis

so that the relative contribution of each level to the overall variation in individual performance can be estimated.

The second type of question addresses differences in psychological meaning across aggregation levels. For instance, Triandis (1995) has argued that the individualism-collectivism dimension may have a somewhat different meaning at individual and country levels. He proposed to use individualism-collectivism to denote the country-level dimension and "idiocentrism-allocentrism" to denote the individual-level dimension. Muthén (1991) has developed a statistical technique, multilevel factor analysis, to compare factor structures across aggregation levels. Similar factor structures at different levels suggest that the meaning of the constructs is similar across levels. An illustration of this approach is given by Van de Vijver and Poortinga (2002), who used exploratory factor analysis to determine whether postmaterialism as measured in the World Values Survey (Inglehart, 1997) has the same meaning at the individual and the cultural levels. Multilevel modeling will be used more frequently as cross-cultural researchers become familiar with this technique.

An Example of a Knotty Cross-Cultural Research Question: Is the Need for Positive Self-regard Universal?

To illustrate the common difficulties encountered in cross-cultural research and the strategies for overcoming them, we review a controversial program of research. As described before, Heine et al. (1999) argued that the need for positive self-regard is culture-specific and is tied to interdependent self-construal (the view that the self is relatively independent of other people), which is characteristic of North America and Western Europe. In contrast, in cultures that emphasize interdependent self-construal (the self is intertwined with other people in terms of social relationships, roles, and duties), the need for positive self-regard is nonexistent, and self-discipline and self-criticism are more prevalent. Heine et al. have provided a range of evidence to support their argument. European Canadians reported a higher level of self-esteem than Japanese, and the more Japanese and Asians were exposed to North American culture, the higher the level of their self-esteem. Self-esteem was found to correlate positively with independent self-construal and individualistic values such as self-direction. Self-esteem is a much more prevalent topic of discourse in North America than in Japan. Self-evaluation is systematically biased in the self-enhancing direction in North America, whereas such a bias is nonexistent in Japan. Self-protective strategies to maintain one's self-esteem are widely documented in North America, whereas such strategies are nonexistent in Japan. In contrast, self-criticism is more prevalent in Japan than in North America. In summary, Heine et al. are able to support their thesis with different types of evidence, and the evidence as a package is impressive.

Given that the need for positive self-regard is widely assumed in Western psychology to be a universalistic attribute of humanity, Heine et al.'s (1999) provocative thesis has naturally sparked a series of heated debates about its validity. Before we examine this controversy, we first describe the nature of the research question based on the framework that we have described. Heine et al.'s argument assumes not only conceptual equivalence but scalar equivalence as well, because they argue that North Americans have the need to maintain positive self-regard, whereas Japanese do not possess such a need. For this argument to hold, the concepts involved (e.g., self-esteem, self-protection) need to have equivalent meanings across the cultural groups concerned. The measurement of these concepts (e.g., self-esteem scores) needs to be comparable as well. In our framework, this type of requirement is perhaps the most challenging of all, and it is easy to understand from a methodological standpoint why this issue is so controversial.

Heine et al.'s (1999) thesis represents a strong form of the argument: Japanese have no need for positive self-regard. A weak form of the thesis is also possible, namely, Japanese have a lower need for positive self-regard than North Americans (Heine, 2003) or they express this need in different ways that are consistent with their cultural milieu, or both (Brown & Kobayashi, 2003). A number of studies have challenged the strong version (e.g., Brown & Kobayahsi, 2003; Kurman, 2003), culminating

in 2003 in the publication of a special issue of the *Journal of Cross-Cultural Psychology* on culture and the self-enhancement bias. Seven empirical papers, some with multiple studies, are included in this special issue. Three papers showed that the emphasis on modesty in collectivist cultures suppressed the self-enhancing bias among East Asians (Kobayashi & Greenwald, 2003; Kudo & Numazaki, 2003; Kurman, 2003, Study 2). Two papers showed that the self-enhancement bias was observable among Japanese in certain contexts (Muramoto, 2003; Takata, 2003). Two studies showed that correlates of self-esteem and self-enhancement were similar for individualistic and collectivistic groups (Kobayashi & Brown, 2003; Kurman, 2003, Study 1). In contrast to other papers in the issue, the final paper in the special issue showed that in a real-world setting, American college students rated their university as better than a rival university, but this bias was not found among Japanese students (Snibbe, Kitayama, Markus, & Suzuki, 2003). Heine (2003) and Brown (2003), a guest editor of the special issue, each provided a commentary on the papers. Heine reviewed the articles critically and concluded that the contradictory data presented do not constitute a strong challenge to the strong form of the thesis advanced by him and his associates. In contrast, Brown regarded such data as strong evidence against the thesis of Heine and his associates. Apparently, this controversy is far from being settled, but this case illustrates the complexity inherent in cross-cultural comparisons and the need to rely on multiple methods to increase the validity of empirical results. Interested readers should consult this special issue and other related articles for a first-hand account of how diverse methods can be used to address cross-cultural research questions.

CONCLUSION

In cross-cultural research, the interpretation of the meaning of research findings is crucial but evasive, because cross-cultural research is essentially different from true experiments. Typically, many interpretations can be generated to explain a cross-cultural difference. In our opinion, the best approach is to formulate a number of rival hypotheses on an a priori basis and design studies that are able to rule out alternative explanations. Cross-cultural research may demand a higher level of methodological sophistication than a conventional monocultural study; but in this globalizing world, we cannot afford to be blind to cultural similarities and differences. A carefully planned, competently conducted cross-cultural study is not only rewarding but highly useful to bringing about productive and enjoyable intercultural contact.

EXERCISES

1. Conceptual Equivalence

This exercise is designed to help you understand the notion of conceptual equivalence. If possible, form a culturally diverse group, ideally with 6–10 members. Identify a construct that is likely to be defined differently by different cultural groups, such as embarrassment, respect, or modesty, and then complete the following tasks:

A. Ask members from different cultural backgrounds to define the chosen concept in simple language independently. Also write down the typical behaviors that serve as markers for this concept. If you have more than one person with the same cultural background, they can work as a team to complete this task.

B. If your group is culturally homogenous, look for a few cultural informants with diverse cultural backgrounds. Select a concept and obtain its definition and behavioral markers by interviewing the informants.

C. Each person or group presents the definition of the concept and the associated behavioral markers.

D. Discuss the similarities and differences in the definitions and behavioral markers presented. Try to identify a common definition and a common set of behavioral markers that are appropriate for the cultural groups involved. Assess to what extent this common definition and the associated behavioral markers are likely to be conceptually equivalent across the cultural groups in question.

E. Discuss research designs that can be used to assess whether the behavioral markers are actually conceptually equivalent across the cultural groups involved.

2. Multimethod Approach

In cross-cultural research, an important strategy is to replicate cultural differences and similarities with different research methods, and if results converge despite the use of diverse methods, we are more certain of their validity. This exercise requires you to first identify a research question and then conduct a literature search to look for the use of different methods in answering this research question. The example on positive self-regard described before could be used as a warm-up exercise to familiarize you with the requirement. A group format with 4–6 members is ideal for this exercise, which involves the following tasks:

A. Identify a research question or topic, which should be clearly defined.

B. Develop a plan to conduct a thorough literature search, and you may limit it to the last 10 or 15 years if there are too many relevant studies. You need to read the papers in detail, so division of labor among members is necessary.

C. Summarize the research findings obtained with different methods and assess to what extent there is convergence in the results.

D. If there is divergence of results, discuss whether certain methods are more trustworthy and the reasons for their higher trustworthiness.

RECOMMENDED READINGS

For a detailed discussion of the various methodological issues encountered in cross-cultural research, consult the book by Brislin, Lonner, and Thorndike (1973). For a detailed discussion of methods and data analysis for cross-cultural research, consult the book by Van de Vijver and Leung (1997). For methodological issues encountered in field research, the book edited by Lonner and Berry (1986) is highly useful. An overview of issues in cross-cultural survey research can be found in Harkness, Van de Vijver, and Mohler (2003).

Computer Resources

www.wwu.edu/~culture

This Web site provides some readings on cross-cultural research.

A number of Web sites provide a variety of data on many nations:

a. www.odci.gov/cia/publications/factbook/index. html

This Web site provides basic information about many nations

b. www.freedomhouse.org/research/

This Web site contains information about political status of many nations.

c. http://laborsta.ilo.org

This Web site provides labor statistics of many nations.

d. http://unstats.un.org/unsd/demographic/products/socind/

This Web site provides data on social indicators of many nations.

e. www3.who.int/whosis/menu.cfm

This Web site provides health statistics on many nations.

f. www.worldbank.org/data/

This Web site provides economic data on many nations.

REFERENCES

Allik, J., & McCrae, R. R. (2002). A five factor theory perspective. In R. R. McCrae & J. Allik (Eds.), *The five-factor model of personality across cultures* (pp. 303–322). New York: Kluwer Academic/Plenum.

Behling, O., & Law, K. S. (2000). *Translating questionnaires and other research instruments: Problems and solutions.* Thousand Oaks, CA: Sage.

Berry, J. W. (1967). Independence and conformity in subsistence-level societies. *Journal of Personality and Social Psychology, 7,* 415–418.

Bond, M. H. (1991). Chinese values and health: A cross-cultural examination. *Psychology and Health, 5,* 137–152.

Brislin, R. W. (1980). Translation and content analysis of oral and written material. In H. C. Triandis & J. W. Berry (Eds.), *Handbook of cross-cultural psychology* (Vol. 1, pp. 389–444). Boston: Allyn & Bacon.

Brislin, R. W., Lonner, W. J., & Thorndike, R. (1973). *Cross-cultural research methods.* New York: Wiley.

Brown, J. D. (2003). The self-enhancement motive in collectivistic cultures: The rumors of my death have been greatly exaggerated. *Journal of Cross-Cultural Psychology, 34,* 603–605.

Brown, J. D., & Kobayashi, C. (2003). Culture and the self-enhancement bias. *Journal of Cross-Cultural Psychology, 34,* 492–495.

Cheung, F. M. (1989). A review on the clinical applications of the Chinese MMPI. *Psychological Assessment, 3,* 230–237.

Cheung, F. M. (1996). The assessment of psychopathology of Chinese societies. In M. H. Bond (Ed.), *The handbook of Chinese psychology* (pp. 393–411). Hong Kong: Oxford University Press.

Cheung, F. M., Leung, K., Fan, R. M., Song, W. Z., Zhang, J. X., & Zhang, J. P. (1996). Development of the Chinese Personality Assessment Inventory. *Journal of Cross-Cultural Psychology, 27,* 181–199.

Cheung, F. M., Leung, K., Zhang, J. X., Sun, H. F., Gan, Y. G., & Song, W. Z. (2001). Indigenous Chinese personality constructs: Is the five-factor model complete? *Journal of Cross-Cultural Psychology, 32,* 407–433.

Chinese Culture Connection. (1987). Chinese values and the search for culture-free dimensions of culture. *Journal of Cross-Cultural Psychology, 18,* 143–164.

Chirkov, V., Ryan, R. M., Kim, Y., & Kaplan, U. (2003). Differentiating autonomy from individualism and independence: A self-determination theory perspective on internalization of cultural orientations and well-being. *Journal of Personality and Social Psychology, 84,* 97–109.

Choi, I., & Nisbett, R. E. (2000). Cultural psychology of surprise: Holistic theories and recognition of contradiction. *Journal of Personality and Social Psychology, 79,* 890–905.

Church, T. A. (1987). Personality research in a non-Western setting: The Philippines. *Psychological Bulletin, 102,* 272–292.

Deregowski, J. B., & Serpell, R. (1971). Performance on a sorting task: A cross-cultural experiment. *International Journal of Psychology, 6,* 273–281.

Earley, C. (1989). Social loafing and collectivism: A comparison of the United States and the People's Republic of China. *Administrative Science Quarterly, 34,* 565–581.

Feldman, S. S., Rosenthal, D. A., Mont-Reynaud, R., Leung, K., & Lau, S. (1991). Ain't misbehavin': Adolescent values and family environments as correlates of misconduct in Australia, Hong Kong, and the United States. *Journal of Research on Adolescence, 1,* 109–134.

Gelfand, M. J., & Realo, A. (1999). Individualism-collectivism and accountability in intergroup negotiations. *Journal of Applied Psychology, 84,* 721–736.

Guida, F. V., & Ludlow, L. H. (1989). A cross-cultural study of test anxiety. *Journal of Cross-Cultural Psychology, 20,* 178–190.

Hambleton, R. K., Merenda, P. F., & Spielberger, C. D. (Eds.) (2004). *Adapting educational tests and psychological tests for cross-cultural assessment.* Mahwah, NJ: Lawrence Erlbaum.

Harkness, J. A. (2003). Questionnaire translation. In J. A. Harkness, F. J. R. Van de Vijver, & P. Ph. Mohler (Eds.), *Cross-cultural survey methods* (pp. 35–56). Hoboken, NJ: Wiley.

Harkness, J. A., Van de Vijver, F. J. R., & Mohler, P. Ph. (Eds.) (2003). *Cross-cultural survey methods.* Hoboken, NJ: Wiley.

Heine, S. H., Lehman, D. R., Markus, H. R., & Kitayama, S. (1999). Is there a universal need for positive regard? *Psychological Review, 106,* 766–794.

Heine, S. J. (2003). Making sense of east Asian self-enhancement. *Journal of Cross-Cultural Psychology, 34,* 596–602.

Hess, R. D., Chang, C. M., & McDevitt, T. M. (1987). Cultural variations in family beliefs about children's performance in mathematics: Comparisons among People's Republic of China, Chinese-American, and Caucasian-American families. *Journal of Educational Psychology, 79,* 179–188.

Hofstede, G. (1980). *Culture's consequences: International differences in work-related values.* Beverly Hills, CA: Sage.

Hong, Y. Y., Morris, M. W., Chiu, C. Y., & Benet-Martinez, V. (2000). Multicultural minds: A dynamic constructivist approach to culture and cognition. *American Psychologist, 55,* 709–720.

House, R. J., Hanges, P. J., Javidan, M., Dorfman, P. W., & Gupta, V. (Eds.). (2004). *Culture, leadership, and organizations: The GLOBE study of 62 societies.* Thousand Oaks, CA: Sage.

Inglehart, R. (1997). *Modernization and postmodernization: Cultural, economic and political change in 43 societies.* Princeton, NJ: Princeton University Press.

Kobayashi, C., & Brown, J. D. (2003). Self-esteem and self-enhancement in Japan and America. *Journal of Cross-Cultural Psychology, 34,* 567–580.

Kobayashi, C., & Greenwald, A. G. (2003). Implicit-explicit differences in self-enhancement for Americans and Japanese. *Journal of Cross-Cultural Psychology, 34,* 522–541.

Kudo, E., & Numazaka, M. (2003). Explicit and direct self-serving bias in Japan: Reexamination of self-serving bias for success and failure. *Journal of Cross-Cultural Psychology, 34,* 511–521.

Kurman, J. (2003). Why is self-enhancement low in certain collectivist cultures? An investigation of two competing explanations. *Journal of Cross-Cultural Psychology, 34,* 496–510.

Leung, K. (1987). Some determinants of reactions to procedural models for conflict resolution. *Journal of Personality and Social Psychology, 53,* 898–908.

Leung K. (1989). Cross-cultural differences: Individual-level vs. Culture-level analysis. *International Journal of Psychology, 24,* 703–719.

Leung K., & Bond, M. H. (1989). On the empirical identification of dimensions for cross-cultural comparisions. *Journal of Cross-Cultural Psychology, 20,* 133–151.

Leung, K., & Bond, M. H. (2004). Social axioms: A model for social beliefs in multicultural perspective. In M. Zanna (Ed.), *Advances in experimental social psychology* (Vol. 36, pp. 119–197). San Diego, CA: Elsevier Academic Press.

Leung, K., & Su, S. K. (2004). Experimental methods for research on culture. In B. J. Punnet, & O. Shenkar (Eds), *Handbook for international management research* (2nd ed., pp. 68–97). Ann Arbor: University of Michigan Press.

Leung, K., & Zhang, J. X. (1996). Systemic considerations: Factors facilitating and impeding the development of psychology in developing countries. *International Journal of Psychology, 30,* 693–706.

Lonner, W. J., & Berry, J. W. (Eds.). (1986). *Field methods in cross-cultural psychology.* Beverly Hills, CA: Sage.

Muramoto, Y. (2003). An indirect self-enhancement in relationship among Japanese. *Journal of Cross-Cultural Psychology, 34,* 552–566.

Muthén, B. O. (1991). Multilevel factor analysis of class and student achievement components. *Journal of Educational Measurement, 28,* 338–354.

Nisbett, R. E., Peng, K., Choi, I., & Norenzayan, A. (2001). Culture and systems of thought: Holistic versus analytic cognition. *Psychological Review, 108,* 291–310.

Raudenbush, S. W., & Bryk, A. S. (2002). *Hierarchical linear models: Applications and data analysis methods* (2nd ed.). Thousand Oaks, CA: Sage.

Schwartz, S. H. (1992). Universals in the content and structure of values: Theoretical advances and empirical tests in 20 countries. In M. Zanna (Ed.), *Advances in experimental social psychology* (Vol. 25, pp. 1–65). New York: Academic.

Schwartz, S. H., Melech, G., Lehmann, A., Burgess, S., Harris, M., & Owens, V. (2001). Extending the cross-cultral vaildity of the theory of basic human values with a different method of measurement. *Journal of Cross-Cultural Psychology, 32,* 519–542.

Snibbe, A. C., Kitayama, S., Markus, H. R., & Suzuki, T. (2003). They saw a game: A Japanese and American (football) field study. *Journal of Cross-Cultural Psychology, 34,* 581–595.

Takata, T. (2003). Self-enhancement and self-criticism in Japanese culture. An experimental analysis. *Journal of Cross-Cultural Psychology, 34,* 542–551.

Trafimow, D., Triandis, H. C., & Goto, S. G. (1991). Some test of the distinction between the private self and the collective self. *Journal of Personality and Social Psychology, 60,* 649–655.

Triandis, H. C. (1995). *Individualism and collectivism.* San Francisco: Westview Press.

Van de Vijver, F. J. R. (2002). Types of cross-cultural studies in cross-cultural psychology. In W. J. Lonner, D. L. Dinnel, S. A. Hayes, & D. N. Sattler (Eds.), *Online readings in psychology and culture.* Retrieved January 4, 2005, from Western Washington University, Department of Psychology, Center for Cross-Cultural Research Web site: http://www.wwu.edu/~culture

Van de Vijver, F. J. R., & Hambleton, R. K. (1996). Translating tests: Some practical guidelines. *European Psychologist, 1,* 89–99.

Van de Vijver, F. J. R., & Leung, K. (1997). *Methods and data analysis for cross-cultural research.* Thousand Oaks, CA: Sage.

Van de Vijver, F. J. R., & Poortinga, Y. H. (2002). Structural equivalence in multilevel research. *Journal of Cross-Cultural Psychology, '33,* 141–156.

Werner, O., & Campbell, D. T. (1970). Translating, working through interpreters, and the problem of decentering. In R. Naroll & R. Cohen (Eds.), *A handbook of cultural anthropology* (pp. 398–419). New York: American Museum of Natural History.

Whiting, B. B. (1976). The problem of the packaged variable. In K. Riegel & J. Meacham (Eds.), *The developing individual in a changing world* (Vol. 1, pp. 303–309). The Hague: Mouton.

32

APPLYING THEORIES TO RESEARCH:

The Interplay of Theory and Research in Science

CHARLES J. GELSO

Ask your typical undergraduate psychology major (who tends to be a good student) what constitutes psychological science, and the reply will almost always include a bottom-line reference to controlled research. Few if any will mention theory. In fact, I must confess that when I was a graduate student, research and science were pretty much the same thing for me. My only consolation in this wrongheadedness is that I was not alone. Buttressed by the radical behaviorism that was ruling the roost in American psychology in the 1960s, many students and even seasoned scholars equated research and science and, implicitly if not explicitly, viewed theory as unnecessary, even impeding, in our search for laws of behavior.

Although things are quite different in the 21st century in psychology, there still tends to be a residue of belief that theory is a second-class citizen in the scientific process. By contrast, in this chapter I shall argue that there is a profound and inevitable connection between theory and research and that science would be impoverished if either were to be relegated to the back seat. Both theory and research are vital and necessary elements of science. Science without controlled, empirical research would consist of only untested ideas and biases, and it would be hard even to think of the result as scientific any more than, for example, witchcraft or astrology. At the same time, science without theory would consist of an array of disconnected observations (which some might call facts) rather than meaningful understandings of the psychological world. To use an example from psychotherapy research, suppose a series of studies has consistently uncovered that therapists' use of interpretations and reflections of clients' feelings (two therapist verbal techniques) are related positively to each other and to therapists' level of experience, but inversely to clients' ratings of their therapy sessions in terms of the depth of their explorations and the rapport they felt with their therapists. Without a theory of how and why therapist techniques, therapist experience level, and clients' experience of the sessions are related to one another, these findings (or facts) are not especially meaningful. They may indeed seem bewildering. Thus, we need theory to explain the findings, and in fact, if no theory exists prior to the research, we must begin to create a theory once the findings have emerged.

Not only is the role of theory in psychological science too often minimized, but what actually constitutes theory is often misunderstood. Because of this misunderstanding, in this chapter I first summarize what I believe to be a useful way of thinking about theory: its definition, its elements, and just what constitutes good scientific theory. Then I examine how theory and research are used in science, how each draws on the other, and how they reciprocally relate to each other (cf. Tzeng & Jackson, 1993, for a useful article on this topic).

WHAT IS A SCIENTIFIC THEORY?

One of the greatest impediments to appreciating the research-theory link in science is the tendency to misunderstand what constitutes theory itself. Many students equate theory with the grand theoretical systems that have been present in psychology for many years, such as psychoanalysis, behaviorism, and humanism. Also, in practice-oriented fields of psychology, theories are often equated with broad therapy systems, such as person-centered therapy, cognitive therapy, and psychoanalytic therapy. As I have elsewhere discussed, these large-scale theories of therapy and the personality theories to which they are wedded are all too often "broad concatenations of (untestable) philosophies of life and humankind, statements of faith, and in some cases loosely stated propositions that were not developed with testability in mind" (Gelso, 1991, p. 212). Such extraordinarily comprehensive theories can probably never be disproved; aspects of them may be disconfirmed, but never the entire theory. Overall, these extremely broad theories are not very scientifically useful. They do not generate research that, in turn, tests their validity.

More useful are what tend to be labeled *minitheories*. These may be parts of the broader systems, or they may be theoretical statements that are separate from existing systems. An example of a theory embedded in a broader system is Carl Rogers' famous statement of the necessary and sufficient conditions for effective counseling and therapy: After years of research and practice, Rogers made a bold, even audacious, theoretical statement that subsequently proved to have enormous heuristic value. He posited that there were certain client and therapist conditions that were both necessary and sufficient for constructive client change. Three of these conditions pertained to the therapist attitudes of empathic understanding toward the client, unconditional positive regard for the client, and congruence with the client. Rogers' theoretical propositions about these three attitudes generated scores of studies over nearly five decades, and recent research syntheses continue to support their importance in therapy (see separate chapters on these attitudes in Norcross, 2002). Rogers' theory was embedded in his theory of client-centered therapy, which in turn was embedded within the even broader humanistic approach to conceptualizing human behavior and counseling.

As I have noted, such minitheories need not be embedded in larger systems. They can stand on their own. A theory emerging from my research program on therapist countertransference management is an example of such a minitheory, and I shall discuss this particular theory later in the chapter. Currently in the field of therapy, Bordin's (1979) minitheory of the components and role of the working alliance in therapy has generated a great deal of research, thus displaying the heuristic value that is so central to good scientific theories (see below). It should be noted, however, that even minitheories appearing to stand alone often are connected at a general level to broader theories. Our countertransference management theory and Bordin's theory of the working alliance are, at a very general level, embedded in psychodynamic theory.

So what is a theory? According to Rychlak (1968), at the most liberal definitional level,

A theory may be thought of as a series of two or more constructions (abstractions), which have been hypothesized, assumed, or even factually demonstrated to bear a certain relationship, one with the other. A theoretical proposition, which defines the relationship between constructions (now termed "variables"), becomes a fact when that proposition is no longer contested by those individuals best informed on the nature of the theory, and dedicated to study in the area of knowledge for which the theory has relevance. Theories vary in their levels of abstraction, objectivity-subjectivity, realism-idealism, perspective, and formality-informality. (p. 42)

Note that by the term, *constructions,* Rychlak is simply referring to constructs or variables.

In essence, then, a theory is a statement of the suspected relationship between and among variables. From this viewpoint, there is a theory behind virtually all of what we do, all of our research. That is, there is some expectation of how the variables in our research ought to relate to each other. As indicated in the above quote, however, theories vary in their degree of formality or informality. Informal theories are those that are not stated explicitly and do not have as a goal "the formulation of a logically consistent and mutually interdependent body of knowledge" (Rychlak, 1968, p. 35). Our goal as scientists ought to be to make our theories explicit, to put them to the test of empirical research, and thus to stimulate research.

Functions and Qualities of Theories

I suggest that for a theory to have much value scientifically, it must go beyond the simple propositional level just described. A theory ought to tell us *why* the variables or constructs are expected to relate to or influence one another. There must be good reasoning, so to speak, behind the expectation of how variables will be interrelated.

It is also useful to think of any theory as serving certain functions, more or less effectively. Rychlak suggests four such functions: descriptive, delimiting, generative, and integrative. It is worth taking at least a brief look at each of these. Regarding the *descriptive function,* most fundamentally any theory will serve to describe phenomena. The fuller the description of the conditions under which the phenomena are said to occur, the closer we get to what is called *explanation* in science. Good theories explain the *why* of things, what causes what. Indeed, full description may be seen as tantamount to a causal explanation. Good theories appear to explain effectively. They have a high degree of what may be termed *explanatory power.*

Theories also *delimit.* In effect, they place limits on what is looked at and seen. To limit is to place boundaries, which also means that there are certain things that any theory will not allow us to see. Limits are necessary, however, for they serve as guides to what may be examined. Perhaps most important, theories serve to *generate* further ideas and examination. Highly generative theories are given the venerable label, *heuristic.* Such theories stimulate investigation; they stimulate research aimed at testing them. Bordin's (1979) aforementioned theory of the working alliance in therapy is an excellent example of a theory with strong heuristic value. Bordin clearly and precisely specified the elements of a sound working alliance, and he offered clear propositions about the role of working alliance in the process and outcome of virtually all forms of therapy. Bordin's propositions were so clear that they allowed for the development of a measure of the working alliance and for the development of clear, testable hypotheses. His statement has generated nearly three decades of research, and because of that, the working alliance is one of the most validated and useful constructs in the field of psychotherapy. Theories that do not have heuristic value tend to stagnate. They essentially have no scientific value. This point, of course, underscores the integral relationship of theory to empirical research.

Finally, theories have an *integrative function.* By this we mean that the theory seeks to bring together propositions and constructs in a consistent, unified picture. In other words, good theories pull together diverse and at times seemingly disparate, even contradictory, facts into a picture that has coherence and a high degree of *internal consistency.*

One type of integration is particularly worthy of note, both because of its importance and because it is all too often forgotten in the current scene. *Parsimony,* a type of theoretical integration, may be seen as an effort by the theorist to introduce *only* as many constructs and propositions as are necessary to explain the phenomena under consideration. In a recent discussion of the concept of parsimony, I asked a group of counseling psychology graduate students how many had heard of "Ockham's razor." None of the six who were present responded affirmatively. This term, dating back to William of

Table 32.1   Ingredients of a Good Scientific Theory

Ingredient	Definition
Descriptive ability	Fully describes the phenomena being theorized about.
Explanatory power	Clarifies the "why" of things—what causes what.
Heuristic value	Generates scientific research.
Testability	Contains propositions that can be tested and disconfirmed through research.
Integration	Organizes ideas into coherent and logically consistent picture.
Parsimony	Includes only the constructs and ideas that are necessary to explain the phenomena in the theory. No excess baggage.
Clarity	States its ideas clearly, explicitly, and precisely.
Comprehensiveness	Thoroughly specifies the relationships within its domain.
Delimitation	Contains clear boundaries as to what is included and studied.

Ockham in the 14th century, implies that the constructs and propositions within a theory that go beyond what is needed to explain the phenomena the theory seeks to explain are "excess baggage." We need to take the razor to them, shaving away the needless excess. Modern-day psychologists would do well to keep Ockham's razor in hand as they construct theories. For further discussion of parsimony in theory development and evaluation, see Nowak (2004) and Fiske (2004).

The Good Scientific Theory

Within the above discussion of the functions of a scientific theory appear several of what may be seen as the necessary ingredients of a good theory. These are now summarized, and a few additional ingredients are also noted.

As implied, the good scientific theory might be said to be *internally consistent, integrative,* and *parsimonious.* It possesses a high degree of *explanatory power.* Within a domain that is *clearly delimited,* a good theory ought to be *comprehensive.* That is, it should thoroughly specify the important relationships within its domain of inquiry. Furthermore, for a theory to be of optimum value scientifically, it should be stated *explicitly* and *clearly* so that its propositions are high in *testability.* A theory that is testable is capable of disconfirmation. If you cannot disconfirm a theory, its scientific value is severely limited. In fact, each and every empirical study that

tests the theory ought to place it in grave danger. In this sense, an endangered theory is a good one! Referring back to a point made earlier, one of the major limitations of the large-scale theories of personality and therapy is that they are not endangered. As Mahrer (1988) noted, this makes theory-testing efforts in relation to such theories next to useless.

Finally, as we have discussed, a bottom line for a good theory is *heuristic value.* The good scientific theory must stimulate inquiry, in the form of both empirical research and further theory. In Table 32.1, I list the ingredients of a good scientific theory and provide a brief definition of each. I should note at this point that, in addition to these ingredients, for a theory to be relevant to the *practice of psychology* (e.g., counseling), it must also be able to guide clinical practice. Thus, the counseling practitioner must be able to use the theory in his or her practice. In this sense, a good clinical theory has an added burden. It must benefit practice as well as science.

As you can see, when we discuss the parameters of theory and the qualities of a good theory, the inherent importance of research to theory becomes evident. As a way of clarifying the roles of these two elements, theory and research, I shall address the question of where scientific ideas come from. Then I shall examine the *cycle of science*—the synergistic relationship of theory and research. In the final section, I shall discuss and exemplify how theories are used early and late in the life of a research piece—in generating ideas and hypotheses and in seeking to explain and interpret findings.

Throughout much of what follows, as a way of personalizing the discussion, I shall use examples drawn from my own research and theory construction in the area of therapist countertransference. As used in this chapter, *countertransference* refers to a counselor or psychotherapist's emotional reaction to a client or patient, which is based on the therapist's issues, often tied to earlier, unresolved conflicts, for example, with parents.

THE ORIGIN OF IDEAS

To begin, let us examine where research ideas come from. In the first study of our counter-transference research program at the University of Maryland, Ann Peabody, a graduate student at the time, became interested in the connection of counselor empathy to countertransference, defined as emotional withdrawal from the client. We had examined psychoanalytic theories about these two constructs, and on the basis of the theories, along with our own impressions as counselors, we reasoned that the more empathic the therapist, the less likely that he (male counselor) would withdraw from or avoid the material presented by a female client who behaved in an aggressive or seductive manner (which theoretically ought to be threatening to the counselor). We expected that the more empathic counselor would also experience countertransference feelings, but the key difference was that he was expected to be more aware of them and consequently to act them out less with the client. When we used taped actresses playing the role of client, with counselors responding to the "client" at certain stopping points on the tape, our hypotheses were generally confirmed (see Peabody & Gelso, 1982). The main point, however, is that the hypotheses came from theory (as well as clinical experience). Although no theory stated the precise hypotheses of our research, these hypotheses were logically derived from theory. The hypotheses would not have been possible if it were not for theories of empathy and theories of countertransference.

We may also ask where theoretical ideas come from. Several years after the Peabody and Gelso (1982) study, my collaborators and I reasoned that although all counselors experienced what could be called countertransference feelings, the most important thing in therapy was how effectively counselors were able to control or manage those feelings. Countertransference feelings could help therapy if managed effectively or hinder therapy if managed poorly. On the basis of this conception, we constructed a theory of the components of therapists' ability to manage their countertransference reactions to clients effectively (Hayes, Gelso, VanWagoner, & Diemer, 1991; VanWagoner, Gelso, Hayes, & Diemer, 1991). The theory drew substantially from the Peabody and Gelso study as described above, studies that built on that initial one, and other studies that were not connected to this program. Our theory posited that countertransference management ability consisted of five interrelated factors (empirical research informing each factor is cited): counselor self-insight (Peabody & Gelso, 1982; Robbins & Jolkovski, 1987), counselor empathic ability (Peabody & Gelso, 1982), counselor anxiety management (Hayes & Gelso, 1991), counselor self-integration (McClure & Hodge, 1987), and counselor conceptualizing ability (Robbins & Jolkovski, 1987). The five factors were described, as was their role in countertransference management. I would be remiss if I did not also note that this theory of countertransference management drew heavily from the authors' experiences in working with clients and how we were best able to manage effectively our own countertransference reactions. When we construct theory, as when we examine where research comes from, we not only rely centrally on research but also make use of our own personal or clinical experiences. This personal part is inevitable and forms a fundamental link in the theory-research-theory-research chain.

THE CYCLE OF SCIENTIFIC WORK

Thus far I have examined how theory generates research and how research generates and refines theory. Further, theory has been defined, and the qualities of a good theory have been discussed. We can now explore what I would suggest is the heart of science: how theory and research reciprocally relate to one another. The relationship of theory and research in science is deeply synergistic. The two go hand in hand, working together to create an optimal product, namely, good science. This synergistic relationship was described nicely by Stanley Strong (1991) in his discussion of "the cycle of scientific work" (p. 208). Strong, like many before him (e.g., Meehl, 1954; Reichenbach, 1938), considered two contexts in which science occurs: the context of discovery and the context of testing. (Others call the latter the context of justification.) He suggested that scientific work cycles between these two contexts. Strong's comments are worth noting:

> In the context of discovery, the scientist invents and constructs concepts of the dynamics that underlie and are expressed in observed events. In this task, the scientist draws on all of the ideas, observations, hunches, and creativity he or she can muster. As concepts emerge, the scientist invents ways to tie them to observable events and specifies how symptoms of the dynamics are to be measured. Equipped with a theory, the scientist enters the context of testing. In this context, the scientist generates observations with which to test the assertions of the theory. Observations inevitably reveal inadequacies in constructs and measures. Armed with more observations, ideas, and hunches, the scientist returns to the context of discovery to alter the theory or invent a new one. (p. 208)

(I should note that Strong's observations were directed at science from one particular philosophical position, what he calls the "Galilean mode," which he contrasts to the "Aristotelian mode." This accounts for his emphasis on theorizing about underlying dynamics. Strong's views, however, are applicable to science more generally.)

Above I discussed how our theory of countertransference management was spawned by several research studies, as well as other theories and ideas. The cycle of science continued in the sense that this theory of countertransference management has itself stimulated a number of investigations aimed at testing the theory and refining the theory. For example, Friedman and Gelso (2000) found that countertransference management ability was negatively related to therapists' undesirable countertransference behavior with clients. In other words, therapists who were good at countertransference management were less likely to behave in ineffective ways with their clients as a result of countertransference. In addition, when this undesirable behavior occurred, we discovered that the client-therapist working alliance was hindered (Ligiero & Gelso, 2002). Finally, we found a beginning link of countertransference to treatment success in that therapists in training who were rated by their clinical supervisors as effectively managing countertransference were most likely to have good treatment outcomes with these clients (Gelso, Latts, Gomez, & Fassinger, 2001). Based on these studies and others, the theory itself has been refined and expanded (Gelso & Hayes, in press).

As suggested by the discussion of our research program, the cycle of science may be seen as unending. Theories become modified based on research, and they eventually give way to other theories. These new theories, in turn, guide research, are tested repeatedly, modified, and so on. The cycle continues.

Some researchers, it should be added, do not appear to believe that an inevitable link and cycle exist between theory and research. For example, in a thoughtful analysis, Mahrer (1988) suggested that hypothesis-testing research (which derives from and tests theory) has not proven to be very fruitful in the area of psychotherapy research. Hypothesis-testing research has been predominant in psychology, according to Mahrer, and has impeded discovery. What is needed is a discovery-oriented approach in which the researcher approaches his or her data free from the biases and constraints caused by hypotheses. Mahrer believes that this "relaxation" will allow fresh understandings to emerge. Much of the current thought about the value of qualitative research in therapy stems from this viewpoint (e.g., Heppner, Kivlighan, & Wampold, 1999, ch. 10).

The scientist is, of course, free to do research that does not seek to test hypotheses. There is nothing about science that dictates the statement and testing of hypotheses derived from theory.

In addition, discovery-oriented approaches may indeed be very fruitful at this point in the history of therapy research. At the same time, I would suggest that the researcher cannot be freed from theory. His or her theories, at times informal rather than formal, about the phenomena being studied will guide the researcher at each and every step in the research process. Discovery-oriented research is probably best at certain points in the scientific process. For example, when theory and hypothesis testing seem to bring us to a dead end and no fresh insights seem forthcoming in an area, discovery-oriented research may be just what is needed. Yet even in this situation, as the findings from discovery-oriented research accrue, they will inevitably be used to create and refine theories about the phenomena under investigation, and these theories will then serve to generate subsequent hypotheses to be tested. In this way, discovery-oriented research may be seen as part of the context of discovery: It discovers relationships that help form theory, which then becomes examined within the context of testing or justification.

FURTHER COMMENTS ON APPLYING THEORIES IN RESEARCH

In this chapter, I have focused mostly on the interplay of theory and research in science. Given scientific psychology's historical tendency to neglect the role of theory in science, I would like to make a few additional comments on how theory is applied in research.

Generally speaking, theories are used at each and every step in the research process (see Hershey, Jacobs-Lawson, and Wilson's discussion of script-based research in Chapter 1 of this book). Theories come into play most centrally, however, at three points: (a) idea generation, (b) hypothesis generation, and (c) interpretation of results. The initial steps in an empirical study involve the first two, generating the idea to be studied and forming hypotheses, or at least research questions. An example of idea and hypothesis generation may be seen in two of the studies in our countertransference research program (Gelso, Fassinger, Gomez, & Latts, 1995; Hayes & Gelso, 1993). In these experiments, we examined the impact of the sexual orientation of

filmed client-actors and actresses on countertransference reactions of therapists in training. On the basis of theory suggesting that people, including counselors, tend to react more negatively to gay and lesbian individuals than heterosexuals (which, in turn, may be seen as based on the broader theory that people react more negatively to those who are different from themselves), we hypothesized that there would be greater countertransference reactions at behavioral, affective, and cognitive levels to gays (Hayes & Gelso, 1993) and lesbians (Gelso et al., 1995) than to heterosexual clients. Theory also suggested the hypothesis that a theoretical construct called *homophobia*, defined as prejudicial attitudes and negative stereotypes toward gay and lesbian individuals, would mediate counselors' countertransference reactions to gay and lesbian client-actors and actresses in the two studies. When counselors responded to the filmed clients at certain stopping points on the films, the results indicated no difference in counselor-trainees' countertransference reactions to filmed gay and lesbian clients than to heterosexual clients, but we did find a significant relationship between counselor homophobia and the behavioral indication of countertransference (i.e., avoidance of the client's feelings involving relationships and sexual problems). The higher the measured homophobia, the greater was the counselor avoidance in both studies.

In the Gelso et al. (1995) study, we also hypothesized that female counselor-trainees would exhibit greater countertransference than male counselor-trainees in response to a filmed lesbian client-actress, whereas we did not hypothesize a difference between female and male counselors toward the heterosexual client-actress. (Male client-actors were not used in this study, but if they had been, we would have expected male counselors to have greater countertransference than female counselors to gay male client-actors.) This hypothesis was based on the theory that people will respond more negatively to homosexuality when it involves members of their own sex than when it involves members of the opposite sex, partly because same-sexed interactions are more likely to stir up subconscious fears in counselors of same-sexed attractions. Our hypothesis was supported for the cognitive measure of countertransference:

errors in recall of the number of sexual words used by the client actress. Female counselors made more recall errors than males with the lesbian client-actress, whereas males and females did not differ in response to the heterosexual client.

You can see that, as is most often the case in psychological research, some of our hypotheses were supported and others were not. The "failed" hypotheses required that we revise our minitheory of the relationship between client sexual orientation, counselor gender, counselor homophobia, and counselor countertransference. The revised theory then stimulated hypotheses for our subsequent studies.

At this point, it might be useful to clarify how the terms *theory* and *theoretical proposition* may be distinguished from the term *hypothesis*. Although there are no absolute distinctions (in fact, in the earlier quote, Rychlak, 1968, appeared to use the terms synonymously), generally theories contain theoretical propositions, and hypotheses are derived from these propositions. Hypotheses tend to be more specific than the propositions, and, as can be seen in the above examples drawn from countertransference research, are the statements that are directly tested in empirical research.

As indicated at the beginning of this section, theory also comes into play most centrally when the experimenter seeks to interpret or explain his or her findings. Findings consistent with hypotheses that were in turn derived from a given theory are, of course, explained by that theory: When unexpected findings occur, however, the researcher tends to search for an existing theory to make sense out of them or create a theory of his or her own to explain the results. This new theory may be embedded in a larger theoretical system. An example of creating a theory to explain unexpected findings occurred with two countertransference studies (Latts & Gelso, 1995; Robbins & Jolkovski, 1987). In both these studies, a classic crisscross interaction was found between therapist-trainees' (a) awareness of countertransference feelings and (b) use of a counseling theory in their work in affecting a measure of countertransference behavior with filmed client-actresses and actors. Both teams of researchers found that countertransference

behavior (avoidance of and withdrawal from the client's material) was least when therapists were high on awareness of countertransference feelings and high in the use of a theory in their counseling. This finding was expected and made theoretical sense to the researchers. If the therapist is sharply aware of his or her feelings and has a theoretical context into which those feelings may be placed, the therapist is less likely to act out countertransference behaviors with the client.

The surprising finding was that high use of theory combined with low awareness of countertransference feelings resulted in the greatest amount of countertransference behavior. In reflecting on these findings, the researchers theorized that when counselors are unaware of countertransference feelings, their use of counseling theory may serve a defensive function. They may intellectualize about the client and the relationship, but there is a lack of emotional understanding. The use of a counseling theory in the absence of emotional self-understanding is ineffective in deterring counselors from enacting countertransference behavior with clients. Although the researchers created this theory, you can see where it is, in turn, based on a broader theory, namely, psychodynamic theory.

As I have suggested earlier in this chapter, we should not forget the role of personal or clinical experience in guiding the theoretician and researcher. Our experiences in the world, and with clients if we are in practice fields (and/or, as clients ourselves, if we are theorizing about and studying therapeutic interventions), guide us in a profound way in our selection of theories to generate hypotheses and explain findings. Although these experiences must be guided by reason and managed (not unlike countertransference management!) if they are to most effectively lead us, they are an inevitable part of the process.

CONCLUSION

In this chapter, I claimed that there is an inevitable, profound, and synergistic link between theory and research in psychological science. The definition and elements of theory, as well as the characteristics of "good theory" were noted. The cycle of science was discussed to exemplify how theory and research interrelate. Finally, the use of theory in early and later stages of the research process was examined, and my research on therapist countertransference was used to exemplify the uses of theory.

EXERCISES

1. Go on the Web and search for sites about scientific theory. Review the various descriptions of what is considered a theory, as well as how to evaluate theories. If you find a particular theory interesting, try to search for a history of the development of that theory. What was the original theory and how did it change over time? What modifications were made and why?

2. Go the library and locate the journal, *New Ideas in Psychology*. Select one of the articles that interest you in that journal and critique that theory in terms of what you have learned from this chapter. In addition, try to devise a study to test the model or theory outlined in the article that you have selected.

RECOMMENDED READINGS

If the student is interested in reading further examples of the theory-research cycle, four references might be most helpful. Strong (1991, pp. 208–209) presents a vivid personal example of his use of theory in research, demonstrating how his research findings required him to modify and at times even scrap his theories. Rotter (1990) clearly displays how a theoretical construct, in this case internal versus external locus of control, is most scientifically useful when embedded in a broader theoretical construct and programmatically studied. McClelland (1993) gives a fascinating summary of the interaction of research and theory in examining the construct of need for achievement and adding to that a second construct, need for power, in an attempt to explain certain behavior patterns. Goldfried (2000), a leading psychotherapy researcher and theoretician, presents some needed cautions about the use of theory in research. Goldfried clarifies the dangers that exist when theoreticians seek to prove their theories through research rather than use research to test, refine, and modify their theories, with the understanding that at some point these theories will be superseded by other, more robust ones. Finally, Kruglanski (2001) has thoughtfully explored social psychology's uneasiness about theorizing and has examined both the reasons for this uneasiness and costs to the field of not being sufficiently theoretical. Although Kruglanski's focus is social psychology, his comments are readily applicable to essentially all areas of psychology. Like few others, Kruglanski explores the question of whether students can be taught to be theoreticians. He answers this affirmatively and examines how this might happen.

REFERENCES

Bordin, E. S. (1979). The generalizability of the psychoanalytic concept of the working alliance. *Psychotherapy: Theory, Research, and Practice, 16,* 252–260.

Fiske, S. T. (2004). Mine the gap: In praise of informal sources of formal theory. *Personality and Social Psychology Review, 8,* 132–137.

Friedman, S. C., & Gelso, C. J. (2000). The development of the Inventory of Countertransference Behavior. *Journal of Clinical Psychology, 56,* 1221–1235.

Gelso, C. J. (1991). Galileo, Aristotle, and science in counseling psychology: To theorize or not to theorize. *Journal of Counseling Psychology, 38,* 211–213.

Gelso, C. J., Fassinger, R E., Gomez, M. J., & Latts, M. G. (1995). Countertransference reactions to lesbian clients: The role of homophobia, counselor gender, and countertransference management. *Journal of Counseling Psychology, 42,* 356–364.

Gelso, C. J., & Hayes, J. A. (in press). *Countertransference and the therapist's subjectivity: A trans-theoretical conception.* Mahwah, NJ: Lawrence Erlbaum.

Gelso, C. J., Latts, M. G., Gomez, M. J., & Fassinger, R. E. (2001). Countertransference management and therapy outcome: An initial evaluation. *Journal of Clinical Psychology, 58,* 861–867.

Goldfried, M. R. (2000). Consensus in psychotherapy research: Where have all the findings gone? *Psychotherapy Research, 10*(1), 1–16.

Hayes, J. A., & Gelso, C. J. (1991). Effects of therapist-trainees' anxiety and empathy on countertransference behavior. *Journal of Clinical Psychology, 47,* 284–290.

Hayes, J. A., & Gelso, C. J. (1993). Male counselors' discomfort with gay and HIV-infected clients. *Journal of Counseling Psychology, 40,* 86–93.

Hayes, J. A., Gelso, C. J., VanWagoner, S., & Diemer, R. (1991). Managing countertransference: What the experts think. *Psychological Reports, 69,* 139–148.

Heppner, P. P., Kivlighan, D. M., & Wampold, B. E. (1999). *Research in counseling* (2nd ed.). Pacific Grove, CA: Brooks/Cole.

Latts, M. G., & Gelso, C. J. (1995). Countertransference behavior and management with survivors of sexual assault. *Psychotherapy, 32,* 405–415.

Ligiero, D. P., & Gelso. C. J. (2002). Countertransference, attachment, and the working alliance: The therapist's contributions. *Psychotherapy: Theory/Research/Practice/ Training, 39,* 3–11.

Kruglanski, A. W. (2001). That "vision thing": The state of theory in social and personality psychology at the edge of the new millennium. *Journal of Personality and Social Psychology, 80,* 871–875.

Mahrer, A. R. (1988). Discovery-oriented psychotherapy research: Rationale, aims, and methods. *American Psychologist, 43,* 694–703.

McClelland, D. C. (1993). Motives and health. In G. G. Brannigan & M. R Merrens (Eds.), *The undaunted psychologist* (pp. 129–141). New York: McGraw-Hill.

McClure, B. A, & Hodge, R. W. (1987). Measuring countertransference and attitude in therapeutic relationships. *Psychotherapy, 24,* 325–335.

Meehl, P. E. (1954). *Clinical versus statistical prediction.* Minneapolis: University of Minnesota Press.

Norcross, J. C. (Ed.). (2002). Psychotherapy relationships that work: Therapist contributions and responsiveness to patients. New York: Oxford University Press.

Nowak, A. (2004). Dynamical mindism: Why less is more in psychology. *Personality and Social Psychology Review, 8,* 183–192.

Peabody, S. A., & Gelso, C. J. (1982). Countertransference and empathy: The complex relationship between two divergent concepts in counseling. *Journal of Counseling Psychology, 29,* 240–245.

Reichenbach, H. (1938). *Experience and prediction.* Chicago: University of Chicago Press.

Robbins, S. B., & Jolkovski, M. P. (1987). Managing countertransference: An interactional model using awareness of feeling and theoretical framework. *Journal of Counseling Psychology, 34,* 276–282.

Rotter, J. B. (1990). Internal versus external control of reinforcement: A case history of a variable. *American Psychologist, 45,* 489–493.

Rychlak, J. F. (1968). *A philosophy of science for personality theory.* Boston: Houghton Mifflin.

Strong, S. R. (1991). Theory-driven science and naive empiricism in counseling psychology. *Journal of Counseling Psychology, 38,* 204–210.

Tseng, O. C. S., & Jackson, J. W. (1993). A common methodological framework for theory construction and evaluation in the social and behavioral sciences. *Genetic, Social, and General Psychology Monographs, 117,* 50–76.

VanWagoner, S., Gelso, C. J., Hayes, J. A., & Diemer, R. (1991). Countertransference and the reputedly excellent therapist. *Psychotherapy, 28,* 411–421.

33

THE RESEARCH SCRIPT:

One Researcher's View

RICHARD E. PETTY

If you are following this book in sequence, many of you have now read a bunch of chapters about the research process. These chapters contain a great deal of wisdom about how you should go about planning and executing a research project. It is probably clear to you by now that there is considerable agreement within the community of science-oriented psychologists about what the appropriate steps are for conducting research. In this final chapter, the editors have asked me to talk about my personal experience in conducting research. Thus, this chapter is a bit different from the rest. Rather than offering you advice about what I think you *should* do in some generic sense, I will offer my personal observations based on my own research experiences.

Before going further, it may be useful to learn a little bit about me to set the background context for my remarks. I am a social psychologist who mostly studies how people's attitudes and beliefs are formed and changed (or resist change) and how these attitudes guide our behavior. In the majority of our studies, we examine the basic underlying psychological processes involved in change, but this work is relevant to all sorts of applied contexts, such as changing people's beliefs in therapy, in an advertising context, in the courtroom, in electoral politics, and so forth.

It is sometimes said that most psychologists are particularly interested in studying what they are really good at or what are particular problems for them. Thus, in the realm of medicine, I have some acquaintances who have selected cancer research or a more rare disease because they or a member of their family has been affected by it. Although I don't know if I am particularly good at social influence or particularly poor; I do know that this is a topic that has interested me since I was on the debate team in high school (a long time ago . . . don't ask). That is, I have always wondered about certain things such as, why do some people become radical liberals and others right-wing conservatives? What causes some people to like Coca-Cola over Pepsi? Why do some people have an abiding faith in God whereas others are atheists? I mention my long-standing interest in these questions because I think that if you are studying something you are truly interested in, you'll be more successful. You'll have better insights when you frame your research questions; and perhaps more important, when your insights prove *wrong* (and they inevitably will), you will have the motivation and ability to come up with a new idea and try something else.

In trying to outline my thoughts for this chapter, I realized that although along with my

465

collaborators and coauthors I have published over 200 research articles of one sort or another, I hardly ever think about the research process itself. Thus, I do not have a handy list of *do*s and *don't*s ready to disseminate. Furthermore, the psychological research literature has convinced me that although I can probably do a pretty good job of telling you *what* we actually do in our research activities, I am unlikely to be able to tell you *why* we do what we do with any degree of accuracy. This is because people in general are typically not very good at coming up with the correct reasons that underlie their behavior (Nisbett & Wilson, 1977). Thus, I may say I like Coca-Cola because of its taste, but it may really be that in a blind taste test I rate the flavor as rather low, and it is the snazzy advertising that has gotten me to like the product. So too it may be that I think my latest research idea came from my astute observations of real life, but instead it came from a television show that I saw last week or a journal abstract I read a month ago. Nevertheless, with this caveat in mind, I will plow forward.

There are some aspects of the research script that appear to be universal. You must come up with a research question, collect some data and analyze it, and report the results to your collaborators and funding agency (if any), and (hopefully) to the world in an archival journal. There are other aspects of the script that may vary from study to study and from person to person. For example, for some projects we spend considerable time reading the relevant prior literature, but for other projects, we do not. Next, I will comment on each of the major steps in the research process with particular attention to the first one.

The Idea for the Project

In my view, deciding what to study is the single most important step in the research process and the one (unfortunately) on which there is the least formal guidance. I would guess that over 90% of what is written about conducting research concerns the ways a study should be designed (e.g., should you use a within- or a between-subjects manipulation), the appropriate ways to analyze the data (e.g., regression vs. ANOVA), the threats to the validity of a study (e.g., internal vs. external),

and how to write it up for publication (e.g., what should be included in a methods section). Relatively little has been written about deciding what to investigate. One notable exception is William McGuire (1997) who has come up with dozens of ways to brainstorm something to research. His handy checklist—with suggestions such as "thinking about a deviant case" or "introspecting about the causes of one's *own* behavior"—is definitely worth examining. McGuire is something of a hero of mine. Not only is he one of the most famous researchers on attitudes (see McGuire, 1985), but his overall orientation toward research fits mine quite well (Petty, 1997; Petty, Tormala, & Rucker, 2004). McGuire is a "contextualist" who believes that virtually *any* result is possible in psychological research. According to him, our job is to determine *when* and *for whom* each result occurs.

Within the various areas of psychology, there are thousands of possible research questions. How can we possibly decide what to investigate? This question may be approached differently at different stages of one's career. As an undergraduate looking for some research experience, you are best off scouring faculty Web pages at your university to look for a faculty member whose substantive interests most closely match your own. The same holds true for graduate students shopping for a graduate program and an initial advisor. The more genuine curiosity and interest in the fundamental research question that *you* can bring to a project, the better. Selecting a faculty advisor will help narrow the domain of possible research questions to some topical area (e.g., attitude change, altruism, memory process, anxiety disorders, and so forth). But within any one of these areas there are still an unlimited set of possible research topics. After considering your own personal interests and those of your advisor, the next most important thing to consider is what kind of contribution the research might make to the field. At the risk of oversimplification, we can consider four fundamental types of contribution that are likely to be valued. I discuss each in turn.

(1) Discover a New Effect

Science is replete with exciting new discoveries: penicillin, nonstick coating for frying pans, the laws of behavioral reinforcement, and so forth. Thus, one way to make a contribution is to discover something new. Although it is statistically unlikely that you will be the one who uncovers the cure for cancer, it is quite realistic to aim to discover a new relationship between psychological variables. The more pervasive the variables are in the world and the more surprising the relationship, the more newsworthy the finding will be. For example, consider the fact that economists have believed since the founding of their discipline that people are basically rational. That is, a fundamental economic assumption is that people carefully weigh the costs and benefits of an option before making a decision. In light of this, the psychological finding that people are sometimes influenced by seemingly irrational cues and heuristics was worthy of a Nobel Prize (see Kahneman, 2003). For example, Tversky and Kahneman (1974) showed that people's numerical estimates could be influenced by a salient and completely irrelevant number that was accessible. Thus, if people were asked about their social security numbers and then asked to estimate the length of the Nile River, people with large social security numbers (e.g., 999–99–9999) would estimate the length of the river to be longer than people with low social security numbers (e.g., 111–11–1111; see Wilson, Houston, Etling, & Brekke, 1996). Thinking about your social security number should have no effect on your estimate of the Nile's length, but it does. This is not rational. Similarly, Johnson and Tversky (1983) showed that the momentary emotions people were experiencing could influence their estimates of the frequency of events. Thus, people who were sad estimated the frequency of negative events (e.g., getting an *F* on a test) to be higher than people who were not sad, but people who were happy provided lower estimates of the frequency of negative events. Again, this effect of experienced emotions is not rational (see Petty, Fabrigar, & Wegener, 2003, for a review of the effects of emotion on judgments).

Within this basic paradigm—looking at how seemingly irrelevant events could bias people's judgments, there are a host of potentially biasing factors that might be investigated. You just need to think of what some of these might be. In my own case, one of the first judgmental biases we investigated was provoked by a personal experience. I was in graduate school, and a fellow student, Gary Wells, and I had just started teaching. We both were struck with how the students' reactions to our lectures were important in determining how good we felt about our performance. If our students were smiling and nodding their heads, we clearly thought we had done a good job, but if they were frowning and shaking their heads, we felt as though we had not performed well. This seemed pretty rational as bodily signals from others can surely convey their impressions of us.

Although it was clear that bodily signals from others could influence our judgments, could our *own* bodily signals influence our own judgments—even if these bodily signals were actually irrelevant to our judgments? We wanted to know, so in an initial study we asked undergraduates to put on headphones and either nod their heads up and down or shake them from side to side while they listened to a radio program (Wells & Petty, 1980). They thought they were doing this in order to test the quality of the headphones. That is, we told the participants that we were trying to scientifically simulate the movements they might make when jogging, dancing, and so forth. While making these movements, they heard an editorial that was either about raising or lowering the tuition at their university. After the message, we asked them what they thought the tuition should be. The primary result was that people who were told to nod their heads while listening to the message agreed with it more than those told to shake their heads. Thus, when the message favored raising tuition, nodders said they favored higher tuition than shakers, but when the message favored lowering tuition, nodders favored lower tuition than shakers. This was one of the early studies showing that a person's own bodily responses could influence his or her judgments.

(2) Extend or Clarify an Effect

In the studies I described above, the primary contribution of the research was to document a new effect. That is, prior to the research, we did not know that an irrelevant number, your mood, or your own head movements could affect your judgments. Once an effect is uncovered, people may wonder how general it is. That is, in any given study, an effect is typically shown with one particular manipulation, for one particular participant population, and for one kind of judgment. Thus, in medical research, a particular drug might be tried out with a particular form of cancer (e.g., liver) in a particular population (e.g., men over 50). If that research uncovers a new effect—the drug reduces cancer—then people might want to extend the research by trying different dosages of the drug (10 vs. 20 mg) on different cancers (e.g., lung) and in different populations (e.g., women). Such extending research is well worth doing once an initial effect is uncovered.

The same is true in psychological research. Thus, after learning about the head movements study just described, you might wonder, for example, if head movements can affect judgments other than monetary ones (i.e., tuition). Thus, some researchers wondered if head movements could affect people's evaluation of consumer products and found that it could (Tom, Pettersen, Lau, Burton, & Cook, 1991). This extending research showed that the impact of head nodding on judgment didn't appear to depend on the particular kind of judgment made or the particular population used in the original research.

Instead of extending the head-nodding effect per se, other researchers might wonder if head movements are a unique bodily response that can affect judgments or whether other bodily movements could make a difference. The answer to this question appears to be a resounding "yes," as subsequent studies have shown that people will like things more if their face is put into a smiling rather than a frowning posture when they are evaluating it (Strack, Martin, & Stepper, 1988) and if they are making the bodily movements associated with pulling something toward them rather than pushing it away (Cacioppo, Priester, & Berntson, 1993). Other possible bodily responses and potential biases remain to be researched.

In our own lab, we were interested in extending the work on emotion and judgment. Recall that Johnson and Tversky (1983) had shown that experiencing a positive or a negative emotion could influence the frequency estimates for events. In the original research, the emotions of

happiness and sadness were used, but these are only two of the several fundamental emotions possible (e.g., Ekman & Friesen, 1971). For example, sadness is a negative emotion, but so too are anger and fear. Given that the emotions are distinct, perhaps different emotions of the same valence would have different links to judgment. In particular, Dave DeSteno, Duane Wegener, Derek Rucker, and I wondered if sad and angry states would increase the likelihood of all negative events, or whether there would be some greater specificity in the effects of the emotions. Thus, in some of our research (see DeSteno, Petty, Wegener, & Rucker, 2000), we had people who were placed in a sad or an angry state estimate the frequency of negative events that had a sad (e.g., loss of a loved one) or an angry (e.g., someone taking your parking place) tone to them. We found that there was a matching of emotion to the tone of the event, such that people made to feel angry were more likely to overestimate the likelihood of angering rather than sad events, but sad individuals were likely to do the opposite. Thus, this work extended or clarified prior work on emotion and judgment because the earlier work treated all negative emotions as having similar effects (i.e., increasing estimates of negative events). Our research was able to build on this earlier finding and show that greater specificity in predictions was possible.

When extending or clarifying a previous finding, others are likely to find it of greater interest if the extension is to important judgments, behaviors, stimuli, and population groups rather than to unimportant ones. Furthermore, extensions that are somewhat surprising or unexpected will likely be valued more than extensions that are somewhat obvious (e.g., if an effect works for 30-year-olds, why wouldn't it work for 40-year-olds?). As one example of a surprising extension of an effect, consider recent work on ostracism or social exclusion (e.g., Williams, Case, & Govan, 2003). It may not be very surprising to you that it is very aversive to be excluded or shunned by others; however, it may be much more surprising to know that who does the ostracizing doesn't matter much if at all. In an extensive program of research on this phenomenon, Kip Williams and his colleagues have shown that the effect is so robust that it is difficult to find qualifications to it. Thus, it doesn't matter if you are ostracized by liked or disliked others—it is equally unpleasant. Furthermore, in one study, college students felt as bad when they were excluded from a game by a "dumb" computer as when they were excluded from the game by living, breathing humans (Zadro, Williams, & Richardson, 2004).

It is important to note that sometimes when you are aiming to show an *extension* of an effect (i.e., show its generality), you may end up showing a *limitation* to the effect. That is, the effect may not work in the population in which you aim to extend the effect, or it may not work for your new manipulation, or for your new measure—although you had initially expected that it would. In this case, if your research procedures are sound, you would have uncovered a *moderator* of the effect, a variable that modifies the basic effect. This strategy is described after I first describe mediation.

(3) Demonstrate Mediation of an Established Effect

In the strategy just described, an investigator starts with an established effect (e.g., emotion affects judgment) and attempts to extend or clarify it in some way. Uncovering new associations among psychological variables and determining how widely applicable new effects are motivate a lot of research. But, in addition to uncovering *how* variables relate to each other, psychologists are often interested in *why* variables have the impact that they do. In fact, this is what theory in psychology is all about—trying to explain why variables relate to each other. Thus, another research strategy is to take an established relationship between variables and try to explain why the variable produces the effect it does.

There are two common strategies for theory testing. One is to specify the underlying mechanism responsible for your effect and then conduct research in which you try to measure this process and see if it is responsible. If the proposed mechanism can be measured, then you can see if the variable of interest affects the proposed mechanism and if this mechanism in turn affects your outcome (see Baron & Kenney, 1986). These days, many seem to think that demonstrating mediation is the only, or the best, strategy for testing one's theory; however, another valuable approach to theory testing is to make a unique prediction from your theory of why something works and show that your theory can predict an outcome that others cannot. For example, you might predict uniquely from your theory that the effect should hold, especially for certain kinds of people or in certain kinds of situations, but not in others. The former is known as the *mediational approach* and the latter is known as the *moderator approach.* I address each of these strategies in turn, beginning with mediation.

Consider first the research on head nodding described above. A number of studies have shown that head nodding can affect a wide variety of judgments. But, this initial research did not address *why* head nodding had its effects. The goal was just to uncover the effect (Wells & Petty, 1980) or extend it to a new domain (e.g., Tom et al., 1991). Various existing theories in social psychology suggest a number of possible mechanisms by which variables such as head nodding could affect judgments. I'll just consider a few of the more obvious ones. First, it may be that people who are nodding their heads are in a better mood than people who shake their heads, and this positive mood generalizes to the topic of the message by a process of classical conditioning (e.g., Staats & Staats, 1958). Or, perhaps nodding one's head in a positive way facilitates access to positive thoughts and shaking one's head facilitates access to negative thoughts. The more positive thoughts one has to the message, the more one is likely to agree with it (see Petty & Cacioppo, 1986).

Pablo Briñol and I were interested in exploring another possibility based on the social signal of head nodding. That is, when other people are nodding their heads at you while you are speaking, you are likely to gain confidence in what you are saying based on this consensual social validation (Festinger, 1954). Likewise, if people are shaking their heads at you, you are likely to lose confidence in what you are saying. We wondered if it could be the case that nodding your own head while thinking could validate your thoughts by giving you greater confidence in them and that shaking would produce doubt in your own thoughts. The possibility that people could validate their own thoughts was something Pablo, Zak Tormala, and I called the *self-validation* effect (Petty, Briñol, & Tormala, 2002).

Each of the possible theories (classical conditioning of mood, biased thoughts, self-validation) of head nodding predicts that nodding your head up and down could increase agreement with a message, but the mechanism is different. In the mediational approach, the mechanisms are compared with each other by trying to measure the presumed mechanisms and seeing which is best at accounting for the results. In the relevant conditions of one study using this approach (Briñol & Petty, 2003), we gave college students in Madrid, Spain, a message containing very strong arguments in favor of a new requirement that students must carry personal identification cards for security purposes. The students were asked to nod or shake their heads while listening to the message. After the message, we assessed their attitudes toward the topic, as well as several of the possible mediators of the effect (e.g., mood, thoughts, and confidence).

First, like the previous head-nodding studies, this experiment found that people who were nodding their heads were more favorable toward the message proposal than people who were shaking their heads. This is a necessary first step in trying to tease apart the mechanisms. The next step is to see if head nodding affected any of the proposed mechanisms. If classical conditioning of a good mood is responsible for the effect of head nodding on attitudes, then people who were nodding should report a more positive mood than people who were shaking. But this did not occur. If nodding one's head leads people to have easier access to positive thoughts, then people who were nodding should have written more positive thoughts, or a greater proportion of positive thoughts, than people who were shaking. But again, this did not happen. Finally, to test the self-validation hypothesis, we asked people how confident they were in the thoughts that they listed. In this case, we found that people who were nodding their heads reported more confidence in their thoughts than people who were shaking. This is a critical finding in establishing mediation. Furthermore, we found that when we controlled for the effect of

head nodding on thought confidence, the effect of head nodding on message attitudes disappeared. Thus, it appears that head nodding increased thought confidence relative to head shaking. When people had confidence in the mostly favorable thoughts that they generated to the message, they were more persuaded than when they had doubt in these favorable thoughts (i.e., when shaking their heads). That is, people used their thoughts in forming their judgments when they had confidence in their thoughts, but they did not use their thoughts when they were held with doubt.

As was the case with the link between head nodding and persuasion, it is generally true that for any given relationship between variables, there will be a number of possible mediating mechanisms. Thus, it is quite useful to try and determine what the mechanism is (e.g., why head nodding affects judgment or why accessible numerical anchors affect judgment). You can be the first to provide evidence for a particular mediator of an effect that already exists in the literature (as we did with the head-nodding effect). Or, you can provide evidence for a *new* mediator of an effect for which people believe the mediation is already known (e.g., Tormala, Petty, & Briñol, 2002). In the case of our head-nodding research, the effect itself was already established in the literature. What made our studies worth publishing was identifying a unique mediator of the effect—people's confidence in their thoughts—and showing that this mediator could account for the effect better than alternative mediators that were plausible prior to our research.

One potential problem with the mediational approach is that you are looking for one mediator to win out over others. Our positive results for thought confidence provide good evidence that this is a plausible mediator of the head-nodding effect. But, our absence of effects for mood and number of positive thoughts is less convincing evidence *against* these theories as possible determinants of the head-nodding effect. This is because null effects are open to multiple interpretations. Perhaps we did not have a very good (reliable or valid) measure of mood or thoughts. Or perhaps the effect of head nodding on mood or thoughts is smaller than its effect on confidence, and thus we would need more participants (power) to detect effects. Nevertheless, providing positive evidence for a new mediator of an established effect is a sensible research strategy combined with negative effects for other plausible mediators assessed with accepted methods. So, when you read the literature on some topic of interest, think about why this effect might have occurred. It may be the case that the authors have suggested one or more possible mediators as accounting for their effect. But perhaps they did not provide evidence of mediation. Or, perhaps they provided evidence of mediation, but did not look at alternative mediators that you believe are possible. These provide avenues for new research (see Exercise 1).

(4) Demonstrate Moderation of an Established Effect

Another potential, and in some ways superior, strategy for theory-testing research is to examine possible moderators of an effect in the literature. Moderation is an alternative means by which you can compare different theories or explanations of an effect. Consider the research on head nodding again. Imagine that proponents of the mood or biased-thinking theories were upset with our mediational research because elimination of their theories relied on null results. An alternative way to compare the mediators is to try and think of some implication of one theory that differs from the others.

This moderation strategy is a favorite of mine and is one that we have used in a large number of studies. For simplicity, let's return to the head-nodding effect one more time. How can our preferred thought confidence explanation be compared with the others using a moderator approach rather than a mediator approach? The key is to think of some third variable that should make a difference according to the thought confidence approach but that would not make a difference (or might predict an opposite effect) from the competing approaches. One aspect of some of the explanations for the head-nodding effect is that they seem to *always* expect vertical (yes) movements to produce more favorable responses than horizontal (no) movements. If vertical movements put people in a good mood and this is simply associated with the message position via classical conditioning, it would always make the message position seem more desirable. Or, if vertical movements increased access to positive thoughts, this too should always make attitudes more favorable. Other possible theories also make this "main effect" prediction. For example, if people simply reason that if they are nodding, they must agree (a "self-perception" account, Bem, 1972), this too always expects nodding to produce more agreement than shaking.

According to the self-validation (thought confidence) account, however, nodding would not always produce more favorable attitudes than shaking. This is because nodding is proposed to enhance confidence in one's thoughts. If the thoughts to the message are favorable (as they generally would be if the arguments are strong), then nodding would produce more favorable attitudes because relying on one's positive thoughts should increase agreement. But, what if the person listening to the message were thinking negative thoughts to the proposal? Here, nodding would increase confidence in these negative thoughts and thereby *reduce* agreement. According to the other theories, because one's thoughts to the message have nothing to do with the effect (e.g., the positive mood from head nodding simply becomes attached to the message position), a manipulation of thought valence (whether the thoughts are positive or negative) should not matter. Thus, one moderator approach to comparing the confidence theory to the others is to have people nod or shake their heads to a message that elicits either mostly favorable thoughts or mostly unfavorable thoughts and see if the effect of head nodding is the same for each kind of message.

According to most of the theoretical accounts of head nodding, the direction of the thoughts should not matter, but it should matter greatly according to the confidence theory. So, to compare these theories, we had participants read a message that either contained very cogent and compelling arguments that were pretested to elicit mostly favorable thoughts (e.g., let's raise tuition at the university so that we can reduce class size) or rather weak and specious arguments that were pretested to elicit mostly unfavorable thoughts (e.g., let's raise tuition so that we can plant exotic tulips rather than common ones on campus; see Briñol & Petty, 2003).

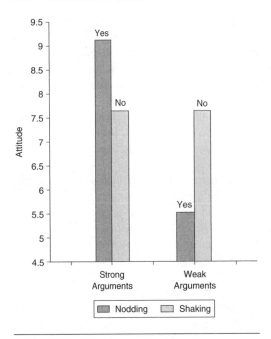

Figure 33.1 Effects of Head Nodding and Argument Quality on Attitudes

Then, the participants were instructed to nod or shake their heads while listening to the message and report their attitudes toward the proposal. Figure 33.1 presents the results. You can see that the effects of head nodding were quite different depending on whether the message presented strong or weak arguments. When the arguments were strong, nodding produced more agreement than shaking—the result found in all of the prior research and expected by all of the theories; however, when the arguments were weak and thoughts were mostly negative, head nodding led to *less* agreement than shaking. This was exactly as the thought confidence explanation expected, but counter to the other theories. Because the self-validation hypothesis predicted a pattern of results that the other theories did not, it was not critical to measure the postulated mediating processes. Indeed, if your theory can predict a pattern of results that all plausible theories cannot, then you can provide very compelling evidence for your theory in the absence of mediational evidence.

In the case of the head-nodding research, we uncovered the initial phenomena in one study (Wells & Petty, 1980) and then many years later conducted mediator and moderator studies to examine a mechanism by which the effect occurs (Briñol & Petty, 2003). This is how research progresses in a long-term research program. Sometimes a research team uncovers a finding and then spends the next several years examining various mediators and moderators of the basic effect. Indeed, according to the contextualist framework, it is unlikely that thought confidence is the *only* mechanism by which head nodding can affect judgments, and future work will likely show that different mechanisms can be responsible for the effect in different situations (Petty & Cacioppo, 1986).

Although sometimes researchers follow up on their own initial findings, at other times it can be quite fruitful to follow up on findings initially reported by others. This was the case in some recent work we have done on what is called the *prime-to-behavior* effect. The basic idea in prime-to-behavior studies (see Dijksterhuis & Bargh, 2001) is that when various traits, stereotypes, or motives are subtly activated, people will often behave in accordance with the activated mental contents even if they are completely irrelevant to them. For example, in one famous study, the investigators wanted to see if college students could be primed to act more elderly (Bargh, Chen, & Burrows, 1996). In this research, undergraduates were asked to make sentences with sets of words that were provided. In the "elderly" prime condition, some of the words in the scrambled sentences they were given were associated with the elderly (e.g., grey, Florida, retired), whereas in the control condition, they were not. Following the sentence generation task, the students were timed as to how long they took to walk down the hallway toward the exit elevator. The key finding was that students primed with the elderly walked more slowly than those not primed. That is, the primed individuals acted in a manner consistent with the stereotype of the elderly. In other studies, people primed with the elderly became more forgetful (Levy, 1996) and became more conservative in their personal attitudes (Kawakami, Dovidio, & Dijksterhuis, 2003). These prime-to-behavior effects are quite robust, but it is not at all clear *why* they occur (see Wheeler & Petty, 2001).

Consider two possible accounts that have been put forward. One account is a *social tuning* explanation, which says that people adopt the traits of primed social categories because it is evolutionarily adaptive to fit in with others (e.g., Kawakami et al., 2003). That is, because people generally like others who are similar to themselves, if people automatically adopt some of the traits and characteristics of others, they will presumably get along better with them. So, if you walked into a room of elderly people and you adopted some of their traits and attitudes, they would presumably like you better than if you did not, and this motivation to fit in could be behind the prime-to-behavior phenomena. Another explanation which Christian Wheeler, Ken DeMarree, and I have called the *active-self* view (Wheeler, DeMarree, & Petty, 2005), says that when traits are subtly primed, they become confused with one's *own* traits. According to this view, you are not trying to fit in with others, but you actually see yourself as having some elderly characteristics and act this way for that reason.

How can these two theories be teased apart? Both theories mostly make the same predictions about what attitudes or behaviors a person would adopt as a result of priming, but they differ dramatically about the motivation underlying the behaviors. One theory says that behavior is enacted because people want to fit in with the activated group (e.g., the elderly), whereas the other says that they are doing it as a reflection of who they are. We employed a moderation approach to distinguish these explanations. It turns out that there is an individual difference measure that taps directly into these divergent underlying motivations. The self-monitoring scale (Snyder, 1974) is a personality measure that separates individuals into those whose behavior is guided by fitting in with others (called high self-monitors) versus those whose behavior is motivated by acting on their inner feelings and traits (called low self-monitors).

It is important that the two different prime-to-behavior theories make opposite predictions about which group should show stronger prime-to-behavior effects. If the motivation underlying the effects is a motive to fit in, then high self-monitors should show the effects more clearly; however, if the motivation is based on a desire to act as oneself, then low self-monitors should show the stronger effects. In a series of studies, DeMarree, Wheeler, and I assessed our participants' self-monitoring tendencies, primed various stereotypes, and measured relevant behaviors. Across these studies, we consistently found that it was the low self-monitors who showed the only significant prime-to-behavior effects (see DeMarree, Wheeler, & Petty, in press, for details). By showing this particular pattern of moderation, we were able to provide support for the active-self view of prime-to-behavior effects. Thus, whether you are following up on an empirical relationship that you uncovered initially or one discovered initially by others, a fruitful research strategy is to use moderator variables to limit the effect and thereby provide evidence for a particular conceptual account of the effect.

Moderation Versus Mediation

When should you use a mediational approach, and when should you use one based on moderator variables? Sometimes a mediation approach might be preferable to a moderation approach, and sometimes the opposite is the case. Which is better can depend on how easy or practical it is to assess the plausible mediators and to ascertain, assess, and/or manipulate the relevant moderators. In the example on prime-to-behavior effects, we thought it was easier to use a moderation approach rather than try to determine if a prime activated a particular motive, which in turn drove the behavior. In other contexts, however, it may be more sensible to try the mediator approach. For example, say that someone has a theory that engaging in exercise reduces heart attacks by reducing inflammation in the blood passageways, whereas another investigator has the hypothesis that exercise works by reducing cholesterol levels. It would be relatively straightforward to assess these possible mediators in high- versus low-exercise groups and then determine which (if either) is the route by which exercise reduces heart attacks.

Finally, it is very important to note that although I have presented the mediator and moderator approaches as independent strategies, it is certainly possible and desirable to examine them together. For example, in one study, you could both manipulate the moderator of interest and measure the mediators of interest.

Such designs are capable of examining moderated mediation and mediated moderation (see Wegener & Fabrigar, 2000, for further discussion).

CHECKING THE IDEA OUT: A LITERATURE REVIEW AND OTHER METHODS

In the previous section, I outlined some major categories of studies that you might conduct. Following the generation of your idea (e.g., I wonder if head nodding affects persuasion) and prior to conducting your study, it is quite common to check your idea out. Why are you checking the idea out? First and foremost, you want to find out if the idea is interesting to others and whether your idea seems plausible and important or not. Although the idea may appeal to you, others may find the idea to be wacky, or it may fly in the face of conventional wisdom. This does not mean that the idea is bad, but it does mean that in writing about your idea, it would be wise to emphasize your awareness of the counterintuitive nature of the idea. Of course, what is counterintuitive to one person may seem mundane to the next. I even had the experience once of a journal editor telling us that a result we reported was so surprising that it was virtually impossible. We were asked to replicate the effect a few times using other manipulations. Once we replicated the effect, however, and resubmitted the paper, the same journal editor now found the effect to be "obvious." Indeed, once we become familiar with something, we may think we knew it all along, so you may need to convince others that your idea is not already accepted by carefully citing prior thinking about the subject matter.

Another important reason for checking your idea out is to find out if the idea (or something close to it) is already out there in the literature. Journal editors and reviewers especially value new or unique ideas, so you want to make sure that this characterizes your proposal. Or, if your idea relates to existing propositions, you want to be sure to indicate what the points of uniqueness are. The literature is already replete with the same basic idea masquerading under different names. You do not want to (deliberately) contribute to this.

There are several ways to check out your idea, but the two most common are asking others and scouring the psychological literature. Researchers vary as to whether they recommend reading the literature intently on a topic before or after you settle on a study idea. Some fear that reading too much literature beforehand might stifle creativity by boxing you in to established ways of thinking. Others fear that a failure to read the literature will lead you to waste your time planning something that will not be a significant contribution. In reality, this is not an either-or decision. Your basic idea may just pop into your head when you wake up in the morning or during a shower. Or, it may be more obviously provoked by reading something in the newspaper or the scientific literature. A moderation or mediation idea likely comes from reading about an established effect or perhaps hearing someone talk about her or his research at a conference or colloquium. There may be no better way to find out what is current and exciting in the field than to attend a major conference in your area. Studies are presented at conferences years before they appear in the journals, and by learning what contemporary researchers are doing right now, you have a leg up on those who merely read about research in a journal. The worst feeling is to spend a year or two working on what you think is a great idea only to find a similar study appears in a journal just as you have finished writing the first draft of your paper. Attending conferences does not preclude this from happening (it has happened to me), but it does make it less likely.

In addition to reading the literature, you should check your idea out with others. Your fellow students and available faculty members (especially your academic advisor) are a critical source of feedback. At a minimum, they can tell you how your idea fits with their way of thinking about human behavior. Or, if they are experts in the domain, they may be able to give you a quick indication of how it fits with the literature. At this point in my career, I still find it highly valuable to check out ideas with others (mostly my graduate students or postdocs, present and former). In addition, they are checking their own unique ideas with me. In the process of checking out your ideas with others, valuable collaborative relationships might be formed.

I had the incredibly good fortune of going to graduate school where there was an enviable collection of generous and expert faculty along with two very talented fellow students who became early collaborators and subsequently went on to become quite famous psychologists: John Cacioppo (now at the University of Chicago and renowned for his contributions to social neuroscience) and Gary Wells (now at Iowa State University and widely recognized for his contributions to psychology and law). Gary and I collaborated on several of my first projects, including the initial head-nodding study mentioned above. John and I have worked together on over 50 published papers and even more individual studies. My collaborations with John greatly influenced the way I think about human nature and set the tone for subsequent successful collaborations. Short-term collaborations (for a project or two) are mostly based on mutual interest in a topic or perhaps some formal advisor-advisee relationship. Successful long-term collaborations also involve mutual interests but are more like a social relationship (e.g., a marriage) in that they require trust, similar work habits, and it sure helps if you really like the person as well! There are a number of famous long-term collaborations in psychology (e.g., see Levine & Moreland, 2004), and when these collaborations are clicking, they are joyous relationships, as they can combine the best of intellectual stimulation with warm comradery. I am highly fortunate to have been the beneficiary of several such long-term collaborative relationships, and they are the part of my career that I find most rewarding.

Early in one's career, one is often advised to avoid too much collaboration or too much work with a particular collaborator. The fear is that it may be difficult to parse the credit. (Is the work yours or your collaborator's?) Although it is certainly important to demonstrate your own independence in a scholarly career by not working *exclusively* with the same people on every project, you can accomplish this without sacrificing any collaborations that you wish to continue (i.e., collaborations that are both enjoyable and productive). In my view, the primary way in which people evaluate fellow scientists is by the *quality* of work in which they are involved. So, if your collaborations are genuine (i.e., all parties are contributing intellectually), are leading to high-quality work, and are fun, then stick with them.

CARRYING OUT THE RESEARCH

Once you have determined that the idea seems sensible and worthy of pursuit, colleagues and the literature will also be helpful in guiding you toward any established ways of conducting the research. All else equal, if you can conduct your study using established manipulations and measures, you will be on safer ground than if you have to invent your own methods. This is primarily because if things do not turn out as intended, you won't know whether to attribute the problem to your conceptualization or to your unique new methodology. Perhaps after reading all you can, however, you find that there are no prior methods or that these methods are too cost prohibitive or impractical. Thus, you might have to come up with something on your own. If this is one of your early research projects, it is at this point that you might abandon the idea unless you can come up with something practical. At a minimum, your new methods might require piloting unless your procedures have such obvious validity that this seems unnecessary (e.g., there are not too many ways to manipulate head nodding).

This book and many others provide much useful advice about conducting and analyzing your data, and I will not dwell on that here. But it may be important to note that if the data came out as you expected all of the time, this stage of the research enterprise would be relatively simple (and boring). In fact, if data always came out as you expected, it might be hard to get excited about collecting and analyzing the data, as you would already know what the results are going to be! But, the data will not always come out as you expect. This is, in fact, one of the parts of research that I enjoy the most. When data do not fit your expectations, you have a puzzle to be solved. Why do the data differ from your expectations? In our own lab, seemingly uncooperative data have sometimes led to totally new lines of research.

If your procedures produce null effects for what was a sensible hypothesis, it is most likely the case that your procedures are at fault (e.g., unreliable measures or insufficiently strong manipulations, or too much psychological "noise" in the experiment). Or perhaps the procedures are fine, but the power of your study was insufficient to detect a significant effect. Much has been written about the statistical *significance* of results. Some authors argue that we should not worry much about whether our results are statistically significant because any two variables will likely be related if you have enough participants (e.g., see Schmidt, 1996). These authors argue that we should be more interested in the size of the effects that we uncover. Although there is undoubtedly too much emphasis placed on whether a statistical test produces a .06 or .05 *p* level, it is important to know if the effect we uncovered is due to chance. Therefore, although I agree that any two conceptual variables of sufficient interest to motivate someone to conduct a study are likely to be related, it will not always be obvious what the *direction* of the relationship will or should be. Until the results can be deemed as not likely due to chance, you'll not be sure what the direction of the effect is. In theory-testing research, establishing a clear direction of an effect is usually more important than the size of that effect.

If you have discovered a direction of effect that is not the one you anticipated, it is important to remember what my first advisor in graduate school, Robert Cialdini, always said: *The data never lie.* That is, assuming the effect is not due to chance, the unexpected effect was produced for a reason. Maybe your theory is right, but your research operations do not represent the concepts you intended, but represent some other concepts. If you believe that this is the case, the natural solution is to try a different method that might better capture your conceptual ideas. But an alternative strategy is to try to figure out what conceptual variables were inadvertently tapped by your procedures and pursue this. The unexpected finding may be as interesting as, or even more interesting than, what you intended to study. Only you can ultimately decide if this *digression* is worthy of pursuit, but discussions with colleagues and a new reading of the literature can once again help you.

REPORTING FINDINGS TO OTHERS

The final stage in the research script involves reporting the research to others. I once knew a psychologist who claimed to conduct research projects simply to satisfy his own curiosity, with no intention of reporting the results; but this is rare. Reporting of your results often occurs first with informal discussions and presentations to colleagues. Making an oral report, either formally at a conference or informally in a seminar or brown-bag series, forces you to try to explain what you did and why you did it. It allows others to ask questions and point out other issues and relevant literature that you might not have considered. Over the years, however, I have learned that the data almost always look better (stronger) in initial oral reports than they will ultimately look when written in manuscript form. This is because in an oral report you can easily gloss over imperfections or irregularities and focus your audience on the key methods and findings. One implication of this idea is that if you can't make a persuasive oral report from your data, then there may be little hope of turning it into a full-fledged publication. So, if you think your results are promising, take any reasonable opportunity to make an oral presentation of your research to some audience.

If your research survives the oral report (i.e., no fatal flaws were uncovered), it is time to prepare a more formal report of your research. My preference in writing research is always to prepare the Methods and Results sections first. In fact, I like to prepare the methods as soon as it is determined that there are some sensible results that might be worth reporting. If you do not write down the methods relatively quickly, you may forget the details. When you are just starting research, this may seem impossible. How can you forget something you've spent so much time thinking about and preparing? But once you've conducted a few studies, the essential details of the methods might become lost. You can end up with a pile of questionnaires, with little recollection of the order in which you administered them, or a big computer data file, with no record of whether this was the study in which you ran the male or the female participants. Mark and label everything clearly. There is no easier time to do this than while you are collecting the data.

Once the Methods and Results sections for each of the relevant studies are prepared, it is time to write the Introduction. The Introduction is probably the most important part of the paper. By the time your readers have read your Introduction, they need to believe that the key question or questions you are addressing are of sufficient importance and interest to publish.[1] How should the Introduction be written? Daryl Bem (2004) has persuasively argued that your manuscript should tell a story. When writing the Introduction, I like to think of myself as a prosecutor in a criminal case. My job is to prove beyond a reasonable doubt that the data support my conceptualization. The evidence in a criminal case (and in the psychological lab) is collected in all sorts of ways in a particular sequence. A good prosecutor would never think of presenting the data to the jury in exactly the order in which it was collected. Yet when I was a journal editor, I would see papers written by (inexperienced) authors who would present their studies in exactly the order in which the studies were conducted. A prosecutor knows that even if the bloody knife was found before the eyewitness, maybe it makes sense to present the information in the opposite order. A prosecutor and a researcher should never make up evidence or be deceptive about the manner in which the evidence was collected, but it is perfectly appropriate to present the information in the order that tells your story the best (see also Bem, 2004).

In the days when research reports consisted of a single study, there was no issue about the order of presentation. Today, when the best journals require at least two or more experiments (with good reason, I think), the order of presentation is a very important issue to consider. Often in a research report, you will begin with a study that reports a basic effect that forms the meat of the paper. Subsequent studies will deal with issues such as showing the generalizability or limitations of the effect or providing evidence of mediation or moderation of the effect that is consistent with your preferred explanation of the effect and inconsistent with alternative accounts. In some cases, when we have conducted five or six studies on a phenomenon, I sit down with our research team and try putting an Introduction together in different ways. Here is how we would tell the story if the studies were ordered in this way. Here is how we would tell the story if the studies were presented in a different way. After playing with different possibilities, we settle on one and begin writing the Introduction. Sometimes, in the course of writing, the sequence that we decided on fails, and we try another one. The process goes on until the story is presented in the most clear and compelling way.

CONCLUSION

In this concluding section, I will add just a few final words of advice about aspects of the research script:

1. *Write your ideas down the minute they occur to you.* Like the methods of your study that you think you will remember forever, but will not, the same is true of your research ideas. Write them down in a reasonable form along with any ideas you have about *why* the idea might be important and to what literature you think the idea relates. You will not pursue all of the ideas that you have, but some of them may be useful later. I recently had the experience of uncovering a folder of research ideas that was over 10 years old. Some of these ideas didn't make any sense to me now, or seemed silly; others were well past their prime. But a few still seemed worthy of investigation.

2. *Be bold.* You can begin thinking in terms of a simple relationship between variables or about one particular mediator or moderator of an effect, but as you progress, you may find that you have invented a whole new theory with multiple mediators and moderators. Very early in my career when I was preparing my dissertation project, I had planned a series of relatively simple studies on a fairly narrow topic (the mediators of the persistence of persuasion over time). When I went to my advisor, Tim Brock, he said my dissertation topic was fine, but that what I really needed to do was to come up with a new theory. I had never contemplated proposing a theory, as that seemed like something one did much later in one's career. But a theory is nothing more than a series of smaller ideas strung together with some conceptual glue, so I

swallowed the bait and tried to come up with something. The point is that I never would have thought of doing this on my own, but it was a valuable lesson in trying to think on a larger scale. So, don't shy away from being grandiose.

3. *Have fun.* There are many careers you can have, and you can be successful in many of them. If you choose a career that involves psychological research, do it because you are truly interested in human behavior, want to contribute to the building blocks of the great human puzzle, and greatly enjoy at least one or more aspects of the research process. As I noted earlier, the aspect of research that I have enjoyed the most is the amazing opportunity I have had

to work with a goodly number of very bright and talented collaborators who are genuinely fantastic people and also cherished friends. My career would not be what it is without them. They know who I'm talking about, even if I could not mention them all by name in this chapter!

NOTE

1. Unfortunately, some readers may not look at your Introduction first, as they will want to know what you did and found, unbiased by your story (e.g., see Oleson & Arkin, Chapter 4, this volume).

EXERCISES

Examine the titles of the articles in the last few issues of your favorite psychology journal. Read the abstracts of studies with appealing titles to find the one article that to you is the most interesting. Assuming the authors present a theory to explain the key effect reported in the article, try to think of a *different* reason why the key effect might have occurred. Think about how you might assess the alternative underlying processes in a mediational study. Then, think about what variable(s) might moderate the effect, according to your alternative theory, that would not make a difference (or would make a different difference) according to the prevailing theory.

RECOMMENDED READINGS

The reference section below provides a wealth of possibilities for additional readings, and the discussions in this chapter indicate what each of them is about. I would recommend paying special attention, however, to the following two readings. These two best exemplify the contextualist framework emphasized in this chapter.

McGuire, W. J. (1997). Creative hypothesis generating in psychology: Some useful heuristics. *Annual Review of Psychology, 48,* 1–30.
Petty, R. E. (1997). The evolution of theory and research in social psychology: From single to multiple effect and process models. In C. McGarty & S. A. Haslam (Eds.), *The message of social psychology: Perspectives on mind in society* (pp. 268–290). Oxford, UK: Blackwell.

REFERENCES

Bargh, J. A., Chen, M., & Burrows, L. (1996). Automaticity of social behavior: Direct effects of trait construct and stereotype activation on

action. *Journal of Personality and Social Psychology, 71,* 230–244.
Baron, R. M., & Kenny, D. A. (1986). The moderator-mediator variable distinction in social psychological research: Conceptual, strategic, and

statistical considerations. *Journal of Personality and Social Psychology, 51,* 1173–1182.

Bem, D. J. (1972). Self-perception theory. In L. Berkowitz (Ed.), *Advances in experimental social psychology* (Vol. 6, pp. 1–62). New York: Academic.

Bem, D. J. (2004). Writing the empirical journal article. In J. M. Darley, M. P. Zanna, & H. Roediger (Eds.), *The compleat academic: A career guide* (pp. 185–219). Washington, DC: APA.

Briñol, P., & Petty, R. E. (2003). Overt head movements and persuasion: A self-validation analysis. *Journal of Personality and Social Psychology, 84,* 1123–1139.

Cacioppo, J. T., Priester, J. R., & Berntson, G. G. (1993). Rudimentary determinants of attitudes II: Arm flexion and extension have differential effects on attitudes. *Journal of Personality and Social Psychology, 65,* 5–17.

DeMarree, K., Wheeler, S. C., & Petty, R. E. (in press). Priming a new identity: Self-monitoring moderates the effects of non-self primes on self-judgments and behavior. *Journal of Personality and Social Psychology.*

DeSteno, D., Petty, R. E., Wegener, D. T., & Rucker, D. D. (2000). Beyond valence in the perception of likelihood: The role of emotion specificity. *Journal of Personality and Social Psychology, 78,* 397–416.

Dijksterhuis, A., & Bargh, J. A. (2001). The perception-behavior expressway: Automatic effects of social perception on social behavior. In M. P. Zanna (Ed.), *Advances in experimental social psychology* (Vol. 33, pp. 1–40). San Diego, CA: Academic.

Ekman, P., & Friesen, W. V. (1971). Constants across cultures in the face and emotion. *Journal of Personality and Social Psychology, 17,* 124–129.

Festinger, L. (1954). A theory of social comparison processes. *Human Relations, 7,* 117–140.

Johnson, E. J., & Tversky, A. (1983). Affect, generalization, and the perception of risk. *Journal of Personality and Social Psychology, 45,* 20–31.

Kahneman, D. (2003). Experiences of collaborative research. *American Psychologist, 58,* 723–730.

Kawakami, K., Dovidio, J., & Dijksterhuis, A. (2003). Effects of social category priming on personal attitudes. *Psychological Science, 14,* 315–319.

Levine, J. M., & Moreland, R. (2004). Collaboration: The social context of theory development. *Personality and Social Psychology Review, 8,* 164–172.

Levy, B. (1996). Improving memory in old age through implicit self-stereotyping. *Journal of Personality and Social Psychology, 71,* 1092–1107.

Nisbett, R. M., & Wilson, T. D. (1977). Telling more than we can know: Verbal reports on mental processes. *Psychological Review, 84,* 231–259.

McGuire, W. J. (1985). Attitudes and attitude change. In G. Lindzey & E. Aronson (Eds.), *Handbook of social psychology* (3rd ed., Vol. 2, pp. 233–246). New York: Random House.

McGuire, W. J. (1997). Creative hypothesis generating in psychology: Some useful heuristics. *Annual Review of Psychology, 48,* 1–30.

Petty, R. E. (1997). The evolution of theory and research in social psychology: From single to multiple effect and process models. In C. McGarty & S. A. Haslam (Eds.), *The message of social psychology: Perspectives on mind in society* (pp. 268–290). Oxford, UK: Blackwell.

Petty, R. E., Briñol, P., & Tormala, Z. L. (2002). Thought confidence as a determinant of persuasion: The self-validation hypothesis. *Journal of Personality and Social Psychology, 82,* 722–741.

Petty, R. E., & Cacioppo, J. T. (1986). The Elaboration Likelihood Model of persuasion. In L. Berkowitz (Ed.), *Advances in experimental social psychology* (Vol. 19, pp. 123–205). New York: Academic.

Petty, R. E., Fabrigar, L. R., & Wegener, D. T. (2003). Emotional factors in attitudes and persuasion. In R. J. Davidson, K. R. Scherer, & H. H. Goldsmith (Eds.), *Handbook of affective sciences* (pp. 752–772). Oxford, UK: Oxford University Press.

Petty, R. E., Tormala, Z. L., & Rucker, D. D. (2004). Resistance to persuasion: An attitude strength perspective. In J. T. Jost, M. R. Banaji, & D. A. Prentice (Eds.), *Perspectivism in social psychology: The yin and yang of scientific progress* (pp. 37–51). Washington, DC: APA.

Schmidt, F. (1996). Statistical significance testing and cumulative knowledge in psychology: Implications for training of researchers. *Psychological Methods, 1,* 115–129.

Snyder, M. (1974). Self-monitoring of expressive behavior. *Journal of Personality and Social Psychology, 30,* 526–537.

Staats, A. W., & Staats, C. K. (1958). Attitudes established by classical conditioning. *Journal of Abnormal and Social Psychology, 57,* 37–40.

Strack, F., Martin, L., & Stepper, S. (1988). Inhibiting and facilitating conditions of the human smile: A nonobtrusive test of the facial feedback hypothesis. *Journal of Personality and Social Psychology, 54,* 768–777.

Tom, G., Pettersen, P., Lau, T., Burton, T., & Cook, J. (1991). The role of overt head movement in the formation of affect. *Basic and Applied Social Psychology, 12,* 281–289.

Tormala, Z. L., Petty, R. E., & Briñol, P. (2002). Ease of retrieval effects in persuasion: A self-validation analysis. *Personality and Social Psychology Bulletin, 28,* 1700–1712.

Tversky, A., & Kahneman, D. (1974). Judgment under uncertainty: Heuristics and biases. *Science, 185,* 1124–1131.

Wegener, D. T., & Fabrigar, L. R. (2000). Analysis and design for non-experimental data: Addressing causal and noncausal hypotheses. In H. Reiss & C. M. Judd (Eds.), *Handbook of research methods in social and personality psychology* (pp. 412–450). New York: Cambridge University Press.

Wells, G. L., & Petty, R. E. (1980). The effects of overt head movements on persuasion: Compatibility and incompatibility of responses. *Basic and Applied Social Psychology, 1,* 219–230.

Wheeler, S. C., DeMarree, K. G., & Petty, R. E. (2005). The roles of the self in priming-to-behavior effects. In A. Tesser, J. V. Wood, & D. A. Stapel (Eds.), *On building, defending, and regulating the self: A psychological perspective* (pp. 245–271). New York: Psychology Press.

Wheeler, S. C., & Petty, R. E. (2001). The effects of stereotype activation on behavior: A review of possible mechanisms. *Psychological Bulletin, 127,* 797–826.

Williams, K. D., Case, T. I., & Govan, C. L. (2003). Impact of ostracism on social judgments and decisions: Implicit and explicit processes. In J. P. Forgas, K. D. Williams, & W. von Hippel (Eds.), *Social judgments: Explicit and implicit processes* (pp. 325–342). Cambridge, UK: Cambridge University Press.

Wilson, T. D., Houston, C. E., Etling, K. M, & Brekke, N. (1996). A new look at anchoring effects: Basic anchoring and its antecedents. *Journal of Experimental Psychology: General, 125,* 387–402.

Zadro, L., Williams, K. D., & Richardson, R. (2004). How low can you go? Ostracism by computer is sufficient to lower self-reported levels of belonging, control, self-esteem, and meaningful existence. *Journal of Experimental Social Psychology, 40,* 560–567.

INDEX

ABOUT THE EDITORS

Frederick T. L. Leong (PhD, Counseling and Industrial-Organizational Psychology, University of Maryland, 1988) is Professor of Psychology and Director of the Counseling Psychology Program at the University of Tennessee at Knoxville. Prior to UTK, he was on the faculty at Southern Illinois University (1988–1991) and The Ohio State University (1991–2003). He has authored or coauthored over 100 articles in various counseling and psychology journals, 45 book chapters, and also edited or coedited six books and two encyclopedias. Dr. Leong is a Fellow of the American Psychological Association (Divisions 1, 2, 17, 45, and 52) and the recipient of the 1998 Distinguished Contributions Award from the Asian American Psychological Association and the 1999 John Holland Award from the APA Division of Counseling Psychology. His major research interests are in cross-cultural psychology (particularly culture and mental health and cross-cultural psychotherapy), vocational psychology (career development of ethnic minorities), and organizational behavior. Currently, he is the President of both the Asian American Psychological Association and the Division of Counseling Psychology of the International Association of Applied Psychology. His latest project is the Sage *Encyclopedia of Counseling* for which he is the Editor-in-Chief.

James T. Austin (PhD, Industrial-Organizational Psychology, Virginia Tech University, 1987) is a Research Specialist 2 at The Ohio State University, specializing in the psychometrics of test creation and evaluation for Career-Technical Education at the secondary and community college levels. He served as Assistant Professor of I-O Psychology from 1991 to 1997 at Ohio State. His research on goal-setting, criterion measurement, and research methodology has appeared in *Psychological Bulletin, Annual Review of Psychology, Journal of Applied Psychology, Personnel Psychology, Organizational Behavior and Human Decisions Processes.* He is currently cowriting a book on analysis and prioritization of needs assessment data in program evaluation.

ABOUT THE CONTRIBUTORS

James W. Altschuld (PhD, Educational Research and Evaluation, The Ohio State University, 1970) is a Professor Emeritus of Education. He received the Alva and Gunnar Myrdal Practice Award from The American Evaluation Association for his contributions to evaluation. He has published extensively, including a pair of widely-cited books on needs assessment (Altschuld & Witkin, 1999; Witkin & Altschuld, 1996), a forthcoming handbook on needs assessment (Altschuld & Kumar, in press) and an edited book on science and technology (Altschuld & Kumar, 2000). His empirical research and provocative commentary appears in prominent journals, including the *American Journal of Evaluation, Evaluation and Program Planning*, and *New Directions in Program Evaluation*.

Michael Arfken is a doctoral student in experimental psychology at the University of Tennessee in Knoxville. He completed his undergraduate work at Texas State University in San Marcos. His research focuses on interpretive and interdisciplinary approaches to social science. He is particularly interested in applying insights from literary criticism, psychoanalysis, and phenomenology to psychological phenomena. He is currently developing a hermeneutic approach for psychology with an emphasis on the social construction of knowledge.

Robert M. Arkin (PhD, Social Psychology, University of Southern California, 1976) is Professor of Psychology, Coordinator of the Social Psychology graduate program, and former Undergraduate Dean at The Ohio State University. He has served as Associate Editor both for the *Journal of Personality and Social Psychology* and *Personality and Social Psychology Bulletin* and is now Editor of the journal *Basic and Applied Social Psychology*. He conducts research on the self, the role of the self in social interaction contexts, and on individual differences in self- and other-perception processes in social interaction. In particular, he is interested in the topics of self-presentation, social identity, and competence appraisals (self and other).

Pam M. Baxter (MLS, SUNY Albany) manages the data archive at the Cornell Institute for Social and Economic Research, Cornell University. She was previously head of the Psychological Sciences Library at Purdue University, a Reference Librarian at the State University College at Geneseo (NY), and a part-time Lecturer at the School of Information Science and Policy, State University of New York at Albany. She is author of *Psychology: A Guide to Reference and Information Sources* (Libraries Unlimited, 1993) and coauthor with Jeffrey Reed of *Library Use: Handbook for Psychology* (American Psychological Association [APA], 2003).

John G. Borkowski (PhD, 1965, Experimental Psychology, University of Iowa) is Andrew J. McKenna Family Professor of Psychology and has been at the University of Notre

Dame for 38 years. He taught for 2 years at Oberlin College. His research interests include metacognitive development, educational interventions for at-risk children, and social-cognitive development in children of adolescent mothers. His research has been supported by National Institutes of Health, Public Health Institute and the Office of Education for over two decades.

Chad S. Briggs is a graduate student in the Applied Psychology program at Southern Illinois University at Carbondale (SIUC). He holds a MA degree in Applied Psychology from SIUC and is a member of the American Evaluation Association, the American Society of Criminology, and APA. He is author or coauthor of a number of articles and conference papers and has had considerable experience in applied research, including survey methodology through Applied Research Consultants (www.arc.siu.edu/). His research interests include corrections, religion and health, and religion and crime.

Robert F. Calderón (PhD, Industrial-Organizational Psychology, The Ohio State University, 1996) is a Senior Research Psychologist at Caliber Associates in Fairfax, VA. He is currently involved in implementation of advanced selection and training interventions for organizations. His research has appeared in *Structural Equation Modeling* and in various conference proceedings.

David Chan (PhD, Industrial-Organizational Psychology, Michigan State University, 1998) is Professor of Psychology at the School of Economics and Social Sciences at Singapore Management University. His research interests include personnel selection, organizational behavior, person-situation interactions in judgment and decision making, and longitudinal modeling. He is the recipient of numerous scholarly awards including the Distinguished Award for Early Career Contributions to Industrial-Organizational Psychology from Division 14 of the American Psychological Association. He is coauthor with Neal Schmitt of the book *Personnel Selection,* and he has published numerous journal articles and handbook chapters. He currently serves as a consulting editor or an editorial board member on seven journals.

Peter Y. Chen (PhD, University of South Florida, 1991) is an Associate Professor of Industrial-Organizational Psychology at Colorado State University. He was a research scientist at Liberty Mutual Research Institute for Safety and an Associate Professor of Industrial-Organizational Psychology at Ohio University. His primary research interests are in occupational health, training, performance evaluation, and methodology. He has published a book, numerous book chapters, and various empirical articles appearing in the *Journal of Applied Psychology, Journal of Management, Journal of Occupational Health Psychology, Journal of Organizational and Occupational Psychology, Journal of Organizational Behavior, Journal of Personality Assessment,* and *Group and Organization Management: An International Journal.*

Madonna G. Constantine (PhD, Counseling Psychology, University of Memphis, 1991) is a Professor of Psychology and Education in the Department of Counseling and Clinical Psychology at Teachers College, Columbia University. Her research and professional interests include the mental health of persons of African descent; multicultural competence issues in counseling, training, and supervision; and the career development of people of color and psychologists in training.

Harris Cooper (PhD, Social Psychology, University of Connecticut, 1975) spent a year as a postdoctoral Fellow at Harvard University and a year teaching at Colgate University. From 1977 to 2002, he taught at the University of Missouri where he was the Frederick A. Middlebush Professor of Psychology and a Research Associate at the Center for Research in Social Behavior. He currently is Director of the Program in

Educational Psychology at Duke University. His research interests follow two paths: research synthesis and the application of social psychology to educational policy issues. He is coeditor with Larry Hedges of the *Handbook of Research Synthesis* (1994).

Don M. Dell (PhD, Counseling Psychology, University of Minnesota, 1972) is a Vice-Chair of the Department of Psychology and longtime faculty member in the Counseling Psychology program at The Ohio State University. He is a former Chair of that university's Behavioral and Social Sciences IRB and currently teaches a required course on professional and ethical issues to graduate students in clinical and counseling psychology.

David N. Dickter (PhD, Industrial-Organizational Psychology, The Ohio State University, 1997) is an industrial-organizational psychologist with Psychological Services, Inc., a provider of employment selection, assessment, licensure, and certification services. He has coauthored several articles and book chapters on various topics. He is a member of the APA, the Society for Industrial and Organizational Psychology, the Society for Human Resource Management, and the Personnel Testing Council of Southern California.

David L. DiLalla (PhD, Clinical Psychology, University of Virginia, 1989) is Associate Professor of Psychology at Southern Illinois University. He completed a postdoctoral residency at the University of Colorado. His research interests include personality and psychopathology, as well as behavioral genetics.

Stephen J. Dollinger (PhD, Clinical Psychology, University of Missouri-Columbia, 1977) is Professor of Psychology and Director of Clinical Training at Southern Illinois University. His research interests include various topics in personality and clinical child psychology.

Nancy Dorr (PhD, Social Psychology, University of Missouri-Columbia, 1997) is an Associate Professor of Psychology at The College of Saint Rose. Her research interests involve social and personality correlates of health.

Charles B. Fields is Professor of Criminal Justice in the College of Justice and Safety at Eastern Kentucky University. He has a BA (1980) and MA (1981) in political science from Appalachian State University, and a PhD in criminal justice (1984) from Sam Houston State University. He has previously taught at Saginaw Valley State, Appalachian State, and California State Universities. He has edited or co-edited four books and numerous articles/reviews. His current research interests include drug policy and comparative justice systems.

Charles J. Gelso (PhD, Counseling Psychology, The Ohio State University, 1970) is a Professor of Psychology at the University of Maryland, College Park. His research and theoretical interests revolve around the client-therapist relationship in psychotherapy and what he terms "the research training environment in graduate education." He is currently Editor of the journal, *Psychotherapy: Theory, Research, Practice, and Training.*

Lucy Gibson (PhD, Industrial-Organizational Psychology, University of Tennessee, 1988) is a licensed Industrial-Organizational Psychologist and Vice President of Resource Associates, Inc., in Knoxville, TN. Having taught at University of Tennessee and Tusculum College, her current interests revolve around testing systems development for employee selection and management as well as design and validation of personality-related assessments for the workplace and developmental systems for adolescents and young adults. In addition, she has worked in the health care field, Oak Ridge National Laboratory, and as a consultant to business and industry in the fields of test validation, managerial assessments, career development, and organization development.

Robert D. Goddard, III (PhD, Organizational Behavior, University of South Carolina, 1981) is Professor of Management at Appalachian State University and founder and President of Organizational Development Associates, a firm providing a variety of management consulting and training services. ODA specializes in employee opinion survey design and administration as a basis of improving the quality of work life for organizations. He is immediate past Chair, Academy of International Business Southeast U.S.A. Chapter (AIB-SE) and serves on its Board of Directors. He is a past Editor of the Southeast Decision Sciences Institute (SE DSI) Proceedings and has been Vice President-Membership, and Vice President-Student Liaison for SE DSI. He has served two terms as Vice President for Educator Programs for Pi Sigma Epsilon (the national professional fraternity for marketing, sales management, and selling) and has also served as its National Secretary for two terms. He currently serves on the Board of Directors of Epsilon Chi Omicron, the international business honor society, and is a member of the editorial board for the *Journal of Global Business*. His current research interests are in the areas of international entrepreneurship education and the business aspects of wind power generation.

Thomas R. Graves, MA, is currently studying for a PhD in phenomenological psychology at the University of Tennessee in Knoxville. He received his MA from University of Chicago in 2000 with a thesis addressing autobiographical accounts of mental illness experiences. He has worked in areas of medical demography and epidemiology for the University of Tennessee Research Centers in partnership with the Tennessee Department of Health. Current research is related to human experiences of exploration; experiences of fate, fortune, or luck; experiences of moral conflict and evil. His areas of specialization include cultural psychology and psychological anthropology, interpretive methods in the social sciences, narrative analysis in phenomenological psychology, and the psychology and anthropology of metaphysical beliefs and religion.

Douglas A. Hershey (PhD, Decision Making, University of Southern California, 1989) is Associate Professor of Psychology at Oklahoma State University. His research on retirement financial planning and goal setting has appeared in several journals, including *Organizational Behavior and Human Decision Processes.*

Kimberly S. Howard (MA, Developmental Psychology, University of Notre Dame) is a graduate student in the psychology program at the University of Notre Dame. Her research is focused on the ways that fathers in high-risk families influence their children's development. She has published her research in the *Journal of Family Psychology.*

Yueng-hsiang Huang (PhD, Industrial-Organizational Psychology, Portland State University, 2000) is a Research Scientist at Liberty Mutual Research Institute for Safety. She was a Senior Research Associate at the Foundation for Accountability (FACCT) Health Care Research Organization and a Supervisor and Consultant at the Survey Research Lab of Portland State University. Her primary research interests are in occupational injury and accident prevention, return-to-work issues, work-life balance, employee selection, training, and performance evaluation. She has authored various empirical articles in the *Journal of Family and Economic Issues; Work: A Journal of Prevention, Assessment and Rehabilitation; Transportation Research Part F: Traffic Psychology and Behavior; Environment and Behavior; Applied Ergonomics; Professional Safety; Journal of Business and Psychology; Accident Analysis and Prevention;* and *Journal of General Internal Medicine.*

Joy M. Jacobs-Lawson (PhD, Oklahoma State University, 2003) is an Assistant Professor in the Graduate Center for Gerontology at the University of Kentucky. Her research interests include cognitive aging and developmental differences in life planning.

Kwok Leung (PhD, Social and Organizational Psychology, University of Illinois, Urbana-Champaign, 1985) is Professor of Management at City University of Hong Kong. His research areas include justice and conflict, international business, and cross-cultural psychology. He is a past Editor of *Asian Journal of Social Psychology* and a Departmental Editor of *Journal of International Business Studies*. He is on the editorial board of several journals, including *Journal of Applied Psychology, Applied Psychology: An international Review, Journal of Cross-Cultural Psychology,* and *Organizational Research Methods.* He is the Chair-Elect of the Research Methods Division of the Academy of Management and a past President of Asian Association of Social Psychology.

Paul E. Levy (PhD, Industrial-Organizational Psychology, Virginia Tech, 1989) is Professor of Industrial and Organizational Psychology at the University of Akron and serves as the Director of the I-O Psychology program. Dr. Levy's research interests include performance appraisal, feedback processes, motivation, and job-related attitudes. His research in these areas has appeared in journals such as *Personnel Psychology, Journal of Personality and Social Psychology, Organizational Behavior and Human Decision Processes,* and *Applied Psychology: An International Review.*

John W. Lounsbury (PhD, Ecological Psychology, Michigan State University, 1980) is a Professor of Psychology at the University of Tennessee. His research interests include personality measurement and predictors of work and school performance, career assessment and development, and psychological sense of community in campus and work settings.

Michele Marks (PhD, Industrial-Organizational Psychology, George Mason University, 1998) is Assistant Professor in the Business College at George Mason University. Her primary research interests are in groups and teamwork and her publications have appeared in such outlets as *Academy of Management Journal, Journal of Applied Psychology,* and *Personnel Psychology.*

Naomi M. Meara (PhD, Counseling Psychology, The Ohio State University, 1967) is the Nancy Reeves Dreux Professor of Psychology Emerita at the University of Notre Dame. With Lyle D. Schmidt, Jeanne D. Day and others, she has written in ethics and related areas on such topics as the ethics of researching the counseling process, ethics and psychoanalytic counseling, principle and virtue ethics, virtues, and the ethics of psychology and the academy. She coauthored *Psychoanalytic Counseling* with Michael J. Patton.

William C. McCready (PhD, Sociology, University of Illinois-Chicago, 1972) is Vice President for Client Development at Knowledge Networks. He works with academic, government, and nonprofit clients to help them design projects that use the Knowledge Networks Panel. In 2000, he worked with the Bureau of the Census and the University of Pennsylvania's Annenberg School of Public Policy on two large national projects for Knowledge Networks. He is currently involved in developing partnerships with academic and government research offices to utilize the national Knowledge Networks panel in a variety of applications. He has worked in the survey research field for more than 35 years, both as the first Program Director at NORC at the University of Chicago and more recently as Director of the Public Opinion Lab at Northern Illinois University. He is the author or coauthor of several books and numerous chapters, articles, and papers and is a sought-after lecturer. He has published several articles concerning work he has done with Knowledge Networks.

Dennis L. Molfese (PhD, Developmental Psycholinguistics and Neuropsychology, The Pennsylvania State University, 1972) is currently Professor at the Department of Psychological and Brain Sciences, University of Louisville. He was formerly Professor of Psychology, Physiology, and Behavioral and Social Sciences and served as Chairman of the Department of Behavioral and Social Sciences in the School of Medicine at Southern Illinois University at Carbondale. In addition to teaching courses in child psychology, neuropsychology, and brain and language, he conducts and publishes research concerned with the relationship between brain function and language and cognition across the lifespan. He is Editor-in-Chief of the journal, *Developmental Neuropsychology* and has edited several books on brain lateralization and the neuropsychology of individual differences.

Douglas J. Muccio (MA, Counseling Psychology, University of Tennessee, Knoxville, 2004) is a graduate student in the counseling psychology program at the University of Tennessee. His research interests include counseling process and sports psychology.

Brett Myors (PhD, Industrial-Organizational Psychology, University of New South Wales, 1996) is Associate Professor at Griffith University in Australia. He has worked as an organizational psychologist in government, industry, and private practice. Among his publications is a comprehensive treatment of statistical power authored by Murphy and Myors (1998).

Donna K. Nagata (PhD, Clinical Psychology, University of Illinois, Urbana-Champaign, 1981) is Professor of Psychology at the University of Michigan, Ann Arbor. Her major research interests focus on the long-term impacts of the Japanese American wartime internment, Asian American mental health, family and intergenerational interactions, and grandparenting. Among her publications are the book *Legacy of Injustice: Exploring the Cross-Generational Impact of the Japanese American Internment* and the recent articles, "Intergenerational Communication of Race-Related Trauma Among Japanese American Former Internees" and "Psychological Reactions to Redress: Diversity Among Japanese Americans Interned During World War II."

Kathryn C. Oleson (PhD, Social Psychology, Princeton University, 1993) is Associate Professor of Psychology and Department Chair at Reed College. She was a National Institute of Mental Health postdoctoral Fellow at The Ohio State University from 1993 to 1995. She is currently Associate Editor of the journal *Basic and Applied Social Psychology.* Her research interests primarily lie in the field of interpersonal perception, including perception of one's self, individuals, and groups. In particular, she is interested in competence appraisals (self and other), achievement strategies and goals, self-concept change and stability, social identity, self-stereotyping, and stereotype formation and change.

Samuel H. Osipow (PhD, Counseling Psychology, Syracuse University, 1959) is Professor Emeritus of Psychology at The Ohio State University. He served as the Editor of the *Journal of Vocational Behavior, Journal of Counseling Psychology,* and *Applied and Preventive Psychology.* He is also the author of *Theories of Career Development* and has coedited seven books. He is a past President of the Division of Counseling Psychology of the APA, past Chair of the Department of Psychology of The Ohio State University, and past Chair of the Board of Directors of the Council for the Register of Health Providers in Psychology.

Christopher Peterson (PhD, Social and Personality Psychology, University of Colorado, 1976) is Professor of Psychology at the University of Michigan, associated with the clinical psychology and personality programs. He respecialized in clinical psychology and experimental psychopathology at the University of Pennsylvania. He is interested in the cognitive determinants of depression and physical illness and is the author of more than one hundred articles, chapters, and books, including *Cognitive Structure* (with W. A. Scott and D. W. Osgood), *Health and Optimism* (with L. M. Bossio), *Learning Helplessness* (with S. F. Maier and M. E. P. Seligman), *Introduction to Psychology,* and *The Psychology of Abnormality.* He has served as Consulting Editor for *Journal of Abnormal Psychology, Journal of Personality and Social Psychology,* and *Psychological Bulletin* and is currently a member of the APA Media Referral Service.

Richard E. Petty (PhD, Social Psychology, The Ohio State University, 1977) is Distinguished University Professor of Psychology at The Ohio State University. He received his BA from the University of Virginia in 1973 and began his career that year as Assistant Professor of Psychology at the University of Missouri. Petty's research focuses broadly on the situational and individual difference factors responsible for changes in beliefs, attitudes, and behaviors. This work has resulted in seven books and over 200 journal articles and chapters. Petty has received several honors for his work including the Distinguished Scientific Contribution Awards from the Society for Personality and Social Psychology (2001) and the Society for Consumer Psychology (2000). After serving as Associate Editor of the *Personality and Social Psychology Bulletin* from 1982 to 1984, he became the journal's Editor from 1988 to 1991. He has also served as Associate Editor for the APA journal, *Emotion,* and has served on the editorial boards of 10 other journals.

Howard R. Pollio (PhD, Experimental Psychology, University of Michigan, 1962) is Alumni Professor of Psychology at the University of Tennessee in Knoxville. He received his bachelor's and master's degrees in psychology from Brooklyn College. His areas of specialization include learning and thinking, college teaching, figurative language, humor, and existential-phenomenological approaches to psychology. He has published over 120 journal articles, book chapters, and books. He was the founding Editor of the journal *Metaphor and Symbol.* He has been President of the Southeastern Psychological Association and a Phi Beta Kappa National Lecturer. He is a Fellow of two divisions of the APA and has received a number of teaching and research awards.

Joseph G. Ponterotto (PhD, University of California Santa Barbara, 1985) is presently Professor of Education in the Counseling Psychology Program at Fordham University, Lincoln Center, New York City campus. His primary teaching interests are in multicultural counseling, career development, qualitative and quantitative research methods, and psychological measurement. He is the coauthor or coeditor of a number of books, most recently the second editions of both the *Handbook of Multicultural Counseling* (also with Sage Publications) and the *Handbook of Multicultural Assessment.*

Jeffrey G. Reed (PhD, Psychology, Kansas State, 1979) currently works for Marian College as an Associate Professor of Business Management. He formerly worked for Xerox Corporation in the Document Production Systems Division as a Process and Planning Manager. Other past positions have included work as a Program Manager, Software Design Manager, User Interface Software Developer, Management Trainer, Assistant Professor of Industrial and Organizational Psychology, Educational Researcher, and College Reference Librarian. He is coauthor of *Library Use: Handbook for Psychology,* published by the APA. He is licensed as a Psychologist in the state of New York, is a Certified Program Management Professional (PMI), holds an MS (Towson State), MLS (Maryland), and BA (Muskingum) and certificates in business (NYU) and program evaluation (Massachusetts).

Jorgianne Civey Robinson is a third-year graduate student in the social psychology doctoral program at Duke University. Her research focuses on the influence of evaluations of physical appearance on self-regulation and self-esteem.

Richard A. Saudargas (PhD, Experimental Psychology, Florida State University, 1972) is Professor of Psychology and Director of Undergraduate Studies at the University of Tennessee and a licensed Psychologist. His current research interests involve the assessment and the development of transition strategies for first-year college students. He has also conducted behavior assessment research to aid in the identification and program planning for developmentally disabled school-aged children, their teachers, and parents.

Charles A. Scherbaum (PhD, Industrial-Organizational Psychology, Ohio University, 2002) is an Assistant Professor of Psychology at Baruch College. His current research focuses on personnel selection, response distortion, work motivation, quantitative methods, and applied psychometrics. His research has appeared in *Personnel Psychology, Leadership Quarterly, Journal of Applied Social Psychology, and Organizational Research Methods.*

Lyle D. Schmidt (PhD, Counseling Psychology, Missouri, 1959) has taught an ethics seminar to graduate students in clinical, counseling, and school psychology for 25 years. He was Chair of the Behavioral and Social Sciences Human Subjects Review Committee at The Ohio State University from 1980 to 1983 and was a member of the university's Policy and Coordinating Committee for Human Subjects Review from 1980 to 1987. He served on the Ethics Committee of the Central Ohio Psychological Association from 1981 to 1983 (Chair in 1982), was Chair of the APA Committee on Accreditation in 1989, and served two terms on the Council of Representatives.

Lisa A. Steelman (PhD, Industrial-Organizational Psychology, University of Akron, 1997) is an Associate Professor of I/O Psychology at Florida Institute of Technology. She also directs the Center for Professional Service, a campus-based management consulting firm. Her research interests include feedback processes, performance appraisal, and employee attitudes.

Steven J. Trierweiler (PhD, Clinical Psychology, University of Illinois, Urbana-Champaign, 1985) is Adjunct Associate Research Scientist at the Institute for Social Research at the University of Michigan, Ann Arbor. His research interests focus on clinical judgment and decision making in psychodiagnostic interviewing in cross-racial/ethnic contexts, interpersonal event memory narratives, and interaction in couples and families. He has a long-standing interest in quantitative and qualitative research methods and in the development of scientific thinking in applied contexts. His publications include articles on African American mental health issues, research training for professional psychologists, and interpersonal memory narratives in psychotherapy. He is lead author of the book *The Scientific Practice of Clinical Professional Psychology.*

Fons J. R. van de Vijver (PhD, Cross-Cultural Psychology, Tilburg University, 1991) holds a Chair in Cross-Cultural Psychology at Tilburg University, the Netherlands, and North-West University, South Africa. His PhD thesis dealt with cross-cultural differences and similarities in inductive reasoning. He has field experience in Southern Africa, Turkey, and Libya. He has published in the areas of methodology of cross-cultural comparisons (bias and equivalence), intelligence, acculturation, and multiculturalism. He is

Editor of the *Journal of Cross-Cultural Psychology* and serves as member of the editorial board of the *European Journal of Psychological Assessment* and the *International Journal of Testing.*

Alan Vaux (PhD, Psychology, Trinity College, Dublin, Ireland, 1979; PhD, Social Ecology, University of California at Irvine, 1981) is Associate Dean, College of Liberal Arts, and Professor of Psychology at Southern Illinois University at Carbondale (SIUC). He is a Fellow of the APA and the American Psychological Society (APS) and has served as an Associate Editor of the *Journal of Social and Personal Relationships* and on the Editorial Board of the *American Journal of Community Psychology.* He is author of *Social Support: Theory, Research, and Intervention,* coeditor of *Independent Consulting in Evaluation,* and coauthor or author of over 50 articles and chapters and 60 conference papers. He has served as Director of Applied Research Consultants, a graduate student–staffed, applied research consulting firm and has supervised over 50 master's and doctoral research projects. His research interests include social support, community psychology, and applied methodology.

Peter Villanova (PhD, Industrial-Organizational Psychology, Virginia Tech, 1987) is a Professor of Management at the John A. Walker School of Business at Appalachian State University. His research interests include employee work attitudes, personnel selection, and performance appraisal. He has published in the *Journal of Applied Psychology; Academy of Management Journal; Personnel Psychology; Human Resource Management Review; Journal of Business and Psychology; Journal of Psychology; Journal of Abnormal Psychology, Educational and Psychological Measurement; Sex Roles;* and *Applied Psychology: An International Review.* He has served as a consultant to numerous public and private organizations in the areas of employee satisfaction, turnover, selection, and performance appraisal.

Bruce E. Wampold (PhD, Counseling Psychology, University of California, Santa Barbara, 1981) is currently Professor and Chair of the Department of Counseling Psychology at the University of Wisconsin, Madison. He is a Fellow of the APA, Diplomat in Counseling Psychology of the American Board of Professional Psychology, and is a Licensed Psychologist in Wisconsin. His area of interest is focused on understanding the benefits of psychotherapy from empirical, historical, and anthropological perspectives. His book *The Great Psychotherapy Debate: Models, Methods, and Findings* (2001) uses the empirical literature to support a contextual model of psychotherapy.

Thomas L. Wilson (PhD, Cognitive Psychology, University of Illinois at Urbana-Champaign, 1989) teaches at Bellarmine University in Louisville, KY.

Stephen J. Zaccaro is a Professor of Psychology at George Mason University, Fairfax, Virginia. He has been studying, teaching, and consulting about leadership and teams for over 20 years. He has written over 100 articles, book chapters, and technical reports on group dynamics, team performance, leadership, and work attitudes. He authored *The Nature of Executive Leadership: A Conceptual and Empirical Analysis of Success* (2001) and co-edited three other books, *Occupational Stress and Organizational Effectiveness* (1987), *The Nature of Organizational Leadership: Understanding the Performance Imperatives Confronting Today's Leaders* (2001), and *Leader Development for Transforming Organizations (2004).* He was co-editor of three special issues of *Leadership Quarterly* on individual differences and leadership (1991). He has also co-edited a special issue for *Group and Organization Management* (2002) on the interface between leadership and team dynamics. He has directed funded research projects in the areas of team performance, shared mental models, leader-team interfaces, leadership training and development, leader adaptability, and executive leadership.

Barbara H. Zaitzow, is professor of criminal justice at Appalachian State University. She has a B.A. in sociology from San Diego State University and an M.S. and Ph.D. in sociology from Virginia Polytechnic Institute and State University. She continues her research in both men's and women's prisons in North Carolina and was co-investigator on a national grant-sponsored study of gangs in prisons. Zaitzow has been involved in local, state, and national advocacy work for prisoners and organizations seeking alternatives to imprisonment. She has served on various editorial boards for nationally-recognized journals and reviews manuscripts for a variety of journals and book publishers. She has published a co-edited book, journal articles, and book chapters on a variety of prison-related topics including HIV/AIDS and other treatment needs of women prisoners and the impact of prison culture on the "doing time" experiences of the imprisoned which appear in the *International Journal of Offender Therapy and Comparative Criminology, Journal of the Association of Nurses in AIDS Care, Journal of Crime and Justice, Criminal Justice Policy Review, Journal of Gang Research*, and *Names*. A member of several regional and national organizations, her primary research areas of interest include female criminality, corrections, and alternatives to incarceration.

Michael J. Zickar (PhD, Industrial-Organizational Psychology, University of Illinois at Urbana-Champaign, 1998) is Associate Professor of Psychology at Bowling Green State University. His research interests range from the field of computational modeling as applied to I-O psychological topics to the history of industrial-organizational psychology and related disciplines.